Handbook of Asset and Liability Management

For other titles in the Wiley Finance series
please see www.wiley.com/finance

Handbook of Asset and Liability Management

From models to optimal return strategies

Alexandre Adam

John Wiley & Sons, Ltd

Telephone (+44) 1243 779777

Email (for orders and customer service enquiries): cs-books@wiley.co.uk
Visit our Home Page on www.wiley.com

Other Wiley Editorial Offices

John Wiley & Sons Inc., 111 River Street, Hoboken, NJ 07030, USA

Jossey-Bass, 989 Market Street, San Francisco, CA 94103-1741, USA

Wiley-VCH Verlag GmbH, Boschstr. 12, D-69469 Weinheim, Germany

John Wiley & Sons Australia Ltd, 42 McDougall Street, Milton, Queensland 4064, Australia

John Wiley & Sons (Asia) Pte Ltd, 2 Clementi Loop #02-01, Jin Xing Distripark, Singapore 129809

John Wiley & Sons Canada Ltd, 6045 Freemont Blvd, Mississauga, ONT, L5R 4J3, Canada

Wiley also publishes its books in a variety of electronic formats. Some content that appears in print may not be available in electronic books.

Anniversary Logo Design: Richard J. Pacifico

Library of Congress Cataloging-in-Publication Data

Adam, Alexandre.
Handbook of asset and liability management : from models to optimal return strategies / Alexandre Adam.
p. cm.
Includes bibliographical references and index.
ISBN 978-0-470-03496-5
1. Asset-liability management. I. Title.
HG1615.25.A33 2007
658.15′5—dc22

2007033392

British Library Cataloguing in Publication Data

A catalogue record for this book is available from the British Library

ISBN 978-0-470-03496-5 (HB)

Typeset in 10/12pt Times by Integra Software Services Pvt. Ltd, Pondicherry, India
Printed and bound in Great Britain by Antony Rowe Ltd, Chippenham, Wiltshire
This book is printed on acid-free paper responsibly manufactured from sustainable forestry in which at least two trees are planted for each one used for paper production.

To Géraldine and to my family

Contents

Preface xiii

Acknowledgments xvii

About the author xix

PART I INTRODUCTION 1

1 The History of ALM 3
- 1.1 The history of the banking industry from antiquity to the Middle Ages 3
- 1.2 The modern banking industry and the history of ALM 5
- 1.3 The history of the insurance industry and ALM 7
- 1.4 The history of other businesses and ALM 9

2 What is Asset and Liability Management Today? 13
- 2.1 ALM and the banking industry 13
- 2.2 Other general ALM questions 14

PART II INTERNAL TRANSFER PRICING, ACCOUNTING AND AUDITING 17

3 Balance Sheet Presentation 19
- 3.1 General balance sheet presentation 19
- 3.2 A/L manager's balance sheet presentation 19
- 3.3 Banking Book and Insurance Book 23
- 3.4 Income statement and statement of cash flows 25

4 "Accrued Accounting" for Interest Rate Instruments Versus "Marked-to-Market" Accounting 29
- 4.1 General principles 29
- 4.2 Accrued accounting examples 30

5 IFRS and IAS Accounting 33
- 5.1 IFRS, international organizations and rule presentation 33
- 5.2 IAS 39 35
- 5.3 Financial disclosures 48

5.4 IFRS and insurance 53
5.5 Other IFRS specificities 54
5.6 Impact of IFRS on ALM and criticism of IFRS 56

6 "Economic Accounting": Fair Value and Full Fair Value 59

7 Internal Transfer Pricing or Fund Transfer Pricing (FTP) 61
7.1 Principles 61
7.2 Advanced transfer pricings including credit risk and expected return on economic capital 64
7.3 The inclusion of implicit options inclusion in the "contract by contract" FTP rules and commercial department arbitrage opportunity 66
7.4 FTP rules based on the "stock" and based on the "flows" 67
7.5 Examples of FTP rules 72
7.6 Perequations 77

8 ALM as a Profit Centre 81
8.1 One profit centre for one financial risk 81

9 Optimal Organization of an ALM Team 83
9.1 The usual ALM organization 83
9.2 The objectives of ALM 84
9.3 ALCO: the ALM committee 87
9.4 The different ALM teams 93

PART III BALANCE SHEET ITEMS AND PRODUCTS MODELLING 99

10 Behavioural Modelling Principles 101
10.1 The constitution of databases 101
10.2 Event driven modelling 103
10.3 Modelling the strategy of the company 104
10.4 Expert advice 105
10.5 Model backtesting 105

11 Deposits and Savings 107
11.1 Deposits, monetary aggregates, money supply and macroeconomics 107
11.2 Demand deposit accounts 111
11.3 Saving accounts: regulated and non-regulated savings versus super-savings 116
11.4 Demand deposits models in the literature 118
11.5 Deposit modelling: the solution through an approach based on customer behaviour modelling 124
11.6 Deposit modelling through a customer behaviour modelling based approach: representation in risk indicators and FTP 132

12	**Loans**	**139**
12.1	Different types of loan	139
12.2	Different definitions and formulae	141
13	**Prepayments**	**145**
13.1	The origins of the prepayment phenomenon	145
13.2	The constitution of the database for prepayment modelling	159
13.3	Different models: historical database-based approaches and MBS-based approaches	166
13.4	Prepayment scoring	178
13.5	Prepayment monitoring	178
14	**Other Examples of Products Needing Behavioural Modelling**	**181**
14.1	Pipeline risk	181
14.2	Margin delay effects such as "whistle effects"	182
14.3	Other volume effects options	183
15	**Examples of Products Partially Correlated with Financial Markets**	**185**
15.1	Presence of correlation between the cash flows and financial markets: examples of credit card	185
15.2	Costs and commissions correlation with financial markets	185
15.3	Examples of embedded options	186
16	**New Production Modelling**	**187**
16.1	New contract production	187
16.2	Commission and cost modelling	192
16.3	Perequation modelling	193
16.4	Future strategies modelling	193
17	**Insurance Products**	**195**
17.1	Unit of account contracts	195
17.2	Mutual funds	195
18	**Hedging Instruments**	**197**
18.1	Derivatives	197
18.2	Bond strategies	197
18.3	Mortgage Backed Securities	198
PART IV	**RISK MANAGEMENT FOR ASSET AND LIABILITY MANAGERS**	**201**
19	**Financial Risks**	**203**
19.1	Liquidity risk	203
19.2	Credit risk	220
19.3	Interest rate risk	235
19.4	Inflation risk	259

19.5 Currency risk 265
19.6 Corporate stock market risk 273
19.7 Real estate risk/property risk 274
19.8 Other financial risks 277

20 Non-Financial Risks 281
20.1 Operational risks 281
20.2 Model risks 282
20.3 Business risk 282
20.4 Risk correlations 283
20.5 "Accounting risk": the risk representation depends on the accounting scheme! 283

PART V TOOLS FOR ASSET AND LIABILITY MANAGERS 285

21 Simulation Tools for Interest Rates and Other Financial Indexes 287
21.1 Stochastic calculation 287
21.2 Equity market simulation 292
21.3 Interest rate simulation 296
21.4 Generic models for joint simulation of inflation, stock index, interest rates, real estate, liquidity and credit spreads 306
21.5 Market simulations including risk premiums 309

22 Delta Equivalent Computation 315
22.1 Principles 315
22.2 Delta, penta, correla and courba equivalents or "Adam equivalents" 322
22.3 Delta equivalent associated break-even point 326
22.4 Examples of delta equivalent computation 327
22.5 Hedging error and gamma equivalent 334

23 Technical Tools Useful in ALM 339
23.1 Risk measures 339
23.2 Optimization methods 344
23.3 Common statistical tools in ALM 347
23.4 Other statistical tools and common ALM functions 355

PART VI ECONOMIC VALUE AND NEW RISK INDICATORS ASSOCIATED WITH THE BASEL II AND SOLVENCY II REGULATORY PERSPECTIVE 357

24 Basel II Regulation and Solvency II 359
24.1 Common regulatory risk constraints 359
24.2 Basel II: normalized regulatory constraints 360
24.3 Solvency II 378

25	**Links Between ALM and Financial Analysis**	**381**
25.1	Performance indicators in the company	381
25.2	Shareholder's equity value, economic value and risk premiums	383
25.3	Capital allocation/attribution and capital consumption	386
25.4	Company valuation and cost of capital with positive tax rate	387
25.5	Merton's model	391
25.6	Financial analysis and ALM implications	391
26	**Towards Economic Capital Indicators**	**393**
26.1	Economic capital and its implications	393
26.2	Economic capital computation main hypotheses	398
26.3	ALM stress testing	401
26.4	Credit risk economic capital computation	406
26.5	Economic capital in ALM	407
26.6	IFRS and regulation implications for ALM	433
26.7	New indicators for the economic value approach	435
PART VII	**OPTIMAL RETURN STRATEGIES**	**441**
27	**Risk Perfect Hedging Using the Delta Equivalent Technique**	**443**
27.1	Micro hedging strategies with structured products	443
27.2	Delta hedging strategies	444
27.3	Example of a bank balance sheet with demand deposits	448
28	**Limits Policy**	**453**
28.1	Economic capital limit	453
28.2	Setting economic capital limits	454
28.3	Gap limit	454
28.4	Income sensitivity limit	455
29	**Income Smoothing Strategies**	**457**
29.1	Important preliminary comment about income smoothing and fraud	457
29.2	Examples of income smoothing	458
29.3	Example of a cumulative AFS bonds income smoothing strategy	460
29.4	ALM and Hawks martingale	461
30	**Economic Value Management: The A/L Manager's Optimization Programme Under Economic Capital Constraints and Accounting Constraints**	**463**
30.1	Point of view of "traditional A/L managers" and criticism of the models	463
30.2	Economic value management	466
30.3	Economic value optimization using grid methodology	470

31 Application to Banking Book Activities 473
31.1 Deposit accounts: valuation and hedging in an economic capital approach using the grid methodology 473
31.2 Application to Stock Market Book 482
31.3 Application to Credit Risk Book 483
31.4 Prepayment risk optimal hedging strategies 484
31.5 Application to a global Banking Book including business and model risk 485
31.6 Direct demand deposit income smoothing through a simple example 487

32 Economic Value Management in Insurance Companies and in Capital Book Management 491
32.1 Economic value management in insurance companies 491
32.2 Application to economic Capital Book management 492

PART VIII CONCLUSIONS ON THE ALM OF TOMORROW 495

33 Conclusions on the Future of ALM 497
33.1 ALM diversity 497
33.2 ALM benchmarking 500
33.3 Conclusions on ALM and models 500

PART IX ANNEXES 507

34 Statistical Advanced Tools 509
34.1 Extreme points 509
34.2 Copulas 509

35 The Basis of Interest Rate Modelling 513
35.1 Yield curve reconstitution 513
35.2 Yield curve stochastic interest rate models 521

Bibliography 533

Index 541

Preface

During the past decade, Asset and Liability Management (ALM) departments have become key departments for balance sheet management and for the profitability management in banks, in insurance companies, in asset management teams and even for financial directions of non-financial companies. Due to the complexity of the subject, it has always appeared difficult to develop a unified vision of what an ALM team should do: optimizing the return, hedging the risk, smoothing the margin . . .

Nevertheless, the external pressure for explanations is growing.

In many countries, the International Accounting Standards (IAS or IFRS) have changed managers' behaviour, obliging them to account their balance sheet in a uniform standard, to better explain their hedging strategies and sometimes to show their residual positions as in the norm IAS 32.

For Banks with Basel II, for insurance companies with Solvency II, the needs for a global understanding of the business is also increasing.

In this context, and in order to prepare the future of ALM, this book tries to give an operational point of view on the business.

This book is written as a handbook for existing or future operational Asset and Liability Managers. It describes all the rules useful for managers to make the activity safe and profitable. It is also meant for all kinds of Asset and Liability managers from banks to financial directors of non-financial companies and on to insurance companies and asset management departments.

The first goal of this book is to explain all the written and unwritten rules of ALM in details, making it easier for everybody to understand the business.

After a presentation of the ALM and of the balance sheet, the new accounting and reporting principles given by IFRS/IAS standards are presented and the FTP (Fund Transfer Price) are introduced. To ensure a better control of results, it is essential to have a basic understanding of the accounting principles.

A large part of the book concentrates on the description of the possible products present in the balance sheet: deposit accounts, prepayments, life insurance contracts . . . The treatment of inflation in balance sheet management is included. Many different up-to-date models are proposed. We propose an operational approach for the management of all these products: from the models to the hedging strategy. The treatment of options in the indicators is described.

Because ALM deals with risk management, the following Parts describe all the inherent risk in a balance sheet. For each risk, we describe:

- the nature of the risk;
- an example;
- the impact on the results;
- the indicator to monitor this risk;
- the better way to simulate this risk;
- the hedging solutions.

We dedicate an entire Part to the useful technical tools used by ALM managers giving a mathematical and statistical background.

The final Parts of the book try to give a global approach for the business using an economic capital approach.

The head of an operational research team (with eight-year's experience including operational management in ALM in one of the best performing ALM Departments in Europe) wrote this book.

Many parts of this book have never been explained in detail. For example, modern models for the demand deposits, for the prepayments are proposed. Developments in economic capital in an ALM context are included. These subjects are only now arising in scientific journals. When we see how the credit risk and the operational risk became of prime importance, with the regulatory pressure of the Basel II Pillar 1, we understand that it will become the same for ALM with Basel II Pillar 2 and 3.

This book first aims to reach Asset and Liability Managers (in banks, insurance companies, financial direction of non-financial companies and asset managers); quantitative ALM researchers, operators and managers, etc.

This book is also written for ALM consultants and advisors, ALM software providers, students in finance their finance lecturers and for actuaries.

This book also seeks to reach many people working with A/L managers:

- risk managers and risk controllers;
- fixed income strategists and sales;
- financial directors;
- auditors and regulators.

The approach is didactical and allows the book to be used as a reference for ALM lecturers. Many lessons provided in universities are not up to date and do not include the latest improvements in this area developed during the last decades. The book tries to fill this gap and to bring the latest findings made by university researchers and professionals.

Whenever it is possible, a quantitative approach is developed. Nevertheless, an economic explanation is provided for each equation, so that the book is understandable by all the people involved in ALM and not only quantitative researchers. The aim of this book is to give a quantitative approach of the subject. Of course, we wrote this book so that a non-mathematician will be able to read it. However, this book includes technical chapters as the job is becoming more and more quantitative.

We took many examples in this book from the ALM banking industry but the main ideas of this book are available to all the other kinds of ALM teams.

As a conclusion, this book is not made for the ALM of yesterday but for the ALM of today (Basel II, IAS/IFRS, etc.) and for the ALM of tomorrow. It will explain which developments the managers have to make in order to improve their competitiveness.

Acknowledgments

I would like to thank all the persons who helped me in the redaction of this book and especially: Barbara, Babette, Géraldine and Jean-Paul.

I would like also to thank all these persons for their help in the comprehension of the ALM topics: Alain, Jean-Louis, Antoine, Carl, Catherine, Christophe, Clément, Erick, Eric, François, Françoise, Julien, Laurent, Martine, Mohamed, Olivier, Stéphane, Valérie, Vincent, and the others . . .

About the author

Alexandre Adam is a French Asset and Liability Manager born in Reims, France. He has a Statistics and Economics Post-graduate Diploma from the École Nationale de la Statistique et de l'Administration Économique, Malakoff; an Advanced Graduate Degree in Engineering from the École Polytechnique, Palaiseau; and a Masters Degree in Mathematics from University Paris-VI.

Since 1997, Alexandre has worked for BNP Paribas, in the ALM and Treasury Department, and is currently Head of the Financial Models Team, contributing to the ALM models and indicators such as Stress Tests, Economic Capital, and Behavioural Models Estimation.

Alexandre is an actuary of the French Institute of Actuaries; a member of the scientific committee of AFGAP, the French Association of Asset and Liability Managers; and since 2005 has been a Master Degree lecturer at University Paris XIII.

Alexandre has published many articles on ALM in specialised journals.

Part I
Introduction

Le rêve est une seconde vie. (Gérard de Nerval)

To introduce Asset and Liability Management (ALM), this part will start with an interesting history of ALM activity. This history is important in order to understand why at the end of the 80s, banks and insurance companies decided to create ALM departments.

The next Part tries to give a brief overview of the existing ALM activity before exposing in detail what the assets and the liabilities of the balance sheet we will discuss throughout the book could be.

1
The History of ALM

Scribitur historia ad narrandum, non ad probandum. (Quintilien)

It is not possible to present ALM history without presenting Banking industry history even if it is possible to make a parallel with the Insurance industry.

This Part is an opportunity to present the links between ALM and the other types of business such as investment management, hedge funds and financial directions of corporate industries, etc.

1.1 THE HISTORY OF THE BANKING INDUSTRY FROM ANTIQUITY TO THE MIDDLE AGES

1.1.1 Origins of banking

The origins of banking go back to antiquity. Historians discovered hints of banking activities dating from 3000 B.C. in Mesopotamia. The temples were places of trades and the priests used to take on the role of banker, taking money as deposits and lending money to the King or to the merchants. Temples were considered as the safest places where gold could be stored.

The first records of loans dating from the 18th century B.C. made by temple priests to merchants were discovered in Babylon.

Remember that in the Bible, Christ drives the moneychangers out of the temple...

In Ancient Greece, the temples conducted not only loans and deposits but also currency exchange and validation of coinage. Each Greek city was independent and minted its own money. Moneychangers appeared in order to develop trade between cities.

The letter of credit made its appearance: in return for a payment, a moneylender in one Greek city would write a credit note and the client would cash the note in another port. Thus, travel was less risky for the client.

In Ancient Rome, banking activities developed greatly and financial operations were established on a juridical basis. The idea of an interest rate on loans and on deposits was born.

1.1.2 The Middle Ages and the Renaissance

After the collapse of the Roman Empire in the late 5th century, monetary circulation slowed down drastically. Economic depression and deflation took place.

The influence of Christianity restricted banking activity: charging interest and usury were seen as immoral.

By the dawn of the 12th and 13th centuries, bankers were grouped into three distinct categories: the pawnbrokers, the moneychangers and the merchant bankers. The cathedral squares remained the centre of the money changers' activity.

At this time, work became a positive virtue: profits were supposed to come from the performance of a duty. The usurer was considered to be a person who earned money without working. The Church condemned usury; in the Third Lateran Council, usurers were excommunicated, usurers' offerings were forbidden as well as their inhumation in Christian ground. Yet, usurers remained in practice.

In the Middle Ages, each Lord or each independent city had the right to strike its own money. Moneychangers changed the money, charging a fixed fee for the transaction. This profession was respectable since it did not involve credit.

Pawnbrokers were considered to be deliberate public sinners, linked to prostitutes. It is at this period that the word "bank" from the Italian word "banca" appeared. "Banca" meant "bench": in the Middle Ages moneychangers or pawnbrokers used to practice their activities on wooden benches. The flat surface of the bench was necessary to display the wares of the lender or the borrower. Note that the term bankruptcy comes from the Italian term "banca rotta" which means that the "banca" has been broken.

At the beginning of the 11th century, the Lombards in Italy introduced new financial techniques and started a new era for the banking activity. The centres of operation were established in Italy: Florence, Genoa, Lucca, Venice and Rome were some of the city-states that gave birth to these banking activities.

That period saw the invention of the customer account: clients received a moderate interest rate on this account on which they could receive and make payments. The depositor was sometimes allowed to overdraw his account within certain limits.

Italian banks developed the letter of credit again; clients could buy a product in a city abroad and see the cash withdrawn on their principal account in their city of origin.

In these times, the notion of liquidity was introduced. The moneylender's business model was simple: lend at a high interest rate and borrow at a usury rate. To survive, banks had simply to ensure the appearance of liquidity and dependability to see the stability of the loans and of the deposits.

1.1.3 From the 17th century to the 20th century

Till the beginning of the 17th century and the invention of the paper check, the value of money was determined by its weight in gold, giving stability to the interest rates.

Trade centres moved to international ports such as Amsterdam or London. Banks started to take risk on the shipping industry: the ships associated with their letters of credit might sometimes not return from the place where they were supposed to carry the exotic goods back from (the voyage to India or America was very uncertain).

Central banks such as the Central Bank of England revolutionized the states' finances before becoming the Bank for the banks in each country.

Napoléon Bonaparte created the French Central Bank, "la Banque de France", on 18 January 1800.

The 19th century was the banks' golden age with the growth and stability of the system and the development of paper money and of scriptural money.

With the First World War, the United States with New York as the new world's leading financial centre became the major lender to the Allied Powers. This resulted in the large growth of the US economy.

After the First World War, the USA started to take a considerable place in the banking system.

1.1.4 The 1929 crisis

In 1929, the crash occurred followed by the "Great Depression". All over the world, markets collapsed and banks were accused of having caused the crash.

In American banking, the reaction was the creation of the Federal Deposit Insurance system and of the Glass–Steagall provisions to separate commercial banking and securities activities.

In the banking industry, from the crisis to the 60s, activity did not grow as fast as before: deposit and loan growth were weak while government influence on financial activity decisions grew faster.

1.2 THE MODERN BANKING INDUSTRY AND THE HISTORY OF ALM

1.2.1 The role of today's bank

Since the Renaissance, banks have been credit institutions providing various types of bank operations:

- receiving deposits;
- granting credits to individuals or corporations;
- providing cash management, means of payment (checks, ATM, credit cards . . .), currency money change;
- storing valuables in safe deposit boxes;
- providing fortune management and financial investment consulting . . .

Banks are the service industry for money, a safe place to deposit money at a moderate interest rate. In banks, we can borrow money so we do not have to wait to make an investment project come true.

Banking activity requires a licence commonly issued by the local bank regulatory authority. This licence gives the right to issue loans and collect deposits. Some financial institutions may provide banking services and are called non-banking financial companies.

The Central Banks of the 18th and 19th century have kept the same role as yesterday: they often control interest rates, inflation rates and money supply. In the case of a liquidity crisis, they may act as "lender of last resort".

An Interbank market has developed to ensure the liquidity of the market: a bank with too many assets may ask other banks for money.

Banking books include reserves and a minimum capital requirement to allow the bank to repay debtors and depositors in case of potential bankruptcy. Basel Committee regulation is the international standard for the calculation of the capital requirements.

Bank profits arise from the fees on financial services and on the difference between the lending rate and the borrowing rate. The overall banking objective is to make profitability on a long-term horizon within the banking system as stable as possible. In fact, the role of regulation is to provide this stability but we will see in this book that his role is also given to ALM.

1.2.2 Types of bank

Nowadays, the banking system recognizes two major types of bank: retail banks and investment banks. It is common to split universal banks between these two different departments: retail and investment banking. In financial service companies, we may find other service types: leasing, factoring, security services and even insurance (in Europe mainly with the "bank-insurance" companies), etc.

Considering retail banking, the customers are individuals or SMEs (small and medium businesses or enterprises).

We may find different types of retail banks: postal saving banks (associated with the national post in the US, in France, etc.), private banks (for wealthy individuals), community development banks (for isolated populations), ethical banks (only investing in socially responsible assets), and mutual bank companies (where shareholders are the customers).

Savings banks are retail banks that took their roots in the 19th century, with the objective of providing saving products to all the categories of savers and usually with a large distribution network.

As for investment banking, the customers are corporations or large businesses willing to act directly with the financial markets. The investment bank may trade for its own accounts but its main activity is to advise corporations on capital markets and to sell financial products to these corporations. Corporations may need advice from investment banks for their mergers and acquisitions, for their financial risk management hedging and for their capital structure refinancing.

The commercial banks are a type of retail bank in the USA that deals with deposits and loans from corporations but not with the capital markets.

1.2.3 The American banking crisis of the 1980s and the necessity of regulation and the implementation of ALM

From 1929 till the mid 60s, the interest rates did not move a lot: bankers used to play according to the 3-6-3 rule: taking deposits at a 3 % rate, lend at 6 % rate and go to play golf at 3 o'clock.

In fact, however, banks are susceptible to many forms of risk: liquidity risk, credit risk, interest rate risk, etc. When a risky scenario becomes true, a banking crisis may follow. Since 1929, prominent examples include the US Savings and Loan crisis in the 80s and early 90s, the Japanese banking crisis during the 90s, etc.

The following figure shows the number of Bank Failures in the United States from 1934 to 1995.

1.2.3.1 The Savings and Loans (S&L) insolvencies

The historically high interest rates between 1980 and 1982 caused insolvencies in the S&L industry.

In 1980, the total assets of S&Ls insured by FSLIC (Federal Savings and Loans Insurance Company) were $ 604 billion. The vast majority of these assets were held in traditional S&L mortgage-related investments. Because of an asset/liability mismatch with a steep ascent of interest rates, net S&L income went down from $ 781 million to negative $ 4.6 billion and $ 4.1 billion in 1981 and 1982.

From 1980 to 1982, 118 S&Ls with $ 43 billion in assets failed, costing the FSLIC an estimated $ 3.5 billion. There were also 493 voluntary mergers and 259 supervisory mergers of S&L institutions.

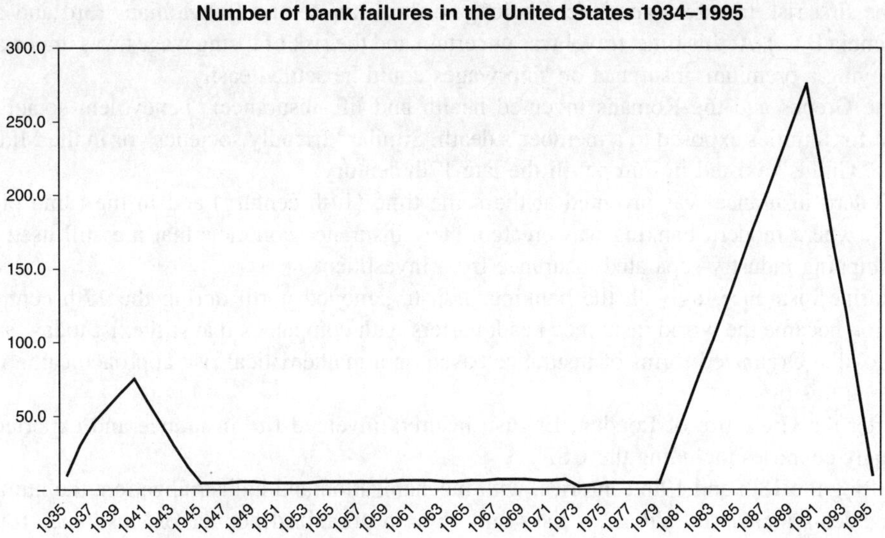

Figure 1.1 Number of bank failures in the United States

The first lesson of the S&L crisis was a regulatory lesson: a need for a qualified, strong, and effective supervision independent from industry with adequate financial resources.

The second lesson of this crisis was the need for indicators to monitor the mismatch risk between assets and liabilities: ALM was born.

1.2.3.2 The real estate crisis

Shortly after, at the end of the 80s, another financial crisis arose with the real estate crisis. Commercial construction activity boomed at the beginning of the 80s due to a large demand for real estate investment. This boom was followed by banks that started to lend within an atmosphere of strong concurrence. Total real estate loans of banks more than tripled. Credit risk taken by banks was very important since the loan-to-values were often close to 100 % and the constraints imposed on customers were weak.

The real estate bubble burst in the late 80s and real estate values collapsed. Loan quality deteriorated and this deterioration caused many banks to fail, especially banks involved in commercial real estate lending.

This crisis was caused by weak credit risk modelling in balance sheet. The Basel regulation framework was a result of this crisis experience.

Consequently, risk management teams and especially credit risk teams found their place in banks' organizations.

1.3 THE HISTORY OF THE INSURANCE INDUSTRY AND ALM

1.3.1 The history of insurance

The will to protect ourselves from the hazards of life is as ancient as human society and leads to the early appearance of the solidarity organization.

The first risk transfer experiences belong to the Chinese and Babylonians (3rd and 2nd Millennia B.C.). At this time, travel was uncertain and the risk of losing wages was important: by paying a premium, insurance on ship wages could be settled easily.

The Greeks and the Romans invented health and life insurance: "benevolent societies" cared for families exposed to a member's death. Similar "friendly societies" or in the Middle Ages "Guilds" existed in Europe till the late 17th century.

Modern insurance was invented at the same time (14th century) and in the same place (Italy) where modern banking was created. New insurance contracts that are still used for the shipping industry separated insurance from investment.

Marine insurance, as with the banking industry, moved north during the 17th century. London became the world insurance headquarters with companies that still exist today, such as Lloyd's. Organized forms of insurance based on a mathematical risk approach came into being at this time.

After the Great fire of London, English insurers invented fire insurance and exported it to many countries including the USA.

During the 18th and 19th centuries, with mechanization and industrialization, the number of accidents increased. With new risks and with an urbanized population, insurance found new areas in which to develop.

In the 20th century, it became an obligation to be insured, with new insurance types such as health insurance, work insurance, etc. Contracting for insurance became common practice after World War II.

In the 70s, with inflationist pressures, individuals started to invest in highly remunerated assets, sometimes using their life insurance as a pledge. In life insurance contracts, many options are sold implicitly to the client. However, it is only at the end of the 70s that insurers began to worry about the risk related to these options.

Options may be of different types:

- option of repayment (right to choose between rent and capital);
- pledge optionality (the client may borrow money on the basis of the market value of his life insurance contracts);
- early prepayment of contracts;
- renewal option (option to extend the term of the contract with its initial terms);
- extra-deposit option (right to invest more than the contractual investment at the initial terms)...

A poor understanding of the options sold implicitly caused the insolvency of some insurance companies: First Capital Holdings and First Executive Corporation in 1991, Baldwin-United in 1983, insurance companies with at least $10 billions of Assets.

1.3.2 Today's insurance industry

Nowadays, insurance is the simplest way to protect against the risk of some uncertain financial losses. Providing this protection against a predictable but significant risk, the insurer charges a premium proportional to the risk.

The risk cannot be an extreme risk in order to provide sufficient solvency for the insurer. Even if insurers may use reinsurance to insure themselves against their extreme risks, customers are protected from insurers' insolvency by systems of Guaranty Funds.

The insurance company's income comes from the premiums and the investment income. Expenses are linked with the incurred losses and the underwriting expenses.

Thus, on the one hand, to become profitable, insurance companies have to calculate the premiums as precisely as possible and to do so they use the actuarial science. Historical databases are used by actuaries to compute the probability and the average cost of the risk arising.

Pricing the premiums should also take into account "anti-selection": customers willing to take insurance are sometimes more exposed to the risk than customers that have the same characteristics in the historical database.

On the other hand, to get profitability, investing the premiums adequately in financial markets is necessary: the premiums are collected before the payment of the claims.

Today's insurance markets are centralized and regulated internationally but the regulation depends on the country. International regulation is derived from the Solvency II regulation framework.

1.3.3 Types of insurance and insurance companies

Among the different types of insurance, we may find auto insurance, health insurance (covering medical bills), liability insurance (for example legal defence in the event of a lawsuit, etc.), casualty insurance (against accidents) or life insurance (providing a sum of money to a family in case of the subscriber's death).

Other types of insurance may be annuities (protecting the retiree from the risk of outliving his financial resources), disability insurance, credit insurance (protecting the bank against the risk of death of the borrower, for example) or environmental liability insurance...

Property insurance protects against fire, weather or theft.

We split insurance companies between three types: life insurance companies (providing life insurance, annuities and pension products), non-life insurance companies and reinsurance companies (highly capitalized companies providing insurance to insurers).

The attractiveness of life insurance products is often due to local tax law regulation: the interest is not taxable under certain circumstances (for example in the UK, in the USA, in France, etc.).

"Producers" usually propose the contracts and "brokers" sell them to the clients. The "brokers" work for many "producers" or directly through the producer's network.

1.4 THE HISTORY OF OTHER BUSINESSES AND ALM

1.4.1 Investment management

Investment management is the management of assets, securities and other various types of investments to meet the objectives of a client (private investor, private banker for the account of their client or institution such as insurance company, pension fund, corporation, etc.).

The investments are usually "mutual funds" managed by a "fund manager". The typical organization is close to the corporate investment bank organization with: research, sales, marketing, middle and back offices, internal audit, controllers, etc.

The relationship between the client and the investment management company is based on the 3 P's rule: Philosophy, Process and People. The investment company fund manager usually works with a Philosophy that has to be explained to the client. Among the possible Philosophies, we may find different types of investment styles:

- "growth" (when deciding to buy stock companies with potentially rapidly growing earnings);
- "value" (when buying stock companies with long-term return);
- market neutral;
- small capitalization, etc.

After having chosen the Philosophy, the Process (i.e. the way the Manager implements the Philosophy) and the People (i.e. the persons that follow the process) there come the other investor's success keys.

Quite often, investment managers work with a benchmark. This benchmark is, for example, the index composed of the proportion of stocks, the proportion of bonds and the proportion of monetary items the client wants his investment's return to look like. A client willing to invest in "aggressive" funds will see his part of stock, for example, around 60 %, bonds around 30 % and monetary items around 10 %. In a "well-balanced" strategy or a prudent strategy, the stock and bond proportion decreases and sometimes goes to zero.

With this benchmark, the asset manager's job is to find the best "asset allocation" with the help of his research teams. The objective is to outperform the peer group of the competing investment funds of the same category (usually working with the same benchmark).

Investment management regulation depends on the country (in the USA, SEC regulates the profession).

Investment Management is a very old ALM problem. Theories about asset allocation go back to the Markowitz Theory (or CAPM). With very simple liabilities (due to the existence of a benchmark), the manager's objective function is to optimize the absolute or the relative performance (compared to the benchmark) of the fund. Markowitz theory invites to use a diversified portfolio in order to benefit from the correlation of the assets.

All this theory is based on the long-term return of the assets. However, the fund accounting is marked-to-market based (the fund "net asset value" is calculated every day or every month): ALM through asset allocation should take into account the risk of underperformance of the funds directly affecting the business revenue (but not the costs, etc.).

1.4.2 Hedge funds

Hedge funds are a new special type of investment fund using unconventional strategies with sometimes a low level of regulation.

Alfred Winslow Jones created the first hedge fund in 1949; his strategy was to sell short stocks and buy others: doing so, a part of the risk present in the fund was "hedged". Many hedge funds still use the long/short strategy but they extend it to the other markets (the bond market, for example).

The main hedge funds strategies include:

- long/short strategy;
- options/derivatives strategy;
- spread arbitrage;
- merger arbitrage (when buying a stock company implied in a merger or acquisition programme, betting on the result of the operation on the stock value);
- event driven strategies;
- global convertible bond arbitrage;

- global macro;
- commodity trading;
- statistical arbitrage, etc.

Another type of hedge funds is the *"fund of funds"* where the hedge fund manager invests in different investments or hedge funds and makes arbitrages among them.

The revenue of the fund management is often a proportion of the amount of assets under management plus a percentage of the fund's net profit. The hedge fund market used to be criticized for its large margins and its weak profitability.

Hedge funds are supposed to have a low risk since the strategies they use contain risk diversification. In fact, however, managers often use what we call the "leverage effect": their strategies use very little cash in order to take strong positions in one risk. For example, when we buy a call option, we get high returns when stocks go up after having paid a very modest premium.

As a conclusion, the extreme risk taken by the manager is important: when tracing the profitability distribution of hedge funds, the graphic often contains a large distribution tail.

Because hedge funds use the same types of strategies, the market is correlated and a systemic risk arises: in unanticipated extreme scenarios, catastrophic losses may occur.

In fact, hedge fund regulation is a major question: a question of methodology (how to regulate such an activity) and a question of regulator training in order to understand this market.

The *failure of Long-Term Capital Management (LTCM)* in 1998 is a good example of what ALM intervention could be in hedge fund management. In 1973, Black, Scholes and Merton developed their famous formula that links the derivative product price with the hedging strategy price. (Two of them received the Nobel Prize for this revolutionary theory in 1997.) Even if they were active members of the hedge fund LTCM, they could not prevent the fund's failure. The fund used the leverage effect on derivatives: it invested a lot of money in order to pay options premiums.

The LTCM example highlights not only the hedge fund systemic risk and the necessity of regulation but also the need for an operational risk management in hedge funds.

2
What is Asset and Liability Management Today?

L'histoire est un perpétuel recommencement. (Thucydide)

The Asset and Liability Management Department is a creation that evolved out of banking and insurance history. The financial crisis of the 80s and 90s (from S&Ls to LTCM) proved the importance of Risk Management in decision taking.

During this period, frightened executive managers created or empowered Risk Management Departments. ALM teams were formed at the same time, bringing organization and strategy into question.

2.1 ALM AND THE BANKING INDUSTRY

2.1.1 Banking Book and Trading Book

We often divide the bank balance sheet in two parts: the Banking Book and the Trading Book.

The Trading Book is made up of all the operations accounted for in marked-to-market coming from the "trading room" businesses: Fixed Income Department, Equity Derivatives Department, Credit Derivatives, Commodity Trading, Forex, etc. It includes derivatives sold to customers, hedging strategy developed in front of these derivatives, Bonds accounted as trading, etc.

The Team responsible for P&L (Profit and Loss) manages the Trading Book.

The usual approach is a "trade approach". For example, the Fixed Income Department through its sales team records a derivative contract with a client. A Fixed Income Trader books the derivative contract presenting a positive valuation. The trader hedges the derivative using futures and may hold a small mismatch position.

The risk taken is minimal and sometimes provides the occasion for provisioning. Managers monitor this risk through technical measures such as VaR (Value-at-Risk) with specialized teams called "Market Risk".

The complexity of the products means higher margins. The implicit "ladder" in the marketplaces lists from the top of the ladder to the bottom: credit derivatives, interest rates exotic products, equity derivatives exotic products, interest rate derivatives, equity derivatives, Forex (foreign exchange) derivatives and finally Treasury Department at the bottom.

The Banking Book is the sum of all the operations recorded by the accountants on an "accrued" basis (including of course the retail banking operations): loans to individuals, to corporations, deposits, investment and debt accounted as available for sale (AFS) or Held to Maturity (HTM).

The ALM objective in banks is to concentrate on the financial position held in the Banking Book.

For accounting and regulatory reasons, the risk management for the Banking Book differs from the one for the Trading Book: nothing is as simple as the delta hedging strategy used by fixed income or equity derivatives. An asset and liability manager needs to know how to manipulate actuarial calculations, statistical modelling, accounting, marketing business model, etc.

2.1.2 Bank organization

In banks, the organization makes a distinction between risk management (RM), treasury and financial direction. The ALM position in the bank organization is often inside the risk management, sometimes inside the Treasury Department and sometimes inside the Budget Department. (The final chapters of this book try to explain the best ALM position in the Bank organization chart.)

Risk management looks after the risks and historically after the credit risk and the market risk included in trading books.

The treasury's objective is often to monitor very short-term liquidity risk and to reduce bid/ask on interbank loans and the cost of deposits. The treasury has a monopolistic access to financial markets with the objective of a better volume/cost arbitrage. The treasury pilots the overall liquidity position.

Financial direction looks after accounting and budgeting.

The implementation of ALM in the Banking Book introduces a set of organizational questions:

- taking of responsibility for AFS and HTM investments;
- differentiation between financial risk taking and commercial risk taking: the objective is to guarantee the businesses their commercial margins through transfer prices;
- refinancing assets and replacing liabilities;
- taking the financial risks related to the refinanced assets and liabilities;
- bank's equity piloting;
- currency risk, interest rate risk and liquidity risk piloting;
- looking after "added value" when working with the interest rate and liquidity markets;
- transmitting to businesses the financial engineering competences when marketing a new product, implementing a new business strategy, etc.

The position of ALM in the organization depends on the orientation decided upon by the Bank's executive management: either more risk oriented, or more investment oriented.

In primitive organizations, ALM is a part of RM and the treasury has the responsibility for investment.

In advanced organizations, ALM acts as a long-term treasury responsible for long-term investments and for associated risk. In such a case, there is a need for an independent team to monitor the accuracy between reports and the position in reality.

2.2 OTHER GENERAL ALM QUESTIONS

In insurance organizations, ALM usually plays the risk management role. The Investment Department plays the role of the Treasury Department.

In Investment funds, the role of ALM is divided between the fund managers (for investment), the financial directors (for strategy and marketing) and sometimes the risk management team.

Perfect positioning in ALM is on its way in all businesses but is considered to be a cyclical activity with a contra-cyclical role. In market equilibrium, ALM seeks to find the points of equilibrium between risk aversion (with preference for the present, for the fixed rate borrowing, etc.) and the risk premium earned when taking positions.

ALM represents the banker, the insurer or the asset manager role in order to take a calculated risk for a premium in front of a market that is risk averse.

This is what we call *"Transformation"*:

- when lending using long fixed rates loans and accepting short floating rate deposits;
- when lending using long-term loans and accepting sight deposits;
- when playing with long/short Equity;
- and when replacing long short-term insurance contracts, etc.

ALM's role is assuming importance at a time of banking system concentration. The Balkanized US banking system, the globalization of the economy, the growth of two-digit emerging markets and the creation of the Euro zone are pushing the banks to merge. The size of the new merged banks implicates to present a faithful comprehension of the assets and the liabilities to the market. Pressure from financial analysts forces the establishment of a successful ALM team.

Regulation, as we will see later, is a key point in the development of ALM: Basel II requirements and Solvency II showed that regulators tend to require a better understanding of ALM risk by the banks.

New IFRS accounting regulation provided the occasion to highlight the ALM profession. During discussions on the adoption of rules, asset and liability managers sat down with accountants to explain financial risk definitions for the operational teams when, for example, deciding upon derivative hedging accounting opportunities. The question was, for example, to know how a swap contract could hedge a demand deposit.

Part II
Internal Transfer Pricing, Accounting and Auditing

Asset and liability managers deal with the balance sheet. The forecasting of future income requires a fine understanding of the accounting standards. The first chapters of this Part are devoted to the balance sheet and to the accrued accounting schemes (or "at historical cost"), to IFRS accounting and to full fair value accounting schemes.

The implementation of an internal system of *internal transfer prices* or of *fund transfer prices (FTP)* is the basis of asset and liability management.

This Part develops the FTP concept and provides some examples of FTP calculation introducing the important *"péréquation"* (or "perequation") concept.

FTP implementation allows us to transform the ALM into an independent profit centre and to differentiate the incomes (financial results) arising from commercial businesses and the incomes arising from financial market risk positions.

3

Balance Sheet Presentation

Tout fait somme.

Assets and liability management means dealing with assets and liabilities, it means dealing with "balance sheet" and "accounting" notions.

A/L managers are not accountants and many of them know very little about the details of accounting standards.

Nevertheless, to understand the whole ALM business, the A/L manager needs to understand his balance sheet and to have some notions of accounting.

3.1 GENERAL BALANCE SHEET PRESENTATION

We will take our balance sheet main example from a financial company example. We have also included an example of an insurance company balance sheet.

In the balance sheet, *the total assets are equal to the total liabilities*. This obvious remark will be very helpful when considering the further product carry cost. *Each asset (respectively each liability) has its liability (respectively each asset); by default the corresponding liability (asset) is a treasury refinancing (at a DD rate cost).*

The asset is a mix of investments, of treasury products and of commercial trades. The liability is a mix of debt, of equity and of commercial trades.

From this accounting presentation, the A/L manager's work will start with the reorganization of the balance sheet.

3.2 A/L MANAGER'S BALANCE SHEET PRESENTATION

ALM book separation is based on trading position isolation and on the differentiation of the commercial book with the capital book.

Book separation by the A/L manager is motivated by the result of separation that *improves company management control*.

3.2.1 Trading Book isolation

The first book to isolate in the balance sheet is the Trading Book. This *trading book* includes all the commercial operations accounted in marked-to-market (i.e. held for trading purpose) with their associated hedge products.

This Trading Book usually belongs to commercial activities; dealt by the trading floor market operators.

This book is usually not within the scope of the A/L manager's study of financial risk (except for the liquidity risk); Market risk analysts study this risk.

	Year Y		Year Y
Cash and amounts due from central banks and post office banks	7 000	Due to central banks and post office banks	1 000
Financial assets at fair value through profit or loss	700 000	Financial liabilities at fair value through profit or loss	600 000
Derivatives used for hedging purposes	4 000	Derivatives used for hedging purposes	1 000
Available-for-sale financial assets	90 000	Due to credit institutions	120 000
Loans and receivables due from credit institutions	45 000	Due to customers	250 000
Loans and receivables due from customers	300 000	Dept securities	85 000
Remeasurement adjustment on interest-rate risk hedged portfolios	−50	Remeasurement adjustment on interest-rate risk hedged portfolios	1 000
Held-to-maturity financial assets	15 000	Current and deferred tax liabilities	2 000
Current and deferred tax assets	2 000	Accrued expenses and other liabilities	43 696
Accrued income and other assets	50 000	Technical reserves of Insurance companies	80 000
Investments in associates	2 000	Provisions for contingencies and charges	4 000
Investment property	5 000	Subordinated debt	16 000
Property, plant and equipment	10 000	**Total liabilities**	**1 203 696**
Intangible assets	1 500	Share capital and additional paid-in capital	10 000
Goodwill	10 000	Retained earnings	20 000
		Net income for the period attributable to shareholders	7 454
		Total capital and retained earnings attributable to shareholders	**37 454**
		Unrealised or deferred gains and losses attribitable to shareholders	5 500
		Shareholders' equity	**42 954**
		Minority interests	−5 200
		Total consolidated equity	**37 754**
Total assets	**1 241 450**	**Total liabilities and equity**	**1 241 450**

Figure 3.1 Balance sheet

3.2.2 Commercial Book and Capital Book differentiation

The main intervention by the A/L manager consists of a separation between the balance sheet analysis and the hedge depending on the product objective. The purpose is to separate the risk and the profitability of the commercial sphere from the risk and the profitability of the financial sphere.

The *commercial book* consists of all the commercial products not accounted as marked-to-market with their associated hedges: the commercial book is made up of instruments measured at "*historical cost*".

The commercial book equilibrium is set through a specific DD rate cost indexed product line. In our example, the commercial book could take the form:

	Year Y		Year Y
Loans and receivables due from credit institutions	45 000	Due to credit institutions	120 000
Loans and receivables due from customers	300 000	Due to customers	250 000
Remeasurement adjustment on interest-rate risk hedged portfolios	−25	Debt securities	85 000
Derivatives used for hedging purposes	2 000	Remeasurement adjustment on interest-rate risk hedged portfolios	500
		Derivatives used for hedging purposes	500
Commercial Banking Book equilibrium	109 025		
Total assets	456 000	Total liabilities	456 000

Figure 3.2 Commercial Book balance sheet

The *capital book* consists of all the other products: equity products, debt products, financial investments products and other non-commercial assets. The hedges associated with these products are of course within this capital book.

In our example, the capital book could take the form:

	Year Y		Year Y
Cash and amounts due from central banks and post office banks	7 000	Due to central banks and post office banks	1 000
Financial assets at fair value through profit or loss	700 000	Financial liabilities at fair value through profit or loss	600 000
Available-for-sale financial assets	90 000		
Derivatives used for hedging purposes	2 000	Derivatives used for hedging purposes	500
Remeasurement adjustment on interest-rate risk hedged portfolios	−25	Remeasurement adjustment on interest-rate risk hedged portfolios	500
Held-to-maturity financial assets	15 000	Current and deferred tax liabilities	2 000
Current and deferred tax assets	2 000	Accrued expenses and other liabilities	43 696
Accrued income and other assets	50 000	Technical reserves of Insurance companies	80 000
Investments in associates	2 000	Provisions for contingencies and charges	4 000
Investment property	5 000	Subordinated debt	16 000
Property, plant and equipment	10 000	Total liabilities	747 696
Intangible assets	1 500	Share capital and additional paid-in capital	10 000
Goodwill	10 000	Retained earnings	20 000
		Net income for the period attributable to shareholders	7 454
		Total capital and retained earnings attributable to shareholders	**37 454**
Equity Banking Book equilibrium	−109 025	Unrealised or deferred gains and losses attributable to shareholders	5 500
		Shareholders' equity	**42 954**
		Minority Interests	−5 200
		Total consolidated equity	37 754
Total assets	785 450	Total liabilities and equity	785 450

Figure 3.3 Capital Book balance sheet

3.2.3 The isolation of the Treasury Book (Funding Book)

It is also possible to create a treasury book within the capital book. The principle is to separate strictly the equity and its hedging from the pure treasury products. The tacit objective of separation is thus to move all the liquidity risk in the simple treasury book.

However, the commercial book also contains liquidity risk. The only way to create a treasury book that concentrates all the liquidity positions is to make *internal transfers between books*.

The A/L manager usually records the debt instruments in this book. Regulators will recognize the Tier 1 and the Tier 2 described in the following figure:

TIER 1: Equity Capital	Shareholder's equity Reserves Minority interests Deeply Subordinated Bonds	
TIER 2: Supplementary Capital	UPPER TIER 2	Subordinated Bond Provisions and other reserves
	LOWER TIER 2	

Figure 3.4 Tier 1 and Tier 2

A/L managers use the terms junior and senior. For example, deeply subordinated bonds (DSB) are junior to all other debt instruments but senior only to any classes of shares.

3.2.4 Book split according to the risk: one risk type/one book

The Commercial Book example shows how *books should be split according to the types of risk* we will develop in further sections:

- Business Book (one book for each business line);
- Liquidity Book (or treasury book);
- interest rate commercial book;
- Interest Rate Capital Book;
- Currency Book, etc.

To ensure the real risk transfer, the A/L manager has to record *internal fictitious operations*:

- FTPs that are developed later are the internal way to compute these transfers;
- internal market operations could also be recorded directly in the systems: swaps, currency forward.

For each book, a profit & loss (P&L) has to be computed. This way, the accountants will measure the risk profitability, risk by risk.

Book	Sub-book	Managed Risk
Commercial Book	Retail Business book Corporate Business book Commercial Interest Rate book Retail Business credit book ...	Retail Business risk Corporate Business risk Interest Rate Risk within Commercial Book Retail Business credit risk ...
Capital Book	Capital Interest Rate Risk ...	Interest Rate Risk within Capital Book ...
Treasury Book	Liquidity Book Currency book ...	Liquidity risk Currency risk ...

Figure 3.5 One risk = One book

3.3 BANKING BOOK AND INSURANCE BOOK

3.3.1 Examples of balance sheet in customer retail banking and in corporate retail banking

The A/L Manager splits the Banking Book between the different currencies, €, USD, GBP, JPY, etc.

Classic retail banking books are made of these different loans:

- mortgages;
- consumer loans;
- overdrafts.

And with these different liabilities:

- demand deposits;
- savings;
- fixed rate deposits.

The Banking Book incorporates many different hedges, such as bonds, swaps, or options.

Across the world, there are many differences between the characteristics of the loans: the balance sheets asset side of the German banks consist of fixed rate loans. This is the same for Dutch, French or Spanish banks also. On the other hand, English banks work essentially with variable rate loans.

The A/L manager will distinguish between:

- the *retail balance sheet* made of retail loans and retail deposits;
- the *corporate balance sheet* made of corporate loans and corporate deposits.

The *off-balance sheet* is made with all the commitments that are still not transformed into effective loans or deposits. The A/L manager distinguishes between:

- disbursement delays when the credit disbursement is predictable (e.g. mortgage disbursement delays);

- lines of credit (when the bank guarantees to the customer an amount of cash he can use as a credit).

3.3.2 The Capital Book in the banking industry

The A/L manager in the banking industry splits the Capital Book by currency.

The Capital Book is made of the equity, the reserves and the net income of the period attributable to shareholders. It contains also goodwill, fixed assets, minority interests and preferred shares.

On the liability side, the book integrates the debts and the subordinated debts. On the asset side, the book incorporates financial assets such as held-to-maturity investments and available-for-sale assets (equity, properties, etc.).

There are also many possible hedges in the balance sheet: swaps, options, etc.

3.3.3 Example of a balance sheet in an insurance company

Liabilities arising from insurance contracts are usually split between:

- life & savings;
- property and casualty;
- international insurance.

There is a strong distinction between liabilities arising from an insurance contract and those arising from an investment contract. In those contracts, it is important to know if the financial risk is borne by policyholders or not.

These liabilities may integrate discretionary participating features. Of course, the resinsurances will take a negative part in the liabilities.

Liabilities arising from insurance contracts	
Future policy benefits reserve Life & Savings	190 000
Unearned premium reserve	7 000
Claims reserve	40 000
Other reserves	60 000
Liabilities arising from insurance contracts	**297 000**
Future policy benefits reserve	90 000
Claims reserve	100
Other reserves	20
Liabilities arising from insurance contracts where the financial risk is borne by policyholders	**90 120**
Reinsurers' share in future policy benefits reserve	4 000
Reinsurers' share in Unearned premium reserve	
Reinsurers' share in claims reserve	4 000
Reinsurers' share in other reserves	100
Reinsurers' share in liabilities arising from insurance contracts	**8 100**
Reinsurers' share in future policy benefits reserve	10
Reinsurers' share in Unearned premium reserve	
Reinsurers' share in claims reserve	
Reinsurers' share in other reserves	
Reinsurers' share in liabilities arising from insurance contracts where the financial risk is borne by policyholders	**10**
TOTAL LIABILITIES ARISING FROM INSURANCE CONTRACTS NET OF REINSURANCE CEDED	**379 010**

Figure 3.6 Insurance Book liabilities

3.4 INCOME STATEMENT AND STATEMENT OF CASH FLOWS

The following table provides an example of an income statement for a financial company.

		Year Y	Year Y−1
Interest Income		**29 935**	**29 063**
	Customer items	**15 005**	**14 568**
	Deposits, loans and borrowings	13 000	12 621
	Repurchase agreements	5	5
	Finance leases	2 000	1 942
	Interbank items	**3 100**	**3 010**
	Deposits, loans and borrowings	3 000	2 913
	Repurchase agreements	100	97
	Debt securities issued	–	–
	Cash flow hedge instruments	**2 000**	**1 942**
	Interest rate portfolio hedge instruments	**400**	**388**
	Trading book	**8 030**	**7 796**
	Fixed-income securities	2 000	1 942
	Repurchase agreements	6 000	5 825
	Loans/borrowings	30	29
	Debt securities	–	–
	Available-for-sale financial assets	**3 000**	**2 913**
	Held-to-maturity financial assets	**800**	**777**
Interest expense		**18 860**	**18 311**
	Customer items	**5 960**	**5 786**
	Deposits, loans and borrowings	5 800	5 631
	Repurchase agreements	80	78
	Finance leases	80	78
	Interbank items	**5 200**	**5 049**
	Deposits, loans and borrowings	5 000	4 854
	Repurchase agreements	200	194
	Debt securities issued	**3 500**	**3 398**
	Cash flow hedge instruments	**800**	**777**
	Interest rate portfolio hedge instruments	**300**	**291**
	Trading book	**7 700**	**7 476**
	Fixed-income securities	–	–
	Repurchase agreements	6 000	5 825
	Loans/borrowings	100	97
	Debt securities	1 600	1 553
	Available-for-sale financial assets		–
	Held-to-maturity financial assets	–	–
Commission income		**9 000**	**8 738**
Commission expense		**4 000**	**3 883**
Net gain/loss on financial instruments at fair value through profit ot loss		**4 500**	**4 369**
	Variable income securities	1 0000	9 709
	Derivatives instruments	6 000	5 825
	Remeasurement of currency positions	500	485
Net gain/loss on available-for-sale financial assets		**1 100**	**1 068**
	Fixed-income securities gains and losses on disposals	100	97
	Equities gains and losses on disposals	1 000	971
Income from other activities		20 000	19 417
Expense on other activities		17 000	16 505
Net banking income		**24 675**	**23 956**
Operating expense		13 000	12 621
Depreciation, amortisation and impairment of property, plant and equipment and intangible assets		1 000	971
Gross operating income		**10 675**	**10 364**
Cost of risk		650	631

Figure 3.7 Banking Book statement of income

Operating Income	**10 025**	**9 733**
Share of earnings of associates	400	388
Net gain/loss on non-current assets	200	194
Change in value of goowill	20	19
Pre-tax net Income	**10 605**	**10 296**
Taxes	2 651	2 574
Net income	**7 954**	**7 722**
of which minority interests	500	485
Net income before minority interests	**7 454**	**7 237**
Basic earnings per share	503	488
Diluted earnings per share	497	483

Figure 3.7 (Continued)

The net income includes taxes and is based on the operating income made of the gross operating income less the cost of risk (i.e. the cost of the credit risk). This operating income is the difference between the net banking income and the operating expenses. The net banking income is made of the net interest income (interest income less interest expenses) and the commission (or fees).

The following table provides an example of an income statement for an insurance company.

CONSOLIDATED STATEMENT OF INCOME	Year Y
Gross written premiums	66 000
Fees and charges relating to investment contracts with no participating feature	500
Revenues from insurance activities	**66 500**
Revenues from other activities	5 000
Total Revenues	**71 500**
Change in unearned premiums of unearned revenues and fees	**500**
Net investment income (from investment property, fixed maturities, equity securities, loans, derivative, etc.)	14 000
Net realized investment gains and losses	3 500
Change in fair value of financial instruments at fair value through profit & loss	16 000
Change in financial instruments impairment	200
Net investment result excluding financing expenses	33 300
Technical charges relating to insurance activities (acquisition costs, staff costs, administrative costs, etc.)	82 000
Net result from outward reinsurance	140
Bank operating expenses	60
Acquisition costs	6 500
Amortization of the value of purchased business in force and of other intangible assets	600
Administrative expenses	8 500
Other income and expenses	84
Other operating income and expenses	**97 884**
Income from operating activities before tax	**6 416**
Income arising form investments in associates – Equity method	20
Financing debts expenses	600
Operating income before tax	**5 836**
Income tax	1 459
Net operating result	**4 377**
Change in goodwill impairment	70
Net consolidated income	**4 307**
Minority interests share in net consolidated result	500
Net income Group share	**3 807**

Figure 3.8 Insurance Book statement of income

In annual reports (or in see further IAS 32 reports), the companies have to publish a statement of its annual cash flows. This type of statement is helpful to financial analysts. Since they wish to verify that their comprehension of financial business is in accordance with the treasury cash flows of the company they study.

An A/L manager, when making a risk analysis, can exploit a great deal of information from this type of table.

The following table provides an example of a statement of cash flows for our example.

	Year
Pre-tex net income	**10 605**
Non-monetary Items included in pre-tax net income and other adjustments	**2 700**
Net depreciation/amortization expense on property, plant and equipment and intangible assets	
Impairment of goodwill and other non-current assets	
Net addition to provisions	
Share of earnings of associates	
Net income/ loss from investing activities	
Net loss income/ from financing activities	
Other movements	
Net decrease in cash related to assets and liabilities generated by operating activities	**10 000**
Net increase in cash releated to transactions with credit institutions	
Net decrease in cash related to transactions with customers	
Net decrease in cash related to transactions involving other financial assets and liabilities	
Net increase in cash related to transactions involving non-financial assets and liabilities	
Taxes paid	
Net decrease/increase in cash and equivalents generated by operating activities	**2 095**
Net decrease in cash related to acquisitions and disposals of consolidated entities	
Net decrease related to property, plant and equipment and intangible assets	
Net decrease in cash and equivalents related to financing activities	6 000
Decrease in cash and equivalents related to transactions with shareholders	
Other increases in cash and equivalents generated by financing activities	
Net increase/decrease in cash and equivalents related to financing activities	6 000
Effect of movements in exchange rates on cash and equivalents	100
Net increase in cash and equivalents	**910**
Balance on cash and equivalent accounts at the start of the period	**7 500**
Net balance of cash accounts and accounts with central banks and post office banks	
Net balance of demand loans and deposits – credit institutions	
Balance on cash and equivalent accounts at the end of the period	**6 590**
Net balance of cash accounts and accounts with central banks and post office banks	
Net balance of demand loans and deposits – credit institutions	
Net increase in cash and equivalents	**910**

Figure 3.9 Statement of cash flows

4
"Accrued Accounting" for Interest Rate Instruments Versus "Marked-to-Market" Accounting

Jamais mal acquit ne profite (Villon)

4.1 GENERAL PRINCIPLES

"Accrued accounting" may be seen as the opposite of "marked-to-market accounting".

"Marked-to-market accounting" refers to a way of measuring products at a fair value price, i.e. at an observable quoted price or at a computed selling price. The P&L (profit and loss) associated with the product on a single day period is the simple difference between the two marked-to-market.

For example, consider a government bond bought at par at date t for a nominal amount of 100 with an annual coupon of 5 % (paid at date t+1). In those conditions, the disbursed amount is of 100 as well.

On date t+1, the government bond market price is of 101.

The P&L associated with the Bond for the period [t; t+1] will be of 6:

- 1 for the market price move from 100 to 101;
- 5 for the coupon paid on t+1.

Of course, each product has to be refinanced. Here comes the notion of *P&L net of carry* (i.e. *free of cost of carry*). *The whole balance sheet is well balanced.* The assets total is equal to the liabilities total. To represent a P&L and to take into account this necessary equilibrium, the P&L free of cost of carry subtracts the cost of the mobilized cash on the period to the simple P&L.

In our example, if the cost of cash on the period [t; t+1] was of 4 % (the average capitalized DD rate on the period plus the liquidity company cost), the marked-to-market P&L free of cost of carry would be of 6 – 4 i.e. 2.

On the other hand, *"accrued accounting"* or *"measurement at historical cost"* refers to a way of measuring products considering only the interests paid or received during the period. The P&L (profit and loss) associated with the product on a single day period is the simple amount of interest paid or received on the period.

In our simple example, the accrued P&L associated with the bond is of 5 and the P&L free of cost of carry is of 1.

The P&L depends highly on the accounting method. As seen in our example, the P&L may vary and sometimes may have a different sign between accrued and marked-to-market accounting (as described in the full fair value section).

In the long-term, at the product end, all the accounting methods are equivalent. This can easily be proven when demonstrating that the marked-to-market is the sum of all the discounted incomes whatever the accounting method is.

Nevertheless, *the hedging strategy will depend highly on the accounting method and on the P&L volatility coming from the method.* For example, the accrued accounting implies a very low volatility in the incomes and does not encourage the hedging.

4.2 ACCRUED ACCOUNTING EXAMPLES

4.2.1 Bonds with premium or discount

In the bond accounting example presented above, the bond was bought at par. When the bond is bought at a price different from par, a *premium* (when the price is above 100) or a *discount* (when the price is under 100) has to be accounted.

If the bond was bought at a price of 110, a premium of 10 is incorporated and smoothed in the P&L incomes. In the past, the smoothing used to be sometimes linear: the negative impact of the 10 was taken uniformly across time.

Today, the premium/discount cost impact on P&L is smoothed using an actuarial method: the impact is computed as if the premium/discount was financed through a loan with fixed monthly payments or though a deposit (with the bond yields as interest).

In our example, the negative impact on the period [t; t+1] is of −1.81 as described on the table below:

	Amount	Interest of 5 %	Constant annuity	P&L impact
Period 0	**10.00**			
Period 1	8.19	0.50	2.31	**1.81**
Period 2	6.29	0.41	2.31	**1.90**
Period 3	4.29	0.31	2.31	**2.00**
Period 4	2.20	0.21	2.31	**2.10**
Period 5	0.00	0.11	2.31	**2.20**

Figure 4.1 P&L impact of bond premium / discount

When selling the bond (for example an "available-for-sale" bond) before its term, the P&L computed is the difference between the cash received from the operation and the remaining cash in the balance sheet: the nominal of the bond plus the amount of premium/discount not yet impacted on the P&L.

4.2.2 A simple example with FTP: demand deposits

The demand deposit accounting example is a simple example that shows the use of FTP in the balance sheet income decomposition.

At the company level, the P&L free of cost of carry arising from demand deposit with zero remuneration is the interest coming at DD rate from the collected cash K less the interest paid to the client (it means zero):

$$\text{Net P\&L (company)} = \text{K . DD} - 0 = \text{K . DD}$$

At the Commercial Department level, the demand deposits have been collected at their FTP price:

$$\text{Net P\&L (Commercial Department)} = K \,.\, FTP - 0 = K.\, FTP$$

At the ALM (or treasury) level, the demand deposits have been collected at the FTP price and refinanced on the market at DD rate:

$$\text{Net P\&L (Commercial Department)} = K \,.\, DD\text{-}\ K \,.\, FTP = K.(DD\text{-}FTP)$$

Two observations come from this example:

- *The company net P&L is the sum of the net P&Ls* of its entities: commercial plus ALM.
- *The company risk on demand deposits is transferred to the ALM through the FTP.*

5
IFRS and IAS Accounting

Brebis comptées le loup les mange. (Virgile)

As seen in the previous chapter, the accounting standard directly affects the hedging behaviour of managers: volatility in the incomes may arise from the chosen accounting method and thus may encourage the manager to hedge his positions or to forget them.

In this context, a new international accounting standard arose by the end of the 90s in order to promote a presentation of company income that was uniform worldwide. The **International Financial Reporting Standards (IFRS)** were introduced to encourage this worldwide harmonization of the accounting rules.

5.1 IFRS, INTERNATIONAL ORGANIZATIONS AND RULE PRESENTATION

5.1.1 International organizations

5.1.1.1 IASB organization

The *International Accounting Standards Board (IASB)* was founded in April 2001 (on the model of American FASB) as the successor of the International Accounting Standards Committee (IASC) founded initially in 1973. IASC is now a non-profit organization with 19 trustees while IASB consists of 14 members ("The Board") with 12 full-time members (five members must be former auditors, three former preparers of accounts, three former users of accounts and one an academic).

The IASB has three main objectives:

- setting International Financial Reporting Standards;
- promoting the IFRS and imposing them as a reference;
- contributing to the international harmonization of accounting practices and of presentation of financial statements.

5.1.1.2 Local accounting organizations

5.1.1.2.1 American organization

It is true that the IFRS are close to the US accounting rules called **US GAAP**. The United States Securities and Exchange Commission (SEC) requires all overseas companies listed in the US to prepare their incomes under US GAAP.

Nevertheless, there are still differences between the IFRS and the US GAAP promoted by the US Financial Accounting Standards Board.

5.1.1.2.2 European organization

All publicly traded European Union companies have been required since 2005 to prepare their consolidated accounts using IFRS. The European version of the IFRS is called IFRS-EU.

In Europe, the EFRAG (European Financial Reporting Advisory Group) is in charge of all the technical questions regarding the elaboration of the rules.

The ARC (Accounting Regulatory Committee) is a regulatory committee presided over by the European Commission; this committee approves and endorses the IAS rules with the recommendation of the EFRAG.

The CESR (Committee of European Securities Regulators) is responsible for the overseeing and for the effective and rigorous application of the IAS rules.

5.1.2 Overview of the rules

The accounting standards consist of the International Financial Reporting Standards (IFRS) along with International Accounting Standards (IAS issued by IASC between 1973 and 2001). IAS rules are no longer produced but they are still in effect unless they were replaced by an IFRS.

The actual norms include:

- a "Framework for the Preparation and Presentation of Financial Statements", this framework provides the basic principles of IFRS;
- the 41 IAS, the standards issued before 2001;
- the IFRS, the standards issued after 2001;
- the 32 SIC interpretations of accounting standards established by the Standing Interpretation Committee (SIC);
- the IFRIC i.e. the newer interpretations issued after 2001.

The major international accounting standards currently in use are the following:

IFRS 1	First-time Adoption of International Financial Reporting Standards
IFRS 2	Share-based Payment
IFRS 3	Business Combinations
IFRS 4	**Insurance Contracts**
IFRS 5	Non-current Assets Held for Sale and Discontinued Operations
IFRS 6	Exploration for and Evaluation of Mineral Resources
IFRS 7	**Financial Instruments: Disclosures**

IAS 1	Presentation of Financial Statements
IAS 2	Inventories
IAS 7	Cash Flow Statements
IAS 8	Net Profit or Loss for the Period, Fundamental Errors and Changes in Accounting Practices
IAS 10	Events After the Balance Sheet Date
IAS 11	Construction Contracts
IAS 12	Income Taxes
IAS 14	Segment Reporting
IAS 15	Information Reflecting the Effects of Changing Prices

Figure 5.1 IFRS standards

IAS 16	**Property, Plant and Equipment**
IAS 17	**Leases**
IAS 18	**Revenue**
IAS 19	**Employee Benefits**
IAS 20	Accounting for Government Grants and Disclosure of Government Assistance
IAS 21	**The Effects of Changes in Foreign Exchange Rates**
IAS 22	Business Combinations
IAS 23	Borrowing Costs
IAS 24	Related Party Disclosures
IAS 26	Accounting and Reporting by Retirement Benefit Plans
IAS 27	Consolidated Financial Statements
IAS 28	Investments in Associates
IAS 29	Financial Reporting in Hyperinflationary Economies
IAS 30	Disclosures in the Financial Statements of Banks and Similar Financial Institutions
IAS 31	**Financial Reporting of Interests in Joint Ventures**
IAS 32	Financial Instruments Disclosure and Presentation
IAS 33	Earnings per Share
IAS 34	Interim Financial Reporting
IAS 35	Discontinuing Operations
IAS 36	**Impairment of Assets**
IAS 37	**Provisions, Contingent Liabilities and Contingent Assets**
IAS 38	**Intangible Assets**
IAS 39	**Financial Instruments: Recognition and Measurement**
IAS 40	**Investment Property**
IAS 41	Agriculture

Figure 5.1 (Continued)

5.2 IAS 39

The most important IAS for A/L managers is IAS 39 (Financial Instruments: Recognition and Measurement). IAS 39 deals with the measurement of financial instruments and with their recognition, i.e. their valuation and their inclusion in financial statements. The rules also proposes special rules for hedge accounting and for impairment.

IAS 39 applies the principle of current value.

5.2.1 Recognition of Financial instruments

5.2.1.1 Scope

IAS 39 applies to all types of financial instruments but excludes:

- loan commitments (generally outside of the scope of IAS 39);
- insurance contracts treated in IFRS 4;
- the financial instruments covered by other norms (pensions, consolidated interests in subsidiaries, employers' rights, own equity, etc.);
- rights and obligations under leases (treated in IAS 17);
- leases treated in IAS 17.

Contracts to buy or sell financial items are within the scope of IAS 39.

Contracts to buy or sell non-financial items are within the scope of IAS 39 if they can be settled net in cash (or another financial asset) and are not entered into and held for the purpose of the receipt or delivery of a non-financial item in accordance with the entity's expected purchase, sale, or usage requirements.

5.2.1.2 Recognition and derecognition

IAS 39 provides a definition of a financial instrument: "A contract that gives rise to a financial asset of one entity and a financial liability or equity instrument of another entity."

A financial asset or liability is recognized when the entity becomes a party to the instrument contract.

A financial liability is derecognized when the liability is extinguished (i.e. when the obligation specified in the contract is either discharged, cancelled, or expired). A gain or loss from extinguishment of the original financial liability is recognized in the income statement.

A financial asset is derecognized in the cases below:

- the contractual rights to the cash flows from the asset expire;
- the entity transfers substantially all the risks and rewards of ownership of the asset;
- the entity transfers the asset, while retaining some of the risks and rewards of ownership, but no longer the ability to sell the asset. The risks and rewards retained are still recognized as an asset.

5.2.1.3 Financial assets

A *financial asset* is any asset that is:

- cash;
- an equity instrument of another entity;
- a contractual right to receive another financial asset from another entity;
- a contractual right to exchange financial assets (or financial liabilities) with another entity under conditions that are potentially favourable to the entity;
- a contract that will or may be settled in the entity's own equity instruments:
  - — a non-derivative for which the entity is or may be obliged to receive a variable number of the entity's own equity instruments;
  - — a derivative that will or may be settled other than by the exchange of a fixed amount of cash or another financial asset for a fixed number of the entity's own equity instruments.

IAS 39 requires the classification of financial assets in one of the following categories:

- *financial assets at fair value through profit or loss*;
- *available-for-sale financial assets* **(AFS)**;
- *loans and receivables*;
- *held-to-maturity investments* **(HTM)**.

Asset recognition and measurement is made under this classification.

5.2.1.3.1 *Financial assets at fair value through profit or loss (trading assets)*

Financial assets at fair value through profit or loss incorporate:

- the financial assets designated to be measured at fair value;
- the financial assets held for trading: derivatives (except hedging instruments and short-term profit objective financial assets).

Those assets will be measured at fair value. The fair value variations will be recognized in the income.

5.2.1.3.2 *Available for sale assets (AFS)*

AFS assets are non-derivative financial assets not held for trading, different from loans and receivables and not necessarily detained till their maturity. In particular, a company may sell its available-for-sale assets.

Equity investments are often recognized as AFS assets. AFS assets are measured at fair value in the balance sheet.

Interest on AFS assets is recognized in income on an effective yield basis. Impairment losses and foreign exchange gains or losses are also recognized in the income. Nevertheless, *fair value changes on AFS assets are recognized directly in equity*, through the statement of changes in equity.

When an AFS asset is derecognized (sold for instance), the cumulative gain or loss that was recognized in equity is recognized in profit or loss.

The *IAS 39 fair value option* provides the opportunity for each AFS asset to recognize fair value changes in income in some cases (asset/liability mismatch or embedded derivatives).

5.2.1.3.3 *Held to maturity investments (HTM)*

HTM investments are non-derivative financial assets with fixed or determinable payments that an entity intends and is able to hold to maturity. These investments cannot be loans or receivables and are not designated on initial recognition as assets at fair value through profit or loss or as AFS assets. The intention and the ability to hold these investments are evaluated at each closing date.

Equity investments cannot be recognized as HTM investments.

Note: If an entity sells a HTM investment, all of its other HTM investments must be reclassified as AFS for the current and next two financial reporting years. This is called the *tainting rule*.

HTM investments cannot be hedged with interest rate derivatives. HTM investments are measured at amortized cost after deduction of impairment.

5.2.1.3.4 *Loans and receivables*

Loans and receivables are non-derivative financial assets with fixed or determinable payments (originated or acquired) that are not quoted in an active market, not held for trading, and not designated on initial recognition as assets at fair value through profit or loss or as AFS. Those assets are issued as a compensation of a transfer of liquidity (or goods or services) to a debtor.

Loans and receivables are measured at amortized cost after deduction of impairment.

5.2.1.3.5 *A note for real estate investments*

For real estate investments, two rules are applicable: IAS 16 for the property and IAS 40 for the investment property.

Properties are not recognized as financial assets. The general rule is to measure them at amortized cost with the component approach for the amortizing calculation (the time to amortize depends on the nature of the components: elevator, building shell, etc.).

Nevertheless, some property investment funds are accounted as financial assets at fair value through profit or loss.

5.2.1.4 Financial liability and equity

A *financial liability* is a financial instrument with a contractual obligation to deliver cash or other financial assets or a contract that will or may be settled in the entity's own equity instruments.

A contract with obligation to exchange financial assets or financial liabilities with another entity under conditions that are potentially unfavourable to the entity is also a financial liability.

A financial instrument is *equity* if it evidences a residual interest in the assets of an entity after deducting all of its liabilities.

Convertible debt is separated into its debt and equity components (debt with premium and option). Note also that liabilities include mandatory redeemable shares, such as units of a mutual fund and some preferred shares.

The finance cost of liabilities is accounted as an expense. Payments on equity are treated as distributions, not as expenses.

IAS 39 requires the classification of financial liabilities in one of two categories:

- Financial liabilities at fair value through profit or loss. As for the financial assets of the same type, these liabilities are either designated at fair value by the entity upon initial recognition or held for trading.
- Other financial liabilities measured at amortized cost using the effective interest method.

5.2.1.5 Derivatives and embedded derivatives

Before the introduction of IFRS, many countries did not recognize derivatives as financial instruments and recognized them as off-balance sheet instruments.

A *derivative* is a financial instrument settled at a future date that requires no initial investment. Its value changes in response to the change in an underlying variable (such as an interest rate, commodity or security price, or index).

The rule recognized many different derivatives: forwards, FRA, interest rate swaps, futures, options, caps and floors, etc.

According to the IFRS, derivatives should appear in the balance sheet and be recognized at fair value unless they correspond to a hedging strategy (cash flow hedge for instance).

The fundamental principle of IAS 39 is that every derivative should be measured at its fair value, even *embedded derivatives*, i.e. derivatives incorporated in non-financial instruments called *host contracts*. An embedded derivative is a feature within a contract, such that the cash flows associated with that feature behave in a similar fashion to a stand-alone derivative. Embedded derivatives should then be separated from their host contracts. IAS 39 requires derivatives that are embedded in non-derivative contracts to be accounted separately at fair value through profit or loss (or at the derivative appropriate standard).

An exception is made for embedded derivatives **closely related** to the host contract. For example, in the following contracts, the derivative should be extracted:

- convertible debts;
- commodity, credit or equity indexed interest or principal payments in host debt contracts;
- contracts with "in-the-money" caps or floors;
- currency derivatives in purchase or sale contracts.

On the other hand, in a debt contract including an interest rate derivative, the embedded derivative will not be extracted:

- if the index is an inflation index (no extraction of inflation derivative in OATi or TIPS, etc.);
- or if the option does not double the yield of a classic debt instrument.

This last rule allows the A/L manager to buy AFS bonds including options but with a cap on the bond yield.

Moreover, embedded derivatives do not have to be extracted in the following cases:

- loans with prepayment option;
- capped loans with "out-of-the-money" caps.

5.2.1.6 Measurement

5.2.1.6.1 General considerations

Initially, financial assets and liabilities should be measured at fair value. For assets and liabilities not measured at fair value through profit or loss, this fair value includes transaction costs.

The table below summarizes the different IAS 39 measurement rules:

	Amortized cost using effective rate method	Measurement at fair value. Gains taken to equity. Losses taken to equity	Measurement at fair value through profit or loss. Gains and losses recognized in profit or loss
Trading assets & liabilities Derivatives (except hedging) Designated assets and liabilities			X
Loans and receivables	X		
Other financial liabilities	X		
HTM	X		
AFS		X	

Figure 5.2 IAS 39 measurement rules

"*Fair Value* is the amount for which an asset could be exchanged, or a liability settled, between knowledgeable, willing parties in an arm's length transaction". Fair value can be obtained through:

- quoted market prices;
- market valuation techniques such as discounted cash flow analysis, option-pricing models.

If these computations are not possible or too uncertain, the fair value measurement is made at cost less impairment. For instance, investments in equity instruments with no reliable fair value measurement should be measured at cost.

The *effective interest rate* is the rate that discounts exactly the estimated future cash payments or receipts through the expected life of the financial instrument to the net book value of the financial asset or liability (i.e. its carrying amount). This is the internal yield rate of the contract.

Note also that on disposal, AFS gains and losses taken previously to equity are recycled to profit or loss.

5.2.1.6.2 IAS 39 fair value option

There is an option to account for any financial asset or liability at fair value through profit or loss if fair value can be measured reliably even if by nature the financial instrument would have been measured at amortized cost.

After long discussions with regulators and practitioners, the IASB limited this option to the financial instruments with conditions:

- the Fair Value option designation eliminates or significantly reduces an accounting mismatch (asset versus liability mismatch);
- or a group of financial assets, financial liabilities, or both is managed and its performance is evaluated on a fair value basis, in accordance with a documented risk management or investment strategy, and information about the group is provided internally on that basis to the entity's key management personnel.

The fair value option can be applied as well to a contract containing an embedded derivative, thereby eliminating the need to separate out the embedded derivative.

Note also that IAS 39 permits to designate loan and receivables as AFS.

5.2.2 Hedging relationships

5.2.2.1 Hedge accounting

A large part of the IAS 39 rules concentrates on *hedging relationships*. There are three recognized hedging strategies in IAS 39:

- **Fair Value Hedge (FVH)** in order to hedge the possible risk on Fair Value changes.
- **Cash Flow Hedge (CFH)** in order to hedge the possible risk on Cash Flow changes.
- **Net Investment Hedge** for currency risk hedging.

Each hedging strategy has to be documented precisely at inception with a precise effectiveness test (80–125 % rules). Indeed, the hedging instrument is expected to offset almost fully changes in fair value or cash flows of the hedged item that are attributable to the hedged risk. All hedge ineffectiveness is recognized immediately in profit or loss.

Hedge effectiveness has to be measurable reliably and be assessed on an ongoing basis. Any forecast transaction being hedged has to be "highly probable".

To avoid this documentation, the alternative is to use the fair value option whenever possible: the natural hedge is to measure the hedged item and the hedging instrument at fair value.

In the FVH, fair value of both the hedging instrument and the hedged item are reported in profit or loss.

In the CFH (as for the net investment hedge), changes in the fair value of the hedging instrument are reported initially in equity and transferred to profit or loss to match the recognition of the offsetting gains and losses on the hedged transaction.

In order to provide discipline, some basic rules are laid down in order to prevent accounting arbitrage (especially for internal hedges).

5.2.2.2 *Hedging instruments*

Hedging instruments are only derivative contracts with an external counterparty. A proportion of the derivative may be designated as the hedging instrument but a set of cash flows in a derivative cannot be designated as a hedging instrument.

Nevertheless, the intrinsic value and the time value of an option contract may also be separated (with only the intrinsic value being designated). In a forward, the interest element and the spot price can also be separated (with the spot price being the designated risk).

5.2.2.3 *Hedged items*

The list of the possible hedged items is the following:

- a single recognized asset or liability, firm commitment, highly probable transaction, or a net investment in a foreign operation;
- a group of these instruments but with similar risk characteristics;
- the credit risk or the foreign currency risk part of an HTM investment;
- a portion of the cash flows or fair value of a financial asset or a financial liability;
- in a portfolio hedge of interest rate risk (macro hedge) only, a portion of the portfolio of financial assets or financial liabilities that share the risk being hedged.

Own equity and Tier 1 cannot be hedged by derivatives. If a company wants to smooth the income arisen from the replacement of this equity, the replacement should be done in HTM or AFS bonds.

5.2.2.4 *Discontinuation of hedge accounting*

Hedge accounting must be discontinued in the following cases:

- the hedging instrument expires or is sold, terminated, or exercised;
- the hedge accounting criteria (including effectiveness criteria) are not respected;

- the future cash flows are no longer expected to occur (for CFH only);
- The hedge designation is revoked by the entity.

In the third case, when a CFH relationship stops, gains and losses deferred in equity must be taken to the income statement immediately.

In other cases of CFH relationship endings, the amounts accumulated in equity will be retained in equity until the hedged item affects profit or loss.

5.2.2.5 *Cash flow hedge*

The *cash flow hedge* objective is to hedge the uncertain flow variations of a hedged instrument to market movements. The exposure to variability in cash flows has to be attributable to a particular risk with a recognized asset or liability (such as a part of the future interest payments on variable rate debt) or a highly probable forecast transaction. The exposure should also affect profit or loss.

Note: with CFH, the future production of contracts cannot be hedged; only the highly probable cash flows arising from existing contracts can be hedged.

When a cash flow hedge exists, the fair value movements, on the part of the hedging instrument that is effective, are recognized in equity until the hedged item affects profit or loss. Any ineffective portion of the fair value movement on the hedging instrument is recognized in profit or loss.

For instance, it means that variable rate cash flows may be transformed in fixed rate cash flows. This analysis makes the cash flow diagram of the financial statements coherent.

Hedging instrument fair value variations go in equity and are progressively amortized in the income. Accruals go into the income. *CFH creates volatility in the equity.* In the following example taken from the banking ALM, the possible transactions to be hedged are variable rate credits. The hedging is made through a fixed rate against short-term rate swap.

Initial date

Assets		Liabilities	
Euribor loan	100	Treasury	50
		Equity	50
		Swap	0

Future date

Assets		Liabilities	
Euribor loan	100	Treasury	50
		Equity	40
		Swap	10

Figure 5.3 CFH hedging

The accrual interests of the CFH are accounted in the income statement symmetrically to the hedged operations.

Any gain or loss on the hedging instrument that was previously recognized directly in equity is "recycled" into profit or loss in the same period(s) in which the financial asset or liability affects profit or loss.

In terms of options, the following instruments can be recognized as CFH:

- purchase of swaption (as a hedge of short-term rate indexed loans/deposits);
- purchase of collar swaption on floating rate (as a hedge of short-term rate indexed loans/deposits);
- purchase of caps (or cap spreads) on short-term indexes (as a hedge of short-term rate indexed loans/deposits);
- purchase of CMS floors (as a hedge of fixed rate loans/deposits highly probable cash flows);
- purchase of CMS collars (as a hedge of fixed rate loans/deposits highly probable cash flows).

The following options are difficult to link as a CFH:

- selling of swaptions;
- selling of cap or floors.

5.2.2.6 Fair value hedge

5.2.2.6.1 General considerations

The objective of the *fair value hedge* is to hedge the possible changes in fair value of a hedged instrument due to market movements. Usual hedged items are AFS assets, loans and receivables or other financial liabilities measured initially at amortized cost.

A financial asset or liability measured initially at amortized cost will change its accounting standard once fair value hedged.

The hedging instrument and the hedged instrument are measured at fair value. The gain or loss from the change in fair value of the hedging instrument is recognized immediately in profit or loss. The corresponding fair value movements on the hedged item are recognized in profit or loss.

At the same time, the book value of the hedged item is adjusted for the corresponding gain or loss with respect to the hedged risk (which is also recognized immediately in net profit or loss).

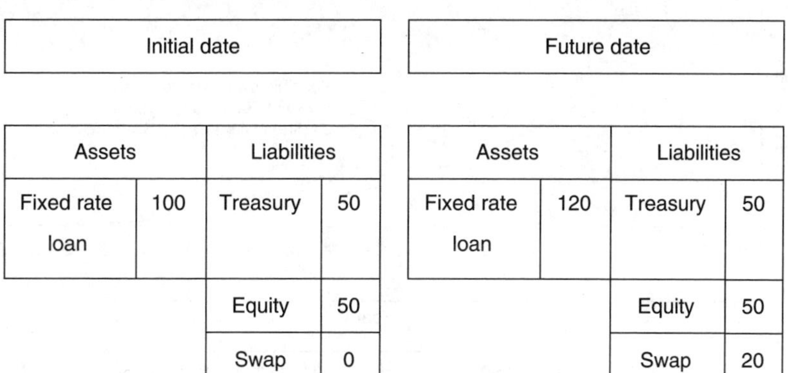

Figure 5.4 FVH hedging

Finally, only the ineffectiveness of the hedging goes into profit and loss.

In the ALM sector, *FVH transforms fixed rate assets or liabilities in floating rate assets or liabilities*.

There is no effect of FVH on the equity. Moreover, in our example, the profit is equal to zero traducing a perfect hedge.

$$[0 = (120 - 100) + (0 - 20)]$$

Note also that fair value hedging means that the entity is able to compute the fair value of the hedged instrument and to measure it in fair value.

5.2.2.6.2 Portfolio hedge of interest rate risk (macro hedging)

The rules allows FVH accounting for a portfolio hedge of interest rate risk (macro hedging). This type of hedging is particularly interesting when working on infinitely granular portfolios when a micro hedging transaction by transaction is impossible (since operations are too small to be analysed one by one).

The analysis starts with an identified portfolio, which can include assets and liabilities. The portfolio analysis is made on the expected (not contractual) repricing schedule. The hedged item is designated by the entity as a percentage of this portfolio repricing date by repricing date.

The entity designates a hedging instrument for each time period and a risk (such as fixed rate against Libor interest rate risk).

The fair value changes of the hedging instrument and of the hedged instrument are recognized as a gain or loss in profit or loss.

Ineffectiveness could come from the difference between the initial hedge ratio (applied to the initially estimated amount in a time period) and that same ratio (applied to the revised estimate of the amount).

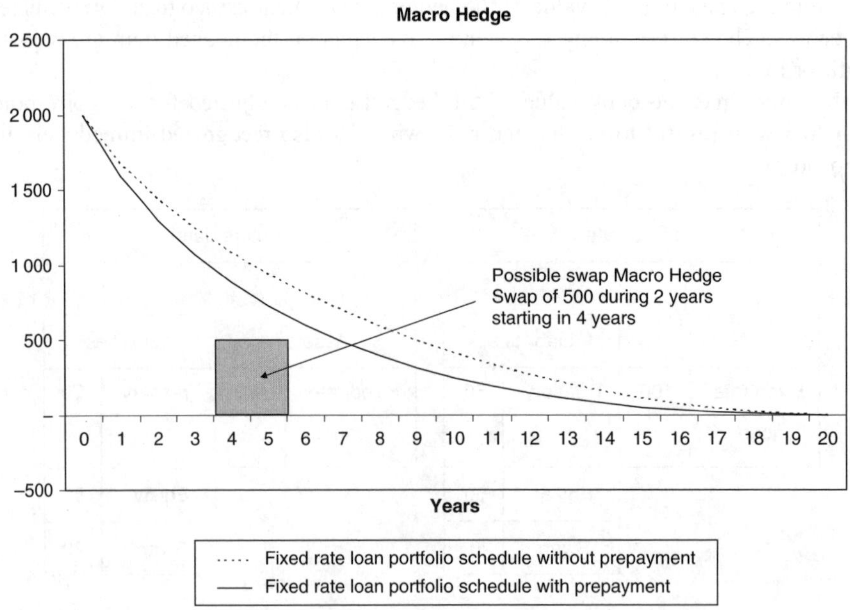

Figure 5.5 Macro hedging

Unfortunately, *demand deposits* and similar items with a demand feature cannot be designated as the hedged item in a fair value hedge. FVH does not recognize deposits payable immediately on demand as a possible hedged instrument.

5.2.2.7 *Carved out fair value hedge (COFVH)*

The carved out fair value hedge **(COFVH)** extends the FVH macro hedge to demand deposits. Demand deposits are represented using their interest rate schedule based on the statistical schedule of the existing demand deposit account.

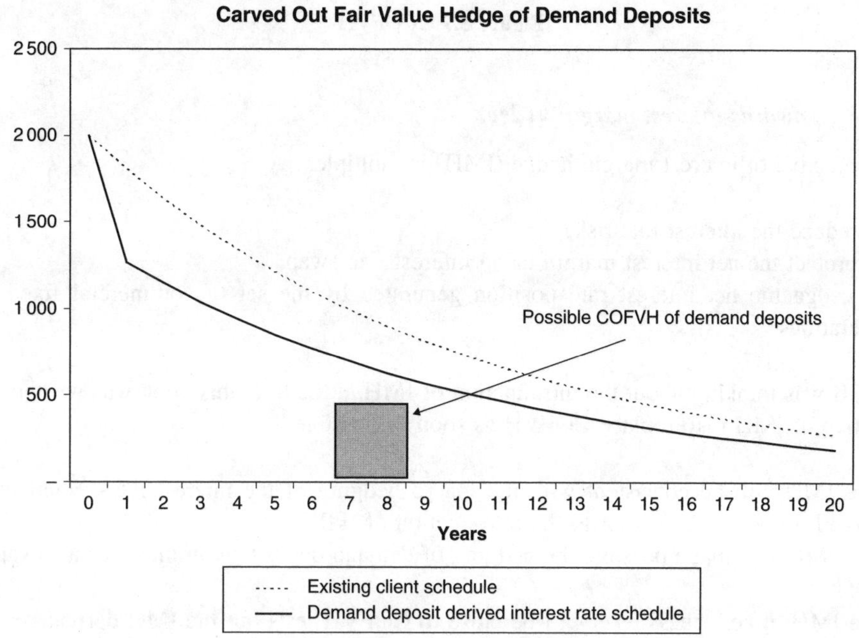

Figure 5.6 Carved out fair value hedge

Unfortunately, for the moment the COFVH is only possible in the EU (and not in the US GAAP).

The COFVH creates a new "adjustment line for the hedged component" as shown in the following example.

In the statement of income, the net income is made of:

- the accruals on the fixed rate loans and on the deposits;
- plus the variation of the fair value of the swap and of the hedged component adjustment (i.e. not very far from the accruals on the swap).

Once a portfolio has been COFVHed, incomes and equity are not sensible to the interest rate moves.

Initial date				Future date			
Assets		Liabilities		Assets		Liabilities	
Fixed rate loan	100	Demand deposit	100	Fixed rate loan	100	Demand deposit	100
		Adjustment	0			Adjustment	20
Swap	0	Equity	0	Swap	20	Equity	0

Figure 5.7 COFVH

5.2.2.8 Towards interest margin hedge?

The objective of interest margin hedge (IMH) is multiple:

- to reduce the interest rate risk;
- to protect the net interest margin using interest rate swap;
- to hedge the net interest rate position generated by the set of commercial fixed rate operations.

IASB was thinking about the introduction of IMH at the time this book was written. The objective of IMH is to replace COFVH as soon as possible:

- The IMH will be consistent with the macro hedging of the interest rates practiced by some European banks prior to the introduction of IFRS.
- The IMH will make possible the hedging of demand deposits with interest rate swaps.

The IMH effectiveness tests will be close to COFVH tests but the IMH derivatives will surely be closer to CFH derivatives accounting.

5.2.2.9 Hedging effectiveness

Every hedging relationship has to be documented explicitly: there is no "hedging presumption".

IAS 39 requires hedge effectiveness to be assessed *prospectively and retrospectively at inception and at each reporting date.*

The changes in the fair value or cash flows of the hedged item must be expected to be highly effective in offsetting the changes in the fair value or cash flows of the hedging instrument.

The effectiveness test should be within a range (confidence interval) of 80 % to 125 %.

All hedge ineffectiveness is recognized immediately in the income statement.

In banking ALM, effectiveness test consists of the comparison between the hedging instruments schedules and the financial hedged assets and liabilities. The test is carried out for each homogeneous hedged instrument.

To justify the CFH, the A/L manager needs enough floating rate assets or liabilities (with constraints on the homogeneous indexations and on the fixing dates):

- Euribor 3 months indexed assets for receiver swaps against payer Euribor 3 months justification;
- Euribor 3 months indexed liabilities for payer swaps against receiver Euribor 3 months justification.

In practice, ineffectiveness will come with the disappearance of the hedged instrument (e.g. excessive loan prepayment, etc.).

5.2.2.10 *Internal contracts*

Hedge accounting for internal hedges is prohibited since, of course, internal transactions are eliminated on consolidation.

The initial idea is to prohibit the double measurement of a same financial instrument. Before the introduction of IFRS, some banks used to book swaps between the banking book and the trading book as follows:

- at amortized cost in the banking book as a banking book hedge;
- at fair value through profit and loss as a "held for trading" in the trading books.

IAS 39 clarifies what needs to be done in order to achieve hedge accounting in this case (when internal hedges are used as a route to the market, via an internal treasury centre).

In practice, the entity has to demonstrate that there is an external compensation for each internal contract.

The other option is to avoid internal contracts and replace them by loans and deposits. Indeed, an interest rate swap can be decomposed in a loan plus a deposit.

5.2.2.11 *Application to senior debt instruments*

Senior debt instruments including options can be fair value hedged if they include embedded options.

It is classic to use the fair value option for a debt instrument, its embedded option and its hedge.

Nevertheless, the fair value may evolve according to the evolution of the company spreads. The impact on the income of the spread volatility is accepted badly by executive management. Consequently, the debt is often measured at fair value except for the liquidity spread part that is still measured at amortized cost (the initial spread is fixed all along the contract life).

The Tier 1 debt is classified as equity and no hedging through derivatives is possible.

5.2.3 IAS 39 (and others): impairment of assets and of loans including credit risk impairment

IAS 39 deals with *impairment on financial assets*. Impairment is another main characteristic of IFRS measurement rules. Impairment occurs when losses should be recognized in profit or loss on those assets that are not accounted at fair value through profit or loss.

Impairment may affect:

- an asset for its *established risk impairment*;
- a group of assets of the same risk type: impairment for *portfolio impairment*. For credit risk impairment, the impairment is made using the default probabilities, the internal notations and the Basel II loss given defaults. The estimations are made on historical bases and eventually corrected by expert advices.

The impairment is computed at each balance sheet date. Impairment should be recognized as soon as there is an evidence of the loss resulting from a past event. *Impairment will not take into account losses that might happen in the future.*

The difference between the present value of the discounted cash flows (using the initial effective interest rate) and the asset book value represents the amount of loss to be recognized.

Impairment is recognized in profit or loss (impairment losses on AFS assets are taken from equity to be recognized in profit or loss). The book value of the asset is reduced.

Impairment in equity investments is recognized once there is objective evidence of the issuer's market position change or once there is a significant or prolonged decline in the investment's fair value.

The impairment could decrease due to an event occurring after the impairment is recognized originally. In such a case, the previously recognized impairment loss is reversed through profit and loss. Nevertheless, impairments relating to investments in available-for-sale equity instruments are not reversed.

Complementary to IAS 39, the A/L manager will find complementary impairment in the following IAS: IAS 2 (inventories), IAS 11 (construction contracts), IAS 12 (deferred tax assets), IAS 19 (employee benefits), IAS 40 (investment property), IAS 41 (agriculture), IFRS 4 (Insurance) and IFRS 5.

IAS 36 delivers accounting rules for the impairment of goodwill, intangible assets and property, plant and equipment in terms of recognition, measure, tests and disclosure. An impairment loss should be recognized whenever the recoverable amount of an asset is less than its book value.

5.3 FINANCIAL DISCLOSURES

IFRS rules do not only look after accounting but also the presentation of financial statements.

5.3.1 IAS 30 and banks' disclosures

Initially, IAS 30 provided for disclosures in financial statements of banks and similar financial institutions. The norm has been applicable since 1991.

Banks are supposed to present:

- an income statement grouping incomes and expenses by type and disclosing the principal amounts of incomes and expenses;
- a balance sheet with assets and liabilities grouped by type and listed according to their relative liquidity (from the more liquid to the less liquid).

Among the other items that should be presented are:

- fair value of each class of financial assets or liabilities;
- residual maturities of assets and liabilities;
- concentrations of assets and liabilities (by geographical area, customer type, etc.);
- secured liabilities and nature and amount of assets pledged as security;
- different information about commitments, contingencies and losses on loans (with their associated impairment or provisions).

IAS 30 is supposed to be replaced by IFRS 7, discussed below.

5.3.2 IAS 32 (disclosure of financial instruments) and IFRS 7 (disclosures checklist)

IAS 32 proposes the disclosure of financial instruments and deals with their presentation in financial statements. The objective is to present to the financial analysts a uniform worldwide presentation of financial instruments and of their associated risks. This will help them to understand the significance of financial instruments in terms of risk, performance and cash flows. The main disclosures of IAS 32 will be:

- risk presentation;
- risk management policies presentation;
- accounting policies presentation with the clarification of financial instrument classification and the presentation of instruments' fair values;
- presentation of the instruments' business purpose.

IAS 32 deals with all the financial instrument types except insurance contracts (IFRS 4), interests in subsidiaries (IAS 27, 28 and 31), share-based payment transactions (IFRS 2), business combinations (IFRS 3) and employee benefits (IAS 19).

Of course, the definitions of the financial instruments used in IAS 32 are the same as those used in IAS 39.

The purpose of IFRS 7 in 2004 was to put all financial instruments disclosures together in a new standard (IAS 32 would then deal only with financial instruments presentation and the disclosures required by IAS 30 would be replaced by IFRS 7). IFRS 7 has been valid since 2007.

The main disclosure requirements of IFRS 7 are:

- the regrouping of similar instruments into classes;
- the disclosure of information about the significance of regrouping and the nature of risk.

5.3.2.1 Balance Sheet (IFRS 7)

The entity should present the balance sheet's significant instruments for each category:

- held for trading assets;
- other financial assets measured at fair value through profit and loss designated at initial recognition;

- HTM investments;
- loans and receivables;
- AFS assets;
- financial liabilities held for trading;
- other financial liabilities measured at fair value through profit and loss designated at initial recognition;
- financial liabilities measured at amortized cost.

5.3.2.2 *Income statement and equity*

IAS 32 requires the disclosure of material items concerning the income statement:

- items of income, expense, gains, and losses, with separate disclosure of gains and losses from:
  - — held for trading assets;
  - — other financial assets measured at fair value through profit and loss designated at initial recognition;
  - — HTM investments;
  - — loans and receivables;
  - — AFS;
  - — financial liabilities held for trading;
  - — other financial liabilities measured at fair value through profit and loss designated at initial recognition;
  - — financial liabilities measured at amortized cost.
- gains and losses resulting from financial assets and financial liabilities (included in profit or loss/included in equity);
- fee income and expense;
- amount of impairment losses on financial assets;
- interest income on impaired financial assets;
- interest income and interest expense for those financial instruments that are not measured at fair value through profit and loss.

5.3.2.3 *Disclosures about the terms and conditions of financial instruments*

Balance sheet disclosure is not enough; the IAS 32 rules require further disclosure for each class of financial asset, financial liability and equity instrument.

The entity should inform about the extent and nature of the financial instruments with the significant terms and conditions (amount, timing and certainty of future cash flows):

- principal;
- scheduled future cash flows;
- date of maturity expiry or execution;
- early settlement options;
- conversion options;

- rate or amount of interest, dividend, or other periodic return on principal and the timing of payments;
- collateral held and pledged liability;
- currency.

The accounting policies and methods adopted have also to be disclosed.

5.3.2.4 *Risk management and hedges disclosures*

The risk management policies of the company have to be disclosed according to IFRS 7:

- qualitatively with the risk exposure for each financial instrument type, management's objectives, policies and processes for managing those risks;
- quantitatively with quantitative data about exposures to each risk (including credit risk, liquidity risk, market risk, interest rate risk and concentration risk, etc.).

Associated with risk management policies, hedges (fair value, cash flow and net investment hedges) have also to be disclosed with the presentation of:

- hedge and its risk nature;
- hedging instruments and their fair values;
- CFH expected cash flows to come;
- Hedge ineffectiveness.

Regarding CFH, the entity has to disclose the amount recognized in equity during the period, the amount removed from equity and included in profit or loss and the amount removed from equity and included in the initial measurement.

5.3.2.5 *Interest rate risk disclosures*

5.3.2.5.1 *General disclosures*

IAS 32 asks for a precise disclosure of interest rate risk for each class of financial assets and financial liabilities. The interest rate risk position is disclosed. The disclosure is now close to the Basel II Pillar 2 regulatory disclosure.

IAS 32 requires information about the risk on cash flows and on fair value.

The entire interest rate risks position has to be taken into account:

- The computation is made at a consolidated level.
- The non-interest bearing demand deposits are scheduled according to their interest rate schedule.
- The calculus includes explicit and implicit interest rate option.
- The presented schedules are real schedules rather than contractual schedules.
- Prepayment risk is included.
- Assets and liabilities without maturity (equity, goodwill, intangible assets, etc.) have to be scheduled.

The rules also describe the form of communication: qualitative and quantitative with the elaborating hypotheses.

The rules propose communication based on the interest rate gap and on the effective interest rates. *The contractual repricing dates and the maturity dates will be disclosed.*

The interest rate gap is often disclosed by maturity bands or by repricing dates.

This indicator is the most appropriate indicator and is not subject to interpretation. This is also its main inconvenience: in the gapping indicator, interest rate schedules (for demand deposits and for equity) and finally the real interest rate position are revealed.

5.3.2.5.2 Other possible disclosures

Instead of presenting the interest rate gap as an indicator, it is possible to choose another risk indicator such as economic value sensitivity or the income sensitivity. Those two indicators will be described in the next chapters.

Economic value sensitivity can be computed under the Basel II framework. Nevertheless, this indicator is easily manipulated.

The "income sensitivity" indicates sensitivity of the net income to interest rate moves on a limited horizon. This indicator integrates the future new productions but it is easy to "manipulate" it.

To avoid such manipulation, financial institutions will have to *disclose all the hypotheses* behind their computations.

5.3.2.6 Credit risk disclosures

Credit risk exposure has also to be disclosed for each class of financial asset and for each other credit exposure:

- maximum amount of exposure;
- description of collateral and pledges;
- concentration of credit risk;
- analytical disclosures for past due or impaired financial assets;
- defaults (details and amounts in terms of principal, interest, etc.).

5.3.2.7 Liquidity risk disclosures (IFRS 7)

Liquidity risk will also be disclosed with these elements:

- a description of the liquidity risk management;
- a liquidity gap (called maturity analysis of financial liabilities).

5.3.2.8 Market risk disclosures (IFRS 7)

Market risks will also be disclosed with the presentation of:

- the sensitivity analysis of each market risk type the entity is exposed and for each combined risk (e.g. the combined interest rate/currency risk);
- a more complex sensitivity analysis (such as VaR) that reflects market risk interdependencies.

5.3.2.9 Fair value of financial instruments disclosures

One of the most important IAS 32 disclosures concerns the *fair value disclosure.*

Even if a financial instrument is measured at cost under IAS 39, the estimate of the fair value has to be disclosed in the annexes of the financial statements. The calculation method of these fair values has to be disclosed (quoted price, discounted cash flows, etc.) with the main calculus hypotheses. The fair value should exclude the credit component of the fair value.

This fair value represents the amount to receive in order to exchange the asset or the amount to pay in order to stop the liability. These amounts are determined between counterparties well informed and without concurrence.

This allows the direct comparison with the book value.

5.3.2.10 Other disclosures

The IAS 32 and IFRS 7 also focus on different disclosures:

- disclosure about derecognition;
- disclosures about compound financial instruments;
- disclosures about financial assets and liabilities at fair value through profit or loss (amounts held for trading and other amounts, etc.);
- disclosures about reclassifications;
- disclosures about market liquidity;
- details about an entity's own equity, an entity's own objectives, policies and processes for managing capital;
- reconciliation of the allowance account for credit losses.

5.4 IFRS AND INSURANCE

IFRS 4 and IAS 39 have a special impact on insurance contracts.

5.4.1 General considerations

The IFRS also affects:

- the classification of financial assets and liabilities;
- the recognition of derivatives and the embedded derivatives (hedging for instance);
- Impairment;
- Consolidation.

The introduction of the IFRS rules is made in two phases: a first phase where only the assets are accounted at fair value (but liabilities at amortized cost) and a second phase where liabilities will also be accounted at fair value.

Strategic allocation is impacted by the introduction of IFRS. Specifically, investments in real estate (usually), deconsolidated entities and investments in asset management funds have to be consolidated.

The use of derivatives is made more difficult due to the complexity of implementing the hedging relationships.

The strategic allocation consists of risk exposures rarely eligible for hedging. Introduction of fair value brings volatility to the income.

The strategic long-term investments will be recognized as HTM investments but they cannot represent the largest part of the balance sheet.

The directional investments will be recognized as AFS assets with a low rotation rate.

The tactical allocation will be accounted at fair value.

5.4.2 IFRS phase 1

During the first phase of the introduction of IFRS, there will be an asymmetric treatment of assets and of liabilities: liabilities are accounted at amortized cost when assets are accounted at fair value (through profit or loss or through equity). It is indeed difficult to recognize assets as HTM investments since these assets cannot be sold.

"IFRS phase 1 improves consistency, enhances transparency and reduces hidden gains and losses on investments." IFRS Phase 1 "applies to insurance contracts as defined, insurance accounting remains, equalization reserves are not permitted; it is not also permitted to increase prudence of reserves, some contracts will require unbundling, increased disclosure requirements, investments will be at Fair Value".

In order to limit the volatility and to limit the asymmetry between assets and liabilities, the IASB introduced the "shadow accounting". Liabilities are retreated to take into account the policyholders' participation in the latent profit and losses. Consequently a large part of the potential latent gains of the assets can be returned on the liabilities once it is assumed that a part of these latent gains belong to the policyholders.

5.4.3 IFRS phase 2

IFRS phase 2 was programmed initially for 2007. The objective of phase 2 is to integrate the value of options and guarantee the liabilities.

On the liability side, the contract should be measured at fair value (with the term of ESV: entity specific value) using models based on the modelling of the policyholder and of the insurer.

The ESV cannot be under the buy-back value to the customer (the price the customer can ask for the reimbursement of his contract).

IFRS phase 2 introduces the question of the market value margin (MVM) and is likely to remove hidden prudential margins and thus to reduce accounting volatility.

Impairment can be accounted if the accounted value of liabilities is insufficient to reimburse the discounted sum of cash flows due to customers.

This impairment is tested at each reporting date and measured through profit and loss.

5.5 OTHER IFRS SPECIFICITIES

5.5.1 Consolidation and securitization

IFRS is computed on a consolidated basis (IAS 27, 28 and 31). All the internal deals disappear, only the external deals are involved.

In IFRS, SPVs (special purpose vehicles) have to be consolidated. An asset is consolidated as soon as the detention percentage is higher than 20 %; between 20 % and 50 %, the consolidation is made with the equity method, above 50 %, the consolidation is global.

This annihilates previous opportunities in past standards to deconsolidate SPVs used for securitization: many companies used to buy back parts issued by a controlled SPV, i.e. buying back their own risks but as a part issued by a SPV.

5.5.2 Stock options

Stock options are now accounted in the balance sheet with IFRS. The option value is measured as an expense when granted to the employees. The expense is smoothed all along the acquisition period of these rights.

This is the same for the differed bonuses paid in equities.

5.5.3 "Smoothing/spreading" and margins

IAS 18 and 39 introduced the effective interest rate method. The idea of this method is to give a constant interest rate including fees and all the cash flows of the financial contracts. In particular, the fees are smoothed in the contract.

This computation is made for all the financial instruments measured at amortized cost.

The fair value computations integrate also a contract margin. The *"day one profit"*, i.e. the margin made on the first day of an operation is smoothed on the expected life of the contract. This margin of course does not exist for the fair values computed with quote prices.

Smoothing is also required when an instrument measured at amortized cost is derecognized before its initial end. The profit or loss then realized is smoothed over the initial residual life of the contract. This is true for prepayment indemnities (for prepayment loans) and for CFH swaps breaks, etc.

5.5.4 Capital Banking Book and IFRS

The Capital Banking Book is also impacted by IFRS norms.

In IFRS 3, goodwill is recognized as a non-amortized asset as long as this goodwill is not overestimated. There are annual depreciation tests to verify the adequacy between the goodwill's accounted value and its "market value".

IAS 16 on properties affects the modelling of the book. Provisions for impairment also affect the capital banking book (when they are included in this book and not in the credit risk book).

Finally with IAS 39, the equity may vary; the CFH derivatives variations go directly into the equity.

5.5.5 Other IFRS items

Among the mass of IAS rules, let us finally cite:

- IAS 37 where the future financial commitments have to be set aside in provision;
- IAS 19 where the retirement pensions have to be provisioned (as a discount of the commitments net of the hedging assets);
- IAS 16, 36 and 40 where the measurement of tangible assets is specified;
- IAS 14 where the results of the business lines are presented analytically.

5.6 IMPACT OF IFRS ON ALM AND CRITICISM OF IFRS

5.6.1 Impact of ALM

For interest rate risk management, *cash solutions will be preferred to derivative solutions*:

- It is easier to replace a swap by a loan plus a deposit (especially for internal contracts).
- Since the embedded options in AFS assets do not have to be extracted (with a condition on the coupon that have not to exceed twice the initial coupon), cash solutions with AFS provide the opportunity not to account at fair value many interest rate options.

Nevertheless, IFRS rules *increase the volatility* (the income volatility and the equity volatility).

Moreover, the introduction of IFRS obliges the A/L manager to be aware of the accounting standard. Before each new hedging operation, each new investment, each new debt issue, the A/L manager has to know how this operation will be recognized.

In terms of income simulation, the A/L manager has to know how each operation is accounted.

With IFRS 7 and the IAS 32, there is more transparency on the internal data and it is more difficult to hide a large interest rate risk position.

The rules oblige one to have a consolidated approach to the balance sheet and then to have *a central ALM group* in order to consolidate all the ALM positions. Consequently managers have set up a new organization taking into consideration the harmonization of the hypotheses at a group level and the necessity of audit trails at a group level to be able to track with the group information system each contract for each subsidiary.

A/L manager systems will also have to be close to accounting systems.

With the IAS 32, the A/L manager will *reveal the real risk position* including its real interest rate risk position. Indeed, not only the position is revealed but also the hypotheses behind the calculation (documentation of conventional schedules for equity and demand deposits, behavioural models, etc.).

Note also that IAS 32 is in "harmony" with the Basel II framework, described later.

Concerning insurance ALM, the rules introduce the notion of fair value in decision taking and then introduce an economic description of the activity.

5.6.2 Criticism of IAS 39

IAS 39 was criticized initially by practitioners because these rules revealed the risk positions that they perhaps wanted to hide. With the rules, derivatives are visible as well as their risk impact.

IAS 39 is a mixed model for accounting and for this reason, it has been widely criticized. IAS 39 is accused of introducing complexity and volatility in the results. However, the rules could not have measured all the financial instruments at cost since this way of accounting is not compatible with trading activities (and with the risk of these activities). On the other hand, measuring all the financial instruments at fair value was a too big change for many industries (including the banking industry due to the existence of demand deposits).

Many improvements were introduced to the initial rule proposal:

- the fair value option with the objective of reducing the volatility of the mismatch between assets and liabilities;
- the portfolio hedge of interest rate risk;
- the definition of impairment on the basis of an "incurred loss" model rather than of an "expected loss" model;
- the loan and receivables category expansion to include purchase loans and deposits, etc.

Many discussions are still taking place to define the evolution of the rules (IMH instead of COFVH for instance). Indeed, many A/L managers hedge the margin more than the cash flows or the fair value.

6
"Economic Accounting": Fair Value and Full Fair Value

Entre trop et trop peu est la juste mesure. (Gilles de Noyers)

The full fair value concept is derived from the fair value concept developed by the IFRS. Indeed, full fair value extends fair value to every product including products accounted at historical cost.

For every product, we compute the full fair values:

- using an available quoted market prices; or
- using a discounted cash flow analysis.

The *discounted cash flow analysis* has to take into account all the flows associated with the product: capital repayments, interests. The A/L manager discounts these cash flows under a risk neutral probability (or under a martingale risk neutral probability minimizing the risk using the Girsanov theorem).

Moreover, full fair value is equal to the expectancy of the sum of all the future discounted incomes. Indeed, on the long-term horizon, all the accounting standards are equivalent.

Nevertheless, many A/L managers fought against the introduction of full fair value in the IFRS rules: they categorically resisted this accounting methodology.

First, they were afraid of the possibility of accounting manipulations by their competitors. However, their main objection was to the risk of income volatility, that full fair value introduces. This volatility comes from the difficulty of computing fair value and achieving a stable formula, i.e. a formula with the least incertitude possible. Moreover, this volatility creates greater complexity for the financial analysts in their work; it is another source of systemic or macroeconomic risk.

Consequently, the method was not adopted for banking activity; such was the conclusion of these A/L managers.

On the other hand, we will see how it is possible to use the full fair value concept for risk measurement. The objective is for the company to smooth the income growth.

The following chapters will give examples of full fair value computation in:

- demand deposit accounts (including the cost of perequation, customer closing probability and links with the other incomes);
- life insurance contracts;
- prepayment options.

6

7 Internal Transfer Pricing or Fund Transfer Pricing (FTP)

Le bon marché coûte cher.

7.1 PRINCIPLES

FTP's main principle is simple: to find a suitable internal fictitious price for the product sold by the different business lines (i.e. by the different Commercial Divisions to the various customers of the company). This FTP exists when the business is the main guide of the activity and when this activity does not depend on the financial markets).

The question arises, for example, for the internal transfer price of loans: at which price should the ALM buy back for the Retail Banking Department each new mortgage loan?

In an insurance company, at which price should each new insurance contract be repurchased internally?

The following sections will explain in details the FTP principles.

7.1.1 Integral financial risk transfer from commercial businesses to ALM

FTP defines the limit between the Commercial Department and the Financial Department (i.e. the ALM Department).

The Commercial Department's goals are simple:

- to sell products;
- to optimize the mix-product;
- to pilot the market share piloting;
- to establish the margin policy.

The Commercial Department has no time to spend on market financial operations, for example managing the interest rate and liquidity risk or earning money with an exposure on the financial markets.

In the ALM committees (ALCO), the Commercial Department representatives may take part in strategic decisions (commercial actions will indeed affect the evolution of the structure of the balance sheet) but it is not their role to profit directly from financial risk exposures.

In conclusion, the FTP rules should *transfer all the financial risk from the Commercial Department to the ALM.*

A corollary of this assumption is that *a Commercial Department that is prepared to keep some financial risks in its business should be charged for the cost of this risk.* The charge could be expressed in terms of capital consumption or in terms of margin reduction.

All types of financial risk should be included in the FTP: liquidity risk, interest rate risk, options, etc.

7.1.2 Risk transfer at market prices

It is imperative that for a FTP system to perform and to avoid any kind of criticism; it has to be transparent and fair. The refinancing price is a deciding factor when computing analytically the profitability of the business.

The FTP should be *based on the real financial costs of the risk*. To avoid any question, the references should be clear and to do so they should be related to market quotations (or to a discounted cash flow analysis).

Whenever it is possible, *the FTP of an operation should be the fictitious price of the fictitious micro hedging of this operation in the market.*

The references to the market should be *explicit* (taking market references such as the Libor, the equity closing indexes, etc.) *or implicit* (market value of the operation calculated at the trading date). In the case of an implicit reference, all the calculations should be done *under the risk neutral probability* (the same probability used in the markets to compute the present value of an instrument).

The risk transfer should be rational and fair in order to avoid the possibility of arbitrage between the ALM Department and the Commercial Department. For example, if a product is associated with a mismatched FTP, this situation could create arbitrage opportunities for the businesses (selling this product with a large margin for the business line but with a small real margin for the company).

7.1.3 The objective of business margin stability

The FTP's purpose is to *let the commercial margin be constant during the life of the refinanced contract.*

To do so, the principle of a *"contract by contract" FTP calculation* is fair. FTP should be calculated for each operation booked in the balance sheet. The FTP rule should be fixed during the entire contract life in order to obtain margin constancy.

For example, a fixed rate loan FTP (at a rate of 5 %, for example) should be fixed (at the rate of 4 %, for example). The margin of this operation is fixed and is equal to 1 %.

On the other hand, a floating rate loan FTP (traded with a rate indexed as Libor +1 %) should be floating (at the rate of Libor +0.10 %). The margin of this operation is fixed and is equal to 0.90 %.

In many other examples, FTP is a bit more difficult to compute but always follows the objective of getting a smoothed margin for the Commercial Department.

7.1.4 The characteristics of FTP

The FTP rationality principle implies that the price should include some key elements:

- *Interest rate risk transfer*

The interest rate reference for the FTP is either the swap curve (interbank rates such as Libor or Euribor rates for maturities from day to day rate to 12 months and swap rates such as "CMS rates" – "constant maturity swap rates", official fixing of Swap rates) or the government curve (government bill yields and government notes yields).

The fund interest rate transfer price principle is to find the swap or the government replication product.

For example, for an amortizing fixed rate loan, the loan FTP should include the price of an amortizing swap with the same liquidity schedule.

- *Liquidity risk transfer*

The same principles apply to the Liquidity Risk transfer.

The liquidity reference is the "liquidity spread" above the swap curve. The liquidity spread curve is the company spread curve.

The liquidity spread represents the "cost of the cash", also called the cost of funding.

The fund liquidity transfer price principle is to find the cost of the loan that replicates the operation liquidity schedule.

For example, in an amortizing fixed rate loan, the loan FTP should include the price above the swap rate of an amortizing debt issue with the same liquidity schedule.

For example, the asset swap price may inform on the liquidity price of a note.

- *Operational costs*

Some operations may include an operational cost integrating, for example, middle or back-office charges.

For example, a specific loan package may be difficult to implement with legal costs to be included in the FTP.

- *Included implicit or explicit options cost*

In the operations the ALM team has to refinance, the Commercial Department may include (voluntarily or not) options in the contract.

For example, the contract may include an explicit option such as a cap in a floating rate loan or an implicit option such as a prepayment option.

Each option has a cost if this option has to be repurchased in the market. The FTP should take into account the operation's virtual repurchase market price.

For example, for the floating rate loan with a 5 % cap and indexed to Libor + 1 %, the FTP rate should be of the form "Libor with a cap at 4 % + a smoothed cap cost of 0.4 %". Doing so, the margin is equal to 60 bps whatever the evolution of the Libor is.

Furthermore, FTP should take into account the *financial characteristics of the operation*:

- *The operation currency*

The operation currency is necessary in order to compute the transfer price. For example, the USD loan FTP will be settled regarding the USD yield curve and not, of course, the Euro yield curve.

- *The trade date*

Knowing the operation trade date is necessary in order to compute the FTP of an operation since the market conditions used to compute the FTP should correspond to the market conditions of the trade date.

- *The trade maturity date and the amortizing profile*

A fixed rate operation has a constant FTP through its entire life.

An amortizing operation FTP is a function of the market conditions in terms of market rates and funding costs.

For amortizing operations, the FTP is often computed as *the operation internal rate of return (with the appropriate yield curve).*

- *Interest rate nature (fixed or indexed, and in that case, the index type)*

When the client rate is Libor indexed, the FTP should be Libor indexed as well (with the same index revision periodicity).

- *Periodicity of repayment or periodicity of interest (if any)*
- *FTP basis*

It is always important to explain the basis on which the FTP is expressed when controlling incomes (in management control teams) or when pricing a commercial product. For example, a 5.00 % FTP on a 30/360 actuarial yearly basis is equivalent to a 4.88 % FTP on a 30/360 linear monthly basis.

7.1.5 FTP as a basis for commercial pricing

The choice for each product of a FTP rule affects directly the way the product is sold. The introduction of a FTP system in a balance sheet means an indexation of the client prices of the new production to the FTP.

Indeed, the Commercial Department uses the FTP to propose *client prices grids.* The Commercial Department fixes a target margin and adds it to the FTP in order to produce those *pricing targets that are called prices grids.*

The margin of the new production is the simple difference between the client prices and the FTP.

The commercials are managed through these margin targets and their evaluation depends on the amounts of products sold and on the effectively obtained margins.

7.2 ADVANCED TRANSFER PRICINGS INCLUDING CREDIT RISK AND EXPECTED RETURN ON ECONOMIC CAPITAL

In large institutions, the FTP calculation needs to be accurate in order to separate as precisely as possible the different costs comprising the FTP.

To explain how precise the FTP calculation can become, we will take the fixed rate mortgage loan FTP calculation as example. To simplify, we will suppose that the mortgage is an eight years bullet loan (without amortization).

The mortgage includes mainly liquidity and interest rate risks but also includes many options.

The primary interest rate risk could be hedged through an amortizing swap. The swap often includes a "forward cost"; when the mortgage contract is signed, the client waits at least two or three months to receive the keys of his new home (two or three months waiting for the administrative signature when buying an existing home, sometimes more than two years when the client builds his own home). We use the term of *"disbursement delays"* in such a case.

For example, the 5 years swap rate against Libor could be of 4.80 % when with a 3 months possible forecasted delay, the 5 years swap rate in 3 months could be of 5.00 % including 20 bps of "forward cost".

The liquidity risk could be micro-hedged through a forward 5 years debt issue at Libor + 10 bps.

However, the loan contains many options sold to the client:

- *Statistical prepayment option* (the customers reasons to prepay are in many cases independent from his wishes such as moving house or invalidity will prepay)

If the A/L manager anticipates a 3 % statistical option independent leg on the market rates, it enables him to compute the most probable schedule (statistically speaking).

For example, the 5 years amortizing swap rate in 3 months is of 4.90 %, showing a negative statistical option cost of *-10 bps.*

- *Financial prepayment option*

In many countries, as we will see it later, the client has the option to prepay his loan with a very small penalty. Of course, when interest rates are going down, the client will exercise this option and will perhaps refinance his loan through another mortgage company.

In our example, this option will cost *30 bps.*

- *Pipeline risk option ("loan offer" option)*

In many countries, another costly option is the pipeline risk option: the client has the right to change his mind between the signature of the loan contract and the payment of the cash to the home seller. Even if a contract has been signed, when rates are going down, the client may sometimes ask for a lower rate or move to another mortgage bank.

In our example, this option will cost *15 bps.*

- *Credit risk*

When providing a mortgage, the bank takes a credit risk. In such a case, the bank has two choices: either to securitize this credit risk (solution often used in the US) or to conserve the risk in the balance sheet.

The securitization price gives the credit risk cost usually transferred in the Credit Risk Banking Book.

The A/L manager has the choice of indexing this credit risk cost over the swap rate or over the risk free rate (i.e. the government rate).

The A/L manager has the opportunity to use the assets including credit risk as collateral.

There is a relationship between the risk free rate, the credit risk and the swap rate with a margin m:

$$\text{Risk free rate} + \text{credit risk cost} + \text{Cost of capital} = \text{Swap rate} + \text{Cost of funding} + m$$

Here the cost of capital includes the gains arising from the collateralization of the risky assets.

• *Capital cost*

The capital manager may charge a capital cost in the FTP. Risk managers allocate a capital in front of the risk: this capital is often a regulatory capital but we recommend in practice an economic computation of the capital (i.e. an economic capital).

The capital cost is the multiplication of the economic capital amount by the cost of the capital recognized by the market. This capital cost is smoothed in the FTP.

The economic capital integrates all the sources of risk, not only the financial risk but also non-financial risks such as model risk and business risk.

• *Operating costs and perequations*

The FTP sometimes integrates operating costs when the executive management wants the Commercial Department to monitor exactly the cost of the operations. The operating costs are smoothed as a charge in the FTP.

• *Disbursement delays*

The FTP has to take into account the disbursement delays, i.e. the delays between the trade date and the operation date.

For example, the FTP of a fixed rate loan is computed at the loan trade date but on the base of the effective schedule of this loan. Indeed, the credit may start with a delay (from 3 months up to 2 years sometimes). FTP is then computed as the internal rate of a forward operation.

7.3 THE INCLUSION OF IMPLICIT OPTIONS INCLUSION IN THE "CONTRACT BY CONTRACT" FTP RULES AND COMMERCIAL DEPARTMENT ARBITRAGE OPPORTUNITY

When incorporating the cost of an implicit option in FTP, we transfer the optional cost from the Commercial Department to the ALM. The transfer cost is computed assuming that the customer will not exercise optimally his option: the optional cost is thus really lower than an explicit optional cost of the same type.

Transferring all the implicit option to ALM is very dangerous: it may cause an arbitrage opportunity for the Commercial Department.

Taking the mortgages financial repayment option transfer example, once the FTP incorporates the optional cost, the Commercial Department is no longer sensitive to the optional cost. If the customer threatens to transfer all his accounts to another bank if the bank does not renegotiate his mortgage rate, the Commercial Department in such a case will follow the customer's desires; finally, the financial prepayment optional cost is transferred integrally to the ALM!

Other examples could be given with "contract by contract" FTP rules on insurance contracts or deposits contracts without maturity.

The solutions to avoid this kind of situation are multiple. However, *the main solution is to penalize contract by contract the Commercial Department for customer behaviour changes from the initial modelling* (the modelling initially used for the pricing of the financial repayment option transfer price).

For the mortgages example, the Commercial Department should pay monthly the differences between the market value of the implicit cost and the market value of the implicit options embedded in the mortgages "still alive" in the balance sheet.

Another solution could be to make sensitive the marketers (from the Commercial Department) to the implicit optional cost, for example indexing their remuneration to a prepayment rate target. If their portfolio prepayment rate is lower than their target and if they do not lose too many clients, they may get extra remuneration.

7.4 FTP RULES BASED ON THE "STOCK" AND BASED ON THE "FLOWS"

7.4.1 Contract by contract FTP calculation principles

The principal basis for FTP calculation is the *"contract by contract basis"*. However, in many cases, the FTP is calculated on a *"pool basis"*:

- when it is difficult in the databases to get the contract by contract information;
- when building up an ALM team, not having so much time to spend on the exact FTP calculations;
- when we do not have enough historical data to provide a perfect contract-by-contract modelling of our product;
- when dealing with a product with a minimal impact on the balance sheet;
- when dealing with an asset or a liability without an apparent contractual maturity.

In those cases, A/L managers may propose a *"pool based" FTP rule*. In practice, this solution should be avoided or should be temporary.

There are two types of such FTP rules called *"conventional schedule rules"*:

- *"FTP rules based on the stock"*;
- *"FTP rules based on the flows"*.

We will see later that *"FTP rules based on the flows" have to be favoured.*

7.4.2 "FTP rules based on the stock"

When computing FTP without using a "pool based" rule, a simple solution is to *affect a smoothed past FTP*.

For example, FTP could be the average 10 years swap rate, the average being calculated on the past 10 years period. The FTP rule affect a whole stock of operations. For this reason, this rule is often called a "FTP rule based on the stock".

Averaging the past Dow Jones indexes on two years could also be a "FTP rule based on the stock".

This kind of FTP calculation is very simple because the computation process does not require the amount to be "repriced".

This kind of FTP calculation is very dangerous when controlling the management.

We take the example of a bank providing 1000 MUSD of deposits without maturity with a 0 % client rate and we assume that the FTP rule is based on the 10 years smoothed government rate.

To simplify the problem, we assume that all the past rates were equal to 5 % and that in order to replicate the FTP rule, the ALM Team has bought 100 MUSD 10 years notes each year during the last 10 years.

On that basis, the annual net interest margin of the Commercial Department of year Y is equal to:

$$\text{Res Commercial (Y)} = \text{Amount deposits.(FTP} - \text{Customer rate)}$$

$$\text{Res Commercial (Y)} = 1000.(5\,\% - 0\,\%) = 50\,\text{MUSD}$$

The Treasury annual net interest margin is equal to zero on year Y because it is the difference between the FTP and the yield of the replacement in bonds:

$$\text{Res Treasury(Y)} = 1000.(5\,\% - 5\,\%) = 0\,\text{MUSD}$$

On year Y+1, if we assume that the rates have gone up to 6 %, the average 10 years smoothed bonds rate moves from 5 % to 5.1 %. The interest incomes move as follows:

$$\text{Res Commercial } (Y+1) = \text{Amount}(Y+1).(5.1\,\% - 0\,\%)$$

$$\text{Res Treasury } (Y+1) = -\text{Amount}(Y+1).5.1\,\% + 900.5\,\% + [\text{Amount}(Y+1) - 900].6\,\%$$

Finally:

$$\text{Res Commercial (Y+1)} = \text{Amount(Y+1)} \;.\; 5.1\,\%$$

$$\text{Res Treasury (Y+1)} = [\text{Amount(Y+1)} - 1000] \;.\; (0.9\,\%)$$

In those conditions, *with a "FTP rule based on the stock", the interest margin of the Treasury (or ALM) Department does not depend on financial parameters but depends on commercial parameters* (such as here the evolution of the amount of deposits sold by the Commercial Department). To avoid such a situation, "FTP rules based on the flows" are a solution.

7.4.3 "FTP rules based on the flows"

In the 90s, many ALM teams started with "FTP rules based on the stock", i.e. the easiest rules to implement. As soon as possible, they moved to "FTP rules based on the flows" or directly to "contract by contract" FTP rules.

We consider "FTP rules based on the flows" as conventional schedule rules. They are still often in use for liabilities (or assets) without maturity or for products correlated imperfectly with financial market indexes.

The "FTP rule based on the flows" is valid for a pool of operations such as a pool of all the deposits without maturity or a provision line of the balance sheet. For this pool, are defined: the stock, the cash flows and the flows to be replaced.

The *stock S(Y)* is the amount of the pool at a date Y.

The stock is made of different *cash flows CF(Y,Y+i),* each cash flow associated with a future date and with *an interest rate ICF(Y,Y+i).*

The stock is the sum of the cash flows at a date Y:

$$S(Y) = \sum_{i=1}^{+\infty} CF(Y, i)$$

The interest rate associated with the stock is the FTP defined as the "sum-product" of the cash flows and of their interest rates:

$$FTP(Y) = \frac{\sum_{i=1}^{+\infty} (CF(Y, i).ICF(Y, i))}{S(Y)}$$

How are the cash flows and their associated interest rates computed?

We call *new production* or *flow*, the difference between the stocks at date Y+1 and the sum of the cash flows already placed after Y+1 at date Y:

$$F(Y+1) = S(Y+1) - \sum_{i=2}^{+\infty} CF(Y, i) = S(Y+1) - S(Y) + CF(Y, 1)$$

The ***"FTP rule based on the flows"*** is, in those conditions, the rule that links the cash flows CF(Y+1, i) with the flow F(Y+1) and with the previous cash flows CF(Y+1, i).

Two constraints remain:

- The sum of the new cash flows should be equal to the new stock S(Y+1).
- The interest rates associated with the flow should be equal to the market rates at date Y+1.

Mathematically speaking, the rule may be represented as a function g that links the flow F(Y+1) to the replacement of this flow on the horizon Y+i+1:

$$CF(Y+1, i) = CF(Y, i+1) + F(Y+1).g(i)$$

$$ICF(Y+1, i) = \frac{CF(Y, i+1).ICF(Y, i+1) + F(Y+1).g(i).MarketRate(Y+1, i)}{CF(Y+1, i)}$$

MarketRate (Y+1, i), the market rate at date Y+1 associated with the horizon i is computed on the adequate yield curve of date Y+1. The market rate may incorporate, as usual, the interest rate risk transfer, the liquidity risk transfer and the operational costs.

The principle is that the FTP rule can be replicated exactly on the market to avoid the problem exposed at the end of the previous paragraph with "FTP rules based on the stock".

If a Treasury/ALM Department wishes to replicate the FTP formula, it has to buy at each period an amount Y of bonds equal to g(i).F(Y) at the market rate of MarketRate(Y, i). In those conditions, the treasury interest income is equal to zero.

Additional definitions

The new production schedule or the *flow schedule* is the amortization of the flow F(Y) using the function g.

The *"stock conventional schedule"* has to be computed as the resultant (i.e. the mathematical consequence) of the past "flow schedules". This schedule will sometimes be used when integrating a product in an interest rate gap. This is nothing but the piling up of the past flows residual schedules.

There are two main types of FTP rules (i.e. the types of choices for the function g):

- *bullet flows rule* (for example the "10 years bullet flows" when $g(i)=1_{\{i=10\}}$: the replicating strategy is to buy 10 years bullet notes);
- *linear flows rule* (for example the "10 years linear flows" when $g(i) = 10\,\%.\ 1_{\{i<11\}}$: the replicating strategy is to buy 10 % of one-year note, ..., 10 % of 10 years notes).

However, of course, it is possible to invent other types of "FTP rules based on the flows".

Please note that the "FTP rule based on 10 years bullet flows" is the improved version of the "10 years smoothed rate FTP rule based on the stock".

7.4.3.1 Application to an example

We take the example of a "FTP rule based on 4 years linear flows".

We suppose that the flow at date Y is equal to 72.5 and that the cash flows of date Y are CF(Y,1) = CF(Y,2) = 22.5, CF(Y,3) = 15.5, CF(Y,4) = 10.

In those conditions, if the stock at date Y+1 is equal to 70, the flow to be replaced is equal to 20 (20 = 70 − 72.5 + 22.5).

The flow schedule is linear 4 years and decreases by an amount of 5 each year. The cash flows at date Y+1 are easy to compute.

	Flow Schedule Y−2	Flow Schedule Y−1	Flow Schedule Y	Stock Y	Cash Flows Y	Flow Schedule Y+1	Stock Y+1	Cash Flows Y+1
Y−2	20.0							
Y−1	15.0	30.0						
Y	10.0	22.5	40.0	**72.5**				
Y+1	5.0	15.0	30.0	50.0	22.5	**20.0**	**70.0**	
Y+2	–	7.5	20.0	27.5	22.5	15.0	42.5	27.5
Y+3		–	10.0	10.0	17.5	10.0	20.0	22.5
Y+4			–	–	10.0	5.0	5.0	15.0
Y+5						–	–	5.0

Figure 7.1 Flows

In terms of interest rates, if the rates were always equal to 5 % and if they are now equal to 6 % at date Y+1, the Table 7.2 represents the evolution of the interest rates associated with the cash flows:

Note that the FTP is increasing as are the interest rates associated with the cash flow.

7.4.3.2 Chart interpretation of Linear and Bullet "FTP rules based on the flows"

In terms of risk analysis, the form of the stock schedule is the source of numerous comments.

Here are some typical forms of stock schedule computed when supposing that the amount to be refinanced is constant or growing at a rate of 5 % per annum.

	Flow Schedule Y–2	Flow Schedule Y–1	Flow Schedule Y	FTP Stock Y	Cash Flows Y	Flow Schedule Y+1	FTP Stock Y+1	Cash Flows Y+1
Y–2	5.00 %							
Y–1	5.00 %	5.00 %						
Y	5.00 %	5.00 %	5.00 %	**5.00 %**				
Y+1	5.00 %	5.00 %	5.00 %	5.00 %	5.00 %	**6.00 %**	**5.29 %**	
Y+2	–	5.00 %	5.00 %	5.00 %	5.00 %	6.00 %	**5.35 %**	5.18 %
Y+3		–	5.00 %	5.00 %	5.00 %	6.00 %	**5.50 %**	5.22 %
Y+4			–	–	5.00 %	6.00 %	**6.00 %**	5.33 %
Y+5						–		6.00 %

Figure 7.2 Flows rate

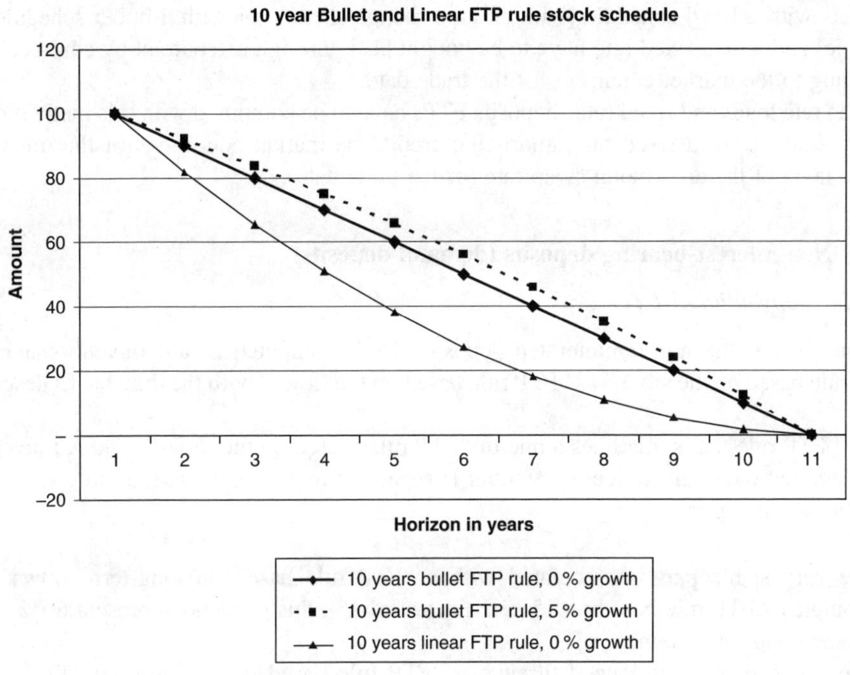

Figure 7.3 FTP schedule

We may note that the 10 years bullet flows rule brings a 10 years linear stock schedule! The stock duration is of 5 years.

The 10 years linear flow rules leads to a convex (or parabolic) stock schedule with duration inferior to 5 years.

When taking into account the amount structural growth, the stock schedule has a longer duration: the last flows are greater than the previous ones.

7.4.3.3 Criticism of "FTP rules based on the flows"

The problem associated with the choice of such a FTP rule is that all the modelling goes back to the choice of the function g. The criticized *"Replicating portfolio"* rule aims to determinate the "appropriate function g" at a given time. The A/L manager's implicit hypothesis is simple: the evolution of the g function across time allows slow convergence for the best refinancing strategy.

Contrary to the "contract by contract" FTP rule, the executive management is not sure that the interest rate risk is transferred properly from the Commercial Department to the ALM or Treasury. For this reason, *"FTP rules based on the flows" should be replaced as often as possible by "contract by contract FTP rules".*

7.5 EXAMPLES OF FTP RULES

7.5.1 Fixed term and fixed rate products

Products with a fixed schedule (with an amortizing schedule or with a bullet schedule, for example) and with a fixed rate have to be bought back through a "contract by contract" FTP according to the market conditions of the trade date.

Fixed rate loans and fixed rates deposits FTPs have to be computed with this methodology.

For example, for a fixed rate amortizing credit, the market conditions of the trade date are the level of the amortizing swap rate (of the trade date).

7.5.2 Non-interest-bearing deposits (demand deposits)

7.5.2.1 Conventional FTP

In many banks, the non-remunerated deposit FTP is computed as a "conventional FTP": "FTP rule based on the stock" or "FTP rule based on the flows" with the drawbacks described above.

Such FTP rules are sometimes a mix of "FTP rules based on the flows". The A/L manager considers that the demand deposit amount is separable in a volatile part, a quite stable part and a very stable part.

- The very stable part is associated with a "FTP rule based on long-term flows" (for example a "FTP rule based on 15 year linear flows"); this part may represent 60 % of the demand deposit amount.
- The stable part is refinanced through a "FTP rule based on medium-term flows" (for example a "FTP rule based on 2 year linear flows"); this part may represent 20 % of the demand deposit amount.
- Finally, the volatile part is refinanced through a day-to-day basis FTP. This part may represent 20 % of the demand deposit amount; this percentage depends on the bank, on the country and on the client type, of course, but it represents the deposit amount that could disappear on a one-day horizon due to a liquidity crisis, for example.

The percentage choices and the horizon choices are the main problems of this FTP methodology: a local convention and implicit rule may exist in some countries but those rules may differ frighteningly from one country to another.

In some countries, the FTP duration may be close to zero (the refinancing strategy is close to a day-to-day basis refinancing strategy). In other countries, the volatile part is close to 0 % and the FTP refinancing duration may approach 10 or 15 years!

Nevertheless, the *amount stability principle* is used everywhere: the more stable the amounts are, the longer the duration should be!

Note also that the longer the flows duration is (or the bigger the very stable amount percentage is), the smoother the FTP is! Therefore, when working with long-term flow FTP, the net interest margin is smoothed since the client remuneration is equal to zero.

The purpose of replicating portfolio strategies (described in chapter 11 on demand deposit modelling) is to compute the optimal percentages (the function g) and the optimal flows duration.

The following chart shows that the 10 year FTP rule based on the stock is often smoother than Euribor or CMS rates; this explains the choices made by many A/L managers:

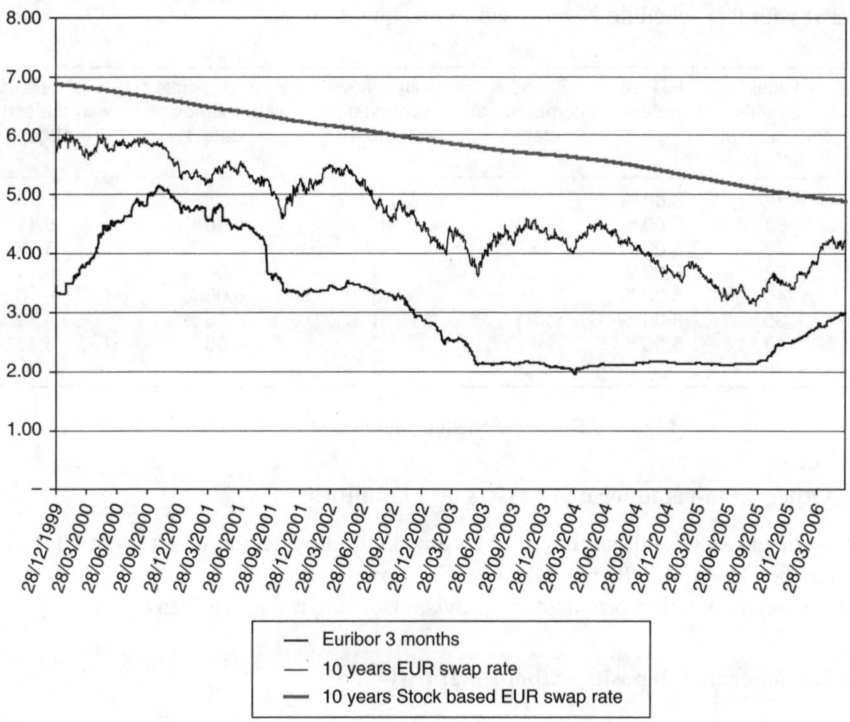

Figure 7.4 FTP rate and market rates

7.5.2.2 Contract by contract FTP

A much better demand deposit FTP computation is based on a contract-by-contract approach. This approach is inspired by demand deposit modelling; those models are developed in the modelling chapter. The most appropriate models are based on a closing rate modelling and on a modelling of the average amount by client.

FTP is computed for a set of demand deposits with the same origination date; for example, the clients produced during the same month are regrouped in a homogeneous cohort.

A schedule is computed for each cohort: the schedule is in fact the prediction of the demand deposit amount in the future.

After the computation of this schedule, the demand deposit cohort may be considered to be a fixed term product with a fixed rate. At the date of the client acquisition, an FTP may be computed according to the expected schedule of the associated cohort. The FTP is fixed for the overall schedule.

Of course, since this methodology requires the implementation of behavioural models, the schedule modelled initially may be different from the evolution of the demand deposit cohort amount. To take into account this evolution, a new schedule modelling may be computed each month; the schedule variation may be refinanced at the market rates of the date of "recomputation".

The following table explains how the 5 % FTP computed with an initial schedule moves to 5.11 % at date 1. The initial schedule supposed that the demand deposit amount at date 1 was 80 when the realized amount is 90. A new schedule is recomputed. The swap rate associated with this schedule is supposed to be equal to 6 %.

Month	Initial schedule computed at date 0	FTP at date 0	Schedule computed at date 1	New flow schedule at date 1	FTP associated with the flow at date 1	FTP associated with the schedule at date 1
M	**100**	**5.00 %**				
M+1	80	5.00 %	**90**	10	6.00 %	**5.11 %**
M+2	70	5.00 %	82	12	6.00 %	5.15 %
M+3	50	5.00 %	58	8	6.00 %	5.14 %
M+4	40	5.00 %	46	6	6.00 %	5.13 %
M+5	30	5.00 %	34	4	6.00 %	5.12 %
M+6	10	5.00 %	12	2	6.00 %	5.17 %
M+7	0		0	0		

Figure 7.5 FTP Schedule and new flow schedule

7.5.3 Other "non-remunerated" assets and liabilities

For many other assets and liabilities, when the client rate is equal to zero, the FTP computation may be close to the demand deposit FTP computation.

Such zero remuneration products are provisions or unproductive loans.

7.5.4 Remunerated deposits without maturity

For remunerated deposits when the remuneration is based on the Libor (Money Market Deposits), FTP is also simply based on the Libor.

When the remuneration is a proportion of the Libor (for example 30 % of Libor), the deposit amount is separated into two parts: 30 % of the amount is refinanced through a Libor FTP and the remaining 70 % is refinanced with the same methodology as the one exposed above for the zero remuneration demand deposit.

For remunerated deposits without maturity and without a remuneration indexation to the Libor (as is mainly the case for savings accounts), the methodology is derived from demand deposit methodology.

When computing savings FTP with a methodology based on the flows, the volatile part is often the most important one and the flows replacements are shorter. Some flows can be invested in real rates (rather than in nominal rates) since the market sometimes supposes a correlation between the savings client rate and the inflation.

Nevertheless, a contract-by-contract FTP computation is a better solution. This FTP will be developed later in the demand deposit modelling chapter.

7.5.5 Capital Banking Book products FTP

Main Capital Banking Book products are usually refinanced through a conventional FTP, often a long-term FTP rule based on the flows (even if some banks use a DD FTP convention).

7.5.5.1 General principles

When looking after the Capital Banking Book, the key elements of this book could be compared with cash instruments available in treasury. The sensitivity of the economic value of these elements to the level of the interest rates is "*a priori*" equal to zero. There is no reason to replace the elements of the Capital Book differently from on a day-to-day basis.

However, many managers will replace their equity in term horizons longer than on a day-to-day basis: the FTP associated with Capital Banking Book products is often a FTP price based on long-term flows such as a 10 years FTP rule based on the flows.

The A/L managers may explain their equity replacement strategy using many reasons:

Possible explication	Contradiction
Wishing to smooth the Capital Banking Book incomes	Analysts could easily take into account the Capital Banking Book incomes volatility when they value the Company.
Wishing to take a pure interest rate position in front of their equity incomes	Taking an interest rate risk position in front of the Capital Banking Book is not profitable on the long-term.
Explaining the existence of an implicit swap contract between shareholders and the Company: the shareholder asking thus the company to produce incomes indexed to the average long-term interest rates rather than on the DD rate.	We will see later that using an economic capital approach, this implicit swap is without value. In case of a Company default, this swap disappears; this swap cannot be taken into account when computing an economic capital or computing an interest gap or a FTP...

Figure 7.6 Equity replacement strategy explanation

For all these possible explanations, a question subsists. Why should we choose a 10 years FTP rule based on the flows rather than a 30 years FTP rule?

In fact, the real reason for using a long-term FTP rule based on the flows is of another nature. When refinancing the Capital Banking Book, not only the Banking Book is refinanced but also the company "economic value". The economic value may take into account some elements like operating costs, human and material investments, etc.

Quite often, those elements are not refinanced through an FTP. However, in order to make the economic value of these elements equal to zero, the Capital Banking Book cash elements are replaced on a horizon that looks like the activity horizon profile.

The horizon of the capital banking book "FTP rule based on the flows" is linked with the horizon of the company activity profile.

Therefore, when an A/L manager chooses a 10 years "FTP rule based on the flows", he supposes implicitly that the activity of the company financed through the equity flow contains a 10 years interest rate risk.

The schedule of the Capital Banking Book FTP rule based on the flows is linked with the company equity economic value duration.

7.5.5.2 Equity: share capital and retained earnings

Share capital is refinanced through the Capital Banking Book long-term "FTP convention based on the flows".

Earnings of the year are often refinanced through a short-term FTP: DD or 3 months Libor average rate.

Net unrealized gains on the securities portfolio and other net unrealized gains may be refinanced through a short-term FTP.

7.5.5.3 Provisions (excepting provision for doubtful loans)

Provisions (country risk provisions, global provisions, etc.) are usually refinanced through the convention for the Capital Banking Book Long-term "FTP rule based on the flows".

Nevertheless, each time it is possible to compute a contract-by-contract FTP, it is better to compute the FTP like this.

7.5.5.4 Property investments, investments in non-consolidated undertakings

Flows associated with property investments are usually refinanced through the capital banking book long-term "FTP rule based on the flows" of the currency.

7.5.5.5 Remark about the other investments (not necessarily in the Capital Banking Book)

Trading books are refinanced through a DD rate FTP. A funding cost can be added easily as soon as a liquidity schedule is computed.

Equities accounted as available-for-sale are usually refinanced through the capital banking book long-term "FTP rule based on the flows".

Fixed rate bonds with a fixed term are refinanced through their interest rate schedule.

7.5.6 Examples of optional cost inclusion in FTP

The example of prepayment showed how the statistical and the financial prepayment cost (the implicit optional cost) could be added in the contract-by-contract mortgage FTP.

For the mortgages indexed to the Libor with a cap, the explicit optional cost can be added at the mortgage origination:

$$\text{FTP}(t) = \text{Libor (revision date before t)} + \text{funding cost} + \text{cap option cost}$$

The cap option cost is the price of an amortizing cap (with the mortgage schedule) expressed in bps.

7.5.7 Doubtful

Doubtful credit amount (net of provisions) could be seen as a quite stable amount through time. For this reason, a FTP rule based on the flows is easily computed for this amount.

Nevertheless, complete modelling can be performed in order to compute a contract-by-contract FTP.

7.5.8 Insurance products FTP

Let us show how it is possible to associate a FTP to a non unit-based life insurance contract.

We will see in the modelling chapter that it is possible to model such a contract with:

- a *liquidity schedule* representing all the future flows the customer is expected to invest or to withdraw. This modelling is made under the assumption that the insurance company will stabilize the portfolio of customers;
- a *tacit agreement with the customers*. In order to stabilize the customers, the normal strategy will oblige the insurance company to pay an interest indexed to long-term smoothed rates.

For example, the interest rate paid on the insurance contract will be indexed to the maximum of the yield of the long-term investment and of the spot long-term investment:

$$Max\,(\text{10 years average rate smoothed on 10 years - m}_1\text{, 10 years spot rate - m}_2)$$

From this modelling of an insurance contract, we will propose a FTP rule. The idea is to consider the price of the derivative instrument that exchanges on the liquidity schedule the tacitly agreed rate for a floating rate (such as a Libor rate) plus a margin m.

In order to provide a constant margin to the Commercial Department, the effective FTP will follow the tacit agreement less the margin m of the derivative product.

$$Max\,(\text{10 years average rate smoothed on 10 years - m}_1\text{, 10 years spot rate - m}_2) - m$$

7.6 PEREQUATIONS

"You will never catch mosquitoes with vinegar"

7.6.1 Principles

The perequation concept is essential to understand a company business. Products are linked one to the other: the perequation links the products' FTPs.

Definition: the perequation is the difference between the Financial FTP and the Commercial FTP. The Commercial Department may ask for FTP lower than the real product cost (financial FTP). This allows the Commercial Department to stick up a positive margin to the marketers. If the Commercial Department pilots the FTP, the margin displayed to the marketers can be also smoothed.

In fact, the commercial FTP is used to motivate marketers (from the Commercial Department) and allow them to follow the market prices (proposed by other competitors) with a stable positive margin. It allows also the Commercial Department to take a bigger market share without changing marketers' politics: when raising the perequation, without changing the marketers' margin objective, the company prices become more competitive and the market share increases.

Of course, the perequation has a cost. This cost should be passed on to the other products.

This way, the perequation represents a potential yield transfer from a balance sheet product to another influencing the pricing of the two products. It is a commercial piloting instrument, in a "price taking" strategy, a potentially cyclical strategy.

7.6.2 Examples

7.6.2.1 Retail banking examples

Perequations mechanisms are a major factor to explain the difference between the observed customer pricing in the UK, in France, in Europe, in the US and everywhere else in the world.

In the American model of the banking business, for example, strong population mobility (geographical mobility or banking mobility) does not ensure a stable demand deposit amount for a bank that markets mortgages.

Consequently, a 300 bps margin on American mortgages is not rare. This margin will take into account all the inherent risks associated with the credit marketing: credit risk, liquidity risk, pipeline risk, business risk, operational costs and economic capital remuneration.

In France, the retail banking business model is based on a customer approach where margin mutualization takes a large place. Since French customers are not mobile, mortgages are highly regarded by the banks: they wish to win future commissions and to collect demand deposits for decades to come.

In France and in many countries in Europe, the mortgage margin can be around 20 bps in front of stable demand deposits. This mortgage margin is made possible due to the presence of a strong perequation from mortgages to demand deposits.

Theoretically, this perequation should be computed explicitly. For example, it should be defined by customer segment. A young high-grade student or a young doctor wishing to contract a mortgage will create more wealth for the bank than will a retiree.

For the same reason, the perequation for a young start-up credit can be different from a traditional SME credit.

This perequation depends on the interest rate level.

This situation is particularly dangerous; indeed, if the perequation is not computed statistically well, it may cause a decrease in the profitability in the long-term.

A "low cost" strategy could become hazardous if customer mobility was not well anticipated or customer profitability was not well calculated.

The risk arises also with the idea of the existence of a *"financial perequation"*. This financial perequation leans on A/L management requirements. Managers may ask for the development of fixed rate assets in their balance sheet. Rather than investing in long-term fixed rates bullet bonds, the Treasury Department may prefer to incorporate amortizing mortgages with implicit options.

Nevertheless, the financial perequation could not explain more than 10 bps.

7.6.2.2 Other examples

In insurance, some products are susceptible to attracting clients. For example, a life insurance contract may become a "loss leader". With a strong commercial advertisement, an attractive out-of-the market rate may convince customers to join the insurance company. Once the customer is "convinced", the insurer may propose products with larger margins (auto insurance, etc.).

A perequation on life insurance contracts FTP is simple to put in place in order to increase the market rate proposed by the competitors.

In asset management, some products may attract clients more than the others.

In banks, Fixed Income Departments used to have smaller margins than Equity Derivatives Departments. However, a bank could not develop an Equity Derivatives Department without a Fixed Income Department. An implicit perequation between the two departments could be put in place.

8
ALM as a Profit Centre

Le bon profit ne se dit pas. (Béroalde de Verville)

FTP is a key part of company management control.

The introduction of FTPs makes possible an essential part of ALM implementation, i.e. transforming the ALM into a profit centre.

Many banks use FTPs to price their products but only the most advanced companies developed an independent ALM as a profit centre. The profit centre is not always the ALM team; it could be the Treasury Department. The most important thing is to *separate the Commercial Department income from the financial ALM income*. Should the opposite occur, it could be easy for the Commercial Department to point the finger at the ALM if the overall incomes are decreasing (even if the diminution is caused by the marketers). Usually, ALM teams are less powerful than the other big commercial departments and computing an ALM income is a simple way to protect ALM teams. On the contrary, a weak ALM team would not promote the idea of becoming a profit centre.

FTP implementation makes the separation easy and possible. The result of ALM is the difference between the FTP and the financial market conditions according to the accounting scheme of the activity.

Moreover, *ALM incomes should be split* between the different risks:

8.1 ONE PROFIT CENTRE FOR ONE FINANCIAL RISK

For example, an ALM team should implement those different profit centres:

- interest rate risk profit centre;
- liquidity risk profit centre;
- currency risk profit centre;
- inflation risk profit centre;
- credit risk profit centre;
- equity risk profit centre;
- volatility risk profit centre;
- model risk profit centre.

Each profit centre receives from the Commercial Department the FTP part associated with the profit centre risk; it pays the financial short-term cost of this risk on the market.

For example, for the interest risk profit centre, the ALM receives the interest rate paid by the Commercial Department on its assets through the FTP and pays the short-term refinancing rate in the market.

In this example, through the FTP, the net interest margin of the Commercial Department is insured. All the interest rate risks are transferred in the interest rate risk profit centre controlled by the ALM team. The ALM committee (the "ALCO", where the Commercial Department is present but is not the specialist of the financial risks) takes the decisions to hedge the risk that are described in this book.

In financial statements, ALM incomes are not presented for the moment. Those incomes are usually *"given back" to the Commercial Departments* in the company incomes presentation.

The redistribution of the ALM incomes is a hard task since it is difficult to explain it to auditors (and of course a bit suspicious): indeed this redistribution may be a possible income-smoothing instrument between the different commercial entities.

9

Optimal Organization of an ALM Team

On ne change pas une équipe qui gagne.

9.1 THE USUAL ALM ORGANIZATION

At the beginning of the 90s, ALM teams in banks were usually integrated:

- in Finance Departments; or
- in Risk Management Departments.

In insurance companies, ALM teams were considered initially to be insurance risk management teams.

The position of ALM teams in Finance Departments was linked with the idea that regulatory reports were to be done by the Finance Department and that bank information systems were usually in the possession of this department.

Risk management teams were also quite often part of the Finance Department for the same reasons. When these teams were emancipated from the Finance Department some of them revived the ALM teams in their organization.

These risk management/ALM teams usually incorporated:

- a simulation team for the computation of risk indicators;
- a financial modelling team;
- a product analysis team.

However, positioning ALM teams in risk management teams appeared to be very dangerous!

- *Nobody controls the risk indicator computation.*
- *Hedging in risk management teams is analysed only from a theoretical point of view.*
- *Risk management teams are not preoccupied by the reconciliation between risk indicators and income management.*

Nowadays, ALM teams tend to be independent from Finance Departments and risk management teams.

9.2 THE OBJECTIVES OF ALM

ALM teams now have a set of responsibilities. The ALCO (the ALM committee) – pays attention to these responsibilities:

- the responsibility for short-term and long-term treasury activities (liquidity risk management);
- other ALM risks management: interest rate risk, optional risks, exchange rate risk, etc.;
- FTP modelling and ALM income computation;
- conformity with local regulations and statutory obligations;
- optimization of risk returns and capital management.

9.2.1 Liquidity management

Liquidity management is the first ALM objective:

- providing cash for all the business lines of the company, giving them full access to liquidity for every kind of liquidity need for each maturity in every country;
- optimizing the short- and long-term funding costs, making the executive management secure about liquidity risk exposures;
- optimizing the cost with a given rating target;
- preparing liquidity contingency plans and being prepared for liquidity crisis;
- monitoring liquidity (volume, cost, liquidity sources, etc.);
- computing liquidity risk indicators (internal and regulatory indicators);
- providing to executive management centralized liquidity management and monitoring.

9.2.2 FTP and modelling

ALM teams are responsible for *FTP implementation and control.* The process has to be validated by the business lines and by the executive management. Executive management guarantees an identical approach for all the business lines.

To implement FTPs, the A/L manager will need *precise financial information about the balance sheet products*. The FTP modelling will take care of:

- transaction schedules or information about the transaction terms;
- behavioural and market option information databases prepayment, etc.

FTP transfers all the risks (liquidity, interest rates, etc.) to ALM: this creates *a separate income for ALM and for business lines.*

This FTP implementation will need precise modelling:

- customer behaviour modelling;
- perequation modelling.

For this reason, ALM will be *responsible for ALM information systems.*

9.2.3 Risk hedging, capital and income management

After the buy-back of all the risks by the ALM teams, it is time to manage those risks. Risk management goes with risk hedging and then with risk positions taking.

9.2.3.1 Risk hedging

ALM is *responsible for all the market risks that are not booked in the trading activities*:

- liquidity risk (as explained above);
- interest rate risk with stable interest rate risk arising from fixed rate FTP transferred operations;
- optional risk: behavioural (embedded or not) options and market options;
- behavioural risk, business risk and model risk;
- capital book risks (versus commercial books risks);
- exchange rate risk: risk on the incomes, risk on investments and on provisions.

For all these risks, *the A/L manager will implement the appropriate indicators*: net open currency positions, liquidity ratios, interest rate gaps, etc. It is also his role to develop more adequate indicators for activity management.

Moreover, ALM will compute its *economic capital consumption*.

The risks transferred by the FTP are easily hedged using the appropriate instruments:

- swaps for interest rate risk;
- cap, floor, swaptions for optional risk;
- spot deals for the net open currency positions.

9.2.3.2 Capital and income management

9.2.3.2.1 ALM risk positions

The role of the ALM teams is not simply to focus on risk hedging.

The definition of the risk taking strategies is an essential part of the A/L managers' task. ALM should contribute to the profitability of the company:

- developing a *contracyclic management* to protect business lines against the cyclicity of the economy;
- taking adequate risk positions.

The business lines margins are protected against market changes and against behavioural risks. *ALM recuperates the financial risks and the volatility on the income* due to those financial risks.

ALM will insure a centralized analysis and a centralized management of the financial risks.

Income optimization is managed by ALM. This optimization requires a delegation of decisions. To make this optimization, the manager will use the same products usually used for risk hedging.

Nevertheless, *ALM income is usually given back to business lines* and is invisible for financial analysts.

9.2.3.2.2 ALM income smoothing

ALM teams have also to concentrate on *income smoothing*. The objective is to stabilize the level of future results. More precisely, the idea is to ensure a stable growth for discounted net income.

The income smoothing strategy may be done using:

- delta hedging techniques in the FTP;
- income smoothing strategies (with AFS bonds, for instance).

9.2.3.2.3 ALM and budget

In the company's budget programme, ALM is essential for *incomes prediction*.

Nevertheless, ALM teams will not have also to concentrate on a 2–3 year budget horizon. Indeed, the risk supported by ALM teams is longer than could be expected. Economic value management will take into account the long-term ALM investments in the budget environment.

Moreover, on a long-term perspective, ALM is linked strongly with business lines through FTP, perequation modelling and strategy optimization. The budget plans for business lines has to be in line with the ALM budget plan.

9.2.3.3 ALM management control

Since an income has to be computed for the ALM department, there is a difficulty for the organization to find an appropriate control for the activity. The control has to be independent and should embrace:

- model control;
- FTP computation control;
- risk indicator computation control;
- performance measure control.

9.2.4 Centralized management

Therefore after FTP risk transfer and after economic value management, *ALM has to be managed as a profit centre.*

A question then arises: should the ALM teams be centralized or decentralized in each business line?

To answer this question let see what the disadvantages of a decentralized ALM are:

- non-uniform modelling quality;
- non-uniform risk transfer;
- non-uniform performance measure.

The advantages of a centralized ALM are the following:

- centralization of the IFRS hedging justifications for cash flow hedge and fair value hedge;
- centralization of the IAS 32 risk indicator;
- centralization of the Basel II Pillar 2 risk indicator.

On the other hand, there is a need for a local ALM in order to be closer to the local modelling practices. This means that *local ALCOs* are required in large corporations to integrate local experts and local business lines in the decision process.

However, there is a need for a *centralized ALM* to:

- define modelling norms;
- define risk indicators/simulation norms;
- validate limits in the local ALCO.

To make this organization possible, *the executive management will invest in ALM teams*, ALM systems and ALM practitioners.

9.3 ALCO: THE ALM COMMITTEE

The *ALM committee or ALCO* is often the heart of the ALM organization.

9.3.1 Different ALCOs

As explained before, in large companies many ALCOs exist:

- *a central ALCO*, which centralizes all the ALM information at the company level. All the other ALCOs report to the central ALCO and the head of Central ALM is present at all these other ALCOs.
- *business lines ALCOs* where the business lines specific ALM problems are studied in detail;
- *local ALCOs* where the ALM problems of a specific country are a studied in details (problems due to a different regulatory environment, to local treasury difficulties, etc.).

9.3.2 ALCO Members

The ALM committee usually consists of:

- a member of the executive management of the company, sometimes the CEO, the Chief Executive Officer (who usually presides the ALCO as a chairman);
- the head of the ALM Department and the executive ALM members;
- the head of the Treasury Department;
- the Chief Operating Officer;
- the head of the Finance Department;
- the heads of the major business lines (consumer banking, corporate banking, etc.) and the head of Marketing Department;
- the Head of the Risk Department and the Compliance director.

The presence of the head of the Risk Management Department is necessary in order to establish a potential source of opposition. This opposition is necessary in order to validate the rules and the strategies proposed during the ALCO.

9.3.3 Frequency and rules

The ALCO's administrative rules should be known by everyone and be reviewed regularly.

The ALCO takes place at least on a monthly basis or on a weekly basis depending on the situation of the company and on the need for intra monthly strategy management.

ALCO crisis committees can convene as soon as the executive management or the head of ALM requires it.

Reporting to the executive management and to the board should be done at least on an annual basis.

9.3.4 ALCO's role and agenda

The board of directors is naturally responsible for:

- financial risk management (including global interest rate risk, liquidity risk, exchange rate risk, etc. but excluding market risk) with delegation to the ALCO;
- credit risk management with delegation to the credit risk committee;
- market risk management with delegation to the market risk committee.

Audit teams and risk teams are usually responsible for consolidated risk reporting:

- economic risk;
- credit risk;
- market risk;
- operational risk.

ALCO will then focus mainly on the *financial risk management* and in particular:

- ALCO will look after procedures and after risk management policies;
- ALCO will verify that the ALM human resources are sufficient to perform all the ALM tasks.

Moreover, ALCO is the occasion to discuss business activity and its link with ALM topics. The usual *ALCO agenda* is the following:

- presentation of the previous ALCO minutes;
- commercial activity and development;
- risk measurement, FTP rules validation and risk limit policy;
- Risk and income Management and customer products pricing.

9.3.4.1 The presentation of ALCO minutes

At the end of an ALCO, key points and action points should be highlighted in the ALCO minutes. These minutes are sent promptly to the ALCO participants.

At the beginning of the next ALCO, the minutes are reread. The action points made in the past ALCO meeting should be reviewed in order to ensure their implementation.

9.3.4.2 *Commercial activity and development*

The Marketing Department is responsible for product innovation and the pricing of existing products. The head of this department is invited at ALCO to present activity and commercial development and in particular:

- evolution of new contract production per customer type;
- evolution of prepayments;
- evolution of customer optional behaviours (closing rates, etc.);
- marketing campaigns;
- overview of customer prices and competitors' prices.

Moreover, the balance sheet should be then presented. For instance in a bank, those figures should be presented:

- for the loans: the average amount, the figures, the average life, the average margin, the average rate, the average FTP and the proportion of fixed rate loans by year of production;
- for the loans: a reporting of the implicit/explicit options (cap, prepayments, etc.), the loan monthly new production and the fixed rate and liquidity schedules;
- the same for deposits by year of production and by deposit type;
- a reporting of all the hedging instruments (including their accounting type: CFH, FVH, trading, etc.);
- a reporting of all the funding instruments and of the possible future funding deals;
- a reporting of the other elements of the balance sheet evolution: equity capital, provisions, AFS bonds, etc.

Finally, the *whole balance sheet should be presented somehow at the ALCO*: in terms of outstanding amounts and flows (past flows and future expected flows through marketing campaign presentation).

9.3.4.3 *Risk measurement, FTP rules validation and risk limit policy*

After the presentation of the balance sheet in an historical way and in a prospective way, it is time to present the balance sheet risks.

For every indicator, the A/L managers will present the *hypotheses* behind this computation. Moreover, the A/L manager will present the *indicator variation* and explain it through the computation of the *indicator sensitivity*.

9.3.4.3.1 FTP rule validation

Regular specific studies will help the ALCO to achieve FTP rule implementation and review. The proposed FTP rules modifications are presented during the ALCO; the ALCO is in charge of their validation.

9.3.4.3.2 Liquidity risk indicators

The ALCO will look after the classic liquidity indicators, the regulatory ones and the internal ones. Of course, the following indicators will be presented:

- liquidity gap: static and dynamic gap;
- current funding composition and provisional evolution;
- historical funding costs and prediction of the funding costs;
- future liquidity needs;
- commitments report, credit lines reporting;
- funding sources (in a diversification perspective);
- rating perspective;
- loan to deposit ratio and other regulatory ratios;
- liquidity contingency plan.

9.3.4.3.3 Interest rate risk indicators

As for liquidity risk, the ALCO is the occasion to present the interest rate risk positions in every currency:

- interest rate gap including delta equivalent computations and break-even rates;
- penta, courba and gamma equivalents ("Adam equivalents");
- income sensitivities;
- economic value sensitivities, earnings-at-risk and value-at-risk;
- Optional risk indicators for explicit and implicit options.

The reporting should also be done for the risk management of the real rate positions.

9.3.4.3.4 The presentation of the other risk indicators

During the ALCO, ALM teams will present the risk indicators for the other financial risks:

- net open currency position for currency risk;
- exchange rate risk hedging portfolio;
- regulatory reporting and constraints;
- transformation policy;
- equity risk positions;
- model and business risk indicators.

9.3.4.3.5 Economic capital

During the ALCO, the A/L managers will discuss the economic risk indicators such as the *economic capital.*

Associated with this reporting, the ALCO should include reporting on the *evolution of economic value*. Economic value and economic capital should be split between the time buckets.

This allows the committee to be aware of the reconciliation between the different risk measures: static gap measures, dynamic gap measures, economic value sensitivity earnings-at-risk and VaR (i.e. economic capital).

This will prevent companies from making the same mistakes as those certain banks experienced in the 90s. These banks were managed with a VaR limit close to zero and with too short a demand deposit schedule; consequently, their income decreased when interest rates decreased.

For this reason, many banks went back to the earning-at-risk indicators or to interest rate gaps instead of investing more in VaR indicators.

Nowadays, ALM teams go back to economic capital indicators (as soon as their ALM modelling teams have developed appropriate business modelling).

In addition, with this capital reporting, the ALCO will evaluate the future economic capital needs.

9.3.4.3.6 Limits

The ALCO fixes the *limits* on the principal indicators:

- gap limits;
- sensitivities limits;
- income sensitivities limits;
- economic capital limits, etc.

These limits should integrate, of course, the regulatory limits.

9.3.4.4 Risk and income management and customer products pricing

9.3.4.4.1 Market situation review

After the presentation of the risk indicators, it is time during the ALCO for presenting the hedging strategies.

However, before taking decisions, the ALCO needs to be informed about the market evolutions:

- short- and long-term interest rates, spot and forward rates;
- CMS forward rates;
- real rates spreads;
- implicit volatility of the interest rates;
- swaps/government bonds spreads;
- CDS spreads;
- exchange rates;
- real estate prices;
- stock index and stock market volatility, etc.

During the committee meeting, the ALCO members will make their predictions as to the evolution of market indexes.

9.3.4.4.2 The presentation of Budget, ALM and commercial income

Associated with risk presentation, the ALM committee is the occasion to present and follow:

- the expected ALM income and the expected commercial incomes;
- the market expectation of the incomes compared to the income presented during the budget sessions.

The presentation can be done with the break-even rates presentation for each book and on an aggregated level.

9.3.4.4.3 Hedging strategies propositions and customer products pricing

After the review of the position and of the predictions, it is finally time to propose actions:

- hedging strategies propositions;
- customer contract pricing decisions (such as deciding the remuneration rate for the savings account).

9.3.5 Specificity of the Insurance ALCO

As an example, we present here some points that should be highlighted during an insurance ALCO:

- *The flows should be presented in an adequate table*:
  - flows on the liability side by product (new contract production in numbers and amounts by duration, etc.);
  - contract closing rates as a function of the contract seniority;
  - marketing campaigns;
  - flows on the asset side (realized hedging strategies: bonds, indexed bonds, equity and real estate);
  - derivatives reporting.
- Benchmarking should be developed through *competitors' campaigns presentation.*
- The committee should spend time on the *presentation of the indicators*:
  - modelling modifications;
  - liquidity gap (with scheduling hypothesis in annex);
  - interest rate gap with the asset and the liquidity interest rate schedule;
  - break-even point (with the asset average rate and the liability average rate by time bucket);
  - the interest rates anticipated by the market (swap rates, bond rates, etc.);
  - the equity portfolio and the equity break-even point;
  - the level of the provisions and the latent capital gains reporting.
- Also in the *income sensitivity simulations* (including stress scenarios):
  - interest rate rises shock;
  - credit risk spread crash;
  - equity crash, etc.
- To finish with the *hedging strategies definition*:
  - market evolution commentary;
  - presentation of the actual strategy;
  - proposition of the possible new strategies: customer price review, provisioning strategies, investments strategies (bonds, derivatives, etc.), etc.;
  - for each proposed strategy, the ALCO is aware of the potential impact of the strategy on the future incomes.

9.4 THE DIFFERENT ALM TEAMS

ALM departments are generally made of these different teams:

- a management team;
- an organization team;
- a production team;
- an operational research team;
- a controllers' team (not managed directly by the Head of ALM);
- a Front Office and analyst team;
- a Middle office team (associated with a Back-Office team);
- an ALM system team.

9.4.1 ALM management

The head of ALM is responsible for the ALM and for ALM management. He is personally in charge of:

- the preparation of the ALCO;
- the evolution of risk management (including the limit system);
- the management of the income evolution;
- the validation of the operations;
- the management of the ALM team human resources;
- the management of the ALM team development projects.

The head of ALM is helped in his work by the senior ALM team members (coordinated usually by an internal ALM team committee).

9.4.2 ALM organization team

An ALM organization team is essential in order to make the development of the ALM efficient. This team should be constituted of senior A/L managers who experienced many ALM jobs (from models to front office posts, for instance).

Their role is to establish a link between the ALM projects decided by the ALM management and the different members of the ALM teams. They are responsible for the *contracting of these ALM development projects*.

Consequently, they are very close to ALM system teams (that are responsible for the project management).

This organization team includes then the function of *business manager*.

Moreover, the organization team usually collects all the *ALM documentation* (for the regulators, the controllers and the auditors).

9.4.3 ALM production team

The ALM production team is responsible for the production of:

- all the ALM indicators exposed during the ALCO;
- all the regulatory indicators;
- all the internal intra-monthly reports;
- all the reports given to the auditors.

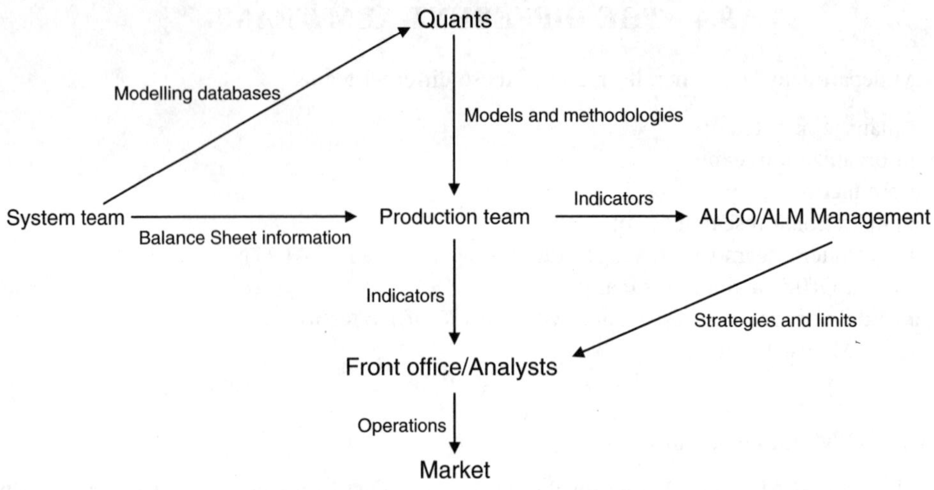

Figure 9.1 ALM organization

The members of this team are usually junior A/L managers even if all the reporting should be checked by a senior manager.

9.4.4 The operational research team: the ALM "quants"

The *ALM operational research team* which is also called the *financial modelling team* consists of graduate A/L managers with an expertise in quantitative modelling. For this reason, they are called the *"Quants"*.

The team is competent in *financial modelling*, in *pricing*, *hedging* and in *optimization methods*.

9.4.4.1 A team responsible for the modelling

This team is *responsible for all the models* used by ALM production team:

- The team incorporates a *"product analysis team"*, responsible for the model construction of the new products.
- Moreover, the team is involved with marketing teams in order to invent new products that respond better to customer desires.
- The team is *responsible for the behavioural models' estimation*, their backtesting and their documentation.

For this reason, the team has a close relationship with risk controllers in charge of modelling control.

- This team is also *responsible for market simulation models and for ALM pricing models*.
- Moreover, these teams are now responsible for *indicators computation methodologies* (including economic capital methodologies).
- Finally, the team works on the *optimization tools*. The team is involved in the determination of the optimal hedging computation.

The team proposes experimental tools with the objective of industrializing these tools and implementing them in front office and in simulation systems.

9.4.4.2 A "research" team

This team is also responsible for *ALM quantitative research projects*.

Technological innovation is a part of the value creation of the company. ALM teams should start long-term research projects and investigate:

- new decision tools;
- the development of innovative products for the marketing teams;
- new modelling methods of estimation;
- new risk indicators.

These projects should be a source of high value creation. However, it takes time to implement these projects. Indeed, this integrates many risks since it is not sure whether these projects can converge or not:

- It is then difficult to compute the team's real productivity and to benchmark the team with competitors' teams.
- It is not easy to explain to the executive management the projects that are followed since the executive management is more involved in the short-term than in the long-term. The only way to do so is to explain how actual indicators and models are derived from past long-term development projects.

Nevertheless, these research projects could be used in order to strengthen the technical image of the company. This image is important in order to attract competent A/L managers.

To do so, the team should be linked with the universities, should integrate graduate students and even PhD students.

Indeed, this kind of team is excellent for the training of the future A/L managers. Nowadays, business specialization (front office operator, production operator, etc.) makes it difficult to train generalist A/L managers. Moreover, the university training courses are more interested in risk management and in financial markets modelling than in ALM. This training is always based on fair value accounting where the risk should be low rather than on an accrued accounting where the issue is to take risks.

There is not so much literature on ALM problems and a part of the role of the modelling team is to *train young A/L managers* and to explain to them the operational principles of the ALM business.

The introduction of *a scientific committee* with the head of ALM could help define long-term research projects.

9.4.5 Model controllers and indicators controllers

ALM activity incorporates many non-financial risk sources:

- an operational risk;
- a model risk.

For this reason, it is necessary to control models and the construction of indicators through a second overview made by the ALM controllers. This expert and independent team role is to highlight modelling weaknesses and potential errors.

To validate the models, the controllers' team will use different techniques:

- benchmarking studies (including bibliographical studies);
- model formal analysis (using the modelling team documentation);
- replication of the modelling with independent tools;
- model backtesting with statistical analysis;
- computation of the sensitivities of the model to its parameters.

9.4.6 ALM front office and analysts

The ALM front office and analyst team have two responsibilities:

- They are responsible for the *proposition and for the execution of the ALM financial risk strategies*.
- For the business lines, they provide *the liquidity and the risk transfer to a centralized ALM*. In particular, they ensure long and short-term treasury management.

To execute their strategies, A/L managers will need advanced front office tools in order to record their operations and be informed of the evolution of the market. Moreover they have to write up the operating rules and procedures.

The analysts report the market information to the ALCO and look after market aberrations. These A/L managers will develop a deep understanding of macroeconomics in order to provide qualitative information about the evolution of the markets.

Their role is to propose investment strategies looking after the risk indicators and their market evolution expectations. They are helped in this task by optimization tools provided by the financial modelling.

These analysts have also to be expert in the IFRS accounting in order to provide adequate propositions to the ALCO.

Nevertheless, the delegation of risk to the front office team is not clear:

- Some companies delegate the determination of strategy to the ALCO and the front office operators obey the ALCO.
- Some companies prefer to delegate the determination of strategy to a group of operators (with risk reporting to the ALCO).

9.4.7 Capital management team

The capital management team computes the economic capital and allocates it. It is not clear whether this function should be incorporated:

- in the ALM Department since this department is close to the markets and able to take risk positions;

- in the Finance Department since the function is linked with budget planning;
- in the Risk Department since this department is able to define the appetite for risk of the company.

9.4.8 ALM systems team

A solid ALM will integrate an advanced ALM system team working in collaboration with the organization team and the other teams.

Indeed, A/L managers use many different systems:

- *front-office and back-office systems* to compute ALM income and record front office operations;
- *historical databases information* for ALM modelling teams and production teams;
- *simulation systems* for the production team (including risk systems).

Nowadays, many ALM teams use an ALM simulation tool developed externally by a specialized system provider.

9.4.9 ALM middle office and back office

For every large business, the back-Office team is responsible for the computation of income (and then reports to the Finance Department) and for payment execution.

The middle office is also responsible for income computation from a management control perspective. Indeed, they act as a control for the income computed by the back-office.

Such an organization allows the A/L managers to perform consistency checks between accounting and financial risks data: process, frequency, etc. The front/middle/back office incidents are recorded by the middle office. This helps in computing the operational risk.

Moreover, the middle and the back office are responsible for the justification of the hedging relationships (under the IFRS accounting rules).

Part III

Balance Sheet Items and Products Modelling

10
Behavioural Modelling Principles

À donner donner, à vendre vendre. (13th century)

Behavioural models propose a modelling of *customers' financial behaviour*: for example their likelihood to break up contracts or to renegotiate them.

Linked to customer behavioural modelling, the A/L manager has to model its own *company behaviour*. It means for example: strategy models, margin modelling, etc.

In many cases, there are *public models* (such as for credit risk) that establish a common framework for A/L managers.

However, sometimes, when there is no public model (or when the public model is source of criticism), the ALM modelling team has to choose a private model. There are three possible model choices:

- *Structural models*: those models focus on utility maximization in a microeconomic framework. Utility maximization provides, for example, the arbitrage function of the customer. Those models are used in very simple microeconomic frameworks.
- *Statistical models*: the behavioural databases will help in the construction of those models (the favourite ones for A/L managers).
- *Mixed or "rational" models*: those models combine the first two approaches supposing that the bahaviour corresponds to an optimal option exercise; the strike of this option depends on customer behaviour. Of course, the A/L manager needs for his simulations some information about the strike distribution function. Traders will use this kind of model for MBS pricing.

In the chapters below, we will explain the most important principles of behavioural statistical models: *database constitution, event driven modelling and backtesting.*

10.1 THE CONSTITUTION OF DATABASES

The construction of historical databases costs a lot but allows for powerful modelling.

Nevertheless, modelling through an historical database may be very *dangerous*: too short a historical database does not allow for the most accurate modelling of the trends (since cycles modify customer sensitivity to economy).

For example, when the A/L manager tries to apprehend the sensitivity of a parameter, such as the growth of his amount of demand deposits, to the level of interest rates, it is important to consider the historical moves of the interest rates. The following graph represents, for example, the German 3 month rate.

During 14 years, the interest rate was mostly decreasing. It means that the economic cycle is longer than 30 years. The A/L manager has to find an historical database longer than 30 years in order to model his demand deposit growth.

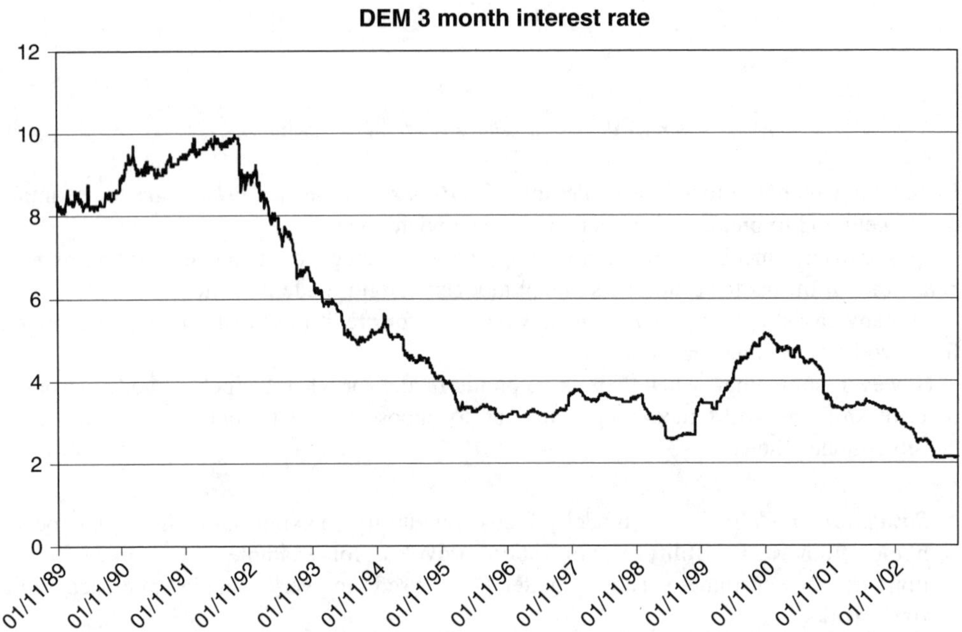

Figure 10.1 Short term interest rate

The historical database has also to apprehend the entire complexity of the customer behaviour. Client by client information is costly (and difficult to analyse statistically or through computers) so *databases often aggregate information* and the A/L manager has to take note of the aggregation:

- *Scoring* is a powerful tool for aggregating clients.
- Customer repartition by year of contract opening is another solution that takes into account the effects of seniority.

If we take the example of demand deposit modelling or the example of insurance non-unit based contracts, the historical database should include:

- the customer rate;
- the number of remaining clients;

- the average amount by client;
- the average amount of cash withdrawn by client;
- the average amount of cash brought by client.

It is necessary to split all these data by at least:

- month of observation;
- year of origination of the deposit;
- client type (client segmentation or scoring);
- Product type (savings, DDA, etc.).

Of course, historical market data will complement this database:

- historical inflation rate;
- historical Euribor rates;
- historical swap rates;
- historical GDP growth rate;
- historical population growth rate, etc.

10.2 EVENT DRIVEN MODELLING

After the database construction, *event driven modelling* can take place. The purpose of event driven modelling is to analyse mathematically the causes of the events in order to be able afterwards to simulate them.

The events are decomposed and often analysed separately. Among them, the A/L manager distinguishes:

- *New contract (or customer) production modelling*

The target is to apprehend how many contracts the customers will sign in the future. This number of future contracts is a function of future market conditions, of marketing campaigns and of average amount by contract.

- *Contract price modelling (such as customer rate modelling)*

The A/L manager needs to know how the contract price conditions will evolve in the future. For example, in insurance companies (for the non unit-based contracts), it is necessary to know how the client remuneration rate varies. This historical remuneration rate has to be regressed over historical market interest rates, inflation rates, and stock index performances.

Sometimes, a public entity will "regulate" the contract price. The modelling will focus on the regulatory price function and on the probability of this regulation disappearing.

- *Contract cost modelling*

Each contract will generate costs and the purpose of this modelling is to link these costs to market conditions such as inflation, GDP, etc.

- *Contract end date modelling*

The objective is to forecast existing contract closing probability. In many cases, the contract end date is contractual but *early redemption* is always possible. Loan prepayment modelling proposes, for example, to link prepayment and interest rates.

In other cases, there is no contract end date. The modelling then proposes to apprehend the closing probability as a function of seniority and of market conditions.

Quite often, the modelling has to introduce a minimal closing rate and a maximal closing rate.

- *Contract life events modelling*

For example, within an insurance contract, the A/L manager will have to model the average amount of withdrawal by client. He will propose a regression of the past withdrawals by contract seniority.

The usual tools to perform this event driven modelling are statistical tools. The statistical approach means:

- a *database cleaning* to remove data seasonality and inflation/GDP trends;
- a *model proposition* (through regression or whatever) and an estimation of the model parameters;
- a *model backtesting*.

10.3 MODELLING THE STRATEGY OF THE COMPANY

The A/L manager has not only to model the customer behaviour but also the behaviour of his own company.

This kind of model will be particularly interesting when computing the company's income sensitivity to market conditions.

Nevertheless, in the economic value framework, the strategy of the company has no impact on the economic value: **the economic value of an "investment strategy" is equal to zero** by definition of the economic value under the risk neutral probability.

For example, in the insurance sector in non unit-based contracts, the A/L manager will propose models for:

- the strategy of the company to remunerate the customers;
- the provisioning strategy of the company as a function of market conditions;
- the investment strategy of the company.

There is a link between investment strategy and new production hedging. Quite often, investment strategy modelling is just a pure replication of the FTP rule. However, it is possible to introduce strategies that are more complex with the introduction of recurrent risk exposures such as a structural interest rate risk exposure.

10.4 EXPERT ADVICE

Expert advice is the last modelling possibility. A/L managers will use this advice when:

- the modelling has not yet been developed;
- the management has strong doubts about the proposed modelling;
- past observations will not reveal the future. For example, when a market deregulates, it is difficult to apprehend what customer reaction will be.

A/L managers will base their expert advice on some comparisons with the existing models. For example, in order to apprehend extreme risks, the A/L manager can base his expert advice on past extreme situations observed in a country different from his country of reference.

Ideally, a group of A/L managers validate the expert advice during the ALCO and the risk managers take part to the discussion.

10.5 MODEL BACKTESTING

Models have to be backtested. The term backtesting means the verification of the pertinence of the models.

We will distinguish two types of backtesting:

- *The month after month backtesting*

The A/L manager has to be aware of the possible spread between the anticipations made, for example, one year ago and what happened in reality.

	Budget	Realised	Backtest	Error
Long-term interest rates	3.00 %	4.00 %	4.00 %	
Prepayments	150	100	120	20 %

Figure 10.2 Backtesting

- *The "out-of-sample" backtesting*

When the A/L manager proposes a model, he has to perform an "out-of-sample" test on the parameters.

Here is a classic procedure for an "out-of-sample" test:

- Estimate model parameters through the entire historical database.
- Estimate the same model parameters using only the first half of the historical database.
- Compare the estimated parameters with a statistical hypothesis test (i.e. testing if the parameters are equal).

	Full historical database 1990–2000	First half used for estimation 1990–1995	Second half used for estimation 1995–2000
Sensitivity of amount to interest rates Estimation	10 %	−5 %	25 %
Sensitivity of amount to interest rates P value	2.4	2.7	2.1

Figure 10.3 Out-of-sample

In the example above, the model has to be refused even if for each estimation period, the P-Value is higher than two. Actually, it could mean that there are not enough variables in the model.

11
Deposits and Savings

Il est bien tard d'épargner sur le tonneau quand le vin est à la lie. (Hésiode)

11.1 DEPOSITS, MONETARY AGGREGATES, MONEY SUPPLY AND MACROECONOMICS

Deposits and savings represent a large part of the bank balance sheet. Nevertheless, their modelling and their hedging have never been as easily analysed as other products.

In this chapter, the usual way those deposits are analysed is explained and discussed. We propose a modern modelling approach providing a perfect hedging of these deposits.

In many western countries, deposits take different forms:

- demand deposit accounts (DDA);
- checking accounts;
- money market savings;
- savings;
- term deposits.

The market is different from one country to the other but some characteristics are common in many places.

The *demand deposit accounts* are ultra liquid deposits. Clients may withdraw their cash at any time without any penalty. The number of transactions (transfers, checks, etc.) allowed each month is not limited. Remuneration is usually equal to zero. The bank may ask for a monthly charge but not necessarily.

Checking accounts are different from demand deposits in that the client usually gets a low remuneration rate with a monthly fee.

Savings are common accounts where the client has the ability to withdraw his cash at any time but the number of transfers is limited within a month. There is no cheque book associated with this account. Remuneration is higher than for checking accounts. In many countries, a public entity "administrates" or "regulates" the remuneration, in the others the remuneration rate is indexed (implicitly or explicitly) to the level of interest rates and of inflation. In the US, remuneration is market driven.

Money market savings are particular type of savings where the rate is indexed to the level of the money market rates (Fed Funds, Libor, etc.). The margin taken by the bank depends on the customer and on his personal fortune.

With *term deposits*, it is not possible to withdraw the cash at any time. Otherwise, a penalty is imposed (sometimes the customer pays a fixed percentage of the withdrawn amount, sometimes he loses all his interest coupons on this amount). Those deposits are indeed "fixed term deposits".

There is an abundance of literature which treats deposit modelling from a macroeconomic point of view. For the money market, supply and the demand go with an equilibrium price (the interest rate) and a quantity (real money balances).

Central banks introduced *monetary aggregates* to monitor the money supply in the economy. The different monetary aggregates are *M0, M1, M2, M3, M4 and MZM*:

- M0: the physical currency (coins and bank notes) and the accounts at Central Bank exchangeable into physical currency;
- M1: M0 plus the amount in demand accounts (checking accounts, current accounts, etc.);
- M2: M1 plus the amount in saving accounts, money market accounts and small certificate of deposit accounts (CDs under 100.000 USD). M2 is called the "quasi-money", i.e. the deposits without maturity that could without any risk and quasi instantly be converted in cash;
- M3: M2 plus large CDs, repurchase agreements and currency deposits (Eurodollars in the US). In some countries, M3 takes into account all the ultra liquid and risky investments easy to sell into the market: institutional money funds, short-term investment funds, term deposits, etc.;
- M4: definition depends on the country but usually M4 is M3 plus medium term treasury bonds;
- MZM: MZM represents the Money Zero Maturity, i.e. all the deposits without any maturity. In the US, MZM is M2 less small-denomination time deposits plus institutional money funds.
- P1, P2 and P4: all the long-term investments are recorded in the P1 to P4 categories.

The chart below represents the monetary aggregates evolution in the US since 1959 showing different growths between M1, M2 and M3.

11.1.1 Money supply and M2 modelling by Central Banks

There is a *link between money supply and inflation* created by the "monetary exchange equation":

$$\text{Velocity} = \frac{\text{NominalGDP}}{\text{Money supply (M2 or MZM)}} \tag{11.1}$$
$$\text{Velocity.Money supply} = \text{RealGDP.GDP deflator}$$

The velocity represents the number of times per year that money changes hands. The GDP deflator is simply the CPI (the inflation) and the real GDP is the nominal Gross Domestic Product divided by the GDP deflator.

Velocity is supposed to be stable across time (according to the monetarists) so if money supply grows faster than real GDP, inflation is likely to follow.

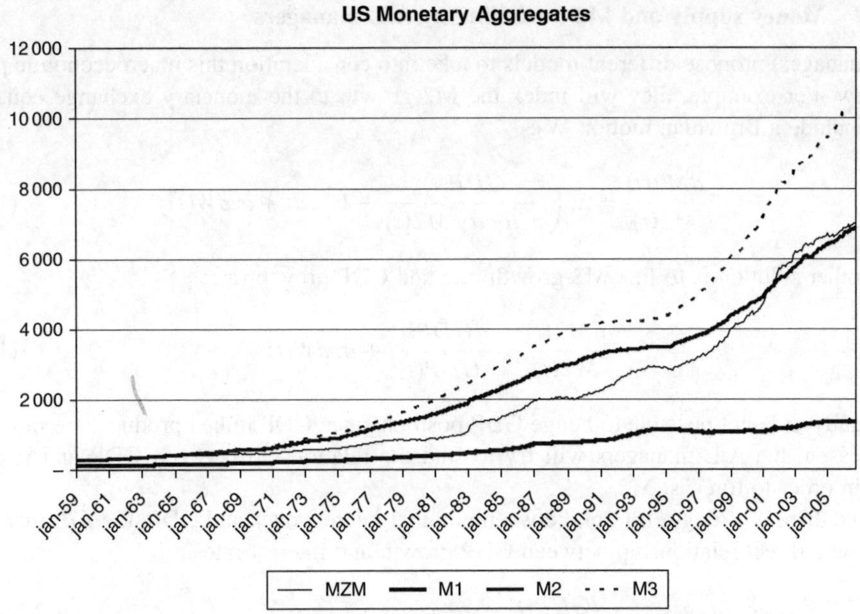

Figure 11.1 Monetary aggregates

Money supply growth is linked to the nominal GDP growth on the long-term.

Central Banks propose a macroeconomic modelling of the money supply. They usually base their analysis on a regression of the money supply growth by the other macroeconomic indicators. Indeed, there is a link between M2 growth, GDP growth, household revenues growth and consumption growth. Actually, they use VAR models (vector autoregressive models) to perform this modelling:

$$(X_t - X_{t-1}) = A.X_{t-1} + E(t)$$

$$X_t = \begin{pmatrix} M2_t \\ CPI_t \\ GDP_t \\ Population_t \\ Revenues_t \\ Consumption_t \\ Interest\ rates_t \end{pmatrix} \tag{11.2}$$

$$E(t) \sim \mathrm{N}(0, \mathrm{Id_N})$$

This kind of modelling does not capture long-term stable relationships between the various parameters.

Interested readers may refer to the "Saint Louis Models" (developed for the Federal Reserve of Saint Louis, USA), to the Central Bank of Canada models or to books about Economics of Money (by Mischkin or Sielbermann).

11.1.2 Money supply and M2 modelling by A/L managers

A/L managers propose different models to take into consideration this macroeconomic point of view. For example, they will index the M2 growth to the monetary exchange equation (and include a Brownian motion W):

$$\frac{dM2(t)}{M2(t)} = \lambda.\left(\frac{GDP(t)}{velocity.M2(t)} - 1\right).dt + \sigma.dW(t) \tag{11.3}$$

Another solution is to link M2 growth rate and GDP growth rate:

$$\frac{dM2(t)}{M2(t)} = \frac{dGDP(t)}{GDP(t)} + \sigma.\,dW(t) \tag{11.4}$$

Usually, it is not possible to hedge GDP position since GDP linked products are rare. For this reason, the A/L managers will try to find the relationship between GDP and interest rates in order to forecast M2.

Since there is a long-term link between nominal interest rates and GDP, the A/L manager may use a direct relationship between GDP growth and interest rates:

$$\frac{dGDP(t)}{GDP(t)} = r(t).dt + \sigma'.\,dW'(t) \tag{11.5}$$

It is also possible to smooth this relationship over time:

$$\frac{dGDP(t)}{GDP(t)} = \lambda'.\left(GDP(t).e^{-\int_0^t r(s).ds} - A\right).dt + \sigma.dW(t) \tag{11.6}$$

11.1.3 Money supply arbitrage: volume effects

Monetary aggregates do not grow at the same speed (as we saw already in the chart above).

Traditional monetary models show:

- a *"technologic effect"*: with the improvement of communication networks, with telephone banking, with the development of internet banking, access to accounts becomes easier. Velocity increases naturally. This explains the observed structural transfers from M1 to M2 and from M2 to M3;
- an "arbitrage between M1 and M2 when rates are going up" since the M1 deposits remuneration rate is quasi-zero. The name given to this form of arbitrage is *"volume effect"*.

Mathematically speaking, the A/L manager will try to model the different ratios representing (M1 over the liquid deposits) or (the liquid deposits over M3):

$$X(t) = \frac{M1(t)}{M2(t)}$$
$$Y(t) = \frac{M2(t)}{M3(t)} \tag{11.7}$$

He will model the technologic effect and the arbitrage effects through a drift on the ratios X and Y depending on the interest rate level r:

$$\begin{aligned}\frac{dX(t)}{X(t)} &= \left(-\alpha_1.e^{-\beta_1 t} + f_1(r_t)\right).dt \\ \frac{dY(t)}{Y(t)} &= \left(-\alpha_2.e^{-\beta_2 t} + f_2(r_t)\right).dt\end{aligned} \tag{11.8}$$

11.1.4 "Credits make deposits"

For several reasons A/L managers quite often use this formula:

- There is a macroeconomic link between deposits and loans: the cash created by loans will be recovered by somebody who will reinvest it somewhere and finally this cash will come back into the banking system.
- When a bank signs a loan contract with a new client, this client will certainly open also a current account. New loan production creates new current account production.
- There is a link between existing current deposits and past productions of credits: past loans production creates the demand deposit amount of today. Quite often, this loan contract no longer exists.

11.2 DEMAND DEPOSIT ACCOUNTS

Interest rate risk management of the demand deposit accounts constitutes the harder task for A/L managers and especially for their ALM modelling teams.

From a basic point of view, these deposits have these characteristics:

- a *client rate close to zero*, i.e. a positive margin wherever the market rate level is;
- a very *stable amount* growing slowly providing a smoothed margin;
- the risk quantification is difficult to apprehend in a quantified way.

With this problem, everything revolves around margin management.

The classic error is to consider that demand deposits are risk free products since the margin is always positive. Actually, the product is much more complex since there is a link between the demand deposits and many other products or functionalities (cheques, ATMs, etc.) providing commissions and costs for the bank. **Demand deposit modelling has to take into consideration the product as a part of the customer commercial relationship and not to forget the presence of fees and costs in this relationship.**

Another classic error comes from the poor use of economic value concepts.

The demand deposit amount is stable or growing slowly when the customer rates are around zero. From an accounting point of view, demand deposit hedging could mean investing in an infinite term fixed rate bond. If we consider the income of each component (after market replacement), calling K the amount of demand deposit (and of infinite bonds) and r the short-term interest rate, the bank overall income is almost constant:

$$
\begin{aligned}
Income_{DD}(t) &= K_{DD}(t).\,(r(t)-0)\\
Income_{\infty BOND}(t) &= K_{DD}(t).\,(F-r(t))\\
Income_{BANK}(t) &= K_{DD}(t).F \approx \text{Constant}
\end{aligned}
\tag{11.9}
$$

Investing in such an infinite bond seems risky for the A/L manager since at any moment, the customer can withdraw its amount of deposits in cash. For this reason, the implicit or explicit replacement in FTPs follows in practice:

- either an amortizing conventional schedule; or
- a very short-term (1-month) replacement schedule.

Very few banks are able to explain their replacement schedule.

Banks tried to provide explanations for their choices of replacement schedule. Two main approaches were tried:

- The *economic value approach* tries to find the strategy that minimizes the economic value sensitivity to the interest rate level.
- The *Replicating portfolio approach* tries to find the strategy that minimizes the net interest income sensitivity to the interest rate movements.

We will see now why we do not recommend these two approaches.

11.2.1 First economic value demand deposit approaches (classic demand deposit modelling mistakes)

When computing the demand deposit economic value, A/L managers presume the demand deposit amount K to be constant. Consequently, the economic value of these demand deposits is equal to their book value:

$$
\begin{aligned}
V &= E\left(\int_0^{+\infty} r(t).K_{DD}(t).e^{-\int_0^t r(s).ds}.dt\right)\\
V &= K_{DD}.E\left(\int_0^{+\infty} r(t).e^{-\int_0^t r(s).ds}.dt\right) = K_{DD}
\end{aligned}
\tag{11.10}
$$

Therefore, the demand deposit economic value sensitivity to interest rates is equal to zero. In this (imperfect) framework, making economic value insensible to interest rates means a short-term demand deposit replacement at day-to-day rates.

On the other hand, with such a strategy the accounted income depends on the interest rate level!

$$
Income_t = K_{DD}(t).r(t) = K_{DD}.r(t) \tag{11.11}
$$

Choosing a replacement longer than a day-to-day rate replacement will allow us to smooth the incomes (as we will see in the replicating portfolio approach).

For example, when considering at date 0, a long-term replacement M at rate r_0, the income at date 1 will vary as follows:

$$\begin{aligned} Income_0 &= K_{DD}(0).r_0 + M.(r_0 - r_0) = K_{DD}.r_0 \\ Income_1 &= K_{DD}(1).r_1 + M.(r_0 - r_1) = K_{DD}.r_1 + M.(r_0 - r_1) \\ Income_1 - Income_0 &= (K_{DD}.r_1 + M.(r_0 - r_1) - K_{DD}.r_0) \\ Income_1 - Income_0 &= (M - K_{DD}).(r_0 - r_1) \end{aligned} \tag{11.12}$$

Here comes the *demand deposit economic value paradox*: if the replacement M is not equal to the demand deposit amount, the income will decrease if the interest rates decrease. Moreover, the economic value insensitivity demands a replacement M equal to zero!

Large Swiss banks encountered this paradox at the beginning of the 2000s. These banks choosed Value-at-Risk (VaR) as a risk measure for interest rate risk management of the balance sheet. VaR is an economic value based risk measure; consequently, the implicit demand deposit replacement was close to zero in these banks.

Swiss interest rates and especially short-term Swiss interest rates came down to less than 1 %. Therefore, the executive management of these companies saw a significant decrease in the net interest income even if they thought they had the best risk management department in the world!

These banks abandoned VaR reporting and switched to traditional earnings-at-risk reporting.

We will see in the next chapters how to reconcile economic value approach and accounting framework through:

- a more appropriate modelling of these demand deposits (with perequations, new production modelling, equilibrium relationships, cost and fees introduction);
- delta hedging strategies.

11.2.2 Replicating portfolio (classic demand deposit modelling mistakes)

11.2.2.1 Description of replicating portfolios

Replicating portfolios methodology is another approach to modelling demand deposits and defining their replacement schedule.

The A/L manager performs the replicating portfolio analysis per product and per segment of customers: stability of deposits is not the same for corporations or for individuals.

The methodology assumes that *there is a portfolio that "replicates" the interest margin dynamics*.

The method is simple: find the replicating portfolio that minimizes the historical net interest margin across time among a set of possible refinancing strategies:

- input: the replicating portfolio strategy;
- output: to minimize the volatility of the net interest margin.

Replicating portfolios aims at building an investment strategy that enables one to achieve a smooth interest rate margin measured as the difference between the interest rate earned on the replicating portfolio and the client rate.

Replicating portfolios enables one to treat non-interest bearing demand deposits as synthetic fixed rate bond issues with specified interest rates and maturities. These models allow us to compute the optimal refinancing strategy, a strategy that smoothes the net interest margin.

The *input* is an on-going investment strategy defined, for instance, as an FTP strategy based on the flows. The objective is to find the proportions X that minimize the margin volatility:

- X_1 % on 1 year;
- X_2 % on 2 years;
- ...;
- X_9 % on 9 years;
- $(1-X_1-X_2\ldots-X_9)$ % on 10 years.

The set of strategies is not always limited to FTP strategies based on the flows but this is often the case.

The purpose of replicating portfolios strategies is to compute the optimal percentages and the optimal flows duration.

The output to minimize is the historical net interest margin across time among this set of possible refinancing strategies that could have been used in the past.

The minimization programme is the following:

$$\underset{X_1,\, X_2,\ldots,\, X_N}{Min} \quad \underset{t=1980 \text{ to } 2000}{HISTORICAL\ VOLATILITY}[\text{Deposit Amount}_t.\,(\text{Resimulated FTP}_t (X_1, X_2, \ldots, X_N) - \text{Client rate}_t)] \qquad (11.13)$$

According to this formula, the replicating portfolio methodology could also be used for remunerated deposits such as savings accounts.

Moreover, here the volatility is computed on the net interest margin but could have been computed on the net discounted interest margin.

A/L managers using replicating portfolios think the calibration will capture these different components:

- partial correlation of client rate and market rate;
- sensitivity of the volume to interest rate movements;
- structural and residual interest rate risk.

In the following example, the replicating portfolio approach leads to an historical FTP rate smoother than the short-term or the long-term interest rates.

However, in our example, with the replicating portfolio technique, the FTP rate is decreasing and the net interest margin is decreasing. The *replicating portfolio methodology does not protect perfectly* the management from the interest rate decreases.

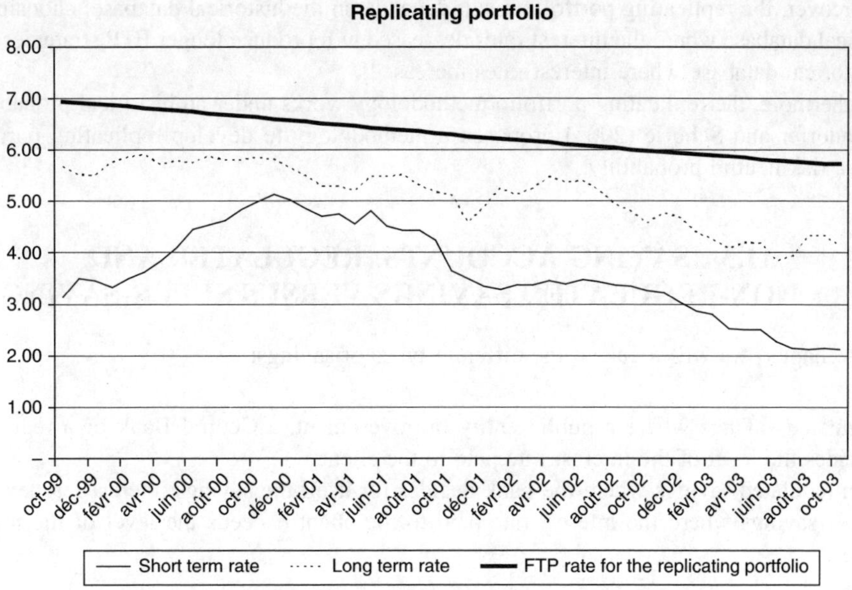

Figure 11.2 Replicating portfolio

11.2.2.2 Criticism of replicating portfolio

Replicating portfolio if often criticized since:

- the set of tested strategies is incomplete. The methodology does not look after the entire universe of possible hedging strategies;
- the methodology imposes constraints (for example liquidity constraints) without justification. Choosing "FTP rules based on the flows", the amount of deposits limits the total sum of investments by. The A/L manager imposes those constraints only to find a non-divergent solution. Consequently, quite often the minimization programme hits the constraints. The computed duration of optimal flows is frequently either zero or infinite.

Some articles such Adam et al. (2004) showed that the optimal strategy is not a strategy based on the flows. Indeed, replicating portfolio reasoning is more heuristic than economic. Its objective is more to obtain a FTP schedule coherent with what the A/L managers are used to do in practice.

Alternatively, the replicating portfolio does not take into account income transfer strategies. Examples of income transfer strategies are legion (and are developed in the final chapters of this book):

- reserves in insurance companies;
- strategies consisting of lending long-term and borrowing short-term and forward.

Somehow, the replicating portfolio methodology does not comprehend the income transfer strategies problem.

Moreover, the replicating portfolio result depends on the historical database: choosing an historical database where the interest rates decreased will produce longer FTP strategies than an historical database where interest rates increased!

Furthermore, the replicating portfolio methodology works under an historical probability. Frauendorfer and Schürle (2003) proposed a methodology to develop replicating portfolio under a risk neutral probability.

11.3 SAVING ACCOUNTS: REGULATED AND NON-REGULATED SAVINGS VERSUS SUPER-SAVINGS

In this chapter, we will focus on the different types of savings:

- regulated savings where a public entity (a government, a Central Bank or a regulator) decides the level of the interest rate paid to the client;
- non-regulated savings where the bank decides for itself the savings interest rate level;
- super-savings where the interest rate paid to the client exceeds the level of the market rates.

11.3.1 Regulated savings

We distinguish two kinds of regulated savings: those where there is an indexation of the customer to a formula and the others.

11.3.1.1 Regulated savings with an explicit interest rate formula: example of French inflation linked savings

In many countries, banks are authorized to sell savings accounts contracts where the remuneration is set explicitly over market financial data by a public entity such as the Central Bank.

For example in France, there is an explicit link between savings remuneration, the inflation level and the Euribor.

$$\text{French Savings rate} = \frac{(\text{Inflation} + \text{Euribor})}{2} + 0.25\% \tag{11.14}$$

The "Banque de France" recalculates the savings rate every 6 months.

The inflation indexation protects customers against inflation movements and the Euribor indexation links the savings rate with market rates.

According to this formula:

- 50 % of the savings amount is indexed to the Euribor rate and will be hedged through Euribor replacements;
- 50 % of the savings amount is indexed to the inflation: in the housewife basket "numéraire" (the real world) this amount is remunerated at an interest rate of 0.5 % (i.e. 0.25 % multiplied by 2).

The strategy to replace this last amount should be the same strategy as the one used for replacing 0 % demand deposit in the nominal world.

In practice, the A/L manager will replace this second amount through:

- long-term inflation indexed bonds;
- long-term inflation swaps against Euribor;
- savings rate against Euribor swaps;
- production of inflation indexed loans.

11.3.1.2 Regulated savings without interest rate formula

The regulated savings rate is not often indexed to a formula, as is the case in France. The savings rate usually varies according to market rates and inflation and also for political reasons.

The A/L manager's task is to determine the regulatory savings rate formula.

Historical analysis provides ideas for modelling and estimating models such as following:

$$
\begin{aligned}
&S_t = f\,(Libor_t, Inflation_t)\\
&\text{Savings Rate}_t = \text{Savings Rate}_{t-1} \text{ if } (\text{Savings Rate}_{t-1} - S_t) \leq Limit\\
&\text{Savings Rate}_t = S_t \text{ if } (\text{Savings Rate}_{t-1} - S_t) > Limit
\end{aligned}
\tag{11.15}
$$

Here the objective is to estimate the function f.

11.3.2 Non-regulated savings and "super-savings"

With non-regulated savings, the bank has the choice of the level of the remuneration rate. When the remuneration rate exceeds the market rates level, the A/L managers give a name to these savings: "*super-savings*". Providing these super-savings, these banks follow an aggressive marketing campaign in order to acquire new customers.

There are three possible strategic options for the remuneration rate of these deposits:

- The remuneration rate is indexed to the market rates level.
- The A/L manager has a replacement strategy providing a variable FTP and the margin is fixed. Consequently, the deposit amount varies accordingly to the proposed rate attractiveness.
- The amount of demand deposit is stabilized across time, the bank providing an adequate interest rate to perform this stabilization (the "savings market rate").

The majority of banks will follow either the first strategy or the third one.

In their choice of strategy, banks will have to optimize their income dependency upon the margin they intend to take. The income is the multiplication of the margin by the deposit amount (that depends also on the margin).

Optimization is in the real world a multi-period optimization since the bank's strategy is often a multi-period strategy. For instance, banks providing super-savings will have to optimize their expected value as a function of their margin strategy:

$$
V = E\left(\int_0^{+\infty} (K\,(t, \text{margin}_t)\,.\text{margin}_t + \text{other income}\,(K\,(t, \text{margin}_t)))\,.e^{-\int_0^t r(s)ds}\,dt\right) \tag{11.16}
$$

This economic value takes into account the other incomes arising from the products other than the super-savings.

11.4 DEMAND DEPOSITS MODELS IN THE LITERATURE

We will develop in this chapter the academic demand deposit models found in the literature:

- Selvaggio (1996);
- Frachot (2001);
- Jarrow and van Deventer (1998);
- Dupré (1996);
- OTS (2001);
- Adam *et al.* (2004).

11.4.1 Selvaggio (1996)

The Selvaggio demand deposit model supposes that there is a target demand deposit amount D^* which verifies the formula:

$$\log D_k^* = \alpha + \beta_1 \cdot \log R_k + \beta_2 \cdot \log Y_k \tag{11.17}$$

Y_k is a vector of macroeconomic variables (revenues, growth, inflation, etc.) and R_k is the level of the interest rates.

The relationship between the target amount and the realized amount is as follows:

$$(\log D_k - \log D_{k-1}) = \lambda \cdot (\log D_k^* - \log D_{k-1}) \tag{11.18}$$

The realized amount converges to the target amount with a speed equal to λ.

In other words, the evolution of the realized amount is as follows:

$$\log D_k = \lambda \cdot \alpha + (1-\lambda) \cdot \log D_{k-1} + \lambda \cdot \beta_1 \cdot \log R_k + \lambda \cdot \beta_2 \cdot \log Y_k \tag{11.19}$$

When he estimated the parameters of this formula over real databases, Selvaggio used a proxy: he supposed that the macroeconomic variables grew at a speed depending on time, adding a seasonal effect (the last term of the equation):

$$\log D_k = \beta_0 \cdot \log D_{k-1} + \beta_1 \cdot \log R_k + \beta_2 \cdot t_k + \sum_{i=3}^{14} \beta_i 1\!\mathrm{I}_{\{month=(i-4)\}} \tag{11.20}$$

Such a model introduces two statistical questions:

- Does this equation work with stationary variables?
- Is macroeconomic variables growth Y really indexed to the time?

11.4.2 Frachot (2001)

Antoine Frachot et al. proposed behavioural demand deposit modelling.

The base of the modelling goes with an analysis of the behaviour of each unitary account d_k. The evolution of each account still converges to a target amount D* with a speed of λ. The target amount is higher when the interest rate R_k is under a level of s, traducing a classic "volume effect".

$$d_k - d_{k-1} = \lambda \cdot (D^* - d_{k-1}) + \beta \cdot 1\mathrm{I}_{\{R_k < s\}} \tag{11.21}$$

When Frachot aggregates this equation over the entire population of the customers, it leads to:

$$D_k - D_{k-1} = \lambda \cdot (D^* - D_{k-1}) + \beta \cdot \int 1\mathrm{I}_{\{R_k < s\}} \cdot f(s) \cdot ds = \lambda \cdot (D^* - D_{k-1}) + \beta \cdot (1 - F(R_k)) \tag{11.22}$$

f is the density of the random variable s and F is the repartition function of this variable. Supposing that this variable follows a normal distribution, it leads to:

$$D_k - D_{k-1} = \lambda \cdot (D^* - D_{k-1}) + \beta \cdot \left(1 - \Phi\left(\frac{R_k - R^*}{\nu}\right)\right) \tag{11.23}$$

The parameters to estimate are λ, β, ν, D* and R* but the estimation is not easy to perform. The model proposes that R* is within the interval [0;15 %] and ν within the interval [0;20 %].

It is perhaps more adequate to estimate a non-parametric model:

$$D_k - D_{k-1} = \alpha_1 + \alpha_2 \cdot D_{k-1} + \alpha_3 \cdot g_{R^*,\nu}(R_k) \tag{11.24}$$

11.4.3 Dupré (1996)

Dupré proposed a continuous time model for non-remunerated demand deposits. The demand deposit amount D grows with a speed correlated with interest rates:

$$\frac{dD_t}{D_t} = (\alpha - \beta \cdot r_t) \cdot dt \tag{11.25}$$

α is the non-financial trend of this amount and β represents the correlation between the trend and the market rate r (still traducing the volume effects).

The continuous version of this model is this:

$$\log D_k - \log D_{k-1} = \alpha_1 + \alpha_2 \cdot R_k \tag{11.26}$$

Once more, the model links a stationary variable with a non-stationary variable R.

When integrating D, the model leads to:

$$D_t = D_0 . e^{\left(\alpha . t - \beta . \int_0^t r(s) . ds\right)} \tag{11.27}$$

The price of the demand deposits V is then easy to compute as the discounted incomes:

$$
\begin{aligned}
V &= E\left(\int_0^{+\infty} D_s.r(s).e^{-\int_0^s r(u).du}.ds\right) \\
V &= E\left(\int_0^{+\infty} D_0.e^{\left(\alpha.s-(1+\beta).\int_0^s r(u).du\right)}.r(s).ds\right)
\end{aligned}
\tag{11.28}
$$

Consequently, it leads to these formulae:

$$
\begin{aligned}
V &= D_0.E\left(\int_0^{+\infty} e^{\alpha.s}.e^{\left(-(1+\beta).\int_0^s r(u).du\right)}.r(s).ds\right) \\
V &= -\frac{D_0}{1+\beta}.\int_0^{+\infty}\left(e^{\alpha.s}.\mu'(s).e^{\mu(s)}\right).ds
\end{aligned}
\tag{11.29}
$$

Dupré gives examples of the function μ according to the interest rate model. For example, if r is constant V is equal to:

$$
V = \frac{D_0.r}{\alpha-(1+\beta).r}
\tag{11.30}
$$

11.4.4 Jarrow and Van Deventer (1998)

Jarrow and Van Deventer deal with the demand deposit problem in a business risk free framework.

They suppose that the market has two actors: financial institutions and investors. The logarithm of the demand deposit grows with a trend indexed to the time, to the interest rates and to the variations of the interest rates:

$$
d\log D_t = (\alpha_1+\alpha_2\cdot t+\alpha_3\cdot r_t)\cdot dt+\alpha_4\cdot dr_t
\tag{11.31}
$$

The continuous version of this equation is the following:

$$
\log D_k-\log D_{k-1} = \alpha_1+\alpha_2\cdot t_k+\alpha_3\cdot R_k+\alpha_4\cdot(R_k-R_{k-1})
\tag{11.32}
$$

When we integrate this equation over time, the demand deposit amount becomes:

$$
D_t = D_0.e^{\left(\alpha_1.t+\alpha_2.\frac{t^2}{2}+\alpha_3.\int_0^t r_s.ds+\alpha_4\cdot(r_t-r_0)\right)}
\tag{11.33}
$$

Once more, it is possible to compute the demand deposit economic value:

$$V = E\left(\int_0^{+\infty} D_s.r(s).e^{-\int_0^s r(u).du}.ds\right)$$

$$V = D_0.E\left(\int_0^{+\infty} e^{\left(\alpha_1.s+\alpha_2.\frac{s^2}{2}+(\alpha_3-1)\cdot\int_0^s r_u.du+\alpha_4\cdot(r_s-r_0)\right)}.r(s).ds\right) \tag{11.34}$$

$$V = D_0.es^{-\alpha_4.r_0}.\int_0^{+\infty}\left[e^{\left(\alpha_1.s+\alpha_2.\frac{s^2}{2}\right)}.E\left(e^{\left((\alpha_3-1)\cdot\int_0^s r_u.du+\alpha_4\cdot r_s\right)}.r(s)\right)\right].ds$$

In other words, the economic value follows:

$$V = D_0.es^{-\alpha_4.r_0}.\int_0^{+\infty}\left[e^{\left(\alpha_1.s+\alpha_2.\frac{s^2}{2}\right)}.\mu_{JD}(s)\right].ds$$

$$\mu_{JD}(s) = E\left(e^{\left((\alpha_3-1)\cdot\int_0^s r_u.du+\alpha_4\cdot r_s\right)}.r(s)\right) \tag{11.35}$$

In the Jarrow and Van Deventer framework, the function μ looks like:

$$\mu_{JD}(s) = [E+\alpha_4\cdot VAR+(\alpha_3-1)\cdot COV].e^{\left\{\alpha_4\cdot E+(\alpha_3-1)\cdot E'+\alpha_4\cdot(\alpha_3-1).COV+\frac{(\alpha_4)^2}{2}.VAR+\frac{(\alpha_3-1)^2}{2}.VAR'\right\}}$$

$$E = E\left(r_t\right) \text{ and } E' = E\left(e^{\int_0^t r_s.ds}\right) \tag{11.36}$$

$$VAR = Variance\left(r_t\right),\ VAR' = Variance\left(e^{\int_0^t r_s.ds}\right) \text{ and } COV = Covariance\left(r_t, e^{\int_0^t r_s.ds}\right)$$

11.4.5 (OTS) Office of Thrift Supervision (2001)

In the US, the *Office of Thrift Supervision (OTS)* supervises "Savings associations" (it includes also "Savings & Loans") and their holding companies.

The OTS's objective is to ensure the safety and the solvency of these savings associations while taking care of the respect of the laws concerning the consumers.

The OTS provided in 2001 a model, the "Net portfolio value model", in order to compute the economic value of the different products of the balance sheet.

For deposit accounts, the OTS distinguishes these different types of accounts:

- transaction accounts (checking accounts, money market checking accounts, etc.);
- Money market deposit accounts (MMDA);
- passbook accounts (other remunerated deposits);
- non-interest bearing demand deposits.

For each account, the method proposes scheduling and remuneration rate modelling.

For demand deposits, this modelling assumes the amount:

$$D_k = D_{k-1} \cdot \left(a + a \arctan\left(d + c \cdot \frac{i_k}{r_k} \right) + e \cdot i_k \right)^{1/2} \tag{11.37}$$

i_k is the deposit remuneration rate and r_k is the interest rate (at date k).

This model helps take into account the asymmetry between market interest rates and remuneration rates. When the interest rates go down, remuneration interest rates tend to amplify this movement; on the other hand, when rates go up, banks tend not to price directly this rise in their remuneration rates.

This formula for non-interest rate bearing demand deposits becomes:

$$D_k = D_{k-1} \cdot \alpha \tag{11.38}$$

α-estimations are easy for savings associations once they have an historical database of their non-interest bearing deposits.

Unfortunately, this model does not take into account volume effects in demand deposit modelling.

Alternatively, the OTS provides a complete modelling formula for interest rate remuneration:

$$\begin{cases} i_k = i_{k-1} + c.(i_{k-1} - i_{k-2}) + d.(R_k - R_{k-1}) + e.(R_{k-1} - R_{k-2}) + C_{k-1} \\ E_k = a + b.R_k (\text{Equilibrium rate}) \\ C_{k-1} = f.(i_{k-1} - E_{k-1}) \text{ if } i_{k-1} \geq E_{k-1} \\ C_{k-1} = g.(i_{k-1} - E_{k-1}) \text{ if } i_{k-1} < E_{k-1} \end{cases} \tag{11.39}$$

The remuneration rate takes into account:

- past movements of interest rates R (3 months forward rate);
- the existence of an equilibrium rate E: deposit rate converges to this equilibrium rate but the speed of convergence depends on the spread between deposit remuneration rates and market rates.

OTS provides regulatory values for the parameters a, b, c, d, f and g for each deposit account type.

This modelling allows the computation of a formula for the valuation of demand deposits.

$$\begin{aligned} V &= E\left(\int_0^{+\infty} D_s.r(s).e^{-\int_0^s r(u).du} .ds \right) \\ V &= D_0 E\left(\int_0^{+\infty} \alpha^s.r(s).e^{-\int_0^s r(u).du} .ds \right) \\ V &= -D_0 \left(\int_0^{+\infty} \alpha^s.\mu(s).\mu'(s).ds \right) \\ \mu(s) &= E\left(e^{-\int_0^s r(u).du} \right) \end{aligned} \tag{11.40}$$

The formula can take into account non-interest costs (NIC) and a discounting spread over zero-coupon rates.

In the US, when a bank acquires a saving portfolio, the accountants report the obtained valuation in the assets under the denomination: transaction account intangible, MMDA intangible or non-interest bearing intangible.

11.4.6 Adam, Laurent and Rebérioux (2004)

Adam, Laurent and Rebérioux introduced a Brownian motion in the modelling of the demand deposit amount K. This Brownian motion is correlated with the Brownian motion of the Libor rate L with a correlation ρ:

$$\begin{aligned} \frac{dK}{K} &= \mu_K.dt + \sigma_K.dW_K \\ \frac{dL}{L} &= \mu_L.dt + \sigma_L.dW_L \\ \langle dW_K/dW_L \rangle &= \rho.dt \end{aligned} \tag{11.41}$$

The correlation represents the volume effect.

The objective is then to compute the optimal hedging strategy. The strategy is made up of a suite of swaplets (or FRA Forward Rate Agreement) exchanging fixed rate against Libor rate on the period going from T to T+1. We call V(t) the amount of swaplets contracted at date t. We call NBJ(T,T+1) the number of days between T and T+1.

It is possible to prove that under theses assumptions the earnings (results) of the period going from T to T+1 can be written as:

$$R(T) = \frac{NBJ\,(T, T+1)}{365} \times \left(L(T,T)K(T) - \int_0^T V(t)dL(t,T) \right) \tag{11.42}$$

The A/L manager's goal is then to maximize a utility function or to minimize a risk measure based on R(T) (i.e. the earnings at date T).

Common risk measures used in quantitative finance are:

- standard deviation (or variance);
- Value-at-Risk;
- coherent risk measures such as expected shortfall.

For example, using the standard deviation as risk measure, the problem can be written as:

$$\min_{V(.)} \operatorname{var} \left(L(T,T)K(T) - \int_0^T V(t)dL(t,T) \right) \tag{11.43}$$

Using stochastic calculations, the optimal solution for V is:

$$V(t) = K(t) \times \left(1 + \rho \frac{\sigma_K}{\sigma_L} \right) \times \exp\left((\mu_K + \rho\sigma_K\sigma_L) \times (T - t) \right) \tag{11.44}$$

If ρ and μ_k are equal to 0 and if there is no correlation between the Brownian motions, the optimal strategy is:

$$V(t) = K(t) \tag{11.45}$$

According to this risk measure, at any horizon t, the A/L manager should replace the deposits in swaps (or bonds).

This conclusion is very different from reality where A/L managers usually replace the demand deposit amounts with a horizon no longer than 15 years.

Moreover, the study proves that the optimal strategy depends on the risk measure chosen by the management. Using expected shortfall or Value-at-Risk as risk measure, the optimal strategy is not to replace all the amount of demand deposits.

Indeed, the real optimal hedge is a bit more difficult to compute than in this model. Indeed, the real optimal hedge should take into account at least:

- demand deposit remuneration;
- servicing costs (usually associated with demand deposits accounts);
- compensation effects between different type of products (other income, other demand deposits and other savings);
- the opportunity to hedge the volatility risk with caplets and floorlets;
- accounting considerations of the hedging;
- multi-period framework.

Nevertheless, the approach introduces:

- a *business risk* (impossible to hedge) on demand deposits through the Brownian motion W_k; and
- a *bank risk aversion* through risk measures. If the risk is expressed in terms of variance, the optimal strategy is to consider that demand deposits have no maturity: it is rational since using the variance as a risk measure, the bank is not sensitive to extreme risk.

11.5 DEPOSIT MODELLING: THE SOLUTION THROUGH AN APPROACH BASED ON CUSTOMER BEHAVIOUR MODELLING

All the proposed models above showed that A/L managers need information about their customer behaviour.

To build this expertise, it is necessary to construct an historical database of customer behaviour before deciding upon a FTP scheduling.

11.5.1 Historical database construction

Databases about customer behaviour have to take into account the longest historical database possible.

These databases will focus on this kind of information:

- *deposit account closing rates*;
- *average amount by account*;

- *customer remuneration rate by account*;
- *new customer production*;
- *operating costs and other incomes linked with the deposit account.*

The A/L manager splits this information according to the deposit account type and by account year of opening.

Additional information could also provide help to the A/L manager: customer internal rating, customer age, average balance segmentation, etc.

Ideally, data are unitary with, for example, for each customer the deposit amount. However, in practice the A/L manager aggregates the data (usually by month of opening and by client type).

Some banks employ a *scoring of their demand deposit*: for each customer, the bank computes an internal score in order to make a distinction between the customers in terms of:

- average monthly amount;
- amount volatility.

11.5.2 Account closing probability modelling

The first element to model is the closing account probability, i.e. the probability for an existing customer to close its deposit account at each future date.

This probability will of course depend on the account seniority.

To begin with, the A/L manager will exclude from this analysis the financial market effects on this closing probability: the "volume effects" category will gather all the effects of this kind.

The initial modelling of this closing probability leads to a parameter P constant and equal to 5 % yearly, for example.

$$\text{P(seniority)} = 5\,\% \qquad (11.46)$$

11.5.3 Average amount by customer account

To be able to simulate the future amount of deposits, it is necessary to model the average amount by account.

This average amount may vary according to account seniority.

To begin with, the modelling will exclude the arbitrage effects gathered later in the "volume effects" category.

Initially, the average amount by account at date 0 is constant and is equal to the total deposit amount divided by the number of accounts.

$$\text{Average Amount}(0, \text{seniority}) = 3.000\,€ \qquad (11.47)$$

11.5.4 Deposit remuneration modelling

11.5.4.1 Classic modelling

The deposit remuneration rate can require specific modelling.

For sight deposits, the remuneration rate is zero. For resources with a regulated rate, there is often a formula as for "Livret A" in France with an indexation to Euribor and to inflation.

For the non-regulated resources, the A/L manager will look after a modelling based on:

- the history of the past remuneration rates;
- the correlation between the remuneration rate and the past market rates;
- the future constraints of the management on the remuneration rate.

The default modelling links the remuneration rate and the market rates as follows:

$$R(t) = A + B\,.\,\text{Libor}(t) + \varepsilon(t) \tag{11.48}$$

If A is equal to 25 bps and B is equal to 30 %, the remuneration will never go under 0.25 % and will follow partially market rates evolution. Improperly, the A/L manager will speak about a 30 % "correlation" between the remuneration rate and the market rates; in other terms, it means that 70 % of the demand deposit "behaves" as a fixed rate product.

Of course, the statisticians will base their advanced modelling on econometrical studies such as the one proposed by the OTS:

$$\begin{cases} R_{(t)} = R_{(t-1)} + c.\left(R_{(t-1)} - R_{(t-2)}\right) + d.\left(Libor_{(t)} - Libor_{(t-1)}\right) \\ \qquad + e.\left(Libor_{(t-1)} - Libor_{(t-2)}\right) + C_{(t-1)} + \varepsilon_{(t)} \\ E_{(t)} = a + b.Libor_{(t)} \text{(Equilibrium rate)} \\ C_{(t-1)} = f.\left(R_{(t-1)} - E_{(t-1)}\right) \text{ if } R_{(t-1)} \geq E_{(t-1)} \\ C_{(t-1)} = g.\left(R_{(t-1)} - E_{(t-1)}\right) \text{ if } R_{(t-1)} < E_{(t-1)} \end{cases} \tag{11.49}$$

In practice, A/L managers will look after the existence of *autocorrelation* between the $\varepsilon(t)$ of one of the two equations above:

$$\varepsilon(t) = h.\varepsilon(t-1) + \eta(t) \tag{11.50}$$

11.5.4.2 Modelling with marketing constraints

In many cases, marketing constraints condition the remuneration rate.

For example, talking about super-savings, the remuneration rate may depend on the asset portfolio of the competitors. It means that if the other super-savings competitors invested their cash in 5 year notes, their asset portfolio rate is indexed to the 5 years smoothed rate on 5 years. Consequently, these competitors will tend to index their customer remuneration rate to this index.

On the other hand, the super-savings are in competition with classic short-term deposits (indexed to the Libor index).

All this means, for example, that the remuneration rate for super-savings is indexed to the maximum of the smoothed rate and of the Libor:

$$R(t) = \text{Max (5 years smoothed rate on 5 years} - \text{A; Libor (t)} - \text{B)} \tag{11.51}$$

Long-term smoothed rates will sometimes replace Libor rates in the regressions and better explain the remuneration rate variations.

11.5.5 Wealth effect modelling

We use the term "wealth effect" for the effect of economic growth (GDP) on liability resources growth. With economic growth, i.e. with GDP growth, the demand deposit collected amount increases.

The collected resources (i.e. the demand deposits) will grow as fast as the economy wealth will grow. However, in the macroeconomic theory, the economy wealth growth converges to the long-term level of the nominal interest rates. Consequently, we will suppose that *the demand deposit growth is indexed to the interest rate level*. However, due to the technologic effect, this growth could be lower than the economy growth:

$$\text{Average Amount (t, seniority)} = \text{Average Amount (0, seniority)}.\, e^{\int_0^t r(s).ds-\alpha.t}.\text{Y(t)} \quad (11.52)$$
$$\text{Y}(0) = 1$$

The variable Y(t) will represent the volume effect described in the next section.

11.5.6 Volume effect modelling

We call "volume effects" all effects of distortion between deposits due to the remuneration rate movements of these deposits.

Initially, banks will avoid the existence of these volume effects. The second time, A/L managers will model this effect proposing a link between the average deposit level and the interest rate level.

It is possible to base the modelling:

- either on the historical evolution of each deposit; or
- on the historical repartition between deposits.

11.5.6.1 Modelling based on deposit historical evolution

We may link the modelling directly with the observations of the variable Y retaining, for example, Frachot's framework:

$$\text{Y}_\text{t} = \lambda.\,(Y_0 - \text{Y}_{\text{t}-1}) + \beta.1_{\{R(t)>Libor(t)\}} \quad (11.53)$$

The arbitrage function may become more complex if we include all the remuneration rates, the inflation rate, etc.

11.5.6.2 Modelling based on deposit repartition historical evolution

On the subject of monetary aggregates, we have already introduced volume effect modelling based upon monetary aggregate ratios.

For example, if we consider an economy with three types of deposits: money market savings, savings and demand deposits, the A/L manager will start to compute these ratios:

$$X_1(t) = \frac{\text{Demand deposits}(t)}{\text{Savings}(t) + \text{Demand deposits}(t)}$$
$$X_2(t) = \frac{\text{Savings}(t) + \text{Demand deposits}(t)}{\text{Money market savings(t)} + \text{Savings}(t) + \text{Demand deposits}(t)} \quad (11.54)$$

Subsequently, the joint modelling of the volume effect and of the wealth effect becomes:

$$\text{Money Market Savings(t, seniority)} = (1 - X_2(t))\,.\,\text{Average Total Amount (0, seniority)}\,.\,e^{\int_0^t r(s).ds}$$

$$\text{Savings(t, seniority)} = (1 - X_1(t))\,.\,X_2(t)\,.\,\text{Average Total Amount (0, seniority)} \times e^{\int_0^t r(s).ds}$$

$$\text{Demand deposits(t, seniority)} = X_1(t).X_2(t).\text{Average Total Amount (0, seniority)} \times e^{\int_0^t r(s).ds} \quad (11.55)$$

The A/L manager's task is then to estimate the relationship between the evolution of X and market rates with, for example, this set of equations:

$$\begin{aligned} \frac{dX_1(t)}{X_1(t)} &= \left(-\alpha_1.e^{-\beta_1 t} + f_1(r_t)\right).dt \\ \frac{dX_2(t)}{X_2(t)} &= \left(-\alpha_2.e^{-\beta_2 t} + f_2(r_t)\right).dt \end{aligned} \quad (11.56)$$

The function f can be regressed using kernel regression.

11.5.6.3 Linking account closing rates and market rates

Theoretically, a volume effect may affect the closing rate. When the remuneration varies, the probability of closing varies as well.

It is common and safe to assume that *the bank will in the future pay the remuneration rate asked by the customer to stay within the bank.* Consequently, the closing probability will not depend on the market rates but the remuneration rate will take into account this constraint (as described for the super-savings accounts example).

Nevertheless, sometimes it is safer to abandon customers when the competitors have a substantial advantage (such as a tax advantage). Thus, the A/L manager will have to model the closing probability as a function of market rates.

11.5.7 New production and perequation modelling

When we compute income sensitivities, it is necessary to project the future number of clients. Models developed above allow the behaviour modelling of future customers. Indeed, the A/L manager needs to know the number of future customers month by month.

Initially, it is possible to choose a number of clients that is constant across time. In practice, an econometrical analysis could help to project this number. New customer production is linked in many countries with:

- the operating cost disbursed to acquire new customers;
- the promotional campaigns;
- the *perequations* (such as the new customer acquisition through low margins on the acquisition of the other products: mortgages, etc.).

Unfortunately, not so many companies decided for the moment to model their perequation system. Indeed the modelling usually shows the real profitablility of the past marketing campaigns (a profitability that some people prefer sometimes to hide).

Perequation modelling follows a simple basis principle:

Economic value produced at time t is independent upon economic conditions of time t

Mathematically speaking this principle becomes:

At least, an equilibrium economic value VE*(t) exists for the production of new clients at date t and follows for example:

$$VE^*(t) = VE^*(0).e^{\int_0^t r(s).ds} \tag{11.57}$$

This economic value takes into account the technologic effects.

The economic value produced by the new clients at date t follows:

$$dVE(t) = \lambda.(VE^*(t) - VE(t)).dt + \sigma.dW_t$$

If the economic value of the new production were a function of the market rates, it would mean that there is no efficiency within the market.

For demand deposits, the economic value **VE(t) is the sum of all the discounted cash flows associated with the deposit account opened at date t.** It means:

- the future incomes arising on the deposit account;
- all the other incomes (fees on future other production to this new customer);
- the perequation (on mortgages, etc.).

For example, in French retail banking, the banks acquire their profitable customers mainly through mortgages. It would mean, for example, that the margin m(t) on mortgages produced at date t depends on the interest rates so that the principle is respected.

11.5.8 Equilibrium relationship between operating costs, other incomes, margins and demand deposits (on existing customers)

The acquisition of future customers introduced the first equilibrium relationship. However, there is also an equilibrium relationship between:

- operating cost growth;
- other income growth;
- demand deposit income.

For example, the net income produced by customer (the sum of all the incomes less the operating costs by customer) explains this relationship:

- If the net income by customer becomes too low (due to an interest rate decrease for instance), the market will compensate for this weakness, creating new fees or new other incomes. For example, in Japan, at the end of the 90s when the short-term interest rates were close to zero, the banks created a new kind of fees, the transaction account fees.

- On the other hand, if the net income by customer becomes too important (due to an interest rate increase for instance), the market in the long-term will compensate for this increase with new banks creation, a negative pressure on the growth of other incomes and a negative pressure on the operating cost growth.

This equilibrium relationship means that the other income evolution will take into account the evolution of the demand deposit interest margin and of the operating cost:

$$Z_t = (\text{Demand deposit interest margin}_t + \text{Other income}_t - \text{Operating cost}_t) \times e^{-\int_0^t r(s).ds} \quad \text{(per client)} \tag{11.58}$$

$$dZ_t = \mu.\left(\tilde{Z} - Z_t\right).dt + \sigma'.dW_t$$

This relationship gives the possible evolution of the other incomes.

For instance, if the banking market replaces demand deposits usually on a horizon of T years, the net interest margins on demand deposits will follow:

$$NIM_t = \left[A + \frac{B}{T}.\int_{t-T}^{t} r(s).ds\right].e^{\int_0^t r(s).ds} \quad \text{(per client)} \tag{11.59}$$

If the average past rates in the formula above are lower than spot rates, a new competitor may come and propose competitive prices on the other incomes. Consequently, the other incomes will follow the equation below:

$$\text{Other income}_t = \left[C - B.\text{MAX}\left(r_t, \frac{\int_{t-T}^{t} r(s).ds}{T}\right)\right].e^{\int_0^t r(s).ds} \quad \text{(per client)} \tag{11.60}$$

$$\text{Operating cost}_t = \text{Operating cost}_0.e^{\int_0^t r(s).ds} \quad \text{(per client)}$$

Alternatively, it is possible to index directly the other income to the interest rates evolution such as:

$$\text{Other income}_t = \text{Other income}_0.e^{(1+\alpha).\int_0^t r(s).ds - \alpha.t.r^*} \quad \text{(per client)} \tag{11.61}$$

$$\text{Operating cost}_t = \text{Operating cost}_0.e^{\int_0^t r(s).ds} \quad \text{(per client)}$$

11.5.9 Sensitivity of the deposit amounts to bank rating

In terms of liquidity, the average amount by client depends on the liquidity risk taken by the customer.

In the emerging markets, a liquidity crisis may provoke important cash withdrawals even if the local bank rating does not change. Expert advisors should consider this point.

Moreover, the average amount by deposit depends on the bank rating. If the bank is downgraded, clients will maybe close their accounts, withdraw a part of their cash or ask for a higher remuneration of their deposits. Expert advisors should also consider this point.

11.5.10 Intraday, intra-monthly and intra-annual seasonality

Over long periods, the demand deposit amount is stable. Nevertheless, this stability varies due to seasonal effects:

- The intraday amount may vary a lot for unpredictable reasons.
- The intra-monthly amount may vary (think about the salaries payment date, the credit card amount withdrawal dates, etc.).
- The intra-annual amount may vary a lot due to the existence of bonuses payment dates, taxes payment dates, etc.

$$\text{Average Amount (t,seniority,month,day)} = \text{Average Amount (t,seniority)}.\ \text{f (month)}.g(\text{day}).\,(1+\varepsilon(t)) \quad (11.62)$$

The analysis of the seasonality helps into computing a minimum amount with a constant α:

$$\text{Minimal average Amount (t,seniority,month,day)} = \text{Average Amount (t,seniority)}.\,(1-\alpha) \quad (11.63)$$

11.5.11 Expert advice

Different expert advice is sometimes necessary in the modelling process.

At long-term horizons, products are exposed to regulatory, market or legal changes. For example, there is a non-zero probability for the demand deposit remuneration to be indexed to the market rates instead of being equal to zero.

This expert advice will of course depend on the country where the business line markets the demand deposits.

11.5.12 Demand deposit modelling backtesting and validation

A/L managers will pay attention to the modelling validation especially if the modelling integrates:

- autoregressive residual terms;
- seasonality;
- lags between market rates and remuneration rates;
- level modelling instead of absolute or relative variation.

The models have to be backtested on different historical periods using, for example, out-of-sample tests.

11.6 DEPOSIT MODELLING THROUGH A CUSTOMER BEHAVIOUR MODELLING BASED APPROACH: REPRESENTATION IN RISK INDICATORS AND FTP

After the modelling of the demand deposit, it is possible to introduce it properly into the risk indicators (liquidity and interest rates schedules, etc.) and into the FTP system.

11.6.1 Representation of Demand deposit in liquidity schedules

The *liquidity schedule of deposits* is the projection over time of the future evolution of the deposits associated with the existing clients.

The A/L manager excludes the future clients from this analysis since the economic value of these clients does not depend on market conditions as well as on the funding costs level.

By construction, the liquidity schedule starts at the actual level of demand deposits and converges to 0 (at an infinite horizon).

To compute this schedule from models, the A/L manager will have to recombine the stock actual photography with the models presented above:

- closing account probability;
- average amount by account;
- wealth effect and volume effect (if needed);
- sensitivity of the average amount to local liquidity conditions (local rating);
- intraday, intra-monthly and seasonality effects.

The most likely amount of deposits at date t, E(t), is deduced from the closing probability P, the initial number of accounts and the average initial amount by account AA. The considered amount is the minimal account taking into account a proportion α of instable deposits:

$$E(t) = \sum_{Generation\, i} \left(NC_i(0).AA_i(0,t).\prod_{j=0}^{t}(1-P_i(j)) \right).(1-\alpha) \tag{11.64}$$

If we consider a simplified modelling, the amount at date t depends only on a unique closing probability P:

$$E(t) = (1-P)^t.E(0).(1-\alpha) \tag{11.65}$$

Note that the average life of the demand deposit amount is equal to (1 − α)/P. For example, the average life is equal to 18 years with α = 10 % and P = 5 %.

11.6.2 Representation of Demand deposit in interest rate schedules

Interest rate schedules may differ widely from liquidity schedules. Banks will only consider the "fixed part" of demand deposits in the interest rate schedules.

The scheduling starts with the liquidity schedule and uses interest rate modelling.

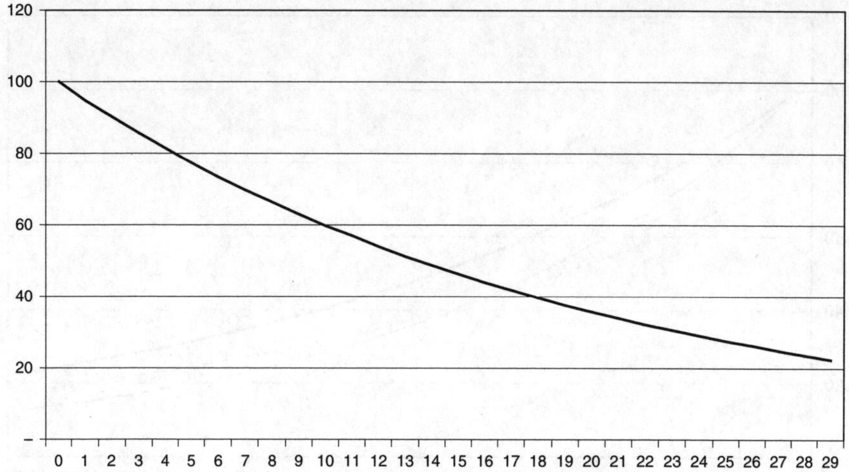

Figure 11.3 Liquidity schedule

Two approaches are possible:

- *Basis approach using a correlation remuneration modelling:*
  - Start with the correlation between remuneration rate and market rates, 30 % for instance.
  - Consider that if the "correlation" is equal to 30 %, the deposit is at 70 % a fixed rate deposit.
  - Consider the interest rate schedule as 70 % of the liquidity schedule.

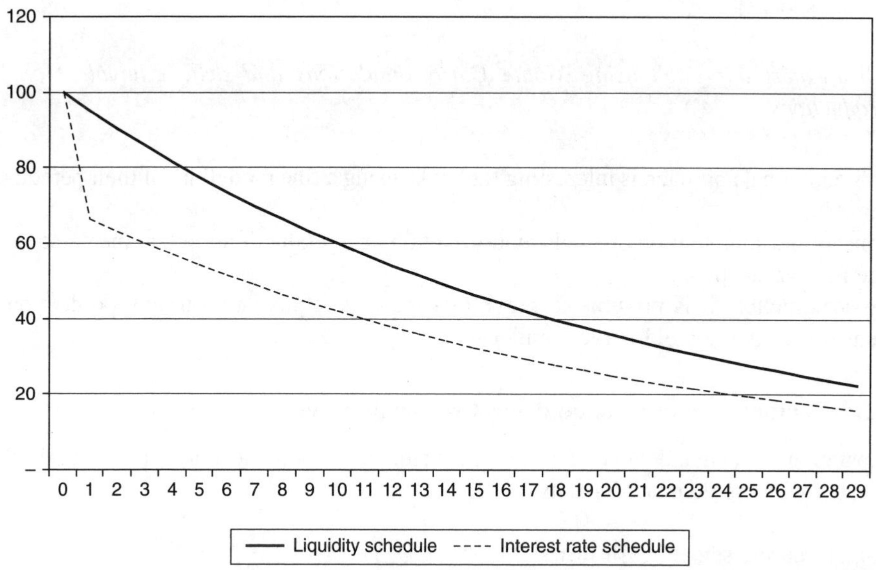

Figure 11.4 Liquidity and interest rate schedule

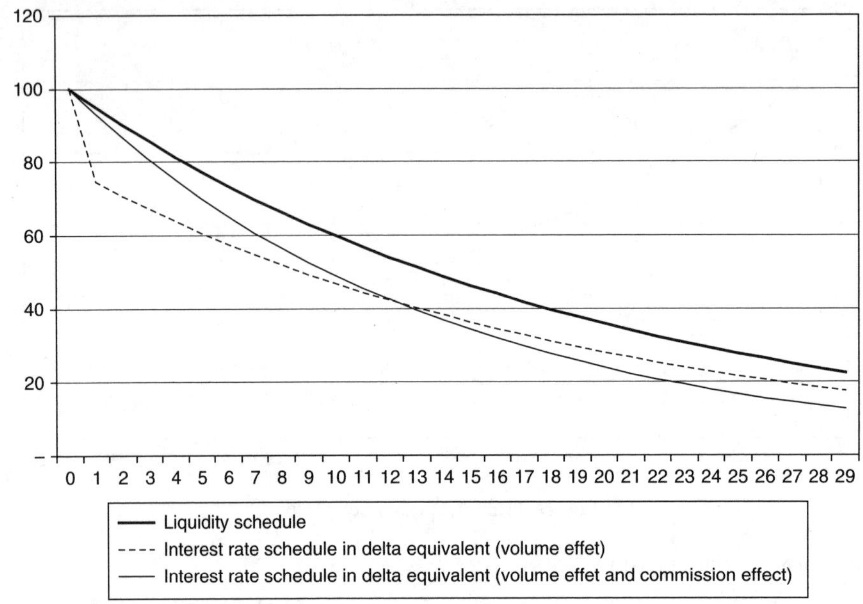

Figure 11.5 Liquidity and interest rate schedule

- *Expert approach using Monte Carlo simulations and delta equivalent:*
  - Simulate market rates with a one or two factors model.
  - Simulate for each scenario the net interest margin from the modelling presented above.
  - Compute the delta equivalent of demand deposits using the "delta equivalent technology" (i.e. the methodology providing the insensibility of the future incomes to interest rate shocks).

- *Ultra-expert approach using Monte Carlo simulations and delta equivalent on new productions.*

This additional approach is interesting for banks using a fine modelling of their perequation system.

It means the computation of a delta equivalent on new productions and on the perequations on the new productions.

By construction, it is possible to prove that the delta equivalent on new production has no sensitivity upon a yield curve parallel shock.

11.6.3 Computation of demand deposit economic value

Computation of demand deposit economic value takes into account all the cash flows associated with the demand deposits:

- capital reimbursement cash flows;
- interest rate cash flows;
- operational costs;
- other incomes.

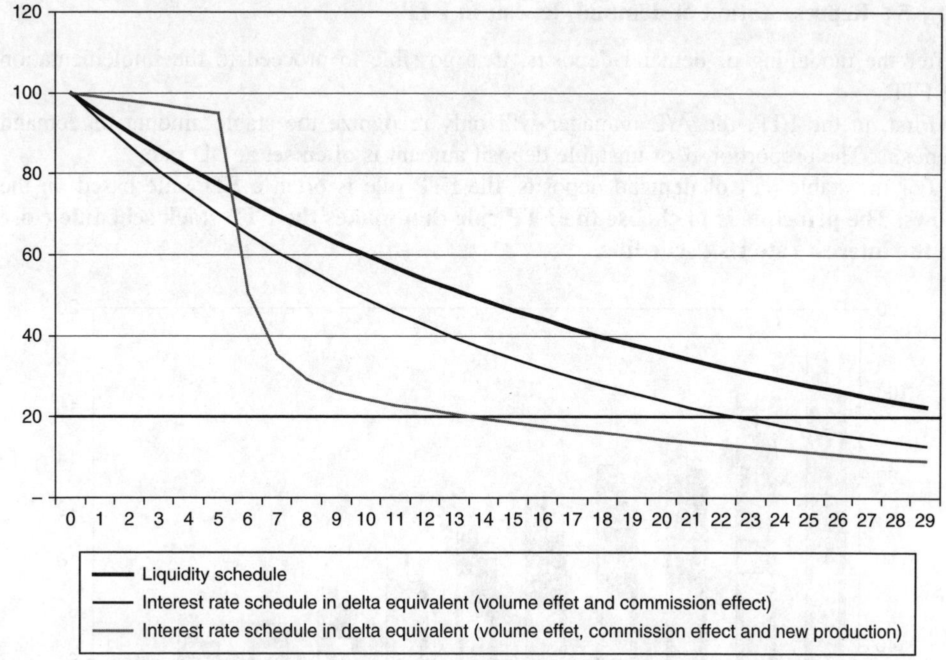

Figure 11.6 Liquidity and interest rate schedule

This computation has to be done over the database of the existing clients.

It is easy to implement analytical formulae according to the modelling. For instance, when closing probabilities are constant and equal to P, the interest rates are equal to r and the economic value is equal to:

$$V = E(0).\frac{r}{(r+p)} \tag{11.66}$$

Nevertheless, the computation can use classical Monte Carlo valuation techniques.

11.6.4 Representation of demand deposit in income sensitivities indicators

When the A/L manager computes income sensitivities, he takes into account all the sources of income using information about:

- deposit closing probability;
- average amount by account;
- client remuneration;
- new production;
- other incomes;
- perequation;
- operating costs.

11.6.5 Representation of demand deposit in FTP

After the modelling of demand deposits, it is possible to proceed to the implementation of FTP.

First, in the FTP, the A/L manager will only recognize the stable amount of demand deposits. The proportion α of unstable deposit amount is often set at DD rate.

For the stable part of demand deposits, the FTP rule is often a FTP rule based on the flows. **The principle is to choose the FTP rule that makes the FTP stock schedule close to the interest rate risk schedule.**

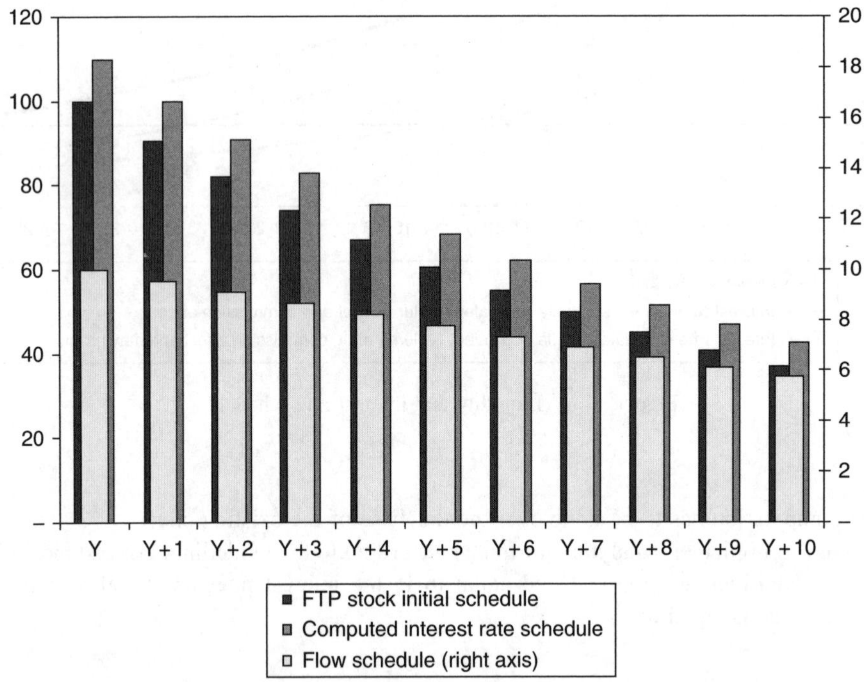

Figure 11.7 FTP stock schedule

The table below shows how the adjustment modifies the FTP:

	FTP stock initial schedule	Initial rate	Flow schedule	Flow rate	Computed interest rate schedule	FTP after adjustment
Y	100	5.0 %	10	6.0 %	110	5.1 %
Y + 1	90	5.0 %	10	6.1 %	100	5.1 %
Y + 2	82	5.0 %	9	6.2 %	91	5.1 %
Y + 3	74	5.0 %	9	6.3 %	83	5.1 %
Y + 4	67	5.0 %	8	6.4 %	75	5.2 %
Y + 5	61	5.0 %	8	6.5 %	68	5.2 %
Y + 6	55	5.0 %	7	6.6 %	62	5.2 %
Y + 7	50	5.0 %	7	6.7 %	57	5.2 %
Y + 8	45	5.0 %	7	6.8 %	51	5.2 %
Y + 9	41	5.0 %	6	6.9 %	47	5.2 %
Y + 10	37	5.0 %	6	7.0 %	43	5.3 %

Figure 11.8 FTP adjustment

Moreover, the modelling showed that the FTP would take into account the perequation effects (i.e. the perequation costs transferred from the FTP of the products including positive perequations).

The Manager will perform a FTP computation product by product. *However, it is also possible to compute the FTP generation by generation (i.e. by generation of demand deposit production).* This way, it allows for a better management control of the income.

11.6.6 Appropriate hedging strategy

The delta hedging gives readily the demand deposit hedging strategy. *After delta hedging, the hedging is quasi perfect* since the residual risks are the business and the model risk.

The delta equivalent chapter will prove how incomes after delta hedging grow with a speed indexed to the interest rate level.

12
Loans

Crédit est mort, les mauvais payeurs l'ont tué.

Ahead of deposits, loans make up the largest part of the asset side of bank balance sheets. Before the definition of the prepayment modelling in the next chapter, we will introduce some basic definitions applied to loans.

12.1 DIFFERENT TYPES OF LOAN

12.1.1 General considerations

To distinguish between loans, it is important to know the reason for which the customer has borrowed money:

- *Mortgage loan*: a loan to an individual using a property as security for the repayment of the loan cash flows.
- *Consumer loan*: another loan to an individual, not a mortgage loan but still with a specific purpose (car, boat, recreational vehicle).
- *Student loan*: a loan proposed to students to assist them in the payment of the costs of education.
- *Corporate loan*: every kind of credit provided to corporations:
    - Investment loan: a corporate loan with a specific investment purpose.
    - Cash credit: a short-term loan proposed to corporations' treasurers.
    - Export credit: a corporate loan for export financing.
    - Buyer credit.
    - Supplier credit.
- *Bridge loan*: a temporary loan (when waiting for a complete established refinancing).
- *Credit card loan or revolving credit*: a credit to an individual without a fixed number of repayments. This credit may be used repeatedly.
- *Overdraft*: an implicit credit when withdrawals from a bank account exceed the available balance.
- *Credit facilities or lines of credit*.
- *Home equity loan*: a loan in which the borrower uses the equity in his home as collateral.

Loans may be *secured* (such as mortgages) when a collateral diminishes the lender credit risk or *unsecured*.

The Commercial Department choose the credit duration and the amortizing schedules according to the financed object duration:

- Consumer loans credit duration is often low since the value of the financed product amortizes very fast (5 years for a car, up to 15 years for a boat, etc.).
- Mortgages loans duration can be higher, up to 50 years in some countries (in Switzerland, duration goes up to 100 years!).
- More generally, credits are often amortized since the value of the financed product decreases with time.

Indeed, credit amortization allows the bank to monitor better its credit risk: the borrower is obliged to repay monthly a fixed sum instead of having to repay a huge amount at the end of the credit.

The A/L manager will distinguish:

- *Bullet loans* when the customer reimburses the principal at maturity and pays the interest on a pre-established basis (usually monthly or annually).
- *Zero-coupon loans* when the customer reimburses principal and interest at maturity.
- *Linear amortizing loans (or P-constant loans)* when the customer reimburses the principal P linearly on a pre-established basis.
- *P+I amortizing loans (or P+I-constant loans)* when the customer reimbursement is fixed on a pre-established basis (usually monthly).

12.1.2 Leasing

Leasing contracts give to the client the "enjoyment" of a material good (car, boat, truck, etc.) without the immobilization of the cash. The lender retains the ownership of the good. The customer pays a fixed or a floating sum that could be a fixed or as an indexed amortizing.

At the end of the contract, the customer has sometimes the opportunity to buy back the material good or to sign a new contract (and to change his car, etc.).

The lessor retains a risk over the price of the material good at the end of the contract: will the lessor be able to sell the good at a price above the credit remaining capital?

In the example below, the price of the material good is equal to 100, the interest rate is equal to 5 %, and the customer will pay an amount of 13 annually.

	Remaining capital	Interest repayment	Capital repayment	Annual payment
Y	100			
Y + 1	92	5	8	13
Y + 2	84	5	8	13
Y + 3	75	4	9	13
Y + 4	66	4	9	13
Y + 5	56	3	10	13

Figure 12.1 Loan repayment

After 5 years, the customer has the opportunity to buy back the material good at a price of 56. If he refuses, the lessor will be obliged to sell this material good with hopefully a price above 56 otherwise he will lose money.

12.1.3 Loans around the world

Around the world, there are many different types of loans. Here are some examples of the diversity of these loans.

In Switzerland, there are mortgage loans with a fixed maturity of 100 years. It means that there is no real repayment of capital in this credit: the loan will be transmitted to the inheritors of the borrower. This allows the customers to take positions on the real estate market without taking a liquidity position.

Libor indexed loans often includes *cap options* in order to protect the borrower against interest rate rises:

$$\text{Interest rate index} = \text{Max}(\text{Libor}; 5\,\%) + 1{,}00\,\%$$

In the 1 % margin is included the cap option cost and the effective margin is under 1 %. The initial interest rate is then higher than the Libor and the monthly repayment is higher than the repayment of the loan indexed to the Libor rates without any cap.

A solution is to propose *maturity cap loans*. These loans are indexed to the Libor rate with a margin. The revision of the monthly repayment of these loans is annual:

- If interest rates are going down, the monthly repayment does not move and the credit duration diminishes.
- If interest rates are going up, the monthly repayment does not grow more than inflation but the credit duration increases.

Nevertheless, there is a cap on the credit duration: the effective maturity cannot exceed the initial contractual maturity plus 3 or 5 years.

This maturity cap option is a real interest rate option: the risk is to see a low inflation with high Libor nominal interest rates so that the residual amount after the duration extension is still positive.

In the Netherlands, at the signature date of a mortgage loan, the customer fixes the interest rate of is loan for a given period. During this period, the borrower cannot prepay his loan without paying an actuarial penalty. However, at the end of the period, the bank will propose a new set of possible interest rates according to the new period he wants to fix his rate. At each end of period, the client will choose either to leave the bank refinancing his loan for another more competitive bank (without penalty) or to accept a new prolongation of his loan (and the associated rate with this prolongation).

In many countries, the banks do not index their loans to interbank rates but to "base rates" or "prime rates". For example, in the UK, we may find "UK base rate loans" or in the US, we may find "US prime rates loans".

12.2 DIFFERENT DEFINITIONS AND FORMULAE

In this chapter, we will describe some formulae often used when working with loans.

12.2.1 Repayment formulae

For a P+I amortizing loan, the repayment formula is not easy to compute. For instance, the periodic payment PMT of a credit of an amount K with an annualized interest rate of r and with a frequency of p payment per annum during N years is:

$$PMT = K.\frac{\frac{r}{p}}{1 - \frac{1}{\left(1+\frac{r}{p}\right)^{N.p}}} \tag{12.1}$$

p is equal to 12 when the customer repays monthly his loan.

The remaining capital K(t) at date t is given by this formula:

$$K(t) = K(0).\frac{1 - \frac{1}{\left(1+\frac{r}{p}\right)^{N.p-t}}}{1 - \frac{1}{\left(1+\frac{r}{p}\right)^{N.p}}} \tag{12.2}$$

We call this amount the *"outstanding amount"*.

Moreover, there is a relationship between the different outstanding amounts (since the periodic repayment includes an interest rate repayment proportional to the previous outstanding amount):

$$K_{t+1} = K_t\left(1 + \frac{r}{p}\right) - PMT \tag{12.3}$$

Consequently, the function K(t) for a credit is *concave*.

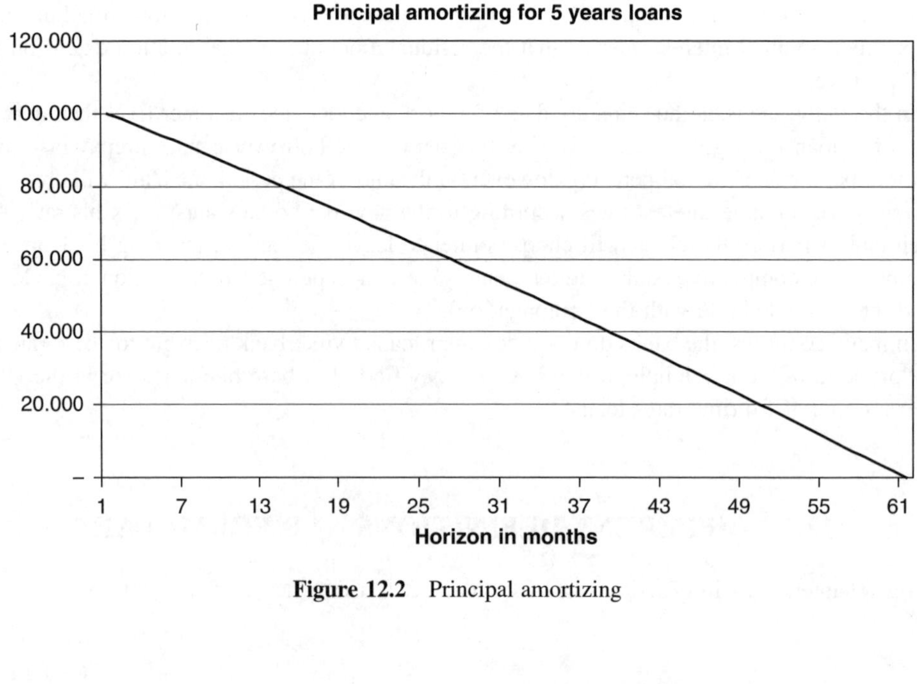

Figure 12.2 Principal amortizing

However, on a portfolio of N credits with different initial maturities or with different initial starting dates, the sum of the principal schedules becomes *convex*.

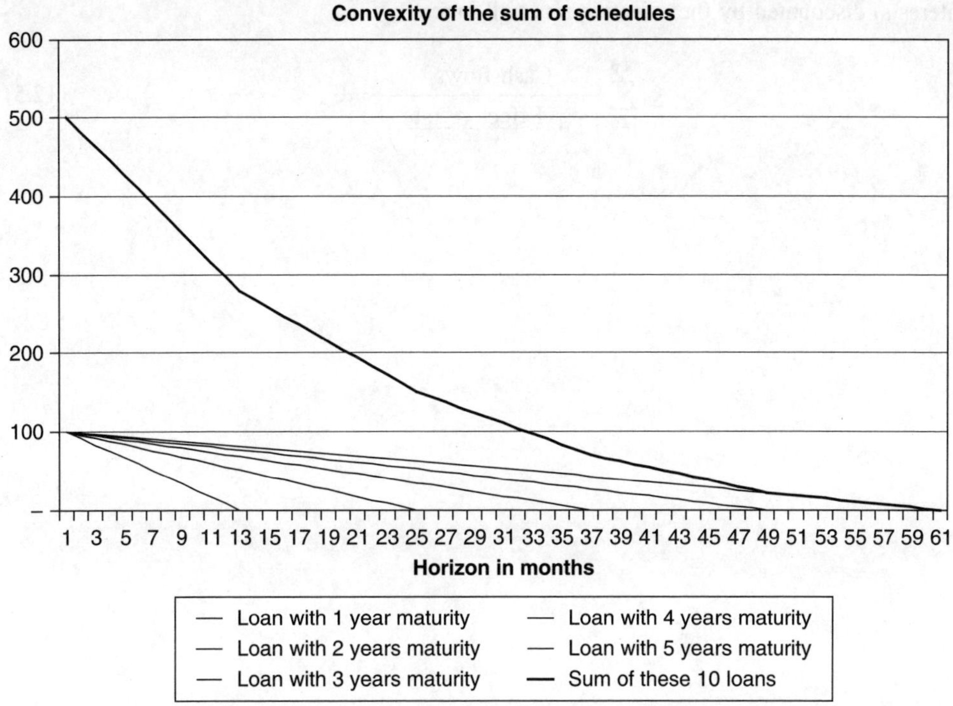

Figure 12.3 Portfolio convexity

12.2.2 Loan weighted average life (WAL)

The loan average life is the sum of the principal repayment weighted by the longevity of each repayment:

$$WAL = \frac{\sum_{i=1}^{N.p} (i.(K(i-1) - K(i)))}{K(0)} \tag{12.4}$$

This is indeed a residual weighted average life.

The weighted average life of a portfolio is the weighted average of the average life of each loan weighted by the loan amount.

12.2.3 Annual effective rate

A loan contract does not only include interest and principal repayments but also sometimes fees.

The IFRS rules ask for the reintegration of the fees inside an effective rate.

Sometimes, local laws ask for the communication to the customer of the effective rate including fees.

The sum of all the cash flows (initial paid amount, received fees, received repayment, and interests) discounted by the effective rate will make 0:

$$\sum_{i=0}^{N.p} \frac{\text{Cash-flows}_i}{\left(1 + \frac{\text{Effective rate}}{p}\right)^i} = 0 \tag{12.5}$$

13
Prepayments

Ami au prêter, ennemi au rendre.

13.1 THE ORIGINS OF THE PREPAYMENT PHENOMENON

13.1.1 Definitions

13.1.1.1 Prepayment

A customer linked to a bank with a mortgage contract has the opportunity to reimburse or to prepay the credit outstanding amount during the credit contractual life. This action modifies the credit schedule and is potentially costly for the ALM.

The prepayment may be *total* or *partial* (when the customer will prepay partially the outstanding amount).

The A/L manager will distinguish between two types of prepayments:

- *Financial* or *rational* prepayments: those prepayments are potentially cyclical.
- *Statistical* prepayments: those prepayments are partially irrational from an economic point of view.

13.1.1.2 Statistical or sociological prepayment

Statistically, there is always a minimum prepayment rate. This statistical prepayment rate is easily modelled or anticipated.

Financial market conditions will not explain those prepayments; the explanations are *sociological*:

- geographic mobility (work, home, etc.);
- decease/disability;
- customer financial situation change (inheritance, divorce, etc.).

They represent the minimal part of prepayments you cannot avoid, those prepayments are observed when the prepayment phenomenon has no economic interest: the statistical prepayment level does not depend on interest rate level. However, it may depend on the contract seniority or on other parameters not linked with the market.

For this reason, A/L managers call also these prepayments "structural prepayments" or "sociological prepayments".

13.1.1.3 Financial prepayment

On the other hand, *financial prepayments* are prepayments linked with the market rates levels. Those prepayments have to be added to statistical prepayments.

The arbitrages (between the market rates level and the customer loan rate) explain the greater part of these prepayments.

A significant interest rate decrease will incite customers:

- either to find a new loan with a lower interest rate and to prepay the existing loan; or
- to renegotiate the existing loan.

Some *penalties* compensate only partially the gains for the customer.

Financial prepayments are arbitrage prepayments and for this reason, they are cyclical prepayments.

Note also that an arbitrage between the amount of credit and the amount of cash may cause financial prepayments: when clients get a new amount of cash (inheritance), they have the choice between investing this cash (and sometimes paying taxes) and prepaying their credit.

13.1.1.4 Renegotiation

In practice, in many countries the lender will be willing to renegotiate the initial rate if the customer is ready to prepay his loan. The bank agrees to reduce the loan interest rate in order to keep the customer away from the idea of moving to another bank. There is a risk for the bank to lose all the other incomes arising from the relationship with the customer (e.g. cash flows on the demand deposit account).

Since the renegotiation does not include the payment of a penalty, the rate after renegotiation is still higher than the rate the customer will find in another bank.

13.1.1.5 Penalties or compensation

In the case of prepayment, the bank will often ask the customer to pay penalties. Indeed, these penalties are more compensation than penalties. They compensate partially for the losses arising from the refinancing of the prepaid loan.

Legal constraints are imposed on penalties usually in order "to inform" or "to protect" the customers. These constraints depend on the country:

- Penalties will be sometimes prohibited.
- Penalties will be prohibited for sociological prepayments (decease, mobility, etc.): those prepayments do not depend on financial market levels.
- *Penalties will be sometimes limited to a fixed amount of the outstanding amount*, for instance 3 % of the prepaid outstanding amount or 10 % of the prepaid outstanding amount.
- *Penalties will be limited to a fixed amount of interest*, for instance limited to 6 months of interest on the outstanding amount.
- *Penalties will sometimes be computed using an actuarial formula.* On mortgages in the Germany, the bank has the ability to ask for an actuarial penalty during the loan's first 10 years.

Actuarial penalties will not cause financial losses for the bank: an actuarial penalty compensates for the loss of economic value arising from the prepayment.

$$\text{Actuarial penalty}_0 = MAX\left(\sum_{i=1}^{N}\left(\frac{\text{Remaining interest and principal cashflows}_i}{(1+\text{Zerocoupon rate}_i)^i}\right) - \text{Outstanding}_0, 0\right) \quad (13.1)$$

For the bank, it is important to introduce an actuarial penalty clause in the contracts wherever it is possible to do it.

Banking market practices impose sometimes conditions on the penalties. If it is not common for the customers to pay penalties, it will be difficult to propose contracts including a penalty clause. This is essentially true for the individual market. Nevertheless, the SME loan market and the corporate loan market will usually include actuarial penalties in the contracts.

13.1.1.6 Example

Let us see how the prepayment will make the bank lose money through an example where the legal constraint imposes a penalty that is not to be higher than 3 % of the prepaid outstanding amount. We will see how this law will offer a free option to the customers.

In 1990, a customer puts his signature on a 20 years mortgage loan contract with bank "A": a loan of € 100.000 with an interest rate of 13 % and with a monthly payment of € 1 171.

The loan FTP is equal to 12 % directly refinanced in the market via a 12 % debt.

In 1996, a rival bank "B" will contact the customer. This bank will propose to buy back the outstanding amount (€ 90 451) and the 3 % penalty (€ 2 714). The customer rate will be of 6 % since market rates have decreased to 5 %. Finally, the monthly repayment will fall to € 821!

If bank "A" lets the customer move to the rival bank "B", the bank will have a debt of 12 % and no more high rate assets in front of this debt. Interest rates have decreased to a very low level of 5 %. The proposed price to buy back the debt contract (with € 90 451 of nominal) is € 134 894. The actuarial cost for bank "A" is then of € 47 247 (including the penalty)!

In order to keep its customer, bank "A" has to react and to renegotiate the loan. The bank will propose a loan with the same monthly repayment of € 821. This means that the loan interest rate after renegotiation is of 6.49 %. Moreover bank "A" will keep a loan with 1 % margin; the actuarial cost for the bank will only be € 35 954.

In this example, the contract includes a non-actuarial penalty and this generates a financial prepayment risk. The bank "A" has no certitude on the event and has not the total financial compensation through the proportional penalty.

The bank's loss is due to the dissymmetry between the assets replaced at the actual market rates and the liabilities that have to be remunerated at the past term rates.

The prepayment makes asset amounts fragile and may create a commercial margin risk and an interest rate risk.

13.1.1.7 The purpose of modelling

Prepayments are an ALM imperative for banks. The objective is first to comprehend the prepayment factors in order to model the customer behaviour. This modelling provides enough elements to determine the best hedging strategy.

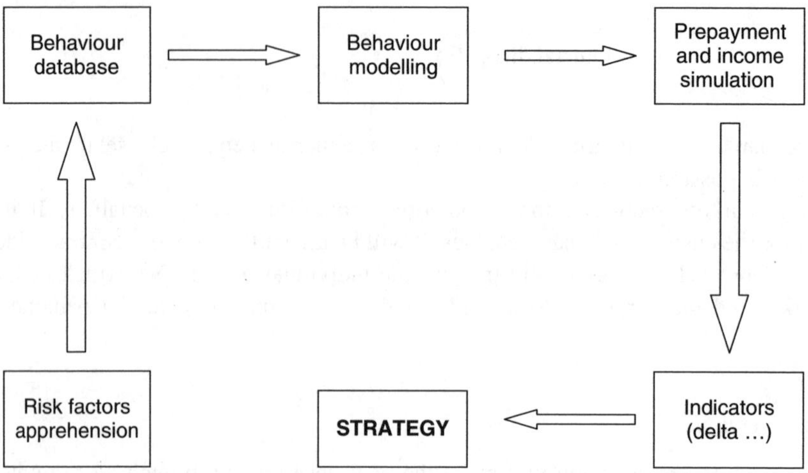

Figure 13.1 Modelling strategy

The modelling objective is to establish predictions on the future amount of prepayments before proposing hedging solutions.

In order to propose a model, the A/L manager will need a precise comprehension of the phenomenon with the associated behavioural database.

13.1.2 The main sources of prepayment

Before going into detail, we will describe briefly all the main sources of prepayment.

First, statistical prepayments are caused by:

- geographic mobility (work, home, etc.);
- decease/disability;
- customer financial situation change (inheritance, divorce, etc.);
- customer civil situation change (birth, marriage, etc.).

Actually, there is a strong link between statistical prepayments and *"turnover"*. For instance, in some States of the United States, citizens move from one house to another every four/five years; this leads to a high level of statistical prepayment.

Many other factors influence prepayments:

- economic context (customer wealth, customer income, etc.);
- turnover cost (real estate agency costs, notary costs, etc.);
- seasonality (higher turnover rates on mortgages between February to September);

- credit structure;
- tax laws on interests (for instance, in the United States, mortgages interest rates are deductible from incomes);
- evolution of the loans types provided by competitors;
- real estate prices (a high real estate price growth would impact positively the turnover);
- original loan size;
- loan to value (LTV);
- credit risk score such as the FICO score: when the scoring gets better, the customer will prepay more easily;
- regional effects;
- customer distribution network.

On the other hand, market financial conditions will influence the level of financial prepayments:

- *Interest rate level evolutions* (prepayments increase with interest rate decrease).
- *Burnout phenomenon*: the progressive diminution across time of the customer reactivity to interest rate decreases.

Some other factors will especially affect the financial prepayments:

- *Interest rate credit type*: Fixed Rate Mortgages (FRM) are more exposed to prepayment than Adjustable-Rate Mortgage (ARM).

Refinancing an ARM by an ARM will have no impact on the interest rate risk but will have an impact on the margin level.

- *Credit options* (such as caps, hybrid credits, etc.).
- *Interest rate revision frequency* (for ARM): the prepayment is higher around the interest rate adjustment dates.
- *Penalties formula.*

13.1.3 Types of prepayment and credit

Prepayment phenomena depend highly on the credit type:

- *Consumer loans*: the short-term maturity of the loan might let us think that the prepayment rate is low since the customer has not a lot of time to prepay. On the other hand, the usually high level of the margin (or the large difference between the consumer loan rate and the deposit rates) makes the statistical prepayment rate higher on the loans with the larger margin. Actually, for customer loans, the prepayment rate depends on the *margin*. Note also that banks rarely renegotiate the interest rate of such a credit.
- *Credits to large corporations*: on those credits, it is usually possible to ask for an actuarial penalty. Consequently, the prepayment rate is usually low and statistical and corresponds to a financial or a tax arbitrage for the corporate company (e.g. if the penalty is taken as a flat loss in the income of the company).

- *Credits to small corporations (SME)*: on the other hand, in small corporations, the actuarial penalty is sometimes difficult to impose for commercial reasons. First, it is difficult to explain the actuarial formula to the customers and secondly, the competitors "offer" the option for free to the client. Sometimes, the penalty is fixed and dissuasive (20 % of the outstanding amount for instance). Occasionally, the penalty does not exist: the prepayment option sell to the customer is then a local market practice.
- *Mortgages*: in the mortgage market, the law regulates the penalty formula: usually, the penalty is limited and fixed at a low level of the outstanding amount.
- *Bridge loans*: the prepayment rate is usually very important in bridge loans since the contractual maturity is indicative and represents only the maximal maturity of the deal. The prepayment rate is statistical on these loans.
- *Leasing:* the prepayment rate is mainly statistical since contracts are frequently short-term contracts with high fixed penalties level.

13.1.4 Transaction costs and penalties

For each customer, there are implicit and explicit transaction costs that limit the arbitrage possibility. Kay et al., and Kelly and Slawson and Peristiani et al. give a description of these costs:

- bank financial prepayment penalties;
- time to be informed about interest rate market evolutions;
- waiting time for the effectiveness of the transaction.

These costs make the option very different from the option usually encountered in the financial options theory.

A classic formulation links costs and customer arbitrage reaction considering:

- CT(t) the unique transaction cost variable (linked to the arbitrage decision) at date t;
- UMB(t) the outstanding amount of capital at date t;
- RP(t,r) the actual value of the loan future cash flows (without prepayment option);
- C(t,r,RE) the prepayment option value at date t depending on the spot interest rate r and for a mortgage credit on the real estate value of the mortgaged good RE. This value is an American call value on the mortgage market value.

The arbitrage condition is the following: the customer will prepay if:

$$\text{UMB}(t) + \text{CT}(t) < \text{RP}(t,r) - \text{C}(t,r,\text{RE}) \tag{13.2}$$

Otherwise, this equation means that the prepayment option has a higher strike (due to the presence of CT(t)) than the classic market option. The customer will wait for an important interest rate decrease before prepaying. If the interest rates decrease, then the variables RP(t,r) and C(t, r, RE) increase. The borrower will prepay if the interest rates decrease sufficiently so that RP exceeds UMB plus CT plus C (and the increase of C).

It is clear that the transaction costs CT(t) will depend on the customer (since each customer has its own perception of time and of the market rates). The prepayment option exercise will depend on the customer characteristics.

Consequently, Kelly and Slawson (2001) also noticed that the prepayment is a function of the penalty type; in their article, they compared different prepayment speeds according to the penalty type (fixed, diminishing, etc.).

Interested readers can read how Fu *et al.* (2003) confirmed this assertion via an econometrical study.

13.1.5 Competing risks

Competing risks such as default risk may affect the prepayment risk. A bias appears when the A/L manager does not estimate jointly default and prepayment risk: the default option exercise annihilates the prepayment option value and vice-versa as indicated by Kelly and Slawson (2001).

When the A/L manager models the prepayment option, the default risk impacting variables have to be included in the modelling; in simulation prepayments and defaults have to be simulated jointly. Since the default risk affects the variables, we might mention:

- the real estate value RE of the mortgaged good;
- the loan to value (LTV) that is the ratio between the borrowed amount and the real estate value;
- the "negative equity probability", i.e. the probability for the customer's net equity to become negative at a certain horizon.

When we take into account P(t,r,RE) the default option value for the customer, the arbitrage condition changes and the customer will now prepay if:

$$\mathrm{UMB(t)+CT(t) < RP(t,r) - C(t,r,RE) - P(t,r,RE)} \tag{13.3}$$

This default option gives to the borrower the opportunity to sell his real estate property at a strike equal to the outstanding amount of the loan. If the customer defaults, the lender takes the mortgaged real estate property and sells it into the market.

We introduce the amount V(t,r,RE) defined as:

$$\mathrm{V(t,r,RE) = RP(t,r) - C(t,r,RE) - P(t,r,RE)} \tag{13.4}$$

This amount is equal to the economic value of the discounted loan cash flows net of the two options (the prepayment and the default options).

We suppose that interest rates follow a Cox Ingersoll Ross (CIR) model:

$$dr_t = \gamma.(\Theta - r_t).dt + \sigma.\sqrt{r_t}.dW_t \tag{13.5}$$

We suppose also that the real estate value RE follows an Itô process with a long-term return of the real estate market equal to a net of the received cash flows "cf" on the real estate property (net rental fees):

$$\frac{\mathrm{dRE}}{\mathrm{RE}} = (\alpha - \mathrm{cf}).\mathrm{dt} + \sigma_{RE}.\mathrm{dW}_t^{\mathrm{RE}} \tag{13.6}$$

We note ρ the correlation between the two Brownian motions above W and $\mathrm{W^{RE}}$.

With these notations, Kelly and Slawson (2001) showed that the amount V is the only solution of the following equation:

$$\frac{\partial f}{\partial t}+(r-cf).RE.\frac{\partial f}{\partial RE}+\lambda.(\Theta-r).\frac{\partial f}{\partial r}+\frac{1}{2}.RE^2.\sigma_{RE}^2.\frac{\partial^2 f}{\partial RE^2}+\frac{1}{2}.r.\sigma^2.\frac{\partial^2 f}{\partial r^2}$$
$$+\rho.RE.\sqrt{r}.\sigma.\sigma_{RE}.\frac{\partial^2 f}{\partial r.\partial RE}=r.f \qquad (13.7)$$

13.1.6 The nature of borrower's

Borrower's rating will influence the likelihood to prepay. Peristiani et al. (1997) and Clapp, Deng et al. (2001) observed that a borrower with a good *rating* was more likely to prepay. A good rating is synonym for solvability and regularity in the loan reimbursement.

The literature shows that the in-life score and the grating score are good indicators for the prepayment modelling.

Moreover, the borrower's personal characteristics may explain the prepayment heterogeneity within a loan portfolio. Among them, we may cite:

- *Education level*: a borrower will be reactive to arbitrage opportunities if he's able to understand financial markets.
- *Salary*: a low salary level will reduce the prepayment probability.
- *Age*: age is negatively correlated with mobility, diminishing the statistical prepayment due to "turnover effects".
- *Personal information*: such as unemployment, divorce, mobility or inheritance may explain statistical prepayments.
- *Ethnical minority status*: this status would diminish the statistical prepayment probability according to South and Crowder (1998). In the United States, Afro-Americans would have a lower mobility than Whites would have for instance. [Note that in many countries, the legislation forbids the storage of the ethnical minority status of the customers into databases and the use of this information.]

A/L managers hardly take such information into account since it requires huge databases for the estimations.

13.1.7 Macroeconomic variables

Macroeconomic variables affect the prepayment phenomenon. Among them, we may cite:

- *Industrial production*: a positive trend in this index means more prosperity and more transactions on the real estate market and then more prepayments.
- *Unemployment rate.*
- *Gross Domestic Product.*
- *Inflation.*

A/L managers will take into account these variables only if they are able to forecast them. It is not easy indeed to predict accurately the unemployment rate on long-term horizons.

Moreover, it is not possible to hedge in the market the prepayment risk arising from the unemployment rate changes: the information given by the model is quite often useless.

Note also that these macroeconomic variables are local variables. For each region where the bank commercializes loans, there is a set of macroeconomic variables.

13.1.8 Seasonality

Statistical prepayments are cyclical.

Mortgages prepayments present a strong seasonality with a peak during summer. Indeed, mobility is greater in summer than in winter as shown by Schwartz and Torous (1989) in their estimations.

Moreover, some months are shorter than the others are and some months contains more weekdays than the others.

Consequently, the A/L manager will model the prepayment as a double function of financial variables and of seasonality:

$$\text{Prepayment Rate} = \text{F1 (month)} . \text{F2 (seniority, interest rate differential, etc.)} \qquad (13.8)$$

13.1.9 Trend effects

Customers are more and more educated and informed. They are less and less afraid to ask for a prepayment or for an arbitrage, more ready to threaten their bankers to move to a rival bank.

For this reason, prepayment probabilities tend to increase naturally.

13.1.10 The three most important variables: interest rate spread, seniority/residual maturity and burnout

13.1.10.1 Interest rate spread

A/L managers define the *re-employment rate* as the rate the customer can find in the market if he wants to refinance it (i.e. the rate of a new loan with the same characteristics as the one of his initial loan). If for instance, the customer has a 6 % rate loan with a 10 year residual maturity, the re-employment rate will be the actual market rate of a 10 year loan.

Many definitions are possible for this rate but usually a shortcut is to choose the government rate or the swap rate of the residual average life of the credit. Another possibility is to take the rate described in the contractual penalty clause.

The chosen rate is often a credit risk-free rate since there is no correlation at first sight between default risk and prepayment risk.

The *interest rate spread* is the difference between the loan initial interest rate and the re-employment rate.

Historically, the interest rate spread is the first variable the prepayment models took into account. The higher is the spread, the higher is the customer interest to prepay; prepaying the outstanding amount, he may ask for a new loan in a rival bank with a lower interest rate. On the other hand, when the interest rate spread is negative, the customer's interest is to keep his initial loan.

The interest rate spread is either an *absolute spread*:

$$\text{Absolute spread} = \text{Initial loan rate} - \text{Re-employment rate} \qquad (13.9)$$

Or a *relative spread*:

$$\text{Relative spread} = \frac{\text{Initial loan rate} - \text{Re-employment rate}}{\text{Initial loan rate}} \text{ or } \ln\left(\frac{\text{Initial loan rate} - \text{Re-employment rate}}{\text{Initial loan rate}}\right) \tag{13.10}$$

For instance, in our example if the re-employment rate is equal to 5 %, the absolute spread is of 1 % and the relative spread is of 16 %.

13.1.10.1.1 Choice between relative and absolute interest rate spread

Usually, A/L managers will choose absolute interest rate spread for its simplicity.

Nevertheless, the relative interest rate spread has a complementary impact since there are links between the periodic repayment spread for the customer and the level of interest rates.

When the interest rates move from 12 % to 11 %, this has a different impact on the monthly repayment of a mortgage from when interest rates go from 5 % to 4 %:

- The repayment decrease is greater (in absolute level).
- The repayment decrease is less important (in relative).

Remaining maturity in years	Outstanding amount	Initial rate	Re-employment rate	Initial annual repayment	Potential repayment after prepayment	Absolute gain	Relative gain
10	€100	12 %	11 %	€17.70	€16.98	€0.72	4.06 %
10	€100	5 %	4 %	€12.95	€12.33	€0.62	4.80 %

Figure 13.2 Relative gain

When looking after discounted gains, the gain is always more important when interest rates are lower.

Remaining maturity in years	Outstanding Amount	Initial rate	Re-employment rate	Initial annual repayment	Potential repayment after prepayment	Discounted gain	Relative discounted gain
10	€100	12 %	11 %	€17.70	€16.98	€4.23	4.23 %
10	€100	5 %	4 %	€12.95	€12.33	€5.04	5.04 %

Figure 13.3 Relative discounted gain

Roll and Richard (1989) analysed why the relative interest rate is also a relatively good proxy for borrower arbitrage decision function modelling. Indeed, they compared the repayment before and after a potential prepayment (when R is the re-employment rate of a mortgage and C the customer initial rate on an initial amount of loan K with a periodicity p).

$$PMT_{before\ prepayment} = K.\frac{\frac{C}{p}}{1 - \frac{1}{\left(1+\frac{C}{p}\right)^{N.p}}}$$

$$PMT_{after\ prepayment} = K.\frac{\frac{R}{p}}{1 - \frac{1}{\left(1+\frac{R}{p}\right)^{N.p}}} \tag{13.11}$$

Consequently, the relative gain in terms of periodic repayment follows if the period p is equal to 1 (annual repayment) this equation:

$$Gain = \frac{PMT_{after\ prepayment}}{PMT_{before\ prepayment}} - 1 = \frac{R}{C}.\frac{1-(1+C)^{-N}}{1-(1+R)^{-N}} - 1 \tag{13.12}$$

The customer gain is indeed a function of the remaining maturity N of the initial rate C and of the re-employment rate R.

$$Gain \approx \frac{R}{C}.\frac{1-e^{-N.\left(C-\frac{1}{2}C^2\right)}}{1-e^{-N.\left(R-\frac{1}{2}R^2\right)}} - 1 \approx \frac{R}{C}.\frac{N.C-\frac{1}{2}N.C^2-\frac{1}{2}.(N.C)^2}{N.R-\frac{1}{2}N.R^2-\frac{1}{2}.(N.R)^2} - 1 \tag{13.13}$$

Consequently, with p = 1 for instance, the relative gain on a periodic repayment for the customer will follow:

$$Gain \approx \frac{1-\frac{1}{2}.C-\frac{1}{2}.N.C}{1-\frac{1}{2}.R-\frac{1}{2}.N.R} - 1 \approx \frac{1-\frac{1}{2}.C.(1+N)}{1-\frac{1}{2}.R.(1+N)} - 1 \approx \frac{1}{2}.(R-C).(1+N) \tag{13.14}$$

It is easy to express the relative gain on the periodic repayment as *a function of the absolute interest rate spread and of the residual maturity.*

On the other hand, let us note that there is a direct link between the absolute economic gain for the customer and the relative gain in terms of periodic repayment:

$$\text{Absolute economic gain} = \sum_{i=1}^{N} \frac{PMT_{before\ prepayment}}{(1+R)^i} - K = K.\left(\frac{PMT_{before\ prepayment}}{PMT_{after\ prepayment}} - 1\right) \tag{13.15}$$

Therefore, the prepayment function should be a function of the re-employment rate R, the initial coupon rate C and the residual maturity N.

$$\text{Prepayment} = \text{F(R, C, N)} \tag{13.16}$$

If the database provided for the estimation of F does not contain enough information, the A/L manager will focus on the interest rate spread as a proxy for modelling still using the residual maturity:

$$\text{Prepayment} = \text{F'}(\text{R} - \text{C}, \text{N}) \text{ or } \text{F''}(\text{R} - \text{C}, \text{R}/\text{C}, \text{N}) \tag{13.17}$$

13.1.10.1.2 Impact of prepayment penalties on the prepayment function

The existence of an actuarial penalty destroys the financial prepayment option.

Alternatively, when the penalty is a percentage p of the outstanding amount, the periodic payment after prepayment is just increased by a percentage p %.

Consequently, there is a translation of the gain by a constant p:

$$Gain \approx \frac{1}{2}.(R - C).(1 + N) - p \tag{13.18}$$

Taking into account penalties, the A/L manager will still use interest rate spreads in order to model the prepayments.

13.1.10.1.3 Non linear terms introduction

Instead of proposing a prepayment function linked directly to the absolute or to the relative interest rate spreads, it is perhaps more clever to use directly a non linear specification as proposed by Schwartz and Torous (1989). The idea is to capture better the prepayment acceleration when interest rates are very low.

Consequently, the prepayment function will become a function of the square or cubic interest rate spreads as follows:

$$\text{Prepayment} = \text{F}_1\left((\text{R} - \text{C}), (\text{R} - \text{C})^2, \text{N}\right) \text{ or } \text{F}_2\left((\text{R} - \text{C}), (\text{R} - \text{C})^3, \text{N}\right) \tag{13.19}$$

13.1.10.1.4 Lag on interest rate spread

A/L managers always noticed the existence of a lag between the market interest rate decreases and the observation of prepayment phenomenon. This lag varies from one country to another, from one credit type to another.

The lag may be important: for instance from 3 months to 1 year for mortgages.

In the prepayment function estimation, the A/L manager should consider this in the re-employment rate R. This rate should be actually a weighted average of the past possible re-employment rates as shown by Belbase (1999).

$$\text{Prepayment} = \text{F}_2\left((\tilde{\text{R}}_\text{t} - \text{C}), (\tilde{\text{R}}_\text{t} - \text{C})^3, \text{N}\right)$$

where

$$\tilde{\text{R}}_\text{t} = \sum_{i=0}^{12} \alpha_i.\text{R}_{\text{t}-\text{i}} \tag{13.20}$$

and

$$\sum_{i=0}^{12} \alpha_i = 1$$

13.1.10.1.5 Volatility impact on prepayment function

Some authors explained that the volatility of interest rates affects the prepayment arbitrage. For instance, Peristiani et al. (1997) showed that a high historical volatility incites customers to prepay because the opportunity to get a favourable interest rate spreads increases.

Moreover, not only the historical volatility but also the implicit volatility (i.e. the markets future volatility) modifies the prepayment value and maybe customer behaviour.

Nevertheless, very few A/L managers will use volatility for the modelling of the prepayment function.

13.1.10.1.6 The impact of tax on prepayments

When customers get an important sum of cash (due to inheritance or whatever), they have the opportunity either to prepay or to invest this cash. The tax collector will naturally tax the investments; at the same moment, the interest rates paid on the loan are not always netted into the customer income (i.e. they do not necessarily reduce the amount of paid taxes). This taxation effect will then depend on the individual country tax laws.

Consequently, the customer has sometimes the opportunity to make an arbitrage between its loan with an interest rate C and some cash he could invest into long-term taxed deposits at a level of R.(1−Tax rate). This leads to a new prepayment function:

$$\text{Prepayment} = F'_2\left((\tilde{R}_t - C), ((1 - \text{Tax rate}).\tilde{R}_t - C), (\tilde{R}_t - C)^3, N\right) \qquad (13.21)$$

13.1.10.2 Credit seniority/residual maturity

Theoretically as shown before, *residual maturity* explains the financial prepayment. On the other hand, loan seniority explains the *statistical prepayments* quite well:

- At the beginning of the loan life, the customer has no real reason to prepay.
- By the end of the loan life, the customer wealth has increased and the customer has more chances to be cash rich: he will statistically prepay more.

This leads to a prepayment function linked to the loan residual maturity N and the loan seniority S:

$$\text{Prepayment} = F_3\left((\tilde{R}_t - C), (\tilde{R}_t - C)^3, \text{residual maturity N, loan seniority S}\right) \qquad (13.22)$$

Nevertheless, in the databases there is sometimes a strong correlation between the two variables. If production has the same initial maturity over time, the relationship between residual maturity and seniority is direct. For this reason, it is sometimes possible to choose a prepayment function depending only on the seniority of the credit:

$$\text{Prepayment} = F_4\left((\tilde{R}_t - C), (\tilde{R}_t - C)^3, S\right) \qquad (13.23)$$

13.1.10.3 Burnout

The "burnout function" is present more and more in prepayment models. The burnout variable gives an idea of the customer reactivity. There is a strong heterogeneity between

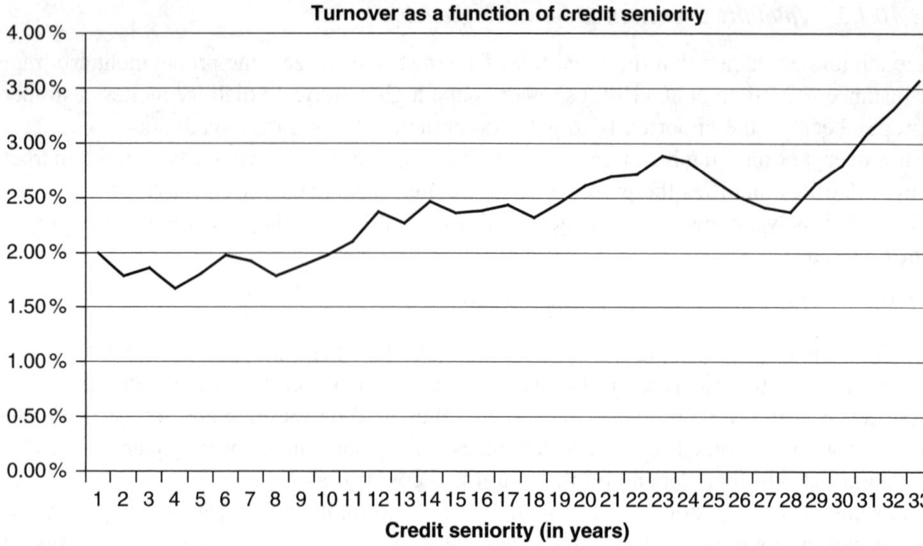

Figure 13.4 Turnover

customers: their reactivity varies. For instance, "rational" customers will prepay as soon as the prepayment is profitable for them, while other customers will wait (with the risk of seeing interest rate rises).

The explicit or implicit costs will in fact vary a great deal from one customer to another.

Consequently, the prepayment option depends on the "market rates path". An interest rate decrease followed by an interest rate rise and then by another decrease will produce less prepayment than two interest rate decreases followed by a rise. In the second situation, non-rational customers will have time to make the decision to prepay; in the first situation, since it takes time to take the decision to prepay, their reaction is too late to be worthwhile.

For this reason, A/L managers talk about a "burnout" phenomenon. The burnout measures as for a candle the "customer capacity to get burned", i.e. their likelihood to react to the interest rate decreases.

There are different activating levels for the prepayment option amongst borrowers. Consequently, it is logical to consider that a customer, who could prepay and did not do so, has a lesser opportunity to prepay than a customer who is exposed for the first time to the prepayment option. The burnout variable will try to capture this phenomenon.

In the literature, LaCour-Little et al. (2002) formalized burnout phenomenon as follows:

- With an *absolute burnout* defined for each loan at each date by:

$$\text{BURNOUT}_{\text{date t, loan rate C and loan start date D}} = \sum_{i=D}^{t} (C - R_i)^+ \tag{13.24}$$

- Or with a *relative burnout* defined for each loan at each date by:

$$\text{BURNOUT}_{\text{date t, loan rate C and loan start date D}} = \sum_{i=D}^{t} \ln\left(\frac{C}{R_i}\right)^{+} \tag{13.25}$$

Those two variables will try to define something that takes into account the path the interest rates followed across time from the loan start date to the current date.

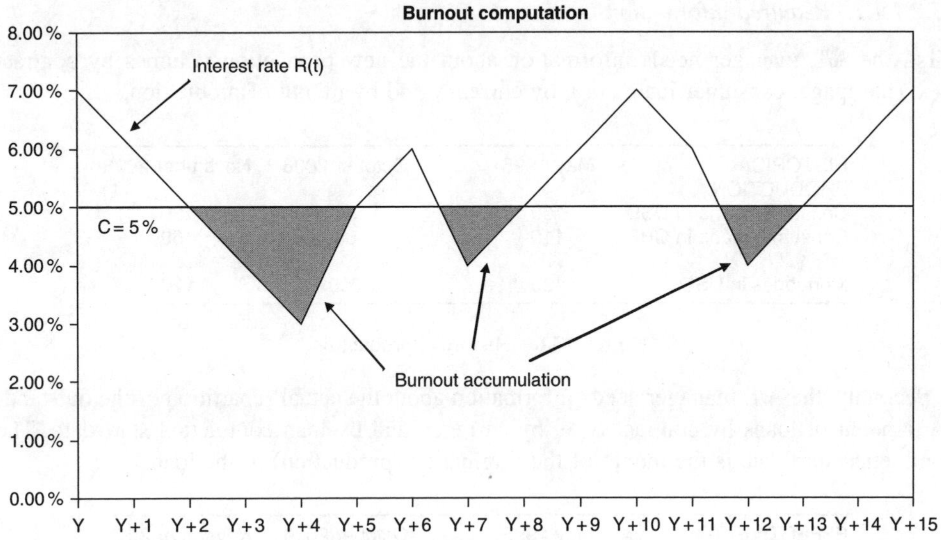

Figure 13.5 Burnout

The graphic above helps to visualize how it is possible to compute the burnout factor.

13.2 THE CONSTITUTION OF THE DATABASE FOR PREPAYMENT MODELLING

This chapter details the required information for prepayment modelling:

- For a rudimentary modelling of statistical prepayments.
- For a more advanced prepayment modelling.

The A/L manager will look after the *prepayment rate*: this is the percentage of prepayment associated with the loan stock. Multiplied by the loan stock, the prepayment rate gives the amount of prepayment. Indeed, it is easier to model the prepayment rates than the prepayment amounts.

The classic convention is to express prepayment rates in an annual linear basis.

$$\text{Prepayment (month)} = \frac{\text{Prepayment rate . Oustanding Amount}}{12} \tag{13.26}$$

13.2.1 Database for rudimentary modelling

It is possible to get an idea about the statistical prepayment rate using some basic information.

There are three possible methods described below.

13.2.1.1 Method 1: Using new production historical database and the repartition of the loan outstanding amount by loan origination date

13.2.1.1.1 Required information

First, the A/L manager needs information about the new production volumes by contract type (mortgage, consumer loan, etc.), by currency and by month of production.

HISTORICAL PRODUCTION	May 1995	...	October 2006	November 2006
Consumer loans in USD	100	...	50	130
Consumer loans in CHF	110	...	80	150
...	...	...	...	...
Mortgages in USD	120		200	120

Figure 13.6 Historical production

Secondly, the A/L manager needs information about the actual repartition of the outstanding amount of loans by contract type, by currency and by loan contractual start date. The contractual start date is the month of the origination (production) of the loan.

EFFECTIVE OUTSTANDING AMOUNT (by year of opening)	May 1995	...	October 2006	November 2006
Consumer loans in USD	10	...	45	130
Consumer loans in CHF	11	...	87	150
...	...	...	...	...
Mortgages in USD	12		198	120

Figure 13.7 Historical outstanding

Thirdly, the A/L manager needs to know contract type by contract type (and by currency) what the new production classic contractual schedule looks like without prepayment.

For instance, he needs to know:

NEW PRODUCTION CONTRACTUAL AMORTIZATION SCHEDULE	Maturity	Contractual amortization
Consumer loans	50 % with 5 years maturity and linear amortization of principal	
	25 % with 2 years maturity without amortization of principal ("bullet loans")	
	25 % with 2 years maturity and "P+I" amortization of principal	
...	...	
Mortgages	100 % with 20 years maturity	Linear amortization of principal

Figure 13.8 New production

13.2.1.1.2 Estimation of statistical prepayment

Using the HISTORICAL PRODUCTION and the NEW PRODUCTION CONTRACTUAL AMORTIZATION SCHEDULE, the A/L manager is able to propose a CONTRACTUAL HYPOTHETIC OUTSTANDING AMOUNT:

HYPOTHETIC OUTSTANDING AMOUNT (by year of opening)	May 1995	...	October 2006	November 2006
Consumer loans in USD	15	...	46	130
Consumer loans in CHF	13	...	88	150
...	...	...	...	...
Mortgages in USD	13		199	120

Figure 13.9 Hypothetic outstanding

We compare this contractual amount with the effective amount:

EFFECTIVE OUTSTANDING AMOUNT (by year of opening)	May 1995	...	October 2006	November 2006
Consumer loans in USD	10	...	45	130
Consumer loans in CHF	11	...	87	150
...	...	...	...	...
Mortgages in USD	12		198	120

Figure 13.10 Effective outstanding

It is then possible to deduce the implicit statistical prepayment rates as the ratio of the effective outstanding over the hypothetical outstanding:

$$\text{Implicit prepayment rate} = -\frac{\ln\left(\dfrac{\text{Effective outstanding}}{\text{Hypothetic outstanding}}\right)}{\text{Loan seniority}} \tag{13.27}$$

This gives an idea for the statistical prepayment rate as a function of the loan seniority and of the contract type.

Implicit prepayment rate (by year of opening)	May 1995	...	October 2006	November 2006
Consumer loans in USD	3.52 %		25.88 %	N.A.
Consumer loans in CHF	1.45 %		13.46 %	N.A.
...				...
Mortgages in USD	0.70 %		5.93 %	N.A.

Figure 13.11 Implicit prepayment rate

It is also possible to deduce from these tables the implicit prepayment rate by contract type (without loan seniority effect) when the above table is weighted (this requires sometimes a statistical treatment):

Implicit prepayment rate	
Consumer loans in USD	4.00 %
Consumer loans in CHF	2.50 %
...	
Mortgages in USD	1.00 %

Figure 13.12 Implicit prepayment rate

13.2.1.2 Method 2: Using two (or more) outstanding amount repartition by contractual opening year

It is also easy to get an idea of the statistical prepayment rate comparing two tables of effective outstanding amount at two (at least) different past dates:

- For instance a table in November 2006:

EFFECTIVE OUTSTANDING AMOUNT (by year of opening) in NOVEMBER 2006	May 1995	...	October 2005	November 2005	...	October 2006	November 2006
Consumer loans in USD	11.5	...	32	38	...	45	130
Consumer loans in CHF	12.5	...	75	87	...	87	150
...	...	...	...	...	...	...	...
Mortgages in USD	14.8	...	158	128	...	198	120

Figure 13.13 Effective outstanding amount

- and a table in November 2005:

EFFECTIVE OUTSTANDING AMOUNT (by year of opening) in NOVEMBER 2005	May 1995	...	October 2005	November 2005	...	October 2006	November 2006
Consumer loans in USD	12	...	33	40	...	N.A.	N.A.
Consumer loans in CHF	13	...	80	90	...	N.A.	N.A.
...	...	...	...	...	...	...	...
Mortgages in USD	15	...	160	130	...	N.A.	N.A.

Figure 13.14 Effective outstanding amount No. 2

There should be a spread of at least 1 year between the two tables to compute the statistical prepayment rate:

$$\text{Implicit prepayment rate} = -\frac{\ln\left(\dfrac{\text{Effective outstanding}_{\text{Date2}}}{\text{Effective outstanding}_{\text{Date1}}}\right)}{(\text{Date 2} - \text{Date 1})} \tag{13.28}$$

This gives also an idea for the statistical prepayment rate as a function of the loan seniority and of the contract type.

Implicit prepayment rate (by year of opening)	May 1995	...	October 2005	November 2005	...	October 2006	November 2006
Consumer loans in USD	18 %	...	10 %	13 %	...	N.A.	N.A.
Consumer loans in CHF	17 %	...	6 %	12 %	...	N.A.	N.A.
...	...	...	...	...	...	...	...
Mortgages in USD	22 %	...	8 %	8 %	...	N.A.	N.A.

Figure 13.15 Implicit prepayment rate

It is also possible to deduce from these tables the implicit prepayment rate by contract type (without any loan seniority effect) when the above table is weighted (this requires sometimes a statistical treatment):

Implicit prepayment rate	
Consumer loans in USD	4.00 %
Consumer loans in CHF	2.50 %
...	
Mortgages in USD	1.00 %

Figure 13.16 Implicit prepayment rate No. 2

13.2.1.3 *Method 3: Using two contractual schedules*

Another idea to obtain the statistical prepayment rate is to compare (for each contract type) the contractual schedules:

- the loan contractual schedule one year ago; and
- the actual loan contractual schedule of all the loans older than 1 year.

There should be a spread of at least 1 year between the two tables to compute the statistical prepayment rate:

$$\text{Implicit prepayment rate (horizon t)} = -\frac{\ln\left(\dfrac{\text{New outstanding amount}_t}{\text{Previous outstanding amount}_t}\right)}{(\text{Date 2} - \text{Date 1})} \tag{13.29}$$

In our example, the statistical prepayment rate is around 25 % per annum.

Note: Sometimes, it is difficult to get the actual loan contractual schedule of all the loans *older than 1 year*. An idea to get this schedule is to start from the actual loan contractual schedule of all the loans and to subtract from it the modelled schedule of loan new production.

13.2.2 Advanced databases for prepayment modelling

Advanced modelling is possible when the A/L manager gets enough information (on the prepayments, prepaid loan by prepaid loan and on the outstanding amounts) and aggregates this information wisely.

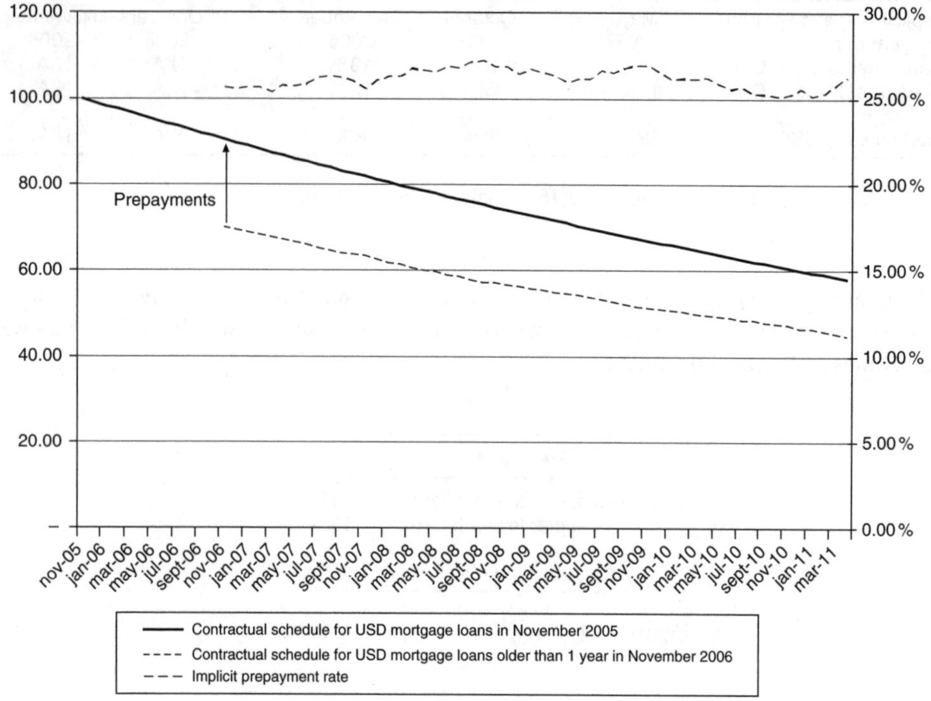

Figure 13.17 Contractual schedule

13.2.2.1 Information on prepayments

It is interesting for the A/L manager to obtain on a monthly basis some information about the prepaid loans on a *unitary basis*. For each prepaid or renegotiated loan within a specified month, the A/L manager should know:

- if the prepayment is total or partial;
- what the amount prepaid is and what the outstanding amount before prepayment is;
- for renegotiated loans at which level the loan rate was renegotiated;
- if the loan is a fixed rate, a floating rate loan or a floating capped rate;
- what the interest rate level is at prepayment/renegotiation date;
- what the credit type of the loan is (mortgage for instance);
- what the currency of the loan is;
- what the penalty type of the loan is;
- what the origination date of the loan is (and its initial maturity date);
- what the prepayment cause is (invalidity, decease, mobility, or financial prepayment);
- what the re-employment rate of the prepaid loan is (the level of the market rates at prepayment date);
- what the rating of the customer who prepaid the loan is.

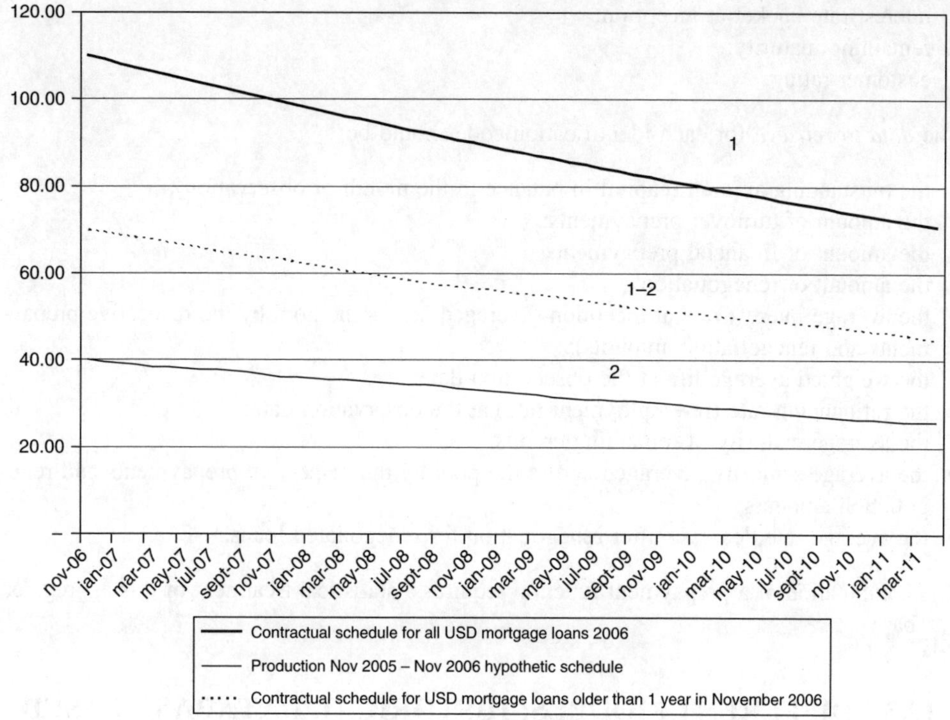

Figure 13.18 Contractual schedule and prepayment schedule

13.2.2.2 Information on the stock of operations

To compute the "prepayment rates", it is necessary to get also enough information about the denominator of the prepayment rate.

The A/L manager needs to know, for instance, on the stock of loans what the repartition of his stock outstanding amount is as a function of:

- the loan start date;
- the loan maturity date;
- the loan interest rate level (segment by segment with segments of 1 % for example);
- the customer rating.

13.2.2.3 Final aggregated information

Using the two information databases above, the A/L manager should be able to constitute an aggregated database with identification codes and observed variables.

The *identification codes* for the database should be the following variables:

- month of observation;
- product type;
- origination year;

- interest rate bucket at inception;
- remaining maturity;
- customer rating.

The *data to retrieve* for each identification code should be:

- the outstanding amount (capital in balance in the month of observation);
- the amount of turnover prepayments;
- the amount of financial prepayments;
- the amount of renegotiation;
- the average interest rate at inception (averaged across the pool by the respective prepayments and renegotiation amounts);
- the weighted average life at the observation date;
- the refinancing rate (re-employment rate) at the observation date;
- the average maturity of remaining credits;
- the average seniority (averaged across the pool by the respective prepayments and renegotiation amounts);
- the average rate decrease after renegotiation for renegotiated loans.

The computation of a prepayment function requires a statistical treatment of this aggregated database.

13.3 DIFFERENT MODELS: HISTORICAL DATABASE-BASED APPROACHES AND MBS-BASED APPROACHES

For prepayment modelling, many models exist in the literature:

- Database-based approaches versus MBS-based approaches.
- Parametric models versus non-parametric models (where the prepayment is linked parametrically or not to the set of explaining variables).

13.3.1 Parametric prepayment modelling

Parametric prepayment modelling may take different forms.

13.3.1.1 Classic prepayment functions

Prepayment modelling could impose a form for the function F that links the prepayment rates with the interest rate spreads.

The prepayment rate to model has to be comprised between zero and one. For instance, it is possible to model the prepayment rate as a double exponential of the interest rate spread and of the cubic interest rate spread:

$$\text{Prepayment Rate} = \exp\left(-\exp\left(A_0 + A_1.(R - C) + A_2.(R - C)^3\right)\right) \tag{13.30}$$

The prepayment rate is still comprised between zero and one when using a normal distribution:

$$\text{Prepayment Rate} = \Phi\left(A_0 + A_1.(R - C) + A_2.(R - C)^3\right) \tag{13.31}$$

A likelihood maximization will give us the estimation of the statistical parameters.

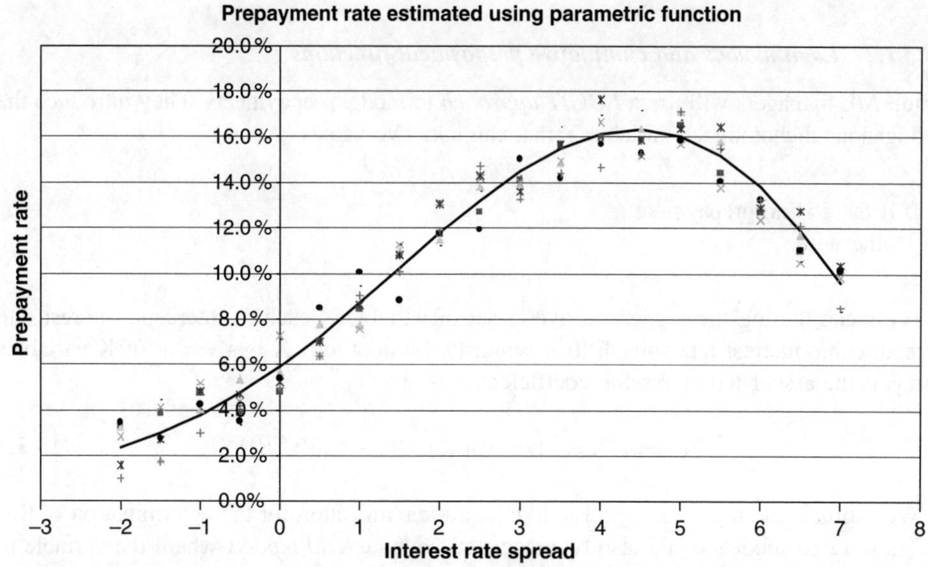

Figure 13.19 Parametric function

The same chart in the double logarithm plan gives:

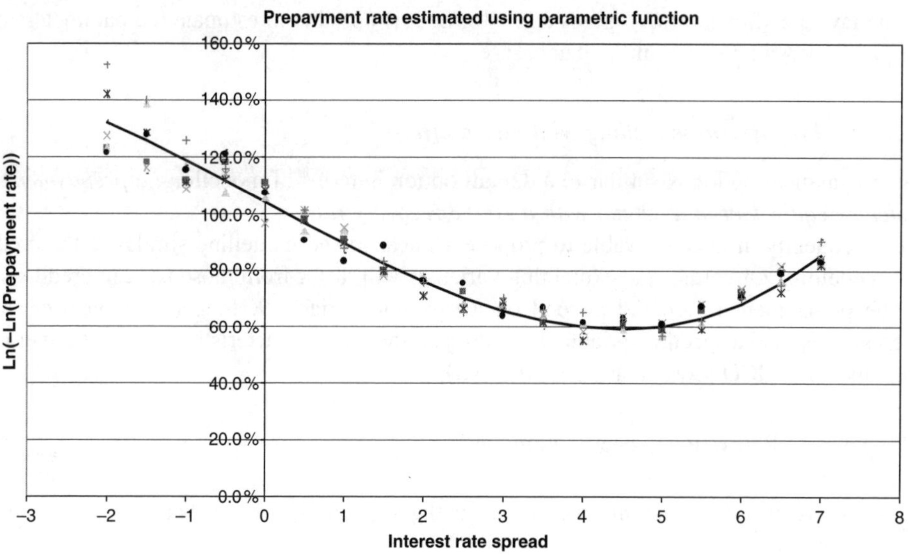

Figure 13.20 Parametric function No. 2

This chart shows the existence of a burnout phenomenon: when the interest rate spread is high, the estimated prepayment rate is low since there is a correlation between the high interest rate spreads and the existence of customers who could prepay before and did not.

There is mean reverting force that brings prepayment rates to lower levels (we modelled this force here with a cubic factor).

13.3.1.2 *Logit models and cumulative prepayment functions*

Some A/L managers will use a *LOGIT approach* to model prepayments. They introduce the endogenous dichotomized variable Y that can take two values (0 or 1):

- 0 if there is no prepayment;
- 1 otherwise.

We make the logistic regression over a set of variable X such as intercept, interest rate spread, cubic interest rate spread, loan seniority, burnout, etc. X is a vector of K variables and β is the associated regression coefficient:

$$P(Y = 1/X = x) = \exp(x'.\beta)/(1 + \exp(x'.\beta)) \tag{13.32}$$

We estimate the model using a log-likelihood maximization for the determination of β.

These Logit models could also be associated with *survival models* where the variable to model is the survival function S such as in *Cox models*.

For a specific loan, we write the survival function:

$$S(t) = P\,(Y_t = 0/\,(Y_{t-1} = 0, X = x)) \tag{13.33}$$

The law specification for Y gives a law for S. It is possible to estimate the parameters on the past observations of S in the database.

13.3.1.3 *Prepayment modelling with mixed effects*

The prepayment option is similar to a default option in terms of modelling: *a prepayment is somehow equivalent to a default with a 100 % recovery rate.*

Consequently, it is conceivable to propose a linear mixed modelling similar to the credit risk modelling. Of course, the explaining variables will differ from those used in credit risk.

The prepayment rate could depend on a systemic variable X (depending on time and interest rates) and a specific variable depending on the loan characteristics (weighted average life, customer FICO score, loan seniority, etc.):

$$\text{Prepayment Rate (t, R, C, specific dummies)} = \Phi\left(\sqrt{\rho}.X_{t,R,C} + \sqrt{1-\rho^2}.\varepsilon_{t,\text{ specific dummies}}\right) \tag{13.34}$$

As for credit risk modelling, we will split the specific variable ε between many other specific variables:

$$\varepsilon_{t,\text{specific dummies}} = \sqrt{\rho_1}.\varepsilon_{\text{first set of specific dummies}} + \sqrt{1-\rho_1^2}.\varepsilon_{\text{second set of specific dummies}} \tag{13.35}$$

13.3.2 Non-parametric prepayment modelling

13.3.2.1 Principles

Non-parametric prepayment modelling means that the A/L manager will not impose a specific parameterized form for the prepayment function.

The "kernel smoothing methodology" allows the A/L manager to estimate directly the function F from the database:

$$\text{Prepayment} = F_4\left((\tilde{R}_t - C), (\tilde{R}_t - C)^3, S\right) \tag{13.36}$$

In practice, the A/L manager will have to look carefully to the estimated function. For instance, he will have to:

- propose a weight for the database information (using a weighted kernel smoothing as shown below);
- backtest the modelling using, for instance, out-of-sample tests.

13.3.2.2 Kernel smoothing

To estimate the function F, the A/L manager will use, for instance, a non-parametric Gaussian kernel smoothing.

The database should for each line i integrate a prepayment rate Y_i, and some regression variables X_i such as the interest rate spread (C-R) and the loan seniority S. Implicitly we write the model like this:

$$Y_i = E(Y_i \mid X_i = x_i) + \varepsilon_i = m(x_i) + \varepsilon_i \tag{13.37}$$

ε_i are the residuals of the regression. The A/L manager's objective is to estimate the function m:

$$m(x) = E(Y \mid X) \tag{13.38}$$

The A/L manager will suppose that the couple (X_i, Y_i) will admit a density f expressed as:

$$\hat{f}(x, y) = \frac{1}{n\,[h(n)]^{k+1}} \sum\nolimits_{i=1}^{n} K\left(\frac{(x, y) - (X_i, Y_i)}{h(n)}\right) \tag{13.39}$$

where:

- K is a Gaussian kernel (or Parzen-Rosenblatt kernel). [Note that there are other kernel types such as the uniform or the beta kernel.]

$$K(x) = (2\pi)^{\frac{n_{axes}}{2}} \exp\left(-\frac{\|x\|^2}{2}\right) \tag{13.40}$$

- h(n) is a *band-with* (or window-with) function depending on the sample size n. This function helps into the selection of the closest observations x_i to x. A rule called "rule of Scott" designs empirically H with the variance-covariance matrix Σ of the explaining variables X and a constant h (taken often equal to 1):

$$H = h \times \Sigma^{\frac{1}{2}} \frac{1}{p^{/(n_{axes}+4)}} \tag{13.41}$$

- k is the dimension of X (2 if the A/L manager chooses seniority and spread).

It is then possible to demonstrate that the better estimation of m follows:

$$\hat{m}(x) = \frac{\sum_{i=1}^{n} Y_i K\left(\frac{x-x_i}{h(n)}\right)}{\sum_{i=1}^{n} K\left(\frac{x-x_i}{h(n)}\right)} = \sum_{i=1}^{n} Y_i w_i(x) \tag{13.42}$$

In this equation, we express the weights w as:

$$w_i(x) = \frac{K\left(\frac{x-x_i}{h(n)}\right)}{\sum_{i=1}^{n} K\left(\frac{x-x_i}{h(n)}\right)} \tag{13.43}$$

For this kind of operation, we use the term of "non-parametric regression" since the estimation of m is the solution of the following minimizing programme:

$$\min_m \frac{1}{n} \sum_{i=1}^{n} \|y_i - m\|^2 K\left(\frac{x - x_i}{h}\right) \tag{13.44}$$

The kernel regression gives a least square estimation weighted by the function K. This estimation is a "local estimation" since in the regression we take only into account the information around the regressed point.

13.3.2.3 Weighted kernel smoothing for granular databases

The information contained in databases is sometimes granular; it means that each observation line does not aggregate enough loans to make the prepayment rate of this line representative of a prepayment rate.

To take into account the granularity into the estimation, the A/L manager will weight the estimation by the outstanding amount J_i at date i. This weighting will give more weight to the most reliable observations.

Thus, we define the minimization programme as follows:

$$\min_m \frac{1}{n} \sum_{i=1}^{n} \|y_i - m\|^2 K\left(\frac{x - x_i}{h}\right) . J_i \tag{13.45}$$

This modifies the estimator as follows:

$$\hat{m}(x) = \frac{\sum_{i=1}^{n} Y_i K\left(\frac{x-x_i}{h(n)}\right) J_i}{\sum_{i=1}^{n} K\left(\frac{x-x_i}{h(n)}\right) J_i} \tag{13.46}$$

13.3.2.4 *Result samples*

The kernel regression gives interesting graphics such as this one where we see the link between the annual prepayment rate, the interest rate spread and the loan seniority:

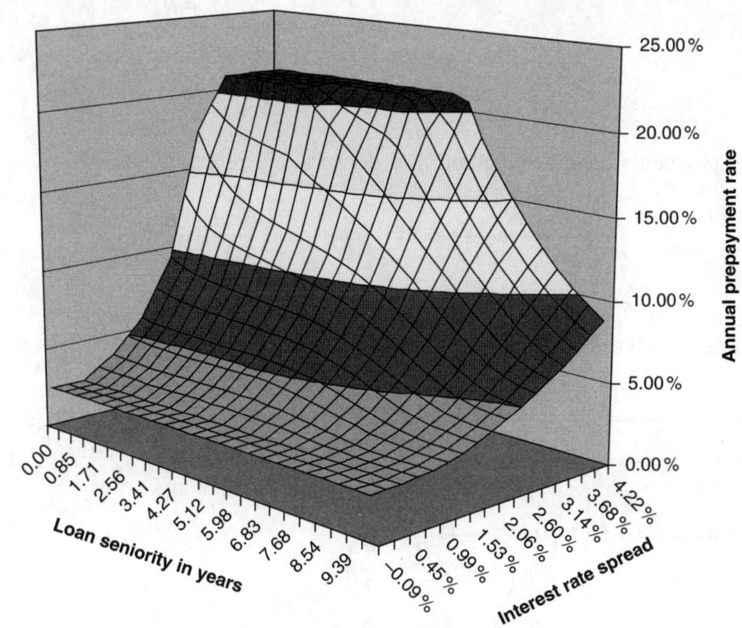

Figure 13.21 Kernel smoothing

13.3.3 Renegotiation modelling

The same principles apply for renegotiation modelling. The idea is that for each customer ready to prepay, the bank will try to propose to renegotiate the loan.

Consequently, the A/L manager will have to model:

- the customer probability to prepay or to renegotiate;
- the customer probability to accept to renegotiate (this probability is a function of the proposed rate after renegotiation);
- the proposed rate after renegotiation.

This task is not easy since the proposition of renegotiation depends on the Commercial Department.

Quite often, the business line will propose a rate after renegotiation so that the customer will not prepay to join another bank.

The monthly payment proposed by other banks will include a penalty p and the bank will compute it according to the re-employment rate R on the outstanding amount K. On the other hand, the new monthly payment proposed by the bank will be based on a new rate R′:

$$PMT_{\text{proposed by other banks}} = K.(1+p)\frac{R}{1-\dfrac{1}{(1+R)^N}}$$
$$PMT_{\text{to propose after renegotiation}} = K.\frac{R'}{1-\dfrac{1}{(1+R')^N}} \tag{13.47}$$

Those two payments have to be equal in order to avoid prepayments:

$$\frac{R'}{1-\dfrac{1}{(1+R')^N}} = (1+p)\frac{R}{1-\dfrac{1}{(1+R)^N}} \tag{13.48}$$

It is possible to make this equation linear:

$$\frac{R'}{1-\left(1-N.R'+N^2.\dfrac{R'^2}{2}+N\dfrac{R'^2}{2}\right)} \approx (1+p).\frac{R}{1-\left(1-N.R+N^2.\dfrac{R^2}{2}+N\dfrac{R^2}{2}\right)}$$
$$\frac{1}{\left(1-N.\dfrac{R'}{2}-\dfrac{R'}{2}\right)} \approx (1+p).\frac{1}{\left(1-N.\dfrac{R}{2}-\dfrac{R}{2}\right)} \tag{13.49}$$
$$R' \approx \left(\left(\cdot\left(\frac{2}{1+N}\right)-\frac{\left(\cdot\left(\dfrac{2}{1+N}\right)-R\right)}{1+p}\right)\right) = \frac{R}{1+p}+\left(\frac{2.p}{(1+N).(1+p)}\right)$$

Of course, this linearization does not work for interest rate levels that are too high.

It is important to compute also the renegotiation acceptance ratio. Not surprisingly, this ratio depends on the Commercial Department reactivity but it could also depend on the difference between the rate proposed to the customers and the theoretical rate R'.

13.3.4 Model backtesting

Prepayment modelling is a good opportunity to present model backtesting. Backtesting provides the opportunity to judge the quality of the models.

First, it is possible to use the model calibrated on the whole database on this same database to compute line by line a "backtested mortgage prepayment". This computed theoretical prepayment could then be projected on the time horizon (see Figure 13.23).

The A/L manager will then be able to compute modelling ratios such as in Figure 13.24. However, this is not really a backtest.

At the opposite, we will consider the "out-of-sample" test as a real backtest. The principle is to separate data sources between two parts: we use one part for the model calibration (the model learns the information present in this first half of the database) and the other for the test.

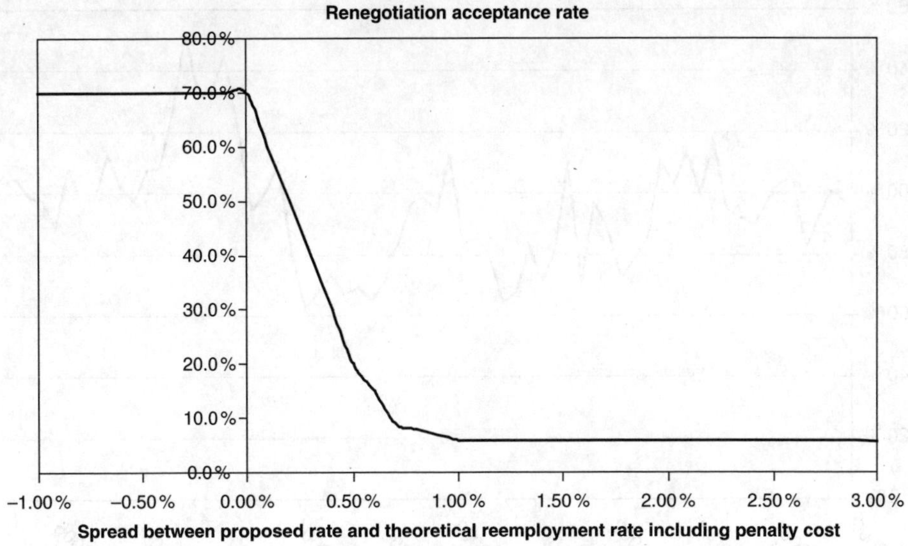

Figure 13.22 Renegotiation

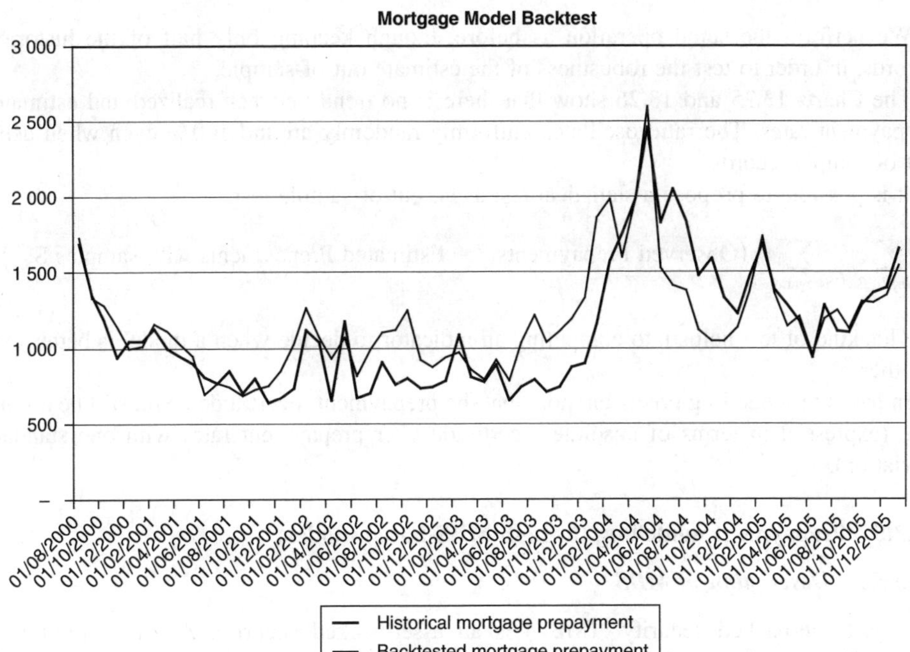

Figure 13.23 Backtesting

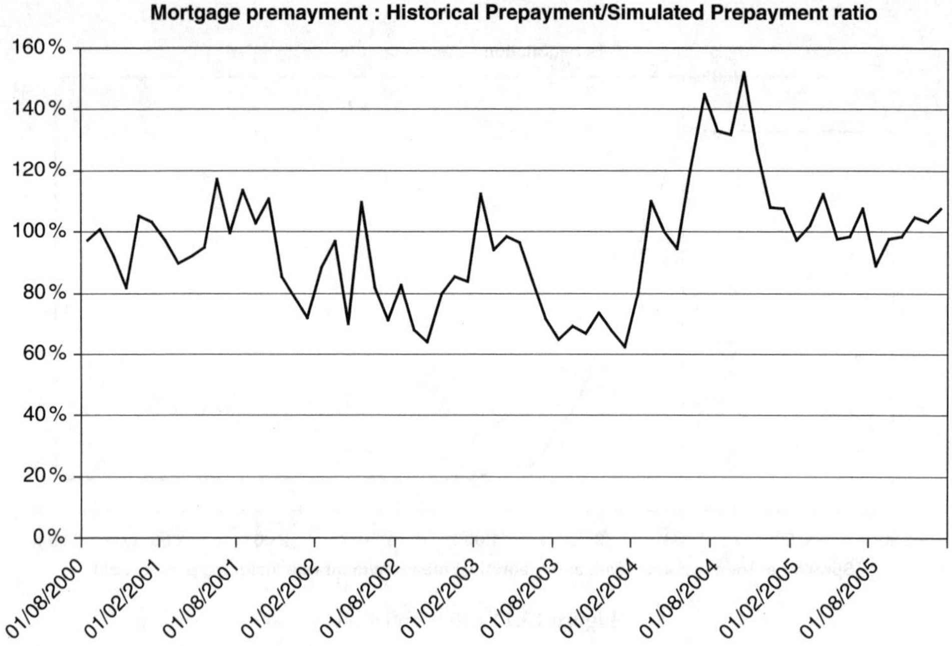

Figure 13.24 Prepayment backtesting

We perform the same operation as before, though keeping only half of the historical records, in order to test the robustness of the estimate out-of-sample.

The Charts 13.25 and 13.26 show that there is no trend between realized and estimated prepayment rates. The ratio oscillates uniformly randomly around 100 % even when using out-of-sample records.

It is possible to propose a statistical test as an out-of-sample test.

$$\sum_{Sample\ S}\ \sum_{\text{Observation } i} \left(\text{Observed Prepayments}_{S,i} - \text{Estimated Prepayments with samples } \mathrm{S}_{S,i}\right)^2 \tag{13.50}$$

This kind of test helps into computing an indicator to decide when a model is better than another.

In terms of modelling precision, note that the prepayment incertitude could still be around 2 % (expressed in terms of absolute incertitude over prepayment rates with one standard deviation).

13.3.5 Prepayment modelling through MBS-based models

13.3.5.1 Description of MBS

A “mortgage-backed security” (MBS) is an asset-backed security. A set of mortgages “backed” the MBS cash flows.

In the USA, Federal Agencies (Freddie Mac, Fannie Mae –FNMA- or GNMA) take the mortgages credit risk but the MBS investor takes the prepayment risk since prepayments are directly transferred to him.

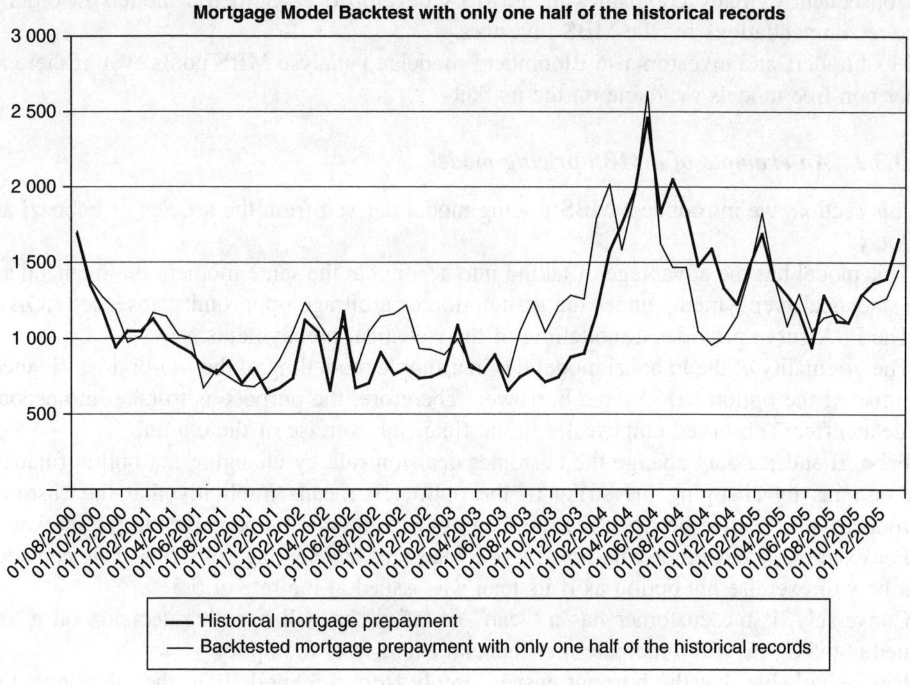

Figure 13.25 Prepayment backtesting

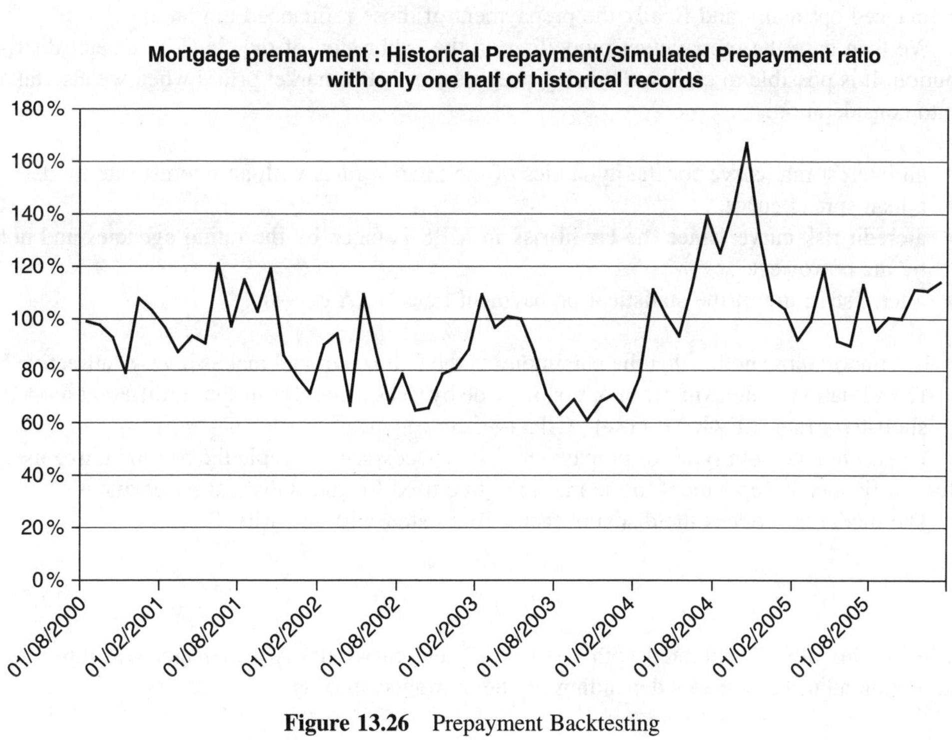

Figure 13.26 Prepayment Backtesting

Consequently, many companies in the USA developed econometric models in order to give recommendations for the MBS investors.

Most traders and investors use Bloomberg models to analyse MBS pools even if there are other non-free models available on the market.

13.3.5.2 An example of a MBS pricing models

In this section, we introduce a MBS pricing model derived from the articles of Fabozzi and Kalotay.

This model has the advantage of taking into account at the same moment the financial and the statistical prepayments under the assumption of arbitrage opportunity absence (AOA).

The PSA curve provides a modelling of the statistical prepayments.

The originality of the Fabozzi model lies in a simple modelling of the sub-optimal financial exercise of the option held by the borrower. Therefore, the purpose is to take into account a "delay effect" observed empirically in the financial exercise of the option.

Fabozzi and Kalotay change the customer decision rule by changing the option financial exercise i.e. by changing the strike of the option. It means implicitly that the customer introduces a difference between the rate he pays and the rate he perceives in the market.

For example, a customer who holds a 6 % loan will have a "lag" of 0.5 % if he considers that he will exercise his option as if its loan was issued at the rate of 5.5 %.

Conversely, if the customer has a "leap" of 0.5 %, he will base his decision on a loan issued at 6.5 %; he will anticipate the financial exercise of the option.

It is remarkable that the burnout ensues simply from this modelling: the lag allows first the prepayment of the loans refinanced too early and then the prepayment of the loans refinanced optimally and finally the prepayment of those refinanced too late.

We then base the prepayment modelling on the calibration of the "lag" parameter distribution. It is possible to calibrate this lag over a set of MBS market prices when we also take into consideration:

- an interest rate curve for the dynamics of the interest rates with an interest rate model;
- a loan spread curve;
- a credit risk curve (since the credit risk in MBS is taken by the rating agencies and not by the borrower);
- a term structure of the statistical prepayment rates (PSA curve).

It is important to notice that the parsimony of the Fabozzi model makes it very "attractive".

The valuation of the American option is made by trees using, for instance, different models of short-term rate (MLG, MLG2 +, CIR ++, etc.).

To accumulate both types of prepayments, it is necessary to couple the trinomial tree used for the financial prepayment to the binomial tree used for the statistical prepayment.

The model introduces the discount factor B at date t with maturity T:

$$B(t, T) = e^{-\int_t^T r_s ds} \tag{13.51}$$

From this model calibrated with a risk free yield curve, the A/L manager will introduce an option adjusted spread s depending on the mortgage such as:

$$r_{mtge} = r + s_{mtge} \tag{13.52}$$

We then price the mortgage as a callable amortizing bond. We price it using classic trading pricing methods with a trinomial tree. The notations are the following:

- t_i are the loan payment dates;
- P_i are the principal cash flows;
- m the loan fixed rate;
- R_i are the loan outstanding amount;
- $C_i = P_i + m.R_{i-1}$ the loan monthly payment;
- c the prepayment cost;
- $S_i = R_{i-1}.(1+c)$ the prepayment option strike;
- $V_m(t_k, Z(t_k))$ the mortgage price at date t_k at the tree node $Z(t_k)$ with a "financial engineer" approach;
- $W_m(t_k, Z(t_k))$ the mortgage price at date t_k at the tree node $Z(t_k)$ without any prepayment.

Those prices have no final value at date N. W is equal to the future cash flows discounted with the mortgage curve taking into account the option value. The minimum of the outstanding amount of capital and the value W gives the value of the option:

$$\begin{cases} V_m(t_N, Z(t_N)) = W_m(t_N, Z(t_N)) = 0 \\ W_m(t_k, Z(t_k)) = B_{mtge}(t_k, t_{k+1}, Z(t_k))(P_{k+1} + mR_k + E(V_m(t_{k+1}, .)\,|Z(t_k))) \\ V_m(t_k, Z(t_k)) = \min(S_k, W_m(t_k, Z(t_k))) \end{cases} \tag{13.53}$$

When the loan customer has a lag "l", this change the value of V:

$$\begin{cases} V_m(t_N, Z(t_N)) = 0 \\ V_m(t_k, Z(t_k)) = \begin{cases} S_k \ if \ S_k < W_{m-l}(t_k, Z(t_k)) \\ W_m(t_k, Z(t_k)) \text{ otherwise} \end{cases} \end{cases} \tag{13.54}$$

Implicitly, the customer makes his prepayment decision on an interest rate of m-l instead of m.

When we price a mortgage pool, we aggregate the cash flows, we aggregate the coupons into a WAC (weighted average coupon) called M with the objective to compute for each lag l the value $V_{m,l}$.

It is necessary to give an idea of the distribution of the lags l with a distribution probability p(l).dl. This will give the mortgage pool value:

$$V_m(t_0) = \int_0^{+\infty} V_{m,l}(t_0)p(l)dl. \tag{13.55}$$

The function p(l) has to take into account the burnout effect.

The prepayment modelling is then based on the calibration of this distribution p(l) using MBS market prices.

Note: the mortgage pools present in MBS are credit risk hedged by the Agencies (Fannie Mae or Freddie Mac) and for this reason the MBS spread is lower than the mortgage spread.

13.4 PREPAYMENT SCORING

Since we can consider the prepayment somehow as a default with a recuperation rate of 100 %, it is possible to apply scoring techniques used in credit risk modelling to prepayment risk.

The idea is to give to each customer a rating that gives his likelihood to prepay whatever the interest rate level is. The rating will allow the A/L manager to regroup in databases customers with close arbitrage reactions.

Scoring techniques take into account the entire customer and loan characteristics:

- geographic position;
- salary;
- age;
- education level;
- payment to income ratio;
- loan to value, etc.

Prepayment scoring allows the A/L manager to reduce significantly the incertitude about its prepayments.

13.5 PREPAYMENT MONITORING

For A/L managers, prepayments are not only a question of modelling; prepayments are also a question of *organization*. Indeed, the A/L manager will have to deal with these questions:

- *How to integrate prepayments in the FTP computation?*

Statistical prepayments will shorten the loan interest rate schedule. When the interest rate curves are not flat, the recognition of a statistical prepayment will change the loan FTP level.

On the other hand, the A/L manager has to introduce the financial prepayment option in the FTPs and this could be very costly for the commercial entities.

- *How to charge internally prepayment costs to commercial entities?*

If the A/L manager charges the prepayment option in the FTP computation, there is no reason for him to charge the Commercial Department for the occurrence of financial prepayments.

Nevertheless, to incite the Commercial Department to charge a penalty to the customer, the ALM could charge to the Commercial Department the maximum contractual penalty the commercials could charge to the customer.

Moreover, once the Commercial Department has transferred the prepayment option to the ALM, this entity wins an arbitrage opportunity. It is then possible to incite customers to prepay and to sign up for a new loan with a lower interest rate level but with a higher margin.

The solution is to transfer to the Commercial Department the result of the prepayment hedging. If the observed prepayment rate is higher than the anticipated one, the ALM team has to transfer this cost (loan by loan) to the commercial entities.

- *How to incite customers to renegotiate rather than to prepay?*

When a customer prepays his loan, the bank loses generally all the relations with this client. On the other hand, when the customer renegotiates his loan the prepayment cost is lower and there are still opportunities to deal with this customer in the future.

To incite renegotiations, the bank internal treatment of a renegotiation should take into account a perequation within a FTP system. The problem is to avoid the creation of arbitrage opportunities for the Commercial Department in front of the ALM. The idea is to find systems where the Commercial Department will encourage customers to renegotiate only if they are close to prepay. Mathematically speaking, it means that the management has to propose a system with the following relationship:

Cost of prepayment for Commercial Department < Cost of renegotiation < 0

- *How to be organized to recuperate the internal data about prepayments?*
- *How to integrate prepayments into risk indicators?*

Delta equivalent techniques will help the A/L manager to compute the prepayment strategy and to integrate prepayments in the risk indicators.

14

Other Examples of Products Needing Behavioural Modelling

Tambour payé d'avance ne fait pas beaucoup de bruit.

14.1 PIPELINE RISK

Pipeline risk defines all the financial risk occurring from the moment a financial product is commercialized (and not of course sold) to the moment the product is booked and hedged.

For instance, *loan offers* may present a pipeline risk. Commercial entities may propose a fixed interest rate to the customer and a decision period (sometimes this is a legal decision period). Actually, there is a kind of option during this decision period: if the interest rates go down, the customer will have the opportunity to ask for another credit in another bank and if interest rates go up, he will accept the credit proposed at the beginning of the decision period (with a lower interest rate).

In terms of modelling, the A/L manager will have to model the ratio of loan offer acceptance as a function of the spread between the proposed interest rate and the level of market rates.

The *uncertainty* between a contract signature and the effective payment start date is another source of pipeline risk. For instance, when a customer needs a construction loan to build up a new home, it could take around two years to finish the construction. Of course, the customer does not get all the money at the loan signature: the bank gives him the money each time he has to pay for the construction:

- At the loan signature, he will pay 30 % to buy the building land for sale.
- Periodically, over two years he will pay the bricklayer, the electrician, the painter, the decorator, etc.
- At the home finishing date ("keys handing over"), the customer will have to pay the outstanding amounts.

The construction of pipeline risk databases helps build up a chart 14.2.

This means that in this example the customer will effectively use only 80 % of the granted amount: customers tend to maximize this amount so as not to be obliged to renegotiate it with banks.

ALM FTPs and indicators have to take into account this pipeline risk.

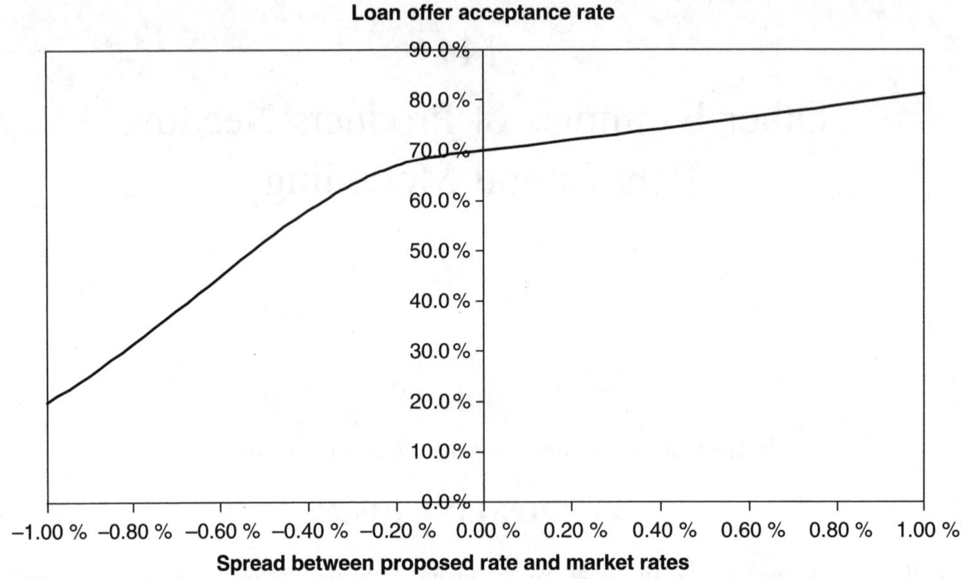

Figure 14.1 Loan offer acceptance rate

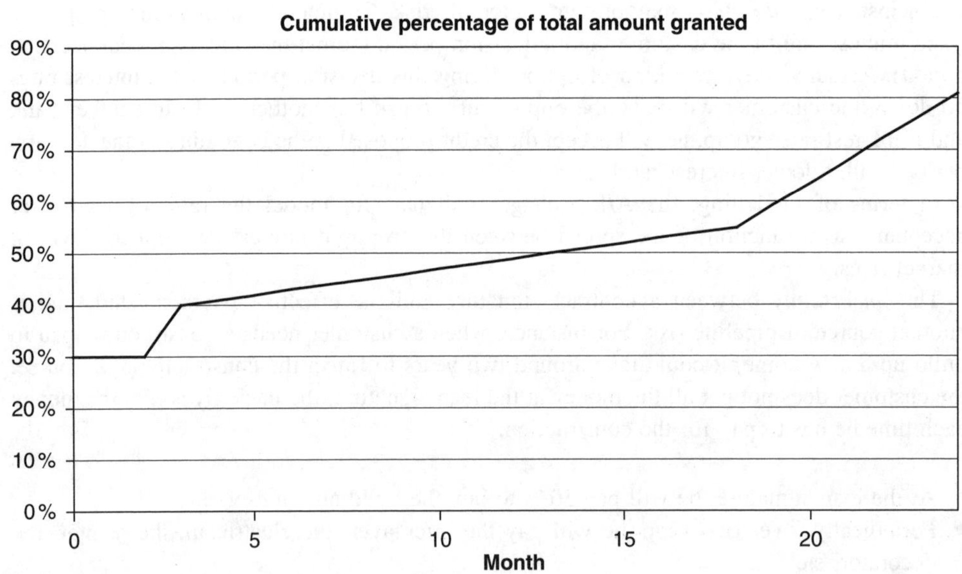

Figure 14.2 Percentage of granted amount

14.2 MARGIN DELAY EFFECTS SUCH AS "WHISTLE EFFECTS"

Delay effects are another type of behaviour that will alter the ALM income. The idea is that there is quite often a delay between the customer prices and market refinancing conditions. There are many examples of these delays:

- Margins on loans will increase when interest rates will go down since the bank introduces the market information in the loan rate proposition with a certain delay. On the other hand, margins on loans will decrease when interest rates will go up.
- Margins on remunerated deposits will increase when interest goes up since the remuneration rate rises take time to happen. On the other hand, when interest rates decrease, the margin decreases also but often more slowly: banks are often quicker to decrease deposit remuneration rate than to increase it. For example, we keep in mind this modelling proposed in the deposit modelling section:

$$\begin{cases} R_{(t)} = R_{(t-1)} + c.\left(R_{(t-1)} - R_{(t-2)}\right) + d.\left(Libor_{(t)} - Libor_{(t-1)}\right) \\ \qquad + e.\left(Libor_{(t-1)} - Libor_{(t-2)}\right) + C_{(t-1)} + \varepsilon_{(t)} \\ E_{(t)} = a + b.Libor_{(t)} \text{(Equilibrium rate)} \\ C_{(t-1)} = f.\left(R_{(t-1)} - E_{(t-1)}\right) \text{if} R_{(t-1)} \geq E_{(t-1)} \\ C_{(t-1)} = g.\left(R_{(t-1)} - E_{(t-1)}\right) \text{if} R_{(t-1)} < E_{(t-1)} \end{cases} \tag{14.1}$$

- In insurance companies, for marketing campaigns, the Commercial Department will advertise a fixed rate on a fixed period that will not vary during the whole promotion campaign.

A/L managers talk about a *whistle effect* since the form of the margin evolution compared with the interest rate evolution may sometimes look like a whistle.

14.3 OTHER VOLUME EFFECTS OPTIONS

Sometimes, commercial risks include a correlation between the amount commercialized and the financial markets: A/L managers use the term of *"volume effects"*.

For instance, we saw that there are clear volume effects between demand deposits (with 0 % remuneration) and savings deposits when interest rates move.

In capped loans, the outstanding amount and then the net interest margin depends on the interest rate path creating a volume effect.

For life insurance products, the insured amounts grow with the market rates. Consequently, the costs charged to the customer (and then the profitability of the insurance company) depend on the interest rate path.

15

Examples of Products Partially Correlated with Financial Markets

C'est une belle harmonie quand le faire et le dire vont ensemble. (Montaigne)

Financial risks may be present in ALM books due to implicit reasons:

- the presence of a correlation between cash flows (interests, commissions or costs) and financial markets; or
- the presence of embedded options in the product.

15.1 PRESENCE OF CORRELATION BETWEEN THE CASH FLOWS AND FINANCIAL MARKETS: EXAMPLES OF CREDIT CARD

There is sometimes a correlation between the interest rates paid to a customer (or received from him) and the market rates but without a direct indexation. We saw the example of savings accounts where the correlation between the savings rate and the market rates is implicit and not explicit.

Credit cards loans (or revolving credits) are another good example of partial correlation between the charged interest rates and the market rates.

The interest rate proposed to the customer is either a free interest rate or a regulated interest rate. The modelling of such an interest rate is similar to the modelling of the savings interest rates.

$$R(t) = A.R(t-1) + B.Libor(t) + C.Libor(t-1) + \varepsilon(t) \quad (15.1)$$

This interest rate has to represent the rate that protects the bank against a customer arbitrage.

The representation of credit cards in indicators will follow the same methodology as for savings. We base the computation of the liquidity schedule on the existing accounts with their closing probability, their average amount evolution.

We compute the interest rate schedule from the liquidity schedule using delta equivalent techniques.

15.2 COSTS AND COMMISSIONS CORRELATION WITH FINANCIAL MARKETS

Fees or costs for existing customers may depend on the financial markets. For instance, bank fees will vary according to the level of the stock exchange. Existing bank customers will

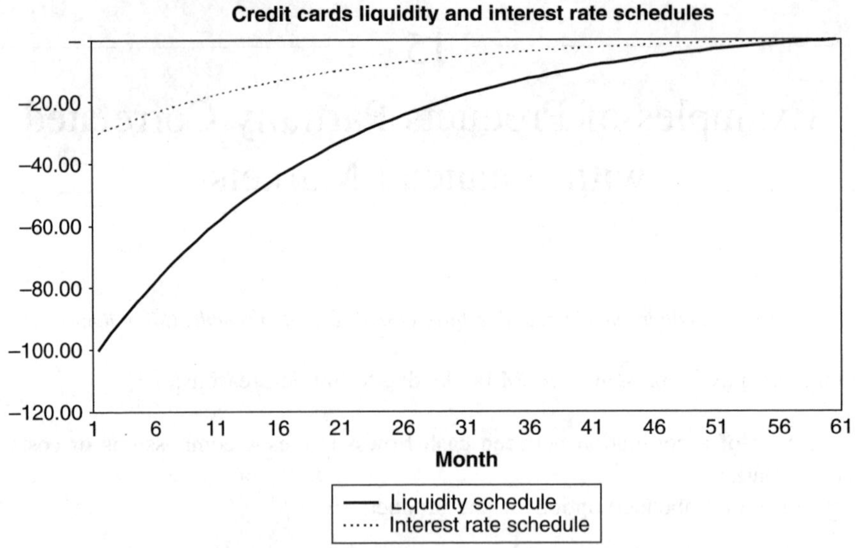

Figure 15.1 Credit card liquidity schedule

conserve stocks and pay regularly fees on these stocks in proportion to the stock exchange level.

On the other hand, there is a possible link between markets rates, inflation, economic growth and the other market variables.

15.3 EXAMPLES OF EMBEDDED OPTIONS

In many contracts, there are embedded options such as prepayment options. Many examples are present in banking books:

- in Libor capped loans;
- in Hybrid ARMs: fixed rate during 3 years and Libor capped after;
- in predetermined rate loan offer: in many countries, some products include loan options with a predetermined rate (Epargne Logement in France, Bauspar in Germany, tontine in Africa, etc.). The customer has the opportunity to borrow at a future date with a predetermined rate. This option is accounted according to IAS 37 and the option price is determined in advance using behavioural databases;
- in life insurance contracts, when the customer has the opportunity to prepay his contract without any penalty in advance.

16

New Production Modelling

Le temps c'est de l'argent.

New production modelling is a source of a lot of work for A/L managers:

- new contracts production modelling;
- commission and cost modelling;
- perequation modelling;
- future strategies modelling.

16.1 NEW CONTRACT PRODUCTION

16.1.1 The general case

Usually A/L managers will use these kinds of hypotheses when they try to model new productions:

- *Constant outstanding*: for example, the stock of the existing contracts will stay the same during the next 3 years.
- *Budgetary outstanding*: for example, the stock of existing contracts will increase by 5 % during the next 3 years.
- *Constant new production*: for example, the new production of contracts will be of 1 billion each year during the next 3 years.

Unfortunately, those hypotheses numbers are not compatible with quantitative modelling. The demand deposit model gave us an example of new production modelling. There is a link in many countries between the new customer production and:

- the operating cost disbursed to acquire new customers;
- the promotional campaigns;
- *the perequation*.

Companies are often afraid of providing a quantitative model of the new production: this modelling shows sometimes to the business lines (or to the Commercial Department) how much the company has lost in badly driven (financially speaking) marketing campaigns.

Nevertheless, quantitative modelling of new customer/contract production follows this simple rule:

The Economic value produced at time t does not depend on the economic conditions at date t

Mathematically speaking this principle becomes:

At least, an equilibrium economic value VE*(t) exists for the production of new clients at date t and follows for example:

$$VE^*(t) = VE^*(0).e^{\int_0^t r(s).ds} \tag{16.1}$$

This economic value takes into account the technologic effects.

The economic value produced by the new clients at date t follows:

$$dVE(t) = \lambda.\left(VE^*(t) - VE(t)\right).dt + \sigma.dW_t$$

If the economic value of the new production were a function of the financial markets, it would mean that there is no efficiency within the market.

In ALM, VE(t) is the sum of ***all*** *the discounted cash flows associated with the customers acquired at date t.* It means:

- the future incomes arising on the existing contract;
- all the other incomes (fees on future other productions linked with the new customers of date t);
- the perequation costs.

16.1.2 Example of new mortgage loan production modelling

In macroeconomic models, the loan production follows the economy growth.

When modelling the new production of mortgage loans, the A/L manager will take into account:

- Loan choices diversity: for each real estate project, the customer has many opportunities to build this project such as "assisted loans" (0 % loans), free of tax investment loans (with rental perspective) and classic private sector loans.
- Prepayments: financial prepayment increases new loan production since a significant part of the new loans comes from competitors' past loans acquisition.
- Geographical factors (city versus suburbs).
- Sociological factors: divorces increases, mobility increases, household increases, "baby boom", etc.
- Household debts.
- Seasonality.
- Customer development.

Usually, there is a link between the new loan production and the household debts level (expressed as a percentage of the personal income). Actually, it is essential to pose the question of the household debts in four terms:

- A generational effect: young versus old customers: 30-year-old customers will need to borrow to buy their home. The borrowed cash is transferred directly to home sellers who are in fact older people. In a same family, the younger generations will borrow when older generations will be cash rich. From this point of view, the household debt is not really a problem since it disappears at a family level.
- Rich population versus poor population effect: a problem will possibly arise when the borrower population does not come from the same family circle as the landowners. In this case, a local market crisis could perhaps affect the household debts of the poorest population.
- Country internal debt versus external debt effect: household debt becomes strategic in new loan production modelling when the country external debts become too important. There is indeed a risk of a prompt economy decrease when this risk occurs: the internal household debt decreases.
- Debt market development is also important. Loan market growth goes with economy growth: loan practice is less developed in emerging markets than in OECD countries but with the rise in globalization, the spreads decrease.

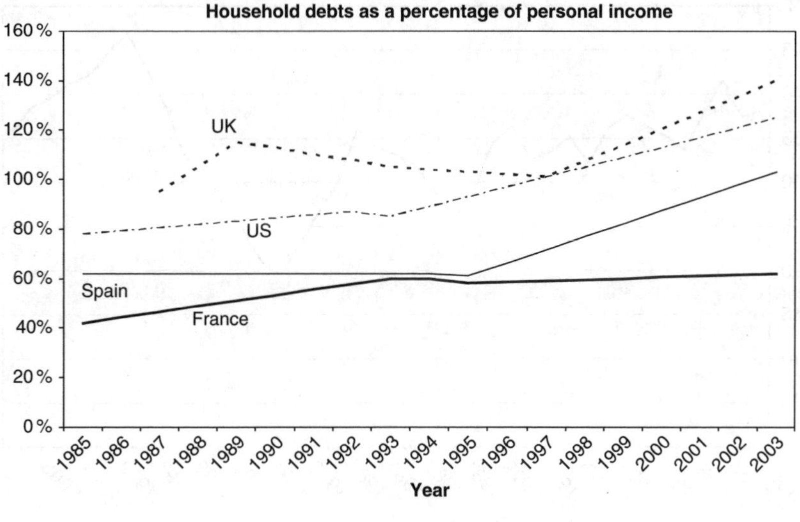

Figure 16.1 Household debts

16.1.2.1 Real estate prices as an exogenous variable

Once all these effects have been taken into consideration, the major effect is simple: *the loan mortgage market grows with real estate prices*. Loan production growth and real estate prices growth are highly correlated on long-term horizons.

Indeed, banks will lend according to the customer personal income. To avoid credit risk, the loan repayment should not be inferior to a certain percentage of this personal income.

If we have to consider the real estate price as an exogenous variable for production modelling, it means that the *loan duration* and the *personal capital contribution* are adjustment variables for the banks.

$$\text{Real estate prices} = \text{Loan production} + \text{Personal capital contribution}$$

$$\text{Loan Production} = \sum_{i=1}^{N} \frac{(\text{Personal income . Percentage})}{(1+R)^{i}}$$

$$\text{Loan Production} = \text{Personal income . Percentage.} \left(\frac{1 - \dfrac{1}{(1+\mathrm{R})^{N}}}{R} \right) \tag{16.2}$$

with constraints:

$$Percentage \leq 30\,\%$$
$$0 \leq \mathrm{N} < \infty$$

This chart shows the stability of the number of affordable square metres in Paris. This number is of course volatile due to cyclic effects but it shows the link between real estate prices and personal income:

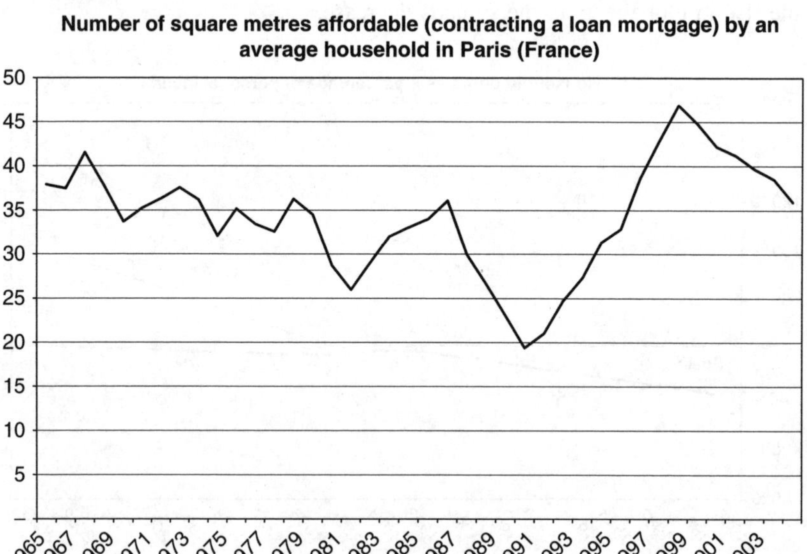

Figure 16.2 Square metres in Paris

Consequently, if the personal capital contribution p is a fixed percentage of the real estate prices, the loan duration proposed by banks will follow:

$$\mathrm{N} = -\frac{\ln\left(1 - \dfrac{(1-p)\,.\text{Real estate prices.R}}{\text{Personal income . Percentage}}\right)}{\ln(1+\mathrm{R})} \tag{16.3}$$

There is a condition for N to exist on the real estate prices:

$$\text{Real estate prices} \leq \frac{\text{Personal income . Percentage}}{(1-p).R} \tag{16.4}$$

However, if this condition is verified, the loan production will follow directly the real estate prices:

$$\text{Loan production} = (1-\text{p}).\text{Real estate prices} \tag{16.5}$$

Nevertheless, in this equation, we have to keep in mind that the real estate prices will grow with the economy growth and consequently the loan production too.

16.1.2.2 Real estate prices as an endogenous variable

The model above imposes a condition on the evolution of the real estate prices:

$$\text{Real estate prices} \leq \frac{\text{Personal income . Percentage}}{(1-p).R} \tag{16.6}$$

If the real estate price saturates this mathematical constraint, it means that the loan production follows:

$$\text{Loan production} = \frac{\text{Personal income . Percentage}}{R}$$

as long as (16.7)

$$\text{Real estate prices} \approx \frac{\text{Personal income . Percentage}}{(1-p).R}$$

When interest rates increase, it is difficult for real estate prices to respect the inequality and consequently loan production is expected to decrease (even if personal income increases).

16.1.2.3 Loan production growth and interest rates

In both models, loan production will grow according to personal income or real estate prices level. Consequently, loan growth will follow a pattern coherent with the interest rates:

$$Loan\_Production^*(t) = Loan\_Production^*(0).e^{\int_0^t r(s).ds} \tag{16.8}$$

This equilibrium production is just an equilibrium relationship and as before, it leads to this kind of equation:

$$dLoan\_Production(t) = \lambda.\left(Loan\_Production^*(t) - Loan\_Production(t)\right).dt + \sigma.dW_t \tag{16.9}$$

16.1.3 Example of new insurance contracts modelling

Exactly as before, new life insurance production follows an equilibrium relationship:

$$Life\_Insurance\_Production^*(t) = Life\_Insurance\_Production^*(0).e^{\int_0^t r(s).ds} \tag{16.10}$$

We use this equilibrium production as a mean reversion for the real life insurance production:

$$dLife\_Insurance\_\Pr od(t) = \lambda.\left(Life\_Insurance\_\Pr oduction^{*}(t) - Life\_Insurance\_\Pr od(t)\right).dt + \sigma.dW_t \quad (16.11)$$

16.2 COMMISSION AND COST MODELLING

The example of demand deposit modelling is once more a good source to comprehend the modelling of fees and operating costs.

At a unitary level, we usually consider that operating costs are growing as fast as the price indexes. In reality, *operating costs will grow as fast as the global economy* since these costs will incorporate the costs of new technologies development and then will grow faster than the CPI index.

On the other hand, *fees and commissions will grow also at economy growth speed* since the new technologies affect also these other incomes.

Moreover, **there is an equilibrium relationship between:**

- **net interest income growth(by customer);**
- **other income growth(by customer);**
- **operating cost growth (by customer).**

In the demand deposit example, we explained this relationship considering the net income produced by customer (the sum of all the incomes less the operating costs by customer):

- If the net interest rate income by customer becomes too low, the market will compensate for this weakness with the creation of new fees.
- On the other hand, if the net interest income by customer becomes too important, the market on the long-term will compensate for this increase (new bank creation, negative pressure on the growth of other incomes, negative pressure on the operating cost growth).

This equilibrium relationship means that the other income evolution will take into account the evolution of the net interest margin and of the operating cost:

$$Z_t = (\text{Net Interest Margin}_t + \text{Other income}_t - \text{Operating cost}_t).e^{-\int_0^t r(s).ds} \quad \text{(per client)}$$

$$dZ_t = \mu.\left(\tilde{Z} - Z_t\right).dt + \sigma'.dW_t \quad (16.12)$$

This relationship gives the possible evolution of the other income as soon as the A/L manager is able to ascertain what the evolution of the net interest margin is for the market.

As for demand deposits, there is a constraint on the value of Z due to the existence of arbitrage possibilities. Consequently, the other incomes cannot exceed a certain level.

16.3 PEREQUATION MODELLING

We will base perequation modelling on this simple idea:

> **Economic value produced at date t will not depend on the economic conditions at date t**

For the banking system, it means that the discounted margins of the new customer production will not depend on the financial markets levels.

Sometimes, it means that the low-level gains on a certain product sold to a certain customer will be compensated for by high-level gains on other products sold to the same customer. Indeed, **perequations come from the cross-selling operations**. The perequation is written in the FTP systems as a cost for one product and as a gain for another product.

We introduced the perequation modelling in the deposit-modelling chapter. We saw for instance, that a margin reduction of 30bps on a 100.000 USD and 20 years amortizing mortgage loan is equivalent to the gains on a 20 years bullet non-remunerated demand deposit of 3.500 USD (when interest rates are around 4 %).

Perequation varies with interest rate level and with customer characteristics.

For instance, for demand deposit and mortgage modelling, the perequation level on mortgages could vary as shown in the next graph depending on the interest rate level.

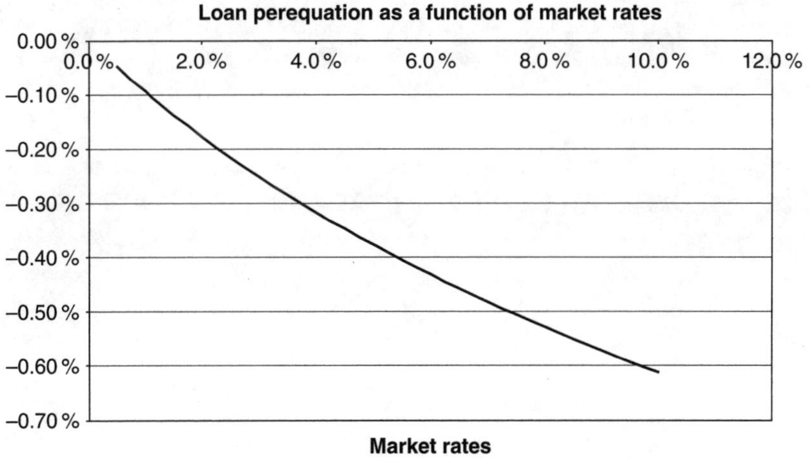

Figure 16.3 Loan perequation

16.4 FUTURE STRATEGIES MODELLING

We will see in the section on economic value computation that trying to model future strategies is not as important as we might have thought initially. Delta equivalent techniques will show how to build a risk free strategy that makes the net income free of risk.

Nevertheless, in income simulations A/L managers will need to implement:

- future hedges;
- future securities purchases;
- future debt issues, etc.

The better idea is to model future strategies as the sum of:

- *a risk free delta equivalent strategy*;
- *plus a constant risk position.*

17 Insurance Products

On ne peut avoir le beurre et l'argent du beurre.

17.1 UNIT OF ACCOUNT CONTRACTS

In unit of account contracts, the insurer does not take a real financial risk since the majority of the risk is transferred to the policyholder.

In terms of modelling, the A/L manager has to model:

- the intermediation margin dependency to the level of the interest rates;
- the new production volumes;
- the contract closing probabilities.

Indeed, these numbers will affect the insurer's income in the long term.

17.2 MUTUAL FUNDS

The modelling of customer behaviour is essential in mutual funds management.

In terms of fair value computation, the A/L manager needs to simulate the future flows arising from the existing customers. More prosaically, it means that there is a need for the modelling of:

- the liquidity schedule;
- the coupon paid to the customers.

For this modelling, the A/L manager will compute his estimation of the parameters in a framework where the client is not exposed to arbitrage opportunities. This modelling is made under the assumption that the insurance company will stabilize the portfolio of customers.

As for the demand deposit modelling, the liquidity schedule is computed with:

- a closing probability;
- an average amount by customer;
- a new payment by existing contract.

The compilation of the liquidity schedule allows us to represent all the future flows the customer is expected to invest or to withdraw.

The coupon paid to the customers is a tacit agreement with them. In order to stabilize the customers, the normal strategy will oblige the insurance company to pay an interest indexed to long-term smoothed rates. For example, the interest rate paid on the insurance contract will be indexed to the maximum of the yield of the long-term investment and of the spot long-term investment:

$$Max\,(\text{10 years average rate smoothed on 10 years-m}_1, \text{10 years spot rate-m}_2)$$

The second part of the coupon protects the insurer from the risk of seeing its clients move to a rival insurance company.

From this modelling of an insurance contract, the FTP rule is priced considering the insurance contract as a derivative that exchanges (on the contract liquidity schedule) the tacit agreed rate (paid to the customer) with a Floating rate (such as a Libor rate) plus a margin m. In order to provide a constant margin to the Commercial Department, the effective FTP will follow the tacit agreement less the margin m of the derivative product.

$$Max\,(\text{10 years average rate smoothed on 10 years-m}_1, \text{10 years spot rate-m}_2) - m \quad (17.1)$$

Of course, the coupon modelling can be a bit more complicated. For example, the modelling can integrate a part of equity risk.

$$Max \begin{pmatrix} \text{90 \%.10 years average rate smoothed on 10 years} \\ \text{+10 \%.Dow Jones growth on 10 years-m}_0 \\ \text{10 years average rate smoothed on 10 years-m}_1 \\ \text{10 years spot rate-m}_2 \end{pmatrix} \quad (17.2)$$

If the A/L manager models the coupon like this, he will have to invest in stock markets in order to hedge his risk on the Dow Jones index.

The *full fair value of the insurance contract* will be computed as the discounted sum of all the cash flows on the liquidity schedule (capital repayment and coupon payments). The economic capital will be computed based on this economic value.

18

Hedging Instruments

L'âne se couvre de la peau du lion. (Ésope)

The balance sheet incorporates many types of hedging instruments:

- derivatives such as swaps or options (caps, floors, swaptions, etc.);
- indirect hedging instruments: bonds such as HTM investments or available-for-sale bonds such as MBS or inflation-linked bonds.

18.1 DERIVATIVES

The financial markets now integrate many different derivative strategies. The diversity of the opportunities is wide:

- equity derivatives;
- swaps (exchanging cash flows as of a specified date or a series of specified dates based on a notional amount and fixed and floating rates);
- futures and forwards (contracts to purchase or sell a specific quantity of a financial instrument, a commodity, or a foreign currency at a specified price determined at the outset, with delivery or settlement at a specified future date);
- inflation and real rate swaps;
- caps/Floors and collars (call less put);
- swaptions;
- CMS swaps (exchanging long term interest rates against short term interest rates);
- CMS caps;
- Knock-in and knock-out caps and floors, etc.

18.2 BOND STRATEGIES

After the introduction of the IFRS, many A/L managers developed cash hedging strategies. These strategies are made of AFS investments including an interest rate option (with a constraint on the maximum level of the coupon in order not to be obliged to extract the potential embedded derivative):

- AFS assets with options on CMS/Libor indexes;
- inflation-linked bonds;

- MBS;
- CDOs, etc.

The strategies may be static or dynamic.

18.3 MORTGAGE BACKED SECURITIES

MBS (Mortgage-Backed Securities) are one of the main possible fixed rate investments in the US market. A MBS is an asset-backed security, a securitization of mortgage loan issued by a government agency without credit risk (i.e. AAA rated). The flows are backed by a set of mortgages.

The bonds replicate portfolios of mortgages in terms of cash flows. They are credit risk free since the mortgages are guaranteed by a governmental agency such as Fannie Mae (FNMA) or Freddie Mac.

The MBS investor takes the prepayment risk since prepayments are directly transferred to him.

For these assets, there are public models for customer behaviour modelling. The issuers are indeed incited to provide to the investors all the required information to model the risk they buy.

There are also private models developed by specialized companies.

The risk is indeed a prepayment risk. The MBS are quoted using the notion of OAS (option adjusted spread): a MBS is quoted for instance with an OAS of 80bps above the risk free rate.

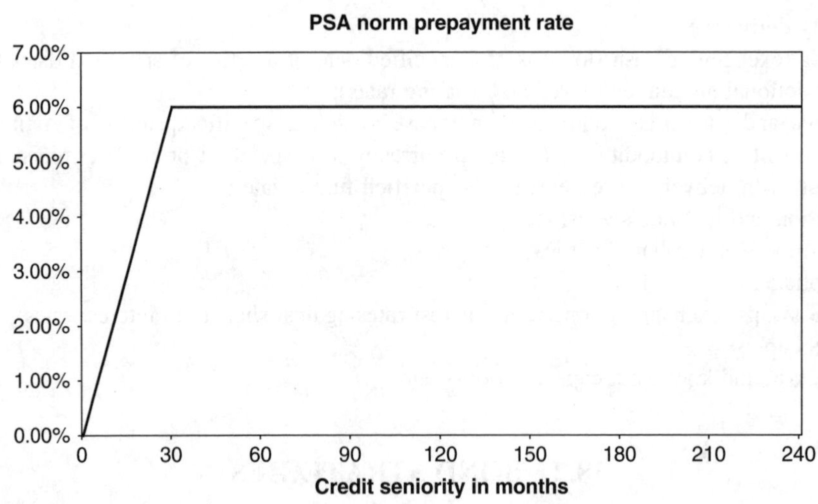

Figure 18.1 PSA norm

The MBS are quoted according to the PSA equivalent. This norm gives a standard for the statistical prepayment rate: with an increase of 0.2 % per month during 3 years to a maximum of 6 %.

A quotation of 130 PSA for a MBS with 5 year loans indicates that the implicit prepayment rate in this MBS is of 7.8 %.

Another factor in pricing is the prepayment speed. Whenever a mortgage refinances or the borrower prepays during the month, the prepayment measurement increases. They are usually measured in units of CPR or PSA.

The duration of the MBS depends on the level of the interest rates; the investor has sold receiver swaptions implicitly in order to get a higher profitability:

- If interest rates decrease, the MBS amortizes faster (at the worst moment).
- If interest rates increase, the MBS duration increases (at the worst moment too).

The A/L manager will distinguish:

- ARM: a MBS in which the mortgages are floating or variable rate mortgages.
- Residential mortgage-backed security (RMBS).
- Commercial mortgage-backed security (CMBS).
- Collateralized mortgage obligation (CMO): a MBS in which the mortgages are ordered into tranches by some quality (such as repayment time).
- Interest-only stripped mortgage-backed securities (IO): a bond with cash flows backed by the interest component of property owner's mortgage payments.
- Principal-only stripped mortgage-backed securities (PO): a bond with cash flows backed by the principal repayment component of property owner's mortgage payments.

Note: The instead of buying a MBS, the A/L manager may invest in another type of ABS (Asset-Backed Security) where the underlying is, for example, a consumer loan or a credit card loan.

Part IV
Risk Management for Asset and Liability Managers

The Risk Management Department is usually a key department in banks and insurance companies. In some banks at the beginning of the 90s, the A/L Management Departments used to be parts of the Risk Management Departments. Nowadays, A/L managers have to become competent in risk modelling when developing their strategies.

Risk management has many objectives:

- stopping bad things happening;
- keeping regulators happy;
- risk reporting;
- risk policy and risk appetite definition in connection with the operational teams and sometimes the presentation of risk taking opportunities;
- risk exposure, risk allocation and limit controlling;
- developing risk measurement methodology (including aggregation and diversification effects modelling);
- new products risk analysis.

To ensure all these objectives, the Risk Management Department should be independent from risk taking operational teams.

In this Part, all the main kinds of risk are described:

- financial market risks (interest rate risk, currency risk, liquidity risk, credit risk, etc.);
- business and model risk;
- operational risk
- accounting risk.

For each risk the nature of the risk is illustrated (occasionally through an example) and the impact of this risk on company incomes. Additionally, the indicator to monitor this risk, the way to simulate it and the hedging solutions are presented.

The regulatory constraints are detailed in the appropriate chapter.

19

Financial Risks

Qui ne risque rien n'a rien.

19.1 LIQUIDITY RISK

Liquidity risk is a difficult issue in risk management. Many definitions may be provided for this risk and very few mathematical risk analyses exist especially in the regulatory environment.

This chapter will try to define the most interesting part of liquidity risk, i.e. how to manage it and how to represent it.

19.1.1 Nature of liquidity risk and examples

When talking about liquidity risk, the A/L manager will distinguish between illiquidity risk and company liquidity risk.

Illiquidity risk is the risk of not being able to sell, on a short-term horizon, an asset (such as a bond, a stock, etc.) at a reasonable market price. Illiquidity comes from the rarity of the asset, the market low level of development, the complexity of the asset, etc.

For example, it could take time to sell a long-term bond with a coupon indexed to a non-interest rate index (such as a non-liquid stock index) issued by a non investment grade company.

Illiquidity has a market price. The bond coupon in our example should include a premium for possible illiquidity. As long as the bondholder keeps the bond, he gets the premium.

However, for A/L managers, *company liquidity risk* is the most important.

Liquidity management is the company's ability:

- *to provide to business lines funding at a reasonable cost; and*
- *to meet company liabilities* on a short, medium and long-term horizon.

The ability to provide funding at a reasonable cost means the monitoring of the firm's economic value exposure to funding costs.

A funding cost represents the company's spread above market rates such as swap rates. The funding cost is a function of the maturity. For example, if the 10 year swap rate is at 5 % and the company possible funding rate on a fixed 10 year bond issued at par is of 6 %, then the company cost of funding (or spread) on the 10 year horizon is equal to 1 %.

The funding cost yield curve is the curve that assigns to each maturity its funding cost.

Liquidity management is essential and strategic for company growth development:

- Liquidity provides a leverage effect for external growth compared with capital increases.
- Funding cost increases with volumes to refinance or market liquidity.
- Funding costs affect directly the profitability of the investments.

For these reasons, liquidity risk has to be included in FTP in order to charge liquidity costs. A liquidity income has also to be computed and monitored with the adequate indicators described below.

A company's ability to meet its liabilities means that many regulatory constraints, many Central Bank constraints or many bank internal constraints will oblige the company to monitor on an intraday and on a daily basis its liquidity position in order to minimize the operational risk.

Banks, for example, have to get a positive Central Bank account at the end of each day. This is an operational risk. Banks should be able, for example, on an intraday basis to monitor their Central Bank position in order to avoid a regulatory sanction or a market sanction (what would the market think about a bank not able to monitor its cash position?).

The problem is that liquidity risk occurs in *crisis environments* and the A/L manager is not usually familiar with these environments. Consequently, the regulators will ask the bank to build *effective contingency plans* in order to prepare the A/L management response to a crisis.

However, when an A/L manager looks over the past events, he discovers that *a liquidity crisis never looks like a past liquidity crisis*. Nevertheless, liquidity crises look like this:

- The market disappears very quickly: no traders, no answers to phone calls, no contacts.
- No forward, no swaps: the entire derivative market disappears.
- It is impossible to use credit lines (even if they were designed to protect us against a liquidity crisis!).
- Central Banks, the "lenders of last resort" do not answer to banks requests... even if in such a crisis they are supposed to!
- Panic is everywhere even if we were supposed to be prepared.

19.1.2 The impact of liquidity risk on net income

After the introduction of a FTP system in the company, it is easy to compute *company liquidity income*. Liquidity risk is then the risk on the future liquidity incomes.

Liquidity income is simply the sum of:

- the funding cost received on each asset;
- the liquidity cost charged on each credit line;
- minus the funding cost paid on each liability (including debt);
- minus the difference between the effective company funding cost on the net treasury.

Liquidity income can be forecast for each time horizon.

Assets				
	Amount	FTP	Liquidity cost	Liquidity income
Loans	80	5.00 %	0.15 %	0.12
Net treasury	20	4.00 %	0.00 %	–
Total assets	100	4.80 %	0.12 %	0.12
Credit lines	20		0.05 %	0.01
Liabilities				
	Amount	FTP	Liquidity cost	Liquidity income
Current accounts	50	5.00 %	0.10 %	0.05
Debt	40	4.00 %	0.10 %	0.04
Equity	10	4.00 %	0.00 %	–
Total Liabilities	100	4.50 %	0.09 %	0.09
	Net liquidity income			0.04

Figure 19.1 Liquidity income

In the eventuality of a liquidity crisis, we can suppose that in this example:

- all the credit lines are used;
- 50 % of term deposits disappear;
- the short-term liquidity cost rises to 10 %.

This affects strongly and negatively the liquidity income:

Assets				
	Amount	FTP	Liquidity cost	Liquidity income
Loans	100	5.00 %	0.15 %	0.15
Net treasury	–25	4.00 %	10.00 %	–2.50
Total assets	75	5.33 %	–3.13 %	–2.35
Credit lines	0		0.05 %	–
Liabilities				
	Amount	FTP	Liquidity cost	Liquidity income
	Amount	FTP	Liquidity cost	Liquidity income
Current accounts	25	5.00 %	0.10 %	0.03
Debt	40	4.00 %	0.10 %	0.04
Equity	10	4.00 %	0.00 %	–
Total Liabilities	75	4.33 %	0.09 %	0.07
	Net liquidity income			–2.42

Figure 19.2 Net liquidity income

Liquidity management will try to avoid such a situation.

Moreover, if this crisis becomes structural, not only is the spot income impacted but also future incomes.

An *economic value* of the future liquidity incomes can also be computed as the mathematical expectation of future liquidity incomes. Economic capital measures will of course focus on this economic value.

19.1.3 Indicators to monitor liquidity risk

Many indicators will help A/L managers to monitor and understand company liquidity risk. Among them, we will describe:

- market liquidity data reporting information;
- liquidity ratios;
- liquidity gaps (static gap or dynamic gap);
- stress scenarios;
- economic value sensitivity to funding costs.

19.1.3.1 Liquidity information

The market provides a lot of information about liquidity:

- company's spread over swap or government rates: this is the funding cost by maturity;
- company's rating;
- securitization structure prices;
- market anticipated funding rates (forward funding rates);
- bid/ask bond spreads, etc.

On the other hand, the A/L manager has to follow many internal indicators:

- historical funding requirements;
- current liquidity position;
- anticipated funding needs (in fact the business plan for the funding activity);
- panorama of all the possible sources of funds with their costs (for example, the securitization cost may be higher than the senior debt funding cost due to market illiquidity different market costs);
- quality of assets in the balance sheet (in term of liquidity: government bonds are easier to sell in the event of a liquidity crisis than corporate bonds, for example);
- present and future earnings capacity of the company;
- present and future capital position of the company.

19.1.3.2 Liquidity ratios

A/L managers have also invented simple ratios to follow their liquidity positions.

19.1.3.2.1 Regulatory ratios such as a 1 month ratio

In many countries, bank regulators ask for ratios computation to follow liquidity risk. These ratios depend on the country but quite often include:

- intraday liquidity ratio (a limit on the treasury position within a day);
- short-term liquidity ratio such as the 1 month liquidity ratio;

- medium or longer-term liquidity ratios such as 1-year cumulative gap ratio (see section 19.1.3.2.3 below).

The intraday liquidity ratio obliges the bank not to be exposed to a violent market liquidity crunch.

To prevent the occurrence of such a crisis, the regulators often focus on a 1-month liquidity ratio in order to oblige the banks to monitor their risk carefully.

The ratio is often defined like this:

$$\frac{\text{Liquid Assets}_{1\text{month}}}{\text{Liquid Liabilities}_{1\text{month}}} \geq 100\,\%,\ 110\,\% \text{ or } 120\,\% \tag{19.1}$$

It has also this quasi-equivalent form (since total assets are equal to the total liabilities):

$$\frac{\text{Illiquid Assets}_{1\text{month}}}{\text{Illiquid Liabilities}_{1\text{month}}} \leq 100\,\%,\ 110\,\% \text{ or } 120\,\% \tag{19.2}$$

If a liquidity crisis happens in the upcoming month and if the bank stops its new production, a non-negligible part of the liabilities will have to be reimbursed within this month: *the liquid liabilities over 1 month*. To get enough cash to reimburse this entire liquidity shortfall, the bank will get money from its assets reimbursements and maybe will have to sell some of these assets in the market: *the liquid assets over 1 month*. If the bank has more liquid assets than liquid liabilities, the bank will survive during this 1-month period.

Companies other than banks could use this kind of ratio to monitor their treasury exposure on liquidity risk.

19.1.3.2.2 Other ratios

Bank regulators provide other types of ratios and create many constraints for liquidity management:

- Loans/deposit ratio: the total amount of loans should not exceed a percentage of the total deposits.
- Loan/capital ratio: the total amount of loans should not exceed a percentage of the total company's capital.
- Ratio of pledged securities to total securities.
- Ratio of anticipated needs for funds to primary resources of attraction of funds.
- Customers' concentration risk ratio: 10 % biggest clients total deposits to total deposits (this ratio measure the company vulnerability to the richest depositors).

19.1.3.2.3 Medium or long-term ratio

Medium or long-term ratios are often derived from the cumulative liquidity gap. For example, the one-year liquidity ratio could be expressed as:

$$\frac{\text{Total remaining Assets}_{1\text{ year}}}{\text{Total remaining Liabilities}_{1\text{ year}}} \leq X\,\% \tag{19.3}$$

The remaining assets in one year are computed without new production. The A/L manager projects its balance sheet in 1 year and compares the total remaining assets and the total remaining liabilities. If the total remaining assets are too important and if there is no liquidity in one year in the market, the bank could at this horizon experience liquidity troubles.

The regulator may impose a limit on X, for example X = 130 %.

Note also that the remaining assets and liabilities are linked with the liquidity gap indicator by a simple difference:

$$\text{Liquidity gap}_{1\text{ year}} = \text{Total remaining Liabilities}_{1\text{ year}} - \text{Total remaining Assets}_{1\text{ year}} \quad (19.4)$$

19.1.3.2.4 Stable liabilities ratio

Some banks use another ratio to compare the amount of "stable liabilities" and the absolute long-term liquidity gap.

$$\frac{\text{Stable Liabilities}}{\left|\text{Liquidity gap}_{1\text{ year}}\right|} \geq Y\,\% \quad (19.5)$$

The stable liabilities include net equity and demand deposits.

In some banks, the 1-year liquidity gap is important but due to the production of new deposits, this is not really a problem: imposing a constraint on the stable part of the liabilities may help in the event of a liquidity crisis: stopping the credit production but using the stable deposits to overcome the crisis.

19.1.3.2.5 Ratio forecasting

All these ratios have to be monitored and to be forecasted!

The A/L manager should be able to compute forward liquidity ratios and of course to compute forward regulatory ratios (to avoid future regulatory problems).

Forecasting should include new production hypotheses and will help into the construction of the liquidity business plan of the company.

19.1.3.3 Liquidity gap

The *liquidity gap* is the main liquidity indicator. This indicator is a generalization of the 1-month liquidity ratio and of the 1-year liquidity gap ratio.

The liquidity gap is the function that assigns to each maturity the projected difference between the total liabilities remaining at this maturity and the total assets also remaining at this maturity. The remaining assets and liabilities exclude new customer productions and future contracts.

If the company has a liquidity gap constant and equal to zero, the company will not experience liquidity problems: in the worst case, such a company will be obliged to stop the new production but the company will survive.

We used once more our example to compute a liquidity gap as in Figure 19.3.

In this example, the 1-month liquidity gap is negative: the bank is exposed to short-term funding cost rises.

The liquidity gap can be computed over different axes:

- consolidated liquidity gap, by branch or by activity;
- *liquidity gap by currency* since liquidity problems may arise in a particular currency and not in others.

	Today	1 month	3 months	6 months	1 year	3 years	5 years	10 years	More than 10 years
Loans	80	80	79	78	76	68	60	34	–
Net treasury	20	–	–	–	–	–	–	–	–
Credit lines	–	20	20	20	20				
Total Assets schedule	100	100	99	98	96	68	60	34	–
Current accounts	50	40	39	38	36	26	20	0	
Debt	40	40	40	40	40	–	–	–	
Equity	10	10	10	10	10	10	10	10	10
Total Liabilities schedule	100	90	89	88	86	38	30	10	10
Cumulative liquidity gap	–	–10	–10	–10	–10	– 30	– 29	–23	10
Periodic gap		–10	0	0	0	20	1	6	33

Figure 19.3 Periodic gap

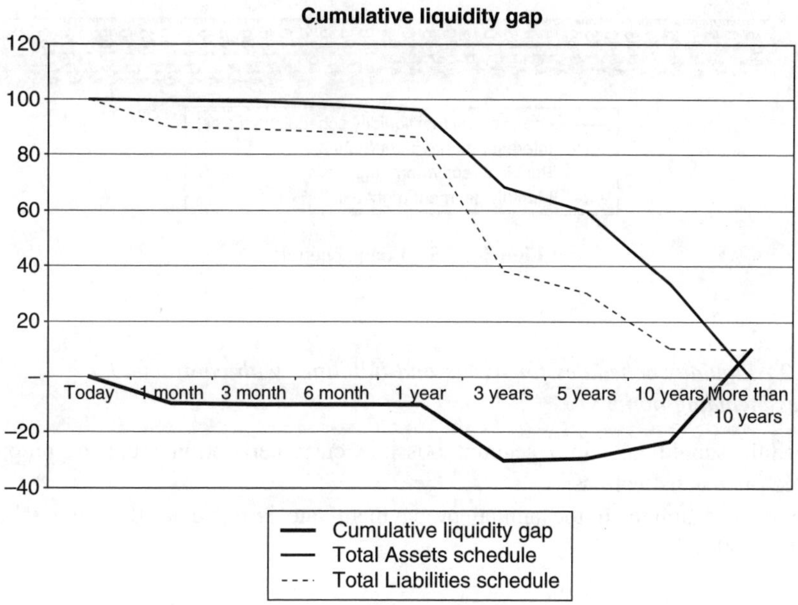

Figure 19.4 Cumulative liquidity gap

19.1.3.3.1 Liquidity schedules for assets and liabilities with contractual maturities

When an asset or a liability gets a contractual maturity, it is easy to compute its principal repayment schedule. This schedule will be used in the liquidity gap. The following assets and liabilities are linked with a direct liquidity schedule:

- company's debt;
- company's loans and borrowings;
- company's deposits.

For example, for an 80 USD 15 year loan with a 5 % interest rate and with constant monthly repayments of 0.61 USD, the liquidity schedule looks like this:

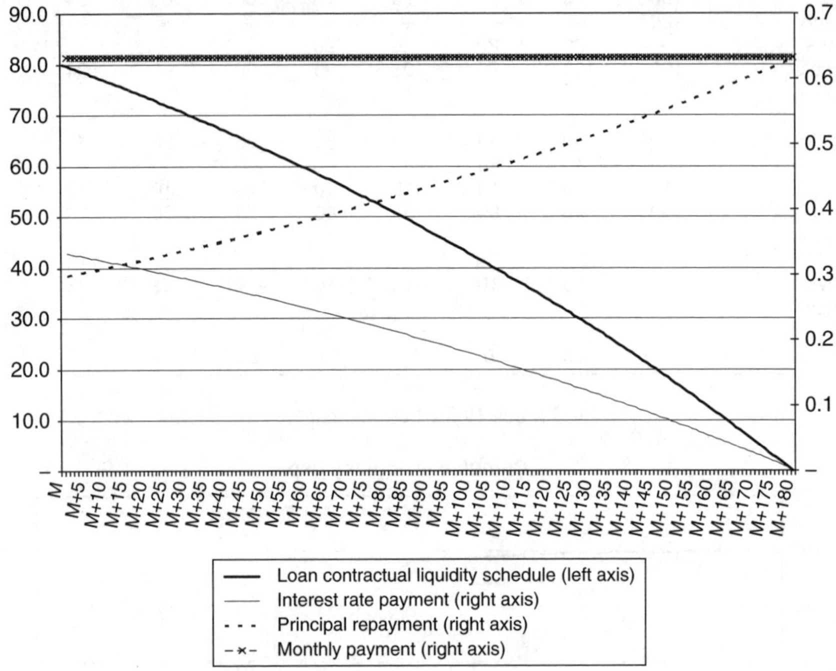

Figure 19.5 Loan schedule

19.1.3.3.2 Liquidity schedules for assets and liabilities with contractual maturities including options

The schedule should take into account possible customer options such as prepayments (computed on a statistical basis).

In the same example, if the annual prepayment rate is equal to 10 % the schedule is modified as follows:

$$\text{Schedule with prepayments (t)} = \text{Schedule without prepayments (t).exp(-t.Prepayment rate)} \quad (19.6)$$

The usual assumption is to take a constant prepayment rate. However, the choice of this prepayment rate should take into account the fact that in the eventuality of a liquidity crisis, the clients will perhaps not prepay their loans. The A/L manager will have to be aware of the sensitivity of prepayment rates to funding costs.

The chosen prepayment rate depends on the credit type (mortgage, investment, etc.) and on the interest rate nature (fixed or indexed).

Prepayments strongly affect the liquidity schedule.

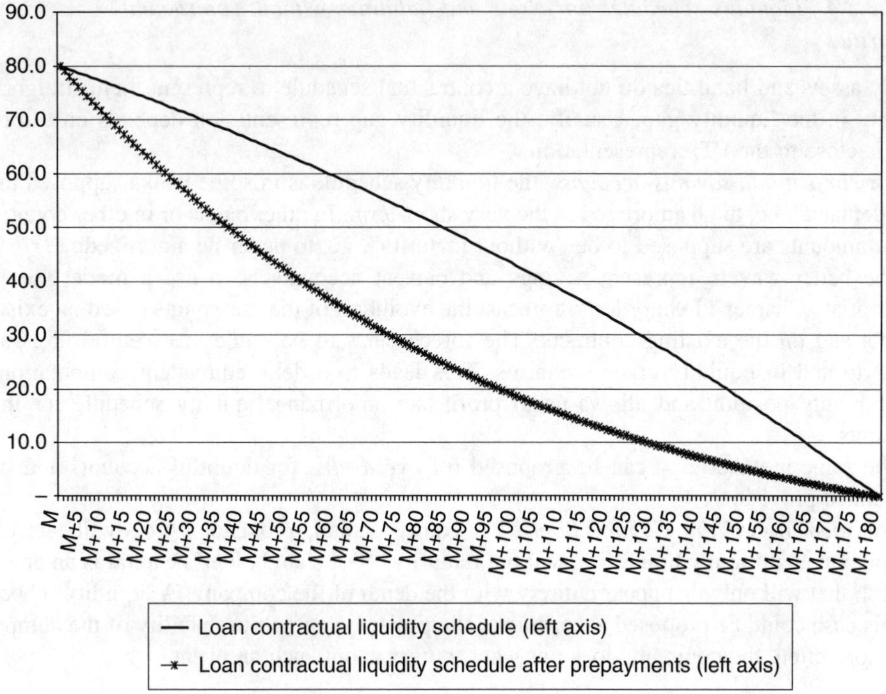

Figure 19.6 Loan schedule with prepayments

19.1.3.3.3 Liquidity schedules for investments

Liquidity representation for bonds depends on many parameters:

- Bonds in trading books are considered to be short-term liquidity investments since they can be sold as soon as possible.
- Bonds that Central Banks may accept as a pledge or as a guarantee are represented conventionally as short-term liquidity.
- Other bonds are represented using their capital repayment schedule.

Some banks do not like to represent as short-term liquidity a bond that can be easily sold in the market or used as a guarantee for a Central Bank refinancing. In fact, in the event of a liquidity crisis, when the bank sells the bond in the market, it will cause damage to the bank "Loss given default" and from a theoretical point of view, it would increase the bank funding cost.

Stock investments usually have a conventional representation depending on their liquidity in the market:

- A large part of these investments may be considered to be short-term liquidity if these investments can be sold easily even in the event of a liquidity crisis.
- The surplus is split between the short-term and medium term buckets in proportion to the probability to sell easily those investments in the market.

19.1.3.3.4 Liquidity schedules for assets and liabilities without contractual maturities

Many assets and liabilities do not have a contractual schedule to represent them straightforwardly in the liquidity gap. Usually, the liquidity gap representation depends on a model that is close to the FTP representation.

For *current and savings accounts*, the liquidity schedule is in some banks supposed to be "on demand", i.e. to be amortized in the very short-term. In other banks or in other countries, those amounts are supposed to be "without maturity", i.e. to never be amortized.

The better way to represent savings and current accounts is to use a model (see the appropriate Chapter 11) in order to forecast the evolution of these amounts based on existing clients and on the existing contracts. The forecast has to be made in a central "forward" scenario and in liquidity crisis scenarios. This leads to a delta equivalent computation of the liquidity position and allows us to profile an amortizing liquidity schedule for those accounts.

The same methodology can be proposed for *overdrafts*, for doubtful accounts and their associated provisions.

The *elements of the Capital Book* (i.e. equity capital, provisions, goodwill, etc.) are considered as infinitely liquid (i.e. without maturity). The shareholder's capital is an amount of cash that will only disappear entirely with the death of the company. A liquidity schedule of this cash could be proposed according to the projected default probability of the company but more often, the company does not want to hear about such an event.

19.1.3.3.5 Credit lines

Credit lines are represented in the liquidity gap according to the probability of their being used in the event of a liquidity crisis:

- Bank credit lines are represented as if they were real credits: during the crisis, the bank counterparties will use these lines to cover their liquidity needs.
- For other credit lines, the probability of their being used is lower and the liquidity schedule representation is a percentage of the maximal amount of the line.

19.1.3.3.6 Cumulative gap and periodic gap

Some banks distinguish between the cumulative and the periodic gap.

The cumulative gap is the projected difference between the total liabilities remaining at each maturity and the total assets also remaining at this maturity.

The periodic gap is the variation of this cumulative gap, often defined "bucket by bucket". In other terms, the *periodic gap* is the difference between the asset schedule amortization and the liability schedule amortization.

Without any new production, the periodic gap represents the amount of money to collect or to replace at each "bucket" or at each maturity to hedge the company cash position.

19.1.3.3.7 Break-even point liquidity gap

The liquidity gap has to be *coherent with the FTP convention*: the funding cost part in the FTP should be based on the same horizon as the projected schedules.

For each balance sheet line, a funding cost present in the FTP is associated. It helps to compute the total asset funding cost and the total liability funding cost.

Funding costs go into the computation of the "Liquidity Book" income.

The liquidity gap allows then to compute the future projected incomes of the "Liquidity Book" (without any new production).

	Today	1 month	3 month	6 month	1 year	3 years	5 years	10 years	More than 10 years
Total Assets schedule	100	100	99	98	96	68	60	34	–
Assets FTP funding cost	0.12 %	0.13 %	0.13 %	0.13 %	0.13 %	0.15 %	0.15 %	0.15 %	
Total Liabilities schedule	100	90	89	88	86	38	30	10	10
Liabilities FTP funding cost	0.09 %	0.09 %	0.09 %	0.09 %	0.09 %	0.07 %	0.07 %	0.00 %	0.00 %
Cumulative liquidity gap	-	−10	−10	−10	−10	−30	−29	−23	10
Break-even FTP funding cost		0.51 %	0.51 %	0.50 %	0.48 %	0.25 %	0.24 %	0.22 %	0.00 %
Forward funding cost		0.01 %	0.02 %	0.03 %	0.04 %	0.05 %	0.06 %	0.07 %	0.08 %
Projected income (annualized)		0.05 %	0.05 %	0.05 %	0.04 %	0.06 %	0.05 %	0.03 %	0.01 %

Figure 19.7 Projected income

The break-even FTP funding cost is the average cost of the liquidity gap. There is a break even for each future maturity:

$$\text{Break Even}_{1\ \text{year}} = \frac{\text{Liabilities}_{1\,\text{year}}.\text{FTP Liquidity Liabilities}_{1\,\text{year}} - \text{Assets}_{1\,\text{year}}.\text{FTP Liquidity Assets}_{1\,\text{year}}}{\text{Liquidity gap}_{1\,\text{year}}} \tag{19.7}$$

If the A/L manager knows the future funding cost of this maturity, he is able to project the (annualized) income of the Liquidity Book:

$$\text{Liquidity Book Income}_{1\,\text{year}_{\text{forecast}}} = \text{Liquidity gap}_{1\,\text{year}} \cdot \left(\text{Forecasted Funding Cost}_{1\,\text{year}} - \text{Break Even}_{1\,\text{year}}\right) \tag{19.8}$$

A large part of the A/L manager's task will then be to project the future funding cost and to monitor its Liquidity Book income.

19.1.3.4 Dynamic liquidity gap

When analysing the liquidity gap, it is difficult to project future liquidity needs since this projection does not introduce the new productions.

Dynamic liquidity gaps introduce this new production and help to build the business plan for the liquidity needs.

The new production is introduced in the static gap on a budget horizon (say 2 years) with the budgeted assets and liabilities.

In the example of Figure 19.8, the cumulative dynamic gap is positive during the first 3 months, but on the 6 months bucket, this gap becomes negative: it means that the budget plan underestimates the liquidity needs on a 6 month horizon. ALCO members should rapidly investigate how to fill the gap!

	Today	1 month	3 month	6 month	1 year	3 years	5 years	10 years	More than 10 years
Cumulative static gap	–	–10	–10	–10	–10	–30	–29	–23	10
Total Assets schedule	100	100	99	98	96	68	60	34	–
Projected new credit volumes	100	101	103	106	110	120	108	50	25
Projected new credit production	–	1	4	8	14	52	49	16	25
Projected Deposit new volumes		10	11	12	14	22	17	14	11
Projected Short term Financement		15	15	–	–	–	–	–	–
Projected Debt emission	–		5	5	5				
Projected Liability new production	–	25	31	17	19	22	17	14	11
Cumulative dynamic gap	–	14	17	–1	–5	–60	–61	–26	–4

Figure 19.8 Cumulative dynamic gap

19.1.3.5 Economic value sensitivity to funding spreads

The liquidity gap break-even helps to forecast the Liquidity Book future incomes. This indicator is computed on a whole set of horizons.

It is possible to reduce this set of indicators into one when using a discounted framework. The sum of the future discounted expected Liquidity Book incomes could be defined as the *economic value of the Liquidity Book.*

This economic value depends on the level of the future estimated funding costs. An interesting indicator for liquidity management is *economic value sensitivity to liquidity spreads.*

	y	y+1	y+2	y+3	y+4	y+5	y+6	y+7	y+8	y+9	y+10
Liquidity Book Projected income (annualized)	0.05	0.04	0.04	0.04	0.03	0.03	0.02	0.02	0.01	0.01	0.00
Discount Factor	1.000	0.952	0.907	0.864	0.823	0.784	0.746	0.711	0.677	0.645	0.614
Liquidity Book Economic value	0.250										
Liquidity Book Projected income (annualized) (funding cost +.1%)	0.04	0.04	0.03	0.03	0.02	0.02	0.02	0.01	0.01	0.01	0.00
Liquidity Book Economic value (finding cost +.1%)	0.200										
Economic Sensitivity to funding spreads Increases (+10bps)	–0.050										

Figure 19.9 Liquidity book sensitivity

This indicator summarizes in only one number the company liquidity exposure.

19.1.4 Simulating liquidity risk

When simulating liquidity risk, the A/L manager will focus on the Liquidity Book income computation. Without any new production, this income looks like:

$$\text{Liquidity Book income (t)} = \text{Liquidity Gap(t)} . [\text{Break-Even (t)} - \text{Funding Cost (t)}] \quad (19.9)$$

It is possible to introduce the new productions in the Liquidity Book income but the A/L manager will have to introduce also his liquidity risk hedging strategies. If his liquidity risk management strategy were a replication of the needs in the market, there would be no difference between the income presented above without new production and the income with new production and strategies.

The A/L manager's task is then to forecast the funding cost. In fact, a complete funding cost curve exists and the task is tougher than expected.

The funding spread depends on:

- market place liquidity;
- company economic value evolution;
- company rating;
- company debt issue strategy;
- company capital level.

Actually, there are two possibilities to simulate the future evolution of the funding costs:

- using interest rate simulation methodologies;
- using company economic value simulation methodologies.

19.1.4.1 Simulation using interest rate simulation methodologies

Company funding cost is the simple difference between the swap interest rate and the funding rate of the company.

An easy way to simulate funding spread is therefore to simulate simultaneously the swap rate yield curves and the company rate yield curves. Methodology uses the interest rate simulation methodology as if it was two different yield curves from two different countries.

For example, using models with one simple factor, the funding spread will be easily modelled using this system of equations:

$$\begin{aligned} &dr_t^{swap} = \lambda^{swap}.\left(\theta^{swap}(t) - r_t^{swap}\right).dt + \sigma^{swap}.dW_t^{swap} \\ &dr_t^{company} = \lambda^{company}.\left(\theta^{company}(t) - r_t^{company}\right).dt + \sigma^{company}.dW_t^{company} \\ &\left\langle dW_t^{swap}; dW_t^{company}\right\rangle = \rho.dt \\ &\text{Funding Spread}_t = r_t^{company} - r_t^{swap} \end{aligned} \quad (19.10)$$

Actually, the model to be used is more complex since the funding spread has to be positive and has a fat tail distribution (see Figure 19.10).

The *forward funding spread* will be the difference between the forward company rate and the forward swap rate: it represents the better estimation for the funding spread.

19.1.4.2 Simulation using economic value simulation methodologies

On the other hand, a link exists between company credit risk and liquidity risk.

The funding spread depends on the company rating. This rating depends on the company probability of default and this default probability depends on the company capital adequacy.

Inversing this analysis, it is possible to simulate the funding spread:

- simulating the company economic value;
- simulating the company economic capital;
- using this capital to comprehend the company rating evolution;
- translating this company rating in a funding spread.

The use of such a model proves that the evolution of funding spreads has a "fat tail distribution". The chart below gives an example of the possible distribution of the funding spread evolution.

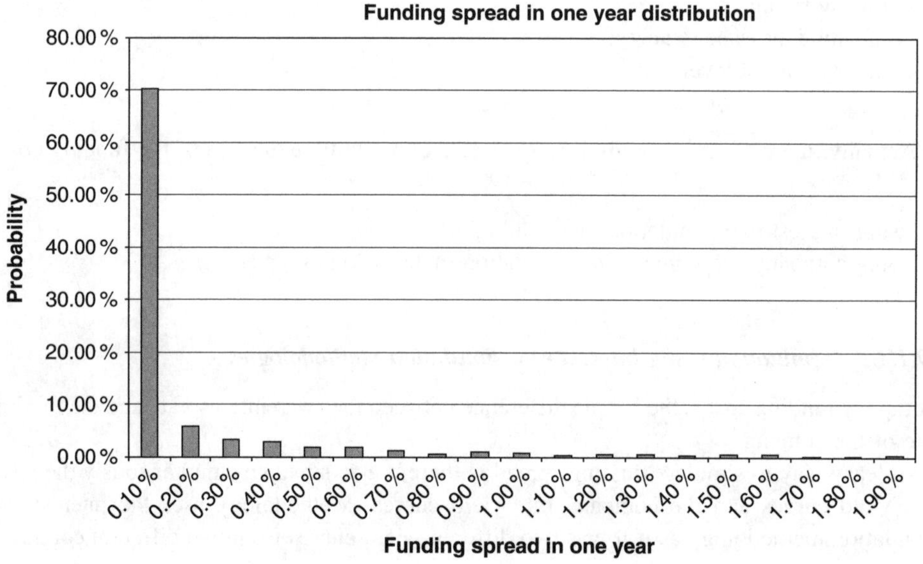

Figure 19.10 Funding spread

19.1.4.3 Other simulations

There are different possibilities offered to the A/L manager to simulate this liquidity risk:

- using random stress scenarios from historical databases;
- using deterministic stress scenarios from the analysis of historical databases;
- using credit risk modelling.

19.1.5 Liquidity risk hedging

Liquidity risk hedging is more complex than the hedging of the other risks since it incorporates strategies that depend not only on the market products. Specifically, liquidity hedging implies:

- effective contingency plan;
- liquidity structuring;
- liquidity sources diversification;
- debt and covered bonds;
- securitization;
- interbank market;
- Central Bank;
- economic capital implementation.

19.1.5.1 Stress tests and contingency plans

Quantitative indicators are not sufficient for the management of the liquidity risk.

Liquidity crises may arise with different forms:

- global economy crisis (like the Great Depression of the 20s);
- local market economy crisis;
- emerging markets economy crisis (like the Asiatic crisis in the 90s);
- liquidity crisis on the specific sector of the company (e.g. an automobile sector crisis or a banking liquidity crisis);
- liquidity crisis on the company name (e.g. a liquidity crisis arising from an event affecting the reputation of the company);
- liquidity crisis due to an operational risk (e.g. a worldwide avian flue event stopping the entire activity of the treasury).

Other stress scenarios may come from:

- a higher sector competitiveness;
- a reduction of the earnings;
- a growth of the non performing assets;
- a too large deposit concentration;
- an unexpected expansion of activities;
- a market liquidity reduction due to Central Bank action;
- an unexpected customer deposit outflow;
- a deposit outflow due to unexpected rising interest rates;
- a larger than expected use of credit lines.

To be prepared for such liquidity events, the A/L manager should prepare a list of possible events affecting liquidity: the *stress scenarios*. For each scenario, the A/L manager has to find the emergency solution: a *contingency plan* has to be prepared for each event type. It could affect:

- the payment system control;
- the liquidity position;
- the funding sources;
- the treasury operation organization;
- stop loss limits;
- new production organization;
- a better information system for intraday liquidity;
- a better information on the company general risk exposure;
- a transformation of the liquidity position information process.

The company has to be prepared to react promptly:

- ready to sell at every moment some assets (bonds, equity investments, etc.);
- ready to use bonds as a pledge (repo transactions, etc.);
- ready to propose securitizations programmes, debt issue programmes (for liquidity needs above 2 or 3 months).

The effective contingency plan is the better response for large liquidity crisis risk.

19.1.5.2 Liquidity structuring

The easiest way to hedge liquidity risk is to change the company asset structure, i.e.:

- changing the debt structure (e.g. proposing longer term debt issues);
- changing the asset structure (e.g. proposing shorter term loans instead of long-term mortgages);
- maintaining or creating reserves of ultra liquid assets (e.g. choosing assets usable as a pledge instead of illiquid assets as investments).

19.1.5.3 Liquidity sources diversification

The diversification of liquidity sources is important for the management of liquidity.

For example, banks with a strong *concentration* of their deposits in one company or in one sector (e.g. the petrol sector or the public sector) are particularly exposed to liquidity risk. If an over concentrated company wishes to withdraw all its cash invested in a bank (Whatever the reason is: economic, relational, etc.), will the bank be able to collect an equivalent amount of liquidity quickly in order to compensate?

Funding sources are various:

- interbank loans;
- classic debt;
- subordinated debt;
- pledged debt;
- international institutions loan (e.g. IFC);
- cross-border loans;
- securitization;
- credit lines or stand-by lines;
- capital increase.

Moreover, the company has to develop its ability to attract funds:

- an easy task for large companies (but exposed to reputation risk);
- a tougher task for small companies (who need to improve their financial communication in order to get the best rating possible).

19.1.5.4 Interbank market and classic debt

For banks, the interbank market is a real source of funding: usually some banks concentrate the liquidity; having good relations with those banks is a key factor of success for liquidity management.

Rumours, supports (e.g. from cross-border banks or from the Central Bank) and reputation make access to liquidity of the Interbank market easier.

Classic debt programmes (fixed or floating debt) are of two forms: public issue or private placements. Dealers are ready to set up these issues programmes.

Debt may also include embedded options (indexing for example coupons to the stock index) or prepayment options.

Debt seniority is important in terms of cost and of capital structuring.

19.1.5.5 Covered bonds and other types of pledged bonds

Many companies use pledged bonds to get better refinancing rates. The possible pledges are assets such as credits or buildings.

At every moment, the assets cover the bond: in the eventuality of a default of the company, the investor may ask for the pledge.

We can use mortgages as a pledge: Pfanbriefe (in Germany), covered bonds, etc.

As long as the debtor is not in default, he pays a coupon (either fixed or indexed), nothing differs from the case of a classic debt. However, in the eventuality of a company default, the covered bond is cancelled and the company has to transfer its mortgages to the investor through a specific vehicle.

Such a market can be regulated (with constraints on the assets or imposing a legal structure) or not (in England, for example, where everything has to be explained in the contract).

The investor's point view is simple: the product is quasi risk free (with a low level of economic capital consumption) and ultra liquid (when the covered bond programme is important).

The debtor's point of view is even simpler: there is no impact on the company capital and this kind of debt is cheaper than classic long-term debt. The covered bonds do not affect the company default probability. So where is the trick?

Lavoisier, the famous chemist, used to say, "Nothing gets lost, nothing gets created, and everything is transformed". Such a programme cause damage to the loss given default of the company. It means that the covered bonds programme affects the classic debt programmes: *a new covered bonds programme theoretically deteriorates the funding cost of the company.*

19.1.5.6 Securitization

In the credit risk chapter, we will explain how securitization helps to hedge credit risk. However, securitization provides also liquidity and is a good source of liquidity diversification.

19.1.5.7 Cross-border funding

In emerging markets, a classic funding is the cross-border funding. The lender sends money from another country and takes the risk not to recover its money due to a political event.

For this reason, cross-border funding could be more expensive than local funding (i.e. it includes a premium): the premium is proportional to the probability of not recovering the funds.

19.1.5.8 Central Bank and regulators

Central Banks plays an important role in market liquidity.

First, Central Banks provide refinancing through the Central Bank interest rate. On the other hand, they ask the banks to constitute reserves in front of their deposit accounts.

The Central Bank is supposed to regulate the liquidity market in an event of a liquidity crisis. Nevertheless, it is hazardous to propose a contingency plan based exclusively on the relationship with the Central Bank. In emerging markets, Central Bank pressure from international organizations is very strong and they are ready to abandon the banks most exposed to liquidity problems.

Moreover, in a context of a more concentrated financial sector with a higher level of correlations between risks (with the development of hedge funds for instance) there is a need for a more regulated liquidity risk.

Across the banking sector, regulators recognize that practices differ in terms of liquidity risk measures, limits, types of scenarios, time considerations and underlying assumptions.

Regulation depends highly on the country but liquidity risk is exposed to *contagion effects*.

The regulation response for the moment is not to impose constraints on liquidity risk (such as the constraints imposed on credit risk). For instance, only Pillar 2 of Basel II treats the question of the liquidity risk through the computation of an economic capital and through supervisory review.

19.1.5.9 Economic capital

For Banks with Basel II and for insurance companies with Solvency II, the regulators ask for the implementation of an "economic capital" computation.

Usually economic capital represents an amount of capital that protects the rating of the company: A/L managers compute the economic capital as an economic value variation over 1 year with a quantile corresponding to a rating target.

Implementing an economic capital (as a basis for the risk management with a rating target) protects against the probability of default of the company; simultaneously the company gets a less volatile funding spread.

In other terms, there is a link between the amount of equity capital and the funding spread; to avoid liquid risk, a high level of equity is indispensable.

Nevertheless, when the liquidity risk occurs, the allocated capital would not solve the liquidity risk issue!

19.2 CREDIT RISK

A/L managers will focus traditionally mainly on the interest rate risk, the liquidity risk and on the inflation risk.

However, credit risk represents the major risk for the banking activity; the Risk Management Department usually performs the analyses of the credit risk exposure. Nowadays, with the introduction of a well-developed derivative market, credit risk has moved from banks to other sectors: insurance companies, asset management, hedge funds, etc. Actually, Basel II reduced the opportunities of credit risk profit in the banking activity with the introduction of an economical link between the risk and the capital needs.

For this reason, credit risk takes a larger place in the core business of every A/L manager and not only the bank A/L managers.

19.2.1 Nature of credit risk and examples

19.2.1.1 General definition

Credit risk may take different forms:

- *Counterparty default risk* when the loan counterparty is unable to honour his duties (unable to repay the capital or the interests).
- *Recovery rate risk.* The recovered capital (when the counterparty goes to default) depends on the debt seniority, the collateral quality, the liquidation and the carry costs. Moreover, this risk is highly correlated with default risk since expected recovery rates decrease as the expected default increases.
- *Credit quality downgrading risk.* When rating agencies upgrade or downgrade the counterparty rating, it affects the quality of the company credit portfolio and the company refinancing costs (a credit portfolio global downgrade may increase the risk of the company and oblige the company to allow more capital or to pay higher coupon on the new refinanced debts).

Credit risk is quite often a *contagion risk*: credit crises are often concentrated in a specific area and touch the entire economy of this area. For this reason, risk managers focus on the diversification of the credit portfolio and recognize different types of credit risk:

- *Geographical credit risk* when the loan portfolio is packed in one region or in one country.
- *Sector concentration credit risk* such as industrial credit risk.
- *Concentration credit risk* when, for instance, 20 % of the portfolio credit risk is concentrated in one company.

For this reason, it is important to distinguish *retail credit risk* and *corporate credit risk.*

We will see that ratings will help us to model the corporate credit risk. On the other hand, *scores* will help us to hedge the retail credit risk:

- *Granting scores* (such as FICO score in the US) allows banks to decide whether the customer will be able to repay its debts or not at the moment when the credit is granted.
- *In-life scores* allow banks to know during the credit life what the level of the customer's credit quality is.

Credit risk depends highly on the wealth of the counterparty, i.e. on the wealth of the economy. The macroeconomic environment helps one to understand credit risk. For this reason, *credit risk follows macroeconomic cycles.* Forecasting credit risk means, for example, forecasting GDP since there is a link between the counterparty's ability to repay and its revenues, i.e. between the ability to repay and the GDP.

For example, Basel II distinguishes two kinds of credit risk estimation:

- *Point in time (PIT)* when, for example, default rates are estimated at their actual expected value.
- *Through the cycle (TTC)* when, for example, default rates are estimated at their average historical expected value.

PIT estimations are more volatile and show less correlation between assets but they are accused of provoking *procyclic effects* (that regulators do not want). If all the banks use PIT default rate estimations, they will increase their credit margins for new credits when the economy will decrease; this will create more difficulties for the companies to repay their loans and then make the economy's decrease stronger.

19.2.1.2 Ratings

Rating agencies provide a wonderful independent analysis of credit counterparties. Their goal is to present "An opinion on the ability of an entity or of a securities issue to meet financial commitments on a timely basis."

They provide ratings for public and private corporations, states, regions or cities. The investors, counterparties and many other interested parties use these ratings.

For each company, rating agencies distinguish long-term rating and short-term rating. They distinguish also individual company rating and rating for the proposed instruments (securitization programme, fixed long-term debt, subordinated debt, etc.).

We already saw how the three major rating agencies (Standard & Poor's, S&P, Moody's and Fitch) distinguish the *"investment grade"* and the *"speculative grade"*. Extremely speculative grade means junk bonds or high yield bonds.

	Investment grade				Speculative or extremely speculative					Default
S&P	AAA	AA	A	BBB	BB	B	CCC	CC	C	D
Moody's	Aaa	Aa	A	Baa	Ba	B	Caa	Ca	C	D

Figure 19.11 Rating

How are these ratings are set? Rating agencies aggregate quantitative and qualitative sources of information. In practice, rating agencies propose multiple company reviews:

- operating environmental review: economic environment, regulatory environment, etc.;
- organizational review: how the company is structured and organized?
- management review;
- financial review: profitability, capital and reserves, debt structure and risk management are reviewed.

The rating agencies "smooth" the ratings across time since their methodologies are more "through the cycle" than "point in time (PIT)". For this reason, ratings will change only as soon as market conditions have changed durably. It is possible to notice an autocorrelation between rating changes:

- Downgrade probability knowing that the company has just been downgraded is higher than upgrade probability.
- On the other hand, upgrade probability knowing that the company has just been upgraded is slightly higher than downgrade probability.

Ratings depend on the company history: the rating of a new created company will not be as significant as the rating of an old company.

Note also that ratings are based on an economic risk approach and do not depend on the accounting standard. IFRS norms have no impact on ratings.

There is a stronger *link between ratings and company default probability* (PD) rather than with the company loss given default (LGD).

For example, rating agencies started to publish "idealized cumulated losses expectancies rates" set for each particular rating, time horizon and for each type of asset.

The table and the chart below give an example of such idealized rates:

Rating	Horizon 1y	2y	3y	4y	5y	6y	7y	8y	9y	10y
AAA	0.0%	0.0%	0.1%	0.1%	0.2%	0.3%	0.5%	0.8%	0.9%	1.0%
AA	0.0%	0.0%	0.1%	0.2%	0.3%	0.4%	0.6%	0.8%	0.9%	1.0%
A	0.0%	0.1%	0.2%	0.4%	0.6%	0.8%	1.0%	1.3%	1.7%	2.1%
BBB	0.2%	0.5%	0.9%	1.5%	2.2%	2.9%	3.5%	4.1%	4.6%	5.0%
BB	1.0%	3.4%	6.3%	9.4%	12.4%	15.7%	17.8%	20.0%	22.1%	23.7%
B	5.5%	12.4%	19.0%	24.3%	28.4%	31.7%	34.7%	37.6%	40.0%	42.2%
CCC	23.7%	33.5%	41.1%	47.4%	54.3%	56.4%	57.9%	58.4%	59.5%	60.9%

Figure 19.12 Idealized rates

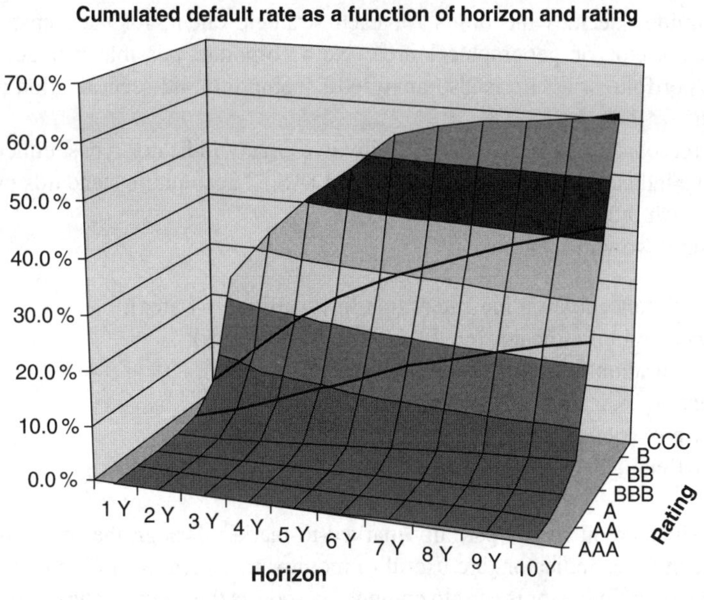

Figure 19.13 Cumulated default rates

These default rates are easy to translate in terms of credit spreads.

For example, a 1-year default rate of 1 % for a BB rating with a loss given default of 60 % and an annual risk free interest rate of 5 % gives:

40 in 1% of the cases
100.(1+5 %+Spread) in 99 % of cases.

The arbitrage free spread is then of (105−40.1 %−99 %.105)/(99 %)=0.65 %.

19.2.2 Impact of credit risk on the incomes

In banking activity, credit risk affects incomes:

- through the constitution of a *credit risk provision*;
- through the regulatory *obligation to allocate capital* in front of the credit risk exposures.

For the other activities, everything depends on the accounting scheme but it is clear that in every activity, credit risk and especially a credit risk contagion can affect income.

As long as a credit is alive, the company earns relatively smoothed margins. However, as soon as the risk increases, income is impacted directly or indirectly by a capital loss through the **"cost of risk" statement of income line.** Somehow, this amount represents a kind of credit exposure marked-to-market variation.

19.2.3 Indicators to monitor credit risk

In the banking sector, Risk Management monitors credit risk through many committees: risk policies committees, credit risk committees, etc.

Each committee decides the limits for each strategic client, for each customer profile line, for each sector or geographical area. New corporate possible production is analysed. Credit portfolio structure is also analysed keeping in mind securitization and hedging programmes.

For these reasons, credit risk monitoring involves many indicator types, either qualitative or quantitative indicators. Basel II regulation and IAS 32 accounting standards provide good examples of such indicators.

Among them, we will mention:

- geographical concentration indicators (credit repartition by area);
- sector concentration indicator (credit repartition by sector);
- name concentration indicator (credit repartition by name);
- stress scenario indicator;
- credit risk provision sensitivity to systemic factor;
- credit risk Regulatory/Economic Capital.

Actually, since credit risk is partially marked-to-market through the provision variation, provision sensitivities indicators are useful to monitor risk such as in Figure 19.14.

Such a sensitivity indicator is easy to compute as soon as the company has a comprehensive model for the computation of the credit risk provision.

			Provision value	Sensitivity	Limit
		Actual provision	100		
Systemic risk factors	Europe	EUR GDP decrease of 1 %	150	50	70
		EUR Inflation increase of 1 %	110	10	30
		EUR Rate increase of 1 %	110	10	30
		EUR Stock index decrease of 10 %	140	40	30
		EUR Petrol price increase of 20 %	105	5	30
		EU external debt to GDP increase of 10 %	130	30	30
		...	...	...	...
	US	USD GDP decrease of 1 %	150	50	70
		USD Inflation increase of 1 %	110	10	30
		USD Rate increase of 1 %	110	10	30
		USD Stock index decrease of 10 %	140	40	30
		USD Petrol price increase of 20 %	105	5	30
		US external debt to GDP increase of 10 %	130	30	30
		...	...	...	...
Geographical risk		Average PD in Germany increase by 0.10 %	110	10	30
		Average PD in the UK increase by 0.10 %	115	15	30
		Average PD in the US (west coast) increase by 0.10 %	113	13	30
		Average PD in the US (east coast) increase by 0.10 %	112	12	30
		...	...	...	...
Sectorial risk		Average PD in Industry increase by 0.10 %	110	10	30
		Average PD in the banking sector increase by 0.10 %	115	15	30
		Average PD in the insurance sector increase by 0.10 %	113	13	30
		Average PD in the public sector increase by 0.10 %	102	2	30
		...	...	...	...
Name concentration risk		Expected PD of client XXX increase by 0.10 %	110	10	30
		Expected PD of client YYY increase by 0.10 %	110	10	30
		Expected PD of client ZZZ increase by 0.10 %	110	10	30
		...	...	...	...
Specific risk		Average PD in mortgages rating X1 increase by 0,10 %	110	10	30
		Average PD in mortgages rating X2 increase by 0.10 %	110	10	30
		Average PD in mortgages rating X3 increase by 0.10 %	110	10	30
		...	...	...	...

Figure 19.14 Credit risk sensitivity

19.2.4 Credit risk factor modelling and simulation

Credit risk modelling became an easier task with the introduction of the Basel II regulation framework.

Models introduce two notions:

- The **Probability of Default (PD)**, i.e. the counterparty probability to default at a given horizon. The probability can be cumulative or conditional.
- The **Loss Given Default (LGD)**, i.e. the loss (taking into account possible capital or interest recover) once the company has gone to default. The LGD can be *expressed either as a percentage of the remaining capital, as a percentage of the remaining cash flows to repay or as a percentage of the marked-to-market of projected cash flows.*

Nevertheless, three classes of model are used by the industry with diverse degrees of sophistication:

- migration models;
- structural models;
- intensity based models.

Migration models such as the CreditMetrics™ model from JP Morgan propose a market based approach of credit risk based on the spreads and the signature risk.

Structural models such as the KMV™ model from Moody's or CreditGrades propose a balance sheet based approach where the asset and liability structure of the counterparty (its economic value) is linked with the counterparty default probability.

Intensity based models are the basis for a market based default probability model. Their objective is to make a link between derivatives (like CDS) market prices and the probability of default.

These models propose different approaches to credit risk in terms of:

- extreme losses events models;
- correlation portfolio effects models;
- risk management indicators computation;
- risk/return comprehension.

19.2.4.1 Migration models: a rating change risk

Migration models base the risk models on ratings: **credit risk is considered as a rating change risk in migration models.**

To perform the model, the risk manager should first compute **transition rating matrices**. Those matrices are either given by rating agencies, either computed on migration historical databases.

Those matrices look like this:

		Rating in one year							
		AAA	AA	A	BBB	BB	B	CCC	D
Initial rating	AAA	91.1 %	8.0 %	0.7 %	0.1 %	0.1 %	0.0 %	0.0 %	0.0 %
	AA	0.7 %	90.5 %	7.8 %	0.7 %	0.1 %	0.1 %	0.0 %	0.0 %
	A	0.1 %	2.3 %	90.9 %	5.5 %	0.7 %	0.3 %	0.1 %	0.1 %
	BBB	0.0 %	0.3 %	6.0 %	87.1 %	5.3 %	1.2 %	0.1 %	0.1 %
	BB	0.0 %	0.1 %	0.7 %	7.7 %	80.7 %	8.8 %	1.0 %	1.0 %
	B	0.0 %	0.1 %	0.2 %	0.4 %	6.5 %	83.4 %	4.1 %	5.2 %
	CCC	0.0 %	0.0 %	0.2 %	1.3 %	2.4 %	11.2 %	65.1 %	19.8 %

Figure 19.15 Rating migrations

These models also assign to each rating a target spread above risk free rate:

	Average spread
AAA	0.16 %
AA	0.20 %
A	0.27 %
BBB	0.44 %
BB	0.89 %
B	1.50 %
CCC	2.55 %
D	x

Figure 19.16 Spreads

$$\text{Rate} = \text{Risk Free Rate} + \text{Credit spread(rating)}$$

This allows the computation for each bond of its bond value in one year. For example, a 5 years maturity bond with a 6 % coupon rate will be priced in one year if its rating is A:

$$6+\frac{6}{(1+5\,\%+0.27\,\%)}+\frac{6}{(1+5\,\%+0.27\,\%)^2}+\frac{6}{(1+5\,\%+0.27\,\%)^3}$$
$$+\frac{106}{(1+5\,\%+0.27\,\%)^4}=108.57 \tag{19.11}$$

The methodology allows then to forecast for each bond its distribution value in one year and for example for an initially BBB bond:

Rating in one year	Average spread	Bond value in one year	Probability
AAA	0.16 %	108.97	0.0 %
AA	0.20 %	108.82	0.3 %
A	0.27 %	108.57	6.0 %
BBB	0.44 %	107.97	87.1 %
BB	0.89 %	106.38	5.3 %
B	1.50 %	104.29	1.2 %
CCC	2.55 %	100.81	0.1 %
D	x	40.00	0.1 %
Average value		**107.80**	

Figure 19.17 Bond value in one year

This model is adapted when forecasting the spread of a specific bond. When dealing with a bond portfolio, it is necessary to introduce correlation effects between rating changes within the portfolio. It means specifying joint probability of rating changes. In other terms, the question is, "what is the probability for firm X to become AAA and for firm Y to become A simultaneously?"

The solution is to divide the risk for each bond into two parts:

- a **systemic risk** function of the sector or the country;
- a **specific or idiosyncratic risk,** function of the bond or company characteristics.

Mathematically speaking, for each bond we consider a latent variable X depending on time t and on bond i. This variable depends on the systemic risk ε and the specific risk η:

$$X_{t,i}=\sqrt{\rho}.\varepsilon_t+\sqrt{1-\rho}.\eta_{t,i} \tag{19.12}$$

The rating of the bond i at date t will be a function of X:

$$\text{Rating}_{t,i}=f(X_{t,i}) \tag{19.13}$$

This allows us to simulate the rating evolution for each bond of a portfolio, i.e. the evolution of the portfolio value.

19.2.4.2 Structural models

19.2.4.2.1 Merton based models

In 1973, *Merton proposed a firm model* to understand how defaults occur. The balance sheet considered in the model was made up of a shareholder's equity and of a unique debt maturing at date T. In this model, the firm goes to default if the value of its assets goes under the debt value at date T.

It means that *the shareholders own a call on the asset value*, the strike of this call is the debt value.

Nowadays, structural models still use this approach based on asset value evolution.

The usual hypothesis is to consider that the variation V of the asset value variation follows a Gaussian Brownian evolution following this optional calculus formalism (Black-Scholes formalism):

$$\frac{dV_t}{V_t} = \mu dt + \sigma dW_t \tag{19.14}$$

19.2.4.2.2 One period models

The initial structural models focused on one period from 0 to T when the default cannot occur before date T.

This lets us compute the *Distance to Default (DD)* as the distance between the asset value and the debt at date T:

$$DD = \frac{E[V_T] - D}{\sigma . V_0} \tag{19.15}$$

For each company, structural models introduce using a Black-Scholes call formula the *Cumulative Expected Default Probability (CEDP)* i.e. the probability to go to default at date T:

$$CEDP_T = 1 - \Phi\left[\frac{\ln(V_0/D) + (\mu - \frac{\sigma^2}{2}).T}{\sigma.\sqrt{T}}\right] \tag{19.16}$$

This indicates the probability of the asset value V to go under the debt level D at date T.

To implement these models, the A/L manager will need large databases with:

- the asset value for each firm; and
- the volatility of this asset value for each firm.

It is possible to use shortcuts to compute the asset value using stock index databases (since equity is a call option on the asset value).

19.2.4.2.3 Multiple date credit risk model

It is possible to enlarge the model for a set of maturity T.

It is possible to compute the cumulative expected default probability (*CEDP*) from date 0 to horizon T as the following probability:

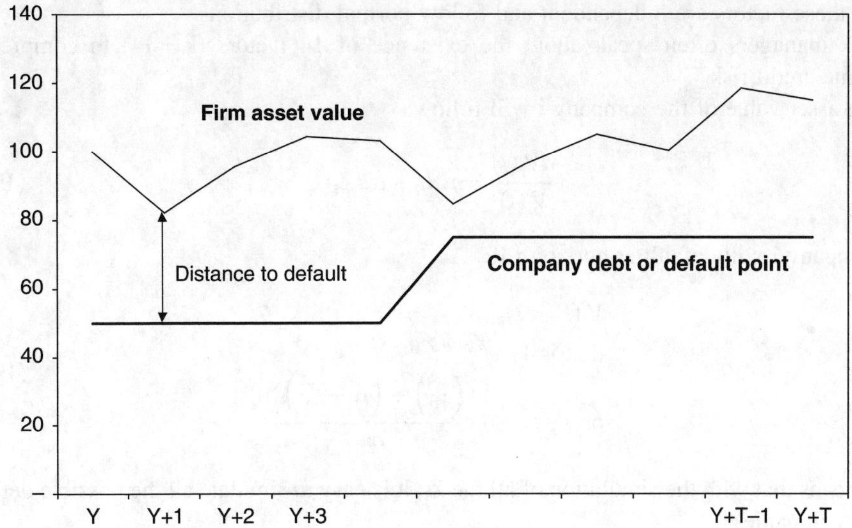

Figure 19.18 Distance to default

$$CEDP(T) = 1 - \text{Probability}\,[V_t > D, 0 \le t \le T]$$
$$1 - CEDP(T) = \text{Survival rate at horizon T} \tag{19.17}$$

The *Expected Default Probability (EDP)* is the annualized version of the CEDP:

$$EDP(T) = 1 - (1 - CEDP(T))^{\frac{1}{T}} \tag{19.18}$$

The *default conditional probability PC(T)* between T−1 and T, knowing that the bond did not default at date T is obtained through cumulative expected default probabilities:

$$PC(T) = 1 - (1 - CEDF(T))/(1 - CEDF(T-1)) \tag{19.19}$$

19.2.4.2.4 Portfolio effect integration

The model can take into account portfolio effects with the integration of correlation effects.

The idea is to divide the asset value between independent systemic risk factors F and idiosyncratic factors ε for each asset i:

$$\begin{cases} Z_I = \sum_{j=1}^{k} \sqrt{\beta_I^j} F_j + \sqrt{1 - \sum_{j=1}^{k} \beta_I^j}\, \varepsilon_I \\ \ldots \\ Z_i = \sum_{j=1}^{k} \sqrt{\beta_i^j} F_j + \sqrt{1 - \sum_{j=1}^{k} \beta_i^j}\, \varepsilon_i \text{ where } (F_1, \ldots, F_k, \varepsilon_1, \ldots, \varepsilon_n) \overset{iid}{\to} N(0; Id) \\ \ldots \\ Z_n = \sum_{j=1}^{k} \sqrt{\beta_n^j} F_j + \sqrt{1 - \sum_{j=1}^{k} \beta_n^j}\, \varepsilon_n \end{cases} \tag{19.20}$$

All these factors are independent and follow normal distributions.

Risk managers often speak about the existence of 14 factors (k = 14) to comprehend systemic credit risk.

The asset value of the company i will follow:

$$\frac{dV_i(t)}{V_i(t)} = \mu dt + \sigma dZ_i(t) \tag{19.21}$$

Company i will default at horizon t if:

$$\begin{aligned} &V_i(t) < D_i \\ &\text{that is } V_0.e^{\mu.t+\sigma.Z_i(t)-\frac{\sigma^2}{2}.t} < D_i \\ &\text{or } Z_i(t) > \frac{\ln\left(\frac{V_0}{D_i}\right) + \left(\mu - \frac{\sigma^2}{2}\right).t}{\sigma} \end{aligned} \tag{19.22}$$

It means that with the simulation of all the Z_i, it is easy to simulate all the possible defaults of the companies.

The default probability of the company i at horizon t follows this expression:

$$PD_t = \Phi^{-1}\left(\frac{\ln\left(\frac{V_0}{D_i}\right) + \left(\mu - \frac{\sigma^2}{2}\right).t}{\sigma}\right) \tag{19.23}$$

Note also that more advanced structural models will integrate a random debt barrier.

19.2.4.3 Basel II regulatory credit risk model

19.2.4.3.1 General framework

The Basel II implicit regulatory model is also a structural model based on Merton's models based on the asset value.

The regulatory model focuses on a portfolio loss distribution over a specified horizon (usually 1 year). It introduces some classic definitions for:

- *Exposure at default (EAD)*: the credit nominal exposed to credit risk at the specified horizon.
- *Loss given default (LGD)*: the loss rate occurred when the counterparty defaults. 1-LGD represents a recovery percentage.
- *Probability of default (PD)*: the probability of default over the horizon.

The Basel framework proposes only one systemic factor ψ instead of 14 factors for each company i:

$$Z_i = \sqrt{\rho}.\psi + \sqrt{1-\rho}\varepsilon_i \text{ where } (\psi, \varepsilon_1, \ldots, \varepsilon_n) \overset{iid}{\rightarrow} N(0; Id) \tag{19.24}$$

We will compute then the Basel II loss L_i for a specific loan i:

$$L_i = 1_{\{i \text{ defaults at horizon}\}} \times EAD_i \times LGD_i = 1_{\left\{\sqrt{\rho}\Psi + \sqrt{1-\rho}\varepsilon_i < \Phi^{-1}(PD_i)\right\}} \times EAD_i \times LGD_i \tag{19.25}$$

For a portfolio, the overall portfolio loss is the following one:

$$L=\sum_i 1_{\{\sqrt{\rho}\Psi+\sqrt{1-\rho}\varepsilon_i<\Phi^{-1}(PD_i)\}}.EAD_i.LGD_i \tag{19.26}$$

19.2.4.3.2 Retail portfolios

In an *infinitely granular portfolio of homogenous credits*, exposures at default are supposed to be equal, the losses given default are independent, and the defaults are independent and equiprobable. For such a scenario, the portfolio loss L becomes:

$$L=\frac{EAD}{N}.LGD.\sum_{i=1}^{N} 1_{\{\sqrt{\rho}\Psi+\sqrt{1-\rho}\varepsilon_i<\Phi^{-1}(PD)\}} \tag{19.27}$$

Conditionally upon ψ, the expected portfolio loss follows:

$$E(L/\Psi)=\frac{EAD.LGD}{N}.\sum_{i=1}^{N} E\left(1_{\{\sqrt{\rho}\Psi+\sqrt{1-\rho}\varepsilon_i<\Phi^{-1}(PD)\}}/\Psi\right) \tag{19.28}$$

Finally:

$$E(L/\Psi)=EAD.LGD.\Phi\left(\frac{\Phi^{-1}(PD)-\sqrt{\rho}\Psi}{\sqrt{1-\rho}}\right) \tag{19.29}$$

This function decreases with the systemic risk ψ and does not depend on the idiosyncratic risk factors.

This formulation on L conditionally upon ψ allows the computation of the risk quantiles used by this Basel II framework.

19.2.4.4 Intensity based models

Intensity based models propose another credit risk description used for credit derivatives pricing.

These models are based on the modelling of the date of default τ.

The default intensity (or hazard rate) λ is defined as the intensity of default i.e. the probability of occurrence of the default between date t and t+dt:

$$\lambda_t dt = P[t<\tau<t+dt\,|\,\tau>t] \tag{19.30}$$

This allows the survival function description:

$$P[\tau>T\,|\,\tau>t]=\exp\left[-\int_t^T \lambda_s ds\right] \tag{19.31}$$

The default intensity λ may be:

- constant;
- time dependent: deterministic (term structure of default) or affine;
- stochastic.

For example, in a stochastic intensity model, we divide the intensity in a CIR (Cox Ingersoll Ross) process plus a deterministic part:

$$\begin{cases} \lambda_t = x_t + \Psi_t \\ dx_t = a(\theta_t - x_t)\,dt + \sigma\sqrt{x_t}dt \end{cases} \tag{19.32}$$

The value at date t of a risk free zero-coupon maturing at date T (value at date t of 1 unit of currency paid at date T by a risk free counterparty) is usually a function of the short-term interest rates r:

$$ZC(t,T) = E_t\left[\exp\left(-\int_t^T r_s ds\right)\right] \tag{19.33}$$

We introduce the notion of *risky zero-coupon* ZCR(t, T) as the value at date t of 1 unit of currency paid at date T by a risky counterparty:

$$ZCR(t,T) = E_t\left[\exp\left(-\int_t^T r_s ds\right) \times 1_{\tau<T}\right] = E_t\left[\exp\left(-\int_t^T (r_s + \lambda_s)\,ds\right)\right] \tag{19.34}$$

This model allows us to evaluate the fair value of the credit risk products such as bonds, CDS or CDOs. The present value of such a product is the sum of the flows discounted with the risky zero-coupons:

$$PV_t = \sum_{j=1}^{T} CF_j \times ZCR(j,T) \tag{19.35}$$

Note also that there is a link between the intensity and the notion of spread since:

$$spread(t,T) \sim \frac{1}{T-t}\int_t^T \lambda_s ds \tag{19.36}$$

This model is then easy to calibrate over market prices with the possible introduction of risk premiums.

For the integration of portfolio effects, the model needs the implementation of copulas (see section 34.2).

19.2.5 Credit risk hedging

Credit risk hedging used to be a superfluous question since credit risk managers used to concentrate more on the new credit risk flows rather than on the management of the stock of operations.

Some banks in the 80s started to *securitize* their credit portfolio, transferring this way their credit exposure to the market.

Nevertheless, with the development of the Basel II regulation, a credit derivative market took shape, providing *credit default swaps (CDS)* and *collateralized debt obligations (CDOs)* permitting an effective management of credit risk exposures in large corporations.

19.2.5.1 *CDS and CDOs*

The credit default swap (CDS) is the most frequent credit derivative. It is an agreement between two counterparties for a precise period:

- The protection buyer pays a periodic fee computed as a percentage of a nominal.
- The protection seller pays the nominal multiplied by the loss given default when a specified company goes to default.

For bondholders, the CDS is a possible and natural protection against credit risk.
The CDS market provides:

- prices for the hedging of the corporate credit risk;
- a source for corporate credit risk introduction in *FTPs*; and
- for the computation of corporate credit risk *provisions.*

19.2.5.2 *Securitization*

Securitization is the most common mode to transfer credit risk from the banking industry to other financial institutions.

19.2.5.2.1 Loan securitization through a SPV

Special purpose vehicles (SPVs) are financial vehicles dedicated to securitization.
The SPV balance sheet consists of:

- Assets: loans portfolio transferred from a bank (potentially recharged and thereafter amortized).
- Liabilities: bonds notes with various ratings from AAA to BBB, the reserve, and an equity part: these are the "tranches" issued by the SPV.

The SPV sells into the market the investment grade bonds and sometimes the bank buys back the equity tranche.

Tranche	Nominal	Rating	Spread
Senior	93	AAA	Libor +0.10 %
Mezzanine	5	A	Libor +0.30 %
Subordinated	2	BBB	Libor +1 %
Equity part	2	NR	...

Figure 19.19 Securitization

The SPV gave an engagement to pay each month to the bondholders following this order:

- commissions and fees;
- past coupons not paid;
- coupons on investment grade notes;
- remaining capital;
- residual coupon (for the equity part).

For capital, there are two amortizing modes:

- Normal mode: notes repayment of capital follows a contractual schedule.
- Accelerated mode once the excess spread (difference between asset rate and liability rate) has become negative over a specified period. First, the SPV repay the senior tranches, then mezzanine tranches and finally the subordinated tranches.

In the normal mode, pass-through securitization means that the notes amortization follows the amortization of the loan portfolio.

The SPV remunerates the residual equity part in the last position. Moreover, when the excess spread decreases, the SPV does not pay the residual coupon associated with the equity part but delays it into the reserve. In the accelerated mode, the SPV does not repay the residual equity part.

When the residual loan amounts are too low, a *"clean-up call"* will usually liquidate the SPV. The bank who securitized the credits buys back the residual loans.

The securitization may include also many "triggers" in order to protect the senior bonds (these triggers ask for reserve increases in some specific cases).

Finally, the SPV balance sheet may include swaps in order to protect the bondholders from interest rate risk changes.

19.2.5.2.2 Securitization and IFRS

IFRS ask for the SPV consolidation in the balance sheet as soon as the bank buys back the majority of the risk (i.e. buys back the equity tranche issued by the SPV).

19.2.5.2.3 Securitization costs, risk hedging and prudential arbitrage

Securitization implies significant costs, indeed much higher than the cost implied by a classic debt issue (these costs are higher than 5 bps, for example, even for the larger securitization programmes). Placement costs are higher and the montage implies fixed cost.

The Basel I regulation framework obliged banks to immobilize capital in front of their credit exposures. The principle was to decrease the banking industry defaults. However, the Accord introduced arbitrage opportunities in retail credit: after securitization, if the bank conserved only the equity part, the capital to immobilize was equal to the amount of this equity part.

The regulatory capital division by a coefficient of 5 or more was a wonderful regulatory arbitrage!

In the Basel II framework, risk managers will compute their capital immobilization economically. Nevertheless, in Pillar 1, the regulators impose many coefficients such as the correlation ρ. For mortgages, ρ is equal to 15 % even if economic estimations show that the real value may be inferior to this level. It means that regulatory arbitrages are still possible in the Basel II framework but are really less interesting: risk managers have to explain to the market how this correlation ρ is inferior to 15 %. Nevertheless, the regulatory arbitrages disappear in the Pillar 2 framework since in this Pillar the regulator does not impose a value for ρ.

19.2.5.2.4 *SPV rating by rating agencies*

Rating agencies focus on different approaches to propose a rating for the notes issued by the SPVs:

- Stress scenarios to see when the bond goes to default (stress on the movement of the excess spread or stress on the prepayment scenarios).
- Cumulative default rate at maturity: the rating agencies ask for the computation of these default rates and translate them into rating using their matrices of "idealized cumulated losses expectancies rates".

19.2.5.2.5 *Synthetic securitization and CDO*

A classic securitization implies a real transfer of loans, i.e. a transfer of all the cash flows to the SPV.

Other montages like synthetic securitization propose only a transfer of the cash flows information.

CDOs (Collateralized debt obligations) represent a new range of market products. On the asset side of the SPV, there is a portfolio of risky bonds (or a portfolio of risk free bonds plus a portfolio of CDS).

CDOs are investment products allowing the A/L manager to take risks or to diversify the credit risk exposure. This market brings a new category of AAA assets into the market.

Investors should pay attention to the strong correlation existing between the existing CDOs: the large corporate debt market is not so wide and the same company names always appear on the asset side of each CDO SPV. This explains why CDO AAA tranches include higher premiums than classic AAA government bonds.

Pricing CDOs is not so easy. Traders use intensity based models with many hypotheses about correlations and copulas. They price each tranche using an implicit correlation and an implicit default probability for the tranche.

The big crisis of May 2005 showed how difficult it was to price CDOs: some credit spreads (e.g. General Motors) increased and at the same time, the correlation used to price mezzanine tranches decreased, showing a negative correlation to CDS spreads. Unfortunately, many traders thought that this correlation was positive and when they recalibrated their model, they had to recognize negative incomes.

Some traders propose "CDO square" (CDO^2) investments: in this case, the asset side of the SPV is already made of CDO investments. There is no real diversification with these products since there is no real difference between the different CDO tranches present in the market.

19.3 INTEREST RATE RISK

19.3.1 Nature of interest rate risk and examples

ALM interest rate risk can be defined as the risk of portfolio marked-to-market change or as the risk of an income stream change in the portfolio (when portfolios are measured on an accrual basis) due to a change in the interest rate level.

Different interest rate risk types exist in ALM risk management:

- *Mismatch risk*: asset and liability interest rate sensitivity difference.

Interest rate sensitivity is a concept directly linked to the duration concept (i.e. the Macaulay duration).

- *Basis risk*: risk of deterioration of two usually highly correlated risk types.

For example, a loan indexed to the Libor 3 months refinanced by a deposit indexed to the Libor 6 months.

- *Embedded option risk*: an embedded option such as a prepayment option included in a loan may include an optional interest rate risk.
- *Interest rate yield curve slope risk*: not only may the level of the interest rates create an interest rate risk but also the interest rate yield curve configuration (its level, its slope, its convexity).

To get a better understanding of the interest rate risk, it is necessary to remember what a yield curve is.

19.3.2 Different types of yield curves

19.3.2.1 General considerations

When talking about yield curves, an A/L manager should explain which yield curve he is talking about. In fact, the yield curves are numerous:

- yield to maturity (YTM) yield curve;
- swap rate yield curve;
- zero-coupon yield curve;
- forward yield curve and instant forward yield curve, etc.

The interest rate designs a placement yield rate of a currency unit for a given period. This rate measures the individual preference for the present and for instant consumption.

The interest rate is positive.

The interest rate level reveals also the *monetary policy*. The Central Bank controls the level of the short-term interest rates. The "Theory of anticipations" links the level of the long-term interest rates with the anticipations of the future short-term interest rates.

A/L managers specify by the term **"interest rate term structure"** or **"interest rate yield curve"** when defining the function that at a *given date* associates a level of interest rate with a *given maturity*. The function is a two variables function.

Yield curves are not unique but multiple. First, the yield curves are associated with a currency such EUR (€, Euro), USD (US Dollar), JPY (Japanese Yen), CHF, GBP, etc. For each country, there is a multitude of yield curves. There is a yield curve for each issuer, according to its rating level or its sector. The interest rates take into account the credit risk of the counterparty. For example, we can find these kinds of yield curves:

- US Federal Reserve yield curve;
- Rating A US Petrol Company yield curve;
- BNP Paribas debt yield curve.

In this context, some considerations about the functioning of the rating system are necessary.

There are not so many rating agencies: Standard & Poor's, Moody's and Fitch for example. Each agency provides a rating, i.e. a notation for the credit risk of a company, of a specific bond issued by a company or of a securitization product.

19.3.2.2 Standard & Poor's Ratings

The ratings provided by Standard & Poor's (S&P) start with the rating "AAA", the best rating, and ends with the "D" rating. The ratings may be modified by the adjunction of the sign "+" or "−" in order to get a more precise relative position in the rating scale.

Long-term ratings may be associated with a perspective "stable", positive" or "negative". The perspective has to indicate the potential rating evolution in the next 2 or 3 years.

The ratings distinguish the investment grade from the speculative grade.

In the investment grade, S&P differentiates:

- AAA: The highest S&P rating, the ability to repay coupons and to reimburse the capital is extremely strong.
- AA: the ability is still very strong; this category is not so different from the AAA category.
- A: high capacity to repay coupons and capital but with a sensitivity to economic conditions and to circumstances changes.
- BBB: still with high capacity to repay interest and capital but with higher sensitivity to these changes.

As for the speculative grade, S&P differentiates:

- BB: the repayment presents an uncertainty since the issuer is vulnerable to bad financial or economic conditions.
- B: the issuer may still face his engagements but is more vulnerable than a BB rating.
- CCC: the repayment is doubtful and depends on propitious conditions (financial or economic).
- CC, C: the repayment is extremely doubtful and depends highly on economic and financial conditions.
- D/SD: the company is already in payment default (interest or capital default) except when a grace period has been granted (a settlement before expiration of this time limit may occur). The D rating points out that the default is general or at least substantial. The SD rating indicates that the default does not alter the normal service of the other commitments.

19.3.2.3 Moody's ratings

Moody's long-term bond ratings constitute opinions about the credit risk of the more than 1-year debt bonds and about the eventuality of seeing a financial engagement not honoured as expected. Those ratings reveal the default probability as well as the financial lost probability.

Moody's ratings are:

- Aaa: best quality obligation debt presenting a minimum credit risk.
- Aa: high quality obligation debt with a very low credit risk.
- A: investment grade obligation debt with an average quality and with a low credit risk level.
- Baa: first speculative grade obligation debt presenting a moderate credit risk.
- Ba: speculative grade obligation with an important credit risk level.
- B: speculative grade obligation with a high credit risk level.
- Caa: bad signature obligation with high credit risk.
- Ca: highly speculative obligation, close to default but still with perspectives of interest or capital repayment.
- C: the rated obligation poorest grade in default situation, with limited principal or interest repayment perspective.

Moody's applies numerical coefficients from 1 to 3. The coefficient 1 indicates that the issuer is one of the best of the rating categories.

19.3.2.4 Market interest rate yield curves and implicit yield curves

Market yield curves are built directly with the instrument markets quotes:

- A swap yield curve is, for example, based on the swap rate and on the Interbank rates (for rate inferior to 12 months).
- A state bond yield curves is another example.

The implicit yield curves are interest rate curves deduced from the market interest rate yield curves:

- the zero-coupon yield curve;
- the forward yield curve;
- the instant forward yield curve.

19.3.3 Different types of interest rate

In the next section we will go more into the different types of interest rate.

19.3.3.1 The Yield to Maturity (YTM) for bonds

Bonds are debt contracts coming from diverse issuers close to loans or deposits excluding the fact that they may be traded on the markets.

Bond flows are made of capital flows (principal flows) and of interest rate flows (coupon flows).

The bonds get a nominal value. The coupon rate is the outstanding capital remuneration at each interest payment date.

For a "bullet" or an "in fine" bond, the capital is reimbursed at maturity.

Zero-coupon bonds do not provide any flow before the bond maturity.

The market quotes bonds in "price" or in "rate". We call this rate the yield to maturity (YTM). It is possible to use this definition for every kind of fixed rate interest rate product.

By definition the YTM(t) is the discount rate of the future flows f(i) that allows us to obtain the bond price V(t):

$$V(t) = \sum_{i=t+1}^{m} \frac{\varphi(i)}{[1 + YTM(t)]^{i-t}} \tag{19.37}$$

The YTM yield curve associates with each maturity the yield of the bond of this maturity. This yield curve will be used in simple models since the discounting factor present in the formula above does not depend on i but only on the horizon t.

19.3.3.2 Swap rates

The swap rate is the interbank reference for interest rates.

A *swap* is an exchange contract between two counterparties. A counterparty (Bank 1) gave an engagement to pay a fixed rate at different dates on a constant nominal to another counterparty (Bank 2); Bank 2 gave also an engagement to pay a variable rate on the same nominal at different dates.

From Bank 1s point of view, this is a two branches (two legs) contract:

- A fixed leg with payment to Bank 2 based on a fixed rate (for example 3 % per annum with a 30/360 basis).
- A floating leg with variable payments from Bank 2 (for example, an Euribor 3 months paid every 3 months on an Exact/360 basis).

The swap rate is the swap fixed rate value where the banks (Bank 1 and Bank 2) accept to trade the deal. This rate is called "swap rate" of the swap maturity. Swaps are quoted this way.

By market definition, the marked-to-market of a standard swap contract is equal to zero at the swap initiation moment. This value will change, may become positive or negative: it is called the swap cancellation value.

Each bank may define at which level the bank will accept swap contracts for each swap maturity available on the market (usually from 1 year to 30 up to 50 years). Each bank may have its own swap curve (slightly differing from other banks yield curves).

For this reason, the *"CMS swap yield curve"* (constant maturity swap yield curve) was designed in order to establish a benchmark swap yield curve. At the fixing hour (11 o'clock usually), the major banks give their swap yield curve and the average of these yield curves is published as the CMS yield curve.

The "CMS Swap yield curve" is also the observation of the "Interbank curve".

In the Euro zone, the swap rate yield curve is defined by:

- the EONIA rate for the one day rate;
- Euribor rates from the maturity 1 week to 1 year;
- CMS swap rate for maturities above 1 year.

For other currencies, *Euribor rates* are often replaced by the *LIBOR rates* (London Interbank Offer Rate).

The swap rates are often the rates of the fixed leg of swaps against Euribor or against Libor. Nevertheless, sometimes it is possible to use fixed rates swaps against short-term capitalized rate (on the floating leg, the coupon is indexed to the annual product of the EONIA capitalization).

In those conditions, another yield curve, the *EONIA swap yield curve* (or the Fed Funds yield curve in the US), is another yield curve option.

19.3.3.3 Zero-coupon rate

A *discount factor* B(0, T) is the value today at date 0 of €1 that will be paid back at date T. This factor is often called *"zero-coupon"* or "zero-coupon discount factor".

The zero-coupon rate ZCR(0,T) is defined as the yield of the zero-coupon bond (without any coupon) repaying a €1 nominal at date T.

Mathematically speaking, the equation below characterizes the link between the zero-coupon price and the zero-coupon rate:

$$B(0,T) = \frac{1}{[1 + TZC(0,T)]^T} \tag{19.38}$$

Common actuarial lessons show that in the absence of arbitrage opportunities, the price V(t) of a bond is the sum of the bond flows $\phi(i)$ discounted with the zero-coupon:

$$V(t) = \sum_{i=t+1}^{m} \frac{\varphi(i)}{[1 + TZC(t, i-t)]^{i-t}} = \sum_{i=t+1}^{m} \varphi(i) B(t,i) \tag{19.39}$$

To evaluate the bond price, knowing the zero-coupon prices is enough. Nevertheless, zero-coupon prices are difficult to obtain directly since zero-coupon bonds are rarely traded on the market. In practice, zero-coupon rates are extracted from the market rates.

From the zero-coupon rates, it will be possible to extract other yield curves such as the forward rate yield curves.

19.3.3.4 Forward rates

The *forward rate* at date t, starting at date x with a maturity y is defined by the following equation:

$$F(t, x, y-x) = \left[\frac{(1 + TZC(t,y))^{y-t}}{(1 \leq TZC(t,x))^{x-t}}\right]^{\frac{1}{y-x}} - 1 \tag{19.40}$$

For a zero-coupon borrowing with a repayment of interests and principal at maturity, starting at date x and with a maturity y, F(t, x, y−x) is the contract market interest rate at date t.

It is possible to build many *forward yield curves* with this definition: each forward yield curve is a function that links x with F(t, x, y−x) for each maturity y−x. For example, we may work with the forward yield curve starting in one month (x=1/12), with the forward yield curve starting in one year, in 10 years.

A special forward rate is also often used: the instantaneous forward rate.

19.3.3.5 *Instantaneous forward rate*

The *instantaneous forward rate* is a special forward rate defined as the first yield curve point. Concretely, it is the forward rate determined at date t starting at date x and finishing after an infinitesimal period of time:

$$f(t, x) = \lim_{y-x \to 0} F(t, x, y - x) \tag{19.41}$$

This rate is often used as a base for interest rate models (HJM models, etc.).

The *instantaneous forward yield curve* associates f(t, x) to x. This kind of yield curve is different from the forward rate yield curves since here x is the variable and not y−x.

Another rate is the "short-term rate" r(t) = f(t, t), i.e. the rate starting at date t and finishing after an infinitesimal period of time (one day usually).

19.3.4 Different forms of yield curve

The yield curve form is the source of recurrent discussions between A/L managers. Usually, the yield curve may take different forms:

- almost flat;
- increasing;
- decreasing;
- decreasing on the short-term and increasing in the long-term;
- increasing on the short-term and decreasing in the long-term.

The increasing form is the most common form. The market trend is to reproduce the present in the future but incorporating a risk premium on the long-term horizons.

The historical study of the yield curves movements shows that:

- Interest rates are positive.

Real interest rates are sometimes negative but nominal interest rates cannot be negative since from an economic point of view it is aberrant to lend money at a negative price. It is healthier to conserve our cash rather to lend it.

- Interest rate movements are associated with a mean reverting effect.

The periods of high interest rate levels tend usually to follow periods of low interest rate levels. Respectively, the periods of low interest rate levels tend usually to follow periods of high interest rate levels.

Moreover, the interest rate movements do not present a trend on the long-term. Their evolution seems to be constrained within a tunnel.

- Interest rate movements of all the yield curve points are not perfectly correlated.

For example, the short-term rate evolution is correlated badly with long-term rate evolution. Nevertheless, these correlations are often positives.

For interest rates simulations, this will lead one to prefer two or three factors models (instead of one-factor models).

- Short-term interest rates are more volatile than long-term interest rates.

Moreover, interest rate volatility seems to be correlated with the interest rate level.

An analysis (the Principal Component Analysis or PCA) shows that mainly *three factors* explain more than 95 % of the interest rate movements:

- Evolution of the interest rate level also called *"translation"*.

The short-term and the long-term interest rates tend to move on the same way with a parallel shift.

- Evolution of the interest rate yield curve slope also called *"rotation"*.

This rotation movement may provoke a yield curve "flattening" or a yield curve "sloping".

- Evolution of the interest rate yield curve convexity also called *"curvature change"* or *"convexity change"*.

This movement provokes yield curve convexity changes when for example, medium term rates move one way when short-term and long-term rates move on the other way.

19.3.5 Impact of the interest rate risk on the incomes

Interest rate risk has various impacts on the incomes.

In a balance sheet where we measure the assets at historical cost, the accountants compute the net income as the difference between the interest income on the assets and the interest expense on the liabilities. Consequently, when there is an *asymmetry between the asset side and the liability side* (i.e. when the assets are fixed rate assets and the liabilities are, for example, floating rate assets), the income varies with the floating rate variations. The interest rate gap (i.e. the gap analysis) will measure this risk.

The interest rate risk is also present in the economic value sensitivity. Of course, when we compute an economic value, we discount the cash flows with an interest rate yield curve. Consequently, the economic value of the balance sheet will depend on the form of the balance sheet.

As a result, the margins always contain an interest rate risk. Even if the margins are fixed, their actual value increases when the interest rates decrease.

19.3.6 Interest rate risk indicators

19.3.6.1 Actual risk indicators

There are different forms of interest rate risk:

- *Firm interest rate risk* due to maturity mismatch between fixed rate assets and fixed rate liabilities (over 1 year).

- *Short-term interest rate risk* due to the fixing risk or to the mismatch between Libor and DD rates.
- *Optional interest rate risk* due to the presence of embedded interest rate derivatives in the balance sheet or behavioural options (such as: prepayments, capped loans, etc.).
- *Structural interest rate risk* due to contractual schedule lack for some Balance Sheet products (demand deposits, equity, etc.) or to partial correlation between market rates and customer rates.

For each risk nature, it is possible to provide a specific indicator:

- *Gap analysis and its associated break-even point.*
- *Short-term position.*
- *Optional indicator.*
- *Income sensitivity/implicit demand deposit or equity placements.*

Each indicator proposes a specific risk measure for an adapted income hedging.

19.3.6.1.1 Gap analysis and "equilibrium point"

19.3.6.1.1.1 Gap analysis

Interest rate gaps present a static vision of interest rate risk. Gaps represent a picture of the balance sheet amounts at a given date and their extinction across time.

Firm interest rate gap is linked with fixed rate products excluding their interest rate coupons based on a contractual schedule or on a conventional schedule.

When a FTP system is implemented in the company, the interest rate gaps represent the firm interest rate risk (transferred from commercial entities to ALM).

The **interest rate gap** is the function that assigns to each maturity the projected difference between the total fixed rate liabilities remaining at this maturity and the total fixed rate assets also remaining at this maturity. The remaining assets and liabilities exclude new customer productions, new contracts, etc.

The usual convention is to *sign positively the liabilities and negatively the assets.* Nevertheless, some companies still use the inverse convention.

If the company has an interest rate gap constant and equal to zero, the company will not be exposed to interest rate moves: without new production, the incomes are then not sensible to the interest rate movements.

There is an interest rate risk gap example of a bank Balance Sheet in Figure 19.20.

The interest rate gap is positive on the short-term. It means that fixed rate liabilities exceed fixed rate assets.

The **cumulative interest rate gap** gives the schedule of the amortizing fixed rate against short-term interest rate swap that hedges the interest rate risk.

In this example, the interest rate gap is negative: the bank is exposed to interest rate decreases.

The interest rate gap has to be computed over different axes:

- interest rate gap *by branch or by activity*;
- interest rate gap *by currency* since the interest rate movements are different in one currency from in another currency.

	Today	1 month	3 month	6 month	1 year	3 years	5 years	10 years	More than 10 years
Fixed rate loans	40	34	34	33	32	20	12	–	–
Floating rate loans	40	27	–	–	–	–	–	–	–
Net treasury	20	–	–	–	–	–	–	–	–
Credit lines	–	–	–	–	–	–	–	–	–
Total Assets IR schedule	100	61	34	33	32	20	12	–	–
Current accounts	50	40	39	38	36	28	20	0	–
Libor based debt	40	27	–	–	–	–	–	–	–
Equity	10	10	10	10	9	7	5	–	–
Total Liabilities IR schedule	100	77	49	48	45	35	25	0	–
Receiver swaps	–	–	–	–10	–10	–	–	–	–
Cumulative interest rate gap	–	16	16	5	3	15	13	0	–

Figure 19.20 Cumulative interest rate gap

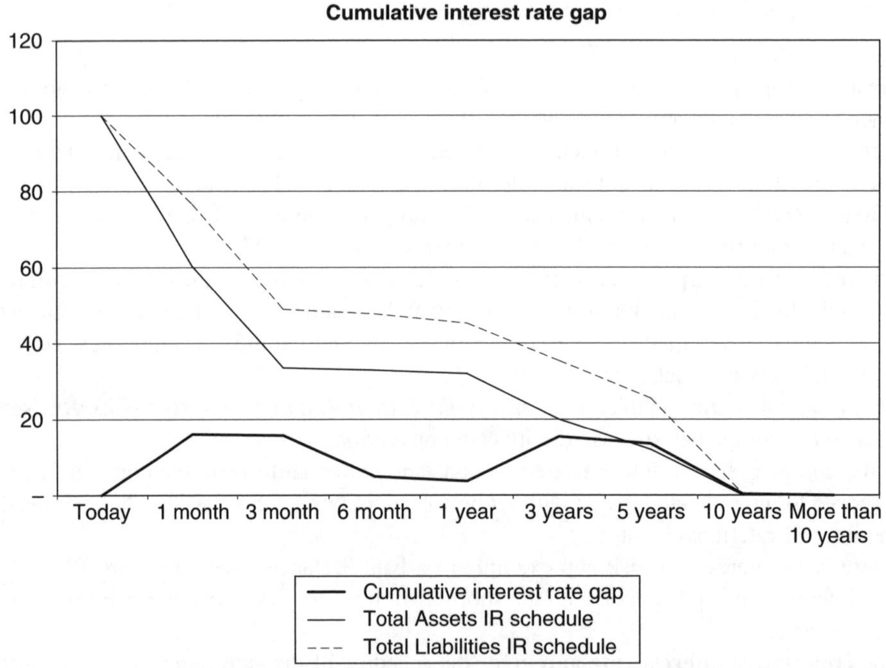

Figure 19.21 Cumulative interest rate gap

The interest rate gap computation makes sense only *for non-trading books*. Interest rate risk in the trading book has to be taken into account in trading book risk measures such as value-at-risk.

Actually, the interest rate gap is a pertinent risk measure for assets and liabilities accounted on an accrued basis (i.e. "at historical cost").

19.3.6.1.1.1.1 *Interest rate schedules for fixed rate assets and liabilities with contractual maturities*

When an asset or a liability gets a contractual maturity, it is easy to compute its principal repayment schedule. This schedule will be used in the interest rate gap as soon as the asset or the liability pays or receives a fixed rate coupon. For example, these assets and liabilities are linked with a direct liquidity schedule:

- company's debt;
- company's loans and borrowings;
- company's deposits;
- interest rate swaps, etc.

For fixed rate liquid products, interest rate schedules looks like liquidity schedules. Some examples of such liquidity schedules are given in section 19.1 on liquidity risk or in Chapter 7 on FTP.

19.3.6.1.1.1.2 *Interest rate schedules for floating rate assets and liabilities with contractual maturities*

For floating rates products, the interest rate gap is equal to the liquidity gap only on the period where the rate is fixed.

In our example above, we represented a Libor 1 month floating rate debt of 40 in the interest rate gap. If the debt is as 5-year maturity debt issued 4 years ago, the interest rate is fixed only for the upcoming month. The interest rate debt representation is thus a 1-month interest rate maturity product as shown in the interest rate gap.

19.3.6.1.1.1.3 *Interest rate schedules for interest rate swaps*

Derivative products such as swaps are represented in the interest rate gap but they will not be represented in the liquidity gaps.

Actually, a fixed rate receiver versus floating rate payer swap is the sum of a fixed rate loan and of a floating rate deposit.

In our example, we used a 1 year fixed versus 3 months Libor swap for an amount of 10.

	Today	1 month	3 month	6 month	1 year	3 years	5 years	10 years	More than 10years
Receiver swaps	–	–	–	−10	−10	–	–	–	–
Fixed rate leg loan	10	10	10	10	10	–	–	–	–
Floating leg deposit	10	10	10	–	–	–	–	–	–

Figure 19.22 Swap representation

19.3.6.1.1.1.4 *Liquidity schedules for assets and liabilities with contractual maturities including options*

Option inclusion in interest rate gap is not an easy task.

Since the interest rate gap represents the amount of swap to contract in order to hedge interest rate risk, option conversion in interest rate gap means *option conversion in their "swap equivalent"*.

The option conversion method in interest rate gaps is called **"delta equivalent method"** (see chapter about delta equivalent computation). This delta equivalent minimizes the volatility of the future incomes.

This method exists for every kind of option:

- *market options* such as caps, floors, collars, swaptions, etc.;
- *"behavioural options"* such as prepayments;
- nonlinearly sensitive interest rate products such as *MBS*, etc.

Options affect durably the interest rate gap. Forgetting them in the interest rate gap is often a dangerous mistake.

It is possible to introduce readily in the interest rate gaps the options that do not depend on the interest rates. For example, the introduction of financial prepayments in gaps is feasible using delta equivalent computation; on the other hand, some "options" do not need such a complex methodology, for instance:

- default rates (if they are supposed not correlated with the level of the interest rates);
- statistical prepayments (i.e. sociological prepayments).

As an example, the statistical part of prepayments implies the following schedule modification:

$$\text{Schedule}_{\text{with statistical prepayments}}(t) = \text{Schedule}_{\text{without statistical prepayments}}(t) \\ .\exp(\text{-t.Statistical Prepayment rate}) \qquad (19.42)$$

19.3.6.1.1.1.5 *Interest rate schedules for assets and liabilities without contractual maturities*
Many assets and liabilities do not have a contractual schedule to represent them straightforwardly in the interest rate gap. Usually, *the interest rate gap representation depends on a model that is close to the interest rate FTP representation.*

For current and savings accounts, the interest rate schedule in some banks is supposed to be "on demand", i.e. to be amortized on very short-term horizons. In other banks or in other countries, those amounts are proposed as "no maturity", i.e. they are represented as very long-term investments.

The better way to represent savings and current accounts is to *use a model* (see Chapter 11) to forecast the evolution of these amounts based on existing clients (and based on the existing contracts) and to forecast customer rate remuneration. Forecasting requires sometimes a delta equivalent computation of the interest rate schedule since many options (volume effects) are present in the product.

The same methodology can be proposed for *overdrafts*, for doubtful accounts and their associated provisions.

The elements of the Capital Book (i.e. equity capital, provisions, goodwill, etc.) are also amortized in the interest rate gap as shown in their interest rate modelling proposed with FTPs. In our example, equity is linearly amortized over 10 years.

19.3.6.1.1.2 "Break-even interest rate point" or "Equilibrium points"
Interest rate gap has to be coherent with the FTP convention: the interest rates taken into account in the FTP should be based on the same horizon as the projected schedules.

For each fixed rate balance sheet line, a fixed rate FTP is assigned. It helps to compute the total asset interest rate cost and the total liability interest rate cost.

Fixed interest rate costs go into the income computation of the "Interest Rate Books".

The interest rate gap allows us then to compute the future projected incomes of the "Interest Rate Books" (without any new production).

	Today	1 month	3 month	6 month	1 year	3 years	5 years	10 years	More than 10 years
Total Assets schedule	100	61	34	33	32	20	12	–	–
Assets FTP IR cost (ann.)	4.3	2.7	1.6	1.6	1.5	1.0	0.6	–	–
Assets FTP IR cost (%)	4.34 %	4.48 %	4.85 %	4.85 %	4.85 %	4.85 %	4.85 %	0.00 %	–
Total Liabilities schedule	100	77	49	48	45	35	25	0	–
Liabilities FTP IR cost (ann.)	4.4	3.4	2.3	2.3	2.1	1.7	1.2	0	–
Liabilities FTP IR cost (%)	4.41 %	4.44 %	4.72 %	4.72 %	4.72 %	4.72 %	4.72 %	4.90 %	0.00 %
Total Swap schedule	–	–	–	–10	–10	–	–	–	–
Swaps FTP IT cost (ann.)	0.1	0.1	0.1	0.4	0.4	–	–	–	–
Swap FTP IR cost (%)	N.S.	N.S.	N.S.	4.00 %	4.00 %	0.00 %	0.00 %	0.00 %	0.00 %
Cumulative liquidity gap	–	16	16	5	3	15	13	0	–
Balance Sheet FTP IR cost (ann.)	0.0	–0.6	–0.6	–0.3	–0.2	–0.7	–0.6	0	–
Break-even FTP interest rate	N.S.	3.66 %	3.80 %	5.33 %	5.62 %	4.55 %	4.61 %	4.90 %	0.00 %
Forward interest rate		3.00 %	3.00 %	3.50 %	4.00 %	4.50 %	5.00 %	5.50 %	6.00 %
Projected income (annualized)		–0.11	–0.13	–0.09	–0.06	–0.01	0.05	0.00	–

Figure 19.23 Liquidity gap

The ***FTP interest rate break-even*** is the average interest rate cost of the assets and the liabilities. There is a break-even for each future maturity:

$$\text{Break-Even}_{1\text{ year}} = \frac{\text{Fixed Liabilities}_{1\text{ year}}.\text{FTP IR Liabilities}_{1\text{ year}} - \text{Fixed Assets}_{1\text{ year}}.\text{FTP IR Assets}_{1\text{ year}}}{\text{Interest rate gap}_{1\text{ year}}} \tag{19.43}$$

Another formulation is possible through the definition of *fixed interest rate costs over the book*; this formulation avoids the divisions by 0:

$$\text{Fixed Book IR costs}_{1\text{ year}} = \left(\text{Break Even}_{1\text{ year}}.\text{Interest rate gap}_{1\text{ year}}\right) \tag{19.44}$$

$$\text{Fixed Book IR costs}_{1\text{ year}} = \text{Fixed IR Liabilities Cost}_{1\text{ year}} - \text{Fixed IR Assets Costs}_{1\text{ year}}$$

In the break-even computation, note that, *swaps are broken down as the sum of a loan (i.e. as an asset) and of a deposit (i.e. as a liability).*

The break-even point has some interesting properties:

- *The break-even point represents the interest rate of the swap that hedges the total gap and sets the monthly income to zero.*
- *The comparison between the break-even point and the market anticipated DD rate allows us to forecast the incomes.* In our example, the forward DD rate (day-to-day short-term interest rate) is below the break-even rate (except on the 10 year horizon) and the interest rate gap is positive: it means that future incomes are expected to be negative.

If the A/L manager knows the future interest rate of a maturity, he is able to project the (annualised) income of the Interest Rate Book:

$$\text{IR Book Income}_{1\,\text{year}_{\text{forecast}}} = \text{IR gap}_{1\,\text{year}} \cdot \left(\text{Forecasted DD rate}_{1\,\text{year}} - \text{Break Even}_{1\,\text{year}}\right) \tag{19.45}$$

A large part of the A/L manager's task will then to project the future interest rate in order to monitor its Interest Rate Book income.

19.3.6.1.2 Income sensitivities

Gapping is a formidable indicator to monitor interest rate risk. Nevertheless, this indicator may provoke mismatches between risk perception and income management. For these reasons, income sensitivities represent a useful complementary risk measure.

19.3.6.1.2.1 Indicator presentation

Interest rate gaps did not introduce new production in the risk measure.

On the contrary, income sensitivities propose risk quantification in a dynamic approach including new productions and new volumes evolution, new margins and new hedging strategies.

The **sensitivity indicator** measures the impact on future net incomes of interest rate movements with a set of possible future scenarios.

Sensitivities are computed around *a central scenario* that could represent the forward market scenario or the internal company budget scenario.

The sensitivities' objective is to summarize all kind if interest rate risks in one indicator:

- firm and optional interest rate risk;
- short-term and long-term interest rate risks;
- structural risks due to balance sheet renewal;
- inflation risk;
- ALM and commercial risks.

The sensitivity indicator allows risk scenarios identification and hedging strategies definition. In a non-trading environment, such anticipation of the income is necessary in order to propose better hedging strategy at the right moment.

Future incomes have to be coherent with actual incomes. Computing sensitivities allows us to backtest the company interest rate income and to comprehend business risk.

Under all these assumptions, the indicator may become very complex. In large companies, an organization is necessary to avoid the computation of *"black box" sensitivity*:

- models and assumption documentation;
- backtest;
- external controls, etc.

The Table 19.24 shows a basic example of sensitivity computation. Here are presented two basic scenarios around the central scenario of a 5-year horizon: a rising rate and a decreasing rate scenario.

The indicator shows the projected incomes in each scenario and the sensitivity decomposition over different products.

Note that the sensitivity is *asymmetric*: the sensitivity to the interest rate decreases is not equal to the sensitivity to the interest rate increases since the products contain embedded options (here we added "volume effects" in the demand deposits).

The indicator presents the sensitivities of the ALM and of the Commercial Department.

Sensitivities are computed according to a *new volumes refinancing strategy*. Here the hypothesis is to suppose that each new production is replaced at its FTP convention:

- Libor based loans are refinanced through Libor based Interbank borrowings.
- Libor based debt is refinanced through Libor based Interbank loans.
- Fixed rate loans are refinanced through fixed rate debts.

In our example when interest rates increase, the ALM income increases too. However, the Commercial Department income increases too and its growth is really higher than the ALM income growth.

The interest rate gap showed an exposure to interest rate decreases and said roughly that a swap on the 5th year horizon for an amount of around 13 could hedge the position.

On the other hand, the sensitivity computation shows a net income sensitivity of 0.43 on the 5th year horizon for a decrease of interest rates of 100 bps; this requires an investment in a swap of an amount of 43 in order to hedge the risk.

This example shows how interest rate gaps and income sensitivities may produce different risk analyses: those analyses are "a priori" difficult to conciliate. In the next chapters, we will explain how to propose a more efficient approach to measure the risk. *The usual source of the observed differences between gap and sensitivity indicators is the lack of modelling or the bad comprehension of the indicators.*

19.3.6.1.2.2 Main hypotheses

19.3.6.1.2.2.1 *ALM incomes and Commercial Department incomes simulation*

A/L managers have to compute income sensitivities for each book and to distinguish the ALM income sensitivity and the Commercial Department sensitivity computation.

Indeed, sensitivities computation allows the A/L manager to *backtest* the budgeted incomes: sensitivities help to explain income variations around the past budgeted incomes.

Moreover, it completes the budgetary computations in a prospective way and not only in a retrospective way.

Month after month, the income sensitivity computation helps to forecast future incomes on a long-term horizon and to verify the coherence between the different books.

Income sensitivities are often computed based on the net interest margins. This is a very noticeable and hazardous mistake. It is worthiest to compute sensitivities *based on the net income* rather than based on the net interest margins. As we will see it later, operational costs and commissions growths are highly correlated with the net interest margins levels.

19.3.6.1.2.2.2 *Horizon*

Horizon computation of the income sensitivities is often close to the company budget horizon. Some companies compute only 1 year or 2 years' income sensitivities.

Others will choose longer horizons such as 5 or 10 years, close to medium or long-term budget plans.

Quite often, companies think that visibility is difficult after 5 or 10 years and that the accuracy of the hypotheses is really lower on the long-term. Especially, replacements hypotheses take a large part of the income in the 5/10 years horizon.

Scenario			Y	Y+1	Y+2	Y+3	Y+4
Standard scenario		Short term rate	3.00 %	4.00 %	4.20 %	4.30 %	4.50 %
		Long term rate	4.00 %	4.10 %	4.20 %	4.30 %	4.40 %
		Inflation	2.00 %	2.00 %	2.00 %	2.00 %	2.00 %
		Projected income	**0.50**	**0.52**	**0.53**	**0.55**	**0.56**
		ALM income	−0.10	−0.06	−0.01	− 0.01	− 0.01
		Commercial income	0.60	0.57	0.54	0.55	0.57
Rising rates scenario		Short term rate	3.50 %	4.50 %	5.20 %	5.30 %	5.50 %
		Long term rate	4.50 %	4.60 %	5.20 %	5.30 %	5.40 %
		Inflation	2.25 %	2.25 %	2.50 %	2.50 %	2.50 %
		Projected income	0.57	0.62	0.80	0.86	0.92
		ALM income	−0.10	−0.06	−0.01	−0.01	−0.01
		Commercial income	0.67	0.67	0.81	0.87	0.93
	Interest income interest expenses	Fixed rate loans	0.02	0.05	0.17	0.24	0.32
		Floating rate loans	0.02	0.20	0.40	0.40	0.40
		Net treasury	0.04	0.07	0.14	0.14	0.13
		Current accounts	–	–	–	–	–
		Libor Based debt	–	−0.20	−0.40	−0.40	−0.40
		Equity	–	–	–	–	–
		Receiver swaps	–	–	–	–	–
		Net interest margin	**0.08**	**0.12**	**0.31**	**0.38**	**0.45**
		Operational costs	−0.01	−0.02	−0.04	−0.07	−0.09
		Net income	**0.07**	**0.10**	**0.27**	**0.31**	**0.36**
Decreasing rates scenario		Short term rate	2.50 %	3.50 %	3.20 %	3.30 %	3.50 %
		Long term rate	3.50 %	3.60 %	3.20 %	3.30 %	3.40 %
		Inflation	1.75 %	1.75 %	1.50 %	1.50 %	1.50 %
		Projected income	0.43	0.37	0.20	0.17	0.13
		ALM income	−0.10	−0.06	−0.01	−0.01	−0.01
		Commercial income	0.53	0.43	0.21	0.18	0.14
	Interest income interest expenses	Fixed rate loans	−0.02	−0.05	−0.17	−0.24	−0.32
		Floating rate loans	−0.02	−0.20	−0.40	−0.40	−0.40
		Net treasury	−0.04	−0.11	−0.20	−0.20	−0.21
		Current accounts	–	–	–	–	–
		Libor Based debt	–	0.20	0.40	0.40	0.40
		Equity	–	–	–	–	–
		Receiver swaps	–	–	–	–	–
		Net interest margin sensitivity	**−0.08**	**−0.16**	**−0.37**	**−0.44**	**−0.53**
		Operational costs	0.01	0.02	0.04	0.07	0.09
		Net income sensitivity	**−0.07**	**−0.14**	**−0.33**	**−0.38**	**−0.43**

Figure 19.24 Income sensitivity

Choosing a sensitivity computation horizon of *5 or 10 years is a minimum.* Choosing a longer horizon is more appropriate but requires more competences in modelling and especially in macroeconomics models for the new production modelling.

19.3.6.1.2.2.3 *Scenario types to perform*

In the presentation of income sensitivity, the choice of the scenarios is of prime importance. The risk is represented only on a few numbers of scenarios that have to be probable for A/L managers. The central scenario is usually a budget scenario (close to the budget scenario presented to the analyst during the company budget presentations). This scenario is close to the forward rates scenario (the average interest rates anticipated by the market).

The *set of proposed scenarios around the central budget scenario* should represent:

- rising rates scenarios;
- decreasing rates scenarios;
- a steeper yield curve (for example a scenario where short-term rate do not move but long-term rates increase);
- a yield curve flattening;
- a margin flattening;
- a customer behavioural change (for example a 10 % demand deposit runoff).

An infinite number of scenarios may be proposed. For each scenario a second axis, the time axis adds more complexity to the scenario choice: for the rising rate scenario, on which horizon have we to put an interest rate rise shock?

- shocks on the initial spot curve (budget curve) and on the implied forwards;
- shocks on the forward rates year by year, etc.

Indeed, a spot shock affecting all the forwards will not produce the same sensitivities results as a *progressive shock* on the forwards. Here are some possible interest rate shocks on the same short-term forward rate:

	Y	Y+1	Y+2	Y+3	Y+4
Budget scenario	3.00 %	4.00 %	4.20 %	4.30 %	4.50 %
Uniform shock	3.50 %	4.50 %	4.70 %	4.80 %	5.00 %
Shock in Y+2 after	3.00 %	4.00 %	4.70 %	4.80 %	5.00 %
Shock in Y+2 only	3.00 %	4.00 %	4.70 %	4.30 %	4.50 %

Figure 19.25 Shocks

All these questions show that income sensitivities are an interesting indicator, but this indicator needs to be described precisely. For this reason, we will introduce in the last chapters of this book different risk measures to capture the entire risk dimension: the stress scenarios and the sensitivities of the expected incomes to Libor forwards.

19.3.6.1.2.2.4 *New production*

The main interest in computing income sensitivities is to introduce the new productions into the indicator.

New productions introduction means the introduction of many different hypotheses:

- hypotheses on the new production volumes;
- hypotheses on the margins on these new volumes;
- hypotheses on the FTP on these new volumes;
- hypotheses on the hedging strategies on these new volumes.

There are three usual hypotheses about new production hedging:

- either the ALM hedges every new production; or
- the ALM has a constant position (for example if the ALM rolls a 1 billion 10 years swap: 100 million each year) and does not hedge new productions; or
- *the ALM hedges every new production but has a constant position.*

The last hypothesis is the more coherent with ALM activity.

19.3.6.1.2.2.5 *Options*

The income sensitivities indicator considers options more precisely than interest rate gaps did:

- In gaps, the options are translated into a static delta equivalent.
- In income sensitivities, the dynamic shows directly the non-linear option impact on the different interest rate scenarios.

19.3.6.1.2.2.6 *Interest rate and/or inflation sensitivities*

The indicator allows us not only to show income sensitivity to interest rate moves but also to inflation moves. A large part of the balance sheet is indeed exposed to concomitant inflation and interest rate moves.

19.3.6.1.2.2.7 *Income simulation*

The income simulation has to take into account all the sources of interest rate risk. For example, the A/L manager has to take into account in his income simulations:

- price/volume effects (correlation between volumes and interest rates);
- margin effects (correlation between margins and interest rates);
- customer behaviour models;
- pipeline effects modelling (differences between market conditions at the contract signature and at the refinancing date);
- prepayments and renegotiations (dependant on interest rates) even in investments such as MBS;
- Capital Book modelling;
- Dynamic hedging strategies;
- basis risk;
- FTP modelling;
- ALM financial risks strategies.

19.3.6.1.2.2.8 *Income discounting*

The large majority of A/L managers compute their income sensitivities on the current money basis.

On the other hand, it seems more coherent to **compute sensitivities based on the discounted incomes.**

For example, the value of an income of 10 in 5 years decreases when the zero-coupon interest rates move from 5 to 6 %. This value moves from 7.78 to 7.41. In other terms, it means that the expectation of return depends on the interest rate level: the company result should increase with interest rates in order to prevent economic value decreases.

If the company objective is to hedge discounted incomes, then *the company return growth will be indexed to the interest rates.*

On the other hand, if the company objective is to hedge incomes expressed in current money basis, the company is exposed to bad return on equity levels compared to the interest rate levels.

19.3.6.1.2.3 Discussion about the sensitivity indicator

Sensitivity indicator implementation implies the construction of a large number of hypotheses. Consequently, the sensitivity indicator is *an easily manipulated indicator*. Changing only one hypothesis, the indicator sign may change effortlessly!

Moreover, the introduction of *strategies* in the indicator allows us to transform the indicator results.

For example, consider the risk free strategy consisting into "investing 100 into long-term bonds borrowing through short-term investments if in one year the interest rates decrease by 1 %". This leads to an impact in the net income simulation as follows:

	Y	Y+1	Y+2	Y+3	Y+4
Standard scenario	–	–	–	–	–
Rising rate scenario	–	–	–	–	–
Decreasing rate scenario	–	0.1	0.4	0.3	0.1

Figure 19.26 Decreasing rate scenario

In other ways, it is possible through strategies (of FTP) to compute a strategy that has a positive sensitivity in every future scenario!

For all these reasons, **imposing a regulatory limit on the sensitivities is very dangerous.**

Only normalized hypotheses amongst A/L managers may form a consensus for correct indicator computation.

19.3.6.1.2.4 Reconciliation between gap analysis and sensitivity

Reconciliation between gap analysis and income sensitivity indicator is possible through many hypothesis:

- working with discounted incomes;
- working with a new production modelling coherent with economy (for example with a new production market value independent upon market rates);
- working with an hypothesis of perfect hedging of new productions;
- working with long-term horizons.

The proper framework to conciliate all these hypotheses is the *economic value framework* described in the last chapters of this book.

19.3.6.1.3 Implicit demand deposit or equity placements

Other complementary indicators are sometimes used by A/L managers. They tend to transpose the interest rate gap in front of the equity or the other liabilities without maturity.

In our example, the interest rate gap could be used to compute the implicit placement of those liabilities without maturity such as in Figure 19.28.

Our example shows that the implicit placement is shorter than the FTP placement.

If the FTP convention may be criticized, the A/L manager may prefer to use such a representation to understand better the company exposure to interest rate risks.

	Today	1 month	3 months	6 months	1 year	3 years	5 years	10 years	More than 10 years
Cumulative interest rate gap	–	16	16	5	3	15	13	0	–
Current account and equity FTP placement	60	50	49	48	45	35	25	0	–
Current account equity implicit placement	60	34	34	43	42	20	12	–	–

Figure 19.27 Current account and equity implicit placement

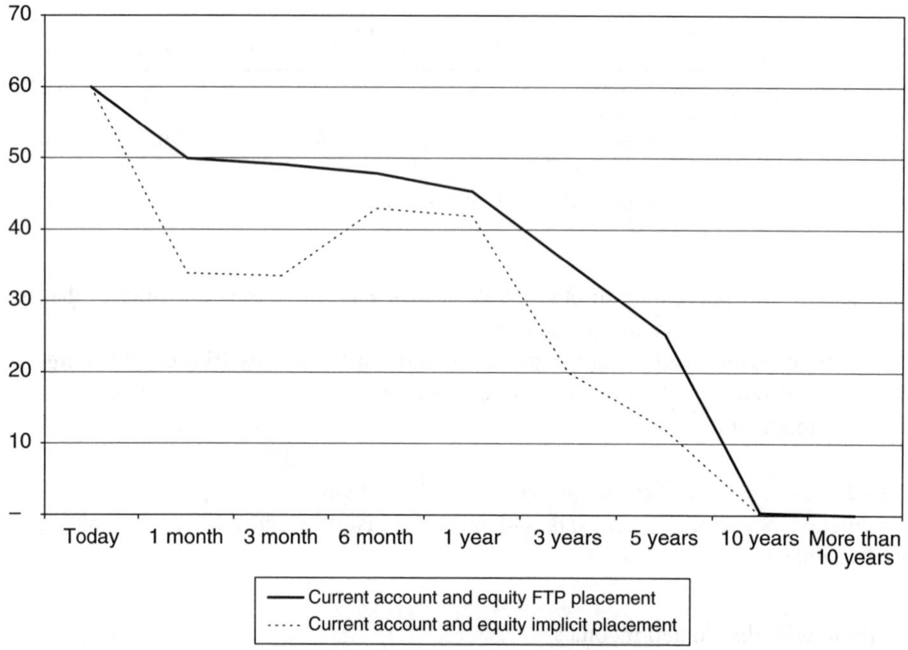

Figure 19.28 Implicit placement

19.3.6.1.4 Optional risk indicator

The optional risk indicator objective is to identify the amount of market interest rate options in order to protect the company against the extreme interest rate moves.

The objective of the delta equivalent computation is to minimize future incomes volatility with a firm hedging. Even if this minimization works, the income is still volatile since the income sensitivity to interest rates is not linear.

The indicator differs from a company to another but its construction principles are simple:

- Computation of the sensitivity of the interest rate gap to the interest rate levels: a *"gamma" sensitivity*.
- Translation of the gamma sensitivity in terms of hedging instruments: caps and floors or swaptions, for example.

	Today	1 month	3 month	6 month	1 year	3 years	5 years	10 years	More than 10 years
Delta equivalent	–	16.1	15.6	4.9	3.4	15.3	13.3	0.3	–
Delta equivalent + 1 %	–	16.2	15.7	4.9	3.5	15.5	13.5	0.3	–
Delta equivalent – 1 %	–	16.4	15.9	5.0	3.5	15.6	13.6	0.3	–
Delta equivalent + 2 %	–	16.5	16.0	5.0	3.5	15.7	13.7	0.3	–
Delta equivalent – 2 %	–	15.7	15.2	4.7	3.4	14.9	13.0	0.3	–
Caps at 6 %	–	24	24	7	5	23	20	1	–
Caps at 5 %	–	16	16	5	3	15	13	0	–
Floors at 3 %	–	32	31	10	7	31	27	1	–
Floors at 2 %	–	73	70	22	16	69	60	2	–

Figure 19.29 Optional risk indicator

The indicator explains the amount of caps and floors to buy for every strike, once the balance sheet is delta equivalent hedged.

19.3.6.1.5 Stress testing

Income sensitivities are typically computed on a set of plausible scenarios. This set of scenarios is restrictive and does not cover all the risk forms. Above all, the indicator does not treat the stressed scenarios.

Basel II provides now a framework for the computation of stress scenarios. Please refer to Chapter 24 for further information.

19.3.6.1.6 Economic value based indicators

Economic value based indicators are also introduced in the Basel II framework. This chapter gives a first approach of these indicators through the duration concept.

19.3.6.1.6.1 Duration and economic value sensitivity

Economic value represents the discounted value, the market value of the existing balance sheet products. This value is easy to compute with the help of the interest rate gap: the value is the discounting of the net incomes (computed on the basis of the interest rate schedules of the interest rate gap).

This determines an economic value for each balance sheet product and also the sensitivity of this economic value to interest rates.

The net economic value is the difference between the economic value and the book value.

The net economic value is decomposed as the sum of the expectations of future net incomes INC discounted with zero-coupons B:

$$NEV = \sum_{\text{month i}} E\,(\text{INC}_{\text{i}}.B(0,i)) \tag{19.46}$$

When breaking down the net incomes, this leads mathematically to the series of equations:

$$
\begin{aligned}
NEV &= \sum_{\text{month } i} E\left(\mathrm{K_i}.\left(\mathrm{FR_i} - \mathrm{DD_i}\right).B(0,i)\right) \\
NEV &= \sum_{\text{month } i} E\left(\mathrm{K_i}.\left(\mathrm{FR_i} - \left(\frac{B(0,i-1)}{B(0,i)} - 1\right)\right).B(0,i)\right) \\
NEV &= \sum_{\text{month } i} E\left(\mathrm{K_i}.\left(\mathrm{FR_i}.B(0,i) - \left(B(0,i-1) - B(0,i)\right)\right)\right) \\
NEV &= \sum_{\text{month } i} E\left(\mathrm{K_i}.\left((1+\mathrm{FR_i}).B(0,i) - B(0,i-1)\right)\right) \\
NEV &= \sum_{\text{month } i} E\left(\left(\mathrm{K_i}.(1+\mathrm{FR_i}) - \mathrm{K_{i+1}}\right).B(0,i)\right) - \mathrm{K_0} \\
NEV &= \sum_{\text{month } i} E\left(\left(\mathrm{K_i} - \mathrm{K_{i+1}} + \mathrm{K_i}.\mathrm{FR_i}\right).B(0,i)\right) - \mathrm{K_0}
\end{aligned}
\tag{19.47}
$$

> The net economic value is the sum of the expected incomes and the sum of the cash flows (interest rates and amortizing cash flows) less the book value.

The economic value follows:

$$
EV = \sum_{\text{month } i} E\left(\left(\mathrm{K_i} - \mathrm{K_{i+1}} + \mathrm{K_i}.\mathrm{FR_i}\right).B(0,i)\right) \tag{19.48}
$$

The sensitivity of the economic value is the derivative of the economic value to interest rate level. In a balance sheet without options, the zero-coupon and its sensitivities are easy to compute:

$$
\begin{aligned}
B(0,i) &= \frac{1}{(1+r_i)^i} \\
\frac{dB(0,i)}{dr_i} &= -\frac{i}{(1+r_i)^{i+1}}
\end{aligned}
\tag{19.49}
$$

Thus, the computation of the economic value sensitivity follows:

$$
\begin{aligned}
S &= \frac{dEV}{dr} = \sum_{\text{month } i} \left(\left(\mathrm{K_i} - \mathrm{K_{i+1}} + \mathrm{K_i}.\mathrm{FR_i}\right).\frac{dB(0,i)}{dr_i}\right) \\
S &= -\sum_{\text{month } i} \left(\left(\mathrm{K_i} - \mathrm{K_{i+1}} + \mathrm{K_i}.\mathrm{FR_i}\right).\frac{i}{(1+r_i)^{i+1}}\right)
\end{aligned}
\tag{19.50}
$$

The *duration* such as the *Macaulay duration* represents a modified version of the average life defined as the division of the sensitivity of economic value by the economic value (with a corrective interest rate term) as follows:

$$
D = -\frac{(1+r).S}{EV} = \frac{\sum_{\text{month } i} \left(\left(\mathrm{K_i} - \mathrm{K_{i+1}} + \mathrm{K_i}.\mathrm{FR_i}\right).\frac{i}{(1+r_i)^i}\right)}{\sum_{\text{month } i} \left(\left(\mathrm{K_i} - \mathrm{K_{i+1}} + \mathrm{K_i}.\mathrm{FR_i}\right).\frac{1}{(1+r_i)^i}\right)} \tag{19.51}
$$

In our example, the duration computation gives the results in Figure 19.30.

Since current accounts have a long duration, our balance sheet is exposed to interest rate increases! Even if the income sensitivity indicator and the interest rate gap showed an exposure to interest rates decreases!

	Book value	Economic value	Sensitivity of economic value to 1% interest rate rise	Duration
Loans	80.00	85.00	8.00	9.79
Net treasury	20.00	20.00	–	–
Total Assets schedule	100.00	105.00	8.00	7.83
Current accounts	50.00	30.00	5.00	17.83
Debt	40.00	40.00	–	–
Equity	10.00	10.00	0.50	5.20
Total Liabilities schedule	100.00	80.00	5.50	7.15
Balance sheet	–	25.00	2.50	

Figure 19.30 Duration

This example shows the inconvenience of such a sensitivity indicator (i.e. an indicator of duration): it summarizes risk in one indicator and does not focus on accounting A/L managers' problems with hedging annual incomes.

19.3.6.1.6.2 Value-at-Risk and spectral risk measures

By the end of the 90s, some companies experienced risk measures (initially developed for trading activities) based on the economic value such as the *Value-at-Risk (VaR)* or *spectral risk measures* (like expected shortfall: ES):

- The VaR represents an economic value variation quantile over a specific time period.
- The expected shortfall represents the expected variation of the economic value below an economic value variation quantile over a specific time period (see section 23.1).

Those indicators have the same inconvenience as duration: they project risk into only one number and do not take into account the accounting perspective.

19.3.6.1.7 Conclusions on interest rate risk measures

The choice of a risk measure is important: it should take into account the accounting perspective, the new production effects, a complete modelling of the balance sheet, etc.

Other interest rate risk measures have to be developed by companies in order to provide a unique risk description to executive managers during the ALCO.

19.3.7 Interest rate risk factor simulation

What we call a yield curve model is an interest rate evolution model, often a stochastic model based on the zero-coupon yield or on the forward yield curves.

The interest rate models require a zero-coupon yield curve reconstitution:

- Evaluate the marked-to-market of fixed flows products (such as fixed rate bond).
- Retrieve the implicit yield curves (forward yield curves for example) from the market yield curves.
- Develop a basis for yield curve deformation in interest rates stochastic models.

Stochastic interest rate models were first developed by interest rate derivative market traders to get:

- market prices for derivative products;
- hedging strategy for those products as soon as they are sold.

Those models were in the beginning used in the trading portfolios with impacts on all the logistic chain:

- front office (traders);
- middle office;
- back office;
- market risk controllers, etc.

However, portfolio managers use also these models:

- managers in Asset Management;
- bank A/L managers;
- insurance A/L managers.

In this context, we use these interest models for their simulation ability:

- The manager wishes to simulate the portfolio return as a function of the interest rate level.
- The manager wishes to analyse the impact of the different interest rate scenarios and the impact of the different strategies on income.

Interest rate models will help income prediction and risk computation.

We develop the main interest rate models in section 21.3.

19.3.8 Interest rate risk hedging

Interest rate hedging products may take various forms:

- fixed rate loans or deposits;
- interest rate swaps;
- forward interest rate swaps;
- CMS swaps;
- caps/floors Libor;
- caps/floors CMS;
- swaptions;
- fixed rate debt issues;
- other structured derivative product types.

19.4 INFLATION RISK

19.4.1 Macroeconomic point of view: the links between inflation, interest rates and economic growth

The Consumer Price Index (CPI) represents in a currency the evolution of the price of an average basket, the "housewife basket". This basket is made of all the products usually bought by the consumers.

For example, the table below gives an example of the weighting used in the CPI constitution.

	Weighting in CPI index
Food	17 %
Tobacco	2 %
Manufactured products	30 %
Energy	7 %
Services	36 %
Housing	7 %

Figure 19.31 CPI index composition

The inflation represents the CPI growth expressed in an annual basis:

$$\text{Inflation}\ (t) = \text{IPC}(t)/\text{IPC}(t-12) - 1 \tag{19.52}$$

Inflation is a highly seasonal and autoregressive variable. The seasonality depends on the country.

The evolution of inflation follows "regimes". It means that this evolution proceeds in stages. However, in practice, regime changes are pretty hard to predict.

Inflation is monitored by Central Banks, especially by independent Central Banks. For example, one of the first targets of the ECB (European Central Bank) is to maintain an inflation level under 2 %.

Macroeconomics and the growth theory prove that *there is a link on the long-term between the real rates and the economic growth*:

$$\begin{aligned} \text{Nominal GDP growth} &= \text{Inflation} + \text{Real GDP growth} \\ \text{Nominal Rates} &= \text{Inflation} + \text{Real Rates} \end{aligned} \tag{19.53}$$

The real rate is by definition the simple difference between the nominal rates and inflation.

The GDP represents the Growth Domestic Product; this is the annual wealth production. The nominal GDP growth is the GDP annual variation and the real GDP growth is netted by the inflation.

Macroeconomics link in fact the wealth evolution and the real rates but on the long-term, the wealth growth is comparable with GDP growth.

Another part of the macroeconomic growth theory links (on the long-term) economic growth with demographic growth and productivity growth:

$$\text{Real GDP} = \text{Demographic growth} + \text{Productivity growth} \tag{19.54}$$

The productivity growth is often linked with the impact of research and of improvements in technology in the economy and in productivity.

Actually, inflation and real interest rates are more linked with the global Wealth W of the economy. GDP characterizes the wealth growth. More precisely, the global economy wealth follows this equation:

$$dW(t) = GDP\ (t)\ .\ dt - \alpha.W(t)\ dt \tag{19.55}$$

The second part of the equation deals with "an economy wealth waste due to time that goes".

As a conclusion, the global wealth follows:

$$W(t) = \int_{-\infty}^{t} GDP(s).\exp\left(-\alpha.\left(t - s\right)\right).ds \tag{19.56}$$

There may be an arbitrage between borrowing money and creating wealth with this money borrowed. For example, the short term interest rate r(t) has to be compared with GDP(t)/W(t) the relative value of GDP over the economy wealth.

It is important to notice that *the computation of inflation takes into account productivity growth*. From one period to another, the statisticians in charge of this computation do not compare the pure evolution of the prices but the evolution of the prices for the existing products at the beginning of the period.

For example, everyone understands that when computing the evolution of computer prices, the statisticians compare the same product each month even if this product becomes easier to produce or to copy: this way the price of computers decreases every month. On the other hand, customers always try to buy new generation of computer and they never see the prices going down.

19.4.2 Balance sheet inflation risk

It is not easy to determine the importance of the inflation risk in the balance sheet.

First, some products get a direct indexation to inflation. For example, in France, banks are used to selling savings with an explicit relationship between the customer remuneration rate and the inflation index. When inflation is growing, the interest rate to be paid to the client increases: this represents a cost for the bank.

Many savings accounts worldwide have an implicit indexation to the inflation rate. The savings rate could be partly correlated with the inflation rate creating the same kind of inflation risk in a balance sheet.

However, more generally, every company is exposed to the inflation risk. Many income statement lines may vary according to the inflation index such as *staff costs* or other operating costs.

On the other hand, many incomes may have an inflation-linked growth.

Sometimes, companies take an inflation risk in their investment portfolio when they invest, for instance, in inflation linked bonds. The portfolio is then better diversified with the introduction of those bonds, and especially the Capital Banking Book portfolio, for instance. On the other hand, a company may issue its debt with an inflation-indexed coupon.

19.4.3 Inflation market

The inflation market started with the introduction of inflation linked bonds in the 80s. The principal characteristics of these bonds are detailed in this table:

	UK Linkers	TIPS (US)	OATi (FR)	OAT€I (FR EU CPI based)	Italy
First issuance	1981	1997	1998	2001	2003
Reference Index	RPI monthly	CPI-U monthly	CPI France ex-tobacco	HICP EMU ex-tobacco (€ harmonized inflation index)	HICP EMU ex-tobacco
Coupon	Semi-annual (prefixed)	Semi-annual	Annual	Annual	Semi-annual
Principal	8 months Lag	3 months Lag	3 months Lag	3 months Lag	3 months Lag
Repayment of principal	No Floor	Floor at 100	Floor at 100	Floor at 100	Floor at 100

Figure 19.32 Inflation linked bonds

This bond pays coupons indexed to a consumer price index. The principal repaid at maturity is indexed to the same consumer price index.

The inflation linked bond price follows:

$$P_{full} = P_{quoted} \cdot \frac{CPI_t}{CPI_0} = \left(\sum_{j=t}^{T} \left(\frac{coupon}{(1+r)^j} \right) + \frac{100}{(1+r)^T} \right) \frac{CPI_t}{CPI_0} \qquad (19.57)$$

"r" is the bond real rate as it is quoted in the market. T is the bond maturity.

P represents the price of the bond. There is also a difference between the quoted market price and the full price (the price effectively paid for one unit of currency of bond nominal).

Thanks to the inflation-linked bond, the inflation market expanded rapidly to inflation swaps and to inflation options. As it is the case for nominal bonds, the introduction of inflation-linked bonds was quickly followed by the introduction of the risk neutral model: it is now possible to simulate interest rates and inflation under the risk neutral probability.

In practice, the inflation market simulation considers *the real rate yield curve as an independent yield curve* as if it was the yield curve of another currency. The currency is the housewife basket and the real rate is the rate available for this currency.

In the interest rate risk chapter, we defined the existence of the forward interest rates. Similarly, it is possible to characterize the existence of the forward inflation rates and of the real forward rates too. Investors may compare directly, for example, the forward real rates and their own anticipation. The investment decision may be driven directly by this comparison. A macroeconomic point of view is often useful when making such an investment decision: investing in real interest rates is often imprudent when the manager anticipates a strengthening of real economic growth.

This inflation market allows new hedging possibilities. The table in Figure 19.33 provides a list of possible hedging strategies.

More than the introduction of new hedging possibilities, the inflation market allows managers to take inflation positions, to diversify their risk exposures and to contribute to

Operation Type	Receiver part	Payer part	Hedging purpose
Classic swap	Fixed rate	Short-term rate	Against short-term rates variation
Real Rate swap	(Real) Fixed rate plus inflation	Short-term rate	Against short-term real rates variation
Inflation swap	(Real) Fixed rate plus inflation	Fixed rate	Against inflation variation

Figure 19.33 Inflation derivatives

market efficiency. This diversification allows one, for instance, to get a higher efficient frontier in the construction of asset management portfolios (see Chapter 23).

In some countries, the inflation market may present arbitrage opportunities with disequilibrium between market players.

The classic inflation market players are:

- inflation linked bonds issuers such as governments or government agencies (i.e. issuers with inflation linked incomes);
- inflation exposed companies such as banks, insurance companies, asset managers, etc.;
- arbitrage market players such as hedge funds or other asset managers, etc.

Disequilibrium between the market players' volume may lead to a very strong risk premium as is often the case for the creation of new inflation markets.

The market for inflation options is becoming more and more developed. Options include inflation caps/floors, inflation or real rate swaptions, etc. The difficulty in this market is to get a proper price since inflation volatility or short-term rate/inflation correlation are traded infrequently among traders.

19.4.4 Inflation linked bonds accounting (at historical cost)

It is more difficult for accountants to measure inflation linked bonds than fixed rate bonds owing to the existence of two special elements:

- a discount or a premium to smooth (the difference between the disbursed cash and the nominal);
- a final reimbursement at maturity indexed to the inflation.

If a bank buys, at date s, an inflation-linked bond, the initial value to smooth will be of:

$$P_{quoted}(s).\frac{CPI_s}{CPI_0} - 100 \tag{19.58}$$

The smoothing is made either actuarially either linearly.

On the other hand, the final capital reimbursement at date T will be of:

$$100.\frac{CPI_T}{CPI_0} \tag{19.59}$$

The difference between this amount and the initial amount of 100 has also to be smoothed (consequently, there is not a too important final cash flow to account at maturity date).

$$100.\left(\frac{CPI_t}{CPI_0} - \frac{CPI_{t-1}}{CPI_0}\right) \quad (19.60)$$

At date t, the accountants will finally measure after refinancing cost (at DD rate r(t)) the difference between the bond real rate and the market real rate:

$$\begin{aligned} & Income_t \approx P_{quoted}(s).\,(\text{Bond Real rate}_s - \text{Market Real rate}_t) \\ & \text{Market Real rate}_t = (r(t) - \text{inflation}(t)) \end{aligned} \quad (19.61)$$

The bond real rate is a function of the coupon and of the quoted price exposed above.

19.4.5 Impact of inflation risk on incomes

As shown above, the impact of inflation on incomes may take different forms:

- Impact on the net interest income due to the presence of inflation linked bonds. A market real rate increase will stress the incomes arising from ILBs. The impact is the same as for classic fixed term bonds but in another currency, the household basket currency.
- Impact on directly/indirectly inflation indexed products. Savings will incorporate a remuneration indexed to inflation and this indexation (if not hedged) introduces directly volatility in the results.
- Impact on the operating costs line. The impact of inflation on this line is cumulative: an increase in inflation has consequences over many periods.
- Impact on income growth: many new production volume growths will depend on inflation and on market technology development. Inflation effect may differ from the real rate effect; such an inflation effect will also last for many years.

19.4.6 Indicators to monitor inflation risk

The A/L manager has to consider inflation as another currency even in risk monitoring. It means that *inflation representation is double*:

- in a real interest rate gap;
- in the net open currency position.

For example, in a balance sheet where all the equity is invested in 5 years inflation linked bonds, the real rate gap is the following:

	Today	1 Y	2 Y	3 Y	4 Y	5 Y	6 Y	7 Y	8 Y
Equity Capital	100	–	–	–	–	–	–	–	–
10 years ILB	– 100	– 100	– 100	– 100	– 100	– 100	–	–	–
Real interest gap	–	– 100	– 100	– 100	– 100	– 100	–	–	–

Figure 19.34 Real rate gap

The net open currency position report will take into account the household basket as another currency:

	EUR	USD	EUR Inflation
Equity Capital	50	50	–
10 years ILB	–	–	– 100
Net open currency position	50	50	– 100

Figure 19.35 Net open currency position

19.4.7 Inflation risk factor simulation

19.4.7.1 Market models

If the household basket has to be considered as another currency, the *inflation simulation* will be equivalent to the interest rates simulation in this other currency.

For instance, in a double one-factor model, the nominal and the real rates will be simulated conjointly as follows:

$$\begin{aligned} dr_t^{real} &= \lambda^{real}.\left(\Theta_t^{real} - r_t^{real}\right).dt + \sigma_t^{real}.dW_t^{real} \\ dr_t^{nominal} &= \lambda^{nominal}.\left(\Theta_t^{nominal} - r_t^{nominal}\right).dt + \sigma_t^{nominal}.dW_t^{nominal} \\ \left\langle dW_t^{nominal} \mid dW_t^{real}\right\rangle &= \rho.dt \end{aligned} \tag{19.62}$$

The model includes two Brownian motions W with a correlation ρ and two mean reverting processes with a speed λ and a long-term mean reversion Θ.

19.4.7.2 Economist models

Economist models will link market rates, inflation, and the other macroeconomic variables. Those models developed by Central Banks are the famous "co-integration models" such as VAR (Vector Auto Regressive models).

A vector variable X will contain all the macroeconomic variables such as inflation, interest rates or GDP. This variable follows the VAR model:

$$\begin{aligned} &(X_t - X_{t-1}) = A.X_{t-1} + E(t) \\ &X_t = \begin{pmatrix} M2_t \\ CPI_t \\ GDP_t \\ Population_t \\ Revenues_t \\ Consumption_t \\ Interestrates_t \end{pmatrix} \\ &E(t) \sim \mathrm{N}(0, \mathrm{Id_N}) \end{aligned} \tag{19.63}$$

The parameters A and B of the matrix models are calibrated over past observations. However, the analysis of historical data shows the presence of *regimes*:

- During long periods, the short-term interest rates evolution will follow the evolution of inflation and brutally, this relation will disappear: the evolution of interest rates will follow the evolution of the interest rates. This creates two regimes.
- Regime changes predictions are problematical. Links are unstable.

Consequently, correlation between inflation and market rates is very volatile.

19.4.8 Inflation risk hedging

The inflation market is a good hedging source:

- Inflation linked bonds protect against real rate risk.
- Issue of inflation linked bonds introduce an opposite real rate risk in the balance sheet.
- Inflation swaps, real rate swaps (cumulative or additive inflation) will introduce leverage effects in the hedging strategy.
- Real rate swaptions will hedge the existing options on the level of the real rates.

19.5 CURRENCY RISK

Currency risk is often split between different risk types:

- trading book currency risk;
- net open currency position in the balance sheet;
- structural currency risk on company investments (investment in cash or through borrowings);
- currency risk on earnings or on incomes.

Currency risk hedging is often driven by:

- spot currency deals called "spot" deals;
- conditional spot (orders given to market players in order to hedge the risk in case of too large market currency move);
- forward deals such as term currency deals;
- non delivery forwards (NDF);
- option such as currency call or put option.

The entire currency risk hedging strategy depends on the IFRS hedging treatment and on the type of currency risk hedged.

19.5.1 Trading Book currency risk

The Trading Book currency positions are directly recorded in the Trading Book at their market prices. Hedging instruments are also recorded at marked-to-market in the earnings report.

The risk arising from a currency position mismatch is regulated through the Basel II Market Risk regulation framework.

19.5.2 Net open currency position in the balance sheet

The net open currency position is for every currency the difference between the total asset amount and the total liability amount in this currency.

To compute this indicator the balance sheet includes all kinds of options, spot contracts, forward contracts, etc.

The table below provides an example of computation of a net open currency position:

	EUR	USD	Total
Assets	113	47	160
Liabilities	– 90	– 50	– 140
Equity	– 20		– 20
Currency forward	– 5	5	–
Net open currency position	– 2	2	
Net open currency position as a % of equity	10.0 %	–10.0 %	

Figure 19.36 Net open currency position

A limit is often set as a percentage of the net total equity. This limit may be regulatory.

The equity line is expressed in the reporting currency. Sometimes, regulators allow banks to set equity in a strong currency such as USD or EURO if the shareholder wants his bank to be hedged in a stronger currency than his local currency.

A currency position may create an important P&L (present in the income statement line called "gain less losses arising from currency trading").

For example, a net open currency position representing 10 % of the equity, associated with a currency volatility of 15 % is associated with a potential 3 % equity potential loss at a 1-year horizon with a 99 % confidence interval.

However, compared to the taken risk, the profit may be important. For example, in some volatile markets, treasurers often take "carry trade positions". The treasurer borrows money in a low rate currency and lend into another currency with higher rates. Quite often, the deal wins since currency exchange rate evolution is slow and the "carry" is important.

The currency exchange rates may evolve very fast as shown in the chart 19.37.

Of course, internal limits should include strong constraints in order to avoid important currency risk positions.

19.5.3 Investments and currency risk

The first specific currency risk position is created by currency company investments. The hedging of this position (also called structural currency risk position) is linked with the initial financing choice of these investments.

19.5.3.1 Relevant assets

The relevant assets are:

- branches' endowments;
- participations in subsidiaries;
- equity securities;
- non equity securities;
- investment securities.

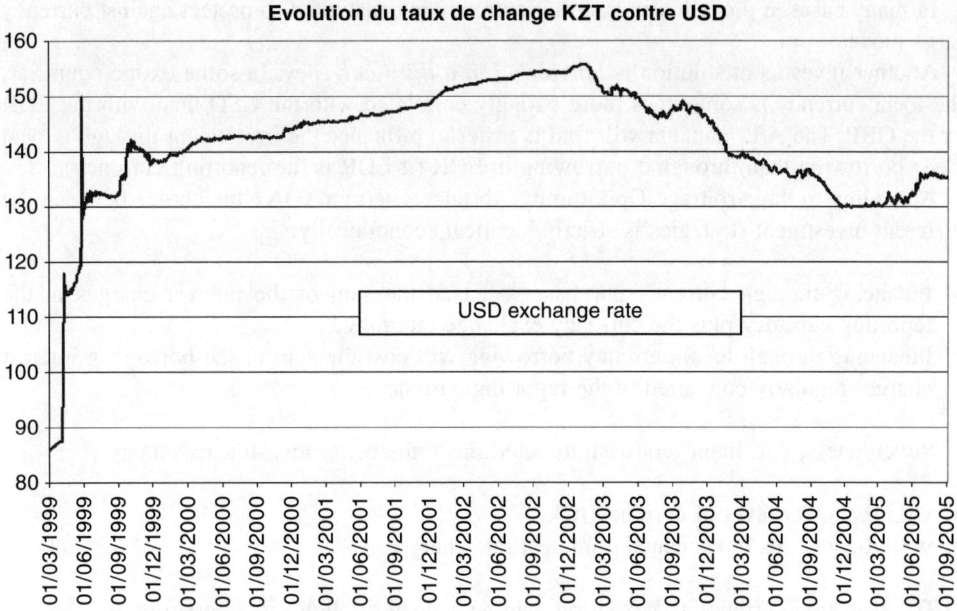

Figure 19.37 Currency exchange rate

All these asset lines are present in the Capital Banking Book.

The currency structural position is the set of all these assets financed initially through a foreign exchange purchase. Of course, if these assets are financed through a borrowing in the investment currency, this does not lead to a currency position.

19.5.3.2 Principles

An investment through borrowing does not produce a currency position. Nevertheless, investments could be done through a foreign exchange purchase. This choice is explained by:

- the currency liquidity;
- the hedging horizon;
- the currency exchange rate level;
- the interest rate level.

Moreover, for investments through borrowing, the A/L manager has to choose the borrowing maturity and to borrow once more after each borrowing maturity date. This investment type creates an interest rate risk position.

Investments in countries where the currency is very liquid are often made through borrowings. The borrowing maturity and the borrowing nature (fixed or Libor based) deals with the Capital Banking Book interest rate hedging position.

When buying currency, not only a direct currency position is taken but also an interest rate risk position since this creates a short-term refinancing in the reporting currency.

Usually, in exotic countries, dealing with non-liquid currencies, the usual practice is to buy the local currency and to consider thereafter equity replacement solutions.

In many cases, a provision in a strong currency is constituted to protect against currency large moves.

Another investment solution is *borrowing in a third currency*. In some exotic countries, the local currency is sometimes more strongly correlated with the USD than with the EUR or the GBP. The A/L manager will find it easier to refinance the investment through a local USD borrowing than through a borrowing in EUR (if EUR is the reporting currency).

According to the Arbitrage Opportunity Absence Theory (AOA), the choice between the different investment strategies is strictly identical economically:

- Financing through currency purchase will cost the sum of the interest charges in the reporting currency plus the currency exchange rate move.
- Financing through local currency borrowing will cost the sum of the borrowing interest charges regularly converted in the reporting currency.

Nevertheless, A/L managers wish to determinate the better investment strategy:

- with the lower level of currency risk;
- with the less costly refinancing interest rate charges.

The structural currency risk position may be hedged through spot operations.

It is also possible to substitute a financing through currency purchase by a financing through borrowing. However, the reciprocal operation is not possible.

19.5.3.3 Regulatory constraints

Regulators usually associate many constraints with the structural currency risk position:

- It is prohibited to finance through borrowings more than the effective recorded assets in the balance sheet.

When the group equity exceeds in a currency the group investment in this currency (due to a local conservation of the previous positives results), it is impossible to hedge through borrowings the net currency position.

- This is also the same at a consolidated level: the total borrowings in a currency cannot exceed the equity total amount in this currency.
- The group borrowing capacity is under liquidity ratios constraints.

19.5.3.4 IFRS treatment

IFRS (with IAS 21, 29 and 39) did not really change the previous accounting treatment for structural currency positions: the P&L impact is still the same but a hedging relationship between the currency borrowing and the investment has to be documented precisely.

19.5.3.4.1 Monetary and non monetary elements

In IFRS, the notion of structural currency position is left behind.

The norm distinguishes monetary instruments (debt instruments) and non-monetary instruments (equity instruments) for the currency moves accounting:

- For the monetary instruments, currency moves are accounted in the earnings report.
- For the non-monetary elements (elements that will be received or paid for non-determinable amounts), the currency moves are accounted at their fair value either in equity (as for available for sale instruments) either in earnings report (as for trading).

Participations in subsidiaries, branches' endowments and equity securities are accounted as AFS.

19.5.3.4.2 Investment hedging

IFRS asks for a hedging demonstration in the eventuality of a subsidiary participation financed through a borrowing. Otherwise, there may be an asymmetrical booking of the currency moves in the earnings report (for the borrowing) and in the equity (for the participation).

IFRS distinguishes two types of hedging relationships depending on the participation characteristics (consolidated or non-consolidated):

- For the consolidated participations, the *Net Investment Hedge (NIH)* is proposed.

Currency moves in the consolidated participation and in the investment are accounted in the equity.

- For the non-consolidated participations, the *Fair Value Hedge (FVH)* is proposed.

Currency moves on the non-consolidated participation and on the investment are accounted in the earnings report.

Every hedging relationship should document (with effectiveness tests) the link between the hedged element and the hedging instrument as soon as this hedging is an internal hedging and not an external hedging.

When investments are financed through currency purchase, this creates a structural currency position: the translation adjustments from the historical purchase rate are recorded in the balance sheet.

When investments are financed through currency borrowings, the translation adjustment is fixed and maintained in the balance sheet.

Special accounting rules apply to the disinvestment or to the cases of negative endowments.

Valuation allowances may be recorded to take into account the value decrease of a structural position asset. Those allowances are recorded in the local currency:

- If the security was financed through borrowings, the provision is recorded through a currency sale on the market.
- If the security was financed through currency purchases, the provision is recorded through a direct record on the earnings report.

19.5.3.4.3 Analytical equity refinancing

At a company/group level, the equity costs are passed directly on to the subsidiaries/branches.

At the subsidiary level, the allocated equity billing currency is often the equity redeployment currency in order to hedge the interest rate risk.

The currency risk may be recharged to subsidiaries in the largest companies.

19.5.4 Currency risk on earnings

Another currency risk component is the risk linked with the results in currencies different from the company reporting currency:

- holding incomes in foreign currencies;
- subsidiaries' incomes in foreign currencies;
- subsidiaries' dividends in foreign currencies.

The results in foreign currencies will affect a group at different levels:

- At a local level: between the result currency and the local currency.
- At the group level: between the local currency results and the company reporting currency.
- At the group level: between the local currency dividends and the company reporting currency.

The currency risk is computed on the net income after taxes. Those results are usually recorded in the holding balance sheet using 1 month smoothed exchange rate. This 1 month smoothed exchange rate becomes then a benchmark for A/L managers in charge of the hedging of currency risk.

Branches incomes of year N are liquidated at the beginning of year N+1. The exchange rate used for the income integration in the holding company is usually the weighted average of the past four quarterly exchange rates (weighted by the income of each quarter).

Subsidiaries dividends are liquidated on their repatriation date.

19.5.4.1 Hedging, limits and model residual risk

Hedging is realized through spot currency purchases/sales, forward currency purchases/sales, non-delivery forwards (NDF) or currency risk options.

Many holding companies hedge currency risk since this risk may affect strongly the income and may cause a large gap between the budgeted incomes and the realized incomes.

Some A/L managers hedge the realized incomes: operations are recorded as soon as the information about the incomes is provided to the ALM front office. Some A/L managers hedge also the budgeted incomes.

The income arising from the hedging is often redistributed at a branch/subsidiary level: it is the difference between the hedging effective exchange rate and the accounting benchmark.

Income often comprises:

- realized income;
- unrealized (latent) income;
- fees;
- running costs;
- endowments;
- highly probable flows.

Of course, there is a residual model risk between the communication date of the income information and the conversion date. The impact of this risk on P&L is often divided in two:

- A position transfer income is computed between the month end exchange rate and the exchange rate of the income information date.
- A real hedged income is computed between the exchange rate of the income information date and the exchange rate of the hedging date.

Statistical studies sometimes allow A/L managers to forecast the future incomes in a certain confidence interval.

In non-liquid currencies, the currency risk position on incomes cannot be hedged because the illiquidity of the currency is too strong.

Limits are often proposed in order to control the currency risk exposure on incomes:

- limit in amount by currency;
- limit expressed in marked-to-market by currency;
- limit in amount for the overall position;
- limit expressed in marked-to market for the overall position.

The A/L manager's strategy often includes the management of these limits:

- "stop-loss limits" on the position (orders given to the market to sell the position if the losses exceed a specified limit);
- "take profit" strategies (inverse of the stop-loss limit);
- option sales.

19.5.4.2 IFRS treatment

It is not possible under the IFRS rules to propose direct hedges based on the income. However, it is possible to use future extremely probable interest rate cash flows (without any link with the currency risk hedging) to justify the currency hedging and then to avoid a marked-to-market in earnings report accounting for the hedging. Nevertheless, some large companies do not justify their hedging and record it directly in their trading portfolios.

Moreover, IFRS does not allow A/L managers to hedge interest rate cash flows in a certain currency when this currency is the subsidiary reporting currency (except for non-consolidated subsidiaries). For example, if the holding company reporting currency is the EUR, the USD interest income could be cash flow hedged through interest rate cash flows in non-US subsidiaries.

Income currency risk hedging instruments are:

- spot deals;
- forward deals;
- non delivery forwards;
- currency options (call/put, vanilla or exotic, etc.).

IFRS restricted the use of such instruments:

- Currency options have to be accounted as trading and are not recognized as hedging instruments.
- Forward deals and NDF are considered as options but are eligible for hedging.
- Spot deals are not eligible for hedging and are accounted as marked-to-market.

IFRS does not recognize internal deals as hedging eligible deals: for example a deal between the Forex dealing room and the ALM. However, to prove that an internal deal is a real hedging, the Forex dealing room has to prove that the deal is sent back to the market through another external deal.

A test of effectiveness of the CFH hedging has to be performed every month:

- on a prospective appreciation at the hedging date;
- on a retrospective appreciation: hedging instrument variations have to hedge the hedged instrument within a confidence interval of 80 %–125 %.

The fair value of the CFH instruments affects the equity but not the income.

19.5.5 Indicators to monitor currency risk

For each currency risk type (trading book, net open currency position, etc.), the A/L manager will propose an indicator in order to monitor the currency risk.

This indicator, as for the net open currency position, may split by currency the difference between the net exposure on this currency and the net hedge on this currency.

In this indicator, options can be introduced at their delta equivalent level:

	EUR	USD	Total
Required currency hedge	3	− 3	0
Currency hedge in the book	− 5	5	0
Forward hedges	− 3	3	0
Call option delta equivalent	− 2	2	0
Net Currency position	− 2	2	0

Figure 19.38 Net currency position

Nowadays, *economic capital* could become, as it is the case for the other risk types, a better indicator for monitoring currency risk exposure. This indicator is based on the computation of the company economic value currency by currency including:

- balance sheet items currency by currency;
- future income results components in fair value.

The economic capital summarizes the exposure level of currency risk in only one number (often calculated as the VaR – Value-at-Risk – of the economic value variation).

19.5.6 Currency risk factor simulation

Currency exchange rate simulation is easier to perform than interest rate simulation.

The exchange rate π follows a Brownian motion plus a drift:

$$\frac{d\pi_t}{\pi_t} = \mu(t).dt + \sigma_\pi.dW_\pi(t) \tag{19.64}$$

In fact using the arbitrage opportunity absence theory (AOA), the drift under a risk neutral probability is directly the difference between the short-term rates of the two currencies r(t) and r'(t). With the two short-term interest rates following a one-factor model, it means:

$$\begin{aligned} dr_t &= \lambda.(\theta_t - r_t).dt + \sigma.dW(t) \\ dr'_t &= \lambda'.(\theta'_t - r'_t).dt + \sigma'.dW'(t) \\ \frac{d\pi_t}{\pi_t} &= (r_t - r'_t).dt + \sigma_\pi.dW_\pi(t) \end{aligned} \tag{19.65}$$

Of course, one of the major difficulties when calibrating the model is to propose a good set of correlation parameters between the three Brownian motions.

19.6 CORPORATE STOCK MARKET RISK

19.6.1 Nature of corporate stock market risk and examples

Balance sheets include many sources of corporate stock market risk:

- The company will possibly detain stocks as investments.
- Banks or insurance companies will sell products implicitly or explicitly indexed to the stock market level.
- Banks gets incomes indexed to the stock market indexes.

For example, banks may ask their customers for a fee for in order to conserve stocks. The fee is proportional to the stock amount detained in the bank; therefore, the bank income is somehow proportional to the stock index level. When the stock index increases, the expected future incomes will increase too.

Consequently, corporate stock prices will affect the incomes level. The accounting impact depends on the accounting scheme.

19.6.2 Monitoring indicators

A/L managers will focus mainly on *sensitivity to the stock market indexes of the future incomes*. Usually, stock market indexes moves affect only the current income. However, sometimes, a stock index increase has a long-term impact on the incomes.

	Expected income					
	Y	Y + 1	Y + 2	Y + 3	Y + 4	Y + 5
Standard scenario	100	105	110	116	122	128
UK stock index increase +10 %	105	110	116	122	128	134
US stock index increase +10 %	103	108	114	119	125	131
Sensitivity to UK index increase	35	5	6	6	6	6
Sensitivity to US index increase	33	3	3	3	4	4

Figure 19.39 Stock index sensitivity

19.6.3 Stock market modelling and hedging

The stock market was of course one of the first markets to get a proper modelling with the Black & Scholes model (1973). In this model, the stock index S follows a Brownian motion with a trend indexed to the short-term interest rate r(t) without any dividends:

$$\frac{dS_t}{S_t} = r(t).dt + \sigma\,(t, S_t)\,.dW_t^{\text{risk neutral}} \tag{19.66}$$

This relationship exists also under real probability with a risk premium μ:

$$\frac{dS_t}{S_t} = (r(t) + \mu)\,.dt + \sigma\,(t, S_t)\,.dW_t^{\text{real}} \tag{19.67}$$

With this formula, stock index simulation is possible and easy. In addition, this formula allows us to price equity derivatives and for this reason, the Black & Scholes model initiated the development of the equity derivatives market.

Nowadays, many options exist in order to hedge the equity risk:

- equity stock acquisition;
- equity swaps; or
- every kind of equity derivatives (e.g. bonds where the coupon is a function of the stock index S).

19.7 REAL ESTATE RISK / PROPERTY RISK

19.7.1 Nature of real estate risk and examples

Balance sheets include many sources of real estate risk:

- The company will retain real estate as property investments.
- The company will retain real estate as an investment used as the company's offices.
- The company will have a risk on the rent paid for its offices.
- Banks or insurance companies will sell products indexed to the real estate indexes or backed with real estate properties. For instance, pension funds will retain real estate as investments for their customers.

In a diversified portfolio, the real estate investments may represent an important part of the total investments; therefore, the evolution of the real estate level affects the company income. The impact depends on the accounting scheme.

19.7.2 Monitoring indicators

As for the stock index, A/L managers will focus mainly on the *sensitivity of future incomes to real estate indexes*. Usually, the movements of the real estate market indexes affect only the current income. Nevertheless, sometimes, a real estate index increase will affect the incomes on the long-term (if the accounting scheme does not account directly the real estate increases but smoothed across time).

	Expected income					
	Y	Y + 1	Y + 2	Y + 3	Y + 4	Y + 5
Standard scenario	100	105	110	116	122	128
UK real estate increase +10 %	105	110	116	122	128	134
US real estate increase +10 %	103	108	114	119	125	131
Sensitivity to UK index increase	35	5	6	6	6	6
Sensitivity to US index increase	33	3	3	3	4	4

Figure 19.40 Sensitivity to real estate index

19.7.3 Real estate modelling and hedging

19.7.3.1 Real estate Black Scholes modelling

Real estate modelling could follow Black & Scholes formula:

$$\frac{dRE_t}{RE_t} = r(t).dt + \sigma^{RE}(t, S_t).dW_t^{\text{risk neutral}} \tag{19.68}$$

However, the market is not as liquid as the stock index market. The market incorporates delays (buying a real estate property take at least three months) and costs (taxes, solicitors' costs, etc.).

When an A/L manager buys a real estate property, the investment will last at least 5/10 years due to the importance of the costs. For this reason, some A/L Managers will develop macroeconomic models in order to comprehend the possible evolutions of the real estate indexes.

19.7.3.2 Macroeconomic modelling

It is possible to develop macroeconomic models for real estate including:

- the modelling of the number of transactions;
- the modelling of the supply and of the demand on the real estate market;
- the arbitrage between the rental market and the real estate market.

Central Banks (FRB, MPS, etc.), international organizations, or economists have developed different equilibrium models. These models will sometimes contain more than 60 equations with many variables:

- the real estate price (with index adjustments and seasonality adjustments);
- macroeconomic variables (inflation, real rates, unemployment rate, etc.);
- household debts, wealth, incomes and solvency;
- demographic factors and sociologic factors (household number increase due to divorces, etc.);
- stock market level;
- average life of real estate properties and their heterogeneity (houses versus flats, etc.);
- tax rates and political forces in the real estate market;
- consumer confidence;
- proportion of rents in the price index;

- mortgage interest rates and mortgage margins;
- mortgage duration;
- mortgage market conditions (bank facility to lend with the loan to value);
- real estate property stock/rental market stock;
- geographic factor, population mobility factors;
- number of transactions;
- comparison between residential and commercial real estate;
- real estate property depreciation (over time a property will depreciate of 2 % each year due to time passing, i.e. each year an investor has to spend 2 % of the property price to restore this property).

These equilibrium models (such as VAR models) will propose long-term equilibrium with disequilibrium on the short-term including:

- autoregressive effects;
- mean reverting effects.

The equilibrium relationship will link indeed:

- real estate prices, interest rates and the new credit production;
- investor preference for real estate compared to other investments (stock market or bond market investments, money market investments, etc.): investing in real estate, investors will consider that they are protected against inflation;
- investor choice between investments and savings;
- cyclic effects including speculative effects;
- arbitrage between the real estate price and the sum of the discounted rents;
- arbitrage between new housing construction and old housing prices;
- links between rents, real estate prices, and new housing construction (housing starts are a classic leading indicator of changes in macroeconomic activity);
- the long-term consistency between the growth of real estate prices, GDP growth and household income growth;
- Arbitrage between the region-by-region real estate prices.

19.7.3.3 Proposed modelling

The A/L manager will use in practice a simplified real estate modelling that links the real estate price and the rental yield.

$$\text{Real estate price}_t = \frac{\text{Rental price}_t}{\text{Rental yield}_t} \tag{19.69}$$

The rental price is usually a percentage of the household income:

$$\text{Rental price}_t = \alpha.\text{Household Income}_t \tag{19.70}$$

This income grows with GDP growth, i.e. with the interest rates r; finally, the rental price will follow this equation:

$$\text{Rental price}_t = \text{Rental price}_0 . e^{\int_0^t r(s).ds + \sigma.W_t - \sigma^2.\frac{t}{2}} \tag{19.71}$$

To model the rental yield, the A/L manager may suppose that this rate uses the interest rates with a risk premium π as a mean reverting objective:

$$d\text{RY}_t = \lambda.[r_t - \text{RY}_t - \pi].dt + \sigma'.\delta W'_t \tag{19.72}$$

These three equations allow the simulation of the real estate price and its link with interest rates. When interest rates increase, rents will increase but this will also increase the rental yield: the overall effect on the real estate price depends on the parameter λ.

19.8 OTHER FINANCIAL RISKS

In this section, we will introduce second-rate financial risks such as cross-border risk or volatility risk.

19.8.1 Cross-border risk

Cross-border risk is a kind of liquidity/credit risk present in emerging markets. "An emerging market is a place from which we cannot emerge in the case of an emergency" (Sigmund Warburg). Liquidity in this market is present on the overnight rate or on floating rates. In these countries, fiscal or prudential costs are important.

For international companies, there is a risk in lending money to a subsidiary abroad. There is always a potential risk that the government of a specific country blocks the cash in this subsidiary (nationalization, currency policy hardening, etc.).

Cross-border risk implies cross-border costs easy to approximate through country CDS prices.

Cross-border risk hedging is possible through external credit lines negotiation, liquidity reserve constitution, securitization, local debt issue, etc. The ALCO committee could also limit the amount of cross-border loans through a legal lending limit.

19.8.2 Counterparty risk

Counterparty risk is another credit risk type present essentially in the derivative market. When contracting a swap, for instance with a specified counterparty and when the swap marked-to-market becomes positive, this creates a credit risk called counterparty risk.

Counterparty risk hedging is possible using derivatives netting agreements.

19.8.3 Volatility risk

19.8.3.1 Volatility risk impact on the incomes

Within the term, "volatility risk", several definitions are possible:

- Economic volatility risk: risk on the income due to the change of the volatility parameter σ (in the Black & Scholes model for the stock market or in the Hull & White model for the interest rate market).

- Accounting risk: risk to see volatility in the incomes for several reasons (and not only the volatility of the economic markets). For instance, demand deposit amount volatility may cause volatility in the income.

In this section, we will describe volatility risk as the economic risk in the incomes of the volatility parameter.

A/L managers will distinguish two kinds of volatility:

- Implicit volatility: the one used in the pricing models representing the market's anticipation of the future volatility.
- Historical volatility: volatility estimated looking after historical databases (the volatility of the residuals of the yields regression, for instance).

Historical volatility is usually lower than implicit volatility since the market pays a risk premium for the person that accepts the volatility risk. Note that the volatility of the volatility parameter is also a kind of a volatility risk.

Before the introduction of IFRS and of Basel II, A/L managers did not hedge their volatility risk well. One of their main strategies was to sell volatility (selling out-of-the money options): these strategies increased not only the incomes but also the extreme risks.

Volatility is present in the computation of economic values. As soon as volatility changes, the economic value changes: the financial companies are sensitive to the variations of volatility. Indeed, volatility risk is present in many products:

- CMS bonds, callable bonds (as investments), mortgages (with prepayment option);
- callable bonds (as debts), insurance life contracts, deposits with guarantees, etc.

Moreover, customer behaviour may depend on volatility. If stock market volatility increases, this may decrease individuals' appetite for risk and consequently increase the amounts of demand deposit.

In life insurance contracts, insurance companies are massively exposed to volatility risk due to the important amount of embedded options in these contracts.

19.8.3.2 Volatility risk representation and hedging

It is possible to represent the exposure to volatility risk in a sensitivity indicator to the parameter of volatility: the *"vega risk representation"*, the sensitivity to the volatility:

	Expected income					
	Y	Y + 1	Y + 2	Y + 3	Y + 4	Y + 5
Standard scenario	100	105	110	116	122	128
Volatility increase +10 %	102	106	110	116	122	128
Sensitivity to volatility	1	1	0	0	0	0

Figure 19.41 Vega risk representation

In mathematics, the vega represents the sensitivity to the volatility. The delta represents the sensitivity to the market level, the theta the sensitivity to the evolution of time and the gamma the sensitivity of the delta itself to the market level.

However, some mathematical considerations will help us to measure the exposure to volatility risk. In stochastic computations, there is a link between vega, gamma and theta. Consequently, the computation of the second derivative of the income (i.e. the gamma) gives the exposure to the volatility:

$$Gamma = \frac{-\partial Income_t}{\partial S_t^2} \tag{19.73}$$

Volatility risk hedging is possible through:

- volatility or variance swaps but these swaps are very costly;
- callable bonds, CMS bonds, CMS caps (but these instruments are exposed to correlation risk).

However, the better hedging is done through delta equivalent/gamma equivalent/vega equivalent techniques as will be discussed in Chapter 22.

20
Non-Financial Risks

Qui sème le vent récolte la tempête.

Companies are not only exposed to the financial risks but also to many other kinds of risk:

- operational risk;
- model risk;
- business risk;
- illiquidity risk;
- reputation risk;
- counterparty risk;
- reputation risk;
- legal and tax risks, etc.

20.1 OPERATIONAL RISKS

The Basel II framework introduced the notion of operational risk and provided a solution to quantify this risk. The Basel Committee defines operational risk "as the risk of loss resulting from inadequate or failed internal processes, people and systems or from external events. This definition includes legal risk but excludes strategic and reputation risk".

General definitions of operational risk include:

- human resources risk;
- system failures risk;
- internal fraud;
- external fraud;
- damage to physical assets risk;
- process management risk;
- legal risk.

The impact of this risk on incomes is clear and rarely smoothed.

The Basel II framework proposes a solution to minimize the impact of the operational risk impact on income with a specific allocation of capital. In order to compute this amount of capital, it is essential to constitute databases. These databases will record the historical costs of the operational risks. Then, a modelling of these costs is possible.

Another solution to minimize this kind of risk is to develop:

- a permanent control of the processes (with the integration of "product controllers" or of "market controllers" in the operational teams); and
- a periodic control of these processes (with the help of an Internal Control Department).

20.2 MODEL RISKS

In the banking sector, the Basel II framework does not recognize model risk as a major risk except in the computation of market risk in the trading books.

Nevertheless, model risk is one of the most important risks in the Banking Book. This risk comes from:

- a lack of data;
- the exploitation of inconsequential data in the modelling;
- an inadequate treatment of the available information.

In trading activities, traders are encouraged to measure provisions in front of their model risk included in their pricing models. Consequently, the pricing models take a large part of the trading books profit and loss (P&L).

In the non-trading books, the model risk will affect the incomes on the long-term horizons. The model risk will be present in:

- customer behaviour modelling;
- financial markets modelling.

For example, if the A/L manager is not able to model his prepayment risk, he will not be able to implement a delta equivalent technique and then the income will vary a great deal.

The demand deposit example will develop a quantification of the model risk.

In practice, we will compute the model risk (i.e. the economic capital consumption for model risk) as a quantile of the economic value variation due to the model's risk parameters variation.

For example, if the A/L manager knows the incertitude of the parameters of the prepayment rate, he will be able to simulate the possible evolution of the economic value and then compute an economic capital.

The information systems are essential in order to reduce the modelling risk. A modelling will perform if the A/L manager has enough information to estimate the model's parameters.

20.3 BUSINESS RISK

Business risk represents the risk of the variation of the economic value due to a variation of the business parameters. Consequently, business risk is not the risk of the variation of the shareholder value due to a variation of the business parameters.

For example, economic value depends upon the number of existing clients: for example in the demand deposit economic value, in unit-based life insurance contracts, etc. With a reduction of the number of the existing customers, the economic value (i.e. the future discounted margins) decreases.

The simulation of the number of customers will allow for the simulation of economic value.

In practice, we will compute the business risk (i.e. the economic capital consumption for business risk) as a quantile of the economic value variation due to the business risk parameters (e.g. the number of existing customers or contracts).

The allocation of economic capital for business risk will incite the Commercial Department to monitor this kind of risk better. This allocation also allows us to improve the economic analysis of the business.

20.4 RISK CORRELATIONS

In the financial markets, there is a strong correlation between risk factors. However, the Basel II framework will merely add risk consumption instead of taking into account its correlations.

Among the possible correlations, we may cite the correlations between:

- the nominal rates and the real interest rates;
- the short term interest rates and the long term interest rates;
- the stock market and the interest rates;
- the credit risk and the real estate risk;
- the credit risk and the interest rate risk (an interest rate decrease is associated with a possible "fly to quality", i.e. a diminution of the credit spreads);
- the different idiosyncratic credit risk factors;
- the credit risk and the macroeconomic factors;
- the business risk factors and the credit risk factors (e.g. the monetary aggregate M1 and the default probability).

Even if there is macroeconomic evidence of the existence of these correlations, they are very difficult to estimate. The CDO correlation crisis of 2005 illustrates the complexity of this estimation.

In practice, we will model the correlations through the correlation between the Brownian motions representing each risk factor.

20.5 "ACCOUNTING RISK": THE RISK REPRESENTATION DEPENDS ON THE ACCOUNTING SCHEME!

Accounting risk represents a final form of non-financial risk. The introduction of the IFRS rules will increase this risk: the accounting standards may introduce volatility in the incomes. These rules do not guarantee the constancy of income growth even in the context of a market risk equal to zero.

Moreover, the introduction of economic risk measures will not eliminate the accounting risk. A Value-at-Risk equal to zero does not imply the end of the accounting risk; it does not imply a constant income growth or an income growth indexed to the level of the market rates.

The A/L manager will focus on this accounting risk in order to provide to the executive management a set of appropriate risk indicators.

Part V
Tools for Asset and Liability Managers

In this Part, we will describe in detail the mathematical tools used by quantitative A/L managers:

- simulation models in order to understand the possible evolution of financial markets;
- delta equivalent techniques used to represent options in risk indicators and to determine risk free strategy;
- other mathematical tools such as risk measures and associated optimization tools, or statistical tools.

21

Simulation Tools for Interest Rates and Other Financial Indexes

Il y a plus d'outils que d'ouvriers. (La Bruyère)

Market prices simulation is the basis of ALM and is required in:

- economic value computations;
- stress testing computations;
- risk measure computations (VaR, economic capital, etc.).

In risk sections, we have already developed some simulation tools for credit risk, stock market risk, etc.

Nowadays the most common simulations are stochastic simulations and for this reason, we start with the presentation of some basic stochastic calculation principles.

21.1 STOCHASTIC CALCULATION

21.1.1 Brownian motion definition

21.1.1.1 Wiener process

The *Brownian motion* is defined in mathematics by the use of a continuous-time stochastic process called the *Wiener process*. The term Brownian comes from Robert Brown and the term Wiener process from Norbert Wiener. This process W_t is characterized by three facts:

- $W_0 = 0$;
- W_t *is almost surely continuous*;
- W_t *has independent increments with normal distributions.*

This means that for $0 < s < t < t_2 < t_3$:

$$(W_t - W_s) \text{ follows } N(0, t-s)$$
$$(W_t - W_s) \text{ and } \left(W_{t_2} - W_{t_3}\right) \text{ are independant variables}$$

In addition, for an infinitesimal increment, the relationship continues:

$$dW_t = (W_{t+dt} - W_t) \text{ follows } N(0, dt) \tag{21.1}$$

To simulate a Wiener process, the A/L manager will use this relationship introducing normal distributions.

21.1.1.2 *Normal distribution*

The normal distribution is also called a Gaussian distribution (after the German mathematician Carl Friedrich Gauss). The *normal distribution* $N(\mu, \sigma^2)$ with a mean μ and a volatility σ or a variance σ^2 follows this probability density function f:

$$f(x).dx = P\,(x < X < x + dx) = \frac{1}{\sigma.\sqrt{2\pi}}.\exp\left(-\frac{(x-\mu)^2}{2.\sigma^2}\right).dx \qquad (21.2)$$

The function f associates with the variable x the probability for the random variable X to be comprised between x and x+dx.

The *standard normal distribution N(0,1)* is the normal distribution with a mean of zero and a variance of one.

The *cumulative probability function* Φ (from $]-\infty; +\infty\,[$ to $]\,0; 1[$) gives the cumulative probability for X to be inferior to x, for a standard normal distribution:

$$\Phi\,(x) = \int_{-\infty}^{x} f(u).du = \frac{1}{\sqrt{2\pi}}.\int_{-\infty}^{x} \exp\left(-\frac{u^2}{2}\right).du = P(X \le x) \qquad (21.3)$$

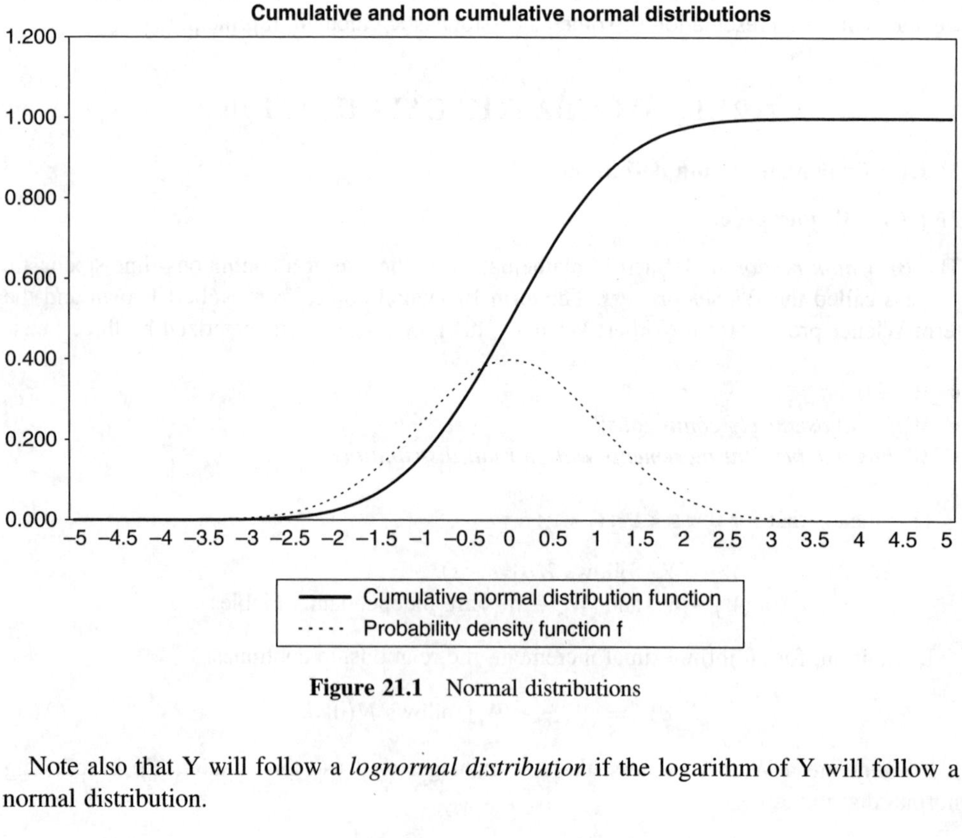

Figure 21.1 Normal distributions

Note also that Y will follow a *lognormal distribution* if the logarithm of Y will follow a normal distribution.

21.1.1.3 Derived processes

The *Wiener process X with drift* μ *and volatility* σ is defined as a stochastic process with this relationship:

$$X_t = \mu.t + \sigma.W_t \tag{21.4}$$

A *geometric Brownian motion Y* will be characterized by the following relationship:

$$Y_t = \exp\left(\mu.t - \frac{\sigma^2}{2}.t + \sigma.W_t\right) \tag{21.5}$$

This process will never take negative values and follows the following differential relationship:

$$\frac{dY_t}{Y_t} = \mu.dt + \sigma.dW_t \tag{21.6}$$

Note that Black & Scholes have modelled the stock market evolution as a geometric Brownian motion.

21.1.2 Laplace transform

The *Laplace transform* will be very interesting in stochastic calculations. Indeed, for a random variable X following a normal distribution N(E(X); V(X)) with a mathematical expectation E(X) and a variance V(X), the Laplace transform will give the mathematical expectation of the exponential of X as follows:

$$E\left(e^{\lambda X}\right) = e^{\lambda E(X) + \frac{1}{2}\lambda^2 V(X)} \tag{21.7}$$

This property will be very useful when computing the mathematical expectation of Brownian motions.

Applied to Brownian motions, this leads to:

$$E\left(e^{\sigma.W_t}\right) = e^{\frac{\sigma^2}{2}.t} \tag{21.8}$$

21.1.3 Martingale notion

In finance, statisticians introduced the notion of *filtration* $(F_s)_{s<t}$. At a given date t, the filtration represents all the known market information at the date t. This information is a set of events. Of course with time passing, the set of information increases and for $s < t$, $F_s \subset F_t$ (F_s is included in F_t).

A random variable X is a F_t*-martingale* if and only if the mathematical expectation of this variable with the financial market information at date s is equal to the value of the variable at date t:

$$E\left(X_t / F_s\right) = E_s(X_t) = X_s \quad s \leq t \tag{21.9}$$

In financial markets, many prices will be martingale prices under a specific probability called risk neutral probability.

If X is defined through an integral of a Wiener process W under the probability P given by the filtration $(F_s)_{s<t}$:

$$X_t = X_0 + \int_0^t \sigma(u, X_u).dW_u \tag{21.10}$$

then X is a F_t-martingale and:

$$E(X_t/F_s) = X_s \quad s \leq t \tag{21.11}$$

21.1.4 Itô lemma

The Itô lemma is the starting point of stochastic calculus and of stochastic simulations: this lemma will allow us to compute the delta. We consider two continuous processes X and U that satisfy the following set of equations:

$$\begin{cases} dX_t = a_X(t, X_t)dt + \sigma_X(t, X_t)dW_t \\ Y_t = f(t, X_t) \end{cases} \tag{21.12}$$

The Itô lemma gives the differential relationship for Y:

$$dY_t = \frac{\partial f}{\partial t}(t, X_t).dt + \frac{\partial f}{\partial x}(t, X_t).dX_t + \frac{1}{2}\frac{\partial^2 f}{\partial x^2}(t, X_t).\sigma_X^2(t, X_t)dt \tag{21.13}$$

Note that compared to classic differential relationships without Brownian motion in the differentiation of X, there is in the differential definition of Y a new term, the last term depending on volatility σ.

21.1.5 Feynman-Kac formula

The Feynman-Kac formula is named after Richard Feynman and Mark Kac. This formula establishes a link between partial differential equations and stochastic processes.

Given a partial differential equation where f is the unknown:

$$\frac{\partial f}{\partial t} + \mu(\mathrm{t, x}).\frac{\partial f}{\partial x} + \frac{\sigma^2(\mathrm{t, x})}{2}.\frac{\partial^2 f}{\partial x^2} = 0 \tag{21.14}$$

and imposing a terminal condition at date T:

$$f(T, x) = \psi(x) \tag{21.15}$$

The solution of this system of equation is given by an expectation:

$$f(t, x) = E(\psi(X_T)/X_t = x) \tag{21.16}$$

with the stochastic process X defined by:

$$\begin{aligned} &X_t = x_t \\ &dX_t = \mu(t, X_t).dt + \sigma(t, X_t).dW_t \end{aligned} \tag{21.17}$$

21.1.6 Girsanov theorem

Associated with the Itô lemma, another theorem is important in stochastic calculus, the Girsanov theorem.

With W_t a Brownian motion under a probability P, we define L_t as follows:

$$L_t = \exp\left\{ \int_0^t \theta(s)dW_s - \frac{1}{2}\int_0^t \theta^2(s)ds \right\} \quad t \leq T \tag{21.18}$$

If the mathematical expectation of L_T under the probability P is equal to 1:

$$E^P(L_T) = 1 \tag{21.19}$$

Then the process L(t) is a P-martingale.

We define a new probability Q as $Q = L_T.P$ if the mathematical expectation of X under Q is equal to the mathematical expectation of X multiplied by L_T under P for each random variable F_T measurable:

$$E^Q(X) = E^P(X.L_T) \tag{21.20}$$

Then the Girsanov theorem says that the variable equal to the difference between the Brownian motion W and the integral of θ will be a Brownian motion under probability Q:

$$\overline{W}(t) = \left(W_t - \int_0^t \theta(s).ds \right) \text{ is a Q brownian motion} \tag{21.21}$$

21.1.7 Historical probability and risk neutral probability in interest rate modelling

In financial markets, A/L managers will start with the definition of an *historical probability P*. This probability represents the real probability of market observations; this probability is called also *real probability*.

We introduce *the zero-coupon B(t,T)* as the price at date t of 1 unit of money paid at date T.

Under the probability P, the zero-coupon will follow (according to the CAPM) this diffusion equation:

$$\frac{dB}{B} = \mu_B dt + \sigma_B dW(t) \tag{21.22}$$

Introducing the short-term interest rate r, the diffusion equation can take this form:

$$\frac{dB}{B} = rdt + \sigma_B \left(\left(\frac{\mu_B - r}{\sigma_B} \right).dt + dW_t \right) = rdt + \sigma_B d\overline{W}(t) \tag{21.23}$$

With a parameter λ following:

$$\lambda = \frac{\mu_B - r}{\sigma_B} \tag{21.24}$$

By application of the Girsanov theorem, we define *a new probability Q called the risk neutral probability*:

$$\frac{dQ}{dP}(T)=\exp\left\{-\int_0^T \lambda dW_s-\frac{1}{2}\int_0^t \lambda^2 ds\right\} \quad t\leq T \tag{21.25}$$

Under this probability, we define a new Q-Brownian motion:

$$\overline{W}_t=\left(W_t+\int_0^t \lambda ds\right) \tag{21.26}$$

This new probability gives the opportunity to introduce *the notion of discounted prices*. A new zero-coupon B* is then introduced:

$$B^*(t,T)=\left(e^{-\int_0^t r(s).ds}\right).B(t,T) \tag{21.27}$$

Using the Itô lemma, this new variable will follow:

$$\frac{dB^*(t,T)}{B^*(t,T)}=\frac{dB(t,T)}{B(t,T)}-r_t dt=\sigma_B d\overline{W}(t) \tag{21.28}$$

Consequently the discounted price B* is a martingale under the probability Q. This implicates that:

$$B^*(t,T)=E_Q\left(B^*(T,T)/F_t\right) \tag{21.29}$$

or using back the notation B:

$$\left(e^{-\int_0^t r_s ds}\right).B(t,T)=E_Q\left[\left(e^{-\int_0^T r_s ds}\right).B(T,T)/F_t\right] \tag{21.30}$$

Since B(T,T) is by definition equal to 1, this leads to this famous equation for the zero-coupon bond:

$$B(t,T)=E_Q\left[e^{-\int_t^T r_s ds}/F_t\right] \tag{21.31}$$

The price at date t of a zero-coupon maturing at T is the expectation under risk neutral probability of the variable $\bar{B}$ defined as:

$$\begin{aligned}\bar{B}(t,T)&=e^{-\int_t^T r_s ds}\\ B(t,T)&=E_Q\left[\bar{B}(t,T)/F_t\right]\end{aligned} \tag{21.32}$$

21.2 EQUITY MARKET SIMULATION

21.2.1 Black & Scholes modelling

The simplest application of stochastic calculus to financial markets is given by the equity market. In the Black & Scholes model (1973), the stock index S follows a Brownian motion with a trend indexed to the short-term interest rate r(t) without any dividends. The initial equation is given under the CAPM real probability P where the stock price varies with a trend μ under a real probability:

$$\frac{dS_t}{S_t} = \mu(t, r(t), S(t)).dt + \sigma(t, S(t)).dW_t^{real} \tag{21.33}$$

We introduce the risk neutral probability using the Girsanov theorem:

$$dW_t^{\text{risk neutral}} = -\frac{r(t) - \mu\,(t, r(t), S(t))}{\sigma\,(t, S(t))}.\,dt + dW_t^{\text{risk real}} \tag{21.34}$$

$W^{\text{risk neutral}}$ is a Q-Brownian according to the Girsanov-theorem with the following choice of function θ:

$$\theta\,(t) = \frac{\mu\,(t, r(t), S(t)) - r(t)}{\sigma\,(t, S(t))} \tag{21.35}$$

Expressed alternatively, this means that the risk premium in the stock markets is given by the following equation:

$$\text{Risk premium}_t = [\mu\,(t, r(t), S(t)) - r(t)] \tag{21.36}$$

This leads to the classic Black & Scholes formula under risk neutral probability:

$$\frac{dS_t}{S_t} = r(t).dt + \sigma\,(t, S_t)\,.\,dW_t^{\text{risk neutral}} \tag{21.37}$$

21.2.2 Arbitrage opportunity absence and risk neutral probability

We consider a product that will pay a flow $\phi(S_T)$ at date T depending on the value of a stock variable S_T at date T. The Itô lemma and the Girsanov theorem give a price for this product for each date $t < T$. For such a product, the price at date t is given by the mathematical expectation of the discounted cash flow under the risk neutral probability.

$$\text{Price}_t = E_Q\left(\phi\,(S_T)\,.\bar{B}(t, T)\right) \tag{21.38}$$

The price of a product is equal to the discounted sum of its cash flows under a risk neutral probability (or risk minimizing probability)

The theory of *arbitrage opportunity absence (AOA)* allows for the demonstration of this equation. This theory assumes the existence of a *risk free auto-financing strategy* that replicates the cash flow $\phi(S_T)$. Of course, the price at date t of this strategy is the price at date t of the product that will pay the final cash flow $\phi(S_T)$ at date T. Otherwise, a trader could build up a risk free arbitrage strategy.

Proof:

We look after an auto-refinancing strategy which allows us to replicate without any risk the final cash flow $\phi(S_T)$ paid at date T.

We consider the marked-to-market price Y_t of this strategy at date t.

The strategy is made of an investment in stock market for an amount of stocks of Δ. The residual cash available in the strategy is put on short-term interest rates:

$$dY_t = r(t).(Y_t - \Delta_t.S_t)\,dt + \Delta_t.dS_t \tag{21.39}$$

And under the risk neutral probability:

$$dY_t = r(t).Y_t.dt + \sigma.S_t.\Delta_t.dW_t \tag{21.40}$$

The problem is to find such a risk free auto-financing strategy that replicates at date T the final cash flow $\phi(S_T)$.

We call Z and $\tilde{\Delta}_t$ the following discounted functions:

$$\begin{aligned} Z_t &= Y_t.e^{-\int_0^t r(s).ds} \\ \tilde{\Delta}_t &= \Delta_t.e^{-\int_0^t r(s).ds} \end{aligned} \tag{21.41}$$

This leads to the following equations:

$$\begin{aligned} dZ_t &= dY_t.e^{-\int_0^t r(s).ds} - r(t).Z(t).dt \\ dZ_t &= \sigma.S_t.\tilde{\Delta}_t.dW_t \end{aligned} \tag{21.42}$$

Finally, our problem is to find a strategy based on the function $\tilde{\Delta}_t$ verifying this set of equations:

$$\begin{aligned} dZ_t &= \sigma.\tilde{\Delta}_t.S_t.dW_t \\ Z_T &= \phi(S_T).e^{-\int_0^T r(s).ds} \end{aligned} \tag{21.43}$$

In terms of stochastic diffusion, applying Itô lemma to Z as a function f of t and W:

$$\begin{aligned} \frac{\partial f}{\partial t}dt + \frac{\partial f}{\partial x}dS_t + \frac{\sigma^2}{2}.\frac{\partial^2 f}{\partial x^2}dt &= \sigma.\tilde{\Delta}_t.S_t.dW_t \\ Z_T &= \phi(S_T).e^{-\int_0^T r(s).ds} \end{aligned} \tag{21.44}$$

In other words it gives:

$$\begin{aligned} \frac{\partial f}{\partial t}dt + \frac{\partial f}{\partial x}.r(t).S_t.dt + \frac{\partial f}{\partial x}.\sigma.S_t.dW_t + \frac{\sigma^2}{2}.\frac{\partial^2 f}{\partial x^2}dt &= \sigma.\tilde{\Delta}_t.S_t.dW_t \\ Z_T &= \phi(S_T).e^{-\int_0^T r(s).ds} \end{aligned} \tag{21.45}$$

With the unicity of the Itô decomposition, this gives this set of equations:

$$\tilde{\Delta}_t = \frac{\partial f}{\partial x}$$

$$\frac{\partial f}{\partial t} dt + \frac{\partial f}{\partial x}.r(t).S_t.dt + \frac{\sigma^2}{2}.\frac{\partial^2 f}{\partial x^2} dt = 0 \quad (21.46)$$

$$Z_T = \phi(S_T).e^{-\int_0^T r(s).ds}$$

Using Feynman-Kac formula this leads to the existence of such a strategy where:

$$Z_t = E\left[\phi(S_T).e^{-\int_0^T r(s).ds} / F_t\right] \quad (21.47)$$

The strategy is finally defined by the investment at each date t into an amount Δ of equity equal to the sensitivity of the expected discounted cash flow.

$$\Delta_t = \tilde{\Delta}_t.e^{\int_0^t r(s).ds} = \frac{\partial E\left[\phi(S_T).e^{-\int_0^T r(s).ds} / F_t\right]}{\partial S_t}.e^{\int_0^t r(s).ds} = \frac{\partial E\left[\phi(S_T).e^{-\int_t^T r(s).ds} / F_t\right]}{\partial S_t} \quad (21.48)$$

For this reason, the above strategy is called *"delta hedging"* in marked-to-market activities.

21.2.3 Stock market simulation with call/put volatility calibration

Consequently, in order to forecast the stock market index, the A/L manager will have to:

- simulate the Brownian motion W;
- calibrate the volatility σ on the call/put equity market (or on a historical database).

The calibration is made by market prices of call or put options. A call option is the right at date T to buy a stock at a given strike K for a nominal N. The put option is the right to sell the stock.

The Black & Scholes formula gives a price for calls and puts. If we call S^*, the discounted price of the stock, this price follows:

$$\begin{aligned} S_t^* &= S_t.e^{-\int_0^t r(s).ds} \\ \frac{dS_t^*}{S_t^*} &= \sigma.dW_t^{\text{risk neutral}} \end{aligned} \quad (21.49)$$

This gives a value for S^* and then for S:

$$S_t = S_0.e^{\int_0^t r(s).ds + \sigma.W_t - \frac{\sigma^2}{2}.t} = \frac{S_0.e^{\sigma.W_t - \frac{\sigma^2}{2}.t}}{\bar{B}(0,t)} \quad (21.50)$$

The price for a call option giving the right to buy one stock at a price K is then given by arbitrage opportunity absence:

$$Call_t = E\left[(S_T - K)^+ .\bar{B}(0,t)/F_t\right] = E\left[\left(S_0.e^{\sigma.W_T - \frac{\sigma^2}{2}.T} - K.\bar{B}(0,t)\right)^+ /F_t\right] \quad (21.51)$$

We consider that the term under brackets is positive when:

$$\left(S_0.e^{\sigma.W_T - \frac{\sigma^2}{2}.T} - K.\bar{B}(0,t) \geq 0\right) \Leftrightarrow \left(W_T \geq \frac{\ln\left(\frac{K.\bar{B}(0,t)}{S_0}\right) + \frac{\sigma^2}{2}.T}{\sigma} \right) \quad (21.52)$$

Then after some stochastic calculations, the call price follows the difference between two cumulative normal distributions:

$$\begin{aligned} Call_t &= S_t.\Phi(d_1) - K.B(t,T).\Phi(d_2) \\ d_1 &= \frac{\ln\left(\frac{S_t}{K}\right) - \frac{\sigma^2}{2}.(T-t)}{\sigma.\sqrt{T-t}} \\ d_2 &= d_1 + \sigma.\sqrt{T-t} \end{aligned} \quad (21.53)$$

The existence of a call/put market gives quotations for the volatility σ. Indeed, with the market price of a portfolio made of calls and of puts, it is possible, inversing the Black & Scholes formula, to compute the volatility σ.

21.3 INTEREST RATE SIMULATION

Interest rate simulation starts in fixed income business lines (accounted as marked-to-market) with the definition of the risk neutral probability Q.

This probability allows for the risk neutral pricing and hedging as it is done for the equity stock market.

Interest rate models will be divided in two sets:

- *models based on the short-term interest rate r*; and
- *market models*: the newest generation of models based on the Libor (*Libor Market Model*) or on the swap rate (*Swap Market model*).

21.3.1 One-factor models: Linear Gaussian Model (LGM) on the short-term interest rate

21.3.1.1 Hull & White modelling

The *Hull & White (1990) one-factor model* is a model where the short-term interest rate r(t) follows a Vasicek dynamic under the risk neutral probability:

$$dr_t = \lambda.(\theta_t - r_t).dt + \sigma.dW_t^{RN} \quad (21.54)$$

θ(t) is the *long-term average of the short-term interest rate*. This term allows the adjustment over the initial yield curve so that a fixed rate product pricing with the model gives the market price of the product.

λ is the *mean reverting force* and gives the speed for the interest rate to return to the level of the long-term average of the short-term interest rates.

σ is a *volatility* and W is a wiener process under the risk neutral probability.

The resolution of the differential equation leads to a simple formula for r(t):

$$r_t = \exp(-\lambda.t).\left(r_0 + \sigma.\int_0^t \exp(\lambda.s).dW_s^{RN} + \lambda.\int_0^t \exp(\lambda.s).\theta_s.ds\right) \tag{21.55}$$

When θ(t) is constant, the model is called a *Vasicek model* (see annexes) and gives for r(t):

$$r_t = \left(\theta + \exp(-\lambda.t).(r_0 - \theta) + \exp(-\lambda.t).\sigma.\int_0^t \exp(\lambda.s).dW_s^{RN}\right) \tag{21.56}$$

It is then possible to compute the zero-coupon price and to prove that *the zero-coupon rate can be written as a linear function of r.*

$$B(t, t+\tau) = E_Q\left[e^{-\int_t^{t+\tau} r(s).ds}\right] = \exp[-\tau.(A_\tau.r_t + B_\tau)] \tag{21.57}$$

It means that simulating the short-term interest rate, the A/L manager is able to simulate the entire yield curve. For this reason, the model is called a *"one-factor model"* since the entire curve B(t,t+τ) at date t depends only on the short-term interest rate r(t).

To be more precise, we introduce the forward spot rate f:

$$f(0, t) = -\frac{\partial \ln B(0, t)}{\partial t} \tag{21.58}$$

To price correctly zero-coupon bonds at date 0, this imposes a value for θ:

$$\theta_t = \lambda.f(0, t) + \frac{\partial f(0, t)}{\partial t} + \frac{\sigma^2}{2\lambda}\left(1 - e^{-2\lambda.t}\right) \tag{21.59}$$

And a correct equation for B follows:

$$B(t, t+\tau) = \frac{B(0, t+\tau)}{B(0, t)} \exp\left\{[f(0, t) - r_t].\frac{1 - e^{-\lambda.\tau}}{\lambda} - \frac{\sigma^2}{4\lambda}\left(1 - e^{-2\lambda\, t}\right).\left(\frac{1 - e^{-\lambda.\tau}}{\lambda}\right)^2 + \frac{1}{2}V(t, t+\tau)\right\} \tag{21.60}$$

$$V(t, t+\tau) = \frac{\sigma^2}{\lambda^2}\left[\tau + \frac{2}{\lambda}e^{-\lambda.\tau} - \frac{1}{2\lambda}e^{-2.\lambda.\tau} - \frac{3}{2\lambda}\right]$$

21.3.1.2 Hull & White modelling weaknesses

Of course, Hull & White modelling has many advantages:

- The model is easy to implement.
- The model allows the computation of yield curve trajectories (short-term and long-term interest rates trajectories).
- The models prices interest rate products using either Monte Carlo simulation, either analytic formulae.

However, the model also has some disadvantages:

- Interest rates can become negative with a non-zero probability.
- The model works with only one factor: interest rate variations are correlated perfectly since the zero-coupons are expressed as pure functions of the short-term interest rate.
- The volatility is constant although a smile effect is observed in the market (the volatility depends on the maturity of the zero-coupon).

21.3.1.3 Hull & White interest rate simulation with trinomial trees

21.3.1.3.1 Example of a binomial recombining tree

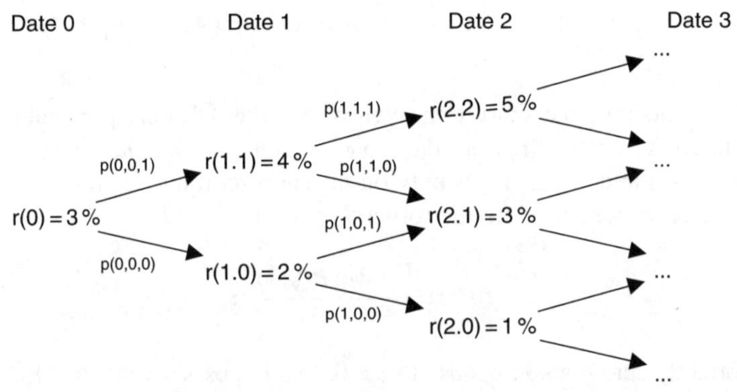

Figure 21.2 Binomial tree

A tree is said to be *binomial* when the short-term interest rate from one date to the next date can just increase or decrease.

The tree is said to be *recombining* when an interest rate increase followed by an interest rate decrease leads to the same *"state"* or "node" as an interest rate decrease followed by an interest rate increase.

We call *node* a couple (i,j) where i represents the date and j the number of times the interest rates increased. At each date i, there are i+1 nodes.

- p(i, j, 1) is the probability for the interest rates to increase starting from node (i, j).
- p(i, j, 0) is the probability for the interest rates to decrease starting from node (i, j). By construction, p(i, j, 0)=1−p(i, j, 1).

In our example, short-term interest rates can increase at date 0 from 3 % to 4 % at node (1,1) with a probability p(0,0,1) or decrease from 3 % to 2 % at node (1,0) with a probability p(0,0,0).

From node (1,1), interest rates may increase to 5 % at node (2,2) or decrease to 3 % at node (2,1).

It is possible to join the same node (2,1) when interest rates increase from node (1,0).

From date 0 to date i, there are 2^i possible paths.

21.3.1.3.2 Example of a trinomial recombining tree

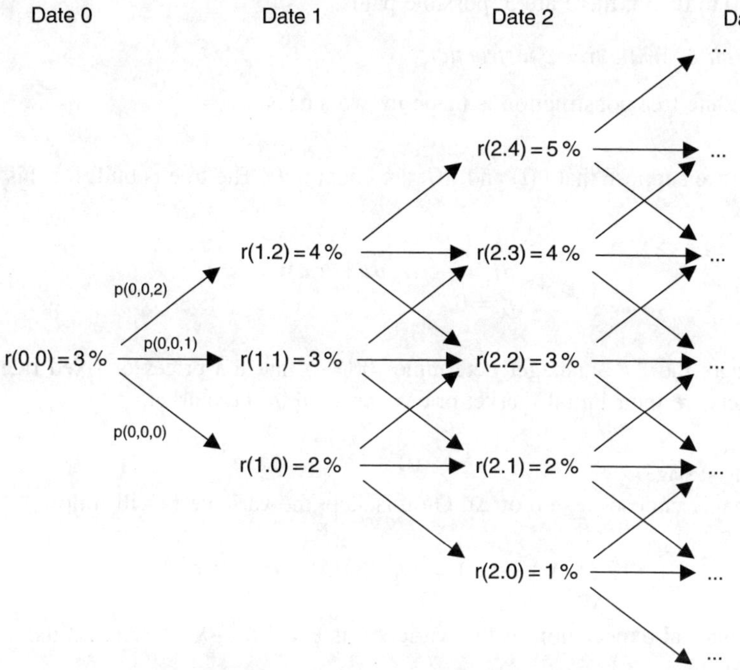

Figure 21.3 Trinomial tree

A tree is said to be trinomial when short-term interest rate evolution from one date to another can evolve only as follows: interest rate increase, decrease or stay stable.

The tree is still said to be recombining when an interest rate increase followed by an interest rate decrease leads to the same "state" or "node" as in interest rate decrease followed by an interest rate increase (or that same "state" as two phases of interest rate stability).

We call node the couple (i,j) where i represents the date and j twice the number of times the interest rates increased and once the number of times the interest rates stayed stable.

At each date i, there are (2.i+1) nodes.

p(i, j, 2) is the probability to see an interest rate increase from node (i, j).

p(i, j, 1) is the probability to see an interest rate stability after node (i, j).

p(i, j, 0) is the probability to see an interest rate decrease from node (i, j).

By construction $p(i, j, 0) = 1 - p(i, j, 1) - p(i, j, 2)$.

In our example, short-term interest rates from date 0 to date 1 can:

- increase from 3 % to 4 % to reach node (1,2) with a probability p(0,0,2);
- decrease from 3 % to 2 % to reach node (1,0) with a probability p(0,0,0);
- stay stable at 3 % to reach node (1,1) with a probability p(0,0,1).

From node (1,1), interest rates may increase to 4 % at node (2,3), stay stable at 3 % at node (2,2) or decrease to 2 % at node (2,1).

It is possible to reach this same node (2,1) when interest rate stay stable after node (1,0).

From date 0 to date i, there are 3^i possible paths.

21.3.1.3.3 Hull & White tree construction

The Hull & White tree construction is made in two stages:

- First stage: we suppose that θ(t) and r(0) are equal to 0. The tree is built for this variable r'(t) satisfying:

$$\begin{aligned} dr'_t &= -\lambda.r'_t.dt + \sigma.dW_t^{RN} \\ r'_0 &= 0 \end{aligned} \qquad (21.61)$$

- Second stage: the A/L manager determines θ(t) so that the prices of fixed rate interest rate products are their initial market prices observed in the market.

21.3.1.3.3.1 First stage

The A/L manager chooses a step of Δt. On this step, the variable r' will follow:

$$\mathrm{r}'(\mathrm{t}+\Delta\mathrm{t}) - \mathrm{r}'(\mathrm{t}) = -\lambda.\mathrm{r}'(\mathrm{t}).\Delta\mathrm{t} + \sigma.\sqrt{\Delta\mathrm{t}}.\varepsilon(\mathrm{t}) \qquad (21.62)$$

The mathematical expectation of this variation is equal to $-\lambda$.r'(t).Δt and its variance is equal to σ^2.Δt.

We impose r'(0) to be equal to 0. If we represent r' in a trinomial tree, a stability condition imposes with t=i.Δt:

$$\mathrm{r}'(i,\mathrm{j}) = (j-i).\sqrt{3.\Delta\mathrm{t}}\sigma \qquad (21.63)$$

The three probabilities p(i, j, 0 1 or 2) will be computed so that the sum of these probabilities i is equal to 1 and so that the variation of r' will have a mathematical expectation equal to $-\lambda$.r'(t).Δt and a variance equal to σ^2.Δt. Consequently, there are *three* conditions and *three* equations for *three* unknown variables.

For instance, with $\sigma = 1\,\%$ and $\lambda = 10\,\%$, we get the tree of Figure 21.4.

21.3.1.3.3.2 Second stage

Once r' has been set up, the objective is to be closer to the reality and to go from r'(t) to r(t).

We note α(t) = r(t)−r'(t) and link it to the node:

$$\mathrm{r}(\mathrm{i},\mathrm{j}) = \mathrm{r}'(\mathrm{i},\mathrm{j}) + \alpha(\mathrm{i}) \qquad (21.64)$$

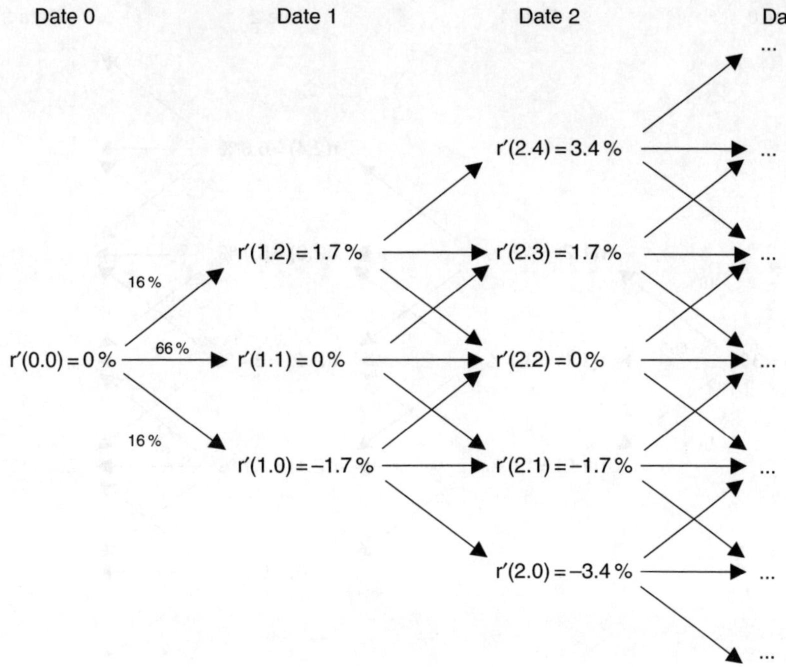

Figure 21.4 First stage Tree

The parameters α(i) are determined by recurrence. The easiest way to calibrate these parameters is to make discount factors computed in the tree B(0,i) equal to the market discount factors B(0,i) (the initial market yield curve is a parameter of the modelling).

Finally, it leads to the tree of Figure 21.5.

21.3.2 Two factor models

21.3.2.1 LGM2+: Linear Gaussian Model with two factors (Hull & White 2 factors model)

The model LGM2+ is a linear Gaussian model with two factors W^X and W^Y and with the integration of the initial curve through an adjustment term ϕ:

$$
\begin{aligned}
&r_t = x_t + y_t + \varphi(t) \\
&\begin{cases} dx_t = -ax_t dt + \sigma dW_t^x \\ dy_t = -by_t dt + \eta dW_t^y \end{cases} \\
&Corr(W_t^x, W_t^x) = \rho
\end{aligned}
\qquad (21.65)
$$

The determinist term ϕ(t) allows the initial yield curve adjustment as the term θ(t) did it in the Hull & White one-factor model. This term is expressed as a function of the model parameters and of the initial zero-coupon rates.

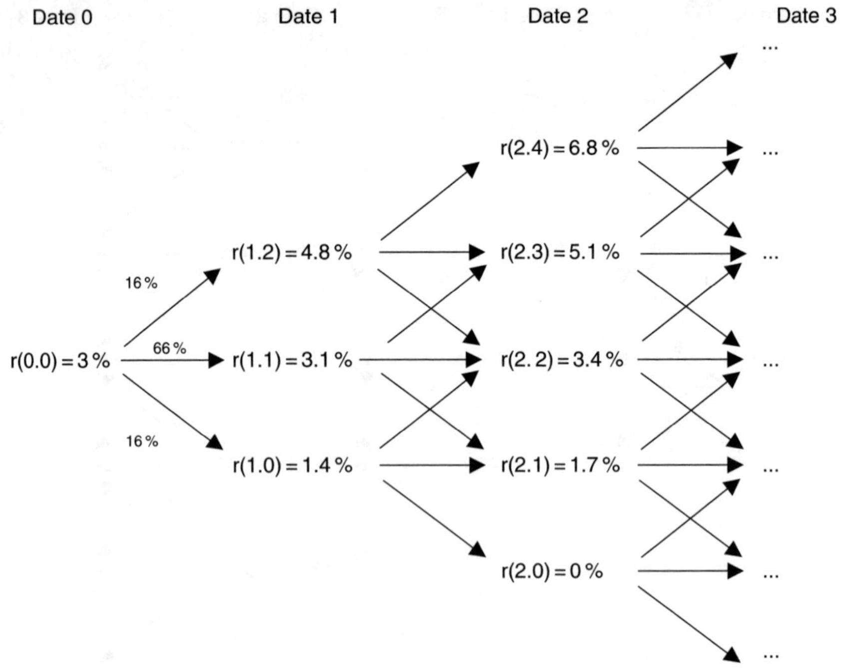

Figure 21.5 Second stage Tree

This model depends on five parameters:

- two mean reverting forces a and b;
- two volatilities σ et η;
- a correlation ρ.

In this model, the zero-coupon interest rate evolution is given by:

$$\frac{dB(t,t+\tau)}{B(t,t+\tau)} = r_t dt - \sigma\frac{1-e^{-a\tau}}{a}dW_t^x - \eta\frac{1-e^{-b\tau}}{b}dW_t^y \tag{21.66}$$

The model is still an affine model: the zero-coupons are expressed as an affine function of the short-term interest rate:

$$B(t,t+\tau) = \exp(A_\tau x_t + B_\tau y_t + C_\tau) \tag{21.67}$$

Consequently, standard interest rate derivatives (caps and swaptions) are priced directly through normal standard distributions.

The risk neutral calibration of the parameters is done minimizing the quadratic spread between market prices and model prices of a set of N caps and swaptions:

$$Error = \sum_{k=1}^{N} (\text{Market price}_\text{k} - \text{Model price}_\text{k})^2 \tag{21.68}$$

The chosen set of caps and swaptions should include out-of-the-money, at-the-money and in-the-money options; this will lead for instance to this set of parameters:

a	50 %
b	7 %
σ	1.4 %
η	1.4 %
ρ	−70 %

Figure 21.6 Set of parameters

As for the one-factor model, the initial variables x and y can be simulated using two independent Brownian motions.

$$\begin{aligned} dW_1(t) &= d\tilde{W}_1(t) \\ dW_2(t) &= \rho \times d\tilde{W}_1(t) + \sqrt{1-\rho^2} d\tilde{W}_2(t) \\ dx(t) &= -a \times x(t) + \sigma \times d\tilde{W}_1(t) \\ dy(t) &= -b \times y(t) + \eta \times \rho \times d\tilde{W}_1(t) + \eta \times \sqrt{1-\rho^2} d\tilde{W}_2(t) \end{aligned} \tag{21.69}$$

The zero-coupon prices can be computed as linear functions of x, y and of the initial market zero-coupons at date 0:

$$B(t, t+\tau) = \frac{B^M(0, t+\tau)}{B^M(0, t)} \exp \left\{ \begin{array}{l} \frac{1}{2}[V(t, t+\tau) - V(0, t+\tau) + V(0, t)] \\ + \frac{\exp(-a.\tau) - 1}{a} x(t) + \frac{\exp(-b.\tau) - 1}{b} y(t) \end{array} \right\} \tag{21.70}$$

Here the function V follows:

$$\begin{aligned} V(t, t+\tau) = {} & \frac{\sigma^2}{a^2}\left[\tau + \frac{2}{a} \times \exp(-a.\tau) - \frac{1}{2a}\exp(-2a.\tau) - \frac{3}{2a}\right] + \frac{\eta^2}{b^2}\left[\tau + \frac{2}{b} \times \exp(-b.\tau)\right. \\ & \left. - \frac{1}{2b}\exp(-2b.\tau) - \frac{3}{2b}\right] + 2\rho\frac{\sigma\eta}{ab}\left[\tau + \frac{\exp(-a.\tau) - 1}{a}\right. \\ & \left. + \frac{\exp(-b.\tau) - 1}{b} + \frac{\exp(-(a+b).\tau) - 1}{a+b}\right] \end{aligned} \tag{21.71}$$

Once more with the notation f for the forward instant rate, this function f will be straightforwardly computed:

$$\begin{aligned} \varphi(t) = {} & f^M(0, t) + \frac{\sigma^2}{2a^2}(1 - \exp(-a.t))^2 + \frac{\eta^2}{2b^2}(1 - \exp(-b.t))^2 \\ & + \rho\frac{\sigma\eta}{2b^2}(1 - \exp(-b.t))(1 - \exp(-a.t)) \end{aligned} \tag{21.72}$$

21.3.2.2 CIR++ (Cox Ingersoll Ross two factors model)

When the interest rate level is very low, the Hull & White model is not recommended: the opportunity to simulate negative interest rates is too important.

The CIR++ model will provide the opportunity to simulate positive interest rates with the following set of equations:

$$r_t = x_t + y_t + \varphi(t)$$
$$\begin{cases} dx_t = -ax_t dt + \sigma.\sqrt{x_t}.dW_t^x \\ dy_t = -by_t dt + \eta.\sqrt{y_t}.dW_t^y \end{cases} \tag{21.73}$$
$$Corr(W_t^x, W_t^x) = \rho$$

21.3.3 Market models: Libor Market Model, Swap Market Model

The last generations of interest rate models are developed in this chapter but the reader is invited to read the specialized books on this topic.

These models are proposed mainly with a pricing purpose:

- The *BGM model* is named after Brace, Gatarek and Musiela and is also called the *Libor Market Model* or *Libor Forward Lognormal (LFL)*.
- The *SMM model* also called the *Swap Market Model (SFL)* or *Jamshidian Model.*

The term market model comes from the fact that these models are priced automatically using option market prices (caps for BGM and swaptions for SMM). Indeed, one and two factors models do not allow the A/L manager to replicate exactly the caps and swaptions market prices. For instance, when pricing a cap with a one-factor model, this may lead to a price different from the price observed in the market.

The principle of the Libor Market Model is to replicate perfectly the European cap prices. The principle of the Swap Market Model is to replicate perfectly the swaption prices. Unfortunately, *those two models are incompatible.*

21.3.3.1 Libor Market Model or BGM

If we denote Libor(t,T_i, T_{i+1}) the Libor at date t going on the period from T_i to date T_{i+1} the Libor follows on a BGM model the martingale diffusion equation:

$$\frac{dLibor(t, T_i, T_{i+1})}{Libor(t, T_i, T_{i+1})} = \sigma_{t,T_i,T_{i+1}} \cdot dW_t^{Q(T_{i+1})} \tag{21.74}$$

The probability used is the forward neutral associated with the date T_{i+1}.

In the BGM model, the volatilities σ are deterministic (i.e. they are not stochastic) and the model is included in the HJM model class (see Chapter 35).

This model is close to the Black model where under the market dynamic the Libor follows:

$$\frac{dLibor(t, T_i, T_{i+1})}{Libor(t, T_i, T_{i+1})} = \sigma_{Black}(T_i).dW_t^{Q_M} \tag{21.75}$$

There is a relationship between the Black volatilities and the BGM volatilities:

$$\sigma_{Black}(T_i) = \sqrt{\frac{1}{T_i - t} \cdot \int_t^{T_i} \sigma_{t,T_i,T_{i+1}}{}^2 \, .dt} \tag{21.76}$$

In practice, to use the BGM model, the A/L manager needs to know the relationship between the different Brownian motions that is the different forward neutral probabilities $Q(T_{i+1})$. It is important to know how to compute the drift changes and the correlations between the different Brownian motions.

The calibration of the volatilities σ is made with calibration models. For instance, we may propose (separable or not, stationary or not) volatility formulae:

$$\begin{cases} \sigma_{t,T_i,T_{i+1}} = f\,(T_i, T_i - t) \\ \sigma_{t,T_i,T_{i+1}} = Cte\,(T_i) \\ \sigma_{t,T_i,T_{i+1}} = [a.(T_i - t) + d]\,.\exp\left(-\lambda(T_i - t)\right) + c \\ \sigma_{t,T_i,T_{i+1}} = Cte\,(T_i)\,.\exp\left(-\lambda(T_i - t)\right) \\ \ldots \end{cases} \tag{21.77}$$

The volatilities calibration is based on cap market prices using the Black formula. When the volatilities are separable, the framework becomes Markovian and explicit pricing formulae are available.

There is the same problem for the estimation of the correlations $\rho(T_i, T_j)$ between the Brownian motions $W_{Q(Ti)}$ and $W_{Q(Tj)}$. Different parametrical or non-parametrical forms are proposed in the literature. For instance, Rebonato propose forms of the following type:

$$\rho_{T_i,T_{i+1}} = \exp\left[-\beta.\left(T_i - T_j\right)\right] \tag{21.78}$$

The correlation calibration is often made using swaption market prices.

21.3.3.2 BGM with smile

The trader observes that *Black cap market price volatility depends on the strike.* The standard BGM model does not answer to this market observation. To correct this, we have to impose a simple constant drift on the Libor:

$$\begin{cases} Libor(t, T_i, T_{i+1}) = X(t, T_i, T_{i+1}) + \alpha \\ \dfrac{dX(t, T_i, T_{i+1})}{X(t, T_i, T_{i+1})} = \sigma_M(T_i).dW_t^{Q_M} \end{cases} \tag{21.79}$$

21.3.3.3 Swap market model

If we call $Swap(t, T_i, T_j)$ the interest rate swap rate at date t for a swap going from date T_i to date T_j, this rate follows in the Swap Market Model, this martingale diffusion:

$$\frac{dSwap(t, T_m, T_n)}{Swap(t, T_m, T_n)} = \sigma_{t,T_m,T_n} \cdot dW_t^{Q(T_m,T_n)} \tag{21.80}$$

The probability used here is the probability under which the swap rates are martingales.

In the framework developed by Jamshidian, the volatilities σ are deterministic (i.e. they are not stochastic) and the model is still included in the HJM model class.

This equation allows us to replicate perfectly the swaption market prices.

As for the BGM model, model volatilities are calibrated using Black market swaption prices:

$$\sigma_{m,n}^{Black} = \sqrt{\frac{1}{T_m - t} \cdot \int_t^{T_m} \sigma_{t,T_m,T_n}^2 \cdot dt} \tag{21.81}$$

21.3.4 Stochastic volatility and SABR

In the modelling above, the volatility is constant and does not vary stochastically. A new range of models appeared by the end of the 90s in order to take into account the volatility "stochasticity". Among those models, we may cite the SABR model. The name of this model comes from the model variables α, β and ρ (alpha, beta, rhô or ABR).

$$\begin{aligned} dLibor(t, T_i, T_{i+1}) &= \alpha_{t,T_i,T_{i+1}} \cdot (Libor(t, T_i, T_{i+1}))^{\beta} .dW_t^{Q(T_{i+1})/1} \\ d\alpha_{t,T_i,T_{i+1}} &= \upsilon.\alpha_{t,T_i,T_{i+1}} \cdot dW_t^{Q(T_{i+1})/2} \\ \left\langle dW_t^{Q(T_{i+1})/1}; dW_t^{Q(T_{i+1})/2} \right\rangle &= \rho.dt \end{aligned} \tag{21.82}$$

With these formulae, one can get the market price immediately and the market risks of many options. Note that the SABR model captures the correct dynamics of the smile.

21.4 GENERIC MODELS FOR JOINT SIMULATION OF INFLATION, STOCK INDEX, INTEREST RATES, REAL ESTATE, LIQUIDITY AND CREDIT SPREADS

21.4.1 General framework

In many ALM teams, the managers will have not only to forecast the interest rate level but also the level of the other risk sources: equity, currency exchange rates, inflation, real estate, interest rates in other currencies, etc.

In our approach, we will show how the *LGM2+ model framework can be extended in practice to the other types of risk sources.*

$$\begin{aligned} & r_t^{nominal} = x_t^{nominal} + y_t^{nominal} + \varphi^{nominal}(t) \\ & \begin{cases} dx_t^{nominal} = -a^n x_t^{nominal} dt + \sigma^n dW_t^{x,n} \\ dy_t^{nominal} = -b^n y_t^{nominal} dt + \eta^n dW_t^{y,n} \end{cases} \\ & Corr(W_t^{x,n}, W_t^{x,n}) = \rho \end{aligned} \tag{21.83}$$

For each risk type, the modelling introduces new Brownian motions that have to be correlated one with the other.

For instance, we will consider inflation as another currency with an exchange rate equal to the household basket price. We will then associate a one-factor model with the real rate curve.

$$r_t^{real} = x_t^{real} + y_t^{real} + \varphi^{real}(t)$$
$$\begin{cases} dx_t^{real} = -a^r x_t^{real} dt + \sigma^r dW_t^{x,r} \\ dy_t^{real} = -b^r y_t^{real} dt + \eta^r dW_t^{y,r} \end{cases} \tag{21.84}$$
$$Corr(W_t^{x,r}, W_t^{x,r}) = \rho$$

The price index π (the household basket price) will be expressed as an exchange rate between nominal zero-coupons and real zero-coupons. The dynamics of this price index are as follows:

$$\frac{d\pi_t}{\pi_t} = (r_t - \bar{r}_t)dt + \sigma_\pi dW_t^\pi \tag{21.85}$$

Note that when introducing a new nominal currency, the A/L manager will proceed as for inflation. The currency exchange rate modelling is also included in this modelling.

When introducing equity stock in the modelling, it will lead to a classic Black & Scholes modelling where the Brownian motions will be correlated with the other Brownian motions. It will be the same for real estate modelling.

$$\frac{dS_t}{S_t} = r(t).dt + \sigma^{equity}(t, S_t).dW_t^{\text{risk neutral, equity}} \tag{21.86}$$
$$\frac{dRE_t}{RE_t} = r(t).dt + \sigma^{RE}(t, S_t).dW_t^{\text{risk neutral, real estate}}$$

Finally, the A/L manager will have to set up a *correlation matrix* between all the Brownian motions.

Of course, the matrix has to be symmetric definite and positive such as a correlation matrix with correlation coefficients comprised between -1 and 1.

21.4.2 Extension to advanced liquidity risk and credit risk simulation

The modelling above can also take into account liquidity risk or credit risk factors.

Indeed, the A/L manager is interested in the modelling of the company spreads i.e.:

- the difference between the A/L manager's company yield curve and the risk free yield curve for liquidity risk;
- the difference between yield curves of other companies (or mortgages yield curves, consumer loans yield curves, etc.) and the risk free yield curve for credit risk.

$$\text{Rate} = \text{Risk Free rate (Government bonds rate)} + \text{spread}$$

Spreads follow a term structure. Intensity based models developed in the credit risk section will help with the modelling of the future evolution of these spreads; the modelling is based on the simulation of a risky zero-coupon rate.

	W^{equity}	$W^{real\ estate}$	$W^{EUR/USD}$	$W^{EUR\ nominal\ I}$	$W^{EUR\ nominal\ 2}$	$W^{USD\ nominal\ 1}$	$W^{USD\ nominal\ 2}$	$W^{EUR\ real\ 1}$	$W^{EUR\ real\ 2}$	$W^{EUR/EUR\ real}$
W^{equity}	100 %	50 %	30 %	...	...	...	...	...	...	...
$W^{real\ estate}$	50 %	100 %	50 %	30 %	...	...	...	...	...	...
$W^{EUR/USD}$	30 %	50 %	100 %	50 %	30 %	...	...	...	...	...
$W^{EUR\ nominal\ 1}$	...	30 %	50 %	100 %	50 %	30 %	...	...	...	...
$W^{EUR\ nominal\ 2}$	...	...	30 %	50 %	100 %	50 %	30 %	...	...	...
$W^{USD\ nominal\ 1}$	...	...	...	30 %	50 %	100 %	50 %	30 %	...	...
$W^{USD\ nominal\ 2}$	...	...	...	...	30 %	50 %	100 %	50 %	30 %	...
$W^{EUR\ real\ 1}$	...	...	...	...	...	30 %	50 %	100 %	50 %	30 %
$W^{EUR\ real\ 2}$	...	...	...	...	...	...	30 %	50 %	100 %	50 %
$W^{EUR/EUR\ real}$	...	...	...	...	...	...	...	30 %	50 %	100 %

Figure 21.7 Brownian correlations

Spreads are positive and will follow these CIR intensity models:

$$d\lambda_t^{liquidity} = a^{liquidity}.\left(\theta_t^{liquidity} - \lambda_t^{liquidity}\right) + \sigma^{liquidity}.\sqrt{\lambda_t^{liquidity}}.dW_t^{liquidity}$$

$$d\lambda_t^{mortgages} = a^{mortgages}.(\theta_t^{mortgages} - \lambda_t^{mortgages}) + \sigma^{mortgages}.\sqrt{\lambda_t^{mortgages}}.dW_t^{mortgages}$$

$$\ldots \tag{21.87}$$

$$d\lambda_t^{X\ company} = a^{X\ company}.\left(\theta_t^{X\ company} - \lambda_t^{X\ company}\right) + \sigma^{X\ company}.\sqrt{\lambda_t^{X\ company}}.dW_t^{X\ company}$$

$$\ldots$$

As for interest rate models, the functions θ are calibrated using the initial spread term structure.

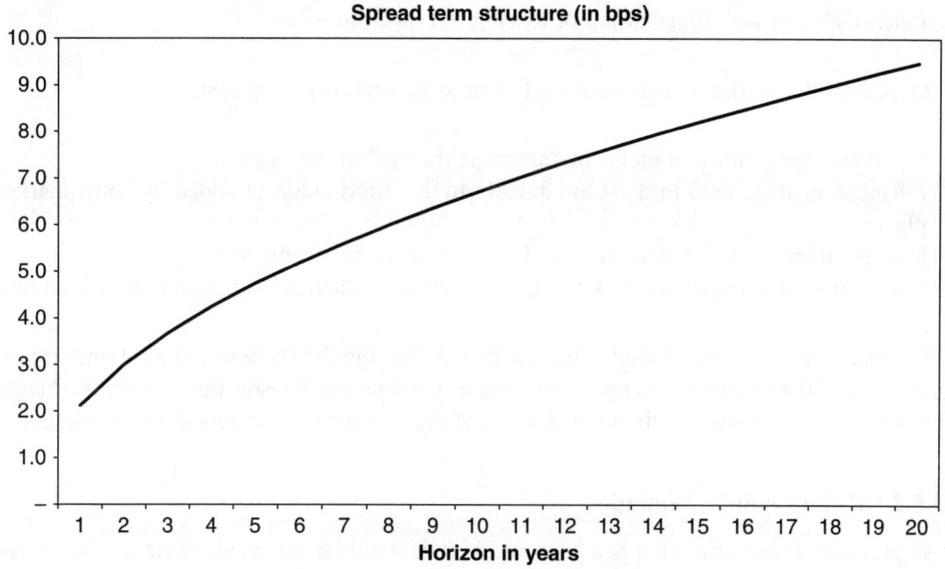

Figure 21.8 Spread term curve

The residual problem is to correlate these Brownian motions with the previous ones.

21.5 MARKET SIMULATIONS INCLUDING RISK PREMIUMS

21.5.1 Sources of risk premium

21.5.1.1 Behavioural finance explains the existence of risk premiums

Traditional finance is based on the following elements:

- individuals' rationality;
- market efficiency;
- equilibrium modelling of financial assets.

The rationality of the individuals follows the *von Neumann-Morgenstern axioms*: each individual maximizes his utility mathematical expectation. The utility is based on the individual wealth with utility functions stable across time. Risk aversion decreases with wealth.

Nevertheless, the *Allais paradox* shows that the choices of individuals are not always transitive. Moreover, the Ellsberg paradox shows that individuals do not allocate subjective probabilities to events but pay premiums to avoid uncertainty. Indeed, individuals are not always rational:

- Individuals play with "heuristics"; for instance, they tend to extrapolate using not enough data to make their decisions.
- Individuals have a less quantitative approach of the wealth than it could be expected.
- Psychology plays its role in individual behaviour.
- Individuals are more likely to assume the existence of "trends".
- Individuals tend to be overconfident (risk underestimation) or to be too much conservative.
- Individuals are sometimes afraid of loosing too much money.

Moreover, the market is not always efficient as it is usually supposed:

- There are many "noise traders" or "arbitrage traders" in the market.
- Financial markets tend to react too quickly to the information provided by some market players.
- Market information is sometimes used too late or in the wrong way.
- Companies tend to increase risk positions when their financial situation is deteriorating.

For example, a statistical study showed that during the 2000s before the internet crisis, more than 150 companies changed their name without any reason but the name change increased by more than two the market value of these companies in less than six months.

21.5.2 Risk premium estimation

Risk premium level estimation is a harder task than could be expected. There are two ways to estimate risk premiums:

- *Ex-post risk premium estimation*: the estimation is made through historical databases (for instance using corporate bonds, stock equity or government bond historical prices).
- *Ex-ante risk premium estimation*: the market prices may indicate the implicit level of risk premiums.

Ex-post estimation is very complex since databases are often polluted (with economic cycles, quotation discontinuities, nationalizations, etc.).

A quick statistical example shows that A/L managers will need very long historical databases to get a risk premium within a reasonable confidence interval. For instance, *for equities with a volatility of 15 %, the A/L manager will need 1 000 years of data to estimate the risk premium within a confidence interval of 1 % and with a probability of 80 %.*

On the other hand, ex-ante estimation is not easier since the estimation depends highly on the chosen model.

Nevertheless, there is a relative consensus on the risk premium levels:

- between 3 to 6 % p.a. on the equity stock market compared to the monetary market;
- around 1 % p.a. on the 10 year government bond market compared to the monetary market;
- around 50 bps p.a. on the 10-year real rate bond market compared to the monetary market.

Indeed, risk premiums increase with the volatility of the underlying (such as in CAPM modelling).

21.5.3 Risk neutral and real probability

As shown before, financial theory distinguishes real probability and risk neutral probability.

Risk neutral probability is linked with the absense of arbitrage opportunity (and this probability is interesting only when developing arbitrage techniques). This probability provides risk neutral market coherent prices but it is not used for risk measurement or for forecasting.

Under this probability, the yield of all the assets is the risk free rate and the discounted value of a set of flows is equal to the sum of flows discounted by the risk free rate. This probability has a pricing objective and realizes the consensus between two counterparties (accepting a risk transfer).

On the other hand, *real probability has a realistic simulation/projection objective*:

- It corrects risk neutral simulation and shows, for instance, that bonds are more profitable on the long-term than monetary investments.
- The real simulation integrates risk premiums for the remuneration of the supported risk.
- It corrects risk indicators calculation (in stress testing, sensitivities computation, etc.).
- It sometimes allows the company to take into account its own market evolution anticipation in the simulations.

Real probability will also be used when trying to optimize the A/L manager's risk exposure.

Risk premium indicates the difference between investors' expected profitability and the risk free rate. Mathematically speaking, we saw that moving from real probability to risk neutral probability means the introduction a risk premium μ:

$$dW_t^{real} = dW_t^{RN} + \mu.dt \tag{21.88}$$

21.5.4 One factor Linear Gaussian Model with risk premiums

When introducing a risk premium in the Linear Gaussian Model, the trajectories are modified as follows:

$$\begin{cases} dr_t = \lambda.(\theta_t - r_t)dt + \sigma\, dW_t \\ dW_t = d\tilde{W}_t + \mu_t\, dt \end{cases} \tag{21.89}$$

When playing with the risk premium μ, the A/L manager may choose either an interest rate yield curve level either a yield curve slope level.

Unfortunately, in this model slope level and interest rate level are directly linked: for instance, an anticipation of an important slope implies a certain short-term interest rate level.

The use of a two-factor model will give more flexibility in order to choose independently a slope and an interest rate level.

21.5.5 Two factors Linear Gaussian Model with risk premiums

The two factors model including risk premiums will be computed when introducing two risk premiums in the Brownian motions:

$$
\begin{aligned}
&r_t = x_t + y_t + \varphi(t) \\
&\begin{cases} dx_t = -ax_t dt + \sigma dW_t^x \\ dy_t = -by_t dt + \eta dW_t^y \end{cases} \\
&dW_t^x = d\tilde{W}_t^x + \alpha_t dt \\
&dW_t^y = d\tilde{W}_t^y + \beta_t dt \\
&Corr(\tilde{W}_t^x, \tilde{W}_t^x) = \rho
\end{aligned}
\tag{21.90}
$$

The risk premiums can be chosen:

- either empirically; or
- when imposing a value for the mathematical expectation for the short-term interest rate level and for a long-term interest rate and imposing it for each future date.

For instance, in risk neutral probabilities, forward short-term and long-term interest rates converge as shown in the next chart.

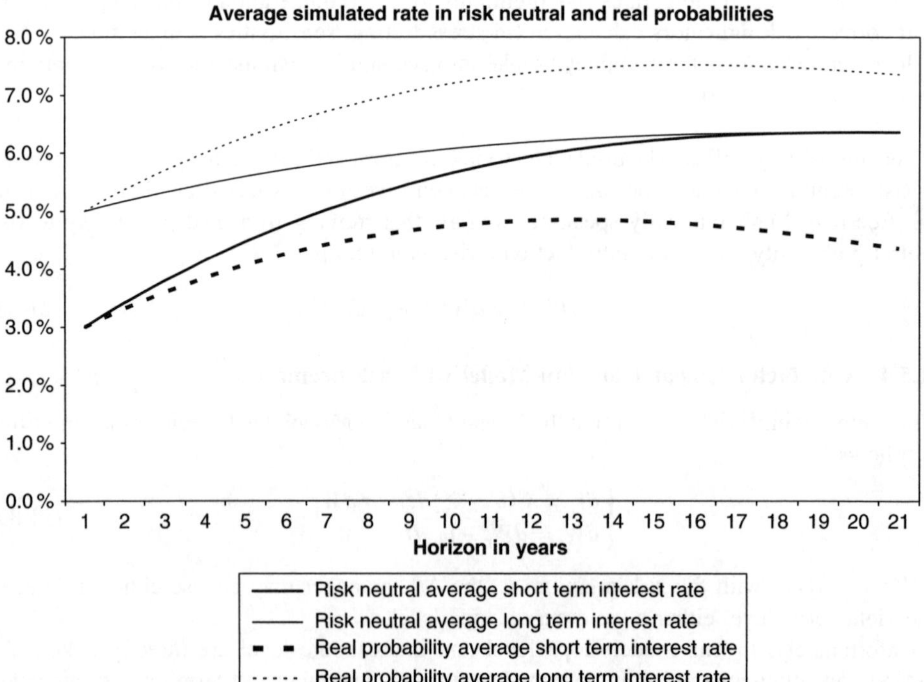

Figure 21.9 Risk neutral and real probabilities

Nevertheless, the A/L manager may impose a risk premium so that the average simulated long-term and short-term interest rates will look like the ones anticipated by the A/L manager. If, for instance, he anticipates that short-term interest rates will not increase greatly and that the interest rate slope will stay stable around 200 bps, he will choose the two risk premiums functions so that he will get the short-term and the long-term yield curves of the following chart.

As a conclusion, the A/L manager is able to simulate (with the LGM2+ with risk premiums) interest rates imposing an average level for the short-term interest rate and for the yield curve slope. This corrects the risk neutral modelling where the forward interest rate slope was converging to almost zero.

Such modelling can straightforwardly be extended to other market simulations.

The other advantages of this modelling are numerous:

- Such modelling illustrates the advantages of long-term investments (compared to short-term investments).
- The model is useful for asset allocation.
- The model is simple and easy to calibrate.
- The model helps the A/L manager to pilot the interest rate level and the slope level in his simulations.
- The model integrates market anticipations (volatility, etc.) and differentiate them from the manager's predictions through a risk premium term structure as presented here:

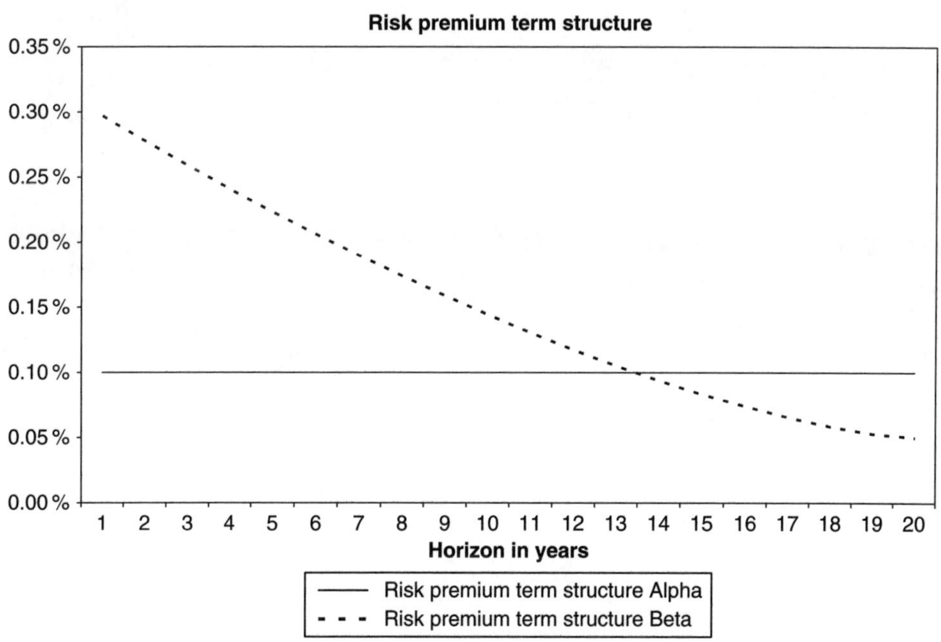

Figure 21.10 Risk premium

22 Delta Equivalent Computation

Mauvais ouvrier ne trouve jamais bon outil.

22.1 PRINCIPLES

The terms *delta equivalent* or *delta hedging* refers to the representation techniques of options in gaps and refers to the hedging techniques used by A/L managers.

The term "delta hedging" means "hedging with derivatives computation" or "first-rate hedging".

22.1.1 Delta equivalent computation in trading activities

These delta-hedging techniques refer to delta hedging practices used by front-office traders in trading books for products accounted as marked-to-market.

Let us show an example to explain how delta-hedging techniques operate in trading activities. We consider a trader selling 10 call options on a company X with these characteristics:

- stock price of company X: 5;
- strike call:5;
- 1-day exercise.

The counterparty who bought the call will receive tomorrow 10 times the maximum between 0 and (S−5) where S is the stock price of company X tomorrow.

We suppose that in one day, there are two possible evolutions for the company stock price:

- State 1: the company stock price is 6 (probability 50 %).
- State 2: the company stock price is 4 (probability 50 %).

The value of the call in the trading book is the expected pay-off of this call, i.e. 5 since:

- in state 1, the pay-off is 10 (probability 50 %);
- in state 2, the pay-off is 0 (probability 50 %).

How will the trader hedge this position?

Before hedging, the trader profit and loss (P&L) will be the following:

- State 1: $5-10=-5$ (probability 50 %).
- State 2: $5-10=+5$ (probability 50 %).

The trader has an access to the stock market and in order to hedge his position, he will buy 5 companies X shares. 5 shares will be his delta hedging. Indeed, after hedging, his P&L becomes:

- State 1: $-5+5.1=0$ (probability 50 %).
- State 2: $+5-5.1=0$ (probability 50 %).

After delta hedging, the trader is perfectly hedged whatever the stock market evolution looks like.

This framework is easy to generalize. It is possible to show that the amount of hedging can be written as a derivative (here comes the origin of the name "delta equivalent"). This amount x is the derivative by S of the expectation of the call price.

$$x=\frac{\partial E\,(\text{Call Price actualized})}{\partial S} \tag{22.1}$$

Indeed, *the option price is replicated completely by the strategy consisting into rebalancing the deltas*. The option price at date T is the sum of the capitalized initial option price (the price paid by the counterparty to buy the option, for example) and of the result of the rebalancing strategy. Mathematically speaking, it means that considering the available cash X for the trader, this cash evolves according to the cash replacement at interest rate r and to the delta strategy replacement:

$$\begin{aligned} X_0 &= \text{Option Price}_0 \\ dX_t &= r(t).X(t)\,.\,dt+\frac{\partial E(\text{Option price actualised})}{\partial S}\,.\,dS \\ X_T &= \text{Option Price}_T \end{aligned} \tag{22.2}$$

The delta hedging strategy allows the trader to replicate exactly the option price evolution and to pay exactly to the option buyer the cash flow of its option.

To summarize, to set up its strategy, the trader needs to know:

- the future possible evolutions of prices, interest rates, etc.;
- how to compute option prices expectancies;
- how to compute derivatives.

22.1.2 Delta equivalent computation in ALM: principles

The ALM delta equivalent technique is derived from the delta neutral technique a trader could use to hedge, at the first-rate, the payoff of a sold option. As shown before, in fixed income activities, the delta equivalent hedging of the position enables one to protect the future earnings from the market rates variations.

In ALM, the technique enables the stabilization and the smoothing of the future earnings that contains optionality (i.e. behaviour or market options accounted in accrued). By the way, it shows that the liquidity schedule is different from the interest rate schedule.

The technique not only takes into account the embedded options but also the impact of this optionality on the earnings. For instance, the impact of a prepayment on a loan with a high client rate is greater than the prepayment of a loan with a lower client rate.

ALM delta hedging's objective is to protect the incomes for each future date T. The protection is based on a suite of swaplets starting in T and maturing in T+1.

The option income translation in terms of a suite of swaplets is called the *"delta equivalent of the option"*.

The expected income (conditionally upon the market information F_t at date t) of a swaplet with nominal value N will vary between t and t+dt as the Libor forward will vary:

$$dE\,(\text{Swaplet Income}_{\mathrm{T}}/F_t) = N.dLibor\,(t, T) \tag{22.3}$$

The initial choice of swaplets is motivated by the accounting perspective and by the use of swaplets by front office A/L managers. (For example, the use of swaps starting from the forward 1st January to the next 1st January allows the hedging of the specific year income.)

The ALM delta hedging strategy is based on the hedging at each time t of the expected income (or result) at date T through forward swaplet.

$$\begin{aligned}&\text{With } \mathrm{X}_0 = 0\\ &\text{and strategy } d\mathrm{X}_t = \frac{\partial E\,(\mathrm{Res}_{\mathrm{T}}/F_t)}{\partial Libor\,(t, T)}.dLibor\,(t, T)\\ &\text{then } \mathrm{X}_{\mathrm{T}} + \mathrm{Res}_{\mathrm{T}} = E\,(\mathrm{Res}_{\mathrm{T}}/F_0)\end{aligned} \tag{22.4}$$

Here the mathematical expectation is computed according to the forward neutral probability.

In this framework, the variations of the interest rates follow a model with only one factor. Next chapters will treat delta equivalent computation with 2 and 3 factor models.

Actually, computing the sensitivity upon the Libor forward rate in a one-factor model is equivalent to compute the sensitivity upon the initial yield curve level. In practice, *delta equivalent in one-factor models will be computed when shifting the initial yield curve.*

At date t, the amount of forward swaplets is equal to:

$$\frac{\partial E\,(\mathrm{Res}_{\mathrm{T}}/F_t)}{\partial Libor\,(t, T)} \tag{22.5}$$

The delta equivalent representation of an option is the function that associates to T this amount. For instance for a 20 years cap with a 3.5 % strike the delta equivalent may look like in Figure 22.1.

The result/income used in the delta equivalent computation is the result/income after cost of carry.

Note that the delta equivalent of a swap is a swap. Indeed, the amount of swaplets computed by the equivalent delta technology is equal to the swap nominal N.

$$\frac{\partial E\,(\mathrm{Res}_{\mathrm{T}}\,(\text{Swaplet nominal N with rate T})\,/F_t)}{\partial Libor\,(t, T)} = \frac{\partial\,(N.\,(T - Libor\,(t, T)))}{\partial Libor\,(t, T)} = -N \tag{22.6}$$

The delta equivalent is the best way to represent option into the interest rate gap. A/L managers often experienced problems with representing options like swaptions, caps or prepayments options in their gap indicators.

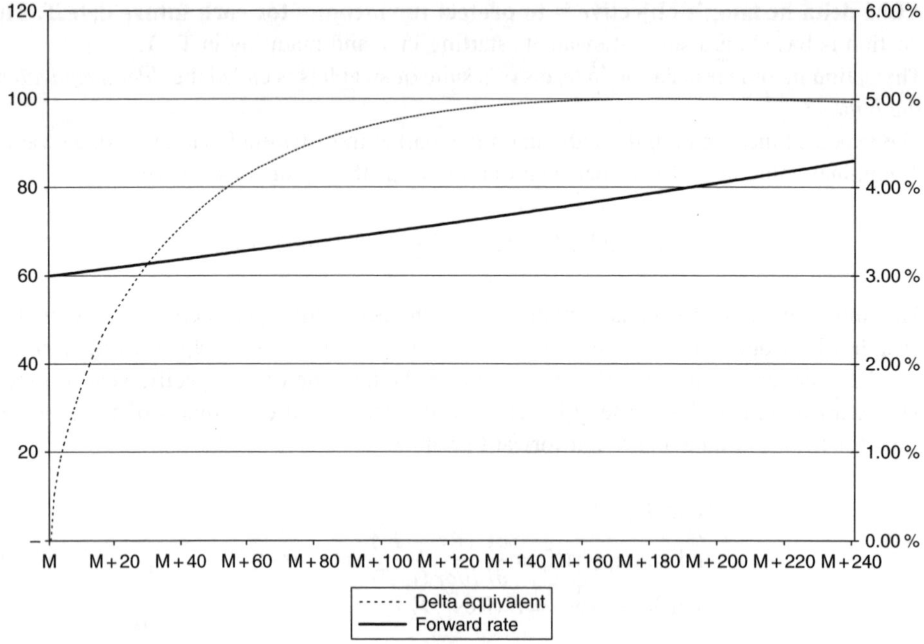

Figure 22.1 Delta equivalent

The delta equivalent of the option is the swap that has the same "first-rate properties": option income sensitivities and the sensitivities of the representation in a delta equivalent swap of the option are identical.

$$\frac{\partial E\left(\mathrm{Res}_{\mathrm{T}}\,(\text{delta equivalent})\,/F_t\right)}{\partial Libor\,(t,T)} = \frac{\partial E\left(\mathrm{Res}_{\mathrm{T}}\,(option)\,/F_t\right)}{\partial Libor\,(t,T)} \tag{22.7}$$

In a first-rate approximation, the equivalent delta is the multiplication of the option nominal by the option exercise probability.

Operationally speaking, the delta equivalent is computed through simulation or using analytic formulae:

- Through simulation, A/L managers simulate incomes with the initial actual yield curve and with a shifted yield curve.
- Using analytic formulas, A/L managers use the "delta" of the option market value (Black & Scholes delta, for instance).

22.1.3 Horizontal and vertical delta equivalent

For A/L managers, there are two possible delta equivalents: the horizontal delta equivalent and the vertical delta equivalent.

The delta equivalent we presented above is the vertical delta equivalent.

The delta equivalent computation follows the hedging instrument logical choice:

- **For vertical delta equivalent, short-term swaplets are the interest rate risk hedging instruments.** For example, the hedging is made through a suite of one-year swaplets each one starting on a future 1st January.

- **For horizontal delta equivalent, long-term swaps are the interest rate risk hedging instruments.** For example, the hedging is made through a suite of 10 years forward long-term swaps each one starting on a future 1st January.

For horizontal delta equivalent, instead of computing the mathematical expectation sensitivity to the translation of the forward swaplet rate, the A/L manager computes the sensitivity to the forward swap rate.

The horizontal hedging (with long-term swaps) affects not only the income of one specific year but of many years; the delta equivalent computation has to consider this.

$$\text{Horizontal Equivalent delta}_{\mathrm{T}} = \frac{\partial E\left(\mathrm{Res}_{\mathrm{T}}/F_t\right)}{\partial 10 \text{ years Forward Swap rate}\,(t,T)} + \int_{T-10}^{T} \text{Horizontal Equivalent delta}_{\mathrm{t}}.dt \tag{22.8}$$

The chart below shows an example of delta equivalent computation with a vertical and with a horizontal delta. For example, for a 2-year swaption the horizontal delta equivalent is a 2-year long-term swap with a constant nominal when the vertical delta equivalent is not constant over the period.

The swaption result in the vertical delta framework is:

$$1_{\{\text{swaption is exerced in one year}\}}.\text{Nominal.(Strike-Libor(t))} \tag{22.9}$$

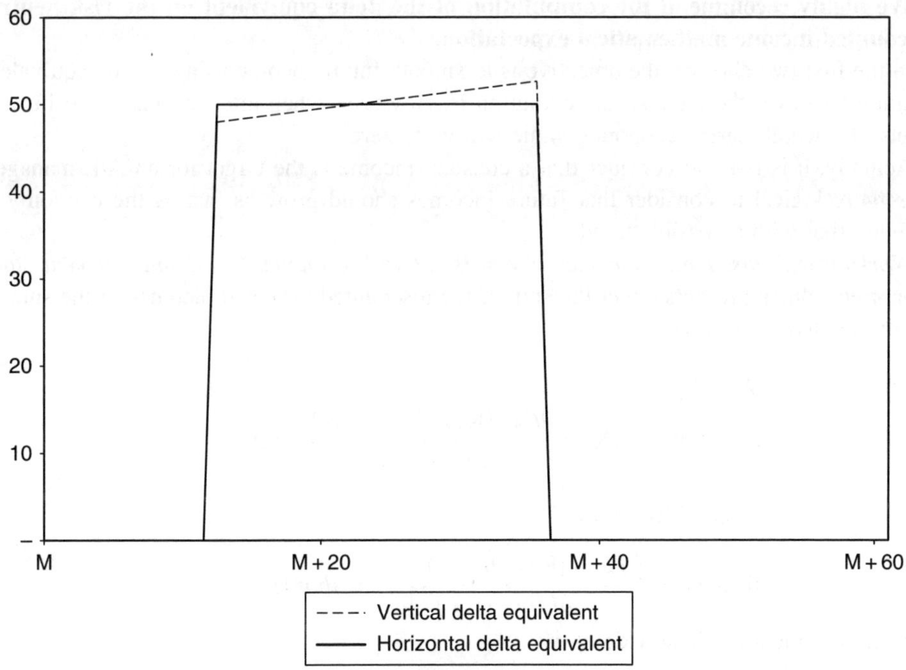

Figure 22.2 Vertical and horizontal delta

In addition, in the horizontal delta framework the result becomes:

$$1_{\{\text{swaption is exerced in one year}\}}.\text{Nominal.(Strike-2 years rate in one year)} \qquad (22.10)$$

This leads to a different delta equivalent according to the methodology choice.

In conclusion, the A/L manager will use the horizontal delta equivalent for a specific product when he is able to compute easily this delta and when his replicating hedging strategy is based on long-term swaps:

- **swaptions;**
- **prepayment options.**

22.1.4 Forward neutral and risk neutral discounted delta equivalent

The previous sections presented a delta equivalent computed under a forward neutral probability. It means that the A/L manager target is to hedge incomes expectancies.

Actually, there are many computation possibilities:

- *hedging risk neutral income mathematical expectation*;
- *hedging forward neutral income mathematical expectation*;
- *hedging risk neutral discounted income mathematical expectation.*

We highly recommend the computation of the delta equivalent on the risk neutral discounted income mathematical expectation.

In the first two choices, the objective is to smooth future income using a delta equivalent hedging whatever the interest rate evolution is. However, when interest rates go to infinite levels, the actual margin economic value will go to zero.

Actually, it is risky to consider that a constant income is the target for an A/L manager. It is more logical to consider that future incomes should grow as fast as the economy is growing (but with a possible trend).

Working with discounted incomes is consistent with economic value management since economic value represents either the sum of the discounted expected incomes or the sum of the discounted cash flows.

$$\begin{aligned}
&\text{With } \mathrm{X}_0 = 0\\
&\text{and strategy } d\mathrm{X}_t = \frac{\partial E_{RN}\left(\mathrm{Res}_\mathrm{T}.\bar{B}(t,T)/F_t\right)}{\partial Libor\,(t,T)}.dLibor\,(t,T)\\
&\text{where } \bar{B}(0,T) = e^{-\int_0^T r(s).ds}\\
&\text{then } \mathrm{X}_\mathrm{T} = \int_0^T \frac{\partial E_{RN}\left(\mathrm{Res}_\mathrm{T}.\bar{B}(t,T)/F_t\right)}{\partial Libor\,(t,T)}.dLibor\,(t,T)
\end{aligned} \qquad (22.11)$$

And the income after delta hedging is:

$$\tilde{\mathrm{X}}_\mathrm{T} = \mathrm{X}_\mathrm{T} + \mathrm{Res}_\mathrm{T} = E\left(\mathrm{Res}_\mathrm{T}.\bar{B}(0,T)/F_0\right).e^{\int_0^T r(s).ds}$$

Risk neutral discounted income delta hedging is equivalent to economic value hedging.

If the A/L manager proposes a solution so that the discounted mathematical expectation of the income decreases exponentially with time:

$$E\left(\mathrm{Res}_{\mathrm{T}}.\bar{B}(0,T)/F_0\right)=e^{-\mu.T} \tag{22.12}$$

Then it is possible to index income growth (after discounted income delta hedging) to the interest rates:

$$\frac{d\tilde{X}_t}{\tilde{X}_t}=(r(t)-\mu)\,.dt \tag{22.13}$$

Consequently, risk neutral delta hedging is the better delta hedging choice since:

- **it allows income growth consistent with the economy;**
- **it allows a direct consistency with economic value hedging.**

22.1.5 Gamma equivalent computation in ALM

Delta hedging proposes a first-rate hedging.

In trading activities, second-rate hedging solutions are necessary. For example, the delta of an option is not constant over time and it is not possible to hedge continuously optional positions.

Usually, traders report their *gamma position*, i.e. the risk of variation of the delta according to the market evolutions.

In ALM, the gamma equivalent is computed as the delta equivalent sensitivity to the interest rate level.

$$\begin{aligned}\Delta&=\frac{\partial E_{RN}\left(\mathrm{Res}_{\mathrm{T}}.\bar{B}(t,T)/F_t\right)}{\partial Libor\,(t,T)}\\ \Gamma&=\frac{\partial^2 E_{RN}\left(\mathrm{Res}_{\mathrm{T}}.\bar{B}(t,T)/F_t\right)}{\partial Libor\,(t,T)^2}\end{aligned} \tag{22.14}$$

The majority of the positions followed by A/L managers are gamma negative since many companies sell more options than they buy: the A/L manager has to borrow when interest rates are rising and to lend when rates are decreasing.

If the A/L manager wants to hedge his delta equivalent, he will replicate the optional cost since he will be penalized at each interest rate movement.

For instance, with the prepayment option example, when interest rates decrease, there are more prepayments than expected and fewer loans: interest rate gap goes up as if there were new fixed rate deposits.

Actually, the delta hedging strategy allows first-rate extreme risk hedging. The second-rate hedging (i.e. the gamma hedging) is accessible only by options selling or buying.

Optional indicators may use this gamma equivalent to compute the amount of options to buy.

22.2 DELTA, PENTA, CORRELA AND COURBA EQUIVALENTS OR "ADAM EQUIVALENTS"

Delta equivalent can be computed in two or three factors models and not only in one-factor models such as in the previous chapter.

It provides the opportunity to develop efficient hedging strategies if we compute a new set of "equivalents" that we will call *"Adam equivalents"*:

- *Penta equivalent: sensitivity to the yield curve slope.*
- *Correla equivalent: sensitivity to the joint movement of the interest rate level and of the yield curve slope.*
- *Courba equivalent: sensitivity to the yield curve convexity.*

We now present these equivalents under the forward neutral probability and under the recommended discounted risk neutral probability.

22.2.1 Under forward neutral probability

We start with the definition of the delta equivalent in a two factors model under the forward neutral probability (i.e. the probability that allows income hedging and not the discounted income hedging).

22.2.1.1 Delta equivalent

We consider the zero-coupon yield curve constituted by the zero-coupon rates r_i expressed in an exponential basis:

$$B(0, i) = e^{-r_i . i} \tag{22.15}$$

We rather define now the forward neutral delta equivalent (on the period T to T+ΔT) as the sensitivity of the expected future income on this period to a translation of the spot zero-coupon yield curve. It means that we have to compute the sum of the sensitivities to the different zero-coupon rates:

$$Eq\Delta_{T\to T+\Delta T} = \frac{\partial E(\text{Res}_{T\to T+\Delta T})}{\partial Translation} = \sum_i \frac{\partial E(\text{Res}_{T\to T+\Delta T})}{\partial r_i} . \alpha_i \tag{22.16}$$

with $\alpha_i = 1$ (∀i)

If we consider a swaplet with nominal N paying a fixed rate F and receiving the day-to-day (DD) rate (on the period T to T+ΔT), its delta equivalent is still equal to the nominal N.

Actually the swap income is easily deconstructed:

$$
\begin{aligned}
&\mathrm{Res}_{T\to T+\Delta T} = N.\left(-F + DD_{T\to T+\Delta T}\right)\\
&E\left(\mathrm{Res}_T\right) = N.\left(-F + E\left(DD_{T\to T+\Delta T}\right)\right)\\
&E\left(DD_T\right) = \frac{1}{\Delta T}.\ln\left(\frac{B(0,T)}{B(0,T+\Delta T)}\right)\\
&E\left(DD_T\right) = \frac{1}{\Delta T}.\left(-r_T.T + r_{T+\Delta T}.\left(T+\Delta T\right)\right)\\
&Eq\Delta_T\left(Swap\right) = \sum_i \frac{\partial E(N.(-F+JJ_T))}{\partial r_i} = \frac{1}{\Delta T}.\left(-T+\left(T+\Delta T\right)\right).N = N
\end{aligned}
\tag{22.17}
$$

Moreover, **the delta equivalent of a zero-coupon CMS swaplet is equal to zero** (a zero-coupon CMS swaplet is a swap that exchange DD rate against a long-term zero-coupon rate with maturity M on the period T to T+ΔT). Here the demonstration is provided assuming that there is no convexity bias in the CMS mathematical expectation computation:

$$
\begin{aligned}
&\mathrm{Res}_{T\to T+\Delta T} = N.\left(CMS(M)_{T\to T+\Delta T} - DD_{T\to T+\Delta T}\right)\\
&E\left(\mathrm{Res}_T\right) = N.\left(E\left(CMS(M)_{T\to T+\Delta T}\right) - E\left(DD_{T\to T+\Delta T}\right)\right)\\
&E\left(DD_T\right) = \frac{1}{\Delta T}.\left(-r_T.T + r_{T+\Delta T}.\left(T+\Delta T\right)\right)\\
&E\left(CMS(M)_{T\to T+\Delta T}\right) = \frac{1}{M}.\left(-r_T.T + r_{T+M}.\left(T+M\right)\right)\\
&Eq\Delta_T\left(SwapCMS\right) = \sum_i \frac{\partial E(N.(CMS(M)_{T\to T+\Delta T} - DD_{T\to T+\Delta T}))}{\partial r_i}\\
&Eq\Delta_T\left(SwapCMS\right) = \left(\frac{(-T+(T+M))}{M} - \frac{(-T+(T+\Delta T))}{\Delta T}\right).N = 0
\end{aligned}
\tag{22.18}
$$

22.2.1.2 Penta equivalent

We are now able to *define the penta equivalent as the sensitivity of the expected income (net of the delta equivalent that is after delta hedging) to the yield curve rotation*:

$$
\begin{aligned}
&\mathrm{Res}^*_{T\to T+\Delta T} = \mathrm{Res}_{T\to T+\Delta T} - Eq\Delta_{T\to T+\Delta T}.\left(-F + JJ_{T\to T+\Delta T}\right)\\
&EqPenta_{T\to T+\Delta T} = \frac{\partial E(\mathrm{Res}^*_{T\to T+\Delta T})}{\partial Rotation} = \sum_i \frac{\partial E(\mathrm{Res}^*_{T\to T+\Delta T})}{\partial r_i}.\beta_i\\
&\beta_i = i\,(\forall i)
\end{aligned}
\tag{22.19}
$$

The rotation means a weighting of long-term zero-coupon interest rates sensitivities higher than the short-term zero-coupon interest rates sensitivities.

The fixed rate F of the delta equivalent is the forward rate that makes the delta equivalent expected profit equal to zero.

By definition, *the penta equivalent of a fixed rate swap against DD rate is equal to zero.*

The penta equivalent of a zero-coupon CMS swap of nominal N against DD rate is equal to the nominal multiplied by the maturity M of the CMS:

$$E\,(\mathrm{Res}^*{}_T) = N.\left(\frac{1}{M}.\,(-r_T.T + r_{T+M}.\,(T+M)) - \frac{1}{\Delta T}.\,(-r_T.T + r_{T+\Delta T}.\,(T+\Delta T))\right)$$

$$EqPenta_T\,(SwapCMS) = \sum_i \frac{\partial E(\mathrm{Res}^*{}_T)}{\partial r_i}.i$$

$$EqPenta_T\,(SwapCMS) = \left(\frac{1}{M}.\,(-T.T + (T+M)\,.\,(T+M)) - \frac{1}{\Delta T}.(-T.T + (T+\Delta T)\,.\,(T+\Delta T))\right).N \tag{22.20}$$

$$EqPenta_T\,(SwapCMS) = \left(\frac{1}{M}.\,(2.T.M + M^2) - \frac{1}{\Delta T}.\,(2.T.\Delta T + \Delta T^2)\right).N = (M - \Delta T)\,.N \approx M.N$$

22.2.1.3 Correla equivalent

Once designed delta and penta equivalents (and therefore delta and penta equivalent hedging), a risk coming from the correlation between translation movements and rotation movements will still exist.

We define *the correla equivalent as the joint sensitivity of the expected income to the rotation and to the translation of the yield curve*:

$$EqCorrela_{T\to T+\Delta T} = \frac{\partial E(\mathrm{Res}_{T\to T+\Delta T})}{\partial Translation \partial Rotation} = \sum_{i,j} \frac{\partial E(\mathrm{Res}_{T\to T+\Delta T})}{\partial r_i.\partial r_j}.i.j^2 \tag{22.21}$$

By definition, *the correla equivalents of a swap and of a CMS swap are equal to zero.*

On the other hand, the correla equivalent of a product mixing interest rate level and slope is not equal to zero. The product that pays at date T+ΔT, the following flow has a correla equivalent close to its nominal:

$$\mathrm{N.[DD(T).(CMS(T) - DD(T))]} \tag{22.22}$$

22.2.1.4 Courba equivalent

Identically, we define *the courba equivalent as the sensitivity of the expected income (net of delta and penta equivalents, i.e. delta and penta hedged) to yield curve convexity moves:*

$$\begin{aligned}\mathrm{Res}^*{}_{T\to T+\Delta T} &= \mathrm{Res}_{T\to T+\Delta T} - Eq\Delta_{T\to T+\Delta T}.(-F + JJ_{T\to T+\Delta T}) \\ &\quad - \frac{EqPenta_{T\to T+\Delta T}.(CMS(M)_{T\to T+\Delta T} - JJ_{T\to T+\Delta T})}{M} \\ EqCourba_{T\to T+\Delta T} &= \frac{\partial E(\mathrm{Res}^*{}_{T\to T+\Delta T})}{\partial Courbure} = \sum_i \frac{\partial E(\mathrm{Res}^*_{T\to T+\Delta T})}{\partial r_i}.\gamma_i \\ \gamma_i &= i^2\ (\forall \mathrm{i})\end{aligned} \tag{22.23}$$

The courba equivalent of a swap or of a CMS swap is equal to zero.

On the other hand, *the courba equivalent is not equal to zero for a convexity product* paying for example on the period going from T to T+ΔT:

$$\mathrm{DD(T)} + \mathrm{CMS(M)} - 2.\mathrm{CMS(M/2)} \tag{22.24}$$

22.2.2 Under risk neutral discounted income delta hedging

It is easy to translate the definitions presented above in the risk neutral framework where the income has to be discounted.

22.2.2.1 Delta equivalent

We define then *the delta equivalent as the expected discounted income sensitivity to a spot yield curve translation*:

$$Eq\Delta_{T\to T+\Delta T} = \frac{\partial E(\mathrm{Res}_{T\to T+\Delta T}.\bar{B}(0,T+\Delta T))}{\partial Translation} = \sum_i \frac{\partial E(\mathrm{Res}_{T\to T+\Delta T}.\bar{B}(0,T+\Delta T))}{\partial r_i}.\alpha_i$$

$$\alpha_i = 1\ (\forall \mathrm{i}) \tag{22.25}$$

$$Eq\Delta_{T\to T+\Delta T} = \sum_i \frac{\partial E(\mathrm{Res}_{T\to T+\Delta T}).\exp\left(-r_{T+\Delta T}.(T+\Delta T)\right)}{\partial r_i}$$

It is possible to establish a link between this delta equivalent and the delta equivalent of the non-discounted incomes:

$$Eq\Delta_{T\to T+\Delta T} = Eq\Delta^{\text{non actualised}}{}_{T\to T+\Delta T}.B(0,T) - T.E(\mathrm{Res}_{T\to T+\Delta T}).B(0,T) \tag{22.26}$$

The risk neutral discounted income delta equivalent of a fixed rate swaplet paying a fixed rate F equal to the fixed rate market rate and receiving the day-to-day rate DD is equal to the discounted nominal N.

Indeed, the computation is as follows:

$$Eq\Delta_T\,(Swap) = N.B(0,T) - T.B(0,T).0 = N.B(0,T) \tag{22.27}$$

The risk neutral discounted income delta equivalent of a CMS swaplet without any margin is still equal to 0:

$$Eq\Delta_T\,(SwapCMS) = 0 - T.0.B(0,T) = 0 \tag{22.28}$$

22.2.2.2 Penta equivalent

Under the same conditions, the *penta equivalent* is in this framework now defined as the net expected discounted income sensitivity to the yield curve rotation. The income is net of the impact of the undiscounted delta equivalent.

$$\mathrm{Res}^*_{T\to T+\Delta T} = \mathrm{Res}_{T\to T+\Delta T} - \frac{Eq\Delta_{T\to T+\Delta T}}{B(0,T)}.(F - DD_{T\to T+\Delta T})$$

$$EqPenta_{T\to T+\Delta T} = \frac{\partial E(\mathrm{Res}^*{}_{T\to T+\Delta T}.B(0,T+\Delta T))}{\partial Rotation} \tag{22.29}$$

$$= \sum_i \frac{\partial E(\mathrm{Res}^*{}_{T\to T+\Delta T}.B(0,T+\Delta T))}{\partial r_i}.\beta_i$$

$$\beta_i = i\,(\forall \mathrm{i})$$

By definition, the penta equivalent of a swap at market rates is equal to zero.

The penta equivalent of a CMS swap of nominal N exchanging a maturity M zero-coupon CMS against DD rate is equal to the discounted nominal multiplied by M:

$$E\,(\mathrm{Res}^*{}_T) = N.\left(\frac{1}{M}.(-r_T.T + r_{T+M}.(T+M)) - \frac{1}{\Delta T}.(-r_T.T + r_{T+\Delta T}.(T+\Delta T))\right)$$

$$EqPenta_T\,(SwapCMS) = \sum_i \frac{\partial E(\mathrm{Res}^*{}_T).B(0,T)}{\partial r_i}.i$$

$$EqPenta_T\,(SwapCMS) = \left(\frac{1}{M}.(-T.T + (T+M).(T+M)) - \frac{1}{\Delta T}.(-T.T + (T+\Delta T).(T+\Delta T))\right).N.B(0,T) - 0 \tag{22.30}$$

$$EqPenta_T\,(SwapCMS) = \left(\frac{1}{M}.\left(2.T.M + M^2\right) - \frac{1}{\Delta T}.\left(2.T.\Delta T + \Delta T^2\right)\right).N.B(0,T)$$

$$= (M - \Delta T).N.B(0,T)$$

$$EqPenta_T\,(SwapCMS) \approx M.N.B(0,T)$$

22.2.3 Replicating portfolio

From these *"Adam equivalents"*, it is easy to deduce the *risk hedging strategy*.

The delta equivalent gives the amount of fixed rate swaplets to contract now.

The penta equivalent gives the amount of CMS swaplets to contract now.

The correla equivalent gives the amount of products mixing interest rate level and slope to contract now.

The courba equivalent gives the amount of convexity products to invest in.

22.3 DELTA EQUIVALENT ASSOCIATED BREAK-EVEN POINT

In interest rate gaps, the assets and the liabilities are represented through their interest rate schedules. The interest rate schedule of options is their delta equivalent.

However, associated to interest rate gaps, we already defined "break-even points". For each asset and each liability, an interest rate is associated: the average rate of the interest rate gap is called the break-even point.

For delta equivalent representation of options, A/L manager has to assign an interest rate allowing the computation of the company break-even point.

In a balance sheet without options, the interest rate associated with a fixed rate product is the product fixed rate, so that the break-even point is computed as the average rate of assets and liabilities applied to the interest rate gap:

$$Break-even_t = \frac{(Liabilities.IRL_{rate})_{\text{fixed rate remaining at t}} - (Assets.IRA_{rate})_{\text{fixed rate remaining at t}}}{\text{Interest rate gap}_t} \quad (22.31)$$

The break-even point is justified as follows: without any new production, the accounted income of period from t to t+dt is computed directly when comparing break-even point and the forward day-to-day rate DD(t):

$$RES_t = -\text{Interest rate gap}_t . (Break\text{-}even_t - DD_t) \quad (22.32)$$

The break-even point indicates the future level of the DD rate that equilibrates the position: if the DD rate is equal to the break-even point, the income is equal to zero.

In order to save this relationship, **we define the interest rate associated with the delta equivalent of an option as the difference between the income mathematical expectation and the forward DD rate:**

$$\text{Option delta equivalent rate}_t = E(DD_t) - \frac{E(RES_t)}{\text{Delta Equivalent}_t} \quad (22.33)$$

Doing so, the expected income is still the difference between the break-even point after option translation in the interest rate gap and the forward DD rate applied to the interest rate gap:

$$E(RES_t) = -\text{Interest rate gap}_t . (Break\text{-}even_t - E(DD_t)) \quad (22.34)$$

22.4 EXAMPLES OF DELTA EQUIVALENT COMPUTATION

22.4.1 Operational delta equivalent computation of prepayment option

Before the computation of the delta equivalent of a prepayment option, we will focus on the principles hidden behind prepayment cost hedging.

22.4.1.1 Principles

We take the example of a set of 100 non-amortizing loans of €100.000 each with 4% interest rates on 5 years without prepayment penalty after 1 year. The total amount of loans granted in year 0 is €10 M.

In our example, the statistical/sociological prepayment rate is of 10% p.a. and the financial prepayment rate is of 20% p.a. if the interest rates are under 4%.

The bank is financed on a 5 years horizon at 4% through an interbank loan. The loan FTP is then equal to 4% and the Commercial Department margin is of 0% during 5 years.

After 1 year, we consider that there are two possible cases:

- either interbank interest rates will go from 4 % to 6 % (case A); or
- they will go from 4 % to 2 % (case B).

In both cases, there are sociological prepayments in one year for an amount of 100*100.000*10 % that is €1 M.

It means that at the loan starting date, the bank will only refinance 90 % of the loan portfolio over 1 year.

However, financial prepayments will also occur and the amount of these prepayments will depend on the interest rate level:

- Case A: there is not a financial prepayment during the first year and the total loan amount after one year is €9 M with a FTP of 4 %.
- Case B: there are financial prepayments during the first year for an amount of 20 %*90 = €18 M; the total loan amount after one year is of €72 M with a FTP of 4 %.

There is no loss in the case A. Nevertheless, in the case B, there is a remaining amount of treasury after one year and the replacement rate is only of 2 %. The net loss is equal to 18*(4 %–2 %) = €360 k p.a. over 4 years!

This example proposes some common conclusions:

- The existence of financial prepayments introduces an optional interest rate risk.
- The statistical prepayments are costless for the A/L manager even if they reduce the profitability for the Commercial Department.

The delta equivalent computation of the prepayment option will help the A/L manager to produce option consistent interest rate gaps and to compute the delta hedging strategy (to smooth over time the prepayment cost).

In our example, the option delta equivalent is equal to €360k/(2 %)/2 = €9 M. Instead of refinancing €90 M, the bank will rather refinance 90−9 = €81 M.

In Case A, the ALM income will be of 90*4 %–81*4 %–9*6 %, i.e. a loss of €180 k p.a. during 4 years.

In Case B, the ALM income will be of 72*4 %–81*4 %+9*2 % that is a loss of €180 k p.a. over 4 years.

After delta hedging, the prepayment option loss does not depend on the interest rate level.

After having presented this example, it is time to introduce the operational delta computation principles, that is:

- **choices of interest rate simulation**;
- **behaviour simulation**;
- **income simulation; and**
- **effective delta computation.**

22.4.1.2 Interest rate simulation

Different interest rate models are used to compute the delta hedging strategy. The most common interest rate model is the one factor Linear Gaussian Model (such as the Hull & White model). With this model, it is necessary to perform a series of at least one thousand Monte Carlo simulations.

A/L managers willing to compute the "Adam equivalents" will have to choose two or three factors models to simulate non-correlated slopes and interest rates.

22.4.1.3 Behaviour simulation

To perform the delta computation, the A/L manager needs also:

- *Information about his stock of loans* (for example the contractual schedule, the client rate and the FTP rate; all this information is given on a monthly basis and aggregated by seniority, by interest rate tranch and by credit type).
- *Behaviour functions* such as the statistical prepayment rate as a function of the seniority, the financial prepayment rate as a function of the seniority and of the spread (the spread between loan rate and market rates) and the renegotiation rate function.
- *Client rate after renegotiation modelling*: the A/L manager needs to know how the client rate is set after renegotiation (as a function of market rates and of the initial client rate).

22.4.1.4 Income simulation

After the simulation of the interest rates through a Monte Carlo simulation, it is possible for each Monte Carlo simulation i to compute date by date the loan ALM income at date t (after replacement and without any hedging strategy):

$$\begin{aligned} &\text{Commercial income}_{t,i} = \text{Remaining capital}_{t,i}.\left(\text{Client rate}_{t,i} - \text{FTP}_t\right) \\ &\text{ALM income}_{t,i} = \text{Remaining capital}_{t,i}.\left(\text{FTP}_t - \text{DD}_{t,i}\right) + \text{Prepayment indemnity}_{t,i} \end{aligned} \tag{22.35}$$

The prepayment indemnity is often an explicit function of the remaining capital so that, the task is to be able to compute for each simulation the remaining capital.

For a loan portfolio, the remaining capital follows the equation below (where the prepayment rate is a function of interest rates and of the client rate):

$$\text{Remaining capital}_{t,i} = \text{Remaining capital}_{t-1,i}.\frac{\text{Contractual remaining capital}_t}{\text{Contractual remaining capital}_{t-1}} \times (1 - \text{Prepayment rate}_{t,i}) \tag{22.36}$$

$$\text{Prepayment rate}_{t,i} = F\left(CMS_{t,i}, \text{Client rate}_{t,i}, seasoning, \ldots\right)$$

Renegotiations are harder to introduce in this framework. The usual shortcut is to recognize renegotiations as prepayments. However, it is better to recognize them as prepayments plus new productions (these new productions are susceptible to be attacked once more by interest rate decreases).

22.4.1.5 Delta equivalent computation

With the methodology presented in the above chapters, we are able to simulate a set of say one thousand scenarios and for each scenario the possible future ALM incomes: ALM $\text{income}_{t,i}$.

The A/L manager knows then what his expected (discounted or not) ALM income is at date t:

$$\begin{aligned} &\mathrm{E}\left(\text{ALM income}_{\mathrm{t,i}}\right) = \frac{1}{\mathrm{N}}\sum_{i=1}^{\mathrm{N}} \text{ALM income}_{\mathrm{t,i}} \\ &or\ \mathrm{E}\left(\text{Actualised ALM income}_{\mathrm{t,i}}\right) = \frac{1}{\mathrm{N}}\sum_{i=1}^{\mathrm{N}} \text{ALM income}_{\mathrm{t,i}}.e^{-\int_0^t DD_i.dt} \end{aligned} \quad (22.37)$$

The set of one thousand scenarios is resimulated with the initial yield curve shifted by one basis point. The ALM incomes are resimulated and it is then easy to compute the sensitivity of the expected income to interest rates and then the delta equivalent:

$$Eq\Delta_{T\to T+\Delta T} = -\frac{E^{+1bp}(\mathrm{Res}_{T\to T+\Delta T}) - E(\mathrm{Res}_{T\to T+\Delta T})}{(0.01\%)} \quad (22.38)$$

The interest rate associated with this delta equivalent (for the break-even point computation) is obtained through the classic formula:

$$\text{Option delta equivalent rate}_t = E\,(DD_t) - \frac{E\,(\text{ALM Income}_t)}{\text{Delta Equivalent}_\mathrm{t}} \quad (22.39)$$

The delta equivalent can be shown in the following chart:

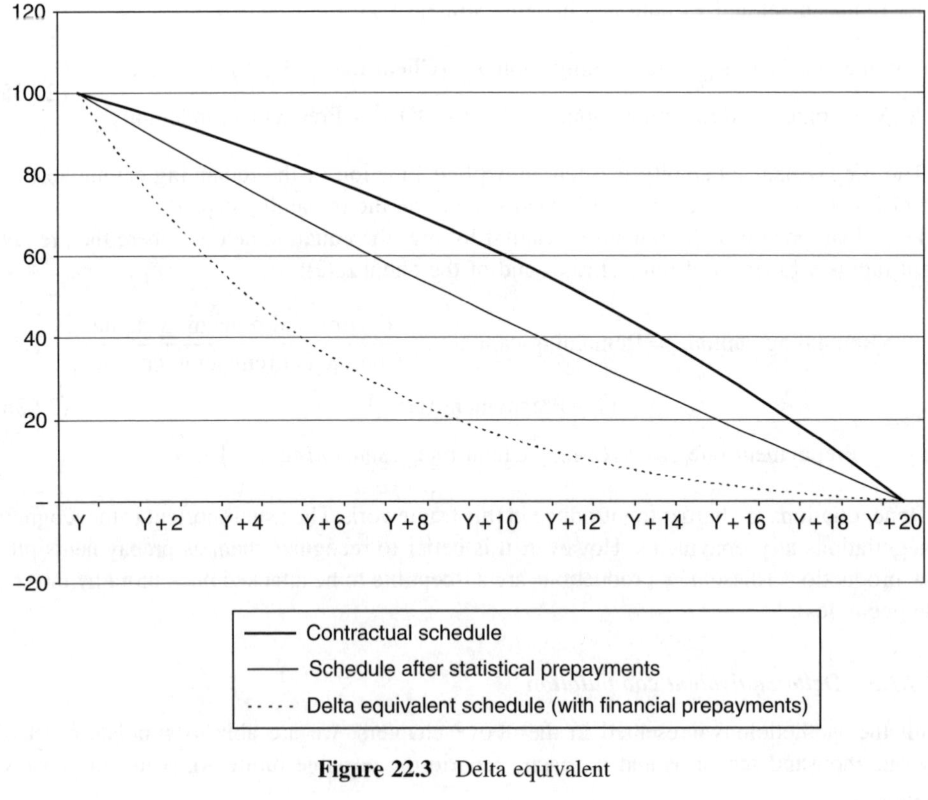

Figure 22.3 Delta equivalent

22.4.1.6 *Delta equivalent and expected prepayment rates*

It is important to notice that the delta equivalent is not equivalent to the expected prepayment rate.

To prove it, let just look after the spot delta equivalent when T is close to zero.

$$Eq\Delta_{0\to 1} = -\frac{E^{+1bp}(Res_{0\to 1}) - E(Res_{0\to 1})}{(0.01\%)}$$

$$Eq\Delta_{0\to 1} = -\frac{E^{+1bp}(\text{Remaining capital}_1.(\text{FTP}_1 - \text{DD}_1)) - E(\text{Remaining capital}_1.(\text{FTP}_1 - \text{DD}_1))}{(0.01\%)} \tag{22.40}$$

So, after having introduced the right formula for the remaining capital:

$$\text{Remaining capital}_1 = \text{Remaining capital}_0.\frac{\text{Contractual remaining capital}_1}{\text{Contractual remaining capital}_0} \times (1 - \text{Prepayment rate}_{0\to 1}) \tag{22.41}$$

$$Eq\Delta_{0\to 1} = -\text{Contractual remaining capital}_1.\frac{\partial E((1 - \text{Prepayment rate}_{0\to 1}).(\text{FTP}_1 - \text{DD}_1))}{\partial translation}$$

$$Eq\Delta_{0\to 1} = -\text{Contractual remaining capital}_1.\left(1 - \frac{\partial E((\text{Prepayment rate}_{0\to 1}).(\text{FTP}_1 - \text{DD}_1))}{\partial translation}\right)$$

If we think that the prepayment rate is indexed to the DD rate as follows (when α is the statistical prepayment rate):

$$\text{Prepayment rate} = \alpha + \beta.\text{Max}\,(0, \text{Client rate} - DD_1) \tag{22.42}$$

Then, the delta equivalent is given by the following equations:

$$\begin{aligned} Eq\Delta_{0\to 1} &= \text{Contractual remaining capital}_1 \\ &\times \left(1 - \frac{\partial E((\alpha + \beta.\text{Max}\,(0, \text{Client rate} - DD_1)).(\text{FTP}_1 - \text{DD}_1))}{\partial translation}\right) \\ Eq\Delta_{0\to 1} &= -\text{Contractual remaining capital}_1 \\ &\times \left(1 - \alpha + \beta.\frac{\partial E((\text{Max}\,(0, \text{Client rate} - DD_1)).(\text{FTP}_1 - \text{DD}_1))}{\partial translation}\right) \end{aligned} \tag{22.43}$$

It means that the delta equivalent is different from the loans liquidity schedule of the loans after prepayment:

$$Eq\Delta_{0\to 1} \neq -\text{Contractual remaining capital}_1.(1 - E\,(\text{Prepayment rate})) \tag{22.44}$$

Moreover, it is possible to prove that the prepayment rate computed implicitly by the loan delta equivalent is often higher than the expected prepayment rate.

In the scenarios where interest rates decrease strongly, the loss is potentially significant. This loss is not compensated by the gains generated in the scenarios where interest rates increase. To compensate this effect, the delta hedging will amplify the prepayment rate. Delta hedging will imply a shorter refinancing to consider this effect.

This example shows also that delta hedging is just a first-rate hedging. Hedging efficiency through delta hedging is not 100 % guaranteed. Here actually the bank has sold swaptions to the borrowers. Hedging through swaps, the bank conserves a volatility risk: if volatility increases, the hedge is imperfect, the A/L manager loses a large amount of money (since its option is gamma negative). To hedge perfectly its position, the A/L manager should buy options.

Note also that prepayment option is a "path dependent" option since the income at date t depends of all the past interest rates from 0 to t.

22.4.2 Insurance contracts

Within insurance contracts, it is possible to compute a delta equivalent.

For example, we may consider that a non unit-based life insurance contract is a contract that pays on a fixed liquidity schedule the following coupon:

$$Max\,(10 \text{ years average rate smoothed on 10 years - } m_1,\ 10 \text{ years spot rate - } m_2) \quad (22.45)$$

Such a coupon formula allows the liquidity schedule K(t) not to depend on the interest rate level:

$$\begin{aligned} \text{RES}_t = K(t).\,(Max\,(&10 \text{ years average rate smoothed on 10 years - } m_1, \\ &10 \text{ years spot rate - } m_2) - DD_t) \end{aligned} \quad (22.46)$$

This formulation allows us to compute a delta equivalent:

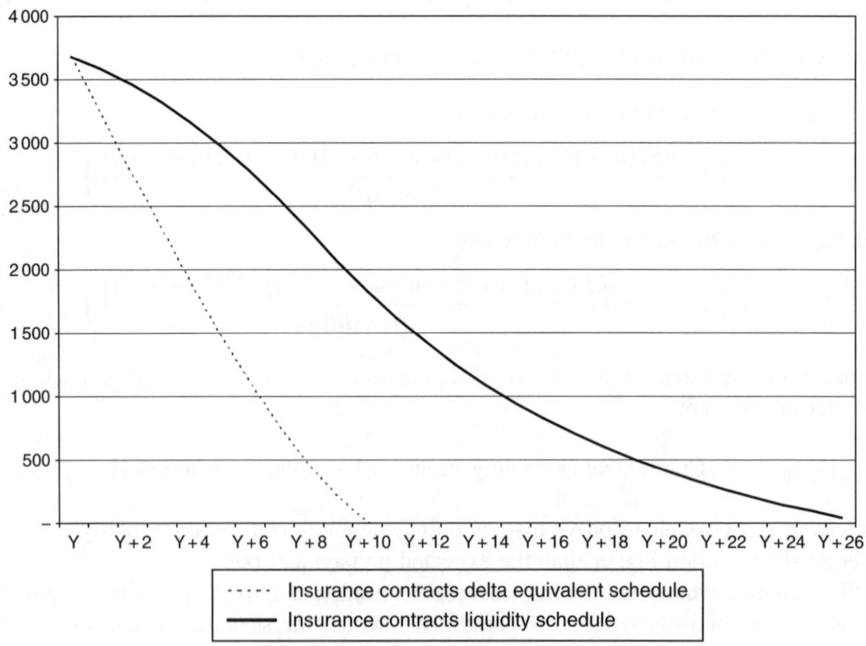

Figure 22.4 Insurance contracts

22.4.3 Market options

Options delta equivalent is computed directly through closed analytic formulae. These formulae are derived from stochastic computations formulae.

For example, for a caplet for date T with strike K and with forward rate F, the valuation formula is:

$$V = B(0,T).(F.N(d_1) - K.N(d_2))$$
$$\textit{where}$$
$$d_1 = \frac{\ln\left(\frac{F}{K}\right) - \frac{\sigma^2}{2}.T}{\sigma.\sqrt{T}} \tag{22.47}$$
$$d_2 = d_1 - \sigma.\sqrt{T}$$

The delta equivalent of the caplet is the "level of the caplet":

$$EqDelta = \frac{\partial V}{\partial Translation} \approx N(d_1)$$
$$\textit{where}$$
$$d_1 = \frac{\ln\left(\frac{F}{K}\right) - \frac{\sigma^2}{2}.T}{\sigma.\sqrt{T}} \tag{22.48}$$

Note that the delta equivalent for a caplet is in fact the probability for the caplet to be exercised.

The same kind of formula is available for swaptions (in horizontal delta hedging).

22.4.4 Multicurrency case and inflation delta equivalent

When the A/L manager deals with options in many currencies, he will calculate a delta equivalent according to each currency.

If the balance sheet incorporates options mixing two currencies, it is necessary to compute a *multicurrency correla equivalent* between the two currencies (even if the currency position is already taken into account in the net open currency position). This correla equivalent is computed as the sensitivity to a joint translation of the two yield curves:

$$MulticurrencyEqCorrela_{T\to T+\Delta T} = \frac{\partial E(\mathrm{Res}_{T\to T+\Delta T})}{\partial Translation_{\text{yield curve 1}}\partial Translation_{\text{yield curve 2}}} \tag{22.49}$$

Note that for inflation-linked products, real rates are represented as another yield curve. In terms of inflation risk, it means for the A/L manager:

- a real rate delta equivalent computation;
- an inflation representation in the net open currency position; and
- a real rate versus a nominal rate correla equivalent computation.

22.5 HEDGING ERROR AND GAMMA EQUIVALENT

22.5.1 Delta hedging error conclusions

In this chapter, we will demonstrate mathematically how important the hedging error is when an A/L manager hedges the income using a delta hedging strategy.

In order to calculate and to explain this error, it is necessary to comment how fixed income or equity derivatives traders manage their delta hedging risk. In these trading activities accounted in marked-to-market, the error is capitalized across time and the error growth is proportional to the product of the gamma by the spread between the realized volatility and the volatility initially expected at the option initiation date.

The gamma is the measure of the sensitivity of the portfolio value to a market shock (an interest rate shock or an equity market shock); this is a second derivative.

These computations can be transposed to ALM: the delta-hedging objective is to make the income accounted in accrual insensitive to the interest rate variations. The demonstration proves that the income after delta hedging is equal to the anticipated income plus a hedging error. This error is proportional to the product of the gamma times the spread between the realized and the anticipated volatility.

$$\text{Income without strategy}(T) + \text{Delta Strategy Income(T)} = \text{Income}_{\text{forecasted at date 0}}(\text{T}) + \text{Gamma.}\,[\text{realized} - \text{anticipated volatility}]$$

Moreover, on the specific path where the interest rates stay constant, the income is equal to the expected income less the product of the gamma times the volatility:

$$Income^{\text{constant rate}}(T) = \text{Income}_{\text{forecasted at date 0}}(\text{T}) - \text{Gamma.}\,[\text{anticipated volatility}]$$

ALM teams tend to sell more volatility than to buy some; the income on this special path overestimates the most probable income.

The conclusion of such an analysis makes us propose:

- the construction of an optional indicator based on the computation of a gamma equivalent associated with a break-even volatility point (as for the delta equivalent and the interest rate equivalent break-even point);
- the computation of the Vega and of the theta equivalent (sensitivity of the expected income to the volatility level or to the time);
- an explanation of the ex-post variation of the expected income.

22.5.2 Hedging error when hedging an equity derivative option accounted in marked-to-market

In the Black & Scholes model, the stock price S follows a Brownian motion with a drift indexed to the interest rate level r with a volatility $\sigma(t)$:

$$\frac{dS_t}{S_t} = r(t).\,dt + \sigma_t.dW_t \tag{22.50}$$

In this model, the price C of an equity derivative option follows this equation according to the Itô lemma:

$$dC_t = \frac{\partial C_t}{\partial t}.dt + \frac{\partial C_t}{\partial S_t}.dS_t + \frac{1}{2}.\frac{\partial^2 C_t}{\partial S_t^2}.S_t^2.\sigma_t^2.dt \qquad (22.51)$$

We apply the Feynman-Kac formula to C since C is solution of the Black & Scholes equation with a volatility $\sigma^{BS}(t)$:

$$\frac{\partial C_t}{\partial t} + r.S_t.\frac{\partial C_t}{\partial S_t} + \frac{1}{2}.\frac{\partial^2 C_t}{\partial S_t^2}.S_t^2.\sigma^{BS^2} = r.C_t \qquad (22.52)$$

The Black & Scholes Partial Derivative Equation (PDE) links the Theta, the Delta, the Gamma, and the option price.

If we consider the autofinancing delta hedging portfolio with value V(t), this value V(t) follows this basic equation:

$$dV_t = r(t).V_t.dt - \Delta_t.(dS_t - r(t).S_t.dt) \qquad (22.53)$$

The delta is by definition equal to the derivative of the option price by the equity stock price:

$$\Delta_t = \frac{\partial C_t}{\partial S_t} \qquad (22.54)$$

The hedging error e(t) between the stock price real evolution and the replicating portfolio is the following one:

$$de(t) = dV_t + dC_t$$

$$de(t) = r(t).V_t.dt - \Delta_t.(dS_t - r(t).S_t.dt) + \frac{\partial C_t}{\partial t}.dt + \frac{\partial C_t}{\partial S_t}.dS_t + \frac{1}{2}.\frac{\partial^2 C_t}{\partial S_t^2}.S_t^2.\sigma_t^2.dt \qquad (22.55)$$

$$de(t) = r(t).(e_t - C_t).dt - \frac{\partial C_t}{\partial S_t}.(dS_t - r(t).S_t.dt) + \frac{\partial C_t}{\partial t}.dt + \frac{\partial C_t}{\partial S_t}.dS_t + \frac{1}{2}.\frac{\partial^2 C_t}{\partial S_t^2}.S_t^2.\sigma_t^2.dt$$

Using the Feyman-Kac formula above, this give this formula for the hedging error:

$$de(t) = r(t).(e_t).dt + \frac{1}{2}.\frac{\partial^2 C_t}{\partial S_t^2}.S_t^2.\left(\sigma_t^2 - \sigma^{BS^2}\right).dt \qquad (22.56)$$

In conclusion, when an option trader follows a delta neutral hedging strategy, *the hedging error*:

- *is capitalized over time*;
- *is proportional to the gamma multiplied by the difference between the realized and the initial volatility* (used for the initial pricing of the option).

22.5.3 Extension to ALM delta hedging (when the income is not accounted in marked-to-market)

The A/L manager focused on the income accounted in accrual at date T. The objective is to replicate the future income at date T under the risk neutral probability; this income is actualized between t and T (knowing the market information F(t) at date t):

$$\tilde{C}_t = E_{RN}\left(Income_T.e^{-\int_t^T r(s).ds} / F_t \right) \tag{22.57}$$

To begin with, we start to focus on the non-actualized income; the expectation of this income is computed under the forward neutral probability associated with T, Q(T).

$$\begin{aligned} \tilde{C}_t &= E_{Q_T}\left(Income_T/F_t\right).B(0,T) = C_t.B(0,T) \\ C_t &= E_{Q_T}\left(Income_T/F_t\right) \\ d\tilde{C}_t &= dC_t.B(0,T) + C_t.dB(0,T) \end{aligned} \tag{22.58}$$

Hedging the second part of this last equation can be done through an independent hedging strategy.

This time instead of using a Black & Scholes model, we prefer to use a Libor Market Model to simulate the interest rates under the forward neutral probability Q(T). Under this probability, the Libor forward rate follows a martingale:

$$\frac{dL(t,T,T+h)}{L(t,T,T+h)} = \sigma_t.\,dW^{Q(T)}(t) \tag{22.59}$$

The expected income follows according to the Itô lemma:

$$dC_t = \frac{\partial C_t}{\partial t}.\,dt + \frac{\partial C_t}{\partial L_t}.\,dL_t + \frac{1}{2}.\frac{\partial^2 C_t}{\partial L_t^2}.L_t^2.\sigma_t^2.\,dt \tag{22.60}$$

C is by application of the Feynman-Kac formula solution of a Black & Scholes equation with volatility equal to $\sigma^{BS}(t)$:

$$\frac{\partial C_t}{\partial t} + \frac{1}{2}.\frac{\partial^2 C_t}{\partial L_t^2}.L_t^2.\sigma^{BS^2} = 0 \tag{22.61}$$

The Black & Scholes PDE links this time the theta, the gamma and the expected income.

We consider the delta-hedging portfolio of the expected income; the hedging is made using forward swaps. By definition, the variation of the expected income V(t) at date T (expected at date t) follows:

$$dV_t = -\Delta_t.dL_t \tag{22.62}$$

The delta is computed as the derivative of the expected income by the Libor forward rate:

$$\Delta_t = \frac{\partial C_t}{\partial L_t} \tag{22.63}$$

The hedging error e(t) between the real evolution of the expected income and of the income of the hedging portfolio is equal to:

$$de(t) = dV_t + dC_t$$

$$de(t) = -\frac{\partial C_t}{\partial L_t}.dL_t + \frac{\partial C_t}{\partial t}.dt + \frac{\partial C_t}{\partial L_t}.dL_t + \frac{1}{2}\cdot\frac{\partial^2 C_t}{\partial L_t^2}.L_t^2.\sigma_t^2.dt \tag{22.64}$$

$$de(t) = \frac{\partial C_t}{\partial t}.dt + \frac{1}{2}\cdot\frac{\partial^2 C_t}{\partial L_t^2}.L_t^2.\sigma_t^2.dt$$

Using the Feynman-Kac formula above, this leads to:

$$de(t) = \frac{1}{2}\cdot\frac{\partial^2 C_t}{\partial L_t^2}.L_t^2.\left(\sigma_t^2 - \sigma^{BS^2}\right).dt \tag{22.65}$$

In conclusion, when an A/L manager follows a delta forward neutral strategy, *the hedging error*:

- *is accumulated across time*;
- *is proportional to the gamma multiplied by the difference between the realized interest rate volatility and the interest rate volatility used at the initiation of the operation.*

22.5.4 Gamma equivalent interpretation

Another way to consider this formula is to write it in an integral form:

$$C(T) = C(0) - V(T) + \int_0^T \left(\frac{1}{2}\cdot\frac{\partial^2 C_t}{\partial L_t^2}.L_t^2.\left(\sigma_t^2 - \sigma^{BS^2}\right)\right).dt \tag{22.66}$$

In other words, *the expected income at date T is equal to*:

- *expected income computed at date 0 under the forward neutral probability*;
- *minus the delta hedging strategy income*;
- *plus the accumulated spread between the realised and the anticipated volatilities* (times the gamma).

$$\begin{aligned} Income(T) = {} & \text{Forecasted income}(0) - \text{Delta Strategy Income} \\ & + \text{Gamma.}\,[\text{realized-anticipated volatility}] \end{aligned} \tag{22.67}$$

$$\begin{aligned} & \text{Income without strategy}(T) + \text{Delta Strategy Income} = \text{Forecasted income}(0) + \text{Gamma} \\ & \quad \times [\text{realized-anticipated volatility}] \end{aligned}$$

For example, on the path where the interest rates stay stable, the delta hedging strategy has no value and the realised volatility is equal to zero:

$$C^{\text{constant rate}}(T) = C(0) - \int_0^T \left(\frac{1}{2} \cdot \frac{\partial^2 C_t}{\partial L_t^2} . L_t^2 . \sigma^{BS^2} \right) .dt \tag{22.68}$$

Finally, on a path where the interest rates stay stable, the final income is equal to the expected income minus the product of the gamma times the volatility.

$$Income^{\text{constant rate}}(T) = \text{Forecasted income}(0) - \text{Gamma.}\,[\text{anticipated volatility}]$$

ALM teams tend to sell more volatility than to buy some, the income on this special path overestimate the most probable income.

22.5.5 Possible ALM application

In ALM, the gamma, i.e. the sensitivity of the delta to an interest rate shock (or the second derivative of the expected income to an interest rate shock) measures the uncertainty of the income delta hedging.

The optional indicator can be a *gamma equivalent*. As for the delta equivalent computation, this gamma equivalent can be associated with a *break-even volatility point.*

This break-even volatility point gives the expected optional income.

This indicator can be associated with a Vega equivalent (sensitivity of the expected income to the volatility level) or with a theta equivalent (sensitivity of the expected income with the time evolution).

The computation of these indicators allows to backtest ex-post the prevision of the income (as for the marked-to-market ex-post evolution in trading activities).

$$\begin{aligned} \text{Income}_{\text{forecasted } i \text{ n } 02/2007}(2010) = \; & \text{Income}_{\text{forecasted } i \text{ n } 01/2007}(2010) \\ & + \text{Interest rate gap}(2010).\,[\Delta\text{Interest rate}] \\ & + \text{P}enta \text{ equivalent}(2010).\,[\Delta\text{Interest rate}] \\ & + \text{Gamma equivalent}(2010)..\,[\Delta\text{volatility}] \\ & + \ldots \end{aligned} \tag{22.69}$$

23
Technical Tools Useful in ALM

À bon cheval, bon gué.

23.1 RISK MEASURES

Nowadays, there are many ways to measure the risk of a portfolio. The approach developed by Markowitz (1952) based on the analysis of variance is still the basis of the risk measurement.

We will start with the presentation of the major risk measures and finish with the presentation of the associated optimization methods.

23.1.1 Variance and standard deviation

Variance is the most simple risk measure in finance. For a random variable X, the mathematical expectation of X is denoted E(X) and the variance V(X). The variance is the mathematical expectation of the square of the difference between X and its mathematical expectation:

$$V(X)=E\left[(X-E(X))^2\right]=E\left[X^2\right]-E[X]^2 \tag{23.1}$$

The wider is the distribution of the possible values of X, the higher is the risk.

Since the variance is by construction positive, the standard deviation defined as the square root of the variance is an equivalent risk measure (also called volatility):

$$SD(X)=\sqrt{V(X)}=\sqrt{E\left[(X-E(X))^2\right]} \tag{23.2}$$

We consider that X has a cumulative distribution function F or a density p:

$$\text{Proba}(x<X<x+dx)=p(x).dx$$

$$F(x)=\int_{-\infty}^{x} p(s).ds \tag{23.3}$$

$$\int_{-\infty}^{+\infty} p(s).ds=1$$

Then the mathematical expectation and the variance will follow:

$$E(X) = \int_{-\infty}^{+\infty} p(x).x.dx$$
$$V(X) = \int_{-\infty}^{+\infty} p(x).\left(x - \int_{-\infty}^{+\infty} p(s).s.ds\right)^2 .dx \tag{23.4}$$

23.1.2 Value-at-Risk

The *Value-at-Risk (VaR)* is characterized by a given probability *threshold* α and a given *horizon* and represents the worst potential loss on this horizon with this probability. For instance, 95 % of the losses will be under a 95 % VaR.

When F is the distribution function of X, the VaR is the quantile of the distribution of X at a given horizon of time:

$$\text{VaR}_\alpha (X) = F^{-1}(\alpha) \tag{23.5}$$

VaR is the potential loss corresponding to a certain level of confidence interval α of the risk distribution.

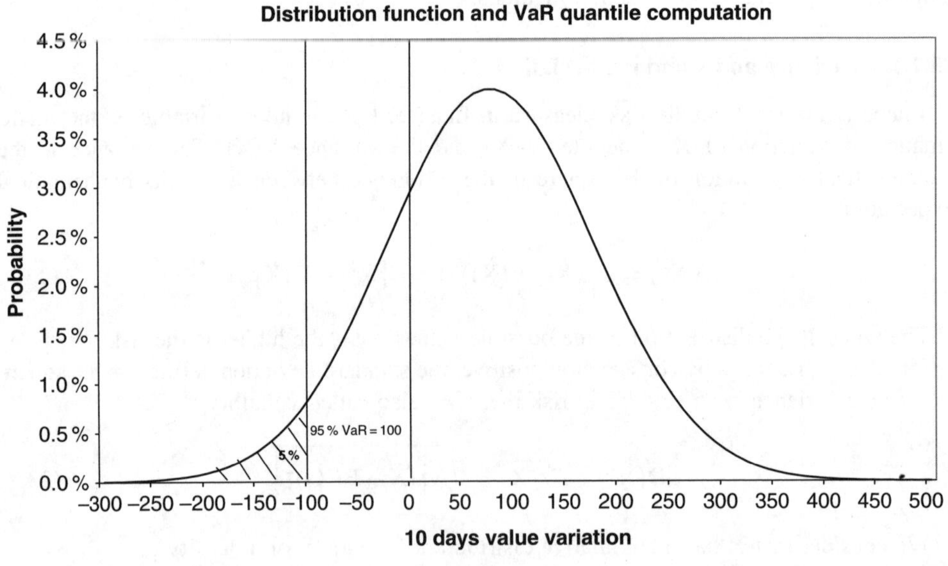

Figure 23.1 Value-at-Risk

When looking after market risks, the risk managers compute a 99 % 10 open days VaR: the computed loss will occur once every 100 open days. The same loss will occur at least twice a year.

The 95 % 10 open days VaR loss will occur 10 times a year.

With this simple definition, VaR constitutes a benchmark risk measure used for economic capital and for regulatory capital.

In terms of risk allocation, the *Euler relationship* allows a simple allocation of risk between different risk contributors.

Nevertheless, VaR as risk measure is not always recommended. First, it is very difficult to optimize under a VaR constraint: the operational utilization for optimization is not clear.

However, the principal weakness of the VaR comes from the "non sub-additivity" of this measure: the aggregated risk of two activities is not dominated by the risk of the sum of the two activities computed on a stand-alone basis. The following relationship is not verified:

$$\text{VaR}(A+B) \leq \text{VaR}(A) + \text{VaR}(B) \tag{23.6}$$

VaR is said not to be a *"coherent risk measure"* such as those presented in the next Section.

23.1.3 Coherent risk measures

Considering other risk measures and extending the classical framework to account for skewness and kurtosis of asset returns has also been discussed. More recently, with Artzner et al. (1999) theoretical properties of a series of risk measures such as VaR have been investigated. This showed how VaR lacked the sub-additivity property.

A risk measure should verify a certain list of properties for portfolios A and B and for the scale factor λ:

- *Law invariance*: two portfolios with the same law will have the same risk.

$$[\text{A and B have the same law}] \Rightarrow [\text{Risk (A)} = \text{Risk (B)}]$$

- *H1 Positive homogeneity*: the risk of a portfolio is proportional to the size of the portfolio ("scale value order respect").

$$\text{Risk } (\lambda.\ A) = |\lambda|.\text{Risk (A)}$$

- *H2 Translation-invariance*: when adding a fixed and certain gain on a portfolio, the portfolio risk is just "translated" by this gain

$$\text{Risk } (\lambda + A) = \text{Risk (A)} - \lambda$$

- *H3 Monotonicity*: when a portfolio is sure to give in every scenario a higher return than another portfolio, this portfolio is less risky.

$$[A \geq B] \Rightarrow [\text{Risk (A)} \leq \text{Risk (B)}]$$

- *H4 Sub-additivity (risk diversification)*: the risk of the sum of two portfolios is lower than the sum of the risks of the two portfolios.

$$\text{Risk (A+B)} \leq \text{Risk (A)} + \text{Risk (B)}$$

- *Risk contribution computation facility*: it should be easy to allocate the risk consumption to every sub-portfolio.

$$\text{Risk (A+B)} = \text{Contribution (A)} + \text{Contribution (B)}$$

The VaR respects the law invariance, the positive homogeneity and is easy to redistribute with Euler relationships.

On the other hand, VaR is not sub-additive and measures partially extreme losses (since VaR is associated with only one risk quantile).

Coherent risk measures are supposed to fulfil hypothesis H1 to H4. From these hypotheses, let us note that a coherent risk measure will verify the following equations:

$$\text{Risk}(0) = 0$$

$$\text{Risk}(r) = -r \text{ where r is the risk free rate}$$

$$-\text{E(A)} \leq \text{Risk (A)} \leq -\text{Inf(X)}$$

The coherent risk measure is more pessimistic than expectation but more optimistic than the minimal return.

The utility theory developed by Von Neumann-Morgenstern states that customer preference is represented by a utility function U. The risk is then evaluated with the mathematical expectation of the utility function:

$$\text{E(U(A))} = \text{E(A)} - \text{Risk(A)}$$

$$\text{Risk(A)} = \text{E(A)} - \text{E(U(A))}$$

This relationship can be developed with an integral form of the density probability p. The risk measure can be seen primarily as a *distortion of probabilities*.

$$\begin{aligned} Risk &= \int_{x=-\infty}^{+\infty} p(x).(x - U(x))\,dx \\ \text{Proba}(x < X < x + dx) &= p(x).dx \end{aligned} \tag{23.7}$$

The quantile function F is defined from the density probability p of x:

$$F(x) = P(X < x) = \int_{s=-\infty}^{x} p(s).ds \tag{23.8}$$

This leads to another form for the risk description with a variable change:

$$Risk = \left(\int_{x=-\infty}^{+\infty} F'(x).(x - U(x))\,dx \right) = \left(\int_{0}^{1} \left(F^{-1}(y) - U\left(F^{-1}(y)\right)\right) dy \right) \tag{23.9}$$

The risk function is also a quantile weighting function.

If we want U to satisfy the law invariance and the positive homogeneity, we will suppose for instance that U verifies:

$$U(x, F(x)) = (1 + \varphi(F(x)))\,x \tag{23.10}$$

Finally, there are two possibilities to represent the risk, either by a *quantile weighting*, either by a *distortion of probability*:

$$Risk = -\int_0^1 \varphi(y).F^{-1}(y).dy = -\int_0^1 x.d\,(g \circ F)(x) \tag{23.11}$$

The deformation of the distribution is equivalent to the deformation of the repartition function (or the deformation of the spectrum of the random variable).

The distortion of the probabilities g represents the risk aversion that is the overweighting of the worst scenarios. The agent represents his risk aversion through a probabilistic risk behaviour modification with the term 1-g.

To each deformation g is associated a risk measure. Indeed, there are two possibilities:

- The manager point of view: probabilities are distorted.
- The risk point of view: the quantiles are weighted.

Spectral risk measures (SRM) will be based on such a quantile weighting by a function ϕ:

$$SRM = -\int_0^1 \varphi(y).F^{-1}(y).dy \tag{23.12}$$

The spectral risk measures will verify the law invariance, H1 to H4 hypotheses and the contribution computation easiness: they are coherent risk measures.

Note that the mathematical expectation is a spectral risk measure (with an equal weighting of the quantiles).

The most common spectral risk measure is the *expected shortfall (or conditional VaR) denoted ES or cVaR*. This risk measure equiponderates all the quantiles exceeding the VaR. This is the mathematical expectation of the loss knowing that the loss is greater that the VaR:

$$\mathrm{ES}_\alpha(\mathrm{X}) = \mathrm{E}[\mathrm{X}/\mathrm{X} \leq \mathrm{VaR}_\alpha(\mathrm{X})] \tag{23.13}$$

Other spectral risk measures were proposed such as the Wang transform, the pH-transform and the absolute Denneberg deviation. Another risk measure, the Fischer semi-variance based risk measure, is well covered in the literature but is not a spectral risk measure.

23.1.4 Earnings at risk

Value-at-Risk measures a risk computed on the economic value. However, A/L managers are more interested in the risk on the incomes.

Earnings-at-Risk (EaR) are the quantiles of the distribution of the incomes year after year. In the following example, the income of the year Y+1 will be higher than 80 with a 95 % confidence interval:

	Year Y	Year Y+1	Year Y + 2	Year Y+3	Year Y+4	Year Y+5
Expected income	100	110	115	115	120	130
Earning-at-Risk (95 %)	90	80	80	75	70	65

Figure 23.2 Earnings-at-Risk

23.1.5 Gaussian framework

Computing the risk under a Gaussian framework is a common assumption. In this context, all the returns follow a normal distribution.

In the Gaussian framework, all the risk measures are equivalent: variance, VaR, Expected shortfall, etc. For instance, the VaR is equal in the Gaussian framework to a multiple of the standard deviation. This multiple is equal to the quantile of the standard normal distribution multiplied by the square root of the horizon.

$$\mathrm{VaR}_{\alpha,T} = Q(\alpha).\sqrt{T}.SD \tag{23.14}$$

Classic quantiles present in the literature are the following ones:

$$Q(95\,\%) = 1.64$$
$$Q(99\,\%) = 2.33$$
$$Q(99.95\,\%) = 3.29$$
$$Q(99.97\,\%) = 3.43$$

Note also that in this context, it is possible to translate one VaR to another very simply. For example, the 10 open days 95 % VaR multiplied by the square of 24 gives the 1-year 95 % VaR (if the year includes 240 open days). The 10 open days 95 % multiplied by 3.43 and divided by 1.64 gives the 10 days 99.97 % VaR.

Usually the value of a portfolio V for which we want to compute the VaR has its sensitivity dV decomposed on the sensitivities dS of the different possible market investments (interest rates, equity, etc.) with a projection vector P:

$$dV = P.dS = \sum_i P_i.dS_i \tag{23.15}$$

The vector dS is supposed to follow a normal distribution N(0,C). This leads finally to the following formula for the VaR:

$$\mathrm{VaR}_\alpha = {}^tP.C.P.Q(\alpha) \tag{23.16}$$

23.2 OPTIMIZATION METHODS

The problem of portfolio allocation optimization will allow us to maximize the portfolio expected gains under a risk constraint. This is linked with the manager's target: to determine the better way to allocate capital between different assets, the risk on the capital being measured by a variance, a VaR or a spectral measure.

23.2.1 Markowitz optimization and CAPM

23.2.1.1 Portfolio returns

The pioneering work of *Markowitz* in 1952 remains a popular tool in quantitative portfolio management. The *Capital Asset Pricing Model (CAPM)* is derived from this analysis (with numerous independent contributors such as Sharpe, Miller, Treynor, Lintner or Mossin).

The model runs with a set of assumptions:

- Returns are distributed normally (Gaussian framework).
- Financial markets are perfectly efficient without any arbitrage opportunity.
- Investors have rational expectations.
- A risk-free rate accessible by everybody exists.
- Transaction costs are absent (no bid-ask spreads).

The CAPM shows the existence of a *"market portfolio"*: the expected return of every portfolio is inferior to the expected return R_m of this market portfolio.

Moreover, within this framework, the CAPM says that the expected return of a portfolio is equal to the risk free rate r plus a multiple of the spread between the expected return on the asset capital $E(R_m)$ and the risk free rate r:

$$E(R) = r + \beta.(E(R_m) - r) \tag{23.17}$$

The multiple is called *the* β *(the "beta") of the CAPM model* and is equal to the covariance between the portfolio return R and the market portfolio return:

$$\beta = \frac{Covariance(R, R_m)}{Var(R_m)} \tag{23.18}$$

Indeed the model introduces the notion of risk premium (above the risk free rate level r):

$$p = \beta.(E(R_m) - r) \tag{23.19}$$

23.2.1.2 Optimal portfolio

In optimization problems, the A/L manager wants to compute how much investment has to be done in every asset i.

Mathematically speaking, the problem is to determine how much he has to invest in every asset i with a proportion invested in this asset equal to an amount w_i, with an expected return A_i, under a risk constraint such as the variance and under an investment constraint.

The expected return of a portfolio is as follows:

$$E(R) = \sum_i w_i.E(A_i) = {}^t W.A \tag{23.20}$$

The variance of the portfolio is linked with the covariance matrix C between the different assets:

$$V(R) = \sum_{i,j} w_i.w_j.Cov(A_i, A_j) = {}^t W.C.W \tag{23.21}$$

The classic constraint on the portfolio is to suppose that the different investments in the different assets are normalised:

$$\sum_i w_i = 1 \text{ or } |W| = 1 \tag{23.22}$$

The A/L manager's optimization programme is then the following:

$$\underset{\substack{|W|=1 \\ {}^tW.C.W \leq M}}{MAX} \quad ({}^tW.A) \tag{23.23}$$

Such a programme is a classic matrix optimization problem and leads to the classic CAPM formulae.

The optimization leads to the existence of an efficient frontier. In the plan mean-variance, the efficient frontier has a parabolic shape:

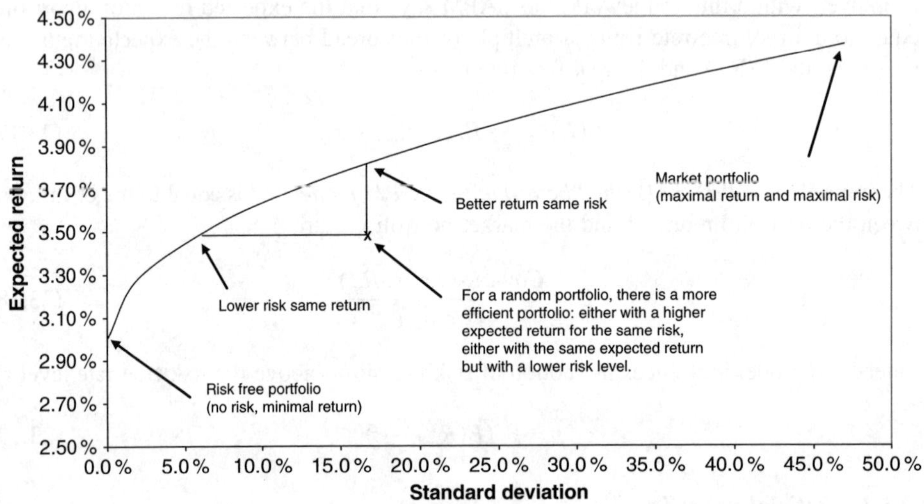

Figure 23.3 Efficient frontier

23.2.1.3 Adding more constraints

In practice, some constraints will be added to the optimization programme. For example, the A/L manager will not wish to invest too much in a specific asset class (due to a shareholder constraint for instance).

This will introduce new linear constraints within the following programme:

$$\underset{\substack{|W|=1 \\ {}^tW.C.W \leq M \\ MIN \leq W \leq MAX}}{MAX} \quad ({}^tW.A) \tag{23.24}$$

Many other extensions of the original setting such as *Black & Litterman model* have been proposed in order to extend the practical use of the method. This last model integrates *priors* in the Markowitz optimization: these priors integrate the A/L manager's anticipation of the expected returns. Indeed, these anticipations may be different from those expected by the market (the "priors").

23.2.2 Optimization under coherent risk measures

Nowadays, the Markowitz optimization under a variance risk measure is still the standard for portfolio optimization.

Nevertheless, the optimization is now possible under coherent risk measures. This leads to a new set of efficient frontiers when the returns are not supposed to be normal.

Acerbi-Simonetti and Uryasev-Rockafellar provided the algorithm in order to perform the optimization.

Optimizing under Value-at-Risk has not yet been developed for technical reasons. However, Alexander and Baptista (2002) showed that the use of VaR leads to portfolios with higher variance returns even for a risk adverse investor.

23.3 COMMON STATISTICAL TOOLS IN ALM

We provide in this chapter some general lessons of statistics for A/L managers with a little statistical background.

23.3.1 Multivariate regression, confidence interval and tests

Regression establishes a linear link between a set of two variables. In this case, the statistician wants to estimate the linear relationship between a variable Y with observations $(Y_i)_{i=1\ldots N}$ and a set of J variables $(X_{i,j})_{i=1\ldots N \text{ and } j=1\ldots J}$.

The objective is to find the vector $A=(a_j)_{j=1\ldots J}$ and the constant b so that:

$$\begin{aligned} Y &= A.X+b \\ Y_i &= \sum_{j=1}^{J} a_j.X_{i,j}+b \end{aligned} \tag{23.25}$$

Regression will estimate these variables through the minimization of the variance of ε, the "*residuals of the regression*" defined by:

$$Y_i=\sum_{j=1}^{J} a_j.X_{i,j}+b+\varepsilon_i$$

The residuals are supposed to follow a normal distribution.

We can write the above equation in a different way with the introduction of a new matrix B:

$$Y = B.\begin{pmatrix} b \\ a_1 \\ \ldots \\ a_J \end{pmatrix} + \varepsilon \tag{23.26}$$

$$B = \begin{pmatrix} 1 & \\ \ldots & X \\ 1 & \end{pmatrix} = \begin{pmatrix} 1 & x_{1,1} & .. & x_{1,J} \\ \ldots & .. & \ldots & .. \\ 1 & x_{N,1} & .. & x_{N,J} \end{pmatrix}$$

This leads to the following estimation of the matrix A and of the vector b also called *"least-square minimization"*:

$$\begin{pmatrix} \hat{b} \\ \hat{a}_1 \\ \ldots \\ \hat{a}_J \end{pmatrix} = ({}^tB.B)^{-1}.({}^tB).Y \tag{23.27}$$

To determine whether the regression is useful or not, the coefficient of determination R^2 will provide the percentage of the variance of Y explained by the regression.

$$R^2 = 1 - \frac{V(\hat{\varepsilon})}{V(Y)} = 1 - \frac{V(Y - \hat{A}.X - \hat{b})}{V(Y)} \tag{23.28}$$

The R^2 is comprised between 0 and 1: a value close to 0 means the model is very poor.

The regression will also give the uncertainty of the estimation, i.e. the standard deviation of the estimators.

If the division of the estimator by its standard deviation leads to a value below 2, the variable is not significantly different from 0; this variable should be excluded from the regression. In the following example, the variable "unemployment" has to be excluded from the regression:

Variable Demand deposit variation	Regression variables			
	Inflation	Unemployment	GDP	Constant
Y	$\hat{a}_1$	$\hat{a}_2$	$\hat{a}_3$	b
Estimator	10.0%	−1.0%	50.0%	30.0%
Variance of estimator	2%	2%	3%	15%
T test (Student)	5.0	− 0.5	16.7	2.0
Accept/Reject	Yes	No	Yes	Yes

Figure 23.4 Regression

23.3.2 Time series

In ALM, many regressions are performed with variables like Y_i where the index i represents the time t. In statistics, the variable Y_t is called a time series.

When working with time series, the statistician will look more carefully after two aspects:

- the autocorrelation of the residual of the analysis;
- the heteroskedasticity of these residuals.

23.3.2.1 *Autocorrelation models*

When looking after a regression analysis of time series, there may be a strong autocorrelation between the residuals ε_t: the correlation between the variables ε_t and ε_{t-1} is maybe too important to be forgotten.

The *autocorrelogram* is a useful tool for the autocorrelation analysis: it represents the correlation between ε_t and ε_{t-j} when j varies.

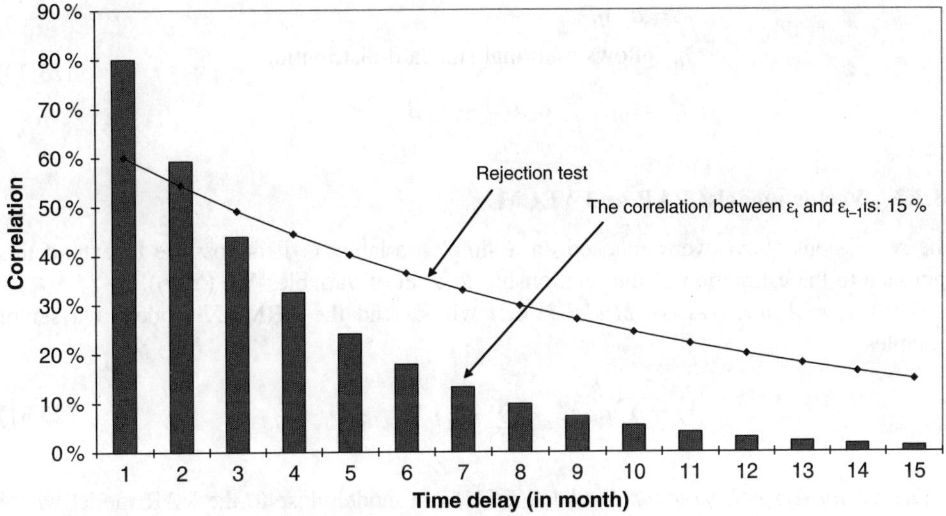

Figure 23.5 Autocorrelogramm

Statistical tools usually compute an autocorrelogram and an acceptance/rejection test to know whether the correlation is important or not.

To take into account the autocorrelation in practice, the statistician will:

- either differentiate the variables introducing new variables: $(Y_t - Y_{t-1})$ and $(X_t - X_{t-1})$; or
- introduce the variable Y_{t-1} or X_{t-1} in the regression; or
- deform the nature of ε_t.

This will lead to the following models:

- AR models (autoregressive models);
- MA models (moving average models where ε_t is autocorrelated);
- ARMA models mixing an AR and a MA model;
- ARIMA models where the variables are integrated.

For example, in the ARMAX model, the regression will try to estimate Y as a function of X as follows:

$$Y_t = \sum_i a_i.Y_{t-i} + \sum_{i,j} a_{i,j}.X_{t-i,j} + b + \varepsilon_t$$
$$\varepsilon_t = \sum_i c_i.\varepsilon_{t-i} + \sigma.\eta_t \qquad (23.29)$$
η_t follows a normal standard distribution

23.3.2.2 *Heteroskedasticity models*

In statistics, a time series is heteroskedastic if the random variables in the sequence may have different variances across time. Instead of supposing that the residuals follow a normal distribution, the GARCH(p, q), for instance, model will suppose that:

$$\varepsilon_t = \sigma_t.\eta_t$$
η_t follows a normal standard distribution (23.30)
$$\sigma_t^2 = \alpha_0 + \sum_{i=1}^{p} \alpha_i.\varepsilon_{t-i}^2 + \sum_{i=1}^{q} \beta_i.\sigma_{t-i}^2$$

23.3.3 Vector models: VAR and VECM

The regressions above were exposed on a simple variable Y. It is possible to extend this approach to the estimation of the relationship to a set of variables $Y = (Y_i(t))$.

The *Vector Autoregressive Model (VAR)* will extend the ARMAX model to a set of variables:

$$Y_t^j = \sum_{i,k} a_i^k.Y_{t-i}^k + \sum_{i,l} a_{i,j,l}.X_{t-i,l} + b_j + \varepsilon_{t,j} \qquad (23.31)$$

The *Vector Error Correction Model (VECM)* is a model close to the VAR model where the variation of the vector variable Y is regressed over past values of Y and past values of this variation:

$$\Delta Y_t = \theta + \Pi Y_{t-1} + \sum_{j=1}^{p-1} \Gamma_j \Delta Y_{t-j} + \varepsilon_t$$
$$\Delta Y_t = Y_t - Y_{t-1} \qquad (23.32)$$
$$\varepsilon_{t,j} \sim MVN(0, \Lambda_t)$$

The VECM integrates an autoregressive model with an error term. It takes into account the non-stationarity of the financial data. This model reduces the probability of simulating extreme scenarios. Moreover, the returns are non-normal.

23.3.4 Backtests and out-of-sample tests

In time series modelling, model backtesting is essential in order to verify the efficiency of the modelling. *Out-of-sample tests* are the more common backtesting tests. The objective is to study for example the stability of the regression coefficients across time.

Here are the principles of a classic and simple out-of-sample test:

Stage 1: We cut the historical database in two: it gives us two samples.

Stage 2: We compare or test the coefficients estimated with the first part of the database and those estimated with the second part of the database.

Stage 3: If the test says the coefficients are statistically different, we should reject the model.

It is possible to represent graphically the out-of-sample test: the evolution of a variable Y modelled with the first part of an historical database is represented on the second part of the database:

- The first "sample" (the first half of the database for instance) will build the model in a training phase.
- The variable Y is simulated using this model on the second sample (this second sample is not used for the calibration).

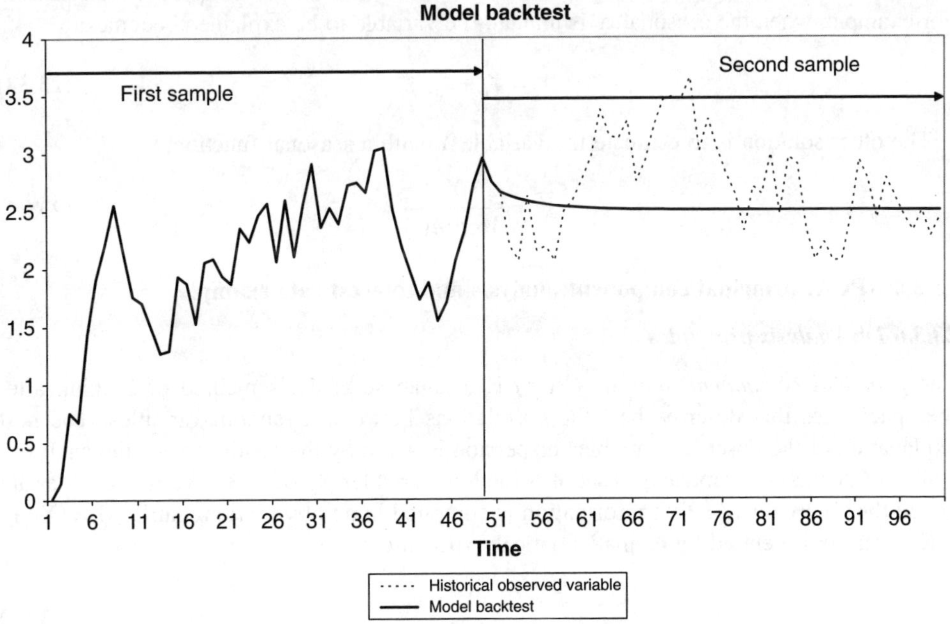

Figure 23.6 Backtest

In practice, A/L managers perform *budget backtesting* in order to verify the efficiency of the modelling used in previous budget assumptions.

Moreover, the out-of-sample test can be used to compare the comparative power of different models.

Nevertheless, A/L managers will pay attention in the use of backtesting for model selection to:

- *Cycle effects*: when the entire historical database is situated within only one economic cycle, the danger is to forget some important variables in the model. For instance in a 10 year historical database where interest rates were only decreasing, it is not certain that the modelling will consider interest rate as a good explanatory variable.
- *Model economic logic explanations*: if two variables seem correlated in an historical database, it does not mean that one explains the other. It is said that if the number of storks and the number of newborn babies decrease simultaneously, it does not mean that the western folk tales are true (the newborn babies are supposed to be brought to their parents by storks).

23.3.5 Seasonality treatments

Seasonality treatments are important for budget planning and for a better calibration of models. In the United States, statistical data are often produced *"NSA"* (non-seasonally adjusted) or *"SA"* (seasonally adjusted). The seasonal adjustments are often made with a process called "X11".

In practice, in time series analysis, the statistician will either distinguish the variable to be modelled Y or estimate directly the seasonality treatment with an appropriate function. For example, when the seasonality is annual, the variable to be explained becomes:

$$\tilde{Y}_t = Y_t - Y_{t-12} \tag{23.33}$$

The other solution is to estimate the variable Y with a seasonal function:

$$\tilde{Y}_t = \frac{Y_t}{Month(t)} \tag{23.34}$$

23.3.6 PCA: principal component analysis and interest rate example

23.3.6.1 Analysis principles

The *principal component analysis (PCA)* is a database analysis method of looking after the space axes that describe best the correlations between n random variables. The best explanation of the observed variables dispersion is given by the result axes of the analysis.

The PCA analysis is made on a set of N random variables $X_1, \ldots, X_N$. These variables are called the "individuals". This information is compiled in an observation matrix $M = (X_{i,j})$.

The matrix is centred by its mathematical expectation:

$$\begin{aligned} &\bar{M} = M - E(X) \\ &{}^t\bar{M}.\bar{M} \text{ is a covariance matrix} \end{aligned} \tag{23.35}$$

However, more often, the matrix M is reduced, i.e. centred and normalized by the standard deviation of the observations.

$$\begin{aligned} &\tilde{M} = \left(\frac{X_{i,j} - E(X_i)}{\sigma(X_i)}\right) \\ &{}^t\tilde{M}.\tilde{M} \text{ is a correlation matrix} \end{aligned} \tag{23.36}$$

The idea is then to find the vector u so that the projection of the observation on u has a maximal variance.

$$P_X(u)=\tilde{M}.u \text{ with variance}^t\left(\tilde{M}.u\right).\tilde{M}.u={}^t u.\left({}^t\tilde{M}.\tilde{M}\right).u \tag{23.37}$$

This last matrix is diagonalizable in an orthonormalized basis with a basis change matrix P and a diagonal (spectrum) matrix Δ.

$$\begin{aligned}{}^t\tilde{M}.\tilde{M}&={}^tP.\Delta.P\\ {}^tP&=P^{-1}\end{aligned} \tag{23.38}$$

The variance of the projection will be then equal to:

$$^t\left(P.u\right).\Delta.\left(P.u\right) \tag{23.39}$$

The diagonalization of the correlation matrix (or the covariance matrix) provides the vectors that explain the best the past observations. The PCA analysis is in fact a matrix diagonalization problem.

The matrix P gives the projection of the past observations on a new space with orthogonal axes.

23.3.6.2 Application to interest rates

A classic financial application of the PCA analysis is made on interest rate variations. The interest rate observation $R_{i,j}$ is, for example, the observation at date i of the interest rate of maturity j. The PCA analysis is made on the following variations of these interest rate observations:

$$X_{i,j}=R_{i,j}-R_{i-1,j} \tag{23.40}$$

The projection gives usually *three main factors for the explanation of the interest rate variation*:

- The *translation*: the short-term and the long-term interest rates tend to move conjointly on the same way with a parallel shift. This usually represents 80 % of the interest rate variations.
- The *rotation*: the yield curve may flatten and this represents around 15 % of the possible interest rate variations.
- The *convexity*: the yield curve convexity may change (for example short-term and long-term interest rate may increase when medium term interest rates decrease).

Every interest rate variation may be projected on these three vectors:

	1 year	2 years	3 years	5 years	10 years	15 years	20 years	30 years
Translation axis	0.10	0.10	0.11	0.11	0.10	0.10	0.10	0.09
Rotation axis	−0.10	−0.07	−0.05	−0.02	0.00	0.03	0.06	0.08
Convexity axis	0.10	0.06	0.02	−0.02	−0.02	0.02	0.06	0.10

Figure 23.7 Axes

23.3.7 Classification

Classification methods are specific statistical methods with aim to regroup individuals into classes.

Prior to classification, a PCA analysis is essential to understand better the database information: this analysis reduces the space dimension of the individuals.

23.3.7.1 Classification by mobile centres

This experimental classification method combines four stages:

- Q individuals are chosen randomly and are called "class centres".
- For each individual, the idea is to find the class centre to which the individual is the closest: each individual is "affected" to the closest class.
- After the classification of the individuals, new class centres are computed as the gravity centres of the Q classes.
- The classification of all the individuals is reprocessed with these new gravity centres.

23.3.7.2 Hierarchical classification

The hierarchical classification algorithm (such as the Ward algorithm) takes more time to be computed.

At each stage, the two closest individuals are aggregated in one. The operation is repeated many times. This leads to a hierarchy of partitions similar to trees called "dendograms" with n-1 partitions (when n is the number of individuals).

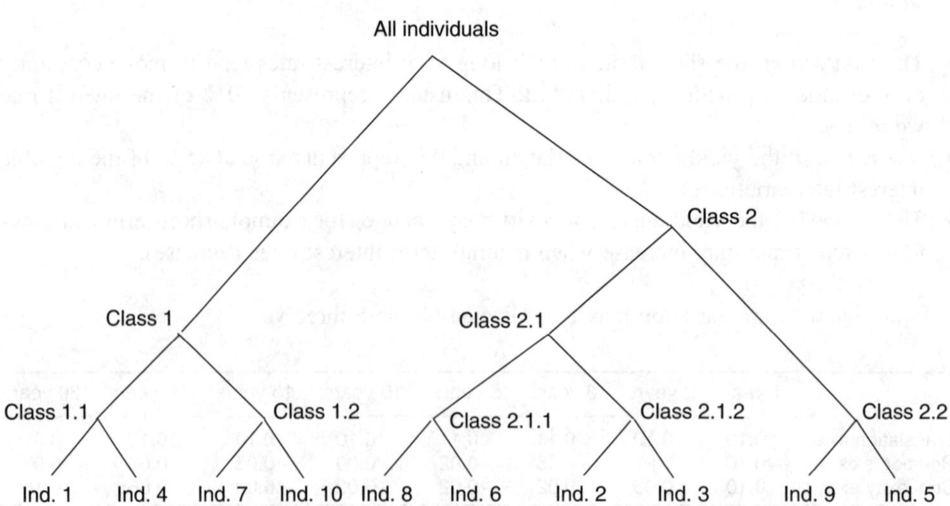

Figure 23.8 Trees

23.3.8 Non-parametric statistics

23.3.8.1 Kernel smoothing

In the prepayment section, kernel smoothing regression techniques were used to build prepayment functions with different explanatory variables (interest rate spread, seniority, etc.). Kernel regression is in fact a smoothing of the density by kernels (such as Gaussian kernels).

The modelling is said be *non-parametric* since parameters are not directly modelled.

Sometimes indeed, economic effects are too complex to be modelled by a simple linear regression.

Note however that kernel smoothing does not give analytic formulae and provides sometimes poor extrapolations in areas where there are not so many observations.

23.3.8.2 Bootstrap methods

In statistics, bootstrapping is a method used to simulate a variable by re-sampling with replacement from the original sample. This method assumes nothing about the distribution of the observed sample. For instance, the Gaussian property of the residuals is not imposed: this is non-parametric simulation method.

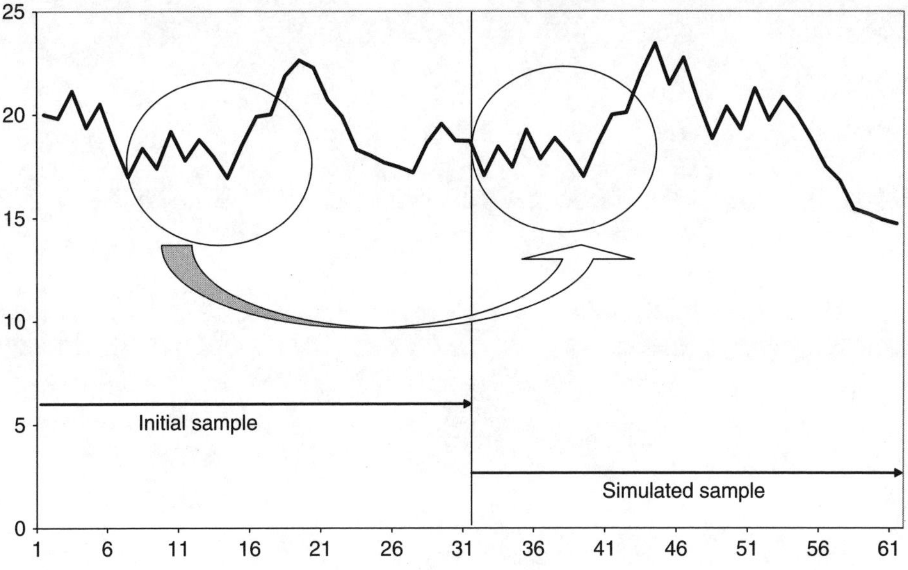

Figure 23.9 Bootstrap

23.4 OTHER STATISTICAL TOOLS AND COMMON ALM FUNCTIONS

This chapter has introduced only the most important statistical tools an A/L manager needs to know about. Among the other statistical tools used less frequently by ALM statisticians, we may cite:

- Lemke algorithm;
- Beveridge and Nelson;
- stochastic control and dynamic optimization through Hamilton Jacobi Bellman;
- regime models;
- scoring methods;
- maximum likelihood maximization programmes, etc.

Readers interested in ALM and statistics should refer to the specialized books.

Moreover, a mathematical background is necessary for ALM modelling. For example, in statistical modelling, variables are often changed using classic mathematical transformations. Among the most common transformations, we may cite:

- Arctangent function to transform a $]-\infty; +\infty[$ variable in a bounded variable in $]-\pi/2; \pi/2[$. Alternatively, inversely the tangent function that transforms a bounded variable into a non-bounded one.
- Ln [- ln( )] function that transforms a]0;1[variable such as a prepayment rate or a default rate into a $]-\infty; +\infty[$ variable.
- Fourier transform function.
- Levy process and Malliavin calculation.

Part VI

Economic Value and New Risk Indicators Associated with the Basel II and Solvency II Regulatory Perspective

In the final chapters of this book we will describe how it is possible to define the optimal ALM strategy. Before that, it is time to explain what are the exogenous constraints imposed upon A/L managers.

First, there are regulatory constraints. With the new regulation (Basel II and Solvency II), banks and insurance companies are encouraged to develop advanced risk indicators such as economic capital.

To better understand those risk indicators, it is necessary to be familiar with financial analysis problems and with the links between ALM and financial analysis. Since executive managers are more interested in the shareholder value of their company than in risk exposure, A/L managers have to propose risk indicators consistant with the company objectives.

All this leads to the proposition of exogenous constraints consistent with regulatory and executive management problems: economic capital constraints.

24 Basel II Regulation and Solvency II

La mesure est la meilleure des choses. (Vléobule de Rhodes)

24.1 COMMON REGULATORY RISK CONSTRAINTS

In ALM activity, regulators tend to play a larger role year after year.

Regulation depends on the country. In the banking sector, the major regulators are, for example: FSA in the UK, "Commission Bancaire" in France, SEC in the US and the Office of Thrift Supervision (OTS) for thrifts in the US.

At a higher level, international regulatory organizations coordinate regulation across countries such as the Basel Committee or the CEBS (Council of European Banking Supervisors) in Europe.

The aim of regulation is to provide stability in the market: customers, government and even market players need this stability.

This leads to a transparent market where market players have nothing to worry about since they are treated equally.

For financial analysts, regulation allows easier risk exposure comparisons.

To perform such a transparent regulation in a market that changes every day, an intensive dialogue takes place between the regulators and the industry. This dialogue is driven by the maximum of flexibility in order to avoid every kind of misunderstanding.

Regulation creates incentives for an improved risk management development in industries that would sometimes prefer not to spend too much money in non-commercial activities (i.e. in financial risk management).

With regulatory pressure, risk management obtains enough power to follow business evolution and even to propose better business strategies considering risk. The regulators' role is to promote risk management as a key to business success and not just as a constraint on business development.

The Basel Committee on Banking Supervision (BCBS) revises the international standards for measuring the adequacy of banks' capital.

The Basel committee members are the G10 countries represented by their Central Banks or by their regulatory authority. The Basel Committee works under the aegis of the BIS (Bank for International Settlements), i.e. the "Central Bank of the Central Banks"; BIS supplies only the secretariat for the BCBS and is not the BCBS itself.

The committee meets four times a year but works with more than 20 workshops and publishes on a regular basis documents about banking regulation.

The committee's purpose is to make recommendations to national authorities. Those authorities later transpose these recommendations into their local laws.

Of course, the committee encourages non-G10 countries to use its recommendations in their local regulation.

The bank local supervisor is the bank interlocutor for internal model validation, the internal ratios examination. In some cases, the supervisor may criticize openly positions that are too risky, give a fine or withdraw banking activity authorization.

The type of constraints usually imposed by regulators relate to:

- liquidity constraints;
- tier 1 ratio;
- interest rate risk constraints;
- currency risk constraints, etc.

24.2 BASEL II: NORMALIZED REGULATORY CONSTRAINTS

24.2.1 The regulatory perspective

24.2.1.1 Basel accord

In the banking sector, *Basel II, also called "The New Accord"* became after the Y2K the new standard for banking regulation. The original document (International Convergence of Capital Measurement and Capital Standards – A Revised Framework) is the second Basel Accord after the first 1988 Accord which was called Basel I. The document, signed in July 2004, proposes an international standard for measuring the adequacy of a bank's capital.

The bank's capital adequacy in the Basel I accord was computed according to the *"Cooke Ratio"*; the new standard suggests replacing the Cooke ratio with the *"McDonough ratio"*.

Banking activity is driven mainly by credit distribution in the economy. The credit risk present in such an activity (since debtors may default) needs to be controlled and measured. On the other hand, the banks may choose between two types of liabilities: equity (capital) or debt. Equity belongs to the shareholders and may disappear if a credit risk crunch occurs; therefore, shareholders will tend to put the minimal amount of equity possible in the balance sheet in order to avoid such a situation. Credit risk occurrence affects directly the shareholder's equity.

Moreover, since banks are usually financed one by the other, a credit risk contagion is possible: this is called *the domino effect or systemic risk*.

From a regulatory perspective, for market regulation, it is more important to protect the bank's debtors from such a credit risk crunch than to protect the shareholders. Banking regulation will impose a minimum capital in front of the credit risk.

The Basel regulators started to control the banking activity in order to allocate capital directly in front of this credit risk. The Cooke ratio was a simple way to allocate capital proportionally in front of credit risk.

Of course, as time went by, the banks wanted the more economic computation of this Cooke ratio that came with the McDonough ratio.

More than 100 countries apply the Basel Accord.

24.2.1.2 Basel I principles

The Basel I regulation took place in 1988 and is often associated with the "Cooke Ratio".

This regulation introduced regulatory capital that was mainly used to:

- Compute bank solvency.
- Communicate company financial results such as the return on regulatory capital (i.e. RAROC) and communicate especially this return subsidiary by subsidiary.

With Basel I, the banks should respect two ratios:

- [Equity + Quasi Equity] / RWA > 8 %;
- [Equity] / RWA > 4 %.

RWA means "Risk Weighted Assets" and these "assets" were the product of the exposure E and the normalized risk weight RW.

$$RWA = RW^{*}E \tag{24.1}$$

For example, for a balance sheet credit, the risk weight was:

- OECD State = 0 %;
- Bank = 20 %;
- Corporations and individuals = 100 %.

Cooke ratio implementation was highly limited by credit exposure definition. The main variable was the total exposure and did not take into account credit fundamental characteristics such as the borrowers' quality. For credit institutions, all the credits were "Cooked" with the same coefficient: credits to banking institutions were supposed to have the same risk even if some of them were close to bankruptcy!

The Basel I model was insensitive to the individual risk of each transaction and poorly adapted to a "micro" piloting of credit risk.

The model was not useful in credit risk pricing.

The Basel I system allowed regulatory arbitrages. For example, credit risk securitization programmes permitted the transfer of all the credit risk exposures to SPVs, i.e. deconsolidated vehicles in order to suppress regulatory capital but to conserve the majority of the risk exposure. (The credit risk was bought back by the bank to the vehicle through equity tranches.)

Moreover, in Basel I, poor consideration was given to derivative products.

As a conclusion, the banking crises of the 80s came at the origin of the Basel I Accord. However, since the market asks always for a higher level of return-on-equity, the banks developed higher return strategies within this simple regulation framework. This resulted in many failures; these failures with large advances in banking technologies and in information technologies came at the origin of the Basel II regulation. Indeed, the risk (i.e. the regulatory capital) has to be computed according to the expected return.

24.2.1.3 Basel II principles

Because of the bank failures of the 80s and 90s, the Basel II accord proposed a new recommendation set with a more precise credit risk representation called the "McDonough ratio".

The two main evolutions proposed by the accord concern:

- regulatory capital computation using new methods more sensitive to the economic credit risk;
- introduction of regulatory capital in front of operational risk.

The Basel II Accord uses a "three Pillars" concept:

- **Pillar 1: Minimum capital requirements (McDonough Solvency Ratio)**:
  - credit risk;
  - market risk (CAD);
  - operational risk.
- **Pillar 2 : Supervisory review**:
  - necessity to compute and allocate an economic capital;
  - economic capital supervisory review and comparison with regulatory capital;
  - equity capital above the minimum capital requirement;
  - interest rate risk in the Banking Book.
- **Pillar 3: Market discipline to promote a greater stability in the financial system**:
  - financial communication improvement;
  - risk profile definition;
  - hedging through capital.

The Basel I accord dealt only with parts of each of these Pillars. For example, for the risks exposed in the first Pillar, market risk was a late addition in the 1988 accord and operational risk was not dealt with at all.

The accord objectives are directly linked with the failures of the Cooke ratio:

- *To ensure a more risk sensitive capital allocation.*

Basel II takes into account risk reduction techniques and introduces risk measures in the operating management. It promotes stress scenarios and the computation of internal risk measures such as economic capital.

- *To separate credit risk and operational risk*

Basel II focuses on the perimeter, on the exposure at default, on the portfolio and on the normalization of credit and of operational risk.

- *To stop regulatory arbitrages with the introduction in banks of an economic capital methodology.*

Indeed the regulators' objective is to develop banks' "best practices".

Basel II wishes to improve governance, risk control, quantitative indicators construction, organization and management processes.

Basel II affects limit policy, hedging strategies and finally business activity.

The accord, of course, fell into imposing minimum capital requirements for many kinds of risks and especially in front of the interest rate risk included in the banking book. However, with the introduction of economic capital in Pillar 2, regulators in fact succeeded in obliging the banks to communicate and to develop risk measurements of their interest rate risk capital.

While the final accord has largely addressed the regulatory arbitrage issue, there are still areas where regulatory capital requirements will diverge from the theoretical economic requirements. For example, US banks will adopt Basel II in 2011; this could provoke a distortion of competition with Europe.

The Basel II fields of application are the following:

- The broadest consolidation is carried out on the holding level (for a holding including a banking group).
- Sub-consolidations are also envisaged at the level of each banking subsidiary company ("banks with international activity").
- Insurance subsidiaries do not take part into the consolidated computation: Solvency II recommendations replace the Basel II recommendations.

24.2.1.4 Basel II glossary

24.2.1.4.1 EAD (Exposure At Default)

To measure the extent of the loss in the eventuality of a borrower's failure, it is necessary to know or to measure which would be the bank's engagement in this case. The engagement at the time of the failure is a direct function of the credit type. The measurement of the exposure is determined simply for a fixed loan but is more complex to determine in the case of a revolving credit, for instance.

The credit risk IRB approach requires the computation of the EAD.

24.2.1.4.2 PD (Probability of Default)

To measure the extent of the loss in the eventuality of a borrower's failure, it is essential to compute the inherent borrower's risk. Usually, default risk is attached to a rating; each rating is linked with a default probability.

The credit risk IRB approach requires the computation of the PD.

24.2.1.4.3 LGD (Loss Given Default)

To measure the extent of the loss in the eventuality of a borrower's failure, it is necessary to measure how much in terms of percentages of the exposure the company would recover. This percentage depends on the credit structure in terms of seniority and on the guarantees attached to the credit.

The credit risk IRB approach requires the computation of the LGD.

24.2.1.4.4 M (Maturity)

To measure the extent of the loss in the eventuality of a failure of the borrower, the effective maturity of the credits exposed to default should be taken into account. This effective maturity is preferred to the credit portfolio economic duration.

In the advanced IRB approach, the Basel Committee proposes an explicit maturity adjustment.

24.2.1.4.5 RA (Risk Assessment)

The risk assessment is the evaluation made by the bank of the amount or of the nature of the operational risks incurred for one or more indicators (KRI, see below).

The regular evaluation of the operational risks incurred by the bank is necessary within the framework of the internal model approach (AMA).

24.2.1.4.6 KRI (Key Risk Indicator)

The key risk indicators are the bank's chosen indicators to evaluate operational risks. Those indicators may be qualitative or quantitative.

KRI construction is necessary in the AMA operational risk approach.

24.2.1.4.7 RWA (Risk Weighted Asset)

The Risk Weighted Asset is the risk amount used as the regulatory capital denominator in the ratio computation.

RWA is the result of the multiplication of the borrower's failure event potential loss by a weight corresponding to the incurred risks.

24.2.1.4.8 EC (Economic capital)

In banks, economic capital is an internal risk measure. Economic capital and regulatory capital follow the same objective: getting a capital measure representative of the risk present in the balance sheet. Quite often, the economic capital framework is close to the regulatory framework but takes into account:

- a less important regulatory credit risk (since many Pillar 1 hypotheses are more regulatory based than economically based);
- second-rate risk not taken into account in Pillar 1.

24.2.1.4.9 VaR (Value-at-Risk)

Economic capital is often computed as a quantile (99.95 % for example) of the economic value variation over a horizon of 1 year for instance. Such a quantile computation is called Value-at-Risk (VaR).

24.2.1.4.10 EL (Expected Loss)

The Expected Loss represents the financial losses the company expects on a given horizon. In credit risk management, the expected loss is the multiplication of the default probability, the exposure at default and the loss given default:

$$\mathrm{EL} = \mathrm{PD.LGD.EAD} \tag{24.2}$$

Expected losses are usually covered by provisions or reserves.

24.2.1.4.11 UL (Unexpected Loss)

On the contrary, the unexpected loss represents on a given horizon, the amount of losses that could occur within a certain confidence interval. Unexpected loss is related to the second moment of the portfolio losses distribution.

A/L managers use Value-at-Risk or coherent risk measures to compute the UL. Usually, the capital hedges a part of the unexpected loss.

24.2.2 Pillar 1: principles for the credit risk

Basel II Pillar 1 focuses mainly on the credit risk and proposes three different methods for credit risk regulatory capital computation:

- *Standard approach*: using rating systems provided by external organizations.
- *Internal Ratings Based – Foundation approach*: using internal rating systems and regulatory data.
- *Internal Ratings Based – Advanced approach*: using a full internal rating system.

Moreover, Basel II recognizes seven principal types of activity:

- Sovereign and non central governmental public sector entities;
- Banks and investment companies;
- Industrial and commercial corporations;
- Individuals and professionals;
- Project finance;
- Securitization;
- Equity.

The advanced approach is often considered to be the one that provides the minimal amount of regulatory capital but it is of course the costliest (in terms of operating costs).

24.2.2.1 Standard approach

The standard approach is the closest to the Basel I Cooke ratio approach: a risk weight is associated with every asset according to the asset counterparty type. However, in the new accord, those weights are more precise.

For *Sovereign* bonds for example, the risk weights follow:

	AAA to AA−	A+ to A−	BBB+ to BBB−	BB+ to B−	Below B	Non rated
Risk Weight	0 %	20 %	50 %	100 %	150 %	100 %

For *Banks*, two risk options are proposed but the option choice depends on the local regulators.

- *Option 1: uniform method*

With this option, the risk weights follow:

	AAA to AA−	A+ to A−	BBB+ to BBB−	BB+ to B−	Below B	Non rated
Risk Weight	20 %	50 %	100 %	100 %	150 %	100 %

- *Option 2: short-term specific method*

With this option, the risk weights follow:

	AAA to AA−	A+ to A−	BBB+ to BBB−	BB+ to B−	Below B	Non rated
Risk Weight	20 %	50 %	50 %	100 %	150 %	50 %

In addition, for operations with maturity under three months:

	AAA to AA−	A+ to A−	BBB+ to BBB−	BB+ to B−	Below B	Non rated
Risk Weight	20 %	20 %	20 %	50 %	150 %	20 %

Securities firms are treated as banks if banking authorities allow it; otherwise, they are treated as corporations.

Non-central governmental public sector entities are treated as banks but in the case of the option 2 choice, the short-term risk weight cannot be applied.

Multilateral development banks follow the option 2 of the banks' treatment but the short-term risk weight cannot be applied to the exposures on these banks.

Corporations are associated with a special risk weight table:

	AAA to AA−	A+ to A−	BBB+ to BB−	Below BB−	Non rated
Risk Weight	20 %	50 %	100 %	150 %	20 %

Claims included in the regulatory retail portfolio are defined through four constitutive criterions:

- The counterparty is either an individual, either a professional, or a SME (Small and Medium Enterprise).
- The product is a standard product such as an amortizing credit or a revolving credit.
- Not a counterparty should exceed 0.2 % of the portfolio total asset.
- The maximum credit amount by counterparty is € 1 M.

The risk weight was chosen for those portfolios at the level of 75 %.

Claims secured by residential property have a risk weight of 40 %.

Claims secured on commercial real estate have a risk weight of 100 %.

Higher risk categories such as risk capital and private equity have a risk weight of 150 % while other assets have a 100 % risk weight.

24.2.2.2 IRB Foundation approach

In the IRB (Internal Rating Based) Foundation approach, banks have to evaluate internally customer default probability (PD: probability of default) in order to determine their risk weight.

The other data required for the capital computation are the Loss Given Default (LGD), the Exposure at Default (EAD) and the maturity M. Those data are provided by the regulators.

IRB Foundation adoption is possible under these conditions:

- PD models should be used for more than 1 year.
- A 5 year historical database of defaults is required.
- A regulator validation is required in order to take into account the diversity of the bank's customers.

24.2.2.3 IRB advanced approach

The IRB advanced approach asks banks to use their internal credit risk evaluations for the PD, the LGD, the EAD and for the maturity M in order to determine their capital needs.

The adoption of this approach (instead of the standard approach) includes more constraints:

- PD, LGD, EAD and M models have to be used for more than three years.
- A seven year PD, LGD, EAD, M history is required.
- A regulator validation is required in order to take into account the bank's customer diversity.

The loss distribution function will follow a normal distribution. A quantile of the distribution function gives the final measurement of capital:

$$\text{RWA} = \text{EAD.f(PD, LGD)} \tag{24.3}$$

The function f follows a normal distribution and takes into account the maturity M of the assets and their granularity.

The capital requirement takes also into account the Expected Loss given directly by the multiplication of the default probability, the exposure at default and the loss given default:

$$\text{EL} = \text{PD. EAD. LGD}$$

24.2.2.4 Risk reduction techniques

Reduction techniques are available for both standard and IRB approach.

Collateralization is considered to be a reduction technique as soon as:

- the contract legal robustness is proved with a low correlation between the exposure and the collateral;
- the collateral is taken into account in the risk systems;
- the collateral is disclosed and published (according to the Pillar III framework).

There are two methods of taking into account the collateral:

- “simple method” where the collateral (cash or bonds, etc.) modify directly the borrower’s exposure;
- “normal method” where the exposure is modified through “hair cuts” and factor “w”.

Guarantees and credit derivatives will modify the exposure weights by substitution also.

Asset and liability balance sheet compensation is open to banking and corporate counterparties as soon as:

- the contract’s legal robustness is proved;
- the risk is managed effectively on a net basis;
- the risk is disclosed and published (according to the Pillar III framework).

24.2.3 Pillar 1 and Market risk

The 1996 amendment (“1996 Amendment to the Capital Accord to Incorporate Market Risks”) to the Basel I Accord concerning market risk is still the reference point for the market risk capital adequacy.

This amendment proposes two methodologies:

- a standardized approach;
- an internal model approach.

The regulator asks for the risk computation with a *Value-at-Risk 99 % 10 open days risk measure* multiplied by a *multiplying factor* above 3.

The methodology implies a backtesting of the computation since the regulator determines the multiplying factor as a qualitative and quantitative function of the modelling performance.

24.2.4 Pillar 1 and operational risk

The Basel Committee defines operational risk “as the risk of loss resulting from inadequate or failed internal processes, people and systems or from external events. This definition includes legal risk but excludes strategic and reputation risk”.

As it is the case for credit risk, the Basel Committee proposes three approaches to treating operational risk:

- *Basic Indicator Approach (BIA)*;
- *Standardised Approach (SA)*;
- *Internal Measurement Approach (IMA)* including the *Advanced Measurement Approach – Loss Distribution Approach (AMA – LDA)*.

The *BIA* approach consists simply of multiplying the gross income over the past three years by a risk weight (15 % for example) called *“alpha factor”* α.

The *SA* approach proposes to divide the banking activity P&L (gross income) into eight categories:

- Corporate Finance $\beta_1 = 18\,\%$
- Trading and sales $\beta_2 = 18\,\%$
- Retail banking $\beta_3 = 12\,\%$
- Commercial banking $\beta_4 = 15\,\%$
- Payment & settlement $\beta_5 = 18\,\%$
- Agency services and custody $\beta_6 = 15\,\%$
- Asset management $\beta_7 = 12\,\%$
- Retail brokerage $\beta_8 = 12\,\%$.

For each category a factor, the *β factor* this time, is imposed by the regulator. The overall capital is the sum for each banking activity of the products of the gross income by the β factor.

The *IMA approach* is based on the construction of an internal database in order to determine the regulatory capital. The approach requires three information types in this database:

- an operational risk exposure indicator;
- data to determine the loss event occurrence probability;
- data to determine the loss occurred during past loss events.

The framework splits this information according to the banking activity decomposition and according to different event types:

- internal fraud;
- external fraud;
- employment practices and workplace safety;
- clients, products and business practices;
- damage to physical assets;
- business disruption and system failures;
- execution, delivery and process management.

As usual, it is important not to forget that *business, strategic and reputation risks are expressly excluded.*

To compute the regulatory capital, bank will apply to these data fixed percentages established by the Basel Committee called *gamma factors* γ (BCBS gives a γ for each business line/Loss type). The formula takes into account an adjustment factor RPI when the bank risk profile differs from the industry risk profile. Thus, the total charge is as follows:

$$Charge = \sum_{activity\ (i)} \sum_{event\ type\ (j)} \left(\gamma_{i,j}.Expected\ Loss_{i,j}.RPI_{i,j}\right) \quad (24.4)$$

The *AMA – LDA approach* (Advanced Measurement Approach – Loss Distribution Approach) links the computation with a loss distribution law. The adoption of this method is contingent to these conditions:

- 5 years historical loss database;
- 1 year model exploitation;
- a regulator validation for the recognition of the bank's operational risk diversity.

24.2.5 Pillar 1 risk aggregation

Once the Risk manager has computed his credit risk requirement, his market risk requirement and his operational risk requirement, it is time for him to aggregate them (without a perfect correlation between these risks):

$$\text{RWA} = \text{Credit risk} + \text{Market Risk} + \text{Operational Risk} \tag{24.5}$$

These RWA represents 12.5 times the capital requirements.

The regulator may then multiply this number by a *scaling factor* in order to broadly maintain the aggregate level of minimum capital requirements.

24.2.6 Pillar 2: implementation of economic capital

The Basel II Pillar 2 introduces a more sophisticated prudential monitoring framework in order to verify capital adequacy and internal risk measure processes.

Pillar 1 focused on the minimum capital requirement with a quantitative approach; on the other hand, Pillar 2 mixes quantitative and qualitative approaches with, for instance, the definition of the relationship with the supervisor (*"Supervisory Review Process"*).

Pillar II recommends an *economic capital implementation* without giving a complete computation guideline (*Internal Capital Adequacy Assessment Process or ICAAP*). In fact, the goal is to let the banks develop an internal risk conscientiousness through:

- an economic capital expertise;
- a constant process analysis;
- partnerships with the supervisor.

Regulators will have to verify that banks work with internal "safe and secure" processes allowing them to verify capital adequacy.

Moreover, regulators will have the opportunity to raise the capital requirements if they think the bank exposure is excessive or if the risk management is not under control.

The second Pillar gives regulators much improved "tools" over those available to them under Basel I. It also provides a framework for dealing with all the other risks that a bank faces: business risk, legal risk, interest rate and liquidity risk (i.e. the "residual risks").

Basel II Pillar 2 introduces *four principles*:

- *First principle: the banks should be able to evaluate their capital needs according to their risk level.*

Bank management should be conscious of its risk exposure and be responsible for the required capital level.

All the main important risk exposures should be taken into account in the economic capital project:

- credit risk (with portfolio effects);
- market risk;
- interest rate risk in the Banking Book;
- liquidity risk;
- residual risks (strategic, business, etc.).

Indeed, an economic capital project has many goals:

- Compare economic capital with the available Tier 1 capital;
- Introduce a risk adjusted performance measurement;
- Allocate economic capital to business lines according to usage;
- Compare return with target return for Tier 1 capital;
- Increase clarity on who is responsible for which risk;
- Focus on return optimization under constraints instead of on risk reduction.

All those risk exposures (and the sensitivity of those risk exposures to hypotheses) should be reported to the bank's management.

The capital computation will require an adequate internal control to make sure that all the risks are taken into account and that the risk exposure is consistent with the bank business plan.

- *Second principle: supervisors will validate the economic capital computation.*

The supervisor will validate the economic capital methodology: this validation takes place in a permanent and continuous relationship:

- internal and external checks;
- regular bank management interviews;
- internal audit and reporting review.

The review will go into the calculus hypothesis details to verify that these details reflect the bank's activity.

Moreover, the regulators will appreciate the capital adequacy and evaluate the bank strategy and its aptitude to watch and respect the regulatory ratios.

- *Third principle: compare required minimum capital and recommended capital.*

Pillar 2 explains that bank will detain more capital than the minimum Pillar 1 regulatory requirement even if a "surplus", an "add-on" or an "excess" could be directly imposed by the supervisor:

- Since the bank would prefer to get a higher solvency level than the minimum level, (a higher solvency level means cheaper liquidity costs and a higher protection for the bondholder and for the shareholder).
- Since the ratio is susceptible to vary due to the activity changes.
- Since new capital issue are often costly.
- Since falling under the minimum capital requirement is very dangerous for the bank's image in the market.
- Since many risks could have been omitted in the risk exposure definition.

- *Fourth principle: supervisors should act for the maintenance of a good capital adequacy*

Regulators should get involved rapidly in the bank management in order to prevent a capital fall under the minimum requirements: in such a situation, they should ask for the adoption of corrective measures:

- o recapitalization;
- o closer bank risk exposure review;
- o dividend distribution blocking;
- o solvency rescue plan definition, etc.

In the long-term, the minimum capital requirement could decrease as soon as risk control and system control is improved: a safer banking industry risk policy will probably lead to softer capital requirements.

As for the capital "add-ons", Pillar 2 explains some particular rules:

- Those "add-ons" could become temporary add-ons and could disappear as soon as the systems and the internal control are improved.
- Supervisors should make publicly available the criteria to be used in the review of banks' internal capital assessments.
- Where the capital requirements are set above the minimum for an individual bank, the supervisor should explain to the bank the risk characteristics specific to the bank, which resulted in the requirement and any remedial action necessary.

Basel II Pillar 2 deals with other regulatory needs. Especially, a certain number of risks not covered in Pillar 1 are described:

- interest rate risk in the Banking Book with an "outlier bank" criterion;
- residual risks;
- securitization risk;
- concentration risk, etc.

24.2.7 Pillar 2 and interest rate risk in the Banking Book

Interest risk in the Banking Book was included in the Pillar 2 and not in the Pillar 1 document since it appeared difficult to construct a homogeneous capital requirement formula: the definition of bank exposure to interest rate risk depends indeed on the country and on the local regulator.

Of course, the supervisor may ask for an interest rate risk capital add-on if the risk is considered to be too important. Eventually, he may ask for a regulatory capital increase or an interest rate risk reduction.

24.2.7.1 Economic capital computation

Usually interest rate risk was measured through classic indicators such as interest rate gap or income sensitivity to interest rate movements. Even if those sensitivities may be computed over a long-term horizon, interest rate risk management focuses on the few years to come. To get information about the interest rate risk taken over longer-term horizons, the Basel

Committee recommends the use of economic capital. In reality, the Basel Committee's objective is to focus on long-term risks and to build a consolidation between Trading and Banking Book.

Of course, there is no general consensus about methodology. The computation should cover the entire balance sheet (assets, liabilities, off-balance sheet instruments, etc.) and all the interest rate risk sources.

The computation needs to be consistent with the accounting sources.

Regulatory methodological requirements are limited once compared with organizational requirements (in term of systems, procedures, documentations, etc.) as if the regulator was interested above all in the implementation of an effective economic capital in the bank management.

Economic capital computation is a delicate exercise including subjective choices. This is particularly the case for interest rate risk where regulatory and conventional aspects complicate the balance sheet economic value computation.

The A/L manager's entire task will be to convince the supervisor of the bank's model choices.

24.2.7.2 Basel II standardized 200 bps shock and the definition of "outliers banks"

In its July 2004 document "Principles for the Management and Supervision of Interest Rate Risk", the Basel Committee proposed a standardized method to determine whether a bank is under capitalized for interest rate risk or not.

The method is proposed but not imposed. Nevertheless, the document defines *outlier banks* as banks where the economic value variation under a 200 bps interest rate shock exceeds 20 % of the bank equity (computed as the net Tier 1 plus Tier 2). Outlier banks should undertake corrective actions. The choice of this 20 % limit means that taking an interest rate risk exposure is usual in the banking activity and allows banks to create value.

Note that the Basel Committee preferred an economic value based computation to an income sensitivity computation.

The +/− 200 basis points shock may be replaced by a 1 % or 99 % annual interest rate variation shock.

This standardized approach includes simple and conservationist hypotheses such as:

- The core deposits maturity should not exceed 5 years.
- Balance sheet elements are taken at their accounted value.
- Fixed rate instruments are split according to their residual maturity and variable instruments according to their next repricing date.
- Derivative contracts are deconstructed using the virtual interest rate position of their components (a receiver swap may be deconstructed in a fixed rate loan and a floating rate deposit, for example).
- Options are included according to their delta equivalent.
- Contract by contract expositions may be aggregated using a statistical repayment schedule.
- Assets and liabilities are split according to 13 maturity tranches. Each tranche is weighted as follows (representing a 200 bps shock):

Maturity Tranche	Risk Weight Coefficient (computed for a 200 basis point shock)
Under 1 Month	0.08 %
From 1 Month to 3 Months	0.32 %
From 3 Months to 6 Months	0.72 %
From 6 Months to 12 Months	1.43 %
From 1 Year to 2 Years	2.77 %
From 2 Years to 3 Years	4.49 %
From 3 Years to 4 Years	6.14 %
From 4 Years to 5 Years	7.71 %
From 5 Years to 7 Years	10.15 %
From 7 Years to 10 Years	13.26 %
From 10 Years to 15 Years	17.84 %
From 15 Years to 20 Years	22.43 %
Above 20 Years	26.03 %

Figure 24.1 Risk weights

The 200 bps economic value sensitivity is the sum of the multiplications of the net exposures on each maturity tranche by the risk weights above.

The 200 bps sensitivity is computed for each currency but the sensitivities are added after all.

Among the many disadvantages included in this method, we may perceive that:

- the economic value does not take into account the asset or the liability remuneration rate;
- the demand deposit exact schedule is not specified: the final result highly depends on this schedule that is not specified to be linear or bullet.

In the future, the supervisor will look after the economic capital methodologies developed internally in order to propose a regulatory method for computing a capital for interest rate risk.

24.2.7.3 Stress tests computation

Pillar 2 asks for a stress test implementation and especially for the implementation of an interest rate stress test.

The stress test's objective is to focus on every unfavourable change. Above all, the interest rate stress tests should take into account:

- interest rate level instant move impacts;
- yield curve profile moves such as slope moves, and yield curve convexity moves;
- inflation and real rate moves;
- correlation among the yield curves of the different currencies;
- customer behaviour changes (such as prepayment speed acceleration, etc.).

24.2.8 Pillar 2 and interest rate risk governance

The following sections summarize the Basel II resolutions about governance and interest rate risk management.

24.2.8.1 *Management implication*

In order to carry out its responsibilities, the board of directors in banks should approve strategies and policies with respect to interest rate risk management and should assure that senior management takes the steps necessary to monitor and control these risks consistent with the approved strategies and policies.

The board of directors should be informed regularly of the interest rate risk exposure of the bank in order to assess the monitoring and controlling of such risk as against the board's guidance on the levels of risk that are acceptable to the bank.

Senior management must assure that the structure of the bank's business and the level of interest rate risk it assumes are effectively managed, that appropriate policies and procedures are established to control and limit these risks, and that resources are available for evaluating and controlling interest rate risk.

24.2.8.2 *Team organization*

Banks should clearly define the individuals and/or the committees responsible for managing interest rate risk and should assure that there is an adequate separation of duties in key elements of the risk management process in order to avoid potential conflicts of interest.

Banks should have risk measurement, monitoring, and control functions with clearly defined duties that are sufficiently independent from the position-taking functions of the bank and which report risk exposures directly to senior management and the board of directors.

Larger or more complex banks should have a designated independent unit responsible for the design and the administration of the bank's interest rate risk measurement, monitoring and control functions.

24.2.8.3 *Processes*

It is essential that banks' interest rate risk policies and procedures are clearly defined and consistent with the nature and the complexity of their activities.

These policies should be applied on a consolidated basis and, as appropriate, at the level of individual affiliates, especially when recognizing legal distinctions and possible obstacles to cash movements among affiliates.

It is important that banks identify the risks inherent in new products and activities and assure that these risks are subject to adequate procedures and controls before being introduced or undertaken.

Major hedging or risk management initiatives should be approved in advance by the board or its appropriate delegated committee.

24.2.8.4 *Internal control*

Banks must have an adequate system of internal controls over their interest rate risk management process.

A fundamental component of the internal control system involves regular independent reviews and evaluations of the effectiveness of the system and, where necessary, ensuring that appropriate revisions or enhancements to internal controls are made.

The results of such reviews should be available to the relevant supervisory authorities.

24.2.9 Pillar 3: market discipline, financial communication and its implications for ALM

Pillar 3 asks for effective financial communication in order to promote safe and sane banking practices. This is called the *market discipline*.

Pillar 3 requires banks to attest of their good management with respect to the market. The Basel Committee wishes to reduce systemic risk by under-capitalized bank identification through the market information. On the other hand, the Committee wishes to create conditions for market best practices rewards.

In fact, the three Pillars are complementary and they support mutually one the others:

- a minimal capital level with Pillar 1;
- an appropriate internal and controlled organization with Pillar 2;
- a market transparency in order to appreciate the banking activity diversity with Pillar 3.

New capital computation implies market transparency in terms of regulatory capital, risk exposures, risk computation processes and capital adequacy management.

Furthermore, regulators will accept the banks' adoption of a credit risk IRB approach and the operational risk AMA approach only if the internal methods used to achieve these approaches are exposed to the market.

The market has to be able to estimate the banks' risk level using:

- qualitative information;
- quantitative information;
- information about risk management organization.

More specifically with relation to interest rate risk, the market needs:

- information about the interest rate risk organization (responsibilities, systems, strategies, limits policy, interest rate risk measure frequency, etc.);
- implicit option treatment hypothesis: prepayment, deposit schedule;
- hypotheses for the computation of the interest rate risk economic capital;
- hypotheses for the computation of income sensitivity or economic value sensitivity.

In the third Pillar, the banks should indicate their interest rate sensitivity publication choice: either they publish their income sensitivity either their economic value sensitivity.

An economic value indicator would be better comfort for the financial analysts and reveal less the predicted income evolution.

	Pros	Cons
Economic Value based indicator	Take into account all the future cash flows will comfort the market	Value insensitivity is incompatible with income stability (see next chapters)
Income based indicator	Closer to the business	Does not reveal interest rate risk on long-term horizons

Figure 24.2 Pros and Cons

Unfortunately, the non-observance of Pillar 3 disclosure is not sanctioned: no additional requirement of capital could be imposed.

24.2.10 Criticism of Basel II

Even as Basel I was often criticized, Basel II produced rapidly its detractors. This chapter will try to explain their point of view.

First, *Basel II seems to favour the larger banks*: those banks are able to develop their own models in order to minimize their capital needs. The introduction of Basel II could lead to banking sector concentration.

Moreover, Basel II implementation costs will favour the larger banks. Using the new regulation, those banks will be able to know better their clients and to propose better-priced credits. Pricing will be more difficult for small sized banks and those banks will tend to acquire only the riskiest clients mispricing their credit spread.

However, the most famous criticism of Basel II surrounds *procyclicity*. Credit models developed for Pillar 1 typically use a one year time horizon. This would mean that, during a downturn in the business cycle, banks would need to reduce lending as their models forecast increased losses, increasing the magnitude of the crisis.

Liquidity risk is a very important risk not recognized in Pillar 1 nor in Pillar 2. Bank should use adequate systems to measure, follow and control their liquidity risk. They should compute an economic capital for their liquidity needs and for the liquidity risk they take on the market where they operate.

On the other hand, economic capital implementation should insure the rating stability of banks and allow better refinancing conditions.

Basel II will perhaps *introduce complexity in the banking activity financial analysis*. Economic capital and internal models may seem to be much too complex for financial analysts. Instead of financial transparency, banks could use their teams to produce too much information with the intention of "losing" financial analysts.

Moreover, currency risk is partially taken into account in Pillar 2. Structural currency risk is not treated separately. Nevertheless:

- Currency risk should be included in the economic capital measurement.
- Interest rate risk has to be computed currency by currency.
- Trading book currency risk is included in market risk capital calculation.

Basel II has consequences for A/L managers:

- Banking Book economic capital computation;
- new economic capital limits to introduce into the business;
- internal indicators conception for communication;
- documentation of the models and of the processes;
- accrued position consolidation at the holding level: risk measure leads to a stronger risk centralization in terms of position and governance.

ALM departments will have to compute their interest rate risk centrally, to make public the A/L norms and be present at all the local ALCOs.

Work is apparently already underway on Basel III, at least in a preliminary sense. The goals of this project are to refine the definition of bank capital, quantify further classes of risk and to further improve the sensitivity of risk measures.

24.3 SOLVENCY II

When we decided to write this book, the Solvency II European directive was not yet published. Nevertheless, we will describe the main chapters included in this project of regulation for the insurance industry.

After many quantitative impact studies, CEIOPS (Committee of European Insurance and Occupational Pensions Supervisors) decided to propose an economic approach to insurance risk measurement close to the one proposed by Basel II. Of course, this new regulation affects only the European insurance companies but it is certain that it will serve as a worldwide standard.

The objective of Solvency II is to:

- improve the protection of the policyholders;
- improve risk management in insurance companies;
- improve the regulatory control;
- provide a harmonized European framework for the solvency risk measurement.

The previous European regulation allowed local regulators to complete the solvency minimal requirements with "complementary requirements" that differed greatly from one country to another.

The framework integrates three Pillars as Basel II did.

Pillar 1 describes the quantitative requirements. This Pillar provides an evaluation formula for the technical provisions. It gives also the opportunity to compute the solvency margin with an internal model. This *solvency margin* is the minimum ratio between the equity of an insurance company and its total activity volume (or its risk). Pillar 1 provides also a standard formula for the smallest insurance companies.

Pillar 2 describes the qualitative requirements. The objective is to make sure that the insurance company is well organized in terms of: risk management, internal control, and governance. The Pillar describes also the supervision process.

Pillar 3 describes the disclosure requirements. The supervisor and the market have to be informed. The Pillar shows which information the insurers have to present.

Moreover, the harmonization of the provision computation methods is one of the main objectives of Solvency II. It seems to be established that the accountants will calculate provisions as the *best estimates of the future cash flows discounted with market rates plus a margin.*

Consequently, with the new regulatory standard and with the introduction of the IFRS rules, the insurance market uses more and more "Full fair value concepts".

The process recognizes two kinds of requirements:

- The Minimum Capital Requirement (MCR): under this minimal level of equity, the insurance company presents an unacceptable level of risk.

- The Solvency capital Requirement (SCR): this is the target amount of equity for the insurance company in order to hedge the possible unexpected losses and to protect the policyholders.

As a conclusion, Solvency II is the transposition of Basel II into the insurance market. It challenges the business culture but includes also a risk of pro-cyclicity.

25 Links Between ALM and Financial Analysis

Mieux vaut ami en place qu'argent en bourse.

Regulatory constraints introduced the notion of economic capital. Economic value and shareholder value are linked; consequently, imposing constraints on economic value has an impact on the income followed by financial analysts.

There is a direct link between ALM and the financial analysis of the company. Indeed, in the past, many ALM teams belonged to Financial Departments before moving into Risk Management or Treasury Departments.

ALM improvement came with the idea that the company performance could be affected by bad market movements. The link between ALM and financial analysis will be described through:

- a brief summary of the financial analysis key indicators;
- an introduction to economic value concepts;
- an introduction to capital allocation and to debt/capital concepts.

25.1 PERFORMANCE INDICATORS IN THE COMPANY

25.1.1 ROE, RONE and ROEC

Financial analysts focus mainly on performance indicators such as:

- *Company ROE (Return on Equity)* based on the Net income (Group share, e.g. before minority interests) divided by the average equity (Group share).
- *Branches RONE* (Return on Normalized Equity) based on the net income (before taxes) divided by the normalized equity.
- *Branches Income contribution computed with Equity set to 0.*
- *Branches Income contribution computed with Normalized Equity.*
- *Branches CVA* (Cash Value Added): net income (before taxes) less Normalized Equity costs (computed as X % *Normalized Equity).

The ROE is often associated with a *ROE Target*, i.e. an ROE objective given by shareholders. The Normalized Equity cost included in the CVA may look like the target company ROE.

The *Normalized Equity* is the amount of Equity allocated to each branch. The allocation can be effective or not due to local capital regulations.

The RONE and the CVA of each branch is computed according to this Equity amount. We will see in the next sections how *Normalized Equity tends to be replaced by economic capital*, a quantitative expression of the Equity. With the economical allocation of capital, the RONE is replaced by the *ROEC (Return on Economic Capital)*. This ROEC ratio refers to the *Risk adjusted return on capital (RAROC)* previously used before economic capital introduction.

The Shareholder's Equity is the definition of equity from an accounting point of view (i.e. in the accountant's "system of reference").

Share Capital	2
Retained earnings	11
Reserves	10
Year's income	5
Shareholder's Equity (Share group)	**28**
Minority interests	5
Shareholder's Equity	33

Figure 25.1 Shareholder's equity

The *Equity capital (or regulatory capital)* is linked with the prudential system of reference and is used for the solvability ratios computation.

Shareholder's equity	**33**
Goodwill	– 5
Equity/regulatory capital	**28**

Figure 25.2 Equity Capital

The *Normalized equity* is the definition of Equity in the analytical system of reference:

Risk Weighted Assets	16
Goodwill	5
Normalized Equity	**31**

Figure 25.3 Normalized equity

Usually, the normalized equity amount has to be inferior to the Equity capital amount.

In terms of ALM, quite often, the company central treasury is used as an income retrocession centre between allocated equity and normalized equity: branches have the opportunity to ask the central treasurer to replace their superfluous equity. On the other hand, ALM's role is to invoice a FTP on shareholder's equity.

25.1.2 Other computed indicators

The *company Market Value (MV)* is the simple multiplication of the number of shares by the share value. This value focuses mainly on a shareholder point of view.

The *Book Value (BV)* is the net worth of the company. This value usually refers to an accounting system of reference (thinking that IFRS is an economic value based framework): the BV is the difference between the Assets Value and the Liabilities Value. The frontier between BV and *Economic Value (EV)* is thin and we will prefer EV to BV.

The *Price to Book (PTB)* is the division of the Market Value by the Book Value.

$$\mathrm{PTB} = \mathrm{MV}/\mathrm{BV} \tag{25.1}$$

The *cost/income ratio (C/I R)* is the division of the operating costs by the net income.

The *price on earnings ratio (P/E ratio or PER)* is the division of the MV by the total earnings (or the price per share divided by the earning per share).

The *gross interest margin (GIM)* in banks is just the ratio between net income and total assets. This indicator is not the best one since it is based on the total of assets and not on bank profitability. In the following example, the GIM rate is lower in the case B only because the total assets is more important.

	Case A	Case B
Credits	100	110
Margin	0.65 %	0.65 %
Deposits	100	100
Margin	2.00 %	2.00 %
Other Liability	0	10
Margin	0.00 %	0.00 %
GIM	2.65	2.715
GIM rate	**2.65 %**	**2.47 %**

Figure 25.4 GIM rate

25.2 SHAREHOLDER'S EQUITY VALUE, ECONOMIC VALUE AND RISK PREMIUMS

Let us formalize the company valuation process in order to introduce economic capital allocation.

25.2.1 At a company level

The company market valuation MV is provided directly by future dividends discounted by the market rates r under a risk neutral probability (the market probability):

$$MV = E_{RN}\left(\int_0^{+\infty} DIVID(t).\exp\left(-\int_0^t r(s).ds\right)\right) \tag{25.2}$$

We neglect the company default probability and we suppose that this company pays a dividend (DIVID) equal to the company net income (INC). Then the shareholders' equity (SE) is constant:

$$\frac{dSE(t)}{SE(t)} = INC(t).\,dt - DIVID(t).\,dt = 0 \qquad (25.3)$$
$$SE(t) = SE(0)$$

Under an historic probability (or a real probability), the income evolution contains a risk premium p that could be supposed to be constant. The income is thus proportional to the interest rate level r and includes a constant growth c:

$$INC(t).dt = SE(0).\left(r(t).dt + p.dt + c(t).dt + \sigma.dW_t^{real}\right) \qquad (25.4)$$

Under the risk neutral probability, the income follows this process without risk premium:

$$INC(t).dt = SE(0).\left(r(t).dt + c(t).dt + \sigma.dW_t^{RN}\right) \qquad (25.5)$$

According to the CAPM, in a Gaussian framework, the risk premium p is equal to the covariance between the income and the optimal market portfolio yield:

$$p = \frac{Covariance(INC, R_M)}{\sigma(INC).\sigma(R_M)} \qquad (25.6)$$

Using this relationship, the MV follows:

$$MV = E_{RN}\left(\int_0^{+\infty} SE(0).\left(r(t).dt + cdt + \sigma.dW_t^{RN}\right).\exp\left(-\int_0^t r(s).ds\right)\right)$$
$$MV = SE(0).\left(\int_0^{+\infty} (E_{FN}(r(t)) + c).B(0,t).dt\right) \qquad (25.7)$$

Finally with a flat yield curve:

$$MV = SE(0).\frac{r_0 + c}{r_0} \qquad (25.8)$$

The company Market Value is derived from its expected growth and its shareholder's equity. The literature provides many examples of MV computations and of P/E ratio computations since in practice the variables such as c, p or r are not constant at all across time.

Nevertheless, our example is interesting when working in a real probability:

$$MV = E_{Real}\left(\int_0^{+\infty} SE(0).\left(r(t).dt + p.dt + cdt + \sigma.dW_t^{Real}\right).\exp\left(-\int_0^t r(s).ds\right)\right)$$
$$MV = E_{Real}\left(\int_0^{+\infty} (INC(t) - SE(0).p).\exp\left(-\int_0^t r(s).ds\right).dt\right) \qquad (25.9)$$

Finally, Market Value may also be considered to be the sum of the discounted incomes less the cost of capital, i.e. the sum of the expected CVAs under historical probability:

$$MV = \int_0^{+\infty} E_{\text{Real}} \left(CVA.\exp\left(-\int_0^t r(s).ds \right) \right) dt \tag{25.10}$$

Indeed, the CVA represents the net income (before taxes) less normalized equity costs.

$$CVA(t) = INC(t) - SE(t).p \tag{25.11}$$

The cost of equity p is also the market risk premium, the covariance between the income and the optimal market portfolio yield:

$$p = \frac{Covariance(INC, R_M)}{\sigma(INC).\sigma(R_M)} \tag{25.12}$$

This framework helps us to link the equity cost at a group level with the company risk premium:

Equity cost (company) = Risk free interest rate + Company risk premium

The company management should thus take into account the CVA and the expected CVAs as a benchmark for budget management.

25.2.2 At a branch or at a risk management level

Company management have to input the CVA computation at the branch level or at the risk level.

Usually the capital is defined as a risk quantile that is somehow an income risk quantile. In the Gaussian framework, it allows us to link the shareholder's equity with the income volatility:

$$SE(t) = SE(0) = \alpha.\sigma(INC(t)) = \alpha.\sigma \tag{25.13}$$

If we suppose now that our company is made of two different branches, the total income is the sum of the branches incomes:

$$INC = INC_1 + INC_2 \tag{25.14}$$

The company overall capital need is computed as:

$$SE = \alpha.\sigma(INC) = \alpha.\sigma(INC_1 + INC_2) \tag{25.15}$$

On the other hand, the company equity cost is computable through the CAPM:

$$SEC = p.FP = \frac{Covariance(INC, R_M)}{\sigma(INC).\sigma(R_M)}.\alpha.\sigma(INC) \tag{25.16}$$

The Shareholder's Equity cost divided over the two branches becomes:

$$p.FP = \frac{Covariance(INC_1, R_M)}{\sigma(R_M)}.\alpha + \frac{Covariance(INC_2, R_M)}{\sigma(R_M)}.\alpha = p_1.FP_1 + p_2.FP_2 \quad (25.17)$$

The Company shareholder's equity cost is simply the sum of the branches equity costs. In terms of economic capital, this has two possible applications:

- Either the capital is computed on a stand-alone basis and the equity cost rate depends on the branch risk exposure:

$$p_1 = \frac{Covariance(INC_1, R_M)}{\sigma(R_M).\sigma(INc_1)}$$
$$FP_1 = \alpha.\sigma(INC_1) \quad (25.18)$$

- *Or the equity cost rate is fixed for the entire company (at the company equity cost rate p) but the capital is computed using this contribution formula:*

$$p_1 = p$$
$$FP_1 = \frac{Covariance(INC_1, R_M)}{\sigma(R_M).p}.\alpha = \frac{1}{p}.\frac{Covariance(INC_1, R_M)}{\sigma(R_M).\sigma(INC_1)}.FP_1^{stand-alone} \quad (25.19)$$

The second solution is quite often the solution decided by (economic) capital managers.

Note that, in this model, if the branch is more diversified than the company is, the final branch capital may exceed the stand-alone capital. To avoid such a situation, risk measures such as *expected shortfall* will be preferred to standard deviation or Value-at-Risk.

25.3 CAPITAL ALLOCATION/ATTRIBUTION AND CAPITAL CONSUMPTION

A/L managers will have to make a distinction between capital consumption and capital attribution or allocation.

Capital consumption is the real ex-post level of taken risk expressed in terms of capital: *capital consumption is an effective solvency measure*. The measure often used is the expected shortfall.

Capital allocation helps in the definition of the effective CVA of the branches. *Capital allocation is made during the budget session*: a level of capital is set branch by branch as a limit for capital consumption. The sum of the allocated capitals is comparable to the total effective capital amount.

Capital allocation should be based on the shareholder risk appetite. Executive managers are depositors of the shareholder directives:

- The level of capital has to guarantee a rating target.
- The capital allocation between risks has to replicate shareholders' choices in terms of risk repartition from business risk to the different financial risks.

There is no proof in the literature for the existence of a company utility function. Indeed, executive managers tend to optimize company profit but, in fact, they act as shareholders wills translators.

The shareholder optimizes his own portfolio between his different investments. In particular, if the company is not "optimized" (not perfectly diversified, too much concentrated in one sector, etc.), the shareholder portfolio will correct this mismatch: the company's objective is not to replicate the CAPM optimized portfolio but to obey to the shareholder risk appetite in certain risks such as banking sector business risk, insurance sector business risk, etc.

Therefore, capital allocation will be based on shareholder risk appetite.

25.4 COMPANY VALUATION AND COST OF CAPITAL WITH POSITIVE TAX RATE

This section summarizes some theoretical backgrounds about company valuation.

25.4.1 Definitions

We will consider a company with the definitions listed below:

- A: total assets;
- D: company debt;
- K: company capital;
- F(A): asset flows over one period;
- F(D): debt flows;
- F(K): capital flows for the shareholder (net income);
- $F(K_0)$: capital flows for the shareholder (net income) if debt was equal to 0;
- TR: tax rate;
- V(A): asset economic value;
- V(D): debt economic value;
- V(K): shareholder value;
- $V(K_0)$: shareholder value if debt was equal to 0;
- Y(A): asset yield;
- Y(D): debt yield;
- Y(K): Yield for the Shareholder;
- RFR = Risk Free Rate.

The variable L (called "economic lever") is characterized by this equation:

$$L = V(D)/(V(K) + V(D)) \tag{25.20}$$

We suppose that the debt is proposed at a risk free rate (e.g. all the risk is concentrated at the shareholder level and the shareholder guarantees implicitly the residual risks with its personal goods, as explained in the next chapter):

$$V(D) = D \tag{25.21}$$

We study the company in a stationary regime: the net income is distributed in dividends to the shareholder every year.

We call *FCF (Free cash flow)* the net treasury flows.

$$FCF = F(A).[1 - TR] \quad (25.22)$$

25.4.2 Company value in equations

The company net income is given by this equation:

$$F(K) = [F(A) - F(D)].(1 - TR) \quad (25.23)$$

This equation gives the following asset flows:

$$F(A) = F(D) + F(K)/(1 - TR) \quad (25.24)$$

The translation in terms of economic values is direct:

$$V(A) = V(D) + V(K)/(1 - TR) \quad (25.25)$$

And using the fact that V(D) = D, finally it leads to:

$$V(A) = D + V(K)/(1 - TR) \quad (25.26)$$

The price to pay to buy an asset depends on the asset acquisition mode.
For example for a company without any debt:

$$V(A) = V(K_0)/(1 - TR) \quad (25.27)$$

So that:

$$V(K_0) = [V(K) + D] - TR.D \quad (25.28)$$

Two conclusions arise from this example:

- *The value of a company without debt is equal to the value of the company with debt less the debt tax economy.* V(K)+D is the economic value of the company with debt.
- *Shareholders will try to saturate their regulatory constraints in terms of debt* (they will try to increase the amount of their debts to the higher level accepted by the regulators) *since debts increase company economic value.*

25.4.3 Cost of capital in equations

The *Weighted Average Cost of Capital (WACC)* is defined so that the company value is equal to the free cash flows discounted with this WACC. WACC includes risk premium.

$$FCF/WACC = V(K) + V(D) \quad (25.29)$$

Using the FCF definition, the WACC looks like:

$$\text{WACC} = \text{F(A)}.[1 - \text{TR}]/[\text{V(K)} + \text{V(D)}] \tag{25.30}$$

$$\text{WACC} = [\text{F(D)}.(1 - \text{TR}) + \text{F(K)}]/[\text{V(K)} + \text{V(D)}]$$

The flows may be expressed in terms of yields in this equation:

$$\text{WACC} = [\text{Y(D)}.\text{V(D)}.(1 - \text{TR}) + \text{Y(K)}.\text{V(K)}]/[\text{V(K)} + \text{V(D)}] \tag{25.31}$$

and then using the economic lever L:

$$\text{WACC} = [\text{Y(D)}.(1 - \text{TR}).\text{L} + \text{Y(K)}.(1 - \text{L})] \tag{25.32}$$

Since the debt yield is equal to the risk free rate, the WACC is classically:

$$\text{WACC} = \text{Y(K)}.(1 - \text{L}) + \text{RFR}.(1 - \text{TR}).\text{L} \tag{25.33}$$

In a perfect economy without taxes, the WACC does not depend on the debt to equity ratio (Modigliani-Miller theorem):

$$\text{WACC}_{(\text{TR}=0)} = \text{Y(K)}.(1 - \text{L}) + \text{RFR}.\text{L}$$

$$\text{WACC}_{(\text{TR}=0)} = [\text{Y(K)}.\text{V(K)} + \text{RFR}.\text{V(D)}]/(\text{V(K)} + \text{V(D)}) \tag{25.34}$$

$$\text{WACC}_{(\text{TR}=0)} = \text{F(A)}/\text{V(A)} = \text{Y(A)}$$

25.4.4 Application to company investments

Let us see how a holding company should reason before investing in a new subsidiary. Before acquisition, the holding company balance sheet looks like this:

<table><tr><td rowspan="2">A</td><td>D</td></tr><tr><td>K</td></tr></table>

We suppose that the price of the new subsidiary is equal to I and that the investment is financed through debt ΔD and capital increase ΔK:

$$\text{I} = \Delta\text{K} + \Delta\text{D} \tag{25.35}$$

After acquisition, the new balance sheet looks like this:

<table><tr><td rowspan="2">I</td><td>ΔD</td></tr><tr><td>ΔK</td></tr></table>

<table><tr><td rowspan="2">A</td><td>D</td></tr><tr><td>K</td></tr></table>

I is the new asset nominal value plus the goodwill.
The new debt is collected at risk free rate:

$$V(\Delta D) = \Delta D \tag{25.36}$$

The new company Weighted Average Cost of Capital (WACC +ΔWACC) follows:

$$(FCF + \Delta FCF)/(WACC + \Delta WACC) = V(K) + \Delta V(K) + V(D) + \Delta V(D) \tag{25.37}$$

Before acquisition, the WACC follows:

$$FCF/WACC = V(K) + V(D) \tag{25.38}$$

We will focus on a particular case where:

- the acquired new subsidiary asset risk is similar to the holding company;
- the new holding company structure is an homothetic transformation of the new subsidiary financial structure, i.e. $V(\Delta K)/V(\Delta D) = V(K)/V(D)$.

Under these conditions, the new holding company WACC is necessarily equal to the WACC before acquisition and:

$$\Delta WACC = 0 \tag{25.39}$$

This means:

$$\Delta FCF/WACC = \Delta V(K) + \Delta V(D) = I \tag{25.40}$$

For the holding company in these conditions, there is wealth creation if the price paid for the new acquisition is inferior to the Free Cash Flows discounted by the WACC.

$$\Delta FCF/WACC > I \tag{25.41}$$

To follow these investments, A/L managers will then promote another indicator, the *ROTE (Return on Equivalent Tangible Equity)*. This operational measure will take into account the goodwill in the capital.

25.4.5 Conclusions on the example

This example showed that:

- *the company's debt to capital ratio should be maximized so that it saturates the regulatory constraints*;
- *assets yield and equity yield are linked and not fixed independently*;
- *the price of an investment should not exceed the free cash flows discounted by the WACC.*

25.5 MERTON'S MODEL

In the previous section, we supposed that the interest rate paid on the debt is the risk free rate as if the shareholder guaranteed implicitly residual risk with his personal goods.

In practice, ***the shareholder owns a put on the company economic value;*** *the put strike is equal to the debt amount*. This put has been sold by the bondholders to the shareholders: in the eventuality of a company default, the bondholder cannot ask the shareholder to "put the money on the table": he is free to leave the company.

The bond spread over risk free rate is equal to the value of this put.

25.6 FINANCIAL ANALYSIS AND ALM IMPLICATIONS

Knowing all these links between ALM and financial analysis, **what is the optimization programme for the A/L manager?**

- Have enough capital to follow the rating target.
- Allocate risk according to the shareholder risk appetite.
- Take positions according to the ALCO market predictions (if the expected income exceeds the cost of capital).
- Decide capital increases or decreases, decide investments if the expected income exceeds the cost of capital.

However, financial analysis affects the A/L manager risk aversion. The IFRS financial statements propose a description of the company risk profile. Nevertheless, financial analysts follow the risk as the volatility of the income.

The A/L manager's error is often to think that company market value is equal to the current income multiplied by a constant. Therefore, A/L managers tend to promote strategies that smooth the net income year after year: "if the projected net income growth is smoothed on a two/three year budgetary horizon, the company won't experience problems . . .".

However, smoothing the income growth may differ from economic value sensitivity hedging. It is not because incomes grow at a constant speed that economic value is not decreasing and this increases the risk to default.

26

Towards Economic Capital Indicators

De leurs ennemis les sages apprennent bien des choses. (Aristophane)

The new regulations (Basel II and Solvency II) introduced a new kind of risk indicator: economic capital. To better understand this risk measure, we described the links between ALM and financial analysis. It is now time to explain in detail the main advantages of economic capital as risk measure.

26.1 ECONOMIC CAPITAL AND ITS IMPLICATIONS

26.1.1 Different systems of reference for economic capital

There is not only one definition for economic capital but many: each definition corresponds to a specific *system of reference*.

Economic capital is different from accounting equity, i.e. the equity according to the IFRS. There is not only one capital but three different capital definitions according to the system of reference: the accounting, the regulatory or the shareholder system.

26.1.1.1 Regulatory system of reference

The regulators defend the interest of the depositors and of the global financial system. To do so, they tend to limit the risk exposures by imposing a minimum regulatory capital.

The rating agencies defend the interest of the debt holders, i.e. solvency. They compute company default probability as a risk measure on the economic value.

From a regulatory perspective, the ratio Cooke introduced:

- *Available regulatory capital* as the sum of the Tier 1, Tier 2 and Tier 3 capital.

Regulatory capital is computed from IFRS consolidated equity capital. Some treatments are done on the latent gains (or losses) on cash flow hedge operations, AFS bonds, real estate investments or debt instruments; fair values. Many elements are deduced such as incorporeal assets and own shares.

- *Used regulatory capital* computed as 8 % of the risk weighted assets (RWA). Those risk weights developed in the Basel II Pillar 1 are based on an economic approach.

26.1.1.2 Shareholder system of reference

The shareholder transmits through the Board its interest in terms of value creation when maximizing the income with a risk exposure computed as the economic equity.

The pure economic approach will be based on a shareholder approach:

- *The available financial resources (AFR)*, i.e. the real available resources on a shareholder point of view. This includes the regulatory capital plus all the elements not recognized by regulators (latent economic capital gains, etc.).
- *The economic equity is the effective consumption of capital.* This represents the amount of risk taken by the company in the past. The computation is made using a quantitative risk measure.
- *The economic capital is the strategic required capital in an allocation approach.* The allocation is the basis for capital management. The perspective is business development and strategic planning.

Economic capital allocation brings for the shareholder an optimization of the value creation with a better risk comprehension: development decisions are healthier, risk is less concentrated.

26.1.2 Economic capital goals

26.1.2.1 Risk protection (capital adequacy) and rating target

Economic capital implementation minimizes risk exposure and secures the regulator, the rating agencies and the shareholders. This capital is an objective capital and a transversal measure of all the risk types for all the business lines.

The capital is computed for each business unit and for each risk type: the ALM financial risks (including credit risk, interest rate risk, etc.), market risk, operational risks, business risks, etc.

All the risk measurements are aggregated in a unique number for the whole company. This capital is used as *a shock absorber for risk taking positions*. The capital allows the banks to take risks (but is costlier than debts).

In banking activity, economic capital is recognized in the *ICAAP (Internal Capital Adequacy Assessment Process)*. The ICAAP is a process for assuring that the executive management identifies adequately measures, aggregates and monitors the risks.

The supervisory authority will review and evaluate this ICAAP and at the same time the internal governance processes.

The ICAAP as a part of the Basel II Pillar 2 will form an integral part of the management process and of the decision-making culture of the institution. It assures the regulators and the shareholders that the company holds an adequate internal capital in relation to the company's risk profile.

The ICAAP should be comprehensive, forward-looking and should produce a reasonable outcome.

Moreover from a rating perspective, when a company introduces an economic capital allocation, it is possible to *link the economic capital with a target default probability*.

When choosing a confidence interval for the economic capital computation equal to 99.95 %, this means, for instance, that the economic value variation within one year is with a

99.95 % confidence interval inferior to the economic capital. Then when the effective capital is greater than the economic capital, the one year default probability is under 0.05 %. This means that *with an economic capital computed as a VaR with a 99.95 % confidence interval, the company rating is close to a AA rating.*

26.1.2.2 Risk performance adjustment with the ROEC

The economic capital framework introduces the risk adjusted performance measurement with the *ROEC (return on economic capital)*. This ROEC is just the division of the return by the economic capital.

In addition to the ROEC, the Capital Manager will implement the *return on economic equity (ROEE)*, that is the ratio of the return on the effective consumed equity.

These indicators give enough information to measure the company profitability. The ROEC provides the basis for a consistent measure of risk-adjusted returns:

- The rating is not affected by the risk position since the economic capital is computed with a rating target.
- The regulatory constraints are respected.
- The computation is the same for every kind of risk.

26.1.2.3 Capital allocation and computation in practice

Capital allocation will contribute to transform the *value management* as the major tool for piloting the company.

Capital management team is headed by the *Capital Manager*.

Capital allocation is a part of the *budgetary process*. Within the Basel I framework, companies had already introduced in the budget sessions the notion of "normative equity" in order to allocate the capital and to compute a ROE (return on equity) for each business line.

During the budgetary session, every business line and every risk portfolio manager will be assigned a *target income* and a *target consumption of capital*:

- To the head of retail banking will be assigned an allocation of capital for the retail business risk.
- To the head of credit risk management will be assigned an allocation of capital for the credit risk.
- To the head of ALM will be assigned an allocation of capital for liquidity risk and for interest rate risks.

Economic equity (or the effective consumption of capital computed as a risk measure of the risk position) should not differ from the economic capital allocated.

As for the target income attribution, the managers will discuss (with the executive management and with the Capital Manager) their allocation of capital since this allocation introduces a limitation on their risk positions.

On the other hand, a high level of economic capital obliges them to take a high risk level; the risk level is indeed linked directly with the target income.

The budgetary discussion will address the expectation of the shareholders in terms of risk exposure and around the expected performance of the manager (or of the business line) compared to the performance of his competitors.

Indeed, the shareholder's judgment (and the judgment of the executive management) will be based on those two points:

For each risk, to be able to get a return higher than the competitors' one
To allocate more in the risks where the Managers' expected return is higher than the one expected by the shareholders

Example

We take the example of a bank with 100 MUSD of capital where the shareholder asks for two types of risk exposure:

- an investment in retail banking business risk of around 80 MUSD; and
- an investment in retail credit risk of around 20 MUSD.

If the credit risk manager is not confident with the market retail credit risk prices, he will ask for a lower allocation of capital: 10 MUSD for example. This credit risk manager will probably securitize a large part of its credit risk portfolio.

The Capital Manager may decide to report this allocation to the head of retail banking in order to take more risks on the business risk.

If the credit risk manager is right, the credit risk will increase and he will get a negative P&L. This could lead to the following P&L table:

	Shareholder's target allocation	Competitors' benchmark return	Benchmark P&L
Credit risk	20	−4 %	−0.8
Business risk	80	15 %	12
Total	100	11 %	11.2
	Effective allocation	**Effective return**	**Effective P&L**
Credit risk	10	−5 %	−0.5
Business risk	90	15 %	13.5
Total	100	13 %	13

Figure 26.1 Capital allocation

Here, the head of credit risk was not able to get a return higher than that of the competitors. However, on the other hand, the company will thank him for not having invested too much in credit risk positions.

26.1.2.4 Other objectives

Economic capital will not only be used in a regulatory or in a budgetary perspective. The management will also use it in:

- financial external communication about the company risk profile;
- risk pricing in FTPs (but taking into account portfolio effects);
- portfolio optimization computations: as we will see it in the next chapters, the A/L manager's objective will be to find the strategy that will maximize shareholder wealth mathematical expectation at date T (under a risk constraint such as the economic capital).

26.1.2.5 Economic capital weaknesses

It is not clear whether the management will really take decisions based only upon economic capital. Indeed, economic capital has some weaknesses:

- *Too new*: the introduction of economic capital revolutionizes management control. Introducing the concept too quickly could lead to dangerous mistakes.
- *Too technical*: the executive management is perhaps not able to understand this concept.
- Too difficult to be piloted by only one person.
- *Economic capital introduces volatility in the balance sheet*: it is not clear whether the economic capital will vary too much or not.
- *Too dangerous for the external communication*: Economic capital introduces risks the management is not used to talking about (such as business risk and model risk).
- The economic system of reference used in economic capital computation is not the IFRS accounting system of reference.

To answer properly all these questions, large companies will create a dedicated *capital management team* (headed by a Capital Manager).

26.1.3 Target ROEC

The economic capital approach introduces from a shareholder perspective the target investment demanded by the shareholder.

The executive management's objective will be to optimize the company's market value with the constraints given by the shareholder in terms of:

- minimal and maximal investments in the different risk sources (business, model, market or credit risks, etc.)
- target return on economic capital.

As we will see it in the final chapters, *the target return is given by the CAPM once the shareholder has given his target investments.*

This target ROEC will be one of the key elements for optimization under the economic capital constraint with the notions of:

- risk premiums;
- risk measures.

26.2 ECONOMIC CAPITAL COMPUTATION MAIN HYPOTHESES

26.2.1 General definition

Many definitions are possible when computing economic capital. Among them, it is possible to find:

- *The "sufficient surplus capital to meet negative cash flows at a given risk tolerance level".*
- *The amount of indispensable equity to absorb the maximal unexpected losses of economic value (within a confidence interval i.e. one maximal probability of occurrence).*
- *The maximal potential loss with a given confidence interval with a given horizon under a global rating target constraint.*

In this definition, *the expected losses are excluded from the economic capital amount.* Indeed, these losses have to be taken into account in the provisions demanded by the IFRS.

With a rating target constraint, the economic capital computation focuses on a bondholder approach not a shareholder approach. Indeed, the shareholder's point of view will be developed when the executive management optimizes the risk allocation.

In practice, the calculation is basically a computation of a loss distribution and a computation of a quantile of this distribution (the VaR or Value-at-Risk) with a given confidence interval and a given time horizon.

For example, the Capital Manager will compare the total maximum loss over all business units over all risk types over a one-year horizon.

The chart below shows an example of computation with a distribution function of the one-year economic value variation cumulative distribution. The expected gain is of 50 but with a probability of 5 %, the management may lose more than 110. The economic capital required for the protection of the debtholder with a confidence interval of 5 % will be of 110.

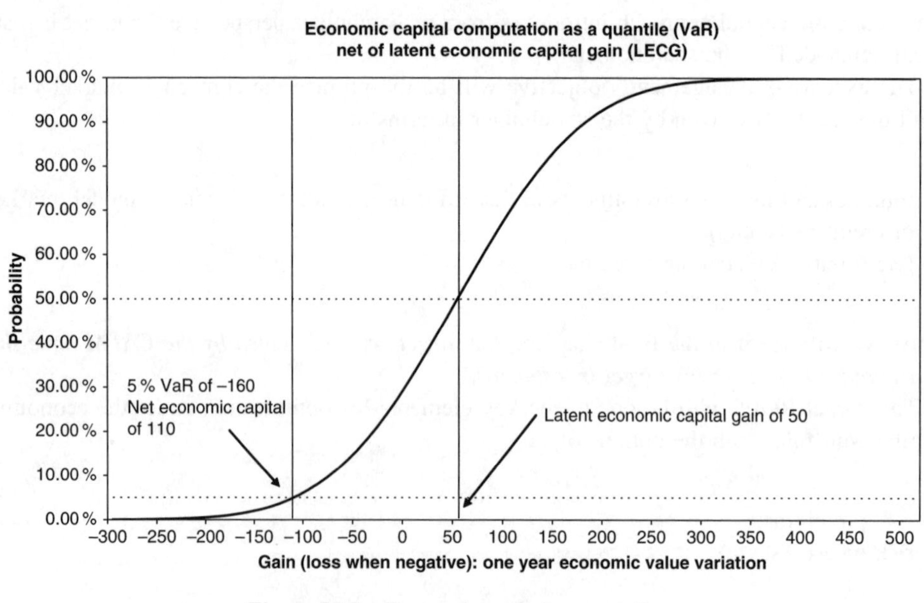

Figure 26.2 Economic capital computation

Using a non-cumulative distribution representation instead of a cumulative one, this leads to this classic representation:

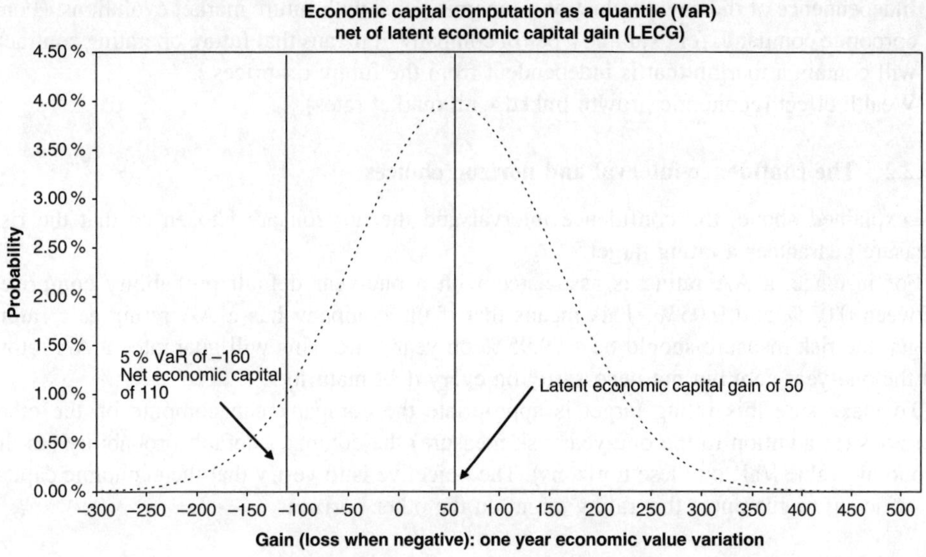

Figure 26.3 Economic capital computation no. 2

In this example, there are no expected losses in the balance sheet. In credit risk management, managers are more used to seeing the following kind of chart where the expected loss is provisioned.

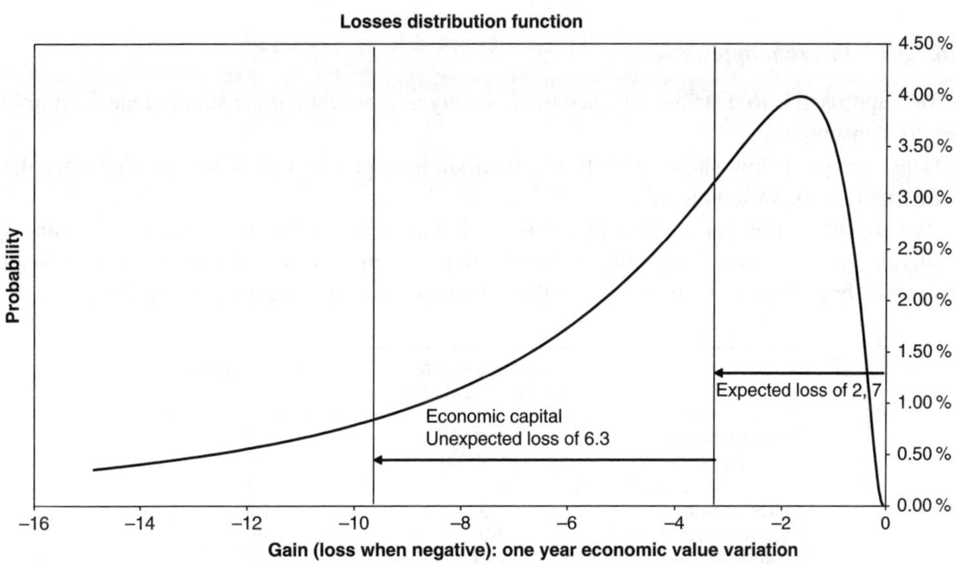

Figure 26.4 Loss distribution

The economic value will have to take into account all the classic points already developed in this book:

- Independence of the new production economic value with future market evolutions. (For a corporate company, for example a petrol company, it means that future operating contracts will contain a margin that is independent from the future oil prices.)
- Wealth effect (economic growth linked with market rates).

26.2.2 The confidence interval and horizon choices

As explained above, the confidence interval and the horizon are chosen so that the risk measure guarantees a rating target.

For instance, a AA rating is associated with a one-year default probability comprised between 0.03 % and 0.05 %. This means that if the company has a AA rating as a rating target, the risk measure should be a 99.95 % on year VaR. This will guarantee a AA rating on the one-year debt but not necessarily on every debt maturity.

To make sure this rating target is appropriate the company can compute on the other horizons (in addition to the one-year risk measure) the company default probability (as the economic value VaR on these horizons). The objective is to verify that the economic capital is sufficient to guarantee this rating target on the other horizons.

26.2.3 The economic equity "distribution"

The real consumption of economic equity is sometimes easy to compute at a company level but harder to redistribute to the different business lines: the risk amount order of height should be accepted by these different business lines.

Problems arise sometimes when the retained economic capital measure is the Value-at-Risk and is non-additive.

26.2.3.1 Pro rata approach

A first approach is to distribute the economic equity as a pro rata of the stand-alone economic equity consumption.

The example below shows how this redistribution is problematic when looking after the redistribution on various levels.

We consider a company including retail, SME and corporate business. The retail business is divided into a "north" and into a "south branch" with a strong diversification between these two branches. This could lead to the following economic equity computation:

	Economic equity stand-alone calculus	Pro rata redistribution
Retail business	100	127
North branch	120	64
South branch	120	64
SMEs business	50	26
Corporate business	50	26
Total company	180	180

Figure 26.5 Stand-alone redistribution

In this example, if the pro rata distribution is made at the more elementary level, then on the aggregated levels the economic equity consumption on a stand-alone basis is lower than after risk pro rata redistribution.

Risk redistribution using the expected shortfall approach will correct this problem.

26.2.3.2 Expected shortfall/spectral risk measure approach

The Value-at-Risk measure integrates many weaknesses: leverage effect, instability of allocation. To correct these problems, the manager might prefer to use a spectral risk measure such as the expected shortfall.

The expected shortfall will indicate which part of the loss is due to which specific business line. For example, the economic equity of a specific business line will be computed as the contribution of this business line to the one year 99.2 % expected shortfall of the company.

Explaining to financial analysts how the risk measure works is a bit harder. Indeed, it is easier to explain the choice of a confidence interval for the VaR than for the expected shortfall. Consequently, the expected shortfall risk measure is for the moment used more often for internal risk redistribution than for the risk computation itself. The idea is to:

- use a VaR 99.5 % for the risk measurement; and
- use an expected shortfall 99.2 % for the risk redistribution (where the 99.2 % level has been chosen so that at the company level, the two risk measures are equivalent).

Of course, every kind of spectral risk measure could be chosen instead of the expected shortfall: Wang transform, pH transform, etc.

26.3 ALM STRESS TESTING

26.3.1 Regulatory framework

In the banking sector, regulatory stress tests were introduced by the January 1996 Basel committee regulation rules. The Basel II framework asks for a more frequent use of stress testing (but does not answer the question of the frequency of the stress test practice).

Stress testing will then complete the computation of economic capital and of sensitivities since the approach is orthogonal (i.e. complementary) to these classic indicators. Nevertheless, stress test methodology will depend highly on the accounting scheme: stress testing will not take the same form for marked-to-market activities as for accrued accounting activities such as those managed by A/L managers.

There are indeed various notions of stress testing and some A/L managers use the term stress test for these different computation types:

- The use of a 200 bps shock sensitivity is considered to be a stress test by Basel II Pillar 2.
- The reproduction of historical scenarios is called historical stress testing. (For instance, using the 1929 crisis scenario as a stress scenario on equity portfolios.)

We will distinguish the *robustness stress test* from the *financial solidity stress test.*

The *robustness stress test* is a local or global level test made either on a specific risk either on a specific product type. The Basel II regulation asks for many tests of this type on the LGDs, on the correlations but many other tests could be performed: stresses on risk concentrations, on warranties, on household local debt ratios, etc.

These tests are performed in Pillar 2 and are complementary to the Pillar 1 VaR computations. In practice, these tests are used for provision computation, for model risk computation and more generally for risk management control.

The *financial solidity stress* test is a more global stress test (demanded by Pillar 2) in order to verify that the company has enough capital and enough other resources to perform its objectives. This stress test integrates all the business expectations in terms of new production from a budgetary perspective.

The idea is to compute the short and long-term sensitivity of the company ratios and to compare these analyses with the business plans. For instance, the company will stress the macroeconomic variables, the margins or the new productions and compare the impact on strategic positioning, on company cost structure and on capital structure.

Of course, *alternative plans, rescue plans or capital contingency plans* are associated with the stress tests in order to propose solutions for the risk revealed by the analysis.

Nevertheless, stress testing is often criticized since this indicator is subjective by nature. Regularly, the stress scenarios are not considered by management as possible scenarios, the management prefer to rule the company with budgetary (highly probable) scenarios rather than with stress scenarios.

26.3.2 Advanced methodology for A/L managers: risk screening

To explain how stress testing can be applied to ALM, let us start with a global approach.

Managers use financial mathematics in practice for economic value computation (the pricing) and for risk or economic capital computation:

- Pricing is in fact a computation of a mathematical expectation, a computation of a set of future cash flows under a pricing probability called risk neutral probability.
- Economic capital is a quantile of a distribution function under a real probability.

Stress testing could be defined as a mathematical expectation of future cash flows under a stressed distribution with only one scenario (a Dirac distribution).

Consequently, the stress test computed as the search for the worst-case scenario is a specific coherent risk measure. The stress test verifies the criteria to become an efficient risk measure.

Note also that stress is definitely not a market extreme evolution scenario:

- The stability may stress.
- The absence of volatility may stress.
- The risk factor is not always one simple variable but a combination of many variables (sometimes under specific dynamics).

Classic stress testing will take various possible forms:

- Computation of sensitivities: when determining the impact of some predefined risk factors on the position (in robustness test).
- Qualitative expertise: when constructing scenarios based on economic previsions. The scenarios are often intuitive or comprehensible and the risk aggregation is easy to perform.
- Historical analysis: the actual positions are stressed using past stress observations (1929 crisis, 1987 crisis, etc.). This analysis is easier to perform too but integrates hypotheses that are too strong.
- Risk screening: the objective is to characterize risk zones by the estimation of the modelled probabilities of risky events. This type of stress test integrates generic techniques for more complex products without any supplementary modelling.

Nowadays, *A/L managers recommend the use of risk screening techniques* for stress testing. This methodology integrates *three classic stages*:

- *Risk economic analysis*: the manager has to choose which risk factors to simulate.
- *Modelling* of all the stress-testing elements: risk factors, models for the balance sheet products, models for customer behaviour and manager's strategies. Stress testing should integrate *extreme values theory (EVT)*. This theory determines the laws that rule the occurrence of the extreme events: for instance, in extreme events, all the market indexes tend to be highly correlated.
- *Analysis*, synthesis and reactions.

This last analysis is itself broken down into four stages:

- *Simulation of the incomes* by the simulation of the risk factors and of the balance sheet (including the company strategy simulation): during this stage, the A/L manager will, for example, simulate thousands of possible future scenarios.
- *Filtration of the risky scenarios* using appropriate risk criterions: the risky scenarios are extracted from the set of simulated scenarios; the risk criterion is defined by the executive management with the help of the risk management teams.
- *Identification of the risky scenarios* with classification methods.
- *Rescue plans definition*/hedging policy elaboration.

In practice, the extreme scenarios are rarely as problematical as is demonstrated in the stress testing: quite often, the A/L manager changes his strategy when the situation becomes difficult to manage. It is important then to integrate the dynamics of management behaviour. In strategy modelling, it is then important to integrate the eventual expert predictions.

The objective is to complete risk indicators with scenarios that are easy to understand and have quantified impacts. The methodology transforms risk indicators into a set of scenarios that have to be watched carefully and sometimes hedged. The hedging could also be defined by the classification of the risk scenarios. Moreover, stress testing allows for the validation of the existing models with robustness testing.

Stress testing completes the indicators and takes into consideration a better risk/profit management.

Stress testing facilitates business apprehension by the risk manager since it obliges him to model the business itself.

26.3.3 Example of Banking Book stress testing

Risk screening methodology can be applied straightforwardly to Banking Books with:

- The mass simulation of interest rate evolution scenarios and consequently of the Banking Book incomes.

The interest rates are simulated with a stochastic model (such as a Hull & White model) on a 20 year horizon in this example. Thus, the incomes can be simulated on the same horizon with the simulation of the interest cash flows on the banking book (demand deposits, mortgages, etc.) and of the A/L manager strategy to hedge those cash flows (simulation of the future open interest rate gap, the future bond investments, the optional strategy, etc.).

In the simulation, the A/L manager should decide what his strategy in front of new production (automatic hedging or no hedging at all) would be.

To be able to make as many simulations as possible with an acceptable computation time, the modelling of the products or of the strategy cannot be too complex.

- The filtration of scenarios with a risk criterion such as the net income level (extraction of all the scenarios where the net income is under a certain level) or as the net income variation (extraction of all the scenarios where the net income decrease in one year by more than 10 % for instance).
- The classification of the filtrated scenarios using short-term and long-term interest rate levels for each scenario as parameters for the definition of each scenario.
- The analysis of the obtained risk classes.

In our example, the interest rate level appears to be the long-term stress factor. The first class of risk consists of scenarios where interest rates decrease in 5 years when the second class consists of scenarios where interest rates decrease in 10 years.

This result is usually common in Banking Book stress testing especially when the compensation effects between fees and net interest margins are not taken into consideration.

The steepness of the yield curve is often a second risk factor with negative effects on prepayment options; the Banking Book stress scenarios are then scenarios where interest rates decrease promptly with a yield curve flattening. The classification methods will have to take into account short-term and long-term interest rate levels as parameters for the classification.

26.3.4 Example of liquidity stress testing

The same methodology can be used for liquidity stress testing:

- simulating the market conditions evolutions (interest rates, currency exchange rate, etc.);
- simulating possible regulation evolution;
- simulating customer behaviour evolution (new contract production, off-balance sheet agreements, correlations between existing products, etc.);

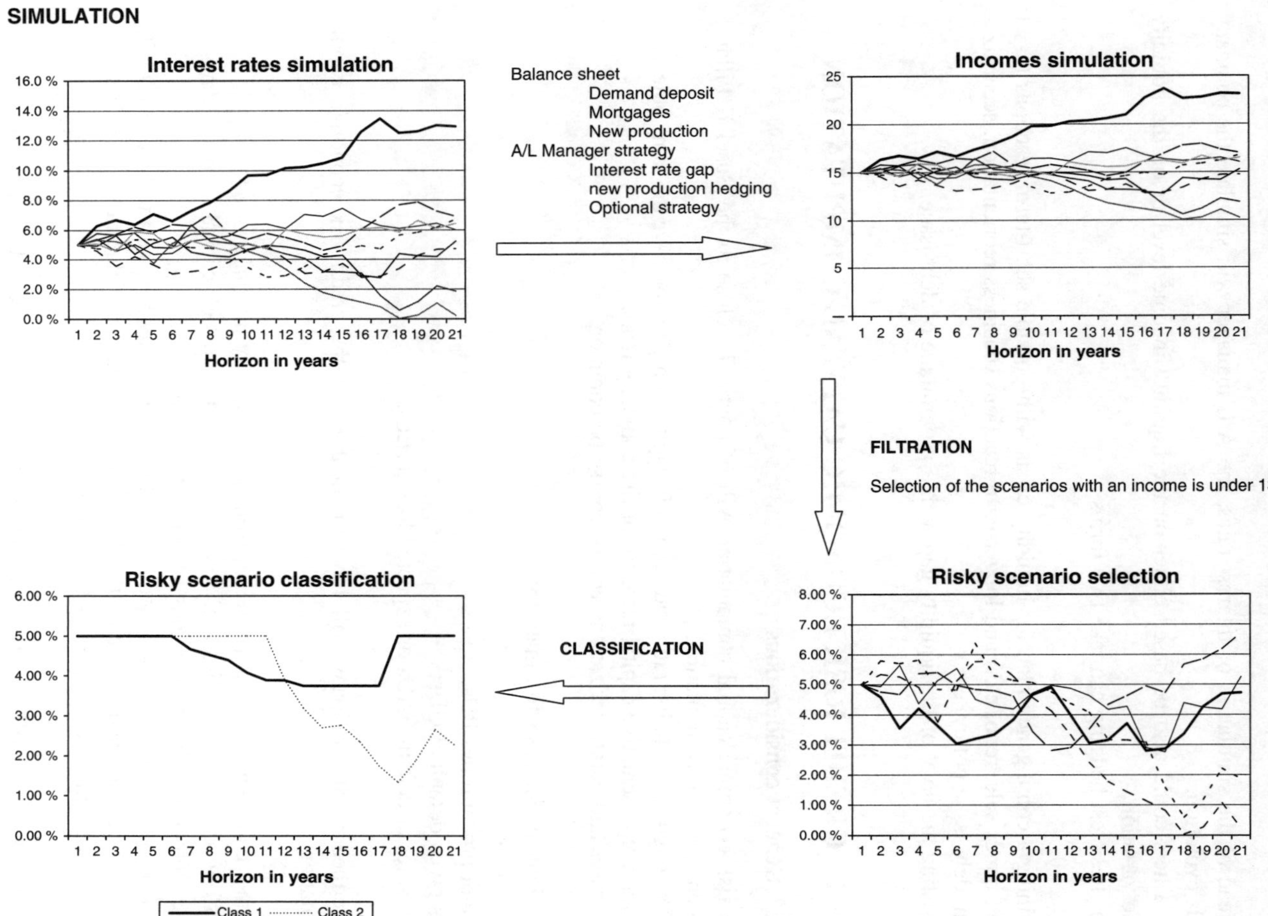

Figure 26.6 Stress testing

- simulating liquidity evolution of the marketplace;
- simulating A/L manager strategy to hedge liquidity risk and to refinance new productions;
- simulating the capital management strategy (since economic capital and liquidity spreads are directly linked).

Instead of the simulation of interest rates, the A/L manager will simulate the company spreads evolution.

The filters could also be based either on the liquidity income level or on the liquidity income variation.

The stress test hedging can take two forms:

- defining a contingency plan for liquidity crisis with possible short-term reactions (asset sale, bonds sale, repo, etc.) and longer-term reactions (business reorientation, securitization, debt issue policy, etc.);
- adjusting the level of the liquidity gap with a programme of debt issue.

26.4 CREDIT RISK ECONOMIC CAPITAL COMPUTATION

26.4.1 General considerations

Credit risk economic capital computation will of course be close to the Basel II Pillar 1 advanced approach computation.

McDonough computation ratio and economic capital computation have the same objective: to obtain a representative capital measure of the company risks.

Databases and parameterizations will of course be common:

- notations, country, sector, maturity;
- migrations;
- default probabilities PDs;
- loss given defaults LGDs;
- exposures at default EADs or expected losses (EL).

Nevertheless, the company will have to integrate in the credit risk economic capital computation:

- another confidence interval (different from the regulatory interval);
- portfolio effects (diversification, concentration): McDonough capital computation supposes sometimes that correlations are equal to 100 %;
- the computation of the risk based on the fair value instead of on the lone EAD. The economic capital has to be computed based on the economic value rather than based on the next year income (such as in Basel II framework).

The A/L manager will start with the computation of the average loss. This average loss is the statistical loss computed with the PDs, the EADs and the LGDs taking into account migration effects. This average loss (or expected loss) is partially hedged with the credit risk margin but it may lead to economic provision or provision for impairment.

The economic capital will represent the unexpected losses above the expected losses taking into account the portfolio effects (diversification, concentration, etc.) within a certain confidence interval.

26.4.2 Retail credit risk economic capital specificities

Retail credit risk economic capital will use the same databases as the regulatory capital computation. The pooling in "cohorts" is made by identical risk components:

- identical marginal default term structure expressed as a specific identical correlation;
- identical LGD (usually expressed as a percentage of the outstanding nominal);
- identical "average" nominal exposure;
- identical maturity, interest rate level and schedule.

If we denote by ψ the systemic risk factor and by X the specific risk factor, the retail portfolio (or cohort) i will default if:

$$\sqrt{\rho_{\text{intra}}}\Psi + \sqrt{1-\rho_{\text{intra}}}X_i < \Phi^{-1}(PD_i) \tag{26.1}$$

Usually, we call ρ_{intra} the intra cohort correlation. The McDonough framework simply adds all the economic capital amounts and does not recognize the portfolio effects. However, in practice, the specific risk factors are correlated among them with a correlation under 100 %. The specific risk factor X can easily be projected on a set of independent risk factors:

$$X_i = a_i + \sum_j \rho_i.\varepsilon_j \tag{26.2}$$

The retail credit risk economic capital computation will take into consideration the inter-cohort correlations and this leads to a lower level of economic capital than the regulatory one. It means as well that there are opportunities for regulatory arbitrage in Basel II.

Moreover, the economic capital could be computed using a temporal correlation between risk factors. For instance, the systemic risk factor could be correlated across time:

$$\begin{aligned}\psi(t) &= \sqrt{\tilde{\rho}}.\psi(t-1) + \sqrt{1-\tilde{\rho}}.Z(t-1)\\ \varepsilon_j(t) &= \sqrt{\tilde{\rho}_j}.\varepsilon_j(t-1) + \sqrt{1-\tilde{\rho}_j}.Z_j(t-1)\end{aligned} \tag{26.3}$$

Such a structure for the correlation allows for the simulation of the defaults and then to value the economic capital.

26.5 ECONOMIC CAPITAL IN ALM

Economic capital computation in ALM is still in discussion in major international banks. Nevertheless, this chapter tries to summarize the main assumptions used by banks in their computations.

26.5.1 General hypotheses

ALM economic capital has to be computed in the company economic capital framework.

This framework often uses the Basel II Pillar 1 "credit risk" approach: economic capital is computed as a VaR, a quantile (at a 99.95 % level for example) of the economic value variation over a time period (1 year for example).

This economic value variation is comparable with the variation of the target asset value of the bank.

This quantile choice is coherent with the company rating target (for example, a AA rating is associated with a 0.05 %/0.03 % default probability over a one-year horizon).

This means the economic capital is the fifth worst loss on a 10,000 year time period! Economic capital goal is to cover the extreme risk with an adequate capital amount; it guarantees a low level of funding costs since the rating target is often very high.

When applying economic capital on ALM, *the computation has to be based on economic value even if the IFRS accounting scheme basis is an accrued accounting basis.*

In fact, this is due to the fact that when looking after company refinancing, the debtholders look after the company economic value and not after the company net income.

A capital computation based only on the next year income (on an accrued basis) could not be judicious: it would not take into account the risks already taken on the future incomes. This capital presents "arbitrage opportunities" for A/L managers (this capital is easily set to zero with a mix of spot and forward options).

The methodology has to produce a stable result coherent with the A/L management practices.

After the optimization of the economic revenue under an economic capital constraint, the A/L manager's optimal position cannot be largely different from the usual positions kept in large banks.

Nevertheless, the economical capital computation leads to a better risk understanding and is profitable for front office A/L managers.

Economic capital order of height should not frighten A/L managers but should only become a new complementary indicator for extreme risks management.

In practice, it helps to understand some "conventions" such as demand deposit FTP conventions and to transpose them into a modelled framework.

In addition, the methodology has to be able to aggregate ALM risks with other risk types such as insurance risk, market risks, credit risk, etc. The *grid methodology* developed at the end of this chapter is a good way to implement economic capital with the ability to aggregate all the risk types.

26.5.2 Banking Book economic value computation

Since economic capital methodology is designed with an "economic value" approach, it means that the entire balance sheet should be accounted at fair value.

Fair value computation, in particular, implies:

- risk neutral probability discounting (i.e. without any risk premiums);
- demand deposit fair value computation;
- capital banking book fair value computation;

- fees and running costs fair value computation;
- Taking into consideration the difference between the book value and the fair value amount in a *latent capital gain (or loss)*.

The A/L manager should be able for each balance sheet line to compute fair values:

- either by the discounting of all the expected cash flows; or
- by the discounting of all the expected incomes.

The two methods lead to the same result since the economic value computation is made under a risk neutral probability.

For a bank, the fair value computation has to take into account various products, which are a bit hard to value:

- Demand deposits and other savings accounts;
  - with volume effects;
  - with wealth effects;
  - with an inflation linked or an interest rate linked remuneration.
- Credits such as mortgages including prepayment options;
- Inflation linked products;
- Future net interest margins;
- Future fees;
- Capital banking book elements;
- Future running costs;
- ALM hedging positions;
- Swaps and options (caps, floors, swaptions, CMS caps, etc.).

For an insurance company, the problem is the same with problems for:

- non unit base life insurance contracts;
- provisions.

To explain how these valuations should be accomplished, the examples below summarize the main possible problems.

26.5.2.1 Simulation horizon

In an economic value computation, the first question is the horizon simulation.

A/L managers were used to simulating their balance sheet on a budget horizon between 1 to 5 years with the revenue sensitivities indicator.

However, since the economic capital is focused on a bondholder point of view, *the simulation horizon has to be set at an infinite horizon.*

Nevertheless, some A/L managers may use a technical shortcut with the computation of the economic value on a 20 year horizon, for example, and then adding a "residual economic value". Economic value controllers have to look carefully after this residual economic value computation and after its sensitivity to market conditions.

26.5.2.2 New productions, income hedging strategies and economic capital

A strong debate centres on the way new productions have to be integrated in the economic value computation.

Many managers consider that new productions smooth the net income and thus have a positive influence on the risk exposure since they provide a kind of insurance across generations.

Nevertheless, when looking carefully after new production models, used in revenue sensitivity computations, those models often do not take into account the market equilibrium.

When you use the hypothesis of "independence of the new production economic value to market conditions", it is equivalent to taking into account new productions in the economic capital computation. Note that the new production economic value takes into account future expenses according to this production (this is a net economic value including running costs).

Therefore, the easiest thing to do is to **avoid new productions in the economic value computation and *a fortiori* in the economic capital computation**.

For a corporate company, for example a petrol company, it means that future operating contracts will contain a margin that is independent from future oil prices.

In practice, all future clients, all future contracts and all "associated" costs are excluded from the economic value computation.

26.5.2.3 Wealth effect

Excluding new production does not involve the exclusion of the *wealth effect*. The wealth effect affects existing client behaviour and some other parameters:

- Demand deposit amount by existing client may grow.
- Fees on existing clients or existing contracts may grow (if this could be statistically proven).

The "wealth effect" has to be taken into account in the economic value computation.

26.5.2.4 Demand deposit economic value

Demand deposit economic value computation is one of the best examples to give for this kind of product valuation.

Trying to define demand deposit valuation means:

- trying to define demand deposit utility for the bank;
- trying to compute the price under a market probability, i.e. a risk neutral probability.

If we call K(t) the total amount of demand deposits arising from the existing clients at date 0 (the economic value computation date), the evolution of this amount could be modelled with a classical Wiener diffusion process associated with a trend μ_K under an historical probability:

$$\frac{dK(t)}{K(t)} = \mu_K dt + \sigma_K dW_K(t) \tag{26.4}$$

Under the risk neutral probability that allows us to compute the demand deposit economic value ("risk minimizing martingale probability" through Girsanov theorem), the amount K follows another diffusion process (i.e. the trend is modified):

$$\frac{dK(t)}{K(t)} = \mu.dt + \sigma_K.dW_Q^1(t) \tag{26.5}$$

The coefficient μ represents the demand deposit closing rate (closing probability) plus the risk premium for demand deposits.

From this formula, it is easy to prove that using a one factor interest rate model with a yield curve flat at the level of r(t), the demand deposit economic value is directly given by the following equation (since it excludes future clients):

$$V(0) = K(0).\frac{\mu}{r_0 + \mu} \tag{26.6}$$

When the level of interest rates r_0 is close to 0 %, the economic value is close to the actual demand deposit amount K(0). The demand deposits associated with the existing clients will not produce so much income.

When the level of interest rates r_0 is infinite, the economic value is close to zero. The money put by clients on their demand deposits has no value for them.

When the coefficient μ is nearby zero, the economic value is nearby zero. Clients' duration is very long, so the money they put on their demand deposit has no value for them.

When the coefficient μ is infinite, the economic value is close to the initial demand deposit amount K(0). Clients will withdraw quickly their money from the bank: this money has no value for the bank.

This valuation formula is important since:

- It will be used in the gross/net economic value computation: *a very important latent capital gain has to be taken in the net economic value computation.*
- *The formula sensitivity will be used in the economic capital computation.*

Of course, the formula needs to be developed taking into account:

- a non flat yield curve;
- the volume effect and the wealth effect;
- the other sensitive flows associated with the deposit account;
- the uncertainty about the evolution of the amount incertitude (i.e. a part of business risk in the valuation).

The FTP schedule quite often sums up all these effects; it traduces the demand deposit interest rate schedule. For this reason, *some banks use the FTP schedule for the demand deposit valuation since it translates the demand deposit sensitivity to interest rates.* Moreover, this schedule is an effective transaction price between the bank's business lines and the A/L managers. *Consequently, the choice of the FTP schedule as the demand deposit schedule has to be validated by a strong modelling review.*

26.5.2.5 Fees and running costs

Fees and running costs have to be included in the economic value computation but only based on the existing clients or on the existing contracts (i.e. excluding "new production of fees and of running costs").

The reason for this inclusion is simple:

- Their value may have a strong sensitivity to market conditions (salaries costs could follow the level of inflation or of interest rates, for example). A hedging strategy is often associated with this risk.
- There may be a diversification between the level of the fees and of the running costs and the level of the net interest margin.

26.5.2.6 How to introduce strategies in the economic capital computation?

When arguing in a "accrued based" environment, the A/L manager thinks that his strategies show an ability to smooth the income and thus to reduce the risk. From this point of view, the A/L manager's strategies should be taken into account in the economic capital computation.

When talking about strategy, one could include:

- FTP refinancing future strategies;
- interest rate gap future position openings or future position shortenings;
- options strategies not already traded in the market
  - for example, the plan to buy caps when interest rates will go down or to sell floors when interest rates will go up.
- possible reductions of provisions in insurance companies when market conditions deteriorate.

From the A/L manager's point of view, decision-making does not rely on pure economic arguments but follows many necessities since hedging decisions may:

- impact the future incomes level;
- impact the future incomes volatility;
- be impacted by market conditions (interest rates, inflation, etc.);
- be impacted by the commercial activity (anticipated production volume, etc.) i.e. the "non hedgeable risk".

Unfortunately, many quantitative approaches did not respond to those imperatives.

At this time, very few research articles have highlighted management practices and economic value arguments. Nevertheless, this book tries to fill this gap and the following chapters explain how to reconcile management and economic capital.

This is a very bad argument! Of course, A/L managers are able to smooth the net interest margin, but economic capital focuses on the extreme risk from a bondholder's point of view not from a shareholder's point of view!

Only existing positions in the A/L manager's hedging strategy have to be incorporated in the economic capital computation. The market value of a "strategy" under a risk neutral probability is equal to zero and does not depend on the market conditions level.

It is the same for the FTP rules: **economic value does not depend on the chosen FTP replacement strategy.**

Of course, the exclusion of this strategy is consistent with the exclusion of the new production in the computation. It is the same with including new production and strategies with an infinite horizon or excluding them all (with the classical new production economic value "independence hypothesis").

This way, economic capital links directly the calculation date hedging position and the calculation date balance sheet risk exposure.

26.5.2.7 Capital Book economic value

The Capital Book economic value computation reveals the same problems as the equity FTP norm description.

Equity economic value has to take into account all the market exposed components of the activity. Of course, this may be considered to be a very hard task, so *quite often the FTP schedule is still used to compute the economic value of the equity* (and its sensitivity to market conditions and especially to the interest rate level).

26.5.3 Economic Provisions (EP), Gross Economic Capital (GEC) and Net Economic Capital (NEC)

Economic capital computation in ALM reveals an important distinction between:

- *gross economic capital (GEC)* that represents the company risk exposure;
- *net economic capital* (NEC), i.e. the subtraction of the difference between book value and full fair value from this gross economic capital.

Securities such as equities are a good example in order to explain the difference between those two capitals. After the presentation of this example, we extend it to the definition of the banking net and gross economic capital (with the demand deposits example).

26.5.3.1 Concepts

Basel II Pillar 1 introduced the "expected loss" concept. This expected loss in the credit risk capital computation was the mathematical expectation of losses (since credit risk focuses mainly on losses and forgets the expected gains integrated in the margins).

The expected loss will not be hedged through capital requirements: expected incomes and/or provisions will cover these expected losses. In the economic system of reference, it leads to the introduction of an *"economic provision"*.

After the definition of the economic provision, the gross and the net economic capital computations may take place.

The gross economic capital is computed in a complete economic framework using full fair values and forgetting the accounting system in place. In fact, this capital reveals the real risk exposure.

A/L managers have to *use this gross economic capital to take optimization decisions*, at a stand-alone level.

Nevertheless, the economic capital measurement cannot be achieved without a reference to the accounting system. The full fair value framework has to be compared to the existing accounting framework in terms of:

- provisions;
- latent capital gains (on AFS bonds, etc.);
- *latent economic capital gains*: the difference between the book value (in the existing accounting system of reference) and the full fair value (in the gross economic capital computation framework).

These latent economic capital gains generate a risk in the gross economic capital framework.

Nevertheless, these latent economic capital gains hedge somehow a part of the gross economic capital.

The net economic capital (NEC) is strictly the gross economic capital (GEC) adjusted with accounting elements including:

- the Latent Economic capital gains (LECG);
- the Provisions (P);
- the Economic Provisions (EP).

$$NEC = GEC - LECG + (EP - P) \tag{26.7}$$

As for the real existence of these LECG, some A/L managers may answer that *securitization programmes are able to materialize in a medium term horizon every kind of economic value in a spot cash payment.* (At the end of the 80s, even singers securitized their royalties on their albums.)

A complementary question sometimes arises: does this LECG really protect the bondholder? Does not a part of this LECG belong to the shareholder?

Of course, in many cases a part of these LECG is "recoverable" by shareholders. In many cases, the net economic value will use only a part of the LECG (using experts' opinions):

$$NEC = GEC - \alpha.LECG + (EP - E) \tag{26.8}$$

The α coefficient is set between 0 and 1 by expert's opinions or through a model depending on the analysed balance sheet product.

26.5.3.2 Application to stock investment portfolios

Stock investment portfolios are the best example to show how the LECG computation works.

For example, we will consider a stock bought for an amount of 100 USD with a market value of 150 USD at the economic capital computation date.

This stock is accounted as Available for Sale (AFS): an amount of 50 USD is accounted in the company equity.

Assets		Liabilities	
Stocks Fair Value	150	Company debt	75
		Shareholder's equity	25
		Stocks potential capital gain	50
Total Assets	**150**	**Total Liabilities**	**150**

Figure 26.7 Balance sheet

If the stock's volatility is of 20 %, the economic capital (computed on a one-year horizon with a 99.95 % confidence interval) gives a gross economic capital of:

$$GEC = 150.[1 - \text{LOGINV}(0.05\,\%;\ 0;\ 20\,\%)]$$

$$GEC = 72\ \text{USD}.$$

Of course, in an unfavourable context, the company may lose those 72 USD. Nevertheless, the stock fair value contains potential capital gains that protect the bondholders strongly.

If such a stressed scenario occurs, the company could sell entirely its stocks, generating an amount of cash of 78 USD (computed as 150–72). The company could reimburse the totality of its debt and even repay 3 USD to its shareholders.

The latent economic capital gain is of 50 USD:

$$LECG = 50\ \text{USD}$$

$$NEC = 72 - 50 = 22\ \text{USD}$$

In our example, the net economic capital is of 22 that is less than the shareholder's equity.

In some banks, the LECG cannot be taken at 100 % since the regulator considers that only an α coefficient of say 50 % can be eligible for the NEC computation.

In our example, it would change the NEC computation as follows:

$$LECG = 50\,\%.50 = 25\,USD$$

$$NEC = 72 - 25 = 47\ \text{USD}$$

In such a case, the NEC is under the shareholder's equity: the risk management may react by either asking for a risk exposure decrease, or asking for a capital increase.

26.5.3.3 Application to the demand deposits example

In a Banking Book balance sheet, many elements are not accounted at their full fair value and especially the demand deposits.

When looking after the overall demand deposit amount, the probability of a major withdrawal on the next day and even on the future dates is very low. A statistical estimation will model easily the withdrawal probability. Demands deposits are stable and durable.

Since the bank will serve no interest on these deposits, an investment consistent with the modelling will create profits for the bank without creating any risk. Thus in an economic perspective, those deposits have an economic value really different from their book value.

Indeed, the IFRS book value does not recognize this difference since it is always possible in a prudential perspective to see all the deposits disappear in just one day.

The full fair value computation described in the chapters above explains the existence of a latent economic capital gains (LECG):

$$\begin{aligned} V(0) &= K(0).\frac{\mu}{r_0+\mu} \\ LECG &= K(0) - V(0) = K(0).\frac{r_0}{r_0+\mu} \end{aligned} \tag{26.9}$$

When the interest rate yield curve is around 0 %, the LECG is equal to zero. However, with for example $\mu = 3\,\%$ and $r_0 = 3\,\%$, the LECG represents 50 % of the demand deposit amount!

As an example, we present the two fictive balance sheets below:

IFRS Commercial Banking Book			
Assets	100	Liabilities	40
		DD	27
		Cash	33
Off Balance Sheet: 0			

Economic Commercial Banking Book			
Assets	110	Liabilities	45
		DD	13
		Cash	33
		$LECG_{DD}$	14
		$LECG_{Other}$	5
Off Balance Sheet: 0			

Figure 26.8 IFRS and economic Banking Books

Here, in this example, the demand deposits (DD) contain a strong LECG representing almost 45 % of their IFRS Book Value.

The main risk for the bank goes around the diminution of this LECG. The chart below represents the evolution of this LECG in different interest rate scenarios.

When interest rates are close to 0, the LECG is low; on the other hand with a high level of interest rates, this LECG converges to the demand deposit initial amount (here 27).

The exact computation of this LECG is difficult to achieve and the quantification demarche has to be prudent.

Nevertheless, this LECG exists. Even in a one-year horizon, in a crisis event, if the bank decided to securitize the future profits on the existing clients on demand deposits (or even to sell the activity), investors would be ready to pay a premium.

This demand deposit LECG allows the bank to take more risks and not only interest rate risk but:

- credit risk;
- business risk;
- operational risk, etc.

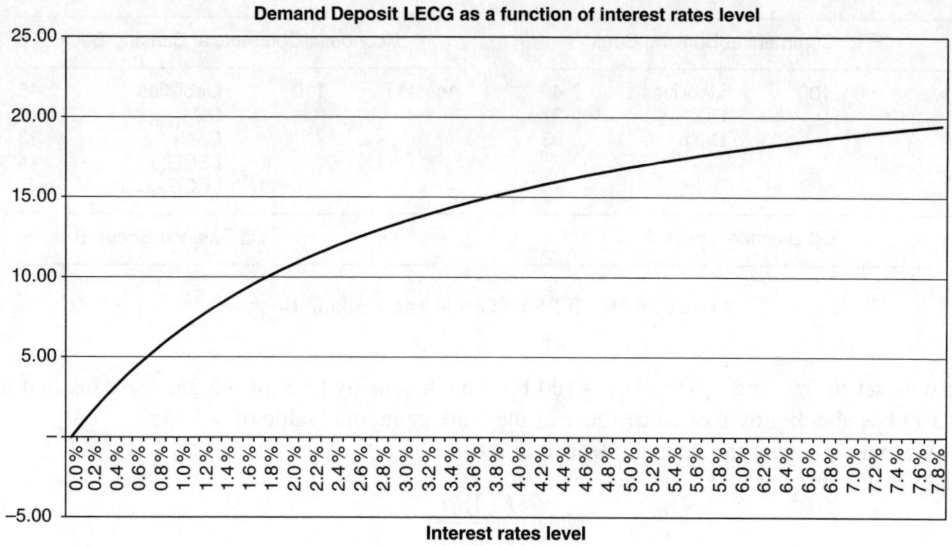

Figure 26.9 Demand deposit LECG

26.5.3.4 Life Insurance example

Life insurance is also a good example for latent economic capital gains computation.

The contracts' full fair value may be different from their book value or their embedded value (refer to Chapter 6 on full fair value). This full fair value contains the client's behaviour and the insurer's behaviour (in terms of provisioning rules, margin choices, etc.).

The existence of an LECG in life insurance produces a more risk consistent net economic capital.

26.5.4 Interest rate risk economic capital using "Sensitivity based technology"

Balance sheet economic capital can be computed using VaR classical techniques such as a direct computation based on the sensitivities of the economic value. For example, in the 90s, JP Morgan introduced RiskMetrics™, a market risk framework, to compute the market capital requirements using the computation of the sensitivities.

26.5.4.1 Simple Sensitivity based computation

Let us consider the Bank Balance Sheet described below:

In our simple model, the sensitivity of the demand deposit value to the interest rate level is easy to draw:

$$S = \frac{\partial V(0)}{\partial r_0} = K(0).\frac{\partial\left(\frac{\mu}{r_0+\mu}\right)}{\partial r_0} = -\frac{K(0).\mu}{(r_0+\mu)^2} \tag{26.10}$$

IFRS Commercial Banking Book			
Assets	100	Liabilities	40
		DD	27
		Cash	33
Off Balance Sheet: 0			

Economic Commercial Banking Book			
Assets	110	Liabilities	45
		DD	13
		Cash	33
		$LECG_{DD}$	14
		$LECG_{Other}$	5
Off Balance Sheet: 0			

Figure 26.10 IFRS and economic Banking Books

μ is set to 3 % and r_0 too. The +100 bps shock sensitivity is of −2.25. It means that a +100 bps shock provokes an increase in the bank economic value of +2.25.

We may compute the demand deposit duration:

$$D = \frac{-S}{V(0).(1+r_0)} = \frac{\dfrac{K(0).\mu}{(r_0+\mu)^2}}{\dfrac{K(0).\mu}{(r_0+\mu)}.(1+r_0)} = \frac{1}{(r_0+\mu).(1+r_0)} \tag{26.11}$$

In our example, the demand deposit economic value duration is of 16 years.

If we suppose that the other liabilities and the cash are not interest rate sensitive, we have just to calculate the assets value and its sensitivity in order to compute the overall balance sheet sensitivity.

If the assets are made of a 5 years zero-coupon bond with a 5 % yield, the assets value takes the form:

$$\text{Asset Value} = 100.\frac{(1+5\,\%)^5}{(1+3\,\%)^5} = 110.1$$

The 100 bps asset sensitivity value is then:

$$\text{Asset Value Sensitivity} = -100.5.\frac{(1+5\,\%)^5}{(1+3\,\%)^6}\% = 5.34$$

Thus, the global sensitivity for a 100 bps shock is 5.34 − 2.25 = 3.09.

The gross economic capital (GEC) is supposed to be computed as the 99.95 % one-year Value-at-Risk of the economic value.

We assume now that the one-year variation of the interest rates follows a normal centred distribution with a volatility of 60 bps.

The 99.95 % one-year quantile of the interest rate variation is Q(99.95 %; 0; 0.6 %) = 1.97 %. It means that the worst (at a 99.95 % confidence interval) variation of interest rates will be of 197 bps.

The GEC is readily computed by multiplying the sensitivity by the quantile of the interest rate variation:

$$\text{GEC} = \text{Sensitivity . Quantile(interest rates)}$$
$$\text{GEC} = 3.09 * 1.97 = 6.1$$

However, in our example, the total LECG is 19 so the net economic capital is directly computed:

$$\mathrm{NEC} = \mathrm{GEC} - \mathrm{LECG}$$

$$\mathrm{NEC} = 6.1 - 19 = -13$$

The net economic capital exposure is negative: this capital need could be subtracted to the other capital needs arising from credit risk or from other risks.

To optimize its NEC, A/L managers could reduce in this example the assets sensitivity.

26.5.4.2 Discrete sensitivity based computation

In the method above, the interest rate yield curve is completely flat. In reality, yield curves are never flat and companies' risk exposure to the interest rate risk does not rely only on the interest rate level but also on the slope or on the convexity of the yield curve.

Therefore, it is better to compute sensitivities on each future date or on each yield curve pillar.

The method starts with the reconstitution of an aggregated schedule on a certain number of yield curve pillars.

Usually, the yield curve pillars are the following ones: 1 month, 3 months, 6 months, 1 year, 2 years, 5 years, 10 years, 15 years, 20 years and 30 years.

Every balance sheet product is then mapped on these pillars. *The mapping is made so that the product's fair value and fair value sensitivity is conserved after the mapping.*

For example, let us consider a simple product that pays on 01/07/2011 a cash flow of 10 and on 01/07/2012 a cash flow of 110. The economic capital calculation date is 01/01/2010.

The first cash flow will be split between the 1 year and the 2 year pillars; the second cash flow will be split between the 2 years and the 3 year pillars.

Each cash flow is mapped so that its sensitivity and its fair value are conserved after mapping. For example, the 01/07/2011 cash flow ($\mathrm{CF}_{01/07/2011}$) is mapped between the 1-year and the 2-year pillars according to:

$$\begin{aligned} \mathrm{CF}_{01/07/2011}\cdot \mathrm{DF}_{01/07/2011} &= \mathrm{CFM}_{1\ \mathrm{year}}\cdot \mathrm{DF}_{1\ \mathrm{year}} + \mathrm{CFM}_{2\ \mathrm{years}}\cdot \mathrm{DF}_{2\ \mathrm{years}} \\ \mathrm{CF}_{01/07/2011}\cdot \mathrm{Sens}_{01/07/2011} &= \mathrm{CFM}_{1\ \mathrm{year}}\cdot \mathrm{Sens}_{1\ \mathrm{year}} + \mathrm{CFM}_{2\ \mathrm{years}}\cdot \mathrm{Sens}_{2\ \mathrm{years}} \end{aligned} \tag{26.12}$$

After the mapping of the entire balance sheet, the A/L manager sums up all the exposures in Figure 26.11.

The last column shows the balance sheet mapped sensitivities on the 10 pillars. Those sensitivities are often called *positions at risk.*

Using those positions at risk P, the balance sheet economic value variation can be approximated through this formula:

$$dEV = \sum_{\text{Pillars i}} P_i.dr_i \tag{26.13}$$

We assume that the vector of the one-year variation of the (zero-coupon) interest rates follows a normal distribution with a variance-covariance matrix C:

$$dr = \begin{pmatrix} dr_1 \\ \dots \\ dr_{10} \end{pmatrix} \approx N(0, C) \tag{26.14}$$

	ZC rate	Discount Factor (DF)	DF 100 bp sensitivity	Cash-Flow (CF)	CF Fair Value (CFFV)	CFFV 100 bp Sensitivity	CF 1 Mapping	CF 2 Mapping	CF Mapping	CF Mapping Fair Value	CF Mapping Fair Value Sensitivity
01/01/2010	3.00 %	1.0000	0.00 %								
01/01/2011	3.10 %	0.9699	0.96%				5.1		5.1	4.9	0.0
01/07/2011	3.20 %	0.9540	1.43 %	10.0	9.5	0.1					
01/07/2012	3.30 %	0.9371	1.91 %				4.9	62.7	67.6	63.3	1.2
01/07/2012	3.40 %	0.9199	2.38 %	1110.0	101.2	2.4					
01/01/2013	3.50 %	0.9019	2.85 %					47.1	47.1	42.5	1.2
Total					110.7	2.5				110.7	2.5

Figure 26.11 Mapping

Pillars	Assets Cash Flow Mapping Fair Value	Liabilities Cash Flow Mapping Fair Value	Balance Sheet Cash Flow Mapping Fair Value	Balance Sheet Cash Flow Mapping Fair Value −100 bps Sensitivity
0 month	− 210	200	− 10	
1 month	50	− 30	20	0.0
3 months	40	− 20	20	0.0
6 months	32	− 10	22	− 0.1
1 year	26	− 20	6	− 0.1
2 years	20	− 20	0	0.0
5 years	16	− 20	− 4	0.1
10 years	13	− 20	− 7	0.5
15 years	10	− 15	− 5	0.4
20 years	8	− 2	6	− 0.6
30 years	7	− 2	5	− 0.5
Total	13	41	54	− 0.3

Figure 26.12 Mapping

Then the gross economic capital is quantified directly:

$$GEC = VaR = Quantile.^{t}P.C.P = Quantile. \sum_{\text{Pillars i, j}} P_i.\sigma_{\text{i}}.P_j.\sigma_{\text{j}}.\rho_{i,j} \tag{26.15}$$

where σ_i is the variance of dr_i the interest rate variation of pillar i and $\rho_{i,j}$ the correlation between dr_i and dr_j.

The VaR computation of our example is presented in Figure 26.13.

The GEC is estimated at a level of 0.35: the taken risk is very low. On the other hand, the LECG is very strong at 54 providing a very negative NEC of −53.

26.5.5 Interest rate risk economic capital using "Grid technology"

The previous method is a possible good methodology for computing economic capital in a balance sheet containing a minimum number of options.

For example, problems arise when trying to compute the sensitivity of a swaption to the interest rate level. This sensitivity is not a linear function of the level of interest rates. The VaR focuses on extreme scenarios where the variation of the swaption value is not a direct product of the sensitivity by the interest rate variation.

In a market risk analysis, the risk manager will add more pillars to correct the computation. For example, the sensitivity to volatility could be added.

Another way to compute economic capital is to project directly the economic value in a one-year horizon. However, from now to next year, too many scenarios are possible!

If we look after a 99.95 % confidence interval VaR, we have to compute 100,000 scenarios from now to take the fifth worst one that gives us the result.

However, for each scenario, the A/L manager has to compute an economic value and for the computation of each economic value, the option value estimation requires at least 1,000 Monte Carlo simulations.

Positions at risk

1 month	0.0
3 months	0.0
6 months	–0.1
1 year	–0.1
2 years	0.0
5 years	0.1
10 years	0.5
15 years	0.4
20 years	–0.6
30 years	–0.5

Covariance Matrix

	1 month	3 months	6 months	1 year	2 years	5 years	10 years	15 years	20 years	30 years
1 month	64 %	58 %	64 %	70 %	58 %	45 %	32 %	32 %	32 %	32 %
3 months	58 %	81 %	72 %	79 %	65 %	50 %	36 %	36 %	36 %	36 %
6 months	64 %	72 %	100 %	88 %	72 %	56 %	40 %	40 %	40 %	40 %
1 year	70 %	79 %	88 %	121 %	79 %	62 %	44 %	44 %	44 %	44 %
2 years	58 %	65 %	72 %	79 %	81 %	50 %	36 %	36 %	36 %	36 %
5 years	45 %	50 %	56 %	62 %	50 %	49 %	28 %	28 %	28 %	28 %
10 years	32 %	36 %	40 %	44 %	36 %	28 %	25 %	20 %	20 %	20 %
15 years	32 %	36 %	40 %	44 %	36 %	28 %	20 %	25 %	20 %	20 %
20 years	32 %	36 %	40 %	44 %	36 %	28 %	20 %	20 %	25 %	20 %
30 years	32 %	36 %	40 %	44 %	36 %	28 %	20 %	20 %	20 %	25 %

Variation volatility

1 month	0.80
3 months	0.90
6 months	1.00
1 year	1.10
2 years	0.90
5 years	0.70
10 years	0.50
15 years	0.50
20 years	0.50
30 years	0.50

99.95 % Quantile	3.29

VaR	0.35

Figure 26.13 Value-at-Risk

Therefore, once we want to compute an economic capital directly we need to simulate 100 million trajectories!

For this reason, *grid technology* or *grid methodology* is a good way to minimize the number of scenarios to simulate.

The methodology includes four steps:

1) The A/L manager determines a grid of possible couples of short-term and long-term interest rates in the one-year horizon. For example, the next year short-term rate could be of 0 %, of 1 % ... or of 9 %; the next year long-term interest rate could be of 0 %, of 1 % ... or of 9 %. This makes only 10*10 = 100 possible couples for the next year short-term/long-term interest rates.
2) The A/L manager projects his balance sheet on the one-year horizon and computes the economic value for each couple of short-term/long-term interest rates.

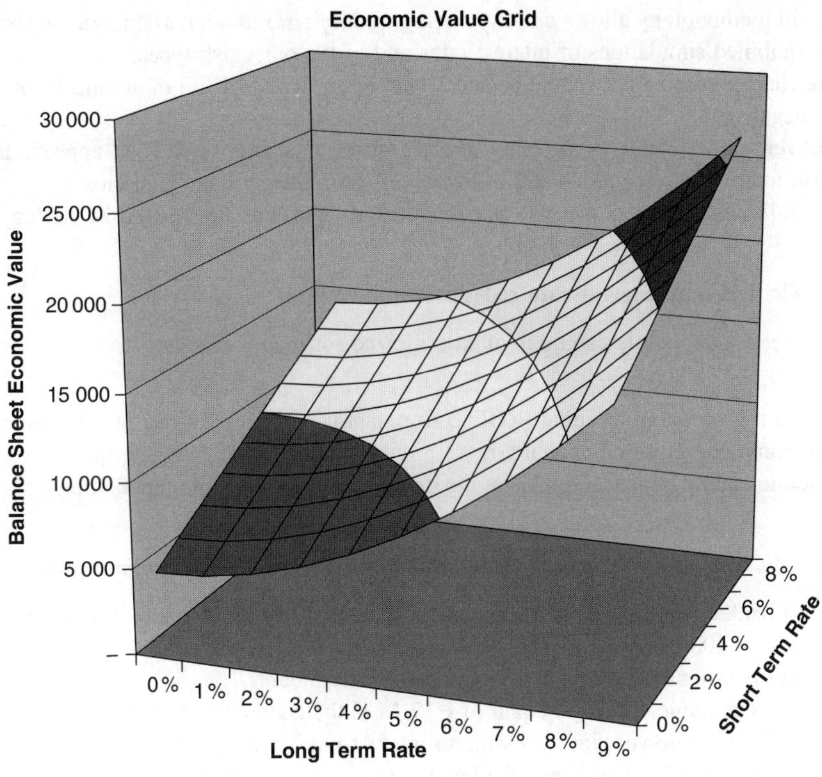

Figure 26.14 Grid

With a couple (short-term/long-term interest rates), it is easy to reconstruct a yield curve with for example Vasicek reconstruction techniques.

The economic values are computed under risk neutral probability as described in the chapters above.

3) The A/L manager computes 100,000 possible couples of short-term/long-term interest rates in a one-year horizon. For each simulation, he interpolates in the grid to determine what the balance sheet economic value is.
   The 100,000 scenarios are sorted under historic probability either:

   - using a normal/lognormal model for the couple (short-term/long-term). This model could be fitted using historical interest rates databases;
   - using bootstrapping methods based on the historical variations of the interest rates.

4) The A/L manager takes the fifth worst economic value as the gross economic capital (if the confidence interval is of 99.95 %) and the mean of the 100,000 simulations as the LECG.

This method needs only 1,000 economic value computations to compute the economic capital instead of hundreds of millions!

The grid methodology allows *an easy aggregation of risks* as soon as a model is proposed for the combined simulations of interest rates and of the other risk types.

In the chart presented above, the balance sheet has a strong LECG of around 10,000. The NEC is negative.

Moreover, this technology informs directly about risk exposure. Risk appears in low long-term interest rate scenarios and in low short-term interest rates scenarios.

In the following chapters, we will use this grid to determine the best ALM strategy.

26.5.6 Criticism of interest rate risk economic capital

Interest rate risk economic capital is often criticized for many reasons:

- The return on economic capital (ROEC) from a structural interest rate position is inferior to the company return on capital target.
- Economic capital depends highly on the demand deposit fair value modelling.

26.5.6.1 Interest rate risk order of magnitude and Return on Economic capital

Consider a bank containing in its assets only a 10 year zero-coupon credit risk free bond for an amount of € 100 M. Bond yield is 5 % and interest rate yield curve level is at 5 %.

The bond is refinanced through equity and short-term debt.

The gross economic capital is equal to € 17 M if the economic capital is computed as a 99.97 % VaR on a one-year interval with an interest rate volatility of 60 bps.

The LECG is equal to zero since the bond value is equal to € 100 M.

Thus, the net economic capital (NEC) is of € 17 M. We suppose that the shareholder's equity is close to the NEC level.

Assets		Liabilities	
Bond	100	Debt	83
		Equity	17

The bank net economic income is equal to the bond fair value variation plus the net income of the year:

$$[\text{Bond Fair Value}_{\text{year1}} - 100] + 100.5\,\% - 83.5\,\%$$

We compute a return on economic capital (ROEC) based on the shareholder's equity:

$$\text{ROEC} = 5\% + \frac{[\text{Bond Fair Value}_{\text{year1}} - 100]}{17}$$

Therefore, if the bank targets a ROEC of 15 %, it means that the bond's fair value has to be above 17*10 % + 100 that is 101.7 in one year.

In terms of interest rates, it means that to get a 15 % ROEC target, interest rates have to be fewer than 4.80 %.

This example shows that to fulfil a 15 % ROEC target, the A/L manager has to plan for a 20 bps interest rates decrease on a one-year horizon to take positions on long-term interest rates.

However, usually, interest rate risk premiums are said to be not so far from 10 bps, so *interest rate risk taking strategies become rapidly incompatible with a very high ROEC target with the economic capital computation.*

An application of the economic capital that is too direct illustrates that taking "structural interest rate positions" (i.e. not changing across time) does not produce a sufficient return compared with the taken risks, with the company rating objective and with its return objectives.

The same conclusion could be drawn for the stock market.

In fact, the problem is more a ROEC target problem: the 15 % ROEC target is not consistent with the economy. We will see in the following chapters how the ROEC target should be set according to the CAPM theory.

With an adequate ROEC target, structural interest rate positions are possible.

26.5.6.2 Economic capital depends highly on the demand deposit model

We return to the example developed in Section 26.5.4.1 on "Simple sensitivity based computation" and we plot the GEC and the NEC as a function of the parameter μ.

When μ becomes important, the NEC becomes positive. *The NEC depends highly on the demand deposit model.*

For this reason, *it is essential to make the demand deposit modelling reliable.* The closer to the client behaviour the A/L manager is, the better will be expressed his economic capital needs and his strategy (cf. Figure 26.15).

26.5.6.3 Rejection of Banking Book economic capital?

Some A/L managers wanted to reject the economic capital computation on Banking Book for the same reason they rejected the full fair value of demand deposits.

The main argument is *"Anyway, there is too much uncertainty to perform this economic capital computation."* A corollary to this argument may also be, *"For the economic capital computation, we will take the rule that fits our plans."*

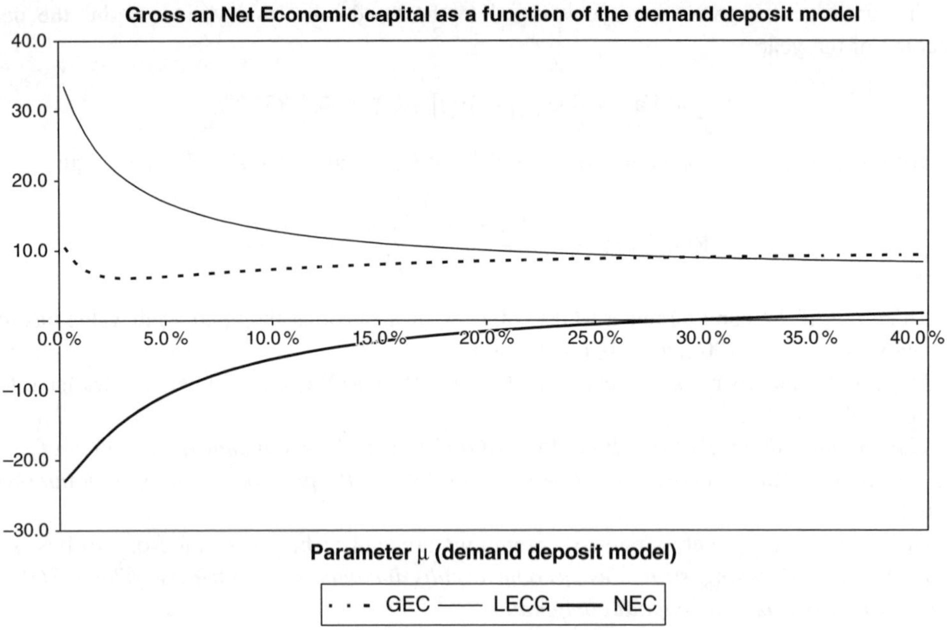

Figure 26.15 GEC

The uncertainty described here is centred on:

- fair value modelling;
- interest rate modelling;
- future regulatory and legal frameworks.

In this context, *economic capital models are not worthy*. Indeed, the chapters above illustrated very well the risk taken when using models.

With such arguments, those A/L managers use models to justify what they want to show to regulators or auditors.

Quite often, they translate this uncertainty into what they call an *"activity structural risk"*. The problem is that giving too much power to this kind of risk, A/L managers tend to take more market risks and to develop income-smoothing strategies.

Forgetting models, A/L management activity focuses more on income smoothing than on risk management.

Furthermore, with this attitude, the A/L manager tends to take positions that are too risky and that very few market traders (with portfolios accounted at marked-to-market and controlled by risk measures such as the VaR) would take.

For these reasons, quantitative A/L managers have to contradict those colleagues who point out the inefficiency of the economic capital concept due to uncertainty that is too strong.

The quantitative reply is to say, **"everything is 'modelable' even uncertainty and even model risk".**

This quantitative approach of economic capital tries to improve management with this new indicator.

26.5.6.4 *Economic capital – other classical mistakes*

A/L managers are susceptible to making mistakes about interest rate economic capital computation:

- when they choose a non infinite horizon;
- when they take into account new productions without any perequation modelling;
- when they do not take into account the Capital Book FTP schedule (i.e. considering for example that the shareholder's equity has no interest rate sensitivity);
- when they do not link the economic value of the product with the hedging front office model.

26.5.7 Liquidity risk economic capital

Liquidity risk has always been very hard to introduce in the quantitative risk management framework.

We propose here a methodology that could be a first draft for liquidity risk integration in economic capital.

First, economic capital is computed from a bondholder point of view. The economic capital methodology's purpose is to give to the company a rating target. When a company sets a 99.95 % one-year horizon VaR for its economic capital, the objective is to get a AA rating. This AA rating is associated with a certain level of liquidity funding cost.

For this reason, *it is always odd to compute an economic capital on the liquidity risk exposures since the economic capital's purpose is to protect the company's bondholder* guaranteeing him a stable rating.

Nevertheless, *the liquidity risk may be modelled as the risk of an economic value shortfall due to funding costs movements.*

Let us remember that funding costs variations distribution is not a normal distribution. This distribution function contains a very fat tail showing probable extreme liquidity events.

The company economic value depends highly on liquidity costs. For example, the liquidity gap may show an exposure on the long-term funding costs.

The grid methodology developed for interest rate risk can also be applied to liquidity risk. Some developments have to be made:

- Short-term and long-term interest rates have to be replaced by short-term and long-term company liquidity costs.
- The economic value formula has to take into account the funding costs for the existing operations (excluding new productions).
- Some balance sheet amounts may vary according to the liquidity costs level: for example in a liquidity crisis, the demand deposit amount may decrease due to "frightened clients' withdrawals". The balance sheet may include *liquidity options.*

The chart 26.16 provides an example of liquidity grid:

In this example, the short-term funding cost may threaten the bank's economic value but the probability of seeing this cost above 10 % in a one-year horizon is perhaps low.

This example shows why it is important to know how to simulate funding costs and how theses costs are distributed, (please refer to Section 19.1.4 on liquidity risk simulation).

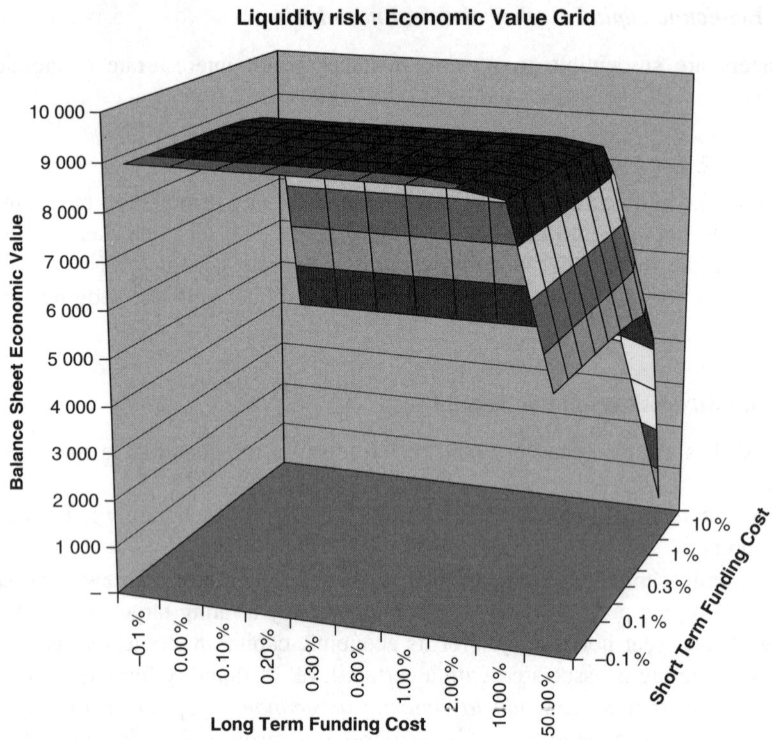

Figure 26.16 Liquidity risk grid

26.5.8 Currency risk economic capital

Currency risk economic capital has of course to be computed currency by currency. For each currency, the exposition is simply the economic value sensitivity to the exchange rate level.

The chart 26.17 represents the possible economic value evolution according to the next year exchange rate. The ten chosen pillars for the USD/EUR exchange rate are 0.2, 0.4 ... and 2.

The currency risk economic capital is defined directly by the 99.95 % confidence interval on the one-year horizon of the exchange rate variation using this chart.

26.5.9 Inflation risk economic capital

The chapter about inflation simulation models described a modelling close to interest rate modelling.

The real rates yield curve is just another yield curve associated with a specific currency: the housewife basket. The same methodology as the one used for interest rates is applicable to real rates/inflation risk economic capital.

A real rates grid is readily computable once the economic value computation takes into account the real rate yield curve possible evolutions.

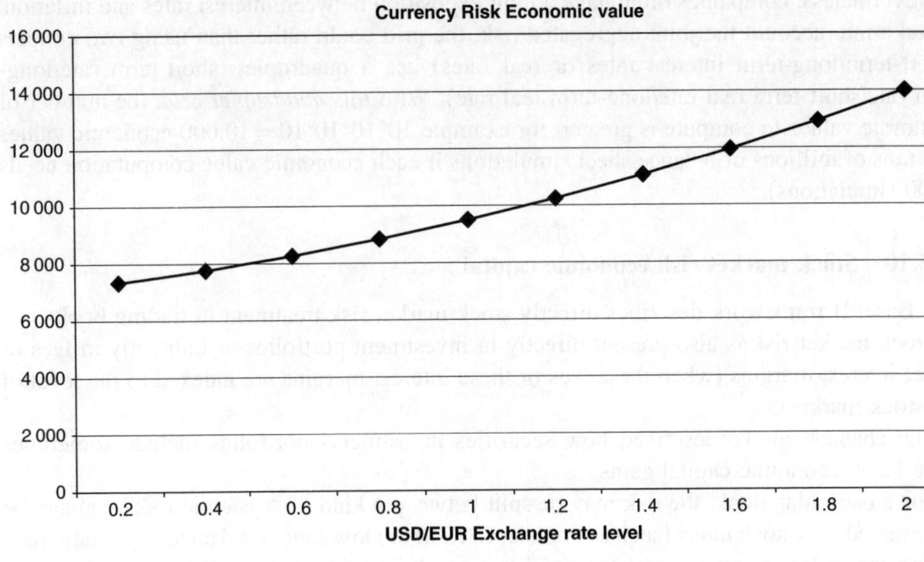

Figure 26.17 Currency risk grid

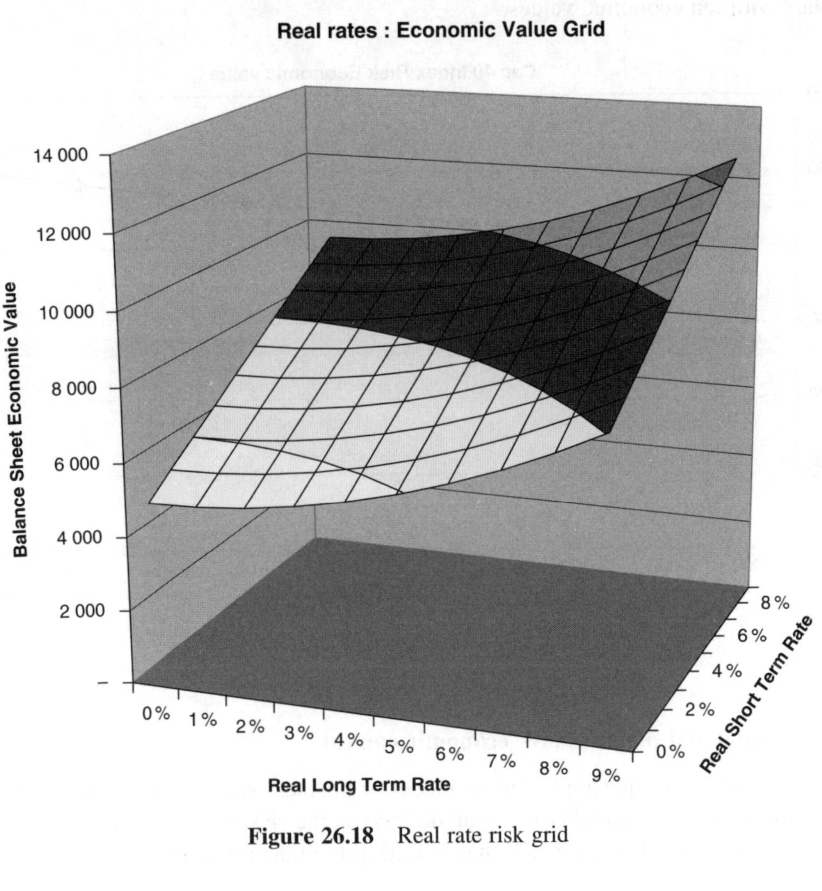

Figure 26.18 Real rate risk grid

Nevertheless, companies often have a joint exposition between interest rates and inflation. To take into account the joint aggregated risk, the grid could rather than using two couples (short-term/long-term interest rates or real rates) use a quadruplet (short-term rate/long-term rate/short-term real rate/long-term real rate). With this *quadruplet grid*, the number of economic values to compute is greater, for example $10^*10^*10^*10 = 10.000$ economic values (i.e. tens of millions of balance sheet simulations if each economic value computation needs 1,000 simulations).

26.5.10 Stock market risk economic capital

The Basel II framework describes directly stock market risk treatment in trading books.

Stock market risk is also present directly in investment portfolios or indirectly in fees or in net interest margins (when these fees or these interest margins are indexed to the level of the stock market).

The chapters above described how securities investments portfolios include sometimes large latent economic capital gains.

For a particular stock, the risk may be split between a kind of "systemic risk" that can be represented by a stock index (such as Footsie, CAC40 or Dow Jones) and an idiosyncratic risk.

The ten pillars for the "systemic risk" have to be representative of the possible future evolutions of the stock index: 1 000, 2 000 ... and 30 000. The grid technology links those ten pillars with ten economic values.

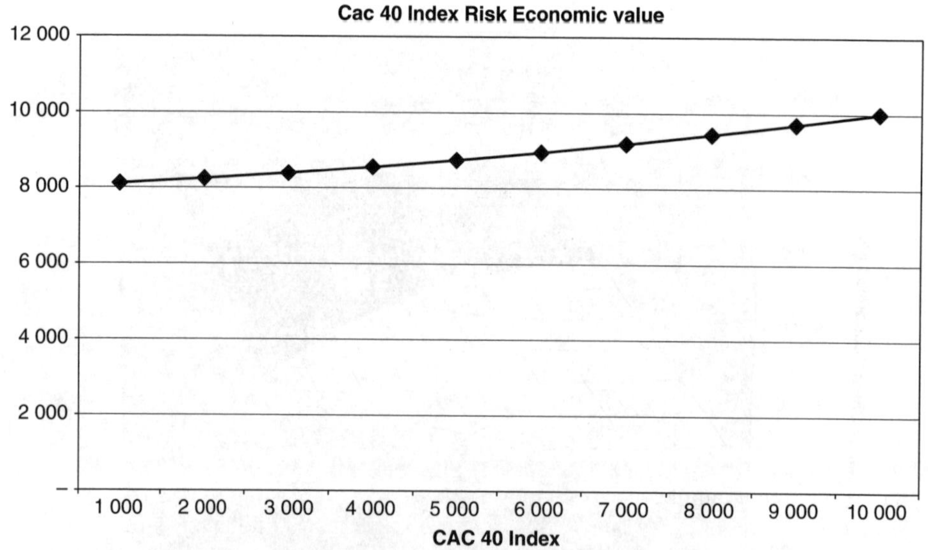

Figure 26.19 Stock index risk grid

26.5.11 Model and business risk economic capital

The grid technology is also applicable to model or business risk capital computation.

Economic capital for model risk can be defined as the risk of an economic value change due to a risk of a model parameter's change during the upcoming year.

For example, in the Banking Book, the economic value could change due to changes in the demand deposit model. If the parameter μ is re-estimated in one year, it will affect strongly the demand deposit economic value. In a full fair value context, a change of this parameter would affect directly the economic income.

Economic capital for business risk can be defined as the risk of a change in the economic value due to a change of the business parameters during the upcoming year.

For example, in the Banking Book, economic value could change due to changes in the amount of demand deposit during the upcoming year. If the parameter K(0) of section 26.5.2.4 decreases during the upcoming year, it will affect strongly the demand deposit economic value and therefore the economic income. The amount of demand deposit in one year K(1) is connected directly to the number of clients in one year.

Those risks are not "hedgeable" but they may contribute to the amount of economic capital since they may affect the bank's economic solvency.

Some A/L managers consider that business risk should not be included in the economic capital computation since the risk belongs to shareholders. However, this risk may affect the company solvency. The economic capital should take into account the business risk affecting the group solvency, i.e. affecting only the economic value and not the shareholder's equity value.

Moreover, A/L management sometimes takes into account the correlation between business risk and market risk. For example, in demand deposit economic value, interest rates sensitivity depends on the demand deposit amount. When computing the derivative of the interest rates sensitivity upon the level K(0) of the demand deposit amount, this derivative is different from 0:

$$\frac{\partial S}{\partial K(0)} = \frac{\partial\left(-\frac{K(0).\mu}{(r_0+\mu)^2}\right)}{\partial K(0)} = -\frac{\mu}{(r_0+\mu)^2} \tag{26.16}$$

The grid technology is directly applicable to model and business risk in the economic capital computation. The chart 26.20 represents the evolution of the economic value in a banking book grid constituted by the couple (μ the model risk parameter/K(1) the business risk parameter).

This chart shows in a retail-banking book the extreme economic value dependence upon the model and upon the business. In this example, a decrease of the number of clients by 3 % impacts the economic value of −0.4.

Consequently, the A/L manager has to model the volatility of the company's number of clients. For example, if in a 99.95 % interval confidence interval on a one-year horizon the number of clients decreases by 15 %; this would lead to a business risk gross economic capital of 2 in our example.

Compared to market risk, business risk may represent in volatile businesses a big part of the economic capital needs.

Model risk implies also the computation of the model parameters incertitude estimation. When preparing a model, an A/L manager has to describe the concurrent possible models and to model the chosen model incertitude.

A risk economic capital model that is too important could lead to:

- greater management implication in the model definition;
- A/L model team enlargement;
- A/L model controllers' increase in power.

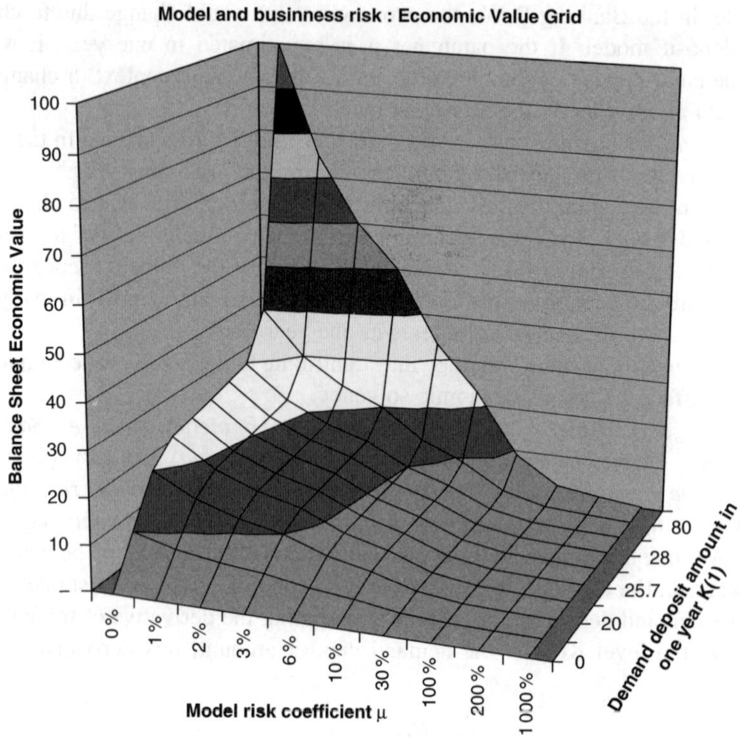

Figure 26.20 Model and business risk grid

To conclude with model and business risks, the strong correlation between market and model/business risk leads to a grid computation using not only projections on those axes. For example in the Banking Book, the use of the following quadruplet is recommended:

(Short-term rate/Long-term rate/Coefficient μ/Demand deposit amount K(1))

26.5.12 Risk aggregation

The chapters above described how each risk could be incorporated in an economic capital computation. However, in practice, the entire company risk has to be computed and all these risks may occur separately or concomitantly.

For the risk aggregation, the A/L manager needs a risk factors simulator. This simulator is not only useful in the fourth step of the computation with the grid technology but is also indispensable for every kind of methodology.

The A/L manager has to perform the simulation of these risk factors under an historical probability; for this reason, four methods are possible:

- using a bootstrap method based on the movements of the historical risk factors;
- calibrating a Gaussian variation model on historical databases;

- calibrating a Copula variation model based on historical databases (especially for arbitrary distributions);
- using a model including a risk premium: risk premiums are extracted from long historical databases and correlations are extracted from market prices.

However, the A/L manager needs also to know the *cross risk exposures*. For example, in the inflation risk economic capital description, we introduced the necessity of computing the economic value grid on four axes (Short-term rates/Long-term rates/Short-term real rates/Long-term real rates).

This is the same for the exposures on the multiple currency interest rate yield curves when, for example, the balance sheet contains quanto options: the balance sheet is then exposed to a joint interest rate risk in the two currencies and in the currency exchange rate. This requires the existence of a five axes grid:

- short-term rates for currency 1;
- long-term rates for currency 1;
- short-term rates for currency 2;
- long-term rates for currency 2;
- currency exchange rate.

Of course, if two risk exposures do not contain a cross risk exposure, there is no need for building cross risk economic value grids.

If not, the cross risk exposure has to be evaluated separately:

- either in a adequate multi-axes grid; or
- in a cross sensitivity computation.

26.6 IFRS AND REGULATION IMPLICATIONS FOR ALM

From a pure theoretical point of view, a direct IFRS, Basel II or Solvency II reading implies radical conclusions for the future of A/L management.

After the computation and the audit of the economic capital, the A/L manager will try automatically to optimize his income under this new constraint. This optimization calculation gives direct conclusions about:

- structural positions;
- arbitrage market positions limits.

Following the new regulatory and accounting framework, the ALM optimal organization would change drastically from classical organizations:

- more rapid balance sheet positions hedging on the market;
- more arbitrage in risk taking decisions;
- more modelling.

One might think that the development of modelling teams would increase the opportunities for A/L managers to "lose" financial analysts (i.e. to provide them deliberately with too large an amount of useless information) and to present a risk exposure in a more flattering light than in reality.

Income smoothing is still possible in the IFRS framework but is more difficult (or impossible) to hide.

The table below summarizes the new opportunities for A/L managers presented by Basel II and IFRS.

	Before IFRS and Basel II	After IFRS and Basel II
What is managed effectively?	Annual social income Expected annual incomes ALM is judged according to business plan realization	Annual social income Expected annual incomes Economic value variation **Return On Economic Capital (ROEC)**
ALM management principles	Budget focus The company market value is based on the annual income and the Price on Earning Ratio (PER): V=PER. Income PER depends on economy growth. A/L manager forgets that analysts know that results are smoothed and that company takes not reported risks	ALM takes into account financial analysts' valuation process: Shareholder's equity valuation Discounted interest income Demand deposits valuation ...
Demand deposit refinancing	Conventional FTP without economic point of view Demand deposit FTP is made for income smoothing	Bank communicates its demand deposit FTP schedule
Shareholder's equity refinancing	Conventional FTP without economic point of view No judgment about risk taking	Economic FTP and hedging
Auditors and regulators relationship	Episodic relationship	More technical relationship (and more presence?)
Indicators	Gaps Sensitivities	Gaps Sensitivities Economic value sensitivities Economic capital Smoothing reserves indicators
Market risk exposure strategy	Important positions not quantitatively analysed Contradictory indicators No real analysis of the company shareholder value exposure to market conditions	Better explained positions Better explained FTP and conventions Less risk taking
ALM net income	Taking risk produces a better income level	Incomes are better explained Lower incomes since market risk exposures decrease?

Figure 26.21 Before and After IFRS and Basel II

ALM income smoothing	Easy to perform	Opportunity to smooth the accrued income, but transparent in the Equity
ALM & financial analysts	Financial analysts are badly informed	Better informed Company valuation includes risk position and business risk
WACC	Higher since risk exposure are explained badly	Lower?
Company share value		Higher?

Figure 26.21 (Continued)

26.7 NEW INDICATORS FOR THE ECONOMIC VALUE APPROACH

In the banking industry, the economic capital was imposed by regulators:

- Pillar 2 of Basel II obliges banks to develop a risk-based approach when they decide to take risk exposures.
- Pillar 3 of Basel II gives more transparency on risk exposures to financial analysts.

This economic capital leads to the introduction of a new kind of indicator in ALM reports.

26.7.1 Economic value evolution

Company management is used to looking after the IFRS company income carefully. Nevertheless, the examples above showed that some balance sheet elements are not recorded at their full fair value, introducing sometimes a difference between the IFRS income and the economic income.

Company management is encouraged to follow not only the IFRS income but also the *economic income* that is the evolution of the company economic value.

Economic value income takes into account many elements that could affect future IFRS incomes:

- Real new production margin value estimation. (For example, taking into consideration not only the impact of the new customers but also all the economic income provided with this new production.)
- Real A/L management hedging effectiveness.

Following economic value evolution is essential and should be included in the ALCO agenda.

Management controllers may also use this economic value evolution report to base a control analysis of the economic value calculation process.

26.7.2 Economic capital indicators

Economic capital needs to be described also during the ALCO. In fact, in terms of economic indicators, the ALCO should describe:

- *economic capital calculation*;
- *economic value sensitivity*;
- *economic value grids* (representing the possible economic value evolution according to the interest rate movements and to the inflation movements as presented in the chapters above).

Those indicators are relevant to risk exposure limits and to the funding requirements strategy since economic capital is linked directly with the company rating target.

26.7.3 Income projection indicators

ALCO does not simply include risk managers or treasurers but also company managers from the board of directors.

Classical indicators such as gaps or income sensitivities will not disappear since they are more income based than economic capital.

An income based indicator related to economic capital has to be provided to the ALCO; this indicator consists of:

- the discounted income predictions;
- the sensitivities of these discounted income predictions to market movements;
- the sensitivities of these discounted income predictions to market movements (including new productions).

	Horizon	2010	2011	2012	2013	2014	2015 / 2020	2020 / 2030	Total
Excl. New production	Expected discounted income	100	80	64	51	41	25	10	**371**
	+100 bps sensitivity	10	5	3	–	–5	–8	–	5
New production	Expected discounted income	–	22	40	55	67	90	145	**419**
	+100 bps sensitivity	10	4	2	–1	–6	–9	–	–
Incl. New production	Expected discounted income	100	102	104	106	108	115	155	**790**
	+100 bps sensitivity	–	1	1	1	1	1	–	5

Figure 26.22 Income projection

Using modelling where the new production economic value does not depend on the market rates, the new production sensitivity is equal to zero.

In this example, the company economic value is of 371: *economic value is the sum of the expected discounted incomes without any new production.*

The case of a company with expected discounted incomes strictly equal to 0:

If for a given company, all the expected discounted incomes sensitivities (including new productions) are forced to zero by a strict hedging, then:

$$
\begin{aligned}
&\frac{\partial \mathrm{E}\left(Income_t.\exp\left(-\int_0^t \bar{r}(s).ds\right)\right)}{\partial \text{Risk Factors}} = 0 \Rightarrow Income_t.\exp\left(-\int_0^t \bar{r}(s).ds\right) = Cst(t) \\
&\frac{\partial \mathrm{E}\left(Income_t.\exp\left(-\int_0^t \bar{r}(s).ds\right)\right)}{\partial \text{Risk Factors}} = 0 \Rightarrow Income_t = Cst(t).\exp\left(\int_0^t \bar{r}(s).ds\right)
\end{aligned}
\tag{26.17}
$$

If the A/L manager creates a hedging forcing the incomes to be homogeneous across time, then:

$$Cst(t) = Cst$$

and

$$Income_t = Cst.\exp\left(\int_0^t \bar{r}(s).ds\right) \tag{26.18}$$

so

$$\frac{dIncome_t}{Income_t} = Cst + \bar{r}(t)$$

In such conditions, income growth is indexed directly to the interest rates (i.e. somehow indexed to the economy growth).

Such a situation where the sensitivity of the discounted incomes is set to zero is perfect for the company since it provides an income growth similar to the economy growth.

26.7.4 Advanced income sensitivity based indicators (interest rate risk example)

In the previous chapter, we introduced an indicator based on income sensitivity. This indicator gives a rough risk approach since it projects the risk on only one risk. It is easy to extrapolate this indicator, for example, in an interest rate risk framework not only to represent the translation yield curve risk but also the rotation or the convexity yield curve risk.

26.7.4.1 Matrix representation

The idea is to represent the interest rate risk sensitivity by a two dimensions matrix C:

- On the horizontal axis, the various income calculation periods are represented (on an annual or quarterly basis).
- On the vertical axis, we represent the future quarterly refinancing period.

In the matrix, cell $C_{i,j}$ represents the sensitivity of the expected income of date i to the level of the forward rate F_j on the period going from j−1 to j. F_j represents a potential refinancing rate.

$$C_{i,j} = \frac{\partial\left(\mathrm{E}_{RN}\left(Income_i.\bar{B}(0,i)\right)\right)}{\partial F_j} \tag{26.19}$$

The risk matrix representation is the following:

$$\begin{pmatrix} C_{1,1} & \cdots & \cdots & \cdots & \cdots \\ \cdots & \cdots & \cdots & \cdots & \cdots \\ \cdots & \cdots & C_{i,i} & \cdots & \cdots \\ \cdots & C_{i,j} & \cdots & \cdots & \cdots \\ \cdots & \cdots & \cdots & \cdots & C_{n,n} \end{pmatrix} \tag{26.20}$$

26.7.4.2 Interpretation

26.7.4.2.1 Diagonal axis

On the diagonal axis, the matrix gives the sensitivity of the income of date i to the refinancing rate of the same date i.

As we will see it later, the weight of this diagonal is important since the expected incomes of many products are impacted only by the diagonal forward rate: swaps, loans, etc.

26.7.4.2.2 Other matrix properties

The lower part of the matrix (below the diagonal) shows the expositions of the expected incomes to future rates, that is long-term rates in fact.

The upper part of the matrix (above the diagonal) shows the expositions of the expected income to past rates. In many cases, some interest rate levels do not only affect the period incomes but also the future incomes. For example, prepayments have a long-term impact on incomes introducing an income dependency on the interest rate trajectory.

The sum of the elements of a column gives the income sensitivity to a parallel yield curve shift. This is in fact the delta equivalent described in previous chapters.

The sum of the elements of a line gives the economic value sensitivity (the economic value is indeed the sum of all the expected incomes) to a special forward interest rate: it is somehow a more "trading based" risk representation.

The sum of all the matrix elements gives the economic value sensitivity to the interest rate level.

The matrix representation has a useful property: *the position matrix of the sum of two balance sheets products is the sum of the position matrices of the two balance sheet products.*

When considering hedging strategies, the A/L manager has to know how hedging instruments may be represented in the matrix.

26.7.4.3 Hedging products matrix representation

Let us see how usual hedging products (swap, CMS, etc.) are represented in this matrix framework.

26.7.4.3.1 Swaplets

A standard swaplet starting at date i-1 and finishing at date i, will be represented in the matrix by just one cell.

$$
\begin{aligned}
C_{i,j}(Swaplet_i) &= \frac{\partial\left(\mathrm{E}_{RN}\left(Income_i.\bar{B}(0,i)\right)\right)}{\partial F_j} \\
C_{i,j}(Swaplet_i) &= \frac{\partial\left(\mathrm{E}_{RN}\left(M_i.\left(F_i-\bar{F}_i\right).\bar{B}(0,i)\right)\right)}{\partial F_j} = -M_i.B(0,i).1_{\{i=j\}}
\end{aligned}
\qquad (26.21)
$$

The swaplet matrix representation will be of the form:

$$
\begin{pmatrix}
0 & 0 & 0 & 0 & 0 \\
0 & 0 & 0 & 0 & 0 \\
0 & 0 & \alpha_i & 0 & 0 \\
0 & 0 & 0 & 0 & 0 \\
0 & 0 & 0 & 0 & 0
\end{pmatrix}
\qquad (26.22)
$$

26.7.4.3.2 CMS Swaplets

A CMS swaplet is just a swap that exchanges an observed long-term interest rate with a floating rate on the period going from i-1 to i.

The CMS swaplet leg is exposed only to the level of the future interest rates: its representation is easily computable and leads to a matrix of the form:

$$\begin{pmatrix} 0 & 0 & 0 & 0 & 0 & 0 \\ 0 & 0 & 0 & 0 & 0 & 0 \\ 0 & 0 & \alpha'_{i,1} & 0 & 0 & 0 \\ 0 & 0 & \alpha'_{i,2} & 0 & 0 & 0 \\ 0 & 0 & \dots & 0 & 0 & 0 \\ 0 & 0 & \alpha'_{i,n} & 0 & 0 & 0 \end{pmatrix} \tag{26.23}$$

26.7.4.3.3 Options: Caps, Floors, CMS options...

Options such as caplets or floorlets are easy to introduce in this matrix framework. For example, a caplet on the forward rate of period i has a sensitivity of the form (using a linearized Black formula for caplets):

$$\begin{aligned} C_{i,j}(Caplet_i) &= \frac{\partial\left(\mathrm{E}_{RN}\left(Income_i.\bar{B}(0,i)\right)\right)}{\partial F_j} = \frac{\partial\left(\mathrm{E}_{FN}(Income_i).B(0,i)\right)}{\partial F_j} \\ C_{i,j}(Swaplet_i) &= \frac{\partial\left(\mathrm{E}_{FN}\left([\bar{\mathrm{F}}_i.\mathrm{N}(\mathrm{d}_1)-\mathrm{K}.\mathrm{N}(\mathrm{d}_2)]-\mathrm{m}\right).B(0,i)\right)}{\partial F_j} \\ C_{i,j}(Swaplet_i) &= \mathrm{N}(\mathrm{d}_1).B(0,i).1_{\{i=j\}} \end{aligned} \tag{26.24}$$

Thus, the caplet representation is not so different from the swaplet representation:

$$\begin{pmatrix} 0 & 0 & 0 & 0 & 0 \\ 0 & 0 & 0 & 0 & 0 \\ 0 & 0 & \alpha_i.N(d_1) & 0 & 0 \\ 0 & 0 & 0 & 0 & 0 \\ 0 & 0 & 0 & 0 & 0 \end{pmatrix} \tag{26.25}$$

26.7.4.3.4 Swaptions

The swaptions representation is a bit harder to compute. In a non cash-settlement swaption, all the incomes are impacted from the fixing date to the underlying swap end date. Moreover, since the swaption execution depends on the long-term swap rate at the fixing date, all the incomes are impacted by the forward rates of this date. The swaption matrix representations that may be calculated analytically or using Monte Carlo simulation have elements on the upper part and on the lower part of the matrix. It looks like this:

$$\begin{pmatrix} 0 & 0 & 0 & 0 & 0 & 0 \\ 0 & 0 & 0 & 0 & 0 & 0 \\ 0 & 0 & \beta_{i,1} & \dots & \beta_{m,1} & 0 \\ 0 & 0 & \dots & \dots & \dots & 0 \\ 0 & 0 & \beta_{i,n} & \dots & \beta_{m,n} & 0 \\ 0 & 0 & 0 & 0 & 0 & 0 \end{pmatrix} \tag{26.26}$$

26.7.4.3.5 Risk free products (or strategies) and matrix representation

This matrix representation entails some disadvantages. Among those disadvantages, *the A/L managers know that some risk-free strategies have a matrix representation different from the empty matrix.*

For example, let us consider a strategy made of:

- a two year loan of 100 with an annual 5 % coupon;
- a one-year borrowing of 100 with an annual 4 % coupon;
- a one-year borrowing forward in one year of 99 with an annual coupon of 6.06 % (that is (105/99–1)).

The strategy is risk free since all the cash flows are matched!

The first year interest income is of 1 (that is 5–4).

The second year interest income is of –B(0,1)/B(0,2) (i.e. 100.5 % −99. 6.06 %−1.F_2).

Once discounted, the first year interest income is of B(0,1) and the second year is of –B(0,1). The matrix representation of this risk free strategy looks like:

$$\begin{pmatrix} \varepsilon_1 & -\varepsilon_1 & 0 & 0 & 0 & 0 \\ 0 & 0 & 0 & 0 & 0 & 0 \\ 0 & 0 & 0 & 0 & 0 & 0 \\ 0 & 0 & 0 & 0 & 0 & 0 \\ 0 & 0 & 0 & 0 & 0 & 0 \\ 0 & 0 & 0 & 0 & 0 & 0 \end{pmatrix} \tag{26.27}$$

Such a representation of a risk free position will be important in the hedging strategy definition: the final income hedging strategy will have to take into account "income smoothing strategies" like this one.

Part VII
Optimal Return Strategies

In this final Part, we describe optimal return strategies.

First, we describe the *risk free quasi-perfect strategy*. This strategy is based on the use of the delta equivalent technique. This technique takes into account the entire complexity of the ALM managers' constraints.

Once the A/L manager knows the risk free strategy, he is able to take risks. Those risks are measured by the economic capital described in the previous Part. To be prepared, the A/L manager has to take into account:

- the necessity of a *limits policy*: these limits will restrict the risk exposure and then restrict the ALM solutions;
- the existence of *income smoothing strategies*: this technical point is important since it resolves the possible divergence between economic risk and accounting risk.

Then, it is time for the economic value management chapter to provide the solution for the optimal risk exposure.

The final chapters apply this economic value management to the Banking Book, to the Insurance Book and to Capital Book management.

27 Risk Perfect Hedging Using the Delta Equivalent Technique

Il n'est si petite chapelle qui n'ait son saint.

In this final Part, we will divide the optimization problem into two problems:

- *Hedging risk strategy definition*: the objective is to define the strategy that minimizes the risk exposure.
- *Risk taking position*: the objective is to determine the optimal risk position that the company can support.

This chapter describes the delta equivalent strategy that hedges perfectly the risk exposures. With the objective of hedging risk perfectly, the company has different choices:

- either to micro hedge risk positions using structured products; or
- to develop indicators such as delta equivalent indicators in order to allow the A/L manager to compute step by step the optimal strategy.

27.1 MICRO HEDGING STRATEGIES WITH STRUCTURED PRODUCTS

The equity derivatives or fixed income teams of large banks will be happy to structure micro hedging strategies for A/L managers in front of their optional risks.

For instance, in front of the prepayment option, they may propose different hedging strategies:

- *Floors*: these strategies contain important residual risks since a short-term interest rate decrease without a long-term interest rate decrease generates positive cash flows without prepayments. Moreover, floor maturities are shorter than mortgages' average life.
- *CMS floors* (with less interest rate slope risk but still with a problem regarding operation duration).
- *Bermudan swaptions*: difficult to exercise, and supposing a rational behaviour of customers.

Many products could be proposed to micro hedge the risk. Another good option is to propose *power options*. When a swap pays a cash flow expressed as (K-Libor), when swaptions pay a cash flow expressed as $(\text{K-Libor})^+$, *power options pay a cash flows equal to* $[(\text{K-Libor})^+]^2$.

For the prepayment risk management, this could be a good option since:

- The prepayment exercise is proportional to the positive difference between the mortgage rate K and the interest rates: $\alpha.(\text{K-Libor})^+$.
- The cost of the exercised prepayments is proportional to the same interest rate difference: (K-Libor).
- And finally the prepayment option total cost is proportional to $\alpha.[(\text{K-Libor})^+]^2$.

This representation has the advantage of showing how prepayment cost is exponential (or parabolic more precisely).

This kind of option introduces *Taylor-made hedging strategies*. It is theoretically possible to structure a hedging product such as *index amortizing swaps* where all the future cash flows are indexed to the prepayment modelling parameters. Taking the prepayment example, the index amortizing swap could look like:

- The counterparty pays monthly a fixed coupon K on an outstanding amount.
- The bank pays a monthly Libor floating coupon on the same outstanding.
- The outstanding varies as the bank estimated prepayment function:

$$\text{Oustanding}_t = \frac{\text{Contractual oustanding witout prepayment}_t}{\text{Contractual oustanding witout prepayment}_{t-1}} \times \text{Oustanding}_{t-1}.(1 - f(K, Libor, \ldots)) \quad (27.1)$$

However, as time passes, this kind of structure has to be renegotiated and this is the problem with this kind of Taylor-made hedging product. Costs for renegotiation are usually important since pricing such a structure is uncommon and since the bank already gave an engagement to a specified counterparty.

27.2 DELTA HEDGING STRATEGIES

In large companies, A/L managers will prefer to put in place a delta hedging strategy.

As shown before, the delta hedging allows:

- a coherent risk representation in the indicators (particularly the interest rate gap);
- an income growth consistent with interest rate levels.

We will see in this chapter how delta hedging works in practice.

27.2.1 Delta hedging principles

In fixed income teams or in equity derivatives teams (i.e. in the marked-to-market world) the option valuation financial theory – based on the Black & Scholes formula – helps to develop replicating strategies in order to:

- replicate option price variations with simple elements (futures, etc.);
- propose a risk free strategy to hedge options selling.

The computation is made by the sensitivities computation and by the computation of the partial derivatives of the sold options: the delta (sensitivity to the interest rate level), the vega (sensitivity to the volatility level).

We recall that the autofinancing strategy V(t) follows the equation:

$$
\begin{aligned}
&P(t) = E\left(\varphi_T.\bar{B}(t,T)/F_t\right)\\
&V(0) = P(0)\\
&dV(t) = \sum_i \frac{\partial P(t)}{\partial Factor_i}.dFactor_i + \left(V(t) - \frac{\partial P(t)}{\partial Factor_i}.Factor_i\right).r.dt
\end{aligned}
\tag{27.2}
$$

Consequently, the strategy V(t) allows us to replicate the option and the final flow V(T) is equal to the option final cash flow:

$$V(T) = \phi_T \tag{27.3}$$

It is easy to translate the option financial theory into the ALM world. An application of this theory proves that **there is a replicating strategy with the following properties:**

- The replicating strategy is *financially risk free*: economic capital for financial risk is equal to zero.
- *The only risk conserved by the company is a business risk* (or cross risks such as business cross financial risks).
- *The company income after costs grows with a speed indexed to the short-term interest rates.*
- *The ALM income is equal to zero if the ALM applies this strategy exactly in the FTP system.*

In this strategy, you have to hedge from now the long-term cash flows. Mathematically speaking, the replicating strategy is similar to the one developed above but this strategy is based on the replication of the income INC:

$$
\begin{aligned}
&P(t) = E_{RN}\left(INC_T.\bar{B}(t,T)/F_t\right)\\
&P(0) = E_{RN}\left(INC_T.\bar{B}(0,T)/F_0\right)\\
&V(0) = 0\\
&dP(t) = \sum_i \frac{\partial P(t)}{\partial Facteur_i}.dFacteur_i + (P(t)).r.dt\\
&dV(t) = \sum_i -\frac{\partial P(t)}{\partial Facteur_i}.dFacteur_i + (V(t)).r.dt\\
&d\left(V(t)+P(t)\right) = \left(V(t)+P(t)\right).r.dt
\end{aligned}
\tag{27.4}
$$

The equations make the replicating hedging possible:

$$V(T) + RES_T = V(T) + P(T) = \frac{V(0)+P(0)}{\bar{B}(0,T)} = \frac{E\left(RES_T.\bar{B}(0,T)/F_0\right)}{\bar{B}(0,T)} \tag{27.5}$$

27.2.2 Putting in place delta hedging instruments

Before implementing the delta hedging technique (or before each delta hedging recalibration), the A/L manager has to rebuild its initial portfolio so that the company projected incomes will not vary too much.

From the date 0, *the A/L manager will project all the discounted expected incomes* (under the risk neutral probability) with the initial hedging stock and an initial strategy S(0).

In this simulation, it is important to take into account:

- all the future productions; and
- to suppose that new production economic values will be independent from future market conditions.

If we call INC(s,t) the income at date t due to the new production of date s, this means mathematically that the new production economic value of date s grows with interest rates with a Brownian W not correlated with the market Brownian motions and with a drift μ:

$$V(s)=\int_{t=0}^{+\infty} E_{RN}\left(\text{INC}(s,t).\bar{B}(0,t)/F_0\right)dt=V(0).e^{\int_0^s r(u).du+\sigma.W_s-\sigma.\frac{s^2}{2}-\mu.s} \tag{27.6}$$

This means that the A/L manager needs a very precise modelling of the activity including perequations and arbitrages.

Under this strategy, it is possible to compute the expected discounted incomes INC(t) and to express them as a function of the initial income at date 0:

$$\begin{aligned} &\text{INC(t)}=\int_{s=-\infty}^{t} \text{INC(s, t).ds} \\ &E_{RN}\left(\text{INC}(t).\bar{B}(0,t)/F_0\right)=\text{INC}(0).\exp(-\alpha(t).t) \\ &\alpha(t)=-\frac{\ln\left(\dfrac{E_{RN}\left(INC(t).\bar{B}(0,t)/F_0\right)}{INC(0)}\right)}{t} \end{aligned} \tag{27.7}$$

The observation of the function α is important since the accrued income volatility will be linked to this function.

The first step of the delta hedging implementation is to modify the initial strategy S(0) so that the function α becomes constant. This will make the initial discounted expected incomes constantly decreasing exponentially:

$$E_{RN}\left(\text{INC}(t).\bar{B}(0,t)/F_0\right)=\text{INC}(0).\exp(-\alpha.t) \tag{27.8}$$

Usually, the function α is already almost constant and there is no need for a modification of the initial strategy. Modifying the function means somehow income smoothing. Therefore, as we will see it later, the transformation of the function could be done:

- by the transformation of the investment strategy S(0) in AFS bonds;
- by the introduction of another refinancing strategy in S(0).

27.2.3 Step by step delta hedging

Under the risk neutral discounting of the incomes, the delta equivalent strategy leads to the scheme already described in the previous two sections:

$$\begin{aligned}
&\text{With } X_0 = 0 \\
&\text{and strategy } dX_t = \frac{\partial E_{RN}\left(\text{INC}_T.\bar{B}(t,T)/F_t\right)}{\partial Libor(t,T)}.dLibor(t,T) \\
&\text{where } \bar{B}(0,T) = e^{-\int_0^T r(s).ds} \\
&\text{then } X_T = \int_0^T \frac{\partial E_{RN}\left(\text{INC}_T.\bar{B}(t,T)/F_t\right)}{\partial Libor(t,T)}.dLibor(t,T)
\end{aligned} \tag{27.9}$$

and the income after delta hedging is:

$$\tilde{X}_T = X_T + \text{INC}_T = E\left(\text{INC}_T.\bar{B}(0,T)/F_0\right).e^{\int_0^T r(s).ds}$$

Consequently, when the A/L manager applies date after date the delta equivalent methodology, the income date t follows:

$$\text{INC}(t) = \frac{E\left(\text{INC}(t).\bar{B}(0,t)/F_0\right)}{\bar{B}(0,t)} = \frac{INC(0).\exp(-\alpha.t)}{\bar{B}(0,t)} \tag{27.10}$$

It means that after the application of the delta equivalent application, the income growth is indexed to the interest rates with a drift α:

$$\frac{d\text{INC}(t)}{\text{INC}(t)} = r(t).dt - \alpha.dt \tag{27.11}$$

After delta hedging, the income growth is consistent with the economy.

To be more precise, since the income incorporates a non-hedgeable model risk and a non-hedgeable business risk, the exact income evolution after delta hedging follows:

$$\frac{d\text{INC}(t)}{\text{INC}(t)} = r(t).dt - \alpha.dt + \sigma.dW_t \tag{27.12}$$

27.2.4 Delta hedging with simple optional products

In the chapter presenting the delta equivalent computation, we saw that behind the term delta equivalent, the A/L manager has to compute several "Adam equivalents":

- The *delta equivalent* itself gives the amounts of swaplets to contract at each date.
- The *penta and the courba equivalents* give the amount of CMS swaps to contract (on the different CMS maturities).
- The *correla equivalent* gives the amount of correlation products to contract.
- The *vega and the gamma equivalents* computation gives the amount of options to contract: swaptions, Libor caps/floors, CMS caps/floors, etc.

At each date, the calibration of the amount of these products is determined so that (after hedging) for each factor the sensitivity of the expected discounted income is equal to 0:

$$\frac{\partial E_{RN}\left(INC_T.\bar{B}(t,T)/F_t\right)}{\partial Factor\,(t,T)} = 0 \tag{27.13}$$

The hedging is made finally with simple elements: swaps, CMS, caps/floors and swaptions are common market elements with low margins. The A/L manager has just to calibrate the strikes and the maturities.

For many "old fashioned" A/L managers, option hedging is "costly": buying options means paying premiums and then losing profitability. However, it is possible to win money when buying options! For instance, buying at-the-money receiver swaptions is a structurally winning strategy (since forward market rates tend to exaggerate future market rates).

Moreover, *optional strategies could be settled at zero cost*. The premium to be paid buying a floor (or a receiver swaption) can be compensated for by the premium to be received when selling a cap (or a payer swaption).

27.3 EXAMPLE OF A BANK BALANCE SHEET WITH DEMAND DEPOSITS

To illustrate delta hedging and income smoothing we will start introducing a simplified balance sheet in a bank that commercializes only demand deposits and mortgages.

27.3.1 Interest rate model

We will suppose that at any time the yield curve is flat and that interest rates at date t are equal to r(t). The discount factor at date 0 with horizon t is equal to:

$$\bar{B}(0,t) = \exp\left(-\int_0^t r(s)ds\right) \tag{27.14}$$

27.3.2 Deposit modelling

We will suppose that the bank produces at each date t, a number PN(t) of new clients. This number of new clients will grow with the population growth. (Actually, the number of new clients would grow with the population growth and the amount by client would grow with the economy growth less the population growth. To simplify we assume that the number of clients grows with interest rates and that the amount by client does not grow.)

$$PN(t) = PN(0)/\bar{B}(0,t).\exp(-\alpha.t) \tag{27.15}$$

Each client will close its deposit account according to an exponential closing law. We denote PN(t,t+u) the number of customers "acquired" at date t already present at date t+u:

$$PN(t, t+u) = PN(t).\exp(-\lambda.u) \tag{27.16}$$

Each new customer opens a demand deposit. The amount of demand deposit at date will not grow with time passing. Consequently, the deposit amount DD(t,t+u) created by the new production at date t and still present at date t+u is as follows:

$$DD(t, t+u) = PN(t, t+u).DAV_0 \tag{27.17}$$

If this deposit amount is replaced in the market at date t+u on short-term interest rates, the income arising from the deposit accounts follows initially:

$$INCDD(t, t+u) = DD(t, t+u).r(t+u) \tag{27.18}$$

The A/L manager can suppose that this amount is hedged integrally according to its liquidity schedule with a swap at date t so that the income becomes:

$$INCDD(t, t+u) = DD(t, t+u).r(t) \tag{27.19}$$

27.3.3 Operating costs and fees

To acquire new customers, to keep them as regular customers and to guarantee them the higher level of services, the bank will pay operating costs in front of the received fees on the diverse operations associated with the demand deposit account.

We will suppose that fees will compensate for these operating costs exactly and that the following relations prevail (between Fee(t,t+u) and OC(t,t+u) the fee and the operating costs at date t+u arising from customers arrived at date t):

$$\begin{cases} OC(t, t+u) = OC(0, u)/\bar{B}(0, t) \\ Fee(t, t+u) = Fee(0, u)/\bar{B}(0, t) \\ OC(t, t+u) = -Fee(t, t+u) \end{cases} \tag{27.20}$$

27.3.4 Mortgage modelling

We suppose that the totality of the new customers is acquired through a new mortgage loan. (This is particularly true in Europe where prepayment rates are low and the incentive to move to another bank is also low.)

We once more write the schedule of the mortgages issued from the new customer production at date t and still present at date t+u. This schedule is decreasing exponentially since it may be a sum of credits of different maturities:

$$P(t, t+u) = A.PN(t).\exp(-\beta.u) \tag{27.21}$$

We call m(t) the margin of the new production at date t. The income *after hedging at the production date* of the credits originated at date t is as follows:

$$INCC(t, t+u) = A.PN(t).\exp(-\beta.u).m(t) \tag{27.22}$$

To determine m(t), we will decide that the economic value creation VEPN on new customer production is independent from market conditions. The margin m(t) will be the adjustment variable to make this condition true.

$$\begin{cases} VEPN(t) = E_t\left(\int_0^{+\infty} (INCC(t, t+u) + INCDD(t, t+u)).\bar{B}(t, t+u).du\right) \\ VEPN(t) = VEPN(0)/\bar{B}(0, t).\exp(-\alpha.t) \end{cases} \tag{27.23}$$

It is easy to show that VEPN(t) is a function of the following constants:

$$VEPN(t) = \frac{A.PN(t).m(t)}{\beta + r(t)} + r(t).\frac{PN(t).DAV_0}{\lambda + r(t)} \tag{27.24}$$

The condition on m(t) becomes directly:

$$m(t) = \frac{(\beta + r(t))}{A}.\left(\left(\frac{A.m(0)}{\beta + r(0)} + r(0).\frac{DAV_0}{\lambda + r(0)}\right) - r(t).\frac{DAV_0}{\lambda + r(t)}\right) \tag{27.25}$$

When plotting this margin m as a function of interest rate, this leads to this kind of chart where logically the margin m decreases with interest rates. When interest rates are low, the gains on the demand deposit are very low and the bank has to compensate for it with a higher level of margins on mortgages.

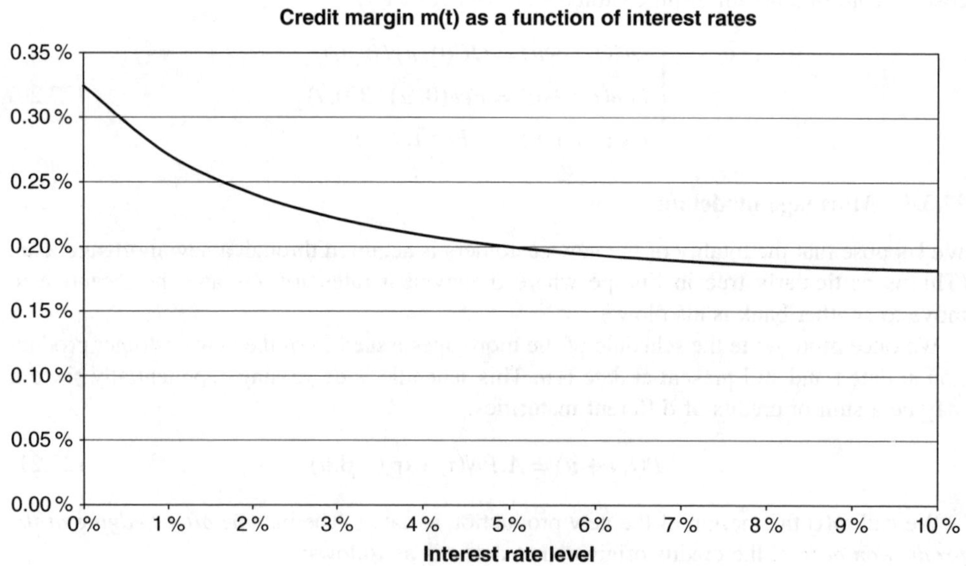

Figure 27.1 Credit margin and perequation

27.3.5 Income simulation

After the parameterization of this model, it is possible to simulate the bank income as the sum of the demand deposit margin and of the mortgage margin on all the existing customers:

$$\begin{aligned}
INC(t,t+u) &= INCC(t,t+u)+INCDD(t,t+u)\\
INC(t,t+u) &= PN(t).(A.\exp(-\beta.u).m(t)+\exp(-\lambda.u).DAV_0.r(t))\\
INC(v) &= \int_{t=-\infty}^{v} INC(t,v).dt = \int_{t=-\infty}^{v} (PN(t).(A.\exp(-\beta.(v-t)).m(t)\\
&\quad +\exp(-\lambda.(v-t)).DAV_0.r(t))).dt
\end{aligned} \tag{27.26}$$

In the equation above, everything is known and this makes the delta hedging feasible.

27.3.6 Delta equivalent computation

On that basis, the delta equivalent technique gives the amount of swaplets to contract on the different horizons. Due to the demand deposit amount growth indexation, the swap amount converges to zero.

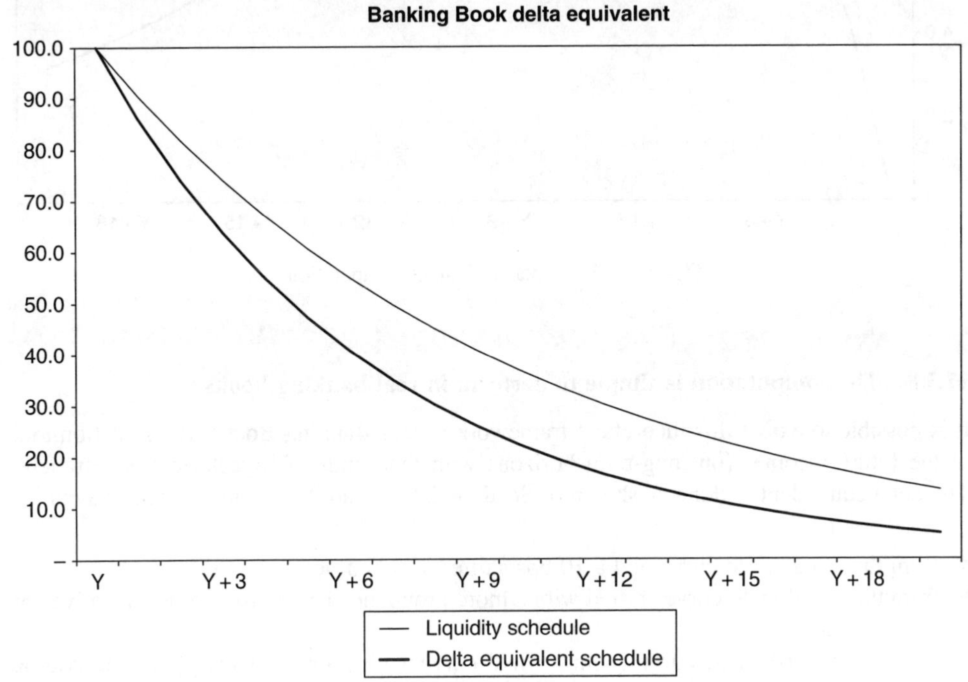

Figure 27.2 Delta equivalent computation

Note that *this delta equivalent is shorter than the liquidity schedule* (the computation is based on the closing probability and on the average amount by client).

The delta equivalent starts at the demand deposit level.

This delta equivalent (computed using past and new productions) could serve as a basis for FTP refinancing.

27.3.7 Penta equivalent computation

The replicating portfolio gives also the CMS swaplets amount to hedge the Banking Book. The computation is done through the delta indicator and the penta indicator.

The CMS equivalent starts at a zero level, becomes positive and converges finally to zero.

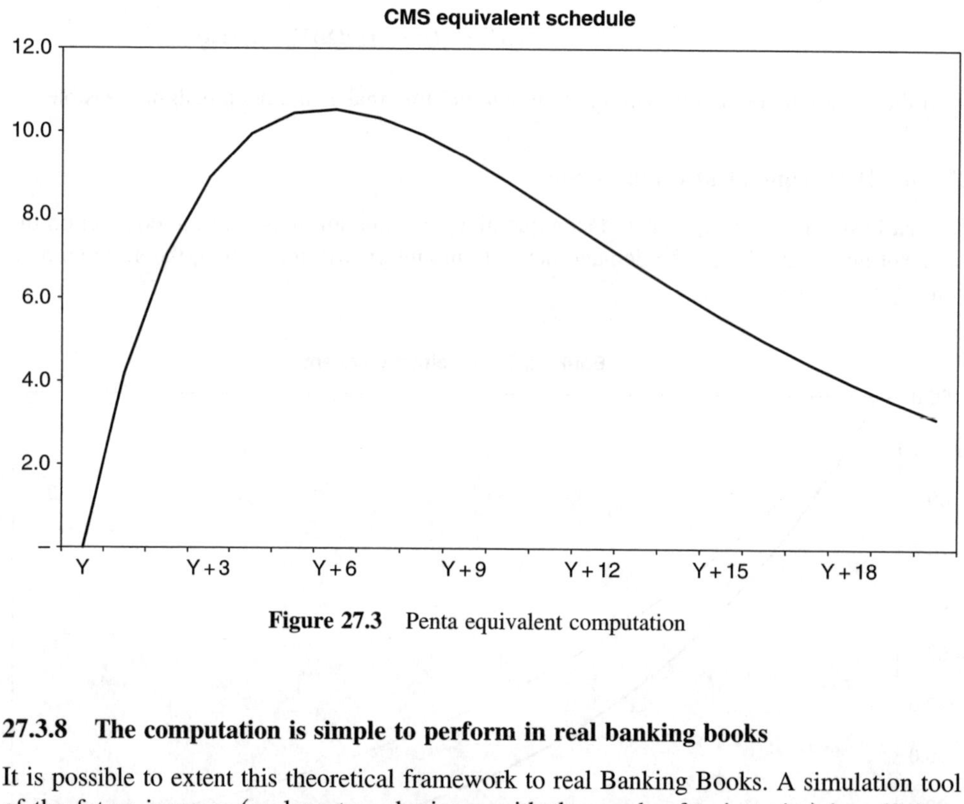

Figure 27.3 Penta equivalent computation

27.3.8 The computation is simple to perform in real banking books

It is possible to extent this theoretical framework to real Banking Books. A simulation tool of the future incomes (on long-term horizons with thousands of trajectories) is sufficient. The delta equivalent is done as shown in Sections 27.2.1 and 27.2.2 on delta equivalent:

- from the initial yield curve and a 10 bps shifted yield curve;
- from the initial yield curve shifted with a more pronounced slope for the penta equivalent computation;
- from the curved yield curve (with a yield curve with more convexity) for the courba equivalent computation.

28
Limits Policy

La vertu même a besoin de limites. (Montesquieu)

Once the risk free strategy has been described with the delta equivalent techniques, the A/L manager is able to measure the risk position. Associated with this risk position, the ALCO may propose a risk limit policy.

This policy usually has the effect that:

- the gross economic capital will not go beyond a certain amount;
- the interest rate (or liquidity) gap has to be in a specified tunnel;
- the interest rate income sensitivities have to be in a specified tunnel.

28.1 ECONOMIC CAPITAL LIMIT

The economic capital allocation process at the group level is incorporated in the company budgetary process.

This economic capital amount may become a constraint for A/L managers: ALCO may set a limit on the economic value exposure to market conditions.

On the other hand, since the capital allocation process contains a strategic risk allocation, this would impose at least a benchmark for A/L managers and sometimes a minimum amount of economic capital by risk type.

	Minimum economic capital	Economic capital benchmark	Computed economic capital	Maximum economic capital
Credit risk	100	150	160	200
Interest rate risk	10	15	12	20
Inflation risk	5	8	11	10
Currency risk	5	8	7	10
Business risk	10	15	19	20
Total risk	**104**	**156**	**167**	**208**

Figure 28.1 Economic capital limit

In the example above, A/L managers have gone beyond the inflation risk economic capital limit: ALCO should decide upon prompt intervention in order to reduce this risk or to review the limit.

28.2 SETTING ECONOMIC CAPITAL LIMITS

Some companies compute their economic capital limits using a model. The idea is to set a confidence interval around the risk taking optimal strategy.

The economic capital benchmark represents the optimal strategy risk exposure. Nevertheless, this optimum is known with incertitude. It is possible to model this incertitude. Once this modelling is performed, the optimal economic capital is known within a confidence interval. This interval may become the economic capital limits.

28.3 GAP LIMIT

When dealing with interest rate risk or with liquidity risk, A/L managers always used limits in their gap reports.

For example, the liquidity gap should be comprised within a tunnel. This tunnel could be expressed in terms of:

- a percentage of the balance sheet total liabilities;
- an economic capital economic limit equivalent.

Limiting the gap means somehow limiting the risk on the stock of operations.

In the following example, the effective liquidity gap is within the limits.

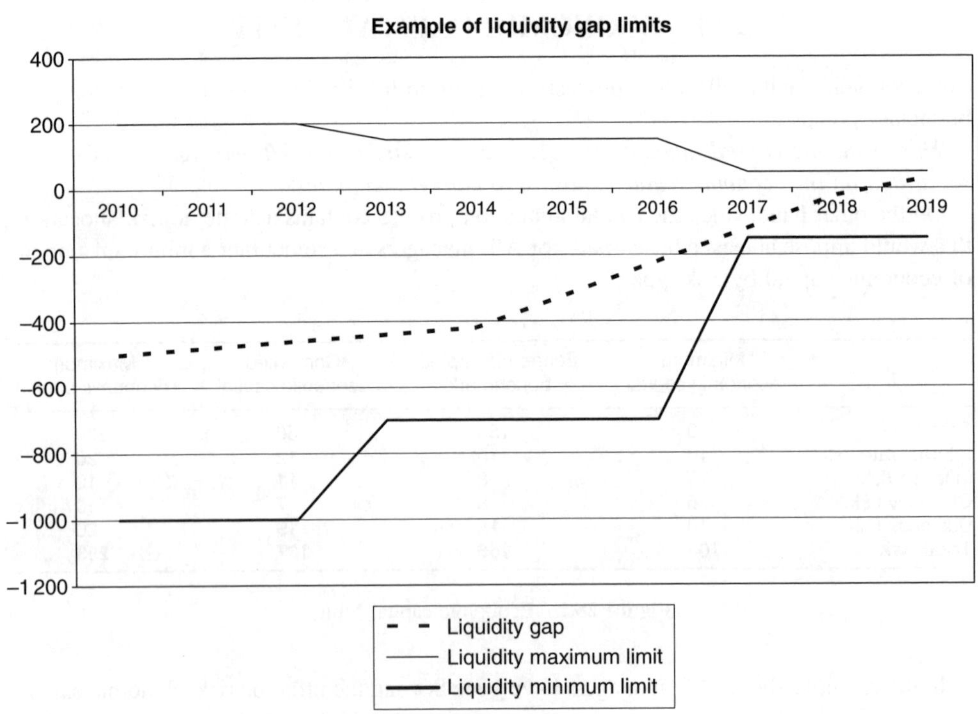

Figure 28.2 Liquidity gap limit

28.4 INCOME SENSITIVITY LIMIT

Income sensitivities limits have also been used by A/L managers from the beginning.

Nowadays, this indicator is criticized because it is possible to build arbitrage strategy with it. Income smoothing strategies may affect the sensitivity computations! *Income sensitivities limits should take into account the smoothing strategies' possible impact on the indicator.*

Nevertheless, net income sensitivities could be comprised within a tunnel and this tunnel could be expressed in terms of:

- a percentage of the interest incomes of the year;
- an equivalent of the economic capital economic limit.

In the example below, all the limits are respected:

	Expected income sensitivities				
Shock/Horizon	2010	2011	2012	2013	2014
+100 bps shock limit	75	75	75	50	50
+100 bps shock	50	30	35	30	50
−100 bps shock	−48	−21	−22	−23	−35
−100 bps shock limit	−75	−75	−75	−50	−50

Figure 28.3 Limits

29

Income Smoothing Strategies

Petit gain est bel quand il vient souvent. (13th century)

One of the A/L manager's objectives is not only to limit financial risk but also to limit accounting risk: the company is seen more stable (by rating agencies, regulators, etc.) when the income is not volatile over time.

The accounting risk imposes constraints on economic value management; income smoothing strategies reduce this risk.

However, the A/L manager will have to make sure he is not to confusing income smoothing with fraud.

29.1 IMPORTANT PRELIMINARY COMMENT ABOUT INCOME SMOOTHING AND FRAUD

Sometimes, even in a Basel II Pillar 3 or in an IAS 32 framework, there is an information asymmetry between the A/L managers and the analysts. Some income smoothing strategies may benefit from this asymmetry and this could be considered reasonably to be a fraud by auditors or by the law.

A/L managers will have to distinguish between income smoothing that includes a risk limitation objective and income smoothing that hides information deliberately from the financial analysts: this second type of income smoothing can be considered to be fraud.

The fraud is characterized by a deliberate will to circumvent the regulation.

As an example, we may cite the structure developed in 2001 by an American gas company we will call Company X, in order to smooth its income. The "Alpha project" was based on the creation of a Special Purpose Entity (SPE) with two stages:

- Stage one: the SPE borrows money from banks, buys natural gas at market price, and sells it to Company X at a discount.
- Stage two: the SPE buys gas at market price but sells it to Company X at a premium and repays creditors.

This kind of operation can create a tax benefit and hedge the gap between net income and cash flows from operations. The analysts were not able to predict the real future cash flows and incomes.

Company X's managers who took part to this project were severely condemned.

Many A/L managers consider now that with IFRS rules and Basel II Pillar 3, there is *no real risk to smooth the incomes* as soon as:

- the income smoothing has a *risk/return optimization objective*;
- the income smoothing is *reported directly or indirectly*. Indirect reporting is done through publication of instrument fair values (in annexes or for AFS instruments and derivatives directly in the balance sheet).

29.2 EXAMPLES OF INCOME SMOOTHING

There are hundreds of types of income smoothing strategies but they can be divided into two: *strategies where the company takes financial risk and risk free income smoothing strategies.*

However, for all the strategies, it is important to note that *economic value is not impacted by income strategies*. Indeed, the economic value of a future strategy is equal to zero under risk neutral probability.

When making an optimization of economic value under an economic risk measure income-smoothing strategies are not present in the optimal strategy.

29.2.1 Libor in arrears investments

A Libor in arrears investment is, for instance, a bond where the investor receives a coupon indexed to the Libor of the previous year plus a fixed margin.

These investments incorporate interest rate risk since the interest is fixed during the first year of the bond.

When interest rates decrease, this investment will delay the interest rate decrease.

29.2.2 Trading investments versus debt accounted in accrued (at historical cost)

A two year fixed rate bond accounted as trading financed by a two year fixed rate bond is theoretically a risk free strategy. This strategy affects incomes when interest rates move: an interest rate decrease affects strongly and positively the income on the asset side while it will affect more slowly but surely the income of the liability side.

29.2.3 Simulated strategies

In simulators, the A/L manager could be tempted to introduce future strategies in the simulator. Here is an example of such a strategy when interest rates are around 3 %:

"If interest rates overcome 5 % in one year, then the bank will contract a payer swap at the future interest rate level"

This kind of operation has no market value since the future operation will be made at future market rates.

The addition of such an operation in income sensitivities indicators modifies profoundly the indicator. It will not change the central scenario when interest rates are around 3 % but it will change the incomes of the other scenarios, consequently it will change the sensitivities:

		Year Y	Year Y + 1
Central scenario	Short-term interest rate	3 %	3 %
	Long-term interest rate	4 %	4 %
	Income	100	100
	Income (with strategy)	100	100
Scenario +1 %	Short-term interest rate	4 %	4 %
	Long-term interest rate	5 %	5 %
	Income	100	90
	Income (with strategy)	100	100

Figure 29.1 Sensitivities

The introduction of this strategy helps the A/L manager obtain income sensitivity on the "scenario +1 %" equal to zero. In this scenario, the strategy wins in year Y+1, the yield curve slope 1 % multiplied by the strategy amount of 1,000 for instance.

This kind of strategy is close to a "Hawks Martingale" as it will be developed later.

29.2.4 Spot mixed with forward deals

When the yield curve has an important slope, there are many opportunities to transfer the income over time mixing spot and forward deals.

For instance, on the one hand, the company borrows €100 M on one year at 3 % and borrows forward one year in one year €100 M at 7 %. On the other hand, the company lends €100 M at 4.93 % on two years.

The first year expected income arising from this strategy is directly 4.93−3 = €1.93 M. The second year expected income is equal to 4.93−7 = €−2.07 M.

This very good example shows how *it is possible to create an income transfer between different accounting years mixing spot and forward deals.*

29.2.5 AFS based strategies

According to the IFRS, companies have the opportunity to account their investments as available-for-sale (AFS). These investments are accounted in marked-to-market in the capital line of the balance sheet but not in the income where they are measured at historical cost.

The company has the opportunity to sell these investments since they are "available for sale". The presence of potential capital gains on AFS investments creates income-smoothing opportunities for the company.

For instance, the company may hold €100 M 5 % bond with a three years residual maturity when the interest rate yield curve is around 3 %.

If the company does not resell the bond, the expected gain is of €2 M per annum on the next three years.

If the company sells the bond, the next year annual income will be a bit less than €6 M and 0 on the following years.

The decision to sell the bond is put in evidence in the capital: financial analysts are aware of the A/L manager's action on AFS bonds.

Fixed rate AFS bonds help the A/L manager to create income when interest rates decrease. On the other hand, an AFS bond that pays a coupon equal to twice the Libor less a fixed rate will create capital gains when interest rates increase.

A portfolio containing fixed rate AFS bonds and AFS bonds paying twice the Libor less a fixed rate is interest rate risk free and creates possible capital gains when interest rate moves. The A/L manager has just to sell one of the two bonds to smooth his income.

29.2.6 Insurance provisions

Insurance provisions are the best example of income smoothing strategies. Insurance regulation is based on the presence of reserves to protect the policyholders against bad management decisions.

On the other hand, *insurance reserves as soon as they are not computed quantitatively are very good sources for the smoothing of incomes.*

One of the major insurance risks is to use the reserves over a long period of time in order to create income for the shareholders, degrading in fact the company's situation for the customers and for the bondholders.

29.2.7 Income smoothing reporting

Because of the existence of all these strategies, the A/L manager may build a synthetic reporting to show to the ALCO members what the solutions for income smoothing are.

This indicator would list all the income-smoothing strategies.

Strategy	Amount	Maximal impact Y	Maximal impact Y + 1	Maximal impact Y + 2
Libor in arrears	1 000	10	0	0
Spot and mixed	500	5	5	0
AFS bonds	2 000	50	25	20

Figure 29.2 Income smoothing reporting

29.3 EXAMPLE OF A CUMULATIVE AFS BONDS INCOME SMOOTHING STRATEGY

We take the example of a portfolio constituted with € 10 MM of 10 years 5 % AFS bonds and with € 10 MM of 10 years bonds paying a coupon equal to twice the Libor rate minus 5 %. This position is theoretically risk free.

When interest rates decrease, the maximum capital gains on this portfolio are potentially huge: after 5 years, if interest rates are equal to 0, the capital gains are around € 2.5 MM. The capital losses also.

When interest rates increase, the maximum capital gains on this portfolio are potentially huge: after 5 years, if interest rates are equal to 10 %, the capital gains are around € 1.9 MM.

The company can take an interest rate risk and smooth the impact of this risk so that using AFS bonds the income stays smoothed. Moreover, with this amount of capital gains, the other kinds of risk (even including business risk) could be incorporated.

Problems arise when interest rates decrease and increase back to 5 %. There are no capital gains at this moment.

29.4 ALM AND HAWKS MARTINGALE

29.4.1 Hawks martingale

Even if an income smoothing strategy affects only the income and not the risk (through economic capital), the smoothing will nevertheless affect the company economic value.

This kind of strategy may refer to martingale strategies cited in game theory such as the "Hawks Martingale". This strategy is used by casino players who play the roulette wheel.

Suppose that we own an amount of £1023 to play and that we bet £1 on "red". If the bowl stops on a red number, we will win £2 and the net gain is £1.

On the other hand, if the bowl stops on a "black" number, we have lost £1 but the strategy is not finished: we will play again and still bet on the "red". We will gamble £2 this time. If the bowl stops on a red number, we will win £4. The total net gain will be £1; indeed we have bet £3 since the beginning of the game.

Alternatively if we lose twice, the strategy will make us bet £8 on red. Moreover, as long as we lose, at the round i, if we have lost (i−1) times, the strategy will make us bet 2^{i-1} on the red.

Theoretically, there will be one round where the red colour will win. Once this round has come up, the strategy gain is £1. We may think that the probability of the "the red colour never winning" is equal to 0 and the expected strategy gain is £1 without any risk.

However, in our example, we have a maximum amount in our pocket at the beginning of the strategy. With our £1023 we cannot play more than 10 times. If the black wins 10 times, the total loss is equal to $2^{10}-1$. To play an 11th time, we will have to borrow £2048 and nobody will agree to lend us this amount of money.

In the Hawks martingale, our capital amount is our strategy limit. This is the same in income strategies. Transferring incomes from one period to another, the A/L manager will play with the company capital, i.e. the company's economic value.

Income smoothing is limited by the company's economic value.

29.4.2 Impact on ALM

The risk of income smoothing strategies: the company loses in one year everything that has been earned on the past 10 years, for instance.

In the 90s, some fixed income traders based their strategies on econometrical models supposing that the market was not arbitrage free. For instance, after a regression they found a relationship between long-term and short-term interest rates:

$$\text{Long term interest rate}_t = 0.8^{*}Libor_t + 2\% + \varepsilon_t$$

Then they would have invested in long-term bonds borrowing on the short-term. This kind of strategy would have won constantly during three, four or five years. However, after a strong interest rate rise, the strategy would have lost in one year, all the gains of the previous five years.

30

Economic Value Management: The A/L Manager's Optimization Programme Under Economic Capital Constraints and Accounting Constraints

Il ne faut pas mettre tous les œufs dans le même panier.

After the presentation of the regulatory constraints and of the risk free strategy, it is time to present the optimal return strategy.

30.1 POINT OF VIEW OF "TRADITIONAL A/L MANAGERS" AND CRITICISM OF THE MODELS

30.1.1 Questions on economic value management

A/L managers were not kind about using models and economic value indicators in company management. Their point of view mixes different approaches:

- *Incertitude in models is so high that they are not useful.*
- *Optimization gives not only one possible strategy but also a full set of strategies where it is not possible to extract "the" optimal strategy.*
- *It is not possible to transform the A/L manager into an automatic pilot.*

Associated with the fear of economic value, there are numerous fears about the fair value accounting concepts:

- Fair value accounting puts in evidence the annual performance of the business lines instead of smoothing it over time.
- Fair value is directly sensitive to small shocks on the market: market positions are put in evidence.

Indeed, if the company income is measured at fair value, this income is computed as a difference of fair values: the income then depends directly on the evolution of the stock of operations, on the margin level of the new contracts and on financial market levels.

Consequently, *according to these "traditional A/L managers", dynamic strategies cannot constitute more than an aid to come to the final decision* since there are too many hypotheses to get the perfect dynamic strategy.

Sometimes, the A/L managers do not want to communicate the real profitability of the ALM Department. Usually the company profitability objective is really higher than the real profitability computed on an economical basis. A/L managers are afraid to communicate an internal return on an economic capital of around 5 % when the company objective is said to be over 20 %.

The fear is not only for internal communication but also for external communication. The idea is that without any communication of the economic value, the income growth is higher.

30.1.2 Replies to this criticism

The modern and quantitative A/L managers' task is to demonstrate that *the company should not be afraid of economic value.*

Insurance workshops on Solvency II or on IFRS phase 2 demonstrated how the use of the fair value concept in embedded value is not as dangerous as it might appear at first sight.

Indeed, nowadays trading activities are satisfied with a marked-to-market accounting as soon as incomes are functions of a large number of parameters (number of factors, number of correlations, etc.) and as soon as there are many accounting instruments (such as model risk reserve) to control the income.

Moreover, fair value accounting has some advantages:

- There is no paradox between financial risk hedging and the hedging of the financial risk on the incomes. This paradox disappears on demand deposit accounting, on Capital Book. Refer to the example given in Section 19.3.6.1.2
- Fair value shows the real value creation of commercial entities: performance indicators are clear and net. The distribution of the roles between A/L managers and business lines is clearer than under accrued accounting.

Internal or external communication of economic capital has in theory a positive impact on shareholder's value since it diminishes the risk premium used by financial analysts in the company valuation. Avoiding the communication of the risk exposure has indeed some theoretical drawbacks:

- higher funding costs;
- higher risk premiums in the valuation and then a lower company valuation;
- risk during the audit of published numbers.

Furthermore, we can draw many lessons from the chapters dedicated to economic value and economic capital:

- *The interest rate directional risk position can be represented exclusively by the interest rate gap.* To do so, the A/L manager needs a precise modelling for each balance sheet product, for the capital, for the fees and the operating costs and for the perequations. New production has also to be modelled with the hypothesis of "new production independence" to the levels of the financial markets. With all these conditions, the risk minimizing strategy is the strategy that gives a sensitivity of the economic value equal to zero: an interest rate gap equal to zero and a convexity of this interest rate gap equal to zero.

- *When the interest rate gap is equal to zero, there is still an accounting risk but this risk can be managed through income smoothing strategies.*
- *Income sensitivities have to be replaced by discounted income sensitivities.* These sensitivities are consistent with the economic value sensitivities as soon as the economic value on the new production does not depend on the market rates. *The economic value sensitivity is equal to the sum of the sensitivities of the discounted incomes.*
    - *A company with a sensitivity of the discounted incomes equal to zero will have an income growth indexed to the interest rate level.*
    - *On the contrary, a company with a sensitivity of the incomes equal to zero will see a depreciation of the economic value when interest rates increase.*

Consequently, the A/L manager's task becomes easier: it is possible for him to *separate the risk free strategy and the risk position on capital markets.* The risk position is determined as a function of:

- risk premium;
- company risk aversion and ALM risk aversion;
- market anticipation;
- the non-hedgeable risk level (and the correlation of this risk with other risks).

The risk position is computed using economic capital methodologies.

The ALM evaluation is given by the economic value growth compared to the ALM economic capital consumption.

Moreover, *the risk position's impact on the volatility of the income could be hedged partially through income smoothing strategies.*

30.1.3 Impact on ALCO communication

All this discussion leads to the implementation of new indicators for the ALCO:

- *gap reports* consistent with the economic value sensitivity;
- *convexity reports* ("Adam equivalents" computation);
- *economic value report* with the justification of the variations from the sensitivities computation;
- *economic value creation on the new production report*: this is actually the real report for the commercial entities and shows the real economic profitability of certain commercial activities;
- *discounted incomes report;*
- *income smoothing strategies possibilities report.*

30.2 ECONOMIC VALUE MANAGEMENT

Modern ALM is built around the basic principle we have just introduced:

Dissociate risk minimizing strategy and risk taking strategy

The next two sections will describe this dissociation.

30.2.1 Conclusions on delta risk hedging

We showed in the previous sections how to conciliate accounting risk on accrued incomes and risk on economic value hedging. The technology called delta hedging is based on trading activities experience and on financial option theory.

Those strategies annihilate the accounting risk on the incomes accounted in accrued basis i.e. at historical cost. After strategy application, the company income growth is indexed to the interest rate level.

Moreover, after delta hedging strategies, the economic value is not sensible to financial markets levels. *The economic capital for financial risk consumed by ALM teams who strictly apply delta hedging is equal to zero.*

Furthermore, *the financial risks* (on the income and on the economic value) *are equal to zero for the business lines* (as soon as the delta hedging is used in the FTP computation).

For instance, the example in the previous chapter showed how the demand deposit interest rate schedule could be computed with delta hedging techniques. This schedule can be used directly to implement the demand deposit FTP rule.

Of course, delta hedging needs an important number of assumptions and each assumption has its importance for the final result:

- hypothesis on the new production;
- hypothesis on the perequation systems;
- precise modelling of the products and of the interaction of these products with fees and operating costs (such as precise demand deposit modelling).

The defined strategy is dynamic but indicates at each date what the A/L manager should do in order to hedge the company financial risks. The hedging strategy is simple to put in place once the A/L manager holds a random path simulator linked with the behavioural models.

The strategy is reset on a periodical basis (the ALCO periodicity) to incorporate new production hedging.

30.2.1.1 Economic value financial risk hedging and company market value financial risk hedging

In this framework, it is important to note that *economic value delta hedging preserves theoretically the company shareholder value from financial risks.*

Indeed, the market value is the sum of all the future incomes under a risk neutral probability and these future incomes could be split between incomes on the stock of customers (or the stock of contracts) and incomes on future new productions. Since new production economic value does not depend on the financial market levels, the economic value delta hedged company is also market value delta hedged.

$$MV = E_{RN}\left(\int_0^{+\infty} Inc_t.\bar{B}(0,t).dt\right) = E_{RN}\left(\int_0^{+\infty}\left(Inc_t^{stock} + Inc_t^{production}\right).\bar{B}(0,t).dt\right)$$
$$MV = EV + E_{RN}\left(\int_0^{+\infty} Inc_t^{production}.\bar{B}(0,t).dt\right) = EV + \text{Constant (financial markets)} \tag{30.1}$$

30.2.1.2 Delta hedging and economic capital for model risks

After the set-up of all the hypotheses, it is necessary to get the incertitude around each hypothesis. This will lead to the definition of an overall incertitude. The incertitude on the economic value and on its sensitivity will give the *model risk capital* (and its correlation with financial market risks).

30.2.2 The company's objectives and the "optimization programme"

After the definition of the replicating strategy, the second role of the A/L manager is to put in place an optimization programme in order to choose which risk expositions he will take. Of course, the company is already exposed to two kinds of risk he cannot hedge: model risk and business risk. However, it is possibly suitable for the shareholder to diversify its risk exposure with other kinds of risks and this is the purpose of the company optimization programme.

30.2.2.1 Company "utility function"

As shown in Section 25.3, there is no proof in the literature for the *existence of a company utility function*. The shareholder himself is able to optimize his own portfolio between his different investments. In particular, if his company is not optimized, the shareholder's portfolio will correct this mismatch: *the company's objective is not to look like the CAPM optimized portfolio but to obey to the shareholder risk appetite* in certain risks such as banking sector business risk, insurance sector business risk, etc.

The company's objective is to *outperform market anticipations or competitors' incomes.*

Then the problem looks like a classic optimization programme found in asset management. The A/L manager will have:

- **a benchmark** (the risk benchmark exposure designed by the shareholder);
- **a risk measure** (usually derived from the economic capital measures but within the shareholder referential);
- **an income measure** (such as an economic value gain);
- **an optimization period** (such as the interval of time between two plenary shareholder sessions);
- **a set of possible investments** (including model and business risk).

30.2.2.2 Company risk measure choice

The company risk measure choice is not an easy task. Of course, when distributions follow normal laws, all the risk measures are equivalent but nevertheless, the quantile choice remains important.

The economic capital gives a first risk measure. This risk measure (quite often a high quantile VaR) allows the company to get a fixed rating.

However, *economic capital is note the only constraint for the A/L manager*. For instance, nobody manages with a 99.95 % Value-at-Risk but with a full set of quantiles.

30.2.2.3 Constraints and benchmark

Due to the presence of a benchmark given by the shareholder, there are constraints on the possible investments: indeed the shareholder imposes implicitly a *minimal investment* and a *maximal investment* for each risk type.

The optimization has to take into account the management constraints: future manager obligations and future manager goals.

For instance, *income-smoothing strategies* will influence also the risk taken by A/L managers. The amount of risk taken by A/L managers will depend on the opportunities the A/L manager has to smooth the income.

Quite often, there are *liquidity constraints* that oblige, for instance, the total amount of investment purchases to be inferior to the treasury account amount. Unfortunately, this mixes liquidity reasoning and risk reasoning; for instance the use of derivatives helps to overcome these constraints.

30.2.2.4 Possible investments in the optimization programme

In the A/L manager programme, the optimization has the objective to find, with the constraints described above, the appropriate investments (in a set of investments):

- Model risk and business risk investment (obligatory investments as soon as the company works!).
- Interest rate investments (in bonds, swaps, etc.): different possible investments (one for each maturity) such as investments in smoothed rates (10 years smoothed rates investments, for instance).
- Real rate investments (in inflation-linked bonds, inflation swaps, etc.).
- Optional or slope investments: collars, CMS swaps, swaptions, etc.
- Corporate stock market investments.
- Real estate investments.
- Alternative investments or structured funds investments.

30.2.2.5 One-period versus multi-period optimization

The whole optimization theory is built for one-period optimization. It is indeed easier to propose a strategy in a one-period framework than in a multi-period framework.

For this reason, the optimization is done for a fixed period of say one year.

However, mean variance frameworks (such as the Markowitz framework) are perfectible when we try to determine the portfolio optimal strategy. The Markowitz strategies are myopic and static strategies. It is called *passive portfolio management*.

On the contrary, active portfolio management makes the A/L manager rebalance the portfolio. This is what we call *dynamic asset allocation*.

In the multi-period framework, the A/L manager provides, date after date, a prediction for market evolution: those anticipations are called priors in the Black Litterman model.

In a multi-period framework, it is possible to reason with trees: at each node of the tree, the A/L manager may optimize its strategy. The problem is that the tree is not a recombining tree and consequently computation times are too important to solve the optimization programme.

Only stochastic programming models and Hamilton Jacobi Bellman optimization will help to compute the multi-period optimal strategy.

Therefore, it is still easier for the moment to propose a mono-period framework for ALM optimization.

30.2.2.6 Value to optimize

Usually the maximization is made on the financial well being of the institution. The objective is to maximize the terminal wealth of the portfolio.

Indeed, the value to be optimized has to be consistent with the risk taken and with the risk premiums inherent to this risk.

The expected gain (or the expected value in the optimization) may be expressed in terms of return on economic capital. This gain expressed in percentages has then to be consistent with the risk premiums levels.

When investing in interest rate bonds, an expected return on economic capital of 5 % computed on a stand-alone basis is more consistent than a 20 % expected return. When taking into account correlations in the economic capital computation, the interest rate risk is merged with all the company risks and the interest rate expected gain moves up.

Consequently, financial risk positions will have a profitability followed more objectively with the introduction of an income maximization programme.

30.2.2.7 Tactical and strategic allocation

Of course, as for the asset management optimization problems, the A/L manager will dissociate two kinds of risk allocation:

- *A strategic allocation*: a large part of the ALM risk position is constant over time. This is a strategic allocation of the economic capital due to the presence of risk premiums. For instance, the presence of a risk premium higher in the bond market than in the monetary market implies a strategic allocation in the bond market.
- *A tactical allocation*: the A/L manager could have a perception of the market evolution different from the anticipated one. This different perception leads to a temporary risk allocation different from the strategic allocation.

For these reasons, tactical and strategic allocation implies *a fine modelling of risk premiums* and then of market models including risk premiums.

Furthermore, the A/L manager's task is to transform himself into an asset manager and to become an expert in the classic asset management questions:

- portfolio selection;
- tactical and strategic allocation;
- bid/ask costs impact on the strategy definition.

30.2.2.8 Efficient frontier and target return on economic capital (target ROEC)

As for asset management problems, portfolio optimization leads to the computation of an *efficient frontier*. This efficient frontier gives a relationship between the optimal expected return, the economic capital and the optimal portfolio composition.

Indeed, there is a full set of optimal portfolios: the portfolio allocation will depend on the company's risk/return preference. For example, the company can have a *target return on economic capital*. This target used with the efficient frontier will give the company's optimal portfolio composition.

30.2.2.9 Portfolio optimization and income volatility

Portfolio optimization could incorporate constraints on the accounted incomes.

Accounting volatility does not always reflect the economic volatility: it comes from an adequacy between assets and liabilities; when reported in financial statements, this provides a lot of information for financial analysts and it gives them the opportunity to comprehend the economic profitability. Analysts look after income volatility through reserves variations: fair value variation reprocessing, reserve variation analysis, etc.

Consequently, taking a risk position affects income volatility. If the company is afraid of having too many unrealized capital losses, the managers may decide to reduce risk positions (or to increase them) in order not to increase these potential losses by too much.

30.2.2.10 Comments about tax and optimization

Theoretically, tax laws have no impact on optimization.

For every company, it is usually equivalent to paying taxes today rather than tomorrow. Indeed, if a company tries to postpone incomes with the objective of postponing taxes, this action just reschedules the tax effect. The future amount of income will be higher since it will include the capitalization of the postponed incomes. For the shareholders of the company, it is equivalent to paying taxes right now or the same amount capitalized later.

30.3 ECONOMIC VALUE OPTIMIZATION USING GRID METHODOLOGY

If the risk measure focuses on the economic value, it is possible to propose directly an optimization programme. This programme will be based on the grid methodology developed for the economic capital computation.

The A/L manager computes the initial grid for the initial book position. To each grid point i, the grid associates a possible economic value in one year EV_i.

The A/L manager can also associate each grid point with P_i the probability of occurrence in one year of this grid point.

The A/L manager is able to compute other grids, one grid for each possible investment strategy J:

- a grid for the interest rate investments;
- a grid for the real rate investments, etc.

The variables $X_{J,i}$ give the value of the economic value in one year of an investment J at grid point i.

We call p_J the risk premium received for an investment J.

$$p_J = E\left(X_{J,i}\right) = \sum_{J=1}^{N} P_i.X_{J,i} \tag{30.2}$$

When investing an amount α_J in investment J, the overall economic value of the company in one year becomes at grid point i:

$$EV_i(\alpha_1, \ldots, \alpha_N) = EV_i + \sum_{J=1}^{N} \alpha_J.X_{J,i} \tag{30.3}$$

The A/L manager objective program is then to find the appropriate set of investments ($\alpha_1 \ldots \alpha_N$) that optimizes the expected economic value in one year under the economic capital constraints.

$$\underset{\alpha_1,\ldots,\alpha_N}{MAX}\ \mathrm{E}(EV_i(\alpha_1, \ldots, \alpha_N)) \text{ with constraint} \begin{cases} \mathrm{VaR}_{99.95\%}(EV_i(\alpha_1, \ldots, \alpha_N)) \le M \\ \alpha_1 = 1(\text{model risk}) \\ \alpha_2 \ge 1(\text{business risk}) \\ \ldots \\ \alpha_N \ge 0 \end{cases} \tag{30.4}$$

The economic expected value can be expressed as a function of the risk premiums and of the investment proportions.

$$\mathrm{E}(EV_i(\alpha_1, \ldots, \alpha_N)) = \sum_{J=1}^{N} \alpha_J.p_J + cons\tan t \tag{30.5}$$

On the other hand, the risk measure constraint can be expressed as a function of investment parameters α.

The problem is a classic asset management optimization problem. When the risk measure is a variance measure instead of a Value-at-Risk measure, the problem is transformed into a CAPM problem (i.e. Markowitz model).

For these reasons, the *grid technology* gives not only information for the economic capital computation but also for allocation optimization.

The computation leads to an efficient frontier that could be compared with, for example, the target ROEC of the company.

Furthermore, let us note that the grid computation is consistent with the delta equivalent technology. When the optimization problem is transformed into a risk minimizing problem, the solution is necessarily the delta equivalent solution.

The following chapters will introduce examples of the use of such a methodology that could be directly applied to:

- banking book income management (including demand deposit and prepayment options);
- Capital Book management;
- insurance books management;
- credit risk management.

31

Application to Banking Book Activities

Qui ne peut moissonner, qu'il se contente de glaner.

In this chapter, we will see through examples how the optimization programme can be applied to Banking Book activities:

- demand deposit hedging;
- prepayment hedging;
- Capital Book hedging;
- credit risk hedging.

31.1 DEPOSIT ACCOUNTS: VALUATION AND HEDGING IN AN ECONOMIC CAPITAL APPROACH USING THE GRID METHODOLOGY

We will start by introducing the optimization programme for a bank constituted only with demand deposits.

We will exclude the perequations from the modelling since our optimization programme will be based on a one period optimization. Indeed, we will consider just the economic value of the existing clients.

31.1.1 Definitions

We denote by K(t) the total amount of deposits without maturity at time t. We assume that no interest is paid to the deposit holders. The total amount of deposits associated with the existing clients (excluding new production) follows a diffusion process under the real historic probability Q_{REAL}:

$$\frac{dK(t)}{K(t)} = \mu_K dt + \sigma_K dW_K(t) \tag{31.1}$$

where W_K is a Brownian motion.

We denote by r(t) the spot interest rate at date t and B(t,T) the discount factor between t and T. Under risk neutral probability, this factor follows:

$$\frac{dB(t,T)}{B(t,T)} = r(t).dt + \sigma_{RN}.dW_{RN}(t) \tag{31.2}$$

31.1.2 Valuation formula

Our first goal is to calculate the market value of the portfolio of deposits. We exclude servicing costs and cross selling. We assume that in the valuation process there is nothing else than the future interest incomes.

The valuation is made under the probability Q, the probability that minimizes the market risk. For the classic interest rate products, this is the same probability as the risk neutral probability.

Under the probability Q, the amount of deposits follows a new diffusion process:

$$\frac{dK(t)}{K(t)} = -\mu.dt + \sigma_K.dW_Q^1(t) \tag{31.3}$$

From this formula, we can obtain a formulation of K(t):

$$K(t) = K(0).e^{-\mu t + \sigma_K W_Q^1(t) - \frac{\sigma_K^2.t}{2}} \tag{31.4}$$

In addition, the discount factor is given by:

$$\bar{B}(0,t) = e^{-\int_0^{+\infty} r(t)dt} \tag{31.5}$$

Thus, we are able to write the economic value of the deposits:

$$V = E_Q\left[\int_0^{+\infty} K(t)r(t)\bar{B}(0,t)dt\right] \tag{31.6}$$

If we assume that W^1 and W^{RN} are independent, we may use the Fubini theorem to obtain this form for the economic value:

$$V = \mu.K(0).\int_0^{+\infty} (1 - B(0,t)).e^{-\mu t}.dt \tag{31.7}$$

31.1.3 Particular case of a flat yield curve

We choose the simple case where the initial yield curve is flat. The interest rates are equal to r_0:

$$\mathrm{B}(0,\mathrm{t}) = \mathrm{e}^{-\mathrm{r}_0.\mathrm{t}} \tag{31.8}$$

This case is very interesting because it gives an explicit formula for the demand deposit portfolio value:

$$V = K_0 \frac{r_0}{r_0 + \mu} \tag{31.9}$$

If r_0 is equal to zero, then the demand deposit value is equal to zero. Demand deposits are then not interesting for the bank since they create no interest income.

On the contrary, when r_0 tends to $+\infty$ then V tends to K_0, the market price of the deposit accounts is at its higher point.

If μ is equal to zero, then the demand deposit value is equal to the initial amount of deposits K_0. Consequently, μ is probably positive in order to assure that the valuation V is inferior to K_0; μ integrates mainly the existing demand deposit account predictable decrease corrected by the probability change.

31.1.4 Basic indicator computation

It is now possible to calculate the deposit portfolio duration and its sensitivity to the interest rate changes:

$$\begin{aligned} S &= -\frac{dV}{dr_0} = -K(0)\frac{\mu}{(r_0+\mu)^2} \\ D &= -\frac{S}{V.(1+r_0)} = \frac{\mu}{(r_0+\mu).r_0.(1+r_0)} \end{aligned} \tag{31.10}$$

The duration is positive. This means that in order to hedge the sensitivity of the market price of the deposit accounts, the A/L manager should buy fixed rate bonds or contract fixed rate receiver swaps.

Once again, we find that the delta equivalent strategy is the risk minimizing strategy.

If we propose a numerical application and set r_0 to 5 % and μ to 3 %, the economic value and its sensitivity follow:

$$V = 5/(5+3).K(0) = 62.5\,\%.K_0$$
$$D = 7.1 \text{ years}$$

The A/L manager should have invested in 7 year bullet bonds if his objective is to hedge its risk exposure.

31.1.5 Grid computations

In the example where the interest yield curve is flat, the A/L manager faces two risks:

- business risk: the initial amount K_0 can vary;
- interest rate risk: the interest rate r_0 can vary.

The computation leads to the grid of figure 31.1; this grid is a function of the value in one year of the demand deposit amount K_1 and of the interest rate level r_1.

The bank cannot change the business risk level but on the other hand, the bank may invest in long-term fixed rate investments.

We consider the grid associated with an investment of an amount of 1 on a 10 year horizon.

The A/L manager's objective is then to optimize his return under a risk constraint such as the economic capital.

To simplify the result presentation, we suppose that the risk measure is a variance measure.

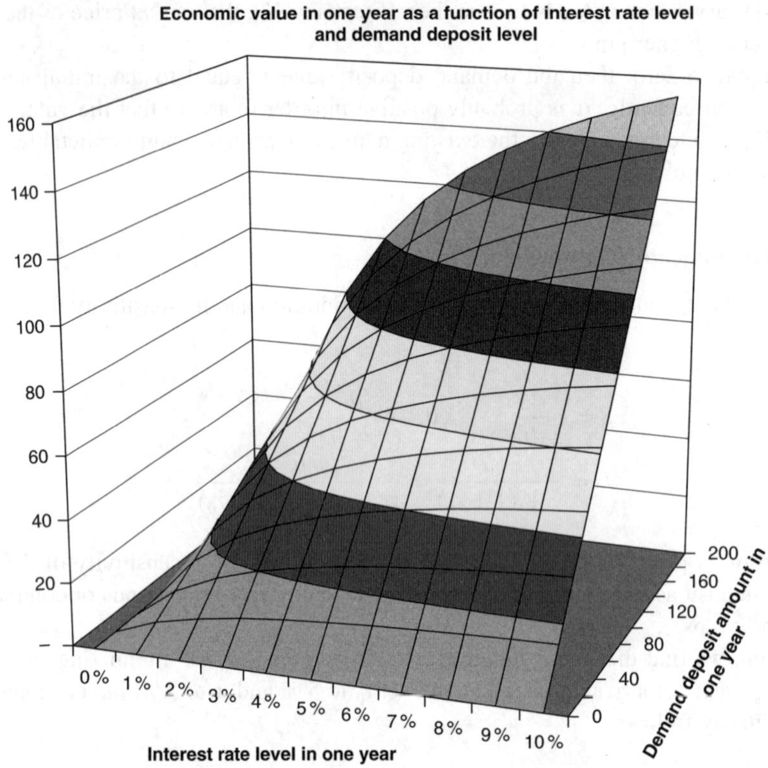

Figure 31.1 Grid

31.1.6 Risk premiums and expected return

In this problem, there are two risk premiums in the real probability:

- *A risk premium on the business risk*: this risk premium is equal to the difference between μ_K and μ. It means that the risk neutral expected demand deposit amount in one year is lower than the real expected amount in one year.
- *A risk premium on the interest rate risk*: there is a risk premium to invest in long-term interest rate bonds rather in monetary markets.

Consequently, the average amount of the interest rates in one year and of the demand deposit amount in one year will be as follows:

$$r_1 = r_0.e^{\sigma.W_1 - \frac{\sigma^2}{2} - p}$$
$$K_1 = K_0.e^{\sigma_K.W_1^K - \frac{\sigma_K^2}{2} - \mu + p_K} \tag{31.11}$$

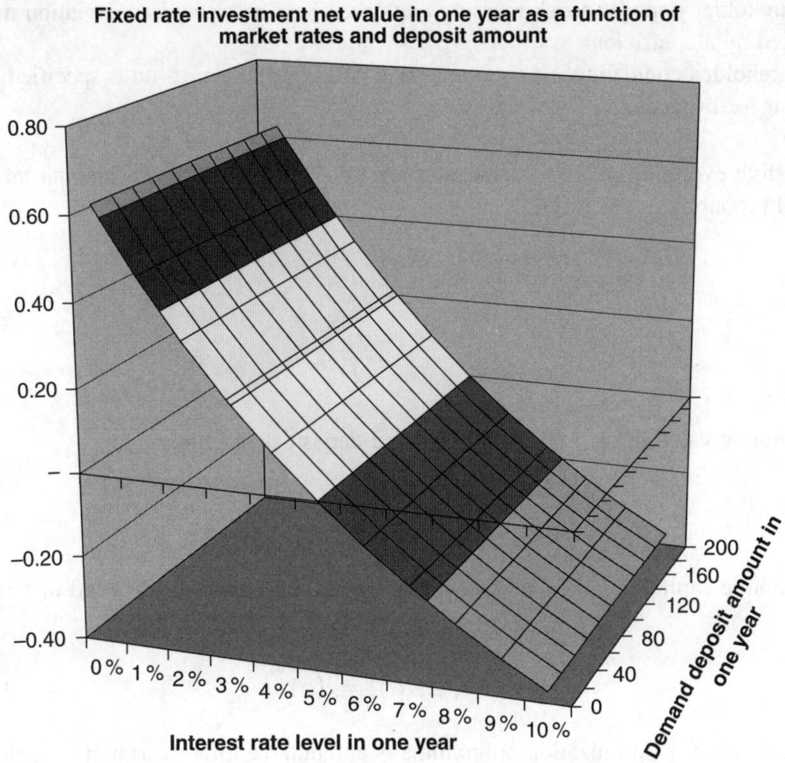

Figure 31.2 Interest rate versus demand deposit amount grid

Therefore, it is possible to compute the value in one year of the demand deposits using the classic valuation formula:

$$V_{1year} = K_1 \frac{r_1}{r_1 + \mu} \tag{31.12}$$

The expected value in one year of the demand deposit value is a function of the amount α invested in the fixed rate bonds:

$$\mathrm{E}\left(EV_{1year}(\alpha)\right) = f(\alpha) \tag{31.13}$$

31.1.7 Shareholder's constraints

In our example, the shareholder will impose some basic constraints:

- The diversifying investments should be made only on interest rate products.
- There could be a maximal investment or a minimal investment in these products: the management could impose the total fixed rate bonds in the portfolio not to overcome a certain amount.

- The shareholder imposes a risk measure expressed here as a standard deviation measure multiplied by a coefficient.
- The shareholder could impose a certain level of expected return on a specified period (one year for instance).

The possible evolution of the interest rates and of the demand deposit amount under the risk neutral probability is as follows:

$$r_1 = r_0.e^{\sigma.W_1 - \frac{\sigma^2}{2}} \qquad K_1 = K_0.e^{\sigma_K.W_1^K - \frac{\sigma_K^2}{2} - \mu + p_K} \tag{31.14}$$

The economic value in one year of the demand deposit then follows:

$$V_{1year} = K_1 \frac{r_1}{r_1 + \mu} \tag{31.15}$$

The economic capital is computable as a function of the amount α invested in fixed rate bonds:

$$\text{EC}\left(EV_{1year}(\alpha)\right) = g(\alpha) \tag{31.16}$$

The A/L manager's optimization programme is computable directly as a maximization of the expected return under an economic capital constraint:

$$\underset{\alpha}{\text{MAX}}\,(f(\alpha)) \text{ under constraints } \begin{cases} g(\alpha) \leq M \\ \alpha \geq N \end{cases} \tag{31.17}$$

This leads classically to an efficient frontier where the A/L manager finds a relationship between the expected return and the economic capital of Figure 31.3.

It is possible to express this efficient frontier as a Return on Economic Capital (ROEC) function of the economic capital such as in Figure 31.4.

We also reproduced in this chart the amount α invested corresponding to the optimal amount invested for a specific economic capital.

Consequently, given a specific return on economic capital target (given by the shareholder), the A/L manager is able to decide in which fixed rate long-term bonds he will invest.

In our example, the A/L manager has a ROEC target of 4.1 %. On the efficient frontier, it means that the economic capital to invest is 160; the optimal amount of fixed rate long-term bonds to invest in is 112.

31.1.8 Tactical versus strategic allocation

With the same example, it is possible to show the difference between a tactical and a strategic allocation.

We suppose now that our A/L manager has a "view" on the evolution of the interest rates. He will suppose, for instance, that the interest rates will decrease more than what the

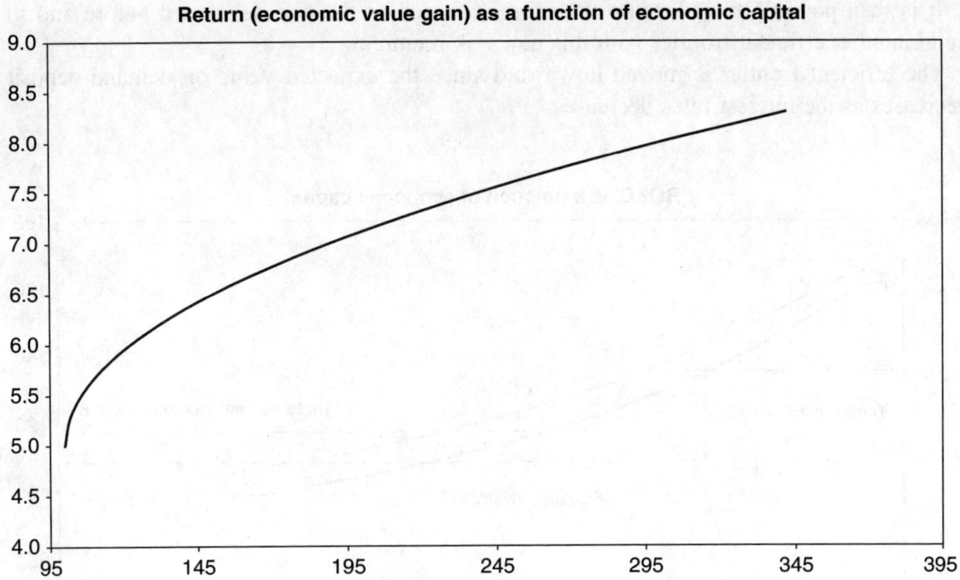

Figure 31.3 Return

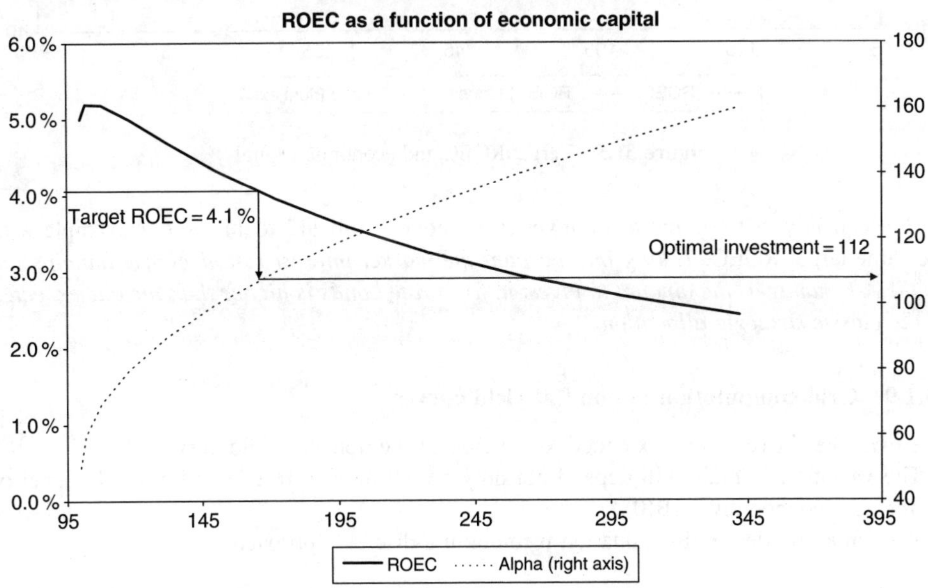

Figure 31.4 Return and target ROEC

market anticipates in the real world. It means that the A/L manager anticipates the interest rate premium in one year to be equal to p+ω rather than equal to p:

$$r_1 = r_0 . e^{\sigma . W_1 - \frac{\sigma^2}{2} - p - \omega} \tag{31.18}$$

It is then possible to redevelop the same approach as the one developed before and to build another efficient frontier with this new risk premium.

The efficient frontier is moved downward since the expected value on demand deposit decreases as the interest rates decreases.

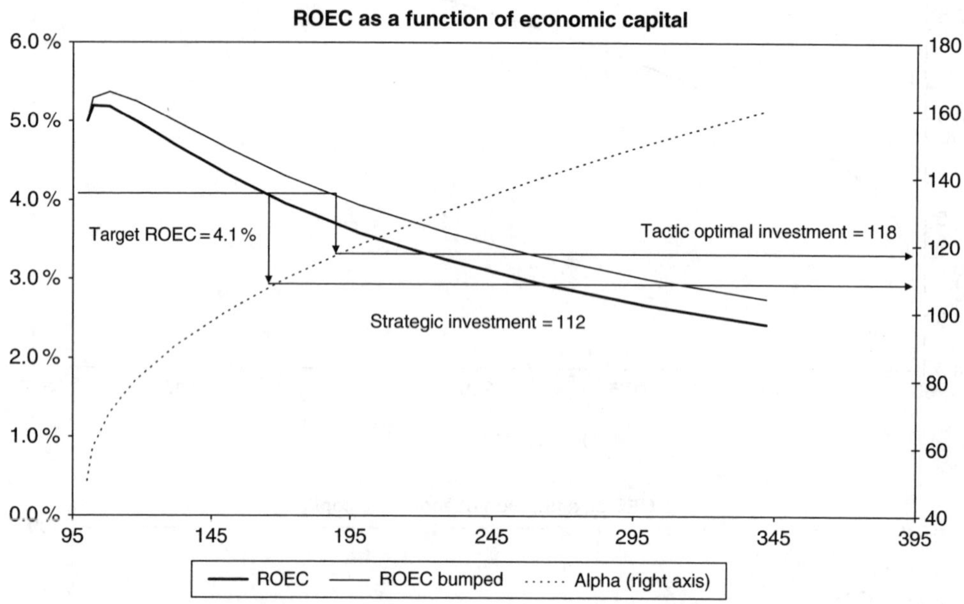

Figure 31.5 Target ROEC and economic capital

Consequently, the optimal tactic investment moves from 112 to 118 in our example with the same target ROEC. *Taking into account the market interest rate decrease anticipation by the A/L manager, the amount to invest in fixed rate bonds is higher than the one expected in the classic strategic allocation.*

31.1.9 Grid computation in non flat yield curves

The example above can be extended to the case of the non-flat yield curves.

The valuation formula will depend not only on the interest rate level but on the level of all the zero-coupon levels B(0,i).

We can easily derive the valuation formula in a discrete approach:

$$V = K_0.\mu.\sum_{i=1}^{+\infty}\left[\frac{(1-B(0,i))}{(1+\mu)^i}\right] \tag{31.19}$$

The sensitivities of the value to the pillars of the yield curve are obtained straightforwardly:

$$\frac{\partial V}{\partial B(0,i)} = -\frac{K_0.\mu}{(1+\mu)^i} \tag{31.20}$$

To hedge this sensibility, the A/L manager should invest in a set of zero-coupon bonds maturing for each date i with an amount of:

$$\frac{K_0.\mu}{(1+\mu)^i}.B(0,i) \tag{31.21}$$

The set of the possible future investments can be the set of zero-coupon bonds of maturity i when i varies from 1 to $+\infty$.

The problem is also easy to solve and leads to the following set of zero-coupons:

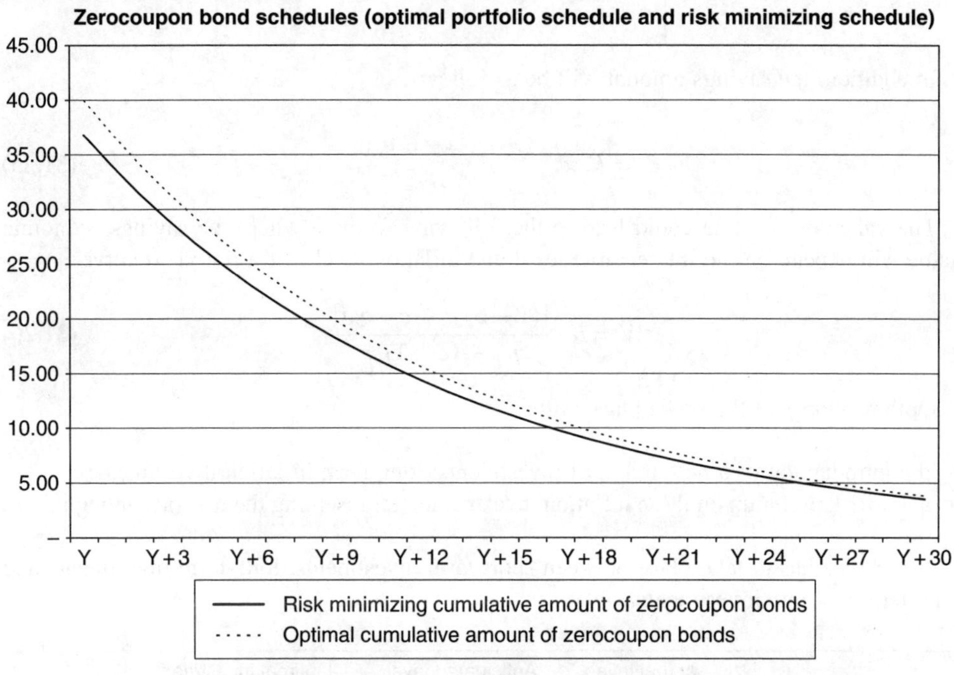

Figure 31.6 Zero coupon bond schedules

31.1.10 Other possible valuations for demand deposits and savings

In practice, the modelling has to be more precise than the one developed before. For instance, we made these various assumptions:

- W^1 and W^{RN} are independent but they could be correlated with a correlation ρ (also called volume effect).
- The demand deposit evolution could take into account a wealth effect where the trend depends on the market rates level with a coefficient δ linking the trend and the interest rate level. This coefficient could be equal to 1:

$$\frac{dK_t}{K_t} = (\mu_K + \delta.r_t).dt + \sigma_K.dW_K(t) \tag{31.22}$$

- The example could be extended to the savings account example where the remuneration rate is correlated with the market rates and the inflation i(t).

$$R_t = c + \beta.r_t + \gamma.i_t \tag{31.23}$$

In this case, the savings economic value will be of:

$$V = E_Q\left[\int_0^{+\infty} K(t).(r(t) - c - \beta.r_t - \gamma.i_t)\bar{B}(0,t)dt\right] \tag{31.24}$$

In addition, the savings amount will be as follows:

$$K_t = K_0.e^{\mu_K.t + \delta.\int_0^t r(s).ds + \sigma_K.W_K(t) - \frac{\sigma_K^2}{2}.t} \tag{31.25}$$

The valuation formula could lead to the following formula where the savings economic value will depend on the interest rate level and inflation level I of a flat yield curve:

$$V = K_0.\frac{[(1-\beta).r - c - \gamma.i]}{\mu_K + (\delta - 1).r} \tag{31.26}$$

Optimization will then take place with:

- the introduction of a new brand of investments: long-term inflation investments;
- a new risk premium on these inflation investments (representing the real rate anticipation).

The choice has to take place between short-term investments, long-term investments and long-term real rate investments.

	Actual level	Anticipated level in one year	Optimal investment
Short-term interest rate	3 %	2.5 %	20 % of savings amount
Long-term interest rate	4 %	3.5 %	40 % of savings amount invested in long-term fixed rate bonds
Long-term real rate	2 %	1.8 %	40 % of savings amount invested in long-term inflation bonds

Figure 31.7 Demand deposit optimal investment

31.2 APPLICATION TO STOCK MARKET BOOK

The optimal portfolio optimization program could very easily be applied to Stock Market Book management. Actually, the problem looks like a problem of portfolio selection mixed with a portfolio optimization problem.

The portfolio is made of equity stock market investments. The portfolio economic value and the portfolio economic capital consumption are not very hard to compute. The harder task is to propose a correlation matrix between each stock market equity possible evolution.

Nevertheless, in the economic capital computation, the A/L manager has to take into account the potential LECG (Latent economic capital gains or losses) that are inherent in such an activity.

The economic capital consumed is a constraint and is also the target ROEC.

The A/L manager has to take into account the risk premiums:

- on the global stock markets (a different risk premium by country);
- on each possible stock investment.

The tactical allocation will be made through the different risk premiums anticipated by the A/L manager.

For instance, the optimization/portfolio selection leads to the following sum of investments:

	Strategic allocation	Tactical allocation
U.S. Market	100.0	105.0
U.S. Company 1	10.0	12.0
...	...	...
U.S. Company N	5.0	5.0
€ Market	50.0	45.0
€ Company 1	10.0	–
...	...	...
€ Company N	2.0	2.0
Emerging markets	50.0	45.0
Company 1	10.0	10.0
...	...	...
Company N	2.0	1.0
Total	200.0	195.0

Figure 31.8 Stock market optimal investment

31.3 APPLICATION TO CREDIT RISK BOOK

The same approach can be applied to the Credit Risk Book optimization. Indeed, credit risk hedging can be done through:

- securitization programmes;
- CDS swaps for large corporate exposures.

The portfolio is made up of credit risk exposures (either large corporate risk exposures or aggregated credit risk exposures in credit risk pools). The portfolio economic value and the portfolio economic capital consumption are a bit harder to compute but the task is easier with Basel II.

The economic capital consumed is still a constraint and is also the target ROEC.

The A/L manager has to take into account risk premiums for its strategic and tactical allocation:

- on the systemic risk;
- on each specific risk.

For instance, the optimization/portfolio selection leads to the following sum of target credit risk exposures:

	Strategic allocation	Tactical allocation
Large corporate	100.0	105.0
Company 1	10.0	12.0
...	...	...
Company N	5.0	5.0
Sovereign Market	50.0	45.0
U.S.	10.0	–
...	...	...
Italy	2.0	2.0
Pools	50.0	45.0
Mortgage rating 1	10.0	10.0
...	...	...
Consumer loans N	2.0	1.0
Total	200.0	195.0

Figure 31.9 Credit risk optimal investment

31.4 PREPAYMENT RISK OPTIMAL HEDGING STRATEGIES

The optimization programme can be used also for the management of embedded option portfolios such as prepayment risk portfolios.

Delta hedging (including gamma, vega and penta hedging) will give the minimizing neutral risk strategy. This hedging leads to the introduction in the balance sheet of:

- interest rate swap positions to hedge the delta risk;
- purchase of swaptions (payer and receiver swaptions) to hedge the vega risk;
- complementary options (if the residual risk is too high).

The model risk is very important when applying such a hedging strategy definition since this risk depends on:

- customer behaviour;
- commercial relationship management with the customer;
- regulations (tax regulation, legal regulation, etc.).

The A/L manager needs a tool for computing the portfolio economic value and its economic capital consumption.

The A/L manager has to take into account risk premiums for its strategic and tactical allocation:

- on the interest rate level risk;
- on the volatility risk.

The optimization/portfolio selection will leads to the following sum of interest rate risk products:

	Strategic allocation	Tactical allocation
Swaps	100.0	105.0
Swap 1	10.0	12.0
...	...	...
Swap N	5.0	5.0
Swaptions	50.0	45.0
Swaption 1	10.0	–
...	...	...
Swaption N	2.0	2.0

Figure 31.10 Optional optimal investment

31.5 APPLICATION TO A GLOBAL BANKING BOOK INCLUDING BUSINESS AND MODEL RISK

On the global Banking Book level, a general optimization can take place. The optimization will take into account all the different possible investments:

- credit risk investment;
- interest rate investment;
- real rate investment;
- business risk investment;
- new incremental business risk including operational risk;
- model risk investment;
- equity investment;
- liquidity investment;
- real estate investment.

The Capital manager will use the economic capital as a risk measure. For each investment, he will ask the concerned front office A/L managers and the concerned business lines managers for their expected risk premium on those investments.

As for business risk, the Commercial Department will compute:

- the economic value of the existing clients (or the existing contracts) and its sensitivity to business risk factors/model risk factors;
- the expected economic value profit in one year on the new contracts (net of operating costs, investment costs, etc.) and the business/model risk associated with it.

	Actual level	Anticipated level in one year	Responsible manager	Risk premium with a 3 % risk free market rate
Equity Market (for a 100 economic capital consumption)	146	151	Equity manager	3 %
Real estate market (for a 100 economic capital consumption)	243	252	Real estate manager	7 %
...	...	...	...	...

Figure 31.11 Banking Book optimal investment

	Actual economic value level	Anticipated economic value level in one year	Responsible manager	Risk premium with a 3 % risk free market rate
Business linked with existing clients (for a 100 economic capital consumption)	1 000	1 010	Commercial manager	10 %
Business linked with future clients (for a 100 economic capital consumption)	0	20	Commercial manager	20 %
...	...	...	...	...

Figure 31.12 Banking Book optimal investments

The commercial managers have to be able to compute the actual economic value (on the existing clients) and the expected economic value in one year (on the base of the existing clients and of the new clients of the forthcoming year). This economic value in one year will depend on the economic capital consumption. In addition, the economic capital consumption will depend on the taken commercial risk.

The capital manager optimization will lead to an economic capital allocation on the following different investments with a target ROEC:

Possible investments economic capital allocation	
Old business risk	300
New business risk	1 000
Model risk	1 000
Interest rate risk	100
Real rate risk	200
Equity risk	200
Liquidity risk	50
Credit risk	1 000
Real estate risk	200
Total	**4 050**

Figure 31.13 Capital allocation

Of course, the optimization will take into account the shareholder constraints on the investment: the shareholder will impose obviously an implicit constraint on the minimal investment in business and model risk.

31.6 DIRECT DEMAND DEPOSIT INCOME SMOOTHING THROUGH A SIMPLE EXAMPLE

We consider the optimal strategy developed in Adam (2004) for demand deposit.

We suppose that the evolution of the amount of deposits follows this random step:

$$\frac{dK_t}{K_t} = \mu_K.dt + \sigma_K.dW_K(t) \tag{31.27}$$

We look after the optimal strategy made of a suite of swaplets (or FRA, i.e. Forward Rate Agreement) exchanging a fixed rate against a Libor Rate on the period going from T to T+1.

The rate L(t, T) of this swaplet at date t follows a drifted Brownian motion:

$$\frac{dL(t,T)}{L(t,T)} = \mu_L.dt + \sigma_L.dW_L(t) \tag{31.28}$$

We call V(t) the amount of swaplets contracted at date t.

There is an additional investment K(T) at date T in the Libor Money Market rate L(T,T).

If we call DAYS(T,T+1) the number of days between T and T+1, Adam and al. prove that with theses assumptions the incomes of the period going from T to T+1 can be written as:

$$INC(T) = \frac{DAYS(T,T+1)}{365}.\left(L(T,T).K(T) - \int_0^T V(t).dL(t,T)\right) \tag{31.29}$$

Thus, the goal of the manager is then to maximize a utility function or to minimize a risk measure based on INC(T) the earnings at date T.

Common risk measures used in Quantitative Finance are the standard deviation, the Value-at-Risk or coherent risk measures such as Expected Shortfall.

31.6.1 Using variance as a risk measure without risk premiums

For example, with the standard deviation as risk measure, the problem can be written as:

$$\underset{V()}{Min}\left[Variance\left(L(T,T).K(T) - \int_0^T V(t).dL(t,T)\right)\right] \tag{31.30}$$

We start the optimization supposing that the drift μ_l is equal to zero. It means for the A/L manager that there is no risk premium.

Using stochastic calculations, with standard deviation as risk measure the optimal solution for V is:

$$V(t) = K(t).\left(1+\rho.\frac{\sigma_K}{\sigma_L}\right).\exp\left((\mu_K + \rho.\sigma_K.\sigma_L).(T-t)\right) \tag{31.31}$$

When ρ is equal to zero, there is no correlation between the two Brownian motions. The variable μ_k will be negative and will represent the liquidity schedule decrease of the demand deposits. The optimal strategy (when risk premiums do not exist) is then equal to the liquidity schedule:

$$V(t) = K(t).\exp(\mu_K.(T - t)) \tag{31.32}$$

31.6.2 Using variance as risk measure with risk premiums

When μ_l is negative, this parameter represents a drift on the interest rates. The market over-evaluates the future level of the interest rates.

$$V(t) = K(t).\exp((\mu_K - \mu_L).(T - t)) \tag{31.33}$$

Taking into account risk premium in the optimization leads to a strategy longer than the liquidity schedule.

31.6.3 Using value-at-risk as risk measure

Adam, Laurent and Rebérioux computed the optimal hedge using a 95 % Value-at-Risk (VaR) as risk measure:

$$X = \text{VaR } 95\,\% \leftrightarrow \text{Probability } (\text{INC(T)} > X) = 95\,\% \tag{31.34}$$

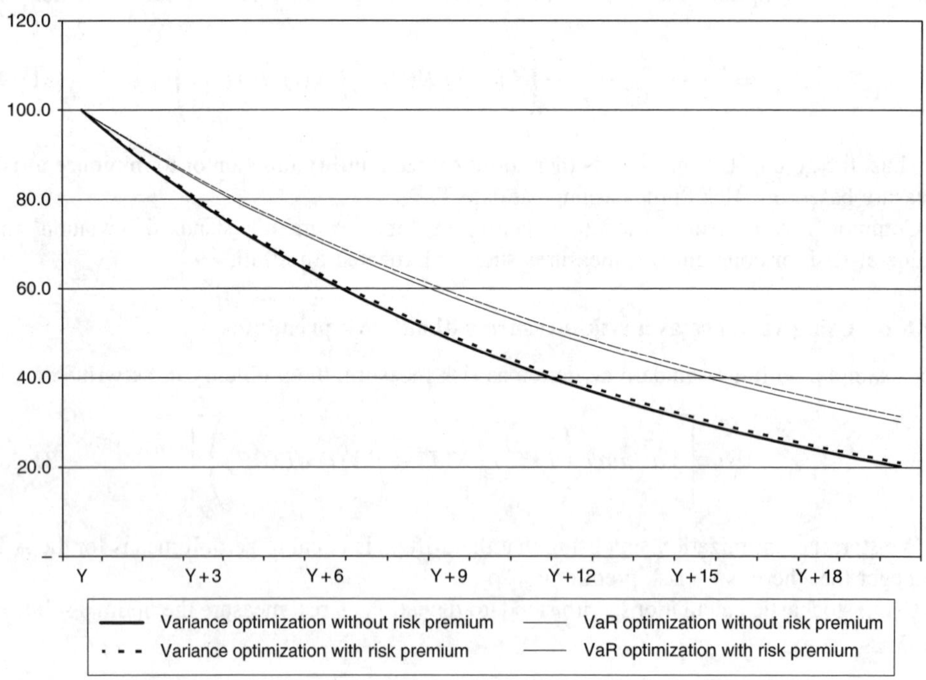

Figure 31.14 Optimal strategy

The optimal hedge was computed on a family of functions V described as:

$$V_{\alpha,\beta}(t) = \beta.K(t).\exp((\alpha + \mu_K - \mu_L).(T - t)) \tag{31.35}$$

Note that $V_{0,1}$ is the optimal hedging using Standard deviation as risk measure when ρ and μ_k are equal to zero.

The optimal α obtained by simulation is equal to $-2\,\%$ but the optimal β is still equal to 1.

This approach provides a general framework in order to compute the optimal strategy to hedge the interest rate risk on demand deposits. The real optimal hedge will be more difficult to compute and should take into account at least:

- servicing costs (usually associated with demand deposits accounts);
- compensation effects between different type of demand deposits;
- the opportunity to hedge the volatility risk with caplets and floorlets;
- accounting considerations of the hedging.

32 Economic Value Management in Insurance Companies and in Capital Book Management

C'est l'imagination qui gouverne les hommes. (Napoléon 1er)

32.1 ECONOMIC VALUE MANAGEMENT IN INSURANCE COMPANIES

The Insurance Book is manageable as a Banking Book. The optimization will take also into account all the different possible investments:

- credit risk investment;
- interest rate investment;
- real rate investment;
- business risk investment;
- new incremental business risk including operational risk;
- model risk investment;
- equity investment;
- liquidity investment;
- real estate investment.

The Capital manager will use the economic capital as a risk measure. For each investment, he will ask the concerned front office A/L managers and the concerned business lines managers for their expected risk premium on those investments.

The margin solvency of the Solvency II regulation provides an economic measurement of risk.

The specificity of the Insurance Book is given by the computation of a full fair value of the non unit-based insurance contracts.

The full fair value of insurance contracts is sensible to the level of the business factor and to the level of the financial markets. This full fair value represents the economic value of the existing clients, since the variations of this economic value are possibly correlated with the variations of the financial markets. For example, the results on the non-unit base life insurance contracts are computed as the multiplication of the liquidity amount of contracts by the net interest margin:

$$\text{RES}_t = K(t).(\mathit{Max}\,(10 \text{ years average rate smoothed on 10 years - } \text{m}_1, \\ 10 \text{ years spot rate - } \text{m}_2) - DD_t)$$

The expected economic value in one year is given by the variation of this economic value. The economic capital consumption will depend on the taken commercial risk. The capital manager optimization will lead to an economic capital allocation on the following different investments with a target ROEC:

Possible investments economic capital allocation	
Old insurance business risk	100
New insurance business risk	300
Model risk	200
Interest rate risk	100
Real rate risk	30
Equity risk	200
Liquidity risk	50
Credit risk	30
Real estate risk	200
Total	**1 210**

Figure 32.1 Optimal insurance portfolio

The optimization will take into account the shareholder constraints on the investment: the shareholder will impose obviously an implicit constraint on the minimal investment in business and model risk.

32.2 APPLICATION TO ECONOMIC CAPITAL BOOK MANAGEMENT

When the A/L manager wants to optimize the economic value of his Capital Book, he needs a precise modelling of the sensitivity of the components of this book. These components are present in the provisions of the FTP rules for equity investments.

The Capital Book is optimized as soon as the full fair value and its sensitivities are computed. These sensitivities take into account the *moral contract* that links the shareholder and the executive management. This contract is at the heart of the FTP rules on the Capital Book. This moral contract is an *implicit swap between the shareholder and the company*: the shareholder asks the bank to produce incomes indexed to the average of the long-term rates (instead of indexed to the level of the DD rate).

The economic value of the equity itself will of course not depend on the interest rate level, since the equity is simply an amount of cash.

However, close to this amount of cash, there are also operating costs and fixed margins sensible to the interest rate level. Their sensitivity corresponds to the activity profile of the company, i.e. the horizon of development of the company. Choosing a long term FTP, the A/L manager supposes implicitly that the activity has a long-term horizon. Let us recall that the choice of a long-term FTP rule leads to an income smoothing of the incomes.

The problem with Capital Book management is then similar to every kind of book management. *The FTP rules provide the benchmark for the A/L manager in this book.* The economic capital is the risk measure and the target ROEC indicates the optimal portfolio composition.

Note however that from a debtholder's point of view, in the case of a default of the company, this implicit swap disappears. The economic capital computation has to take into account the fact that the shareholder has an option on his moral contract with the executive management.

The optimization of the Capital Book will lead to an effective placement of the net equity longer than the FTP rule (as soon the risk premiums in the long-term interest rate investments are positive). The optimization leads to a portfolio invested mainly in fixed rate assets.

[illegible]

Part VIII
Conclusions on the ALM of Tomorrow

33 Conclusions on the Future of ALM

Il faut attendre à cueillir la poire qu'elle soit mure.

Of course, many ALM teams do not apply at this time all the recommendations presented in this book. Indeed, this book gives a large panel of the future developments in the ALM field.

33.1 ALM DIVERSITY

This book provides the occasion to present the diversity of ALM activity: the diversity of the products sold to the customers, the diversity of the possible ALM organizations and the diversity of the different ALM risk profiles. Nowadays, with the new regulatory environment and under the international IFRS rules, the diversity of the ALM activity has tended to diminish.

33.1.1 Product diversity

The diversity of the products the A/L managers deal with explains the diversity of ALM practices.

On the asset side, it is clear that the class of assets the A/L manager can invest in may differ from one country to the other. In the banking sector, the types of commercialized loans differ also:

- Some customers prefer fixed rate mortgages with fixed repayments (in France, Belgium) while others prefer floating rates mortgages (in the UK, Spain).
- Some banks propose floating rate mortgages with fixed repayments. Therefore, the maturity of the loan depends on the interest rate evolution: if the interest rates decrease, the loan maturity decreases.

Moreover, the prepayment option differs from one country to the other:

- In the US, there is no penalty when a customer prepays his mortgage.
- In France, the penalty cannot exceed 3 % of the prepaid amount.
- In Germany, there is no penalty after the first ten years of the credit. During the first ten years, the customer can prepay but with an actuarial penalty.
- In the Netherlands, the customer fixes the loan rate for a given period. During this period, the customer cannot prepay without paying an actuarial penalty. At the end of the period, the customer can fix another rate for another period.

The legislation also has an impact on the mortgage loan offer. In many countries, the customer has the right to change his mind and finally to refuse (for one month, for example) the loan offer he signed. Moreover, in the Netherlands, the bank has the obligation to decrease the mortgage loan rate when interest rates decrease between the loan signature date and the loan disbursement date.

For liabilities, it is the same. For example, in the banking sector, the types of deposit account vary a lot from one country to the other:

- The type of account may be different: current accounts, savings, deposit accounts, etc.
- The remuneration rate is different, either equal to 0 %, or fixed but low, or indexed to the floating interest rates, or indexed to the inflation rate.
- The remuneration rate can be decided by the bank with or without an explicit link with the Interbank market rates.
- The options linked with the account will also differ: in France, cheques are free, while in many other countries customers prefer to pay using the Internet or with a direct fund transfer since cheques are not free.

33.1.2 Geographic diversity

The diversity of ALM practices comes from regional specificities:

- legal differences;
- tax issues;
- regulation differences, etc.

In the emerging markets, ALM teams spend more time on the liquidity risk than on the interest rate risk:

- The funding spread is more volatile than in the OECD countries.
- The risk coming from the new production is more important than the risk coming from the stock of operations.
- The interest rate hedge possibilities are reduced.

33.1.3 Organization diversity

To take into account this diversity, executive managers propose different ALM organizations; in practice, ALM teams are linked with:

- the Finance Department;
- the Risk Department;
- the Treasury Department;
- the board of directors or the Executive Committee.

The relationship between ALM and Risk Management departments varies from one company to the other. The "Four eyes" rules tend to impose management control and model risk control with a distinction between the ALM teams and the ALM control teams.

33.1.4 Strategy diversity

In connection with the diversity of the ALM organizations, the objectives of the ALM team may differ: some teams will work as profit centres while others will transfer the market risk to the market. The diversity of the organizations deals with the diversity of the risk indicators:

- economic value sensitivity;
- interest margin sensitivity to different interest rate shocks;
- earning-at-Risk, Value-at-Risk;
- interest rate gaps, etc.

There is no real convergence on the choice of the perfect indicator. This goes along with the technical competences of the A/L managers. The large international banks develop these competences when in the small local banks the A/L managers tend to be naturally more conservative when dealing with the newest indicators.

It is less and less common for companies to choose a decentralized ALM organization instead of a centralized ALM organization. With the regulatory constraints, it is now necessary to build centralized reporting. Nevertheless, a local knowledge of the customers is necessary and there is also a need for local ALM teams.

Each choice of risk indicator is connected with a choice of an ALM strategy: some ALM teams transfer all the market risks into the market when the others act as risk taking profit centres.

There is also a link between the choice of strategy and local hedge opportunities. For instance, in the US, with the importance of the MBS market, investments are concentrated on those assets where the prepayment risk is essential.

The strategy is linked with the information system. The introduction of a FTP system takes time; and without FTP, the effectiveness of a strategy is hard to measure.

In terms of IAS 32 publications, banks tend to present different types of interest rate risk indicators. Some banks do not apply the IAS 32 rules yet. Some banks mix market risk and ALM risk in their economic capital reporting. At this time, the interest rate risk represents between 1 % and 40 % of the banks' economic capital risk consumption. Consequently, the financial analysts are a bit lost when they try to understand company risk exposures.

33.1.5 ALM practices convergence

Nevertheless, in the future all of these differences will disappear. The Basel II regulatory rules and the IFRS accounting rules (with IAS 32) will accelerate this convergence.

Even if in some countries the Basel II regulation will be effective only in the next decade, the convergence is predictable. (In the United States, the Basel II regulation will be applied only after 2010.)

Moreover, the globalization of the economy makes the banks larger with multinational positions. European and American A/L managers meet one with the other; they meet also emerging markets A/L managers and help them put into place adequate ALM solutions.

The convergence of ALM practices is on its way.

33.2 ALM BENCHMARKING

It is hard nowadays to benchmark an ALM team with another ALM team from a concurrent company. The task is not easy and sometimes quite impossible from a qualitative point of view. From a quantitative point of view, the only way to compare the two teams would be to compare the different ROEC of the two ALM teams (not only the last ROEC but more the track record of the past ROEC). Unfortunately, this information is rarely public.

To perform this benchmarking, it is necessary to look at competitors' reports (annual or periodic reports such as SEC reports), at their observed financial communication changes and at their communications in ALM seminars, conferences in ALM workgroups. Benchmarking is therefore a limited task, limited by the quality and by the quantity of the information. To understand the quality of an ALM team, we should understand the nature of the bank's customers, its economic and competitive environment. This kind of analysis is by nature erroneous since the information is of poor quality.

Nevertheless, with the available information, the first task of the benchmarking team is to backtest the competitors' performance once one has constituted a *"peer group"* of these competitors.

The second benchmarking task is to reveal competitors' best practices in terms of hedging strategies, choices of indicator and ALM organization. The benchmarking will also focus on the ALM function organization (position, link with other departments, control process). The objective is to introduce, as soon as possible, these best practices into the management of the company.

33.3 CONCLUSIONS ON ALM AND MODELS

In this chapter, we will try to summarize all the answers (and all the questions) raised by this book.

33.3.1 Classic criticism of ALM

33.3.1.1 In terms of interest rate risk measurement

In this book, we tried to demonstrate how classic ALM measures have to be replaced by more economic risk measures.

For instance, the chart in Figure 33.1 represents the current evolution of the interest rate risk measurement.

The table in Figure 33.2 explains why the classic interest rate gap and income sensitivities have to be completed nowadays by economic value based indicators.

The "Hawks martingale" explains how the income sensitivity (once the income smoothing strategies have been taken into account in the computation) is not such a good risk measure.

33.3.1.2 In terms of interest rate risk strategies

The classic ALM strategies are based on the classic martingales techniques:

- taking volatility risk;
- lending long-term and borrowing short-term.

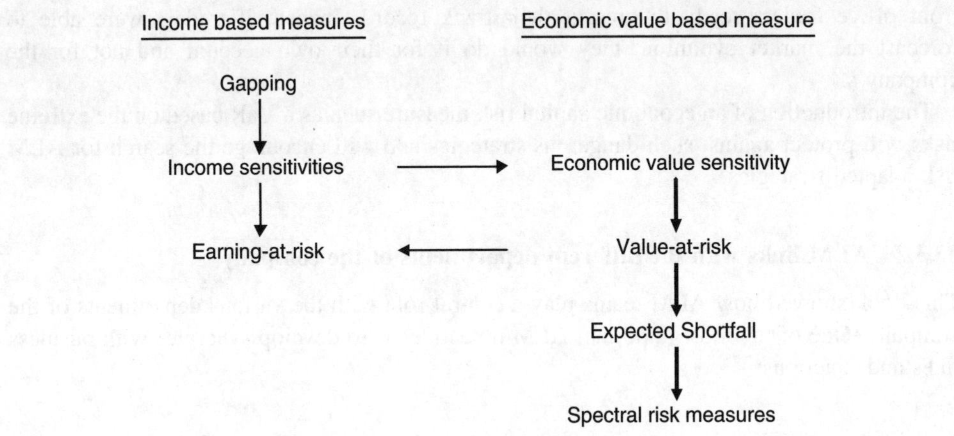

Figure 33.1 Risk measures

	Inconvenient	Advantages
Interest rate gaps	Does not take into account new productions	ALM income simulation with break-even point
Income sensitivities without income smoothing strategies on a set of 5 scenarios	Does not integrate income smoothing strategies	ALM and business lines income simulation
Income sensitivities with income smoothing strategies on a set of 5 scenarios	Shows no difference between the 5 scenarios Does not show risk real localization	Better income simulation
Income sensitivities with income smoothing strategies on a set of 1000 scenarios	Shows no more difference between the 1000 scenarios than between the previous 5 scenarios	Better comprehension of extreme accounting risk
Economic value sensitivity	Does not focus on the income	Better risk measurement once all the risks have been taken into account
Economic capital (Value-at-risk)	Does not focus on the income	Better extreme risk measurement
Earnings-at-risk	Risk sources bad understanding	Focus on the income
Economic capital Future income expectation Interest rate gap with delta equivalent Income smoothing reserves indicator	To determine	Full risk representation: economic and accounting risk

Figure 33.2 Pros and Cons

The classic strategy is to think that interest rates “follow cycles”: the A/L manager waits for the interest rate rises to lend money.

The problem is then to ignore the existence of catastrophic scenarios. The risk is present in extreme scenarios when interest rates decrease or increase on long term periods.

Moreover, in these extreme scenarios, the classic managers tend to take more risk in their search for higher yield returns. The executive management should pay attention to front office traders ready to present their track record. Indeed, if traders were able to forecast the market evolution, they would do it for their own account and not for the company's.

The introduction of an economic capital risk measure such as a VaR based on the extreme risks will protect against such dangerous strategies and will encourage the search for ALM risk adapted strategies.

33.3.2 ALM links with the different departments of the company

This book showed how ALM teams play a central role with the various departments of the company. One of the most important ALM objectives is to develop synergies with business lines and functions:

- With business lines: the business line income is computed when deducing the ALM income from the company income. Perequations are a classic ALM/business line discussion. ALM plays a central role in product pricing and in business development.
- With system teams since ALM plays a large role in the system management: FTPs impact accounting systems, ALM provokes a need for the front office systems, the simulation and the computation systems.
- With accounting teams since hedging strategies implicate IFRS hedging justifications and since ALM income may represent a large part of the company income through FTPs.
- With all the teams working within financial risks: ALM insurance teams, ALM banking teams, fixed income teams, etc. For example, insurance interest rate risk has to be consolidated with other sources of interest rate risks.
- With fiscal teams for the fiscal income optimization.
- With budget and management control teams.
- With economic research teams (their role is to help the ALM Teams to build their investment decisions).

ALM teams should also develop synergies with asset management teams since company portfolio optimization is close to customer portfolio optimization.

However, in banks, the most predictable evolution will see the transformation of credit risk management teams so that they will more look like ALM teams than is the case now with:

- portfolio management teams comparable with front office investment teams;
- credit risk simulation teams;
- credit modelling teams controlled by risk management teams;
- introduction of credit risk in FTPs.

33.3.3 ALM and accounting

A/L managers will now pay more and more attention to accounting standards since hedging justifications may limit investment strategies and since accounting standard knowledge limits accounting risk.

It is essential before proposing a hedging strategy to verify how this strategy can be integrated in the risk indicators and in the balance sheet as a hedging strategy.

IFRS standards affect ALM strategies. With the introduction of IFRS, many banks stopped their optional risk hedging; for instance, some of them were not able to justify under the IFRS their Bermudan swaptions contracted in front of their prepayment risk.

Moreover, the introduction of IFRS modified accounted incomes and then the valuation of the company. For example, this introduction created more volatility in the income presentation of some companies (Fannie Mae for instance).

Consequently, it is not clear whether IFRS does not lead to a lower level of transparency.

Maybe, ALM will be impacted more by the accounting standards if in the future full fair value concepts are applied to every line of the balance sheet. With IFRS phase 2, insurance companies will account for their liabilities at their fair value.

For the banking sector, full fair value is not applied to demand deposits neither to loans. The introduction of full fair value is ineluctable but the horizon is not clear.

A/L managers should not to be afraid of full fair value since this will not increase the income volatility neither the risk. Nevertheless, the introduction of full fair value will revolutionize the organization (with more developed information systems) and the need for a more precise modelling (including perequations, fees modelling, etc.).

33.3.4 ALM and model risk

Finally, the book asks the question of the place of model risk in ALM.

When looking after the example of the parameters presented for demand deposit modelling, it is not clear whether the most important risk is the model risk or not. Indeed, model risk and business risk will play a greater role in risk management and consequently in business management.

33.3.5 Practical conclusions

Asset and liability management is the basis for financial risk management and takes its name by reference to the two sides of the balance sheet.

ALM teams are present in the banking sector and in the insurance sector. The creation of ALM teams in the financial directions of non-financial companies takes time but is clearly in progress.

The objective is to ensure the equilibrium between the different financial resources and the different investments limiting liquidity or solvency risk under a return optimization objective. ALM teams have now a set of responsibilities usually followed by the ALCO (the ALM committee):

- the responsibility of short-term and long-term treasury activities (liquidity risk management);
- the responsibility of the management of the other ALM risks: interest rate risk, optional risks, exchange rate risk, etc.;
- the obligation to comply with local regulations and with statutory obligations;
- the responsibility of the optimization of the risk versus return profile (including capital management).

A performing ALM starts now with a precise modelling performed by a specific modelling team:

- modelling of the perequation;
- modelling of customer behaviour;
- modelling of the new production with the hypothesis of independence of the new production economic value upon market conditions across time.

The modelling allows for balance sheet dissociation in different books by type of risk:

- commercial Book for the business risk;
- model Risk book;
- ALM books such as liquidity book, interest rate risk book, etc.

ALM income is made possible through the introduction of FTPs between business lines and ALM. The FTPs are linked with the modelling so that there is no transfer value from the Commercial books to the ALM books. Finally, this leads to the general ALM rule:

$$1 \text{ book} = 1 \text{ risk} = 1 \text{ income}$$

ALM then becomes a *profit centre* and has to be managed as a profit centre.

Moreover, the *delta equivalent techniques* allows for the *perfect transfer of the risk*, if this risk is replicated exactly in the market, *the income grows at the speed of the economy modified only by the business risk not by the financial markets*. The delta equivalent technique is *the basis for the FTP transfer* between ALM and the business lines.

This reconciles the economic value approach with the income approach. This allows the computation of a risk measure based on the economic value such as economic capital. *Economic capital is the main risk measure for the risk computation and for the risk allocation.* This measure is consistent with other indicators (such as gaps) as soon as this indicator is computed adequately when simulating the discounted cash flows under a risk neutral probability.

Economic capital is also associated with a set of "Adam equivalents": penta equivalent, courba equivalent, etc.

Nevertheless, there is still a place for complementary risk measures such as *stress tests*.

The Capital manager will allocate economic capital and the ALM teams will optimize their portfolio:

- under this economic capital risk constraint;
- with income smoothing strategies;
- under IFRS accounting;
- under regulatory constraints;
- with a benchmark allocation given by the shareholder;
- with the risk premiums anticipated by the market and by the managers.

ALM teams will integrate *income smoothing strategies* and the existence of a *target ROEC* in order to define their optimal ALM strategies.

The risk management and the value management of ALM portfolios leads to a specific organization of ALM teams in connection with the *ALCO* (the ALM committee):

- front office teams;
- middle and back office teams;
- model team;
- simulation team.

This organization will integrate *numerous controls* in order to ensure a low level of operational or model risk.

Nevertheless, this book leaves some *open questions for the future of ALM*:

- **Can ALM be piloted automatically?** With management based more and more on economic value, an automatic risk transfer to markets could be planned. The ALM head's task would be then to optimize the ALM system's costs and to minimize the ALM model risks when transferring all of the risk position to a set of asset managers under a target ROEC and under risk constraints.
- **Will large non-financial corporate companies develop their ALM teams?**
- **Will ALM teams find enough human resources to satisfy their ongoing development?** The training of A/L managers takes time, from one to two years. This training is done in ALM teams since few universities offer training courses in this field.

Part IX
Annexes

34

Statistical Advanced Tools

Qui veut voyager loin ménage sa monture. (Racine)

34.1 EXTREME POINTS

The "80/20 rule" was invented by Vilfredo Pareto by the end of the 19th century. As an economist and as a landowner, he discovered that 80 % of the land belonged to 20 % of the population. Moreover, he found that 80 % of pea production came from 20 % of his plantation.

He decided then to apply this "rule" to economy: *extreme movements explain 80 % of the yields of the portfolios.*

During the crash of 1987, the Dow Jones index lost 22.6 % and every value of the index was affected. This shows that *in extreme market movements, the correlations between assets change radically.*

Managers introduced indicators to monitor this extreme correlation moves such as the *"Spearman rhô"* or the rank statistical correlation. This is indeed the linear correlation between the random variables X and Y considering their statistical laws F:

$$\rho_{SPEARMAN} = \frac{Cov(F_X(X), F_Y(Y))}{\sqrt{Var(F_X(X)).Var(F_Y(Y))}}$$

This correlation can easily be computed and it takes only into account the dependence structure between the two variables.

34.2 COPULAS

Copulas are used more and more often in modern ALM modelling.

We call $X_1 \ldots X_n$ a set of n random variables with a joint law $F(x_1 \ldots x_n)$ and with marginal laws $F_i(x)$. Then, we define the copula by the following formula:

$$F(x_1, \ldots, x_n) = C(F_1(x_1), \ldots, F_n(x_n))$$

Or equivalently:

$$C(u_1, \ldots, u_n) = F(F_1^{-1}(u_1), \ldots, F_n^{-1}(u_n))$$

When there are only two variables concerned, we define the density repartition for U and V by the form:

$$c(u, v) = \frac{\partial^2 C(u, v)}{\partial u . \partial v}$$

This gives the density repartition for X and Y:

$$f(x, y) = f_X(x) . f_Y(y) . \frac{\partial^2 C(F_X(x), F_Y(y))}{\partial u . \partial v}$$

Copulas properties:

Copulas will verify a certain number of equations:

$$C(u, 0) = C(0, v) = 0$$
$$C(u, 1) = u$$
$$C(1, v) = v$$

Moreover, the copulas are bounded by two functions:

$$\text{Max}(0, u + v - 1) \leq C(u, v) \leq \text{Min}(u, v)$$

If two variables U and V are independent, the associated copula with these two variables is:

$$C(u, v) = u.v$$

If two variables are perfectly correlated, the associated copula is equal to:

$$C(u, v) = \min(u, v).$$

Modelling with copulas:

The statistical modelling of the relationship between two variables may be proposed using copulas:

- either with a non-parametric modelling (using kernel smoothing, for instance); or
- with a parametric modelling.

Among the possible parametric copulas, we may cite the Archimedean copulas:

$$C(u, v) = \phi^{-1}(\phi(u) + \phi(v))$$

Such as the Gumbel copula:

$$\phi(u) = (-\ln(u))^{\theta} \text{ for } \phi > 1$$

Such as the Clayton copula:

$$\phi(u) = u^{-\theta} - 1 \text{ for } \theta > 0$$

The *Gaussian copula* is also a common copula used in finance and is defined through the Gaussian distribution function Φ with a correlation ρ between the variables X and Y.

$$C_\rho(u, v) = \Phi_{U,V,\rho}\left(\Phi^{-1}(u), \Phi^{-1}(v)\right)$$

$$c_\rho(u, v) = \frac{\phi_{U,V,\rho}\left(\Phi^{-1}(u), \Phi^{-1}(v)\right)}{\phi\left(\Phi^{-1}(u)\right).\phi\left(\Phi^{-1}(v)\right)}$$

$$\phi_{X,Y,\rho}(x, y) = \frac{1}{2\pi.\sqrt{1-\rho^2}}.\exp\left(-\frac{1}{2.(1-\rho^2)}.\left[x^2+y^2-2.\rho.x.y\right]\right)$$

35

The Basis of Interest Rate Modelling

Bonne semence fait bon grain.

This chapter will describe yield curve evolution modelling in order to propose a practical implementation.

First, A/L managers do not speak about the yield curve model but about **the modelS of the yield curveS**. There is not only one model and of course, there is not only one yield curve.

Interest rate models are developed in order to:

- price and hedge (and delta hedge);
- compute economic values and economic value sensitivities;
- simulate interest rates and diffuse interest rate trajectories.

35.1 YIELD CURVE RECONSTITUTION

In this section, we will reconstitute the initial zero-coupon yield curve, i.e. we will model the market information in order to get a zero-coupon yield curve. Interest rate models will try to simulate the evolution of this curve as time passes.

To begin with, let us recall that the zero-coupon rates TZC introduced in Section 19.3 allowing for the computation of a fixed rate bond price V as the sum of its discounted cash flows ϕ:

$$V(t) = \sum_{i=t+1}^{m} \frac{\varphi(i)}{[1 + TZC(t, i-t)]^{i-t}} = \sum_{i=t+1}^{m} \varphi(i)B(t,i)$$

There are indeed three major types of zero-coupon yield curves:

- The *government bond yield curve* or risk free yield curve built from the quotations of the government bonds (i.e. usually G7 countries not exposed to default).
- The *Interbank yield curve (or swap yield curve)* built from Interbank rates, prices of futures and swap rates.
- The *corporate yield curves*. There is a corporate yield curve for each corporate, for each sector and for each rating. For example, we may find a corporate yield curve for the Media sector with a BB rating or for a specific oil company on the Dow Jones index. These curves are built from concerned corporate bond quotations.

The last two yield curves are not risk free yield curves since banks and corporations are not rated AAA as government bonds.

35.1.1 Government bond yield curve reconstitution

The government bond yield curve is built from government bonds quotations.

The first stage is to select the appropriate set of fixed rate government bonds to build the curve. A poor selection could lead to aberrant yield curves. The selection will eliminate:

- bonds with optional clauses (call option, for instance);
- illiquid or over liquid bonds (their price is not in the market);
- bonds with price error.

It is important to select a continuum of bonds including many different maturities and bonds with long-term maturities.

After the bond selection, there are two methods of reconstituting the government yield curves:

- the theoretical method not used in practice (but this method will be used for the Interbank yield curve reconstruction).
- the bootstrap method.

35.1.1.1 Theoretical method

The theoretical method allows us to deduce zero-coupon rates from the coupon bond prices. This method requires the following two conditions:

- All the coupon bonds should have the same coupon dates.
- All the coupon bonds should have maturities equal to a multiple of the coupon frequency.

For instance, on 15.01.10 the A/L manager should recuperate the information table:

	Price	Coupon	Maturity	Next coupon date	Following coupon date	...
Bond 1	110.2	5.0 %	15.04.10	15.04.10	Ø	...
Bond 2	110.1	5.1 %	15.07.10	15.04.10	15.07.10	...
...	...	...	...	...	...	...
Bond N	109.5	5.5 %	15.01.41	15.04.10	15.07.10	...

Figure 35.1 Bond portfolio information table

It is understandable that in practice, the two conditions above are rarely observed. Nevertheless, if we note:

- The vector price at date t of the N bonds $P = (P_1, \ldots, P_i, \ldots, P_n)$ where P_j is the price of the ith bond.
- The N.N matrix of the bonds flows F at date i for the bond j $F(t)=(F(i,j))$ where $F_{i,j}$ is the cash flow (of interest and of capital) reimbursed at date j by the bond i.
- The N vector B of the discount factors $B = (B_1, \ldots, B_j, \ldots, B_n)$ where B_i is the discount factor between date 0 and date j.

By the usual "property of arbitrage opportunity" absence, it is possible to link the prices, the flows and the discount factors (prices are discounted sums of cash flows):

$$P = F \, . \, B$$

Then inverting the matrix F, it leads to the relation:

$$B = F^{-1} \, . \, P$$

35.1.1.2 Bootstrap method

The bootstrap method is the method used in practice. The methodology builds the reconstitution step-by-step, i.e. maturity segment by maturity segment.

First step: for the segment under 1 year. A set of zero-coupon rates is extracted directly from the prices of zero-coupon bonds quoted in the market. A continuous curve is obtained by linear or cubic interpolation between these points.

Second step: for the segment going from 1 year to 2 years. Among the set of bonds whose maturity is comprised between 1 and 2 years, the method makes us choose the bond with the smallest maturity. The discount factor associated with the first coupon of the bond is known through step 1. The discount factor of the second flow is known as the solution of the non linear equation that links the bond price P and the sum of the discounted cash flows (coupon C and reimbursement of capital of 100 at date t_2):

$$P = CB(0, t_1) + (100 + C)B(0, t_2)$$
$$\text{with } t_1 <= 1 \text{ and } 1 < t_2 \leq 2$$

This gives the first point of this curve segment. The process is reiterated for the next bond with a maturity inferior to 2 years.

The yield curve is then interpolated between 1 and 2 years using an interpolation method.

Third step (and the same for next steps): for the segment going from 2 years to 3 years. The A/L manager reiterates the second step procedure for bonds with maturities comprised between 2 and 3 years.

Finally, the chart 35.2 summarizes the methodology.

At each stage of the methodology, the A/L manager needs an interpolating method to obtain a smoothed and continuous yield curve.

35.1.1.3 Direct interpolation methods

There are two types of direct interpolations:

- *Linear interpolation*: with the zero-coupons TZC(t_1) and TZC(t_2) for maturities t_1 and t_2, the zero-coupon TZC(t) for a date t comprised between t_1 and t_2 is given linearly by:

$$TZC(t) = \frac{(t_2 - t)TZC(t_1) + (t - t_1)TZC(t_2)}{(t_2 - t_1)}$$

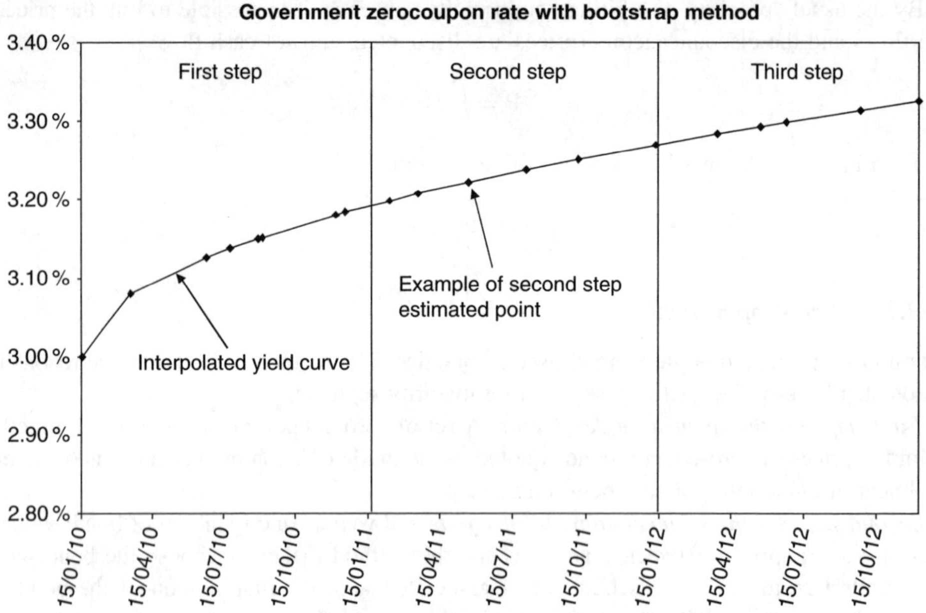

Figure 35.2 Bootstrap method

- *Cubic interpolation*: with $TZC(t_1)$, $TZC(t_2)$, $TZC(t_3)$ and $TZC(t_4)$, the zero-coupon interest rate TZC(t) is defined by a polynomial function of degree three (imposing the function to be consistent with the observed values of TZC(t) at dates t_1, t_2, t_3 and t_4):

$$TZC(0,t) = at^3 + bt^2 + ct + d$$

$$\text{with constraints} \begin{cases} TZC(0,t_1) = at_1^3 + bt_1^2 + ct_1 + d \\ TZC(0,t_2) = at_2^3 + bt_2^2 + ct_2 + d \\ TZC(0,t_3) = at_3^3 + bt_3^2 + ct_3 + d \\ TZC(0,t_4) = at_4^3 + bt_4^2 + ct_4 + d \end{cases}$$

35.1.1.4 *Indirect interpolation methods*

The indirect interpolation methods are more often used in practice. The principle is simple: the A/L manager will try to minimize for a set of coupon bonds the sum of the square spreads between the observed market prices and the theoretical reconstituted market prices once either a zero-coupon rates function has been specified or a discount factors function has been specified.

With the notation P_i for the market price of the ith bond, the objective is to optimize the following minimizing program where β is the set of parameters in the specified function:

$$\underset{\beta}{Min} \sum_{j=1}^{n} \left(P_j - \hat{P}_j(\beta)\right)^2$$

Let see now the different classes of possible models for these functions:

- Nelson-Siegel functions;
- Vasicek functions;
- and spline models.

35.1.1.4.1 Nelson Siegel indirect interpolation models

Nelson Siegel models (1987) are based on a modelling of the zero-coupon rates where the zero-coupon rate TZC(θ) of maturity θ follows:

$$TZC(\theta) = \beta_0 + \beta_1 \left[\frac{1-\exp(-\theta/\tau)}{\theta/\tau} \right] + \beta_2 \left[\frac{1-\exp(-\theta/\tau)}{\theta/\tau} - \exp(-\theta/\tau) \right]$$

The model introduces many parameters:

- β_0: the interest rate level factor since an increase of β_0 will increase all the zero-coupons.
- β_1: the interest rate rotation factor since an increase of β_1 will increase the long-term zero-coupons only.
- β_2: the interest rate convexity factor since an increase of β_2 will increase the medium term zero-coupons only.
- τ: the scale factor.

Nevertheless, in this modelling, the yield curve can only take certain types of forms and the obtained yield curve is not well adjusted for the long-term maturities.

Consequently, the "augmented Nelson-Siegel" or "Svensson model" will correct this model with a new parameter β_3 in order to influence the intermediate yield curve segments and with a new scale parameter τ_2:

$$\begin{aligned} TZC(\theta) = \beta_0 + \beta_1 \left[\frac{1-\exp(-\theta/\tau_1)}{\theta/\tau_1} \right] + \beta_2 \left[\frac{1-\exp(-\theta/\tau_1)}{\theta/\tau_1} - \exp(-\theta/\tau_1) \right] \\ + \beta_3 \left[\frac{1-\exp(-\theta/\tau_2)}{\theta/\tau_2} - \exp(-\theta/\tau_2) \right] \end{aligned}$$

35.1.1.4.2 Vasicek indirect interpolation models

With the same idea as Nelson-Siegel, there are other models to interpolate zero-coupon yield curves. For example, Vasicek (1977) proposed a new set of functions compatible with the one factor stochastic modelling:

$$TZC(\theta) = R_\infty - (R_\infty - r_0) \left[\frac{1-\exp(-\lambda.\theta)}{\lambda.\theta} \right] + \frac{\sigma^2}{\lambda^2} \left[\frac{(1-\exp(-\lambda.\theta))^2}{4.\lambda.\theta} \right]$$

This formula will be consistent with a Vasicek interest rate modelling:

$$dr_t = \lambda.(\theta - r_t).dt + \sigma.dW_t$$

As for Nelson-Siegel, there is also an augmented Vasicek model to take into account every kind of yield curve.

35.1.1.4.3 Spline models

Spline models are based on a modelling of the discount factor function. Either the discount factors are directly expressed as a function f of a set of parameters β or the discount factors are expressed as exponentials of a function g. We call P_j the price of the bond j paying a set of cash flows F_s^j at date s.

$$\hat{P^j} = \sum_s F_s^j B(0,s) = \sum_s F_s^j . e^{-s.g(s;\beta)}$$

$$\text{or } \hat{P^j} = \sum_s F_s^j B(0,s) = \sum_s F_s^j f(s;\beta)$$

There are constraints on the functions f and g since B is a decreasing function converging to 0 with B(0,0)=1.

The most famous splines are: *polynomial splines* (McCulloch, 1975) and *exponential splines* (Vasicek and Fong, 1982).

For instance, the polynomial spline will express the zero-coupon as polynomial functions on the different intervals called "splines".

$$B(0,s) = \begin{cases} B_0(s) = d_0 + c_0 s + b_0 s^2 + a_0 s^3, s \in [0,1] \\ B_1(s) = d_1 + c_1 s + b_1 s^2 + a_1 s^3, s \in [1,2] \\ \ldots \\ B_N(s) = d_N + c_N s + b_N s^2 + a_N s^3, s \in [20,30] \end{cases}$$

The A/L manager will impose this function to be continuous, twice derivable and twice continuously derivable.

This will impose the function B to have a special form:

$$B(0,s) = 1 + c_0 s + b_0 s^2 + (a_1 - a_0).(s-1)_+^3 + (a_2 - a_1).(s-2)_+^3 + \ldots$$

with the classic notion:

$$(s-\theta)_+^3 = [Max\,((s-\theta),0)]^3$$

For this reason, the zero-coupon discount factor is said to be projected on the *B-Spline base* constituted with those cubic positive functions.

In practice, the A/L managers will use from 5 to 8 splines:

- 0–1 year: very short-term;
- 1–2 years: short-term;
- 2–5 years: short-medium term;
- 5–10 years: medium-long-term;
- 10–20 years: long-term;
- 20–40 years: very long-term.

The number of splines will influence residual quality and yield curve smoothing; with more splines, residuals are less important but the yield curve is less smoothed.

The estimation of the parameters (c_0, $b_0 \ldots$) will be done when minimizing the sum of the square spreads between market prices and theoretical prices given by this discount factor function B.

$$\hat{P}^j(c_0, b_0, \ldots) = \sum_s F_s^j B(s; c_0, b_0, \ldots)$$

The minimizing programme is written directly as:

$$\underset{c_0, b_0, \ldots}{Min} \sum_{j=1}^{n} \left(P_j - \hat{P}^j(c_0, b_0, \ldots)\right)^2$$

Alternatively, if the manager supposes that the regression residuals are heteroskedastic (instead of homoskedastic), the regression will integrate weights w:

$$\underset{c_0, b_0, \ldots}{Min} \sum_{j=1}^{n} \left(\frac{P_j - \hat{P}^j(c_0, b_0, \ldots)}{w^j}\right)^2$$

Usually, the weights are chosen equal to the duration of the bond to better estimate the short-term part of the interest rate yield curve.

Statistically speaking, the heteroskedasticity just means that the longer is the term of a bond, the harder it is to determinate the price of the bond:

$$P_j - \hat{P}^j = \varepsilon_j$$
$$\varepsilon_j \text{ follows } N(0, \sigma^2.w_j^2)$$
$$Cov(\varepsilon_j, \varepsilon_k) = 0$$

To conclude on splines, these models will bring more flexibility on the zero-coupons but will also introduce too many non-interpretable parameters financially speaking.

35.1.2 Corporate yield curve reconstitution

Corporate yield curves will be used in liquidity risk and credit risk management.

Instead of speaking about corporate yields, managers prefer to speak about "spreads": the difference between corporate yields and government risk free yields. The idea is to build *the term structure of the zero-coupon spreads*. There are two methods of doing so:

- The disjoint method where the corporate yield curve is estimated independently using directly the prices of corporate bonds.
- *The joint method where the government bond yield curve and the corporate yield curve are estimated jointly.*

The joint method idea is to impose a spline on the spread so that the price of the corporate bonds will be broken down as follows:

$$\hat{P}^{j}_{corporate} = \sum_{s} F^{j}_{s}.e^{-s.g(s;\beta)-spread(s,\gamma)}$$

$$or\ \hat{P}^{j}_{corporate} = \sum_{s} F^{j}_{s} B(0,s) = \sum_{s} F^{j}_{s}\left(f(s;\beta) + Spread\,(s,\gamma)\right)$$

The objective of global spline estimation is then to minimize the sum of the square of the differences between market prices and model prices on a set of government bonds and corporate bonds.

35.1.3 Swap interbank yield curve reconstitution

The Interbank yield curve is built from *monetary interbank rates, future contracts prices and swap rates.* This curve is the basis for the operations between banks.

35.1.3.1 Monetary Interbank rates

Monetary market rates such as Libor (London Interbank offer rate) and Euribor (€ Interbank offer rate) are linear interest rates expressed usually in an Exact/360 basis. These rates are the average of the Interbank loans rates. For instance, every day at 11 o'clock, a panel of the major banks in London is asked to provide its Interbank lending rates when lending money on a 3 month horizon in US dollars. The average of the provided rates gives the Libor 3 month USD rate of the day.

This 3 month Libor USD rate will be available for a loan starting in two open days and ending 3 months later where the interest rate paid is equal to:

$$\text{Nominal.Libor.}\frac{\text{Exact number of days of the lending period}}{360}$$

From this Libor rate, it is then possible to deduce the Exact/365 zero-coupon rate and for instance, if the Libor rate is equal to 3 % and the number of days of the period is equal to 91 days:

$$TZC(3\text{ month}) = \left(1 + 3.0\,\% \times \frac{91}{360}\right)^{\left(\frac{365}{91}\right)} - 1$$

The monetary market rates will help to reconstitute the Interbank yield curve on the segment from 1 day to 6 months.

35.1.3.2 Future contracts

On the segment going from 6 months to 1 or 2 years, the A/L manager will prefer to use future contracts. These contracts give the price to pay to buy right now the future level of, for instance, the Euribor 3 months.

From the price of the future contracts, using interpolated zero-coupon prices from the Interbank monetary rates on the first segment 0–6 months, it is possible to recuperate the zero-coupon rates on the segment 6 months–2 years.

35.1.3.3 Swaps contracts

Let us recall that *a swap* is a market contract between two counterparties where:

- a counterparty pays periodically fixed rate coupons on a nominal N on a "fixed rate leg";
- the other counterparty pays periodically on a "floating rate leg" floating rate coupons indexed to the same nominal N. The floating rate index will be usually a Libor (or Euribor) rate or an overnight rate. The periodicity of the payments is usually the periodicity of the Libor rate: 3 months, for a Euribor 3 months, for instance.

The contract maturity is the same for the both legs.
The standard swap value is equal to the difference between:

- a fixed rate bond with the same maturity and the same nominal, the same coupon frequency and the same coupon rate as for the swap;
- the nominal swap.

At date t, we call *swap rate* or *CMS swap rate* (constant maturity swap rate), the value of the coupon rate that makes the swap contract value equal to zero.

Standard swaps are annual 30/360 fixed rate against Euribor 3 month rate swaps. They are used to build the zero-coupon yield curve for maturities above 2 years.

It is possible to use the *theoretical method* proposed in the government bond yield curve reconstitution.

With the one-year zero-coupon rate, it is possible to deduce the 2 year zero-coupon rate using the 2 year swap rate.

Knowing, the 2 year zero-coupon rate and the one-year zero-coupon rate, it is possible to deduce the 3 year zero-coupon rate using the 3 year swap rate.

35.1.3.4 Final yield curve reconstitution

At the end of the previous section, the A/L manager is in possession of N zero-coupon rates or N discount factors B(0,i) for i = 1 day to 40 years.

To obtain a final yield curve and a function B(0,s) for each s under 40 years, the A/L manager will use once more interpolation methods.

The classic idea is to write zero-coupon rates as a sum of cubic B-splines choosing more splines than in government bond reconstitution.

35.2 YIELD CURVE STOCHASTIC INTEREST RATE MODELS

The reconstitution above allows us to model the initial yield curve at date 0. The objective of the yield curve stochastic models is to simulate the future interest rates.

Those models are presented in Chapter 21 on simulation tools. In this chapter, we will concentrate on a more precise presentation of:

- the Black model;
- the Vasicek model (as an introduction to the one factor Hull & white model); and
- the HJM models.

35.2.1 Black Model (1976)

The Black model provides a direct pricing for caps, floors, collars and swaptions.

35.2.1.1 *Application to caps and floors*

We call $L(t,T_j,T_{j+1})$ the forward rate from date T_j to date T_{j+1} seen from date t. This rate will follow a martingale under a forward neutral probability $Q(T_{j+1})$:

$$\frac{dL_{t,T_j,T_{j+1}}}{L_{t,T_j,T_{j+1}}} = \sigma_j.dW_t^{Q(T_{j+1})}$$

σ_j is called the forward rate volatility.

The caplet formula is similar to the Black & Scholes formula:

$$CAP(t) = B(t, T_{j+1}).\left[L_{t,T_j,T_{j+1}}.\Phi(d_j) - Strike.\Phi\left(-d_j + \sigma_j.\sqrt{T_j - t}\right)\right]$$

$$d_j = \frac{\ln\left(\frac{L_{t,T_j,T_{j+1}}}{Strike}\right) + \left(\sigma_j^2.(T_j - t)\right)/2}{\sigma_j.\sqrt{T_j - t}}$$

By the inversion of the caps market price, this formula gives the market volatility quotation: caps are quoted in volatility.

The formula is also available for floors:

$$FLOOR(t) = B(t, T_{j+1}).\left[-L_{t,T_j,T_{j+1}}.\Phi(-d_j) + Strike.\Phi\left(-d_j + \sigma_j.\sqrt{T_j - t}\right)\right]$$

35.2.1.2 *Application to swaptions*

The Black model gives also a valuation formula for swaptions. In this model, the forward rate $SWAP(t,T_j,T_k)$ from date T_j to date T_k seen from date t will follow a martingale under a swap forward probability $Q(T_j, T_k)$:

$$\frac{dSWAP_{t,T_i,T_j}}{SWAP_{t,T_i,T_j}} = \sigma_{T_i,T_j}.dW_t^{Q(T_i,T_j)}$$

The price of a payer swaption will readily follow:

$$SWAPTION(t) = \sum_{k=1}^{N-1} B(t, T_{k+1}).\left[SWAP_{t,T_i,T_j}.\Phi(d) - Strike.\Phi\left(d - \sigma.\sqrt{T_i - t}\right)\right]$$

$$d = \frac{\ln\left(\frac{SWAP_{t,T_i,T_j}}{Strike}\right) + \left(\sigma^2.(T_i - t)\right)/2}{\sigma.\sqrt{T_i - t}}$$

and for a receiver swaption too:

$$SWAPTION(t) = \sum_{k=1}^{N-1} B(t, T_{k+1}).\left[-SWAP_{t,T_i,T_j}.\Phi(-d) + Strike.\Phi\left(-d + \sigma.\sqrt{T_i - t}\right)\right]$$

35.2.2 Vasicek models

35.2.2.1 Vasicek initial model (1977)

In 1977, Vasicek proposed a stochastic model for the evolution of interest rates with one factor. In practice, this model is not used anymore but it helps us to understand the other models such as the Hull & White one-factor model presented in Section 21.3 on interest rate simulation.

In the Vasicek model, there is only one factor for the yield curve deformation. This unique factor is a short-term interest rate modelled under the form of an Ornstein-Uhlenbeck process.

$$dr(t) = a\left[\theta - r(t)\right] dt + \sigma.dW(t)$$

This model links:

- the short-term interest rate r(t) (close to the DD rate);
- θ the long-term average of the short-term interest rate;
- a the mean reverting speed;
- W(t) a Brownian motion under a real probability.

This modelling takes into account the observed mean reverting of interest rates: high interest rate levels tend to be followed more frequently by decreases than by rises, for instance.

35.2.2.2 Risk neutral probability introduction preparation

As we did it in the simulation section, we will show how a risk neutral probability can be introduced in the modelling above.

We will suppose that it is possible to constitute a risk free portfolio constituted with two zero-coupon bonds of different maturities.

We will suppose also that the zero-coupon B of maturity T at date t is a function of t and of the short-term interest rate r(t):

$$B(t,T,r(t))$$

We consider a risk free portfolio P constituted with:

- one zero-coupon bond with maturity t_1 and with price $B(0,t_1)$;
- ϕ zero-coupon bonds with maturity t_2 and with unitary price $B(0,t_2)$.

The portfolio price will be of:

$$P = B(0, t_1) + \phi.B(0, t_2)$$

The quantity ϕ is chosen so that the portfolio price sensitivity to a short-term interest rate shock is equal to 0:

$$\phi = -\frac{\dfrac{\partial B(0,t_1)}{\partial r}}{\dfrac{\partial B(0,t_2)}{\partial r}}$$

It is then possible to compute the portfolio variation from t to t+dt:

$$dP = dB(0,t_1) - \frac{\dfrac{\partial B(0,t_1)}{\partial r}}{\dfrac{\partial B(0,t_2)}{\partial r}}.dB(0,t_2)$$

Applying the Itô lemma (cf. simulation section) on the zero-coupons B, the terms in dr disappear:

$$dP = \left(\begin{array}{l} \left[\dfrac{\partial B(0,t_1)}{\partial t} + \dfrac{\partial B(0,t_1)}{\partial r}.a.(\theta - r_t) + \dfrac{\sigma^2}{2}.\dfrac{\partial^2 B(0,t_1)}{\partial r^2}\right] \\ -\dfrac{\dfrac{\partial B(0,t_1)}{\partial r}}{\dfrac{\partial B(0,t_2)}{\partial r}}.\left[\dfrac{\partial B(0,t_2)}{\partial t} + \dfrac{\partial B(0,t_2)}{\partial r}.a.(\theta - r_t) + \dfrac{\sigma^2}{2}.\dfrac{\partial^2 B(0,t_2)}{\partial r^2}\right] \end{array} \right).dt$$

The portfolio integrates a simple trend. This portfolio is said to be risk free, so that if we call r the risk free rate:

$$\frac{dP}{P} = r.dt$$

This means:

$$\left(B(0,t_1) - \frac{\dfrac{\partial B(0,t_1)}{\partial r}}{\dfrac{\partial B(0,t_2)}{\partial r}}.B(0,t_2) \right).r = \left(\begin{array}{l} \left[\dfrac{\partial B(0,t_1)}{\partial t} + \dfrac{\partial B(0,t_1)}{\partial r}.a.(\theta - r_t) + \dfrac{\sigma^2}{2}.\dfrac{\partial^2 B(0,t_1)}{\partial r^2}\right] \\ -\dfrac{\dfrac{\partial B(0,t_1)}{\partial r}}{\dfrac{\partial B(0,t_2)}{\partial r}}.\left[\dfrac{\partial B(0,t_2)}{\partial t} + \dfrac{\partial B(0,t_2)}{\partial r}.a.(\theta - r_t) \right. \\ \left. + \dfrac{\sigma^2}{2}.\dfrac{\partial^2 B(0,t_2)}{\partial r^2}\right] \end{array} \right)$$

When separating the terms around t_1 and t_2:

$$\frac{B(0,t_1).r - \left[\dfrac{\partial B(0,t_1)}{\partial t} + \dfrac{\partial B(0,t_1)}{\partial r}.a.(\theta - r_t) + \dfrac{\sigma^2}{2}.\dfrac{\partial^2 B(0,t_1)}{\partial r^2}\right]}{\dfrac{\partial B(0,t_1)}{\partial r}}$$

$$= \frac{B(0,t_2).r - \left[\dfrac{\partial B(0,t_2)}{\partial t} + \dfrac{\partial B(0,t_2)}{\partial r}.a.(\theta - r_t) + \dfrac{\sigma^2}{2}.\dfrac{\partial^2 B(0,t_2)}{\partial r^2}\right]}{\dfrac{\partial B(0,t_2)}{\partial r}}$$

This means that the following quantity λ is at date t constant whatever the zero-coupon maturity T is:

$$\lambda(t) = -\frac{\left(B(t,T).r - \left[\frac{\partial B(t,T)}{\partial t} + \frac{\partial B(t,T)}{\partial r}.a.(\theta - r_t) + \frac{\sigma^2}{2}.\frac{\partial^2 B(t,T)}{\partial r^2}\right]\right)}{\sigma.\frac{\partial B(t,T)}{\partial r}}$$

Then applying the Itô formula, this gives the following formulas:

$$\frac{dB(t,T)}{B(t,T)} = \frac{\left(\frac{\partial B(t,T)}{\partial t}.dt + \frac{\partial B(t,T)}{\partial r}.a.(\theta - r_t).dt + \frac{\sigma^2}{2}\frac{\partial^2 B(t,T)}{\partial r^2}.dt\right) + \frac{\partial B(t,T)}{\partial r}.\sigma.dW_t}{B(t,T)}$$

$$\frac{dB(t,T)}{B(t,T)} = \frac{\left(B(t,T).r + \lambda(t).\sigma.\frac{\partial B(t,T)}{\partial r}\right)}{B(t,T)}.dt + \frac{\frac{\partial B(t,T)}{\partial r}}{B(t,T)}.\sigma.dW_t$$

$$\frac{dB(t,T)}{B(t,T)} = r.dt + \frac{\left(\lambda(t).\sigma.\frac{\partial B(t,T)}{\partial r}\right)}{B(t,T)}.dt + \frac{\frac{\partial B(t,T)}{\partial r}}{B(t,T)}.\sigma.dW_t$$

We introduce a volatility variable:

$$\sigma_B = \frac{\frac{\partial B(t,T)}{\partial r}}{B(t,T)}.\sigma$$

The zero-coupon follows then:

$$\frac{dB(t,T)}{B(t,T)} = (r_t + \lambda(t).\sigma_B).dt + \sigma_B.dW_t$$

Finally, it leads to this classic formulation for B:

$$\frac{dB(t,T)}{B(t,T)} = \mu_B.dt + \sigma_B.dW_t$$
$$\mu_B = r_t + \lambda.\sigma_B$$

This equation shows that *the excess return of the zero-coupon bond (over the risk free rate r) is proportional to the risk of the bond measured by the volatility σ with a multiplying factor λ*. The parameter λ can be interpreted as the risk unitary market price (the higher is the volatility, the higher is the excess return).

35.2.2.3 Risk neutral probability introduction and zero-coupon pricing with martingale approach

35.2.2.3.1 Zero-coupon generic formula

The modelling above has been developed under a real probability.

Using the Girsanov theorem, we introduce a new probability, the risk neutral probability, i.e. an appropriate probability to price zero-coupons. To do so, we define a new process using the following drift change:

$$\overline{W}_t = W_t + \int_0^t \lambda_s.ds$$

With the Girsanov theorem, this Brownian motion is a Q-Brownian motion where the probability Q is defined by the Radon-Nykodym derivative:

$$\frac{dQ}{dP}(t) = \exp\left\{-\int_0^t \lambda_s.dW_s - \frac{1}{2}\int_0^t \lambda_s^2 ds\right\}$$

This allows us to write the zero-coupon price:

$$\frac{dB(t,T)}{B(t,T)} = r_t.dt + \sigma_B.d\overline{W}_t$$

In addition, we introduce the discounted zero-coupon prices:

$$B^*(t,T) = \left(e^{-\int_0^t r_s ds}\right).B(t,T)$$

We use once more the Itô lemma to obtain:

$$\frac{dB^*(t,T)}{B^*(t,T)} = \sigma_B.d\overline{W}_t$$

These discounted prices are martingales under Q and this implies:

$$B^*(t,T) = E_s^Q\left(B^*(T,T)\right)$$
and
$$\left(e^{-\int_0^t r_s ds}\right).B(t,T) = E_s^Q\left(\left(e^{-\int_0^T r_s ds}\right)\right)$$

Finally, it leads once more to the *classic formula for the zero-coupon prices*:

$$B(t,T) = E_s^Q\left(e^{-\int_t^T r_s ds}\right)$$

35.2.2.3.2 *Vasicek formulae*

We will focus now on the case developed by Vasicek where λ is constant and does not vary with time passing.

Moreover, in the Vasicek model, the *short-term interest rate r* is easy to simulate under the risk neutral probability Q:

$$dr_t = a.\left(\overline{\theta} - r_t\right).dt + \sigma.d\overline{W}_t$$
$$\overline{\theta} = \theta - \sigma.\frac{\lambda}{a}$$

The solution of this classic stochastic equation is given by:

$$r_t = r_0 . e^{-at} + \overline{\theta} . (1 - e^{-at}) + \sigma . \int_0^t e^{-a(t-s)} d\overline{W}(s)$$

We will use now stochastic calculations in order to write the zero-coupon as a function of r. Using the Laplace transform, the zero-coupon follows:

$$B(t, t+\tau) = E_s^Q \left(e^{-\int_t^{t+\tau} r_s ds} \right) = E_s^Q \left(e^{-\int_t^{t+\tau} r_t . e^{-a(s-t)} . ds + \overline{\theta} . \left(1 - e^{-a(s-t)}\right) . ds + \sigma . \int_t^s e^{-a(t-u)} d\overline{W}(u) . ds} \right)$$
$$B(t, t+\tau) = e^{-\int_t^{t+\tau} r_t . e^{-a(s-t)} . ds + \overline{\theta} . \left(1 - e^{-a(s-t)}\right) . ds} . E_s^Q \left(e^{-\int_t^{t+\tau} \sigma . \int_t^s e^{-a(t-u)} d\overline{W}(u) . ds} \right)$$
$$B(t, t+\tau) = e^{-\left((r_t - \overline{\theta}) . \left[\frac{e^{-a.\tau} - 1}{-a} \right] + \overline{\theta} . \tau \right)} . E_s^Q \left(e^{-\sigma . \int_t^{t+\tau} \int_t^s e^{-a(t-u)} d\overline{W}(u) . ds} \right)$$

From zero-coupon bond prices, it is possible to extract zero-coupon rates TZC expressed as exponential functions when introducing the infinite zero-coupon rate:

$$TZC_\infty = \overline{\theta} - \frac{\sigma^2}{2a^2}$$

We return to the formula used in the yield curve reconstruction (Vasicek direct interpolation method) as a formula for the zero-coupon rate:

$$TZC(t, t+\tau) = TZC_\infty - (TZC_\infty - r_t) . \left(\frac{1 - e^{-a\tau}}{\tau} \right) + \frac{\sigma^2}{4a^3 \tau} (1 - e^{-a\tau})^2$$

As for the Hull & White model, the zero-coupon rate is expressed as a linear function of the interest rates. The model calibration is made minimizing the difference between the market prices and the model prices for a set of bonds.

35.2.2.4 Criticism of the model

This model is simple, easy to understand and to implement. The model provides explicit formulae for pricing the standard interest rate products: zero-coupons, caps, fixed rate products, floors, swaptions, etc.

The model has nevertheless some weaknesses (and for these reasons, the model is not used in practice):

- The model can give negative rates with a non-zero probability.
- Interest rate variations are perfectly correlated between them. This will be corrected with the introduction of other factors such as in the Hull & White model with two factors.
- The zero-coupon yield curve is not exactly the same as the zero-coupon yield curve observed in the market. Consequently, *the pricing of fixed rate products with the Vasicek model does not give exactly the observed market price for these products.* The Hull & White models will correct this problem.

To avoid the possibility of negative rates, the *Cox-Ingersoll-Ross model (CIR)* will propose another approach for the short-term interest rate modelling:

$$dr_t = a . \left(\overline{\theta} - r_t \right) . dt + \sigma . \sqrt{r_t} . dW_t$$

Under this assumption, the interest rates will take positive values and the zero-coupon rate is still expressed as a linear function of r.

Among the other models present in the literature, we may cite also the *Merton model* where the short-term interest rate is as follows:

$$dr_t = a.dt + \sigma.dW_t$$

The zero-coupon rate is written is this model in a too simple manner:

$$TZC(t, t+\tau) = r_t + \frac{a}{2}.\tau - \frac{\sigma^2}{6}.\tau^2$$

When the maturity increases, the zero-coupon rate converges to $-\infty$.

35.2.3 From Vasicek to HJM models (including Hull & White models)

35.2.3.1 The general framework of the HJM model

In 1992, Heath Jarrow and Morton proposed an interest rate model class where the model is not always based on a short-term interest rate modelling. These models are based on the forward rates f(t,T) defined by:

$$f(t,T) = -\frac{\partial \ln(B(t,T))}{\partial T}$$

Note that the short-term interest rate is a special forward rate:

$$r(t) = f(t,t)$$

The HJM modelling may include many factors but here the presentation will be done using only one factor.

The dynamics of the forward rate will only depend in HJM models on the spot observed yield curve $f^{obs}(0,T)$ at date 0 and on the volatility structure $\sigma(t,T)$.

Adding a hypothesis of arbitrage opportunity absence, the dynamics under a risk neutral probability Q is written (using here only one factor):

$$\begin{cases} df(t,T) = \alpha(t,T).dt + \sigma(t,T).dW_t^Q \\ f(0,T) = f^{obs}(0,T) \end{cases}$$
$$\alpha(t,T) = \sigma(t,T).\int_t^T \sigma(t,s).ds$$

Heath, Jarrow and Morton show that the discount factor B(t,T) follows simply:

$$\begin{cases} \dfrac{dB(t,T)}{B(t,T)} = r(t).dt + \Gamma(t,T).dW_t^Q \\ \Gamma(t,T) = \int_t^T \sigma(t,s).ds \end{cases}$$

It is then possible to write in this model those zero-coupon prices, the zero-coupon rates and the forward spot rates as functions of the initial observable values at date 0 of these variables:

$$B(t,T)=\frac{B(0,T)}{B(0,t)}.\exp\left(-\tfrac{1}{2}\int_0^t\left(\Gamma(s,T)^2-\Gamma(s,t)^2\right).ds+\tfrac{1}{2}\int_0^t\left(\Gamma(s,T)-\Gamma(s,t)\right).dW_s^Q\right)$$

$$TZC(t,T)=TZC(0,t,T)+\frac{-\tfrac{1}{2}\int_0^t\left(\Gamma(s,T)^2-\Gamma(s,t)^2\right).ds+\tfrac{1}{2}\int_0^t\left(\Gamma(s,T)-\Gamma(s,t)\right).dW_s^Q}{T-t}$$

$$f(t,T)=f^{obs}(0,T)+\int_0^t\left(\sigma(x,T).\int_x^T\sigma(x,s).ds\right).dx+\int_0^T\sigma(x,T).dW_x^Q$$

$$r(t)=f(t,t)=f^{obs}(0,t)+\int_0^t\left(\sigma(x,t).\int_x^t\sigma(x,s).ds\right).dx+\int_0^t\sigma(x,t).dW_x^Q$$

where:

- B(0,T) divided by B(0,t) is the forward discount factor from t to T seen from date 0;
- TZC(0,t,T) is the zero-coupon rate associate at date 0 with this discount factor;
- f^{obs}(0,T) is the spot forward instant rate at date 0.

35.2.3.2 The HJM Markov condition

The modelling above is incomplete. For instance, the yield curve movements are not always Markovian.

In practice, Caverhill showed in 1994 that it is sufficient for the volatility function σ to be separable so that the interest rates will respect this Markov condition.

$$\sigma(t,T)=f(t).g(T)$$

35.2.3.3 Application to Ho and Lee Model

The Ho and Lee model is a Markovian HJM model where:

$$\sigma(t,T)=\sigma$$

In this model, the short-term interest rate is easy to implement and the zero-coupon prices depend on this short-term interest rate:

$$r(t)=f^{obs}(0,t)+\sigma^2.\frac{t^2}{2}+\sigma.\int_0^t dW_x^Q$$

$$f(t,T)=f^{obs}(0,T)+\sigma^2.\left(T.t-\frac{t^2}{2}\right)+r(t)-f^{obs}(0,t)-\sigma^2.\frac{t^2}{2}$$

$$B(t,T)=\frac{B(0,T)}{B(0,t)}.\exp\left((T-t).\left(f^{obs}(0,t)-r_t\right)-\frac{1}{2}.\sigma^2.t.(T-t)^2\right)$$

35.2.3.4 Application to Hull & White model

The *Hull & White model* is a Markovian HJM model where:

$$\sigma(t,T)=\sigma.\exp\left(-\lambda\,(T-t)\right)$$

In this model too, the short-term interest rate is easy to implement and the zero-coupon prices still depend on this short-term interest rate:

$$r(t) = f^{obs}(0, t) + \frac{\sigma^2}{\lambda^2}.\frac{(1-\exp(-\lambda.t))^2}{2} + \sigma.\int_0^t \exp(-\lambda.(t-x))dW_x^Q$$

$$f(t, T) = f^{obs}(0, T) + \int_0^t \sigma^2.\frac{\left(1-e^{-\lambda.(T-x)}\right).e^{-\lambda.(T-x)}}{\lambda}.dx + e^{-\lambda.(T-t)}\left(r(t) - f^{obs}(0, t) - \sigma^2.\frac{\left(1-e^{-\lambda.t}\right)^2}{2.\lambda^2}\right)$$

$$B(t, T) = B^f(0, t, T).\exp\left(\frac{\left(1-e^{-\lambda.(T-t)}\right)}{\lambda}.\left(f^{obs}(0, t) - r_t\right) - \sigma^2.\frac{\left(1-e^{-2.\lambda.t}\right).\left(1-e^{-\lambda.(T-t)}\right)^2}{4.\lambda^3}\right)$$

Moreover, in this model, the short-term interest rate variation follows:

$$dr(t) = \left(\frac{\partial f^{obs}}{\partial y}(0, t) + \frac{\sigma^2}{\lambda^2}.\frac{(1-\exp(-2.\lambda.t))}{2} + \lambda.\left(f^{obs}(0, t) - r_t\right)\right) + \sigma.dW_t^Q$$

This finally leads to the classic Hull & White formulation:

$$dr(t) = \lambda.(\theta_t - r_t) + \sigma.dW_t^Q$$

The parameter θ follows in this expression:

$$\theta_t = f^{obs}(0, t) + \frac{\left(\frac{\partial f^{obs}}{\partial y}(0, t) + \frac{\sigma^2}{\lambda^2}.\frac{(1-\exp(-2.\lambda.t))}{2}\right)}{\lambda}$$

35.2.3.5 Forward measure notion

The Vasicek or Hull & White models were developed under the historical probability P then under the risk neutral probability Q.

Some models are based under other probabilities such as the *forward neutral probability* associated with date T also called Q^T.

The *probability change* between the risk neutral and the forward neutral probability is the following:

$$dW_{Q_T}(s) = dW_Q(s) - \Gamma(s, T).ds$$

where Γ is the function presented in the HJM modelling.

Under this probability, the price of an asset paying a flow X(T) at date T is known as:

$$\text{Price}(t; X) = E_Q\left(X(T).\overline{B}(t, T)\right) = E_Q\left(X(T).\exp\left(-\int_t^T r(s).ds\right)\right) = B(t, T).E_{Q_T}(X(T))$$

Under this forward neutral probability, the forward rate is the mathematical expectation of the spot rate:

$$f(t, T) = E_{Q_T}(r_T)$$

Under the forward neutral probability associated with date T_{i+1} the forward Libor rate seen from date t going from T_i to T_{i+1} follows a martingale:

$$\frac{dLibor(t, T_i, T_{i+1})}{Libor(t, T_i, T_{i+1})} = \sigma_{t,T_i,T_{i+1}}.dW_t^{Q(T_{i+1})}$$

since:

$$E_{Q_{T_{i+1}}}(Libor(t, T_i, T_{i+1})) = \frac{B(t, T_i)}{B(t, T_{i+1})} - 1$$

35.2.3.6 CMS convexity adjustment

CMS convexity adjustment is essential in stochastic calculations. Quite often, the A/L manager needs to compute the mathematical expectation of:

- a Libor paid with a lag;
- a CMS indexed coupon.

The forward rate is different from the anticipated CMS rate due to the existence of a *convexity bias*. This bias is given by the following drift:

$$dW_{Q_T}(s) = dW_Q(s) - \Gamma(s, T).ds$$

When a Libor (or a CMS rate) is paid at date T_l, the A/L manager will need to simulate this Libor under the forward neutral probability $Q(T_l)$:

$$\frac{dLibor(t, T_i, T_{i+1})}{Libor(t, T_i, T_{i+1})} = \sigma_{t,T_i,T_{i+1}}.\left(dW_t^{Q(T_l)} + (\Gamma(t, T_l) - \Gamma(t, T_{i+1})).dt\right)$$

Bibliography

Un livre défendu est un feu sur lequel on veut marcher, et qui jette au nez des étincelles. (Voltaire)

In English:

Acerbi, C. (2002) Spectral measures of risk: a coherent representation of subjective risk aversion, working paper, Abaxbank.

Acerbi, C. and Tasche, D. (2001) On the coherence of Expected Shortfall, working paper, Technische Universität München.

Acerbi, C., Nordio, C. and Sirtori, C. (2001) Expected Shortfall as a tool for risk management, working paper, Abaxbank.

Adam, A. (2003) Hot electron bolometers for Far Infrared detection using Low or High Temperature Superconductors, PhD Thesis, Supelec.

Adam, A. and Chouillou, A. (2005) From loss to value: economic capital in retail banking, GARP Risk Review.

Adam, A., Laurent, J.-P. and Rebérioux, C. (2004) How should we hedge deposit accounts?, Banque et Marchés.

Adam, A., Chouillou, A. and Scaillet, O. (2005) Implementing Basel II in retail banking: a simple statistical approach, Default risk.

Adam, A., Houkari, M. and Laurent, J.-P. (2006) New Frontiers of Asset Management, working paper.

Andersen, L. and Sidenius, J. (2004) Extensions to Gaussian copula: random recovery and random factor loadings, working paper, Bank of America.

Ang, A. and Piazzesi, M. (2003) A no-arbitrage vector autoregression of term structure dynamics with macroeconomic and latent variables, *Journal of Monetary Economics* **50**, 745–87.

Artzner, P., Delbaen, F., Eber, J.-M. and Heath, D. (1997) Thinking coherently, *RISK* **10** (11), 68–71.

Artzner, P., Delbaen, F., Eber, J.-M. and Heath, D. (1999) Coherent measures of risk, *Mathematical Finance* **9**(3), 203–28.

Ashley, W.J. (2006) *An Introduction to English Economic History and Theory*, Kessinger Publishing.

Basel Committee on Banking Supervision (2001a) Potential modifications to the Committee's proposals.

Basel Committee on Banking Supervision (2001b) Results of the second Quantitative Impact Study.

Basel Committee on Banking Supervision (2001c) The Internal Ratings-based Approach, Consultative Document, Supportive Document to the New Basel Capital Accord.

Basel Committee on Banking Supervision (2002) Results of Quantitative Impact Study 2.5.

Basel Committee On Banking Supervision (2004a) Principles for the Management and Supervision of Interest Rate Risk.

Basel Committee on Banking Supervision (2004b) International convergence of capital measurement and capital standards: a revised framework.

Belbase, E. (1999) Fixed rate mortgage prepayment model, Quantitative Perspectives.

Berkovec, J., Mingo, J. and Zhang, X. (1997) Premiums in private versus public branch sales, Finance and Economic Discussion Series, 97-33, Federal Reserve Board.

Bessis, J. (2002) *Risk Management in Banking*, John Wiley & Sons Ltd.

Black, F. and Karasinski, O. (1991) Bond and Option Pricing when short rate are LogNormal, Financial Analysis Journal, July–August, 52–9.

Black, F. and Litterman, R. (1990) Asset Allocation: Combining Investor Views With Market Equilibrium, Goldman, Sachs & Co., Fixed Income Research, September.

Black, F. and Litterman, R. (1992) Global Portfolio Optimization, Financial Analysts Journal, 28–43, September–October.

Black, F. and Scholes, M. (1973) The Pricing of Options and Corporate Liabilities, *Journal of Political Economy* **81**(3), 637–54.

Black, F., Derman, E. and Toy, W. (1990) A One-Factor Model of Interest Rates and its Application to Treasury Bond Options, Financial Analyst Journal.

Blondel, S. (2002) PhD thesis, University of Nantes, N-2002-130.

Bouezmarni, T. and Scaillet, O. (2003) Consistency of Asymmetric Kernel Density Estimators and Smoothed Histograms with Application to Income Data.

Brace, A., Gatarek, D. and Musiela, M. (1997) The market Model of Interest-Rate Dynamics, Mathematical Finance **7**, 127–55.

Brigo, D. and Mercurio, F. (2001) *Interest-Rate Models: Theory and Practice*, Springer-Verlag, Germany.

Chabaane, A., Laurent, J.-P., Malevergne, Y. and Turpin, F. (2006) Alternative Risk Measures for Alternative Investments, *Journal of Risk* **8**(4), 1–32.

Chabaane, A., Chouillou, A. and Laurent, J.-P. (2004) Aggregation and credit risk measurement in retail banking, *Banque & Marchés* **70**, 5–15.

Chabaane, A., Salomon, J. and Laurent, J.-P. (2004) Double impact: credit risk assessment for secured loans, *Finance* **25**, 157–78.

Chamberlain, G. and Rothschild, M. (1983) Arbitrage and Mean Variance Analysis on Large Asset Markets, *Econometrica* **51**, 1281–304.

Chen, S. (1996) Understanding Option-Adjusted Spreads: The Implied Prepayments Hypothesis, *Journal of Portfolio Management* **22**, 104–13.

Cheyette, O. (1996) Implied Prepayments, *Journal of Portfolio Management* **23**, 107–113.

Chouillou, A. (2005) Retail banking credit risk modelling with application towards computation and allocation of regulatory and economic capital, Thesis Evry University.

Clapp, J.M., Deng, Y. and An, X. (2001) *Alternative Models for Competing Risks of Mortgage Termination.*

Clapp, J.M., Deng, Y. and An, X. (2006) Unobserved heterogeneity in models of competing mortgage termination risks, *Real estate economics* **34**(2), 243–73.

Cox, J., Ingersoll, J. and Ross, S. (1985) A theory of the Term Structure of Interest Rates, *Econometrica* **53**, 385–408.

Davidson, A. and Hershovitz, M. (1987) *The Refinancing Threshold Pricing Model: An Economic Approach to Valuing MBS, Merrill Lynch Mortgage-Backed Research*, November.

de Beco, S. (2005) PhD thesis. University of Nantes, N-2005-080.

de Beco, R. (2006) *Hedge Funds*, IPAG.

de Beco, G. (2007) *Design and Economy*, ENSCI.

de Jong, F. and Wielhouwer, J. (2003) The valuation and hedging of variable rate savings accounts, *ASTIN Bulletin* **33**, 2, 383–97.

Delbaen, F. (1974) Convex games and extreme points, *Journal of Mathematical Analysis and Applications* **45**, 210–33.

Dembo, A., Deuschel, J.-D. and Duffie, D. (2002) Large portfolio losses, Stanford University, working paper.

Demey, P., Jouanin, J.-F., Roget, C. and Roncalli, T. (2004) Maximum likelihood estimate of default correlations, *RISK* **17** (11).

Demidenko, E. (2004) Linear Mixed Models, John Wiley & Sons Inc.

Demidenko, E. and Massam, E. (1999) On the existence of the maximum likelihood estimate in the variance components model and some aspects of the computations. *Sankhya*, ser. A **61**, 431–43.

Denault, M. (2001) Coherent allocation of risk capital, working paper, Ecole des HEC, Montréal.

Deng, Y., Quigley, J.M. and Van Order, R. (2000) Mortgage Terminations, heterogeneity and the exercise of mortgage options, *Econometrica* **68** (2).

Dermine, J. and Bissada, Y. (2002) *Asset & Liability Management: A Guide to Value Creation and Risk Control*, Editions Financial Times/Prentice Hall.

DeRoover, R. (1963) The organization of trade, in Postan, M.M., Rich, E.E. and Miller, E. (eds) *The Cambridge Economic History of Europe 3: Economic organization and policies in the Middle Ages*, 42–118.

Dhaene, J., Vanduffel, S., Tang, Q.H., Goovaerts, M., Kass, R. and Vyncke, D. (2003) Risk measures and comonotonicity, working paper.

Duffie, D. (2001) *Dynamic Asset Pricing Theory*, Princeton University Press.

Duffie, D. and Kan, D. (1996) A Yield Factor Model of the Term Structure of Interest Rates, *Mathematical Finance*, **6/4**, 379–406.

Düllmann, K. and Scheule, H. (2003) Determinants of the asset correlations of German corporations and implications for regulatory capital, Banca d'Italia.

Dunn, K. and McConnell, J. (1981a) A Comparison of Alternative Models for Pricing GNMA Mortgage-Backed Securities, *Journal of Finance* **36**, 471–83.

Dunn, K. and McConnell, J. (1981b) Valuation of Mortgage- Backed Securities, *Journal of Finance* **36**, 599–617.

Egebo, T., Richardson, P. and Lienert, I. (1990) *A Model of Housing Investment for the major OECD Economies*, OECD Economic Studies, Spring, 14.

Ellis, D. and Jordan, J. (2001) The evaluation of Credit Union non-maturity deposits, working paper, National Credit Union Administration.

Fabozzi, F.J. (1988) *The Handbook of Mortgage Backed-Securities*, Probus Publishing.

FED Reserve Website. History of the Eighties – Lessons for the Future.

Finnerty, J., Kalotay, A. and Farrell, F. (1988) *Evaluating Bond Refunding Opportunities*, The Institutional Investor Series in Finance, Ballinger.

Fisher, J.D.M., Liu, C.T. and Zhou, R. (2002) *When Can We Forecast Inflation*?, *FRB* Chicago Economic Perspectives (1Q), pp. 30–42.

Föllmer, H. and Schied, A. (2004) *Stochastic Finance*, Berlin: de Gruyter, Germany.

Frauendorfer, K. and Schürle, M. (2003) Management of non-maturing deposits by multistage stochastic programming, *European Journal of Operational Research* **151**, 602–16.

Frey, R. and McNeil, A. (2001) Dependence modelling, model risk and model calibration in models of portfolio credit risk, working paper, University of Leipzig.

Fu, Q., LaCour-Little, M. and Vandell, K.D. (2003) Commercial mortgage prepayments under heterogeneous prepayment penalty structures, *Journal of Real Estate Research* **25**(3), 245–75.

Gagliardini, P. and Gouriéroux, C. (2004) Stochastic migration models with application to corporate risk, working paper, CREST.

Gordy, M. (2000) A comparative anatomy of credit risk models, *Journal of Banking and Finance* **24**(1/2), 119–45, 136.

Gordy, M. (2002) A risk-factor model foundation for ratings-based bank capital rules, working paper, Board of Governors of the Federal Reserve Systems.

Gordy, M. (2004) Procyclicality in Basel II: can we treat the disease without killing the patient?, working paper, Board of Governors of the Federal Reserve System.

Gouriéroux, C., Laurent, J.-P. and Scaillet, O. (2000) Sensitivity analysis of Value at Risk, *Journal of Empirical Finance* **7**, 3–4, 225–45.

Gregory, J. and Laurent, J.-P. (2003) I Will Survive, *RISK*, June, 103–7.

Gregory, J. and Laurent, J.-P. (2004) In the Core of Correlation, *RISK*, October, 87–91.

Hagan, P.S., Kumar, D., Lesniewski, A.S. and Woodward, D.E. (2002) Managing smile risk, *WILMOTT Magazine*, September, 84–108.

Hannan, T. and Berger, A. (1991) The rigidity of prices: evidence from the banking industry, *American Economic Review* **81**, September, 938–45.

Hartley, H. and Rao, J. (1967) Maximum Likelihood Estimation for the Mixed Analysis of Variance, *Biometrika* **54**, 93–108.

Harville, D.A. (1974) Optimal procedures for some constrained selection problems, *Journal of the American Statistical Association* **69**, 446–52.

Harville, D.A. (1977) Maximum Likelihood approaches to Variance Component estimation and to related problems, *Journal of the American Statistical Association* **72**, 320–38.

Hayre, L. (2001) *Salomon Smith Barney Guide to Mortgage-Backed and Asset-Backed Securities*, John Wiley & Sons Inc.

Heath, D., Jarrow, R. and Morton, A. (1992) Bond Pricing and the Term structure of Interest rates: a new Methodology for contingent claims Valuation, *Econometrica* **60**, 77–105.

Henderson, C. (1953) Estimation of Variance and Covariance Components, *Biometrics* **49**, 226–57.

Hilliard, J., Kau, J.B. and Slawson, C. (1988) Valuing Prepayment and Default in a Fixed- Rate Mortgage: A Bivariate Binomial Options Pricing Technique, *Journal of Real Estate Economics* **26**, 431–68.

Hördahl, P., Tristani, O. and Vestin, D. (2006) A joint econometric model of macroeconomic and term structure dynamics, *Journal of Econometrics*, **131**(1-2), 405–44.

Howard, C.D. and Kalotay, A.J. (1988) Embedded Call Options and Refunding Efficiency, in *Advances in Futures and Options Research*, Vol. 3, Elsevier.

Hu, J. (1988) An Alternative Prepayment Projection Based on Housing Activity, *The Handbook of Mortgage Backed-Securities*, Frank J. Fabozzi, editor, Probus Publishing.

Hull, J. and White, A. (1990) Princing interest rate derivative securities, *Rev. Financial Stud.* **3**, 573–92.

Hull, J. and White, A. (2004) Valuation of a CDO and an nth to default CDS without Monte Carlo simulation, working paper, John L. Rotman School of Management, University of Toronto.

Hutchison, D. (1995) Retail bank deposit pricing: an intertemporal asset pricing approach, *Journal of Money, Credit, and Banking* **27** (1) 217–31.

Hutchison, D. and Pennacchi, G. (1996) Measuring rents and interest risk in imperfect financial markets: the case of retail bank deposits, *Journal of Financial and Quantitative Analysis* **21**, 399–417.

Jamshidian, F. (1997) Libor and Swap Market Models and Measures, *Finance and Stochastic* **1**, 293–330.

Jamshidian, M. and Jennrich, R.I. (1993) Conjugate gradient acceleration of the EM algorithm, *Journal of the American Statistical Association* **88**, 221–28.

Janosi, T., Jarrow, R. and Zullo, F. (1999) An empirical analysis of the Jarrow van Deventer model for valuing non-maturity demand deposits, *Journal of Derivatives* **7** (1) 8–31.

Jarrow, R. and van Deventer, D. (1998) The arbitrage-free valuation and hedging of demand deposits and credit card loans, *Journal of Banking and Finance* **22**, 249–72.

Johnston, E. and Van Drunen, L. (1988) Pricing Mortgage Pools with Heterogeneous Mortgagors: Empirical Evidence, Working Paper, University of Utah.

Joint Working Group of Standard Setters (1999) Financial instruments: issues relating to banks, mimeo, August 31, 72 pages.

Jonhson, N. and Kotz, S. (1972) *Continuous Multivariate Distributions*, John Wiley & Sons, Inc.

Kalkbrener, M. and Willing, J. (2004) Risk management of non-maturing liabilities, *Journal of Banking and Finance* **28**, 1547–68.

Kalotay, A., Yang, D. and Fabozzi, F.J. (2004) An Option-Theoretic Prepayment Model for Mortgages and Mortgage-Backed Securities, *International Journal of Theoretical and Applied Finance* **7**(8), 949–78.

Kalotay, A.J., Williams, G.O. and Fabozzi, F.J. (1993) A Model for Valuing Bonds and Embedded Options, *Financial Analysts Journal* **49**, 35–46.

Kau, J.B., Keenan, D.C., Muller III, W.J. and Epperson, J.F. (1992) A generalized Valuation Model for Fixed Rate Residential Mortgages, *Journal of Money, Credit and Banking* **24**(3), 279–99.

Kau, J.B., Keenan, D.C., Muller III, W.J. and Epperson, J.F. (1994) The Value at Origination of Fixed-Rate Mortgages with Default and Prepayment, *Journal of Real Estate Finance and Economics* **11**(1), 5–36.

Kau, J.B. and Slawson, V.C. (2002) Frictions, Heterogeneity, and Optimality in Mortgage Modelling, *The Journal of Real Estate Finance and Economics* **24**, 239–60.

Kelly, A. and Slawson, C. (2001) Time- Varying Mortgage Prepayment Penalties and the value of Delaying Prepayment, *Journal of Real Estate Finance and Economics* **23**(2), 235–354.

Klotz, R. and Shapiro, A. (1993) Dealing with Streamlined Refinancings: New Implied Prepayment Model, Merrill Lynch Mortgage Product Analysis.

Kusuoka, S. (2001) On law invariant coherent risk measures, *Advances in Mathematical Economics*, **3**, 83–95, Springer, Tokyo.

LaCour-Little, M., Marschoun, M. and Maxam, C.L. (2002) Improving Parametric Mortgage Prepayment Models with Non-parametric Kernel Regression, *Journal of Real Estate Research* **24** (3), 299–327.

Laird, N. and Ware, J. (1982) Random effects models for longitudinal data, *Biometrics* **38**, 963–74.

Levin, A. (2001) Active-Passive Decomposition in Burnout Modelling, *Journal of Fixed Income* **10**, 27–40.

Lindstrom, M.J. and Bates, D.M. (1988) Newton-Raphson and EM algorithms for linear mixed effects models for repeated-measures data, *Journal of the American Statistical Association* **83**, 1014–22.

Maes, K. (2003) Modelling the term structure of interest rates: Where do we stand?, Working Paper No. 42, National Bank of Belgium.

Maes, K. and Timmermans, T. (2005) Measuring the interest rate risk of Belgian regulated savings deposits, Financial Stability Review, National Bank of Belgium, June, 137–51.

Magnus, J.R. (1988) *Linear Structures*, Oxford University Press.

Magnus, J.R. and Neudecker, H. (1988) *Matrix Differential Calculus with Applications in Statistics and Econometrics*, John Wiley & Sons, Inc.

Markowitz, H. (1952) *Portfolio Selection: Efficient Diversification of Investments*, Yale University Press.

Marrison, C. (2002) *The Fundamentals of Risk Measurement*, McGraw Hill.

Mawa, M. and Papouny, T. (1974) *Random Simulations*, Didi University press, Vol. 18, 200.

McCulloch, J.H. (1975) The Tax-Adjusted Yield Curve, *Journal of Finance* **30**, 811–30.

Merton, R. (1974) On the Pricing of Corporate Debt: The Risk Structure of Interest Rates, *Journal of Finance* **29**, 449–70.

Musiela, M. and Rutkowski, M. (1997) *Martingale Methods in Financial Modelling: Theory and Applications*, Springer.

Nelsen, R.B. (1999) An introduction to copulas, Lecture Notes in *Statistics* **139**, Springer Verlag.

Neuberger, J.A. and Zimmermann, G.C. (1990) Bank pricing of Retail deposit Accounts and the "California Rate Mystery", *Economic Review*, Federal Reserve Bank of San Francisco, Spring, volume 2.

Niandbob, A. (1977) The second mistake of our history, *Champex* **17**, 19–45.

O'Brien, J.M. (2000) Estimating the Value and Interest Rate Risk of Interest-Bearing Transactions Deposits. Division of Research and Statistics Board of Governors Federal Reserve System.

O'Brien, J., Orphanides, A. and Small, D. (1994) Estimating the interest rate sensitivity of liquid retail deposit values, conference proceedings Bank Structure and Competition.

Office of the Thrift Supervision (2001) *Net Portfolio Value Model Manual*, OTS.

Pagan, A. and Ullah, A. (1999) *Nonparametric Economics*, Cambridge University Press.

Patterson, H. and Thompson, R. (1971) Recovery of inter-block information when block sizes are unequal, *Biometrika* **58**, 545–54.

Peristiani, S., Bennett, P., Monsen, G., Peach, R. and Raiff, J. (1997) Credit, Equity and Mortgage Refinancings, FRBNY Economic policy review.

Rebonato, R. (2002) *Modern Pricing of Interest-Rate Derivatives: The Libor Market Model and Beyond*, Princeton University Press.

Rebonato, R. (2004) *Volatility and Correlation, The Perfect Hedger and the Fox*, John Wiley & Sons Ltd.

Richard, F. and Roll, R. (1989) Prepayment on Fixed-Rate Mortgage-backed Securities, *Journal of Portfolio Management* **15**(3), 73–82.

Rockafellar, R. and Uryasev, S. (2002) Conditional value-at-risk for general loss distributions, *Journal of Banking & Finance* **26**, 1443–471.

Roll, R. and Richard, S. (1989) Modelling Prepayments on Fixed Rate Mortgage Backed Securities, *Journal of Portfolio Management* **15**, 73–82.

Sandmann, K. and Sondermann, D. (1997) A Note on the Stability of Lognormal Interest Rate Models and the Pricing of Eurodollar Futures, *Mathematical Finance* **7**, 119–28.

Schoenmakers, J. (2004) *Robust Libor Modelling and Pricing of Derivative Products*, Chapman & Hall.

Schwartz, E.S. and Torous, W.N. (1989) Prepayment and the valuation of Mortgage-Backed-Securities, *Journal of Finance* **44**(2), 375–92.

Scott. D. (1992) *Multivariate Density Estimation: Theory Practice and Visualization*, Wiley – Interscience.

Searle, S., Casella, G. and McCullosh, C. (1982) *Variance Components*, John Wiley & Sons, Inc.

Selvaggio, R. (1996) Using the OAS methodology to value and hedge commercial bank retail demand deposit premiums, Chapter 12 in Fabozzi and Konishi, ed., *The Handbook of A/L Management*, Chicago: Probus Publishing, USA.

South, S.J. and Crowder, K.D. (1998) Leaving the Hood: Residential Mobility Between Black, White and Integrated Neighbourhoods. *American Sociological Review* **63**, 17–26.

Stanton, R. (1995) Rational Prepayment and the Valuation of Mortgage-Backed Securities, *Review of Financial Studies* **8**, 677–708.

Stanton, R. and Wallace, N. (1988) Mortgage Choice: What's the Point? *Real Estate Economics* **26**, 173–205.

Tasche, D. (1999) Risk contributions and performance measurement, working paper, Technische Universität München.

Tasche, D. (2000) Conditional expectation as quantile derivative, working paper, Technische Universität München.

Tasche, D. (2002) Expected Shortfall and beyond, *Journal of Banking and Finance* **26**(7), 1519–33.

Timmis, G.C. (1985) Valuation of GNMA Mortgage-Backed Securities with Transaction Costs, Heterogeneous Households and Endogenously Generated Prepayment Rates, Working Paper, Carnegie-Mellon University.

Tsanakas, A. (2003) Dynamic capital allocation with distortion risk measures, *Insurance: Mathematics and Economics* **35**(2), 11 October 2004, 223–43.

Uyemura, D. and van Deventer, D. (1993) *Financial Risk Management in Banking: The Theory and Application of Asset and Liability Management*, Probus Publishing Company.

van Deventer, D. and Messler, I. (2004) *Advanced Financial Risk Management*, John Wiley & Sons Inc.

Vasicek, O. (1977a) An equilibrium Characterization of the Term structure, *Journal of Financial Econometrics* **5**, 177–88.

Vasicek, O. (1997b) The loan loss distribution, working paper, KMV corporation.

Vasicek, O. (1998) A series expansion for the bivariate normal integral, working paper, KMV corporation.

Vasicek, O.A. and Fong, H.C. (1982) Term Structure Modeling Using Exponential Splines, *Journal of Finance* **37**, 339–48.

West, G. (2005) Calibration of the SABR model in illiquid markets, *Applied Mathematical Finance*, **12**(4), 371–85.

Wielhouwer, J.L. (2003) On the steady state of the replicating portfolio: accounting for a growth rate, *OR Spectrum*, Vol. 134.

Wilde, T. (2001) Probing granularity, *RISK* **14**(8), 103–6.

Wilkie, A. (1995) More on a Stochastic asset Model for actuarial use, Brit. *Actuarial Journal* **1**, 777–964.

Yaari, M.E. (1987) Dual theory of choice under Uncertainty, *Econometrica* **55**, 95–115.

Zenios, S. (2005) *Handbook of Asset and Liability Management*, Elsevier.

Zenios, S. and Ziemba, W. (1992) Financial modelling, *Management Science*, **38**, 1642–664.

Zenios, S. and Ziemba, W. (1998) *Worldwide Asset and Liability Modelling*, Cambridge University Press.

In French:

Demey, P., Frachot, A. et Riboulet, G. (2003) *Introduction à la Gestion Actif-passif bancaire*, Economica.

Dupré, D. et El Babsiri, M. (1997) *ALM: techniques pour la gestion actif-passif*, Editions Eska.

Gourieroux, C. et Montfort, A. (1995) *Séries temporelles et modèles dynamiques*, Economica.

Gourieroux, C. et Montfort, A. (1996) *Statistique et modèles économétriques*, Economica.

Le Vallois, F., Palsky, P., Paris, B. et Tosetti, A. (2003) *Gestion Actif – Passif en assurance vie: Réglementation – Outils – Méthodes*, Editions Economica.

Roncalli, T. (2001) *Introduction à la Gestion des Risques*, 3rd year ENSAI course.

Index

80/20 rule 509

Accounting risk 283–4
Accrued accounting
  examples 30–1
  general principles 29–30
Adam, Laurent and Rebérioux demand deposit model 123–4
Adam equivalents 322–6, 447
AFS based income smoothing strategies 459–60
A/L manager presentation, of balance sheet
  splitting of books 22
  trading book isolation 19
  treasury book isolation 22
ALCO (ALM committee) 87–92
Allais paradox 310
ALM book separation, *see* A/L manager presentation, of balance sheet
American banking crisis of the 1980's
  real estate crisis 7
  savings and loans insolvency crisis 6–7
Amortizing profile 63–4
Amortizing swap 64
Annual effective rate, of loan 143–4
Arbitrage opportunity absence (AOA) 176
Asset and liability management (ALM)
  and accounting 502–3
  ALM committee (ALCO) 87–92
  American banking crisis of the 1980's and 6–7
  backtests and out-of-sample tests 350–2
  benchmarking 500
  capital consumption and capital attribution or allocation 386–7
  classic criticism of 500–2
  classification methods 354
  coherent risk measures 341–3
  company valuation process 383–6
  delta equivalent in 316–18
  departments 93–7
  diversity 497–8, 497–9
  earnings-at-risk (EaR) 343–4
  and financial analysis 391
  gamma equivalent in 321
  Gaussian framework 344
  and Hawks Martingale 461
  insurance industry and 7–9
  Markovitz optimization and CAPM 345–7
  Merton's model of financial options 391
  and model risk 503
  modern banking industry and 5–7, 13–14
  multivariate regression, confidence interval and tests 347–8
  non-parametric statistics 355
  objectives of teams 84–7
  organization 83–4
  other businesses and 9–13
  other indicators 383
  other statistical tools 355–6
  and performance indicators of a company 381–2
  principal component analysis and interest rate example 352–3
  as profit centre 81–2
  relation with other departments 502
  seasonality treatments 352

Asset and liability management (ALM) (*Continued*)
stress testing 401–6
theoretical backgrounds about company valuation 387–90
time series 348–50
value-at-Risk (VaR) 340–1
variance and standard deviation 339–40
vector models 350
Autocorrelogram 349
Available-for-sale financial assets (AFS) 36–7

Backtests and out-of-sample tests, for ALM 350–2
Balance sheet 20
delta hedging example of 448–52
in insurance industry 24–5
presentation by A/L manager 19–23
presentation in general 19
Bank net economic income 425
Banking Books 5, 13, 23
and balance sheet presentation by A/L manager 23–4
economic value computation 408–13
statement of income 25–6
Banking industry
1929 crisis 5
and ALM 5–7, 13–14
modern times 5
origin 3
in the 12th and 13th centuries 3–4
17th century to 20th century 4
types of banks 6
Basel Committee regulation 5, 15
Basel accord 360
Basel I principles 360–1
Basel II glossary 363–5
Basel II Pillar 1 365–70
Basel II Pillar 2 370–5
Basel II Pillar 3 376–7
Basel II principles 361–3
for credit risk 222, 224–5, 230–1
criticisms 377–8
operational risk 281–2
stock market risk treatment in trading books 430
Basis risk 236
Behavioural modelling principles
backtesting of models 105–6
database constitution 101–3
event driven modelling 103–4
expert advice 105
model choices 101
strategy of the company 104
Bermudan swaptions 443
Black & Scholes formula, for stock price 295–6
Black & Scholes model, for financial market 292–3
Black market swaption prices 306
Black model, for caps, floors, collars and swaptions 522
Bond accounting 30
Bond strategies 197–8
Book split 22–3
Book value (BV) 383
Bootstrapping method 355
Brace Gaterek Musiela Market Model (BGM) 304–6
Break-even FTP funding cost 213
Break-even point liquidity gap 212–13
Bridge loan 139
Brownian motion
defined 287
of the Libor rate 123
Budgetary outstanding 187
Bullet loans 140
Burnout phenomenon 157–9
Business risk economic capital 430–2
Business risks 282–3

Cap or floors 43
Capital allocation 386, 395–6
Capital Asset Pricing Model (CAPM), measure for ALM 345–7
Capital Banking Book
products through FTP 75–6
Capital Banking Book and IFRS 55
Capital book 21, 24
Capital consumption 386
Capital cost 66
Capital management team 96–7
Carved out fair value hedge (COFVH) 45
Cash flow hedge (CFH) 40, 42–3
Cash flow statement 27
Cash flows and financial markets 185
CESR (Committee of European Securities Regulators) 34
Checking accounts 107
CIR++ (Cox Ingersoll Ross two factors model), of interest rate simulation 304
Classic debt programmes 219

Classification methods, of ALM 354
CMS floors 443
Coherent risk measures, for ALM 341–3
Collateralized debt obligations (CDOs) 232
Collateralized mortgage obligation (CMO) 199
Commercial banks 6
Commercial book 20–1
Commercial mortgage-backed security (CMBS) 199
Commissions 192–3
Community development banks 6
Company Market Value (MV) 383
Concentration credit risk 221
Confidence interval 400
Consolidation and IFRS 54–5
Constant maturity swap yield curve 239
Constant new production 187
Constant outstanding 187
Consumer loan 139
Contract cost modelling 103
Contract end date modelling 104
Contract life events modelling 104
Contract price modelling 103
Conventional schedule rules 67
Convertible debts 38, 39
Convexity change 242
Cooke ratio 360–1, 365
Copulas 509–11
Corporate balance sheet 23
Corporate loan 139
Corporate stock market risk 273–4
Corporate yield curve reconstitution 519–20
Correla equivalent
  under forward neutral probability 324
Cost/income ratio (C/I R) 383
Counterparty default risk 221
Counterparty risk 277
Coupon paid, to the customers 195–6
Courba equivalent, under forward neutral probability 324–5
Covered bonds 219
Credit cards loans 185
Credit default swaps (CDS) 232–3
Credit lines 212
Credit quality downgrading risk 221
Credit risk
  cost 65
  disclosures 52
  economic capital computation 406–7
  hedging of 232–5
  impact on incomes 224
  modelling and simulation of 225–32
  monitoring of 224
  nature and examples 221–4
  sensitivity 225
Credit seniority/residual maturity, of prepayment 157
CreditMetrics™ model 226
Cross-border funding 220
Cross-border risk 277
Cubic interpolation 516
Cumulative gap 212
Cumulative interest rate gap 243–4
Cumulative probability function 288
Currency risk
  on earnings 270–2
  economic capital 428
  indicators for 272
  investments and 266–9
  net open currency position 266
  simulation of 272–3
  trading book 265
Curvature change 242
Customers' concentration risk ratio 207

Deeply subordinated bonds (DSB) 22
Delay effects 182–3
Delta equivalent computation
  Adam equivalents 322–6
  in ALM 316–18
  associated break-even point 326–7
  examples 327–33
  and expected prepayment rates 331–2
  forward neutral and risk neutral discounted 320–1
  gamma equivalent computation in ALM 321
  hedging error and gamma equivalent 334–8
  horizontal and vertical delta equivalent 318–20
  in trading activities 315–16
Delta equivalent method, for option conversion 245
Delta hedging error conclusions 334
Delta hedging strategies 444–8
Delta hedging techniques 315–16
Demand deposit accounting 30
  application of LECG 415–16
Demand deposit accounts 107
  modelling 111
  replacement schedules 112–16

Deposit modelling, elements in
average amount by account 125
backtesting and validation 131
closing account probability 125
computation of demand deposit economic value 134–5
equilibrium relationships 129–30
expert advice in 131
FTP, representation in 136–7
hedging strategy 137
historical database construction 124–5
income sensitivities indicators, representation in 135
interest rate schedules, representation in 132–4
liquidity schedules, representation in 132
projection of customer production and perequation 128–9
remuneration 125–6
seasonal effects 131
sensitivity 130–1
volume effects 127–8
wealth effect 127
Deposits and savings
academic demand deposit models 118–24
demand deposit accounts 111–16
forms of 107
modelling based on customer behaviour modelling 124–37
and money supply 108–11
role of monetary aggregrates 108
savings accounts, *see* Savings accounts
valuation formula for deposits 474
Derivatives 38, 197
Disbursement delays 64, 66
Discounted cash flow analysis 59
Diversification, of liquidity sources 218–19
Doubtful credit amount 76
Dupré demand deposit model 119–20
Dynamic liquidity gaps 213

EAD (Exposure At Default) 363
Early redemption 104
Earnings-at-risk (EaR), measure for ALM 343–4
EC (Economic capital) 364
Economic capital 220
allocation process and limit setting 453–4
in ALM 407–33
computation of 398–401
credit risk computation 406–7
goals 394–7
IFRS and regulation implications for ALM 433–5
implications of 393–7
indicators for the economic value approach 435–40
target investment demanded by the shareholder 397
Economic equity distribution 400–1
Economic lever 387
Economic value (EV) 383
approach for replacement of deposit 112
of the future liquidity 206
of the liquidity book 214
produced by new clients 188
Economic value management
A/L managers' views 463–5
applications to capital book 492–3
company's objectives and the "optimization programme" 467–70
delta hedging strategies 466–7
grid technology 470–1
impact on ALCO communication 465
in insurance companies 491–2
Effective interest rate 40
EFRAG (European Financial Reporting Advisory Group) 34
EL (Expected Loss) 364
Embedded derivatives 38–9
Embedded option risk 236
Embedded options 186
EONIA swap yield curve 240
Equity cost (company) 385
Ethical banks 6
Euler relationship 341
Euribor rates 116, 240
Event driven modelling 103–4
Expert advice, by A/L managers 105
Extreme correlation points 509

Fair value
defined 40
of financial instruments disclosures 53
Fair value hedge (FVH) 40, 43–5
Fair value option, IAS 39 40
Fannie Mae (FNMA) 198
Feynman-Kac formula 290, 295, 337
Financial asset, defined 36
Financial assets at fair value through profit or loss (trading assets) 36–7

Financial instruments, under IFRS
derivatives and embedded derivatives 38–9
financial assets 36–8
financial liability and equity 38
measurement 39–40
recognition and derecognition 36
scope 35–6
Financial liability 38
Financial markets
and cash flows 185
costs and commissions with 185–6
Financial prepayment option 65
Financial risks
corporate stock market risk 273–4
counterparty risk 277
credit risk 220–35
cross-border risk 277
currency risk 265–73
inflation risk 259–65
interest rate risk 235–58
liquidity risk 203–20
real estate risk/property risk 274–7
volatility risk 277–9
Fire insurance 8
Firm interest rate risk 242
Fixed Income Trader 13
Fixed term deposits 108
Floating rate loan 63
Floors 43, 443
Forward rates 240
Frachot demand deposit model 119
Freddie Mac 198
French Savings rate 116
FSLIC (Federal Savings and Loans Insurance Company) 6
FTP interest rate break-even 247
FTP rule based on the flows 68–9
FTP rule based on the stock 67–8
Fubini theorem 474
Full fair value, of the insurance contract 196
Fund transfer pricing (FTP)
advanced, including credit risk and expected return on economic capital 64–6
examples of rules 72–7
incorporating the cost of an implicit option in 66–7
perequation concept 77–9
principles 61–4
rules based on "stock" and "flows" 67–72
Fund transfer pricing (FTP), in the balance sheet income 30–1
Funding book, *see* Treasury book
Future contracts 520

Gap analysis 243–4
Gap limit 454
Gaussian distribution, *see* Normal distribution
Gaussian framework, of ALM 344
GDP growth and interest rates 110
Geographical credit risk 221
Geometric Brownian motion 289
Girsanov theorem 291, 293
Government bond yield curve reconstitution
bootstrap method 515
direct interpolation method 515–16
indirect interpolation method 516–19
theoretical method 514–15
Granting scores 221
Grid technology computing, of interest rate risk capital 421–4
Gross economic capital (GEC) 413, 418
Gross interest margin (GIM) 383
Guaranty Funds 8

H3 monotonicity 341
H1 positive homogeneity 341
H4 sub-additivity (risk diversification) 341
H2 translation-invariance 341
Hawks Martingale 461
Hedge accounting, discontinuation of 41–2
Hedge funds 10–11
Hedging and IAS 39
application to senior debt instruments 47
carved out fair value hedge (COFVH) 45–6
cash flow hedge 42–3
discontinuation of hedge accounting 41–2
effectiveness 46–7
fair value hedge 43–5
hedge accounting 40–1
instruments 41
interest margin hedge (IMH) 46
internal contracts 47
Hedging effectiveness 46–7
Hedging instruments 41
bond strategies 197–8
derivatives 197
MBS (Mortgage-Backed Securities) 198–9
Held-to-maturity investments (HTM) 36–7
Heteroskedasticity models 350
Historical cost measuring, *see* Accrued accounting
Historical databases, construction of 101–3

Home equity loan 139
Horizon choices 400
Horizon computation, of the income sensitivities 249–50
Horizontal Equivalent delta 319
Host contracts 38
Hull & White interest rate models 528–31
Hull & White one-factor model, of interest rate simulation 296–301

IAS 39 35–48, 56–7
IAS 30 and banks' disclosures 48–9
IAS 32 (disclosure of financial instruments) and IFRS 7 (disclosures checklist) 49–53
ICAAP (Internal Capital Adequacy Assessment Process) 394
Idealized rates 223
IFRS-EU 34
Impairment and IAS 39 47–8
Implicit or explicit options cost 63
Implicit prepayment rate 161–3
Implicit yield curves 238
Income projection indicators, of economic capital 436–40
Income sensitivity limit 455
Income smoothing strategies
  comments 457–8
  examples 458–60
  Hawks Martingale 461
Inflation and money supply 108–9
Inflation risk
  in balance sheet 260
  of bonds linked 262–3
  factor simulation 264–5
  hedging 265
  impact on incomes 263
  indicators 263–4
  macroeconomic point of view 259–60
  market 261–2
Inflation risk economic capital 428–30
In-life scores 221
Instantaneous forward rate 241
Insurance book 24–7
  statement of income 26
Insurance contracts 332
Insurance industry
  history 7–8
  and IFRS 53–4
  in modern times 8–9
  types of 9
Insurance products
  FTP 77
  mutual funds 195–6
  unit of account contracts 195
Insurance provisions 460
Intensity based models, for credit derivatives pricing 231–2
Interbank market 219
Interest margin hedge (IMH) 46
Interest rate risk
  forms of yield curve 241–2
  hedging 258
  impacts on the incomes 242
  indicators 242–57
  nature and examples 235–6
  simulation 257–8
  types of interest rate 238–41
  types of yield curves 236–8
Interest rate risk capital
  criticism 424–7
  grid technology computation 421–4
  sensitivity based computation 417–21
Interest rate risk transfer 62–3
Interest rate schedules, estimation of 245
Interest rate spread, on prepayment
  absolute 153
  comparison between relative and absolute 154–6
  impact 156, 157
  lag on 156
  non linear terms 156
  relative 154
  volatility impact 157
Interest rate yield curve slope risk 236
Interest risk profit centre 81–2
Interest-only stripped mortgage-backed securities (IO) 199
Internal transfer pricing, *see* Fund transfer pricing (FTP)
International Accounting Standards Board (IASB) 33
International Accounting Standards (IAS 39)
  criticisms of 56–7
  financial disclosures 48–53
  hedging relations 40–7
  impact on ALM 56
  impairment of assets and loans including credit risk impairment 47–8
  and insurance 53–4
  other specifications 54–5
  recognition of financial instruments 35–40

International Financial Reporting Standards (IFRS)
financial disclosures 48
international organizations 33–4
rules 34–5
Intraday liquidity ratio 206–7
Investment banking 6
Investment management 9–10
Investment strategy modelling 104
IRB advanced approach 367
IRB (Internal Rating Based) Foundation approach 367
Italian banks 4
Itô lemma 290

Jarrow and Van Deventer demand deposit model 120–1
JP Morgan introduced RiskMetrics 417

Kernel smoothing 169–70
KMV™ model 226
KRI (Key Risk Indicator) 364

Laplace transform 289
Law invariance 341
Leasing 140
Least-square minimization 348
Letter of credit 3
LGD (Loss Given Default) 363
Libor in arrears investment 458
Libor indexed loans 141
Libor indexed rate 64
LIBOR rates 240
Life insurance companies 9
application of LECG 417
Limits policy
economic capital allocation process 453–4
gap limit 454
income sensitivity limit 455
Linear amortizing loans 140
Linear Gaussian Model with risk premium 311–13
Linear Gaussian model with two factors, of interest rate simulation 301–3
Linear interpolation 515–16
Liquid deposits 110
Liquidity book income 213
Liquidity crisis 205
Liquidity gap 208–9
Liquidity income 204–5
Liquidity information 206
Liquidity risk
funding cost 203–4
hedging 217–20
illiquidity 203
impact on net income 204–6
monitoring of 206–14
simulation of 215–16
Liquidity risk disclosures (IFRS 7) 52
Liquidity risk economic capital 427
Liquidity risk transfer 63
Liquidity schedule 195
Loan offers 181
Loan/capital ratio 207
Loans
definitions and formulae 141–4
types 139–41
Loans and receivables 36–7
Loans/deposit ratio 207
Lognormal distribution 288
Lombards, of Italy 4
Long-Term Capital Management (LTCM) 11
Loss given default (LGD) 223, 225

M (Maturity) 363
Macaulay duration 256
Marine insurance 8
Marked-to-market accounting
general principles 29–30
Market models, of interest rate simulation 304–6
Market options 333
Market risk 13
Market risk disclosures (IFRS 7) 52
Market yield curves 238
Markowitz optimization, measure for ALM 345–7
Markowitz Theory 10
Martingale notion 289–90
Maturity cap loans 141
MBS (Mortgage-Backed Securities) 198–9
McDonough ratio 361
Medium or long-term ratios 207–8
Merton's model of financial options 391
Micro hedging strategies, with structured products 443–4
Migration models, for rating credit risk 226–7
Mismatch risk 236

Model and business risk economic capital 430–2
Model backtesting 105–6, 172–4
Model risks 282
Modigliani-Miller theorem 389
Monetary aggregates 108
Monetary interbank rates 520
Monetary policy 236
Money market savings 107
Money supply
A/L manager formula 111
and M2 modelling by A/L managers 110
and M2 modelling by Central Banks 108–9
volume effects 110–11
Money Zero Maturity (MZM) 108
Moneychangers 4
Monte Carlo simulation 329
Moody's long-term bond ratings 237–8
Mortgage loans 139
new production of 188–91
Mortgage-backed security (MBS) 174
Multicurrency correla equivalent 333
Mutual bank companies 6
Mutual funds 195–6

Nelson Siegel indirect interpolation models 517
Net economic capital (NEC) 413, 414
Net income 26
Net investment hedge 40
New insurance contracts modelling 191–2
New production modelling
commission and cost modelling 192–3
new contract production 187–92
perequation modelling 193
strategies 193–4
Non-financial risk
accounting risk 283–4
business risks 282–3
model risks 282
operational risks 281–2
risk correlations 283
Non-interest-bearing deposits (demand deposits) 72–4
Non-parametric prepayment modelling
kernel smoothing 169–70
principles 169
weighted kernel smoothing 170
Non-parametric statistics, of ALM 355
Normal distribution 288
Normalized equity 382

Off-balance sheet 23
Office of Thrift Supervision (OTS) demand deposit model 121–3
Operating income 26
Operation currency 63
Operational costs 63
Operational risks 281–2
Optimization programme, applications
banking book activities 473–82
credit risk book 483–4
for demand deposit income smoothing 487–9
global Banking Book including business and model risk 485–7
prepayment risk optimal hedging strategies 484–5
stock market book 482–3
Optional interest rate risk 243
Optional risk indicator, for market interest rate options 254–5
Outstanding amount 444
Overdrafts 139, 246

P & L impact, of bond premium / discount 30
Parametric prepayment modelling
classic prepayment functions 166–8
logit models and cumulative prepayment functions 168
with mixed effects 168
Pawnbrokers 4
PD (Probability of Default) 363
P/E ratio computations 383
Penta equivalent
computation of bank balance sheet 452
under forward neutral probability 323–4
under risk neutral discounted income delta hedging 325–6
Perequation concept 77–9
Perequation modelling 193
Perfect positioning, in ALM 15
Periodic gap 212
P+I amortizing loans 140
Pillar 1, of Basel II regulation
and market risk 368
and operational risk 368–70
risk aggregation 370
Pillar 2, of Basel II regulation 394
implementation of economic capital 370–2
and interest rate risk governance 374–5
and interest rate risk in the banking book 372–4

Pillar 3, of Basel II regulation 376–7
Pipeline risk 181
Pipeline risk option 65
P&L net of carry, notion of 29
Point in time (PIT) 222
"Pool based" FTP rule 67
Positions at risk 419
Postal saving banks 6
Power options 443
Premium/discount cost 30
Prepayment modelling
  advanced databases for 163–6
  database for rudimentary modelling 160–3
  expression of prepayment 159
  model backtesting 172–4
  non-parametric 169–71
  parametric 166–8
  rationale 148
  renegotiation 171–2
  through MBS-based models 174–7
Prepayments
  application of optimization programme 484–5
  borrower rating 152
  burnout variable 157–9
  competing risks 151–2
  credit seniority/residual maturity 157
  example 147
  financial or rational 145, 146
  interest rate spread 153–7
  macroeconomic variables affecting 152–3
  modelling, *see* Prepayment modelling
  models 166–77
  monitoring 178–9
  penalties or compensation 146–7
  renegotiation 146
  scoring techniques 178
  seasonal 153
  sources of 148–9
  statistical or sociological 145
  transaction costs and penalties 150
  types of 149–50
Price on earnings ratio (P/E ratio or PER) 383
Price to Book (PTB) 383
Prices grids 64
Principal-only stripped mortgage-backed securities (PO) 199
Private banks 6
Probability of default (PD) 225
Procyclic effects 222
Quantitative modelling, of new customer/contract production 188

RA (Risk Assessment) 364
Real estate crisis 7
Real estate investments 38
Real estate prices 191
Real estate risk/property risk 274–7
Real probability 291
Recovery rate risk 221
Regulated savings rate 116–17
Regulatory capital 393
Remunerated deposits without maturity 74
Renegotiation prepayment modelling 171–2
Repayment formula, of loans 142–3
Replicating portfolio approach, for replacement of deposit 112
Residential mortgage-backed security (RMBS) 199
Retail balance sheet 23
Retail banking books 23
Risk adjusted return on capital (RAROC) 382
Risk aggregation 432–3
Risk contribution computation facility 341
Risk correlations 283
Risk free auto-financing strategy 293
Risk management 14
Risk management, for assets and liability managers 201
Risk neutral delta hedging 321
Risk neutral probability 292
Risk premium level estimation 310–11
Risk reduction techniques, under Basel II regulation 367–8
Risk transfer, a market price 62
ROE (Return on Equity) 381
ROEC (Return on Economic Capital) 382, 425, 478
  risk adjusted performance measurement with 395
Rome and banking activities 3
RONE (Return on Normalized Equity) 381
Rotation 242
RWA (Risk Weighted Asset) 364

Saint Louis Models, of money supply 109
Savings accounts
  non-regulated 117–18
  regulated 116–17
Savings and loans insolvency crisis 6–7
Savings banks 6

Schedule with prepayments 210
Scoring 102
Seasonality treatments, of ALM 352
Sector concentration credit risk 221
Securitization 219, 232–5
Securitization and IFRS 54–5
Securitization price 65
Selvaggio demand deposit model 118
Senior debt instruments 47
Sensitivity based computation, of interest rate risk capital 417–21
Sensitivity indicator 248–54
Shareholder system of reference, of economic capital 394
Shareholder's constraints 477–8
Shareholder's equity 382
Short-term interest rate risk 243
Short-term liquidity ratio 206
Simulating liquidity risk 215–16
Simulation tools, for interest rates and other financial indexes
  equity market simulation 292–6
  generic models 306–9
  interest rate simulation 296–306
  market simulations including risk premiums 309–13
  stochastic calculation 287–92
Solvency II European directive
  objective 378
  and pillars of Basel II 378–9
Spearman rhô 509
Special purpose vehicles (SPVs) 232
Spectral risk measures (SRM) 343
Spline models 518–19
Spot mixed with forward deals 459
Stable liabilities ratio 208
Standard and Poor's (S&P) ratings 237
Standard normal distribution 288
Statement of income 25–6
Statistical prepayment option 65
Stock conventional schedule 70
Stock investment portfolios and latent economic capital gains (LECG) 414–15
Stock market risk economic capital 430
Stock options and IFRS 55
Stress testing, of ALM 401–6
Structural interest rate risk 243
Structural models, for estimating defaults 228–30
Student loan 139
Super-savings 117–18
Swap contracts 521
Swap interbank yield curve reconstitution 520–1
Swap rates 239–40
Swaptions 43

Term deposits 107–8
Theory of arbitrage opportunity absence (AOA) 293–5
Through the cycle (TTC) 222
Tier 1 and Tier 2 capital 22
Time series assessment, of ALM 348–50
Trade date 63
Trade maturity date 63
Trading books 13
  isolation of 19
Transformation, defined 15
Translation 242
Treasury book 22

UL (Unexpected Loss) 364
Unit of account contracts 195
United States Securities and Exchange Commission (SEC) 33
US GAAP 33

Value-at-Risk (VaR), measure for ALM 340–1
VaR (Value-at-Risk) 13, 364
Variance and standard deviation, measure for ALM 339–40
Vasicek indirect interpolation models 517–18
Vasicek stochastic model, for the evolution of interest rates 523–8
Vector models, of ALM 350
Volatility risk 277–9
Volume effects 183
von Neumann-Morgenstern axioms 310

Weighted Average Cost of Capital (WACC) 388
Weighted average life (WAL), of loan 143
Weighted kernel smoothing 170
Whistle effect, *see* Delay effects
Wiener process 287

Yield curve evolution modelling
  reconstitution of 513–21
  stochastic interest rate models 521–31
Yield to Maturity (YTM) for bonds 238–9

Zerocoupon bond schedules 481
Zero-coupon loans 140